Out of Step

Books by the same author

Second to None: The Royal Scots Greys 1918–1945
El Alamein
Tobruk
The War Lords (ed.)
Harding of Petherton
The Apostles of Mobility
War Since 1945
A Policy for Peace
The Seven Ages of the British Army
Dilemmas of the Desert War
Twentieth Century Warriors

OUT OF STEP

STEP

Memoirs of a Field Marshal

Michael Carver

HUTCHINSON
LONDON SYDNEY AUCKLAND JOHANNESBURG

To Our Children
Susanna, Andrew, Alice and John

This edition first published in Great Britain by
Hutchinson, an imprint of Century Hutchinson Ltd,
Brookmount House, 62–65 Chandos Place, London WC2N 4NW

Century Hutchinson Australia Pty Ltd, 89–91 Albion Street,
Surry Hills, NSW2010

Century Hutchinson New Zealand Ltd, PO Box 40–086,
Glenfield, Auckland 10, New Zealand

Century Hutchinson South Africa (Pty) Ltd, PO Box 337,
Bergvlei, 2012 South Africa

Printed and bound in Great Britain by
Mackays of Chatham PLC, Chatham, Kent

Contents

ILLUSTRATIONS

(Note: Maps 1 to 5 are taken from *Dilemmas of the Desert War* by the author, published by Batsford in 1986)

Prologue

How true is this story? As true as I could make it. The only period for which I kept a diary – other than engagement diaries, which have proved invaluable to check dates and movements – was 1931–33, my last three years at Winchester. Most of the entries were trivial: those that were not proved embarrassing, but useful as revelations of my feelings at the time. Apart from these, the only detailed diaries I wrote were of my travels in Europe and to Greece before the Second World War.

The story of my experiences in that war is based partly on the brief histories I wrote, of 7th Armoured Division after the end of the North African campaign, and of 4th Armoured Brigade at the end of the war; on detailed accounts of the operations of 1st Royal Tanks in North Africa, Italy and Normandy, when I commanded the regiment, which I wrote at the time; partly on detailed accounts provided by the regiments of 4th Armoured Brigade, on which I based my history; and partly on the extensive research I made in compiling my three books on the North African campaign, *Tobruk, El Alamein* and *Dilemmas of the Desert War*, published by Batsfords in 1964, 1962 and 1986 respectively. My service in the desert from 1940 to 1943 was a significant period of my life, which had a decisive influence on all that came after. As I have already written three books about that desert war, I have not attempted in this account to describe the operations in detail.

For the post-war period until I assumed command of the 3rd Division in 1962, I have relied largely on my extensive correspondence with Sir Basil Liddell Hart and Major-

General Sir Percy Hobart, and also with others on the subject of armoured warfare. The research involved in writing my book *War Since 1945*, published by Weidenfeld and Nicolson in 1980, also helped to remind me of my time in Kenya and the various problems with which I was concerned as Director of Army Plans and of Army Staff Duties.

I wrote detailed accounts at the end of my time as a peacekeeper in Cyprus and as Commander-in-Chief Far East as official despatches to the Chiefs of Staff, and of my involvement in the affairs of Rhodesia, as Resident Commissioner (Designate), to the Foreign Secretary. Before leaving the post of Chief of the General Staff, I wrote an account of my involvement in the affairs of Northern Ireland, and a similar one covering my stewardship of the post of Chief of the Defence Staff. Both were based on the official papers to which I had access at the time, and all have proved invaluable as sources.

The rest is based on memory. As an amateur historian, I know how treacherous that can be; but contemporary sources and subsequent research have acted both as stimulants and correctives to the self-deception to which the memories of old age are prone. I claim therefore that what the reader will find in the pages which follow is the truth, if not the whole truth.

I am grateful to my wartime scout-car driver, Peter Roach, for permission to quote from his war memoirs, *The 8.15 to War*, and to my agent, Bruce Hunter, for his help and encouragement with this and previous books.

M.C.

1

Shades of the Prison-house

Shades of the prison-house begin to close
Upon the growing boy.
William Wordsworth (1770–1850),
Ode: *Intimations of Immortality*

I was born on 24 April 1915, the day before the landings at
Gallipoli, at the Manor House, Bletchingley, Surrey, which
my grandmother, Nora Wellesley, rented from her brother-
in-law, William Bell, who lived in Pendell Court, the large
Elizabethan house next door. I was my parents' second son,
Antony having been born in 1913. I was to be followed by
two others, Rodney in 1916 and Paul in 1919. My father,
Harold Carver, had met my mother, Anne Wellesley, eight
years younger than himself, through his acquaintance with
her brother Richard, who was an officer of the Egyptian
Police, my father being employed by the family firm of
Carver Brothers Ltd, Egyptian-cotton merchants.

My father's family can be traced as far back as a William
Carver, who was a farmer and churchwarden at Ruddington,
a few miles south of Nottingham, at the beginning of the
eighteenth century. His eldest son went to farm at Hungarton
near Leicester, and his son, having farmed first at Braunston
near Oakham, returned in 1790 to Hungarton and leased the
house and farm of Ingarsby from Lord Maynard. He had
three sons, William, who later took on Ingarsby, Robert, who
farmed at Queniborough nearby, and John, the youngest,
who did not care for farming. John was 20 when his father
died in 1809, and, a few weeks later, left Ingarsby to try his

hand in business in Manchester. He did well there and started a firm of his own, John Carver Ltd, later to be renamed Carver Brothers Ltd, dealing in the import of cottonseed from Morocco. As a base from which to organize this, he set up an office in Gibraltar. Having no children of his own at that time, he offered employment to his nephews. This was the start of the Carver family's association with Gibraltar, the business expanding from the import of cottonseed to that of raw cotton, grown mostly in Egypt, especially after the American Civil War had cut off supplies from their cotton-growing states in the south.

One of the nephews, who later joined the office in Gibraltar, was Benjamin, fifth of the six sons of John's brother Robert. At the age of 27 he arrived there in 1861, destined to become head of the office and spend his life on the Rock. In 1864 he married Emily Jane Power, of an Irish family who lived in Malaga, engaged in the liquor trade. Her grandfather, Michael Power, of the same name as her father, had married Juana, one of the daughters of the Belgian consul, the Baron de Grivégnée, her sisters marrying respectively the French, the Polish and the American consuls, the last named being a Scotsman, William Kirkpatrick. His daughter married the Count of Teba, later Count of Montijo, and was the mother of Napoleon III's Empress Eugénie.* The youngest of Benjamin's six children was my father, christened Harold Power, born in 1878. After attending boarding schools in England, he went to work in Egypt and later joined the family firm there.

My mother's father, Courtenay Wellesley, was a direct descendant of the Marquess Wellesley, the first Duke of Wellington's eldest brother. The Marquess had met the lady who was to become his wife, Hyacinthe Rolland, on the stage in Paris in 1786, she herself almost certainly being the illegitimate daughter of an Irishman named Fagan, who had served as a cavalry officer in the French army before the revolution, and Madame Rolland, who had previously been the mistress of an Englishman, Mr Lambert. Wellesley had five children by Hyacinthe before he married her in 1794, three years before he went to India as Governor-General without her.

* The Powers, Kirkpatricks and de Grivégnées were all in the wine business.

After his return in 1805, they quarrelled and separated, and his children were never legitimized. His titles, which included also Earl of Mornington and Viscount Wellesley, passed on his death to his brother the Duke of Wellington, Lord Maryborough, the second brother, having no male heir. The Marquess's eldest son, Richard, had four sons, the eldest of whom, another Richard, had no children, and the second of whom, Edward, was Courtenay's father. He died in the Crimea in 1854, when serving as a major on Lord Raglan's staff. Courtenay spent his working life with the Texas Land and Mortgage Company in Dallas, Texas, but does not appear to have been a successful man of business, unlike his brother-in-law, William Bell, who went to America at about the same time, in the early 1870s, and made a fortune in railways, mining and property, based on Colorado Springs. My grandmother, Nora Scovell,* was Courtenay's second wife, his first having died in 1879 after only five years of marriage, leaving him with two young children. Nora was at that time staying with her sister, Cara Bell, at Manitou near Colorado Springs, where William had built an imposing Victorian house of red granite, called Briarhurst, which, when I visited it in 1974, was a restaurant. Courtenay and Nora had first met at the wedding of his sister Hyacinthe to Dr William Dalby, a close friend of William Bell, who had been a fellow medical student. They were married in 1885 and my mother, their second child, was born in England in 1886.

Courtenay retired from America in 1910, assisted by the sale of a Hoppner portrait of Hyacinthe Wellesley, and died in 1912, the year after my parents were married. Soon after the wedding, my father took on the post of agent for Carver Brothers on the continent of Europe, in which his command of languages, particularly his fluency in French and Spanish, was an asset. He, my mother and my elder brother Antony were living in Zurich when the First World War broke out, and he was recalled to Egypt. My mother returned to England, having just conceived myself. My father, unlike most of his relations in the company, joined the British army in Egypt and served in the Camel Transport Corps, a branch of the

---

* Her father, Whitmore Scovell, member of a London wharfinger firm, and his wife had been killed in a railway accident at Abergele in Wales in 1868.

Army Service Corps. After my birth, my mother left Antony and me in my grandmother's care and went out to Egypt to help run a convalescent hospital in Alexandria, caring for sick and wounded officers from Gallipoli. Almost immediately she became pregnant again and returned to England, where Rodney was born. She then rented Pyt House Cottage near Tisbury in Wiltshire, where we were joined by my father before the end of the war. He had contracted severe dysentery in the Palestine campaign and was invalided to England. My earliest memories are of Pyt House Cottage; of seeing German prisoners of war marching to work in the fields; of putting my handkerchief over the end of the vertical exhaust pipe of the mechanical saw across the road and seeing it fly high into the air; of travelling in Mr Jukes's wagonette through the lovely woods of Fonthill to Hindon; of being placed in a large stone urn in the gardens of Hatch House to protect me from Mrs Bennett's horrid, yapping Pekinese; of travelling pillion on my mother's bicycle. The great event of my life there was bursting through the bars of the nursery window to try and get at a toy I had dropped on to the sloping roof outside, down which I rolled, landing in a rose-bed, while my mother was carving the Sunday joint. I was unharmed, but was said to have screamed my head off.

When the war ended in 1918, my father was sent to the firm's Manchester office, of which later he became managing director. We lived in a succession of rented homes, first in Buxton, then Disley – a thatched house, the roof of which caught fire – Wilmslow and Alderley Edge; until, finally, in 1922, we came to rest in an attractive house called Turner Heath at Bollington Cross, a village adjoining the cotton-spinning town of Bollington, near Macclesfield in Cheshire. My parents rented it unfurnished, and it became our first real home. It was a pleasant red-brick house, probably built in the eighteenth century, to which Victorian and later additions had been made. One side fronted on the road on the edge of the village: the other faced a large garden with a paddock, which overlooked open fields.

We had plenty of room to play in, with a tennis court as well as a croquet lawn. Our obstinate Welsh pony, Peggy, pulled the lawn-mower and the pony cart, as well as providing a mount for all of us, as we grew up and learned to ride, our favourite hack being on to the moors on the far side of the Macclesfield canal. My riding career suffered a setback when, riding round the paddock under my uncle Dick Wellesley's expert tuition, the saddle slipped round underneath the pony's belly, my foot caught in the stirrup and Peggy took fright, galloping round and round the paddock, dragging me behind her. After one or two circuits, she slipped up, caught her foot under the iron railing, swung the back of my head against it and sat on me. I was naturally frightened. Fortunately my injuries were not serious, although I had to have some stitches in the back of my head. It was a long time before I felt really confident in the saddle again, and was naturally ever thereafter very sensitive about tightening girths and the safety of stirrups.

As a family of four boys close in age, all, certainly Antony and myself, fairly hot-tempered, we were naturally up to all sorts of tricks and fought each other a good deal. Rodney, delicate in health as a young child, received special protection from us, as did Paul, the youngest by a gap of three years. We got through governesses in quick succession, as we had done nurses and nursemaids. When they could not deal with us, we were beaten either by our mother with her hairbrush, which was not painful, or, if very bad, by our father with his shoe, which was. In spite of our fights with each other and tearful scenes over one thing or another – I was very easily provoked to tears and rage – we lived a happy family life and loved our parents dearly. We did not regard ourselves as well off, and certainly not as rich; but, with about four servants, as well as a governess, in the house, and a gardener, Bretherton, and a boot-boy, Arthur Brooks, outside, we led a comfortable life, though not at all a luxurious one. It was not until 1925 that we acquired a car, a bull-nosed Morris-Oxford. Until then the pony-cart took us shopping in Macclesfield, visiting our friends and meeting my father at the station at Prestbury on his return from the office. He was not a partner in the firm, but was, I believe, employed on a five-year contract on a fixed salary, augmented by a bonus based on the firm's profit. This seemed satisfactory in the early 1920s, but, when the world recession started, cotton, particularly high quality Egyptian cotton, was one of the first trades to feel the pinch, and, from 1928 onwards, the firm began to go downhill.

My father's side of the family, the descendants of Robert's Benjamin, felt that the best jobs had all gone to the descendants of the eldest, William, and there was a constant undercurrent of resentment between my father and his richer cousins, for whom he worked in Manchester. Their relations were not improved by my mother's Wellesley-worship, with which we were imbued, and her determination not to be thought of as a Manchester businessman's wife. My father longed to be, and to be thought of as, a country gentleman. As a young man he had stayed with one of his sisters, Emmie, who had married a rich Lancashire brewer, Hubert Wilson, whose family had many connections with the Carvers. They lived in a large house in Cheshire, hunted with the fashionable Cheshire Hunt and shot with the squires. My father, who was a good games-player and sportsman, was greatly attracted by the life and longed to escape from the business world.

It was perhaps partly this desire on the part of my parents to bring us up in a circle divorced from Manchester business which prompted them to send us to a preparatory boarding school as far away as possible, to St Peter's Court at Broadstairs in Kent. The other reason for their choice was that the school had been evacuated during the war to Pyt House in Wiltshire, and, when we had lived in Pyt House Cottage, my mother had come to know and like Janet Richardson, sister of one of the joint headmasters, an Old Harrovian bachelor. The school specialized in sending boys to Eton and Harrow, and most of the parents were rich or aristocratic. Two of the Royal princes, the Dukes of Gloucester and of Kent, had been to school there, giving it a special snob cachet as a result. In retrospect I believe it was a serious error. It implanted in us, certainly in Antony and myself, a feeling of being outsiders. It certainly left us with a strong aversion to the arrogance and self-satisfaction of the rich, the aristocratic, the establishment. In spite of my mother's Wellesley-worship, we were none of these. Unlike my father, I was not good at games. I was sensitive, good at my books and keen on music. All in all, I, like Antony before me, was an easy butt for teasing and bullying. An outsider to begin with, I was driven further outside the pale and deeper inside myself. I had few friends.

I do not know when my parents decided that we should aim for Winchester as our next step on the scholastic ladder. I believe that my father had struck up a friendship before or during the war with a Wykehamist, whom he greatly admired and who was later killed. He himself had been to Malvern, and Dick Wellesley and his father to Wellington, where, as Wellesleys, they paid less, I believe, than the normal fees. My father may have been influenced by the fact that Antony and I were good at our books. St Peter's Court sent hardly any boys to Winchester and contented itself with seeing that they could pass the Common Entrance examination well enough to enter Eton and Harrow. If they failed that, they were likely to go to the newly established school at Stowe. Whether it was because the school left the decision too late, because it did not know the rules, or because we were not accepted, neither Antony nor I was 'down for' a house at Winchester and had to attempt the scholarship examination, known as Elections. Neither of us was successful, but we both did well enough to gain Headmaster's nominations to a house. A certain number of places in the houses, to which some 400 of the 472 boys at Winchester were assigned, were reserved for nominations by the headmaster from those who took the scholarship examination and failed to gain either a scholarship or an exhibition.

The five years I spent at St Peter's Court from 1923 to 1928 were not, in general, happy ones, although the periods of unhappiness were no doubt short in relation to the total; but they seemed intense at the time, and still do in retrospect. Holidays were certainly a blessed contrast. Being so far away, our parents did not often visit us and the long train journey home was always a welcome release. On our way through London we were generally looked after by my mother's delightful half-sister, Hyacinth, married to a terrifying retired brigadier-general of the Royal Engineers, Philip Maud, who looked after the London County Council parks. Tea on the Euston to Macclesfield express of the London and North Western Railway, later the London, Midland and Scottish, was one of the highlights, with its delicious chocolate biscuits of which we took a handful. One

letter from me to my mother, dated 4 March 1927, survives.
It is headed 'Memoirs of M. R. P. Carver. Rather Rotten day'
and continues:

> On Friday March 4th I felt jolly good, the game went quite
> well. I felt very fit, but everyone talked so frightfully, I got
> quite angry.
>   Then I got fairly raging, inside, but outside I kept
> up a smile, because they would take my ball out of the
> shed and take it away; if I hadn't given it up in Lent, I
> would have lost my bait. Then the last string was broken.
> Thompson bagged Olley's (Rodney's) Baby Tractor and
> *would* not give it up.
>   Then I could not control myself. I'd had enough already,
> I lost my bait; Fawcus ma tried to bend the wheels but I
> stopped him: I got it back but felt rotten most of the time;
> the only time I bucked up a bit was when Burnell (one of
> the masters) congratulated me on my French Paper.

The ease with which I could be provoked to 'lose my bait' was
a permanent cause of trouble at St Peter's Court, the effort
required to overcome it laying the foundations of a future
ability to exercise a pretty firm control of my emotions,
although I was not so successful in concealing the visible
expression of my inner feelings.

It must have been about the time that I left St Peter's Court
and went to Winchester that our parents had started the
habit of spending part of the summer holidays on Exmoor
at the Dunkery Beacon Hotel at Wootton Courtenay near
Minehead in Somerset. We all looked forward eagerly to this
annual event. We rode ponies, provided by a remarkable
bearded old man, Mr Dascombe, whose broad Somerset
accent was almost incomprehensible. The hotel was run
by a cheerful, friendly family, the Taplins, assisted by our
favourite Miss Hunter, who clearly came from Scotland.
When we did not ride, we walked for miles over the moors
or followed the Devon and Somerset Staghounds by car.
By the time I had gone to Winchester, I graduated to a
better type of mount than Mr Dascombe's rough Exmoor
ponies, but began to suffer severely from an allergy when
in contact with horses. One year I was severely stricken by

it, could hardly breathe and had to give up riding altogether.

I had taken the Winchester scholarship examination in June 1928 and got my headmaster's nomination to 'G' house, known as 'Sergeant's' or 'Phil's', of which Antony had been an inmate for the previous two years. It was a prison-like Victorian building, and still is, presided over by the Reverend W. D. Monro, known as 'The Munner', a strict Evangelical parson, son of an officer of the Indian Police. He was a lover of all things French and classical. His first wife had died many years before and he had married the nurse who had looked after her. Under the system then current, they had to feed and care for the 70 boys in the house, as well as themselves and their family, from within the same limited sum. Mrs Monro was not a good manager and, as a result, the food and general standard of living in the house were among the worst in the school.

As I reached the top of St Peter's Court, the pressures of unpopularity and the sense of being an outsider had eased off, but now, back at the bottom again, they returned and seemed more intense than ever. The extraordinarily complicated ritual of Wykehamical society hedged one around at every step. Not only was there a special school language, known as 'notions', which one had to learn and in which one had to prove oneself proficient after one's first month, but life was determined by a complicated set of taboos and restrictions about what one could wear, where one could walk, what one could say and to whom. It was almost impossible not to put a foot wrong in some way or another, making one liable to punishment by the house prefects, whose whole aim seemed to be to catch one out. The weekly 'Ekker Roll', a statement of the physical exercise one had taken, which had to add up to a total of seven hours, was the main imposition. The rules about what counted as an hour's exercise were complicated and somewhat illogical. If one wanted any time to oneself at all, one had either to cram an almost impossible amount of exercise into one afternoon, in order to free another, or to cheat by stating that one had taken exercise when one had not. Life seemed to be one long fight against the system. It was not that I disliked taking exercise. I much enjoyed physical activity in the open air, particularly walking, bicycling and cross-country running. I liked fives and enjoyed football and cricket, if they were not taken too seriously, but rebelled against the obsession about winning games competitions and the all-pervading assumption that prowess and success at games were to be achieved above all else.

The time spent 'up to books', that is in the class-room, was a welcome relief. I was good at it, although not outstanding by the very high standards of Winchester. The teaching was excellent and the dons, as the masters were called, with few exceptions, were men who knew how to inspire their pupils and develop their minds and characters. I progressed rapidly up the school, with the exception of one disastrous term under a horrid old man called Blakeney. I was lucky to escape from his division after only one term. My forte was the classics, and I gravitated to that speciality, although the enlightened curriculum of the time saw to it that every-one had a grounding in moderately advanced mathematics, including the theory of relativity, and in biology, physics and chemistry. Time that was not spent in the classroom or on the playing field was spent in one's 'toys', a small open-sided cubicle in the main room of the house. Only the house prefects had studies, and even those were diminutive. One's work was done, one's whole life passed, in a crowd. My 'toys' was close to the house gramophone, which, in the hours when it was allowed to be in use, blared out the current popular tunes close to my left ear. In later years the ability to concentrate my mind and get on with my work in spite of the distraction of a high level of noise was to come in very useful. My other two assets were a photographic memory and an ability to read at high speed. The latter, I believe, was acquired by starting to read at an exceptionally early age, which included reading Shakespeare avidly before I understood much of what I read. As a result I acquired the valuable habit of taking in a broad span of words at one glance.

The impression left on me is that my first two years at Winchester were as unhappy as my time at St Peter's Court had been, except that, to a limited extent, one could escape. I loved the buildings, the river and its water-meadows, the magnificent cathedral and the surrounding countryside.

One's passport to freedom was the bicycle. Once one had fulfilled the imposed norm of exercise (bicycling and walking did not count), and provided that one kept out of the town of Winchester itself (unless one had been given permission by the housemaster to go there to do some shopping) and did not visit that sink of iniquity, Southampton, one was free to go anywhere. The only limit was the need to be back in time for the next roll-call. I was a keen and energetic cyclist and became an expert map-reader as a result.

At about this time, in 1930, we left Cheshire and moved to a smaller house in Shropshire. I suspect that there were several reasons for this. Business was poor and the firm of Carver Brothers was in difficulties. The bonus, which had added significantly to my father's salary, had dwindled, if not totally disappeared. There were now four of us at expensive boarding schools. I have no idea what the situation was about the rent of Turner Heath, or even whom it belonged to; but the house and garden could not be managed without several servants. As we grew up, sport and social life in Cheshire tended to be expensive. My parents were therefore probably considering a move when they went to stay with an old friend from Egypt days, Lindsay Bury, who lived in a large imitation of a Roman villa, Millechope Park, in southern Shropshire. While they were there, they discovered that a house which, although small, had six bedrooms and two paddocks, stables and a tennis court, was to let. It was said at one time to have been a public house, the Three Horseshoes, although I doubt it. Now it was called Bank House, being near the bank of a stream, a few miles from Millechope, in the hamlet of Ticklerton three miles south-east of Church Stretton; and thither we moved in the autumn of 1930. We were to be very happy there. Field sports were cheap: the countryside was beautiful, and we were in easy reach of glorious walks, on Wenlock Edge, the Long Mynd, Caer Caradoc and others. We could indulge to our hearts' delight in what became our principal activity, following hounds on foot and by car. Our parents took risks, which today would seem high, by letting us drive the car long before we were old enough to qualify for a driving licence. In Cheshire we had been close to the Derbyshire moors and learned to drive on their open roads, on which anyone approaching could be seen from a long

way off. I was driving the car at the age of thirteen, and
continued to do so regularly away from towns until, at
seventeen, I could do so legally. There was no test in those
days. Fortunately we never got into trouble, although there
were one or two anxious moments.

After the move, my father lived as a paying guest with a
doctor at Chelford, 15 miles south of Manchester, and came
home for weekends. He was going through a difficult time.
Business was bad and relations with his cousins in the firm
were sour. Although keen on sports – real and lawn tennis,
cricket, riding and shooting – he had become very fat. I
suspect that this may have been connected with his relations
with my mother. She had given birth to four sons in fairly
quick succession, although separated from my father for
most of the war. In 1921 she had suffered an attack of
angina, and I suspect had decided to have no more children.
She was extremely reticent in matters concerning sex, and I
doubt if she had any knowledge of contraceptive measures.
Although I have no proof of it, apart from the fact that
they slept in separate beds, I suspect that at this time my
father was sexually frustrated, and that this contributed to
his obesity, for which, one year, he had to undergo a cure. He
may not, therefore, have objected too strongly to a régime
which brought him home only at weekends. Unfortunately
it meant that we saw less of him in the holidays, and our
relationship with him was not as close as with our mother.
Looking back, I regret this. We had much in common. He
took a cynical but tolerant view of life and his fellow human
beings, and was much more realistic about the former and
sympathetic to the latter than my mother. She had never
been to school. As a result she combined romanticism and
naïveté about life and people with a priggish, prudish and
unsympathetic attitude to those with whom she had little or
nothing in common. She did not readily make friends, but
was devoted to the few she counted as such, as she was to
her family and we to her. My father was sparing in his
advice to us as we grew up. I think he felt he had been
a failure and had no right to impose his views on us or
influence us strongly. 'The only vice is excess' was one of the
few precepts he recommended. 'Keep off married women'
was another.

The year of 1931, when I was 16, was a decisive one in my life. It determined both my general outlook and my future career. Up to that time I had wished to conform, to be accepted by my contemporaries as one of them. Antony, who had had an even unhappier time than I had, both at St Peter's Court and at Winchester, influenced me in the opposite direction; to reject the conformism and conventions of the majority and to lay great emphasis on originality, on taking a different line from the crowd. He himself had decided to go into the Royal Air Force, itself an act of originality at that time, and he left Winchester for Cranwell, the RAF College, that summer. A second influence was that of religion. I had always been inclined to take religion seriously, and this was greatly intensified by preparation by my housemaster for confirmation that autumn. I became fairly intensely religious, and the emphasis in so many sermons that one must reject the world and the low moral standards of the crowd reinforced my tendency to despise the habits, values and conventions of the common herd. There is no doubt that I became a prudish prig, and it is not surprising that I was not very popular.

While I was struggling with these problems of adolescence, I was under increasing pressure to decide on my future career. Rodney had gone into the navy and was at Dartmouth. Paul would soon be following Antony and myself to Winchester. Carver Brothers' business was going from bad to worse, and the burden of school bills was weighing heavily on my father. He made it clear to me that he could not afford to pay for a long training in a profession, nor would he be able to afford to send me to a university, unless I won a scholarship which defrayed most of the cost. I would have liked to follow my uncle, Dick Wellesley, to Clare College at Cambridge and was attracted to the idea of journalism or possibly the law. However it was thought that my chances of gaining such a scholarship were doubtful, although I was well up the school for my age. School life was beginning to open up more horizons and interests. I was a keen member of the debating society, speaking in which had helped me to master a stammer from which I had always suffered. I was also a keen member of the literary society and, although not a skilful singer, of the choral society,

Glee Club. I tried my hand at poetry and generally enjoyed the varied cultural activities which Winchester provided, both in the class-room and outside. Interest in the arts had been encouraged at home. Both my parents were keen on music, my father having an excellent baritone voice, and both appreciated the visual arts and literature, my mother rather more than my father. As far as sport was concerned, I played unskilful football and cricket, the only sports in which my performance was any better than average being cross-country running, swimming and fives.

It was therefore a surprising decision that I made in February 1932, two months before my seventeenth birthday, that I would go into the army. In the diary which I kept at the time, the entry for 27 February 1932 reads:

> Letter from Antony. He says that Mum and Dad have been discussing my career again and are more earnestly set on Sandhurst than ever, and are bound to put it to me soon. It either means giving in and conforming oneself to a life which is not of one's own choosing, or else leaping into the dark and making oneself look at any rate as if one was content with a life, which after all is after one's own choosing, in an attempt to justify oneself, whether or not one is in fact content with it. He thanked God that his leap had been so satisfactory.

My comment on his letter was that the worst thing about my case was that there was nowhere, except the Church, to leap to. Having turned it over and over in my mind, I decided to write to my parents next day and say that I had decided to go for the army, which I said to myself was 'not so bad and at least secure', and apologized for the delay in making up my mind. My recollection, although it is not recorded in my diary, is that I thought of it as a way of becoming financially independent at an early age, and, as I understood that one did not have to work very hard in the army, a secure base from which I could study for another profession. My parents warmly welcomed my decision. They had practically no capital and my father would not earn any pension. His five-year contract was nearing its end and he suspected, correctly, that it might not be renewed. At that time of severe recession and high unemployment, they attached great importance to security. I believe that it was this emphasis on security, combined with a desire for social status, that led them to encourage us all to become officers in the armed forces, as all but Paul did.

The decision having been made, I could relax. I was exceptionally fortunate in my 'div dons' or form masters, first Cyril Robinson (The Bin), one of the most inspiring of teachers, and later, when I moved up into 'Sixth Book', Mr Philip, a much younger man. The latter, appreciating that the Sandhurst examination would pose me no problem, allowed me to follow my own bent, provided that I complied with the basic curriculum, fundamentally the classics. That summer of 1932 seemed a blissful interlude. I was high enough up in the school to have escaped from the feeling of oppression. I was free to do what I liked in many different fields. The requirement to take military drawing in the Sandhurst examination brought me into contact with one of the most interesting of Winchester's outstanding body of teachers, Richard Gleadowe, art master and Slade Professor. One might have thought that he would have regarded teaching military drawing as far beneath him. Not at all. Through it he taught me to analyse what I really saw, and opened up to me not only a fresh appreciation of the visual arts, but also the joy of attempting to put on paper, or canvas, one's own perception of an object. Drawing from memory a saddle lying on the ground was one of the tasks he set me.

Having decided to enter the army, I had to turn my mind to the choice of corps or regiment I should join. Being a poor mathematician, the Royal Engineers or Artillery, involving Woolwich instead of Sandhurst, seemed to be ruled out. The only army contacts we had were my godfather and cousin, Gerald Dalby, at that time a colonel, whose regiment was the 60th Rifles (The King's Royal Rifle Corps), and another colonel, Hugh Hibbert, son of Admiral Hibbert, one of our great friends, whose house at Longparish was an ever-popular refuge from Winchester. Hugh Hibbert was in the King's Own Yorkshire Light Infantry. Both these regiments expected one to have some private income to supplement one's pay, the 60th's expectation being the higher. The choice I made was influenced by my contact with the Royal

Air Force at Worthy Down, a few miles outside Winchester. One of the officers there was a nephew of Admiral Hibbert, Dick Barlow, who had been influential in persuading Antony to join the RAF. He had taken me for my first flight, an alarming and very cold one in the tail-gunner's seat of a Vickers Virginia night-bomber. A brother officer of his, McGill, told me that he had started off in the infantry and been intensely bored: he recommended the Royal Tank Corps. His advice was reinforced by a friend of a friend, Derek Hutchinson, who was seconded from the Royal Tank Corps to the RAF. The fact that it was a corps with its eyes very much on the future; that it would, I hoped, be less bound by tradition and convention; that it would provide an interest in its mechanical side, and not expect me to have a private income, all influenced me to decide towards the end of 1932 to apply to join it.

At that time I was still as serious about religion as I had been at my confirmation a year before, but my priggishness had abated somewhat, thanks to the advice of one of Winchester's noted dons, Budge Firth, who, at about that time, took holy orders himself. He was a tubby, short-sighted bachelor with a high voice, who ran both the debating and the literary societies. He was also a notable cricketer. Antony had spent a considerable time in his division and had found him more sympathetic than any other don. In the course of a discussion, in which I had held forth about the need for a radical reform of Wykehamical society, Firth suggested that I should stop complaining about other people's faults and concentrate on curing my own. He put it in such an understanding way that, instead of resenting it, I resolved to accept his advice and do my best to follow it. As a result my personal relations with my contemporaries improved.

These were years of high unemployment, a fact which had been brought home to us when we had lived on the edge of the cotton-spinning town of Bollington, and of which we were reminded whenever we visited Manchester, which we did to go to Gilbert and Sullivan operettas, to the tailor or the dentist, and when we drove through the towns of the Midlands, such as Wolverhampton, where we would meet my father on Friday evenings, if he did not come to Shrewsbury. One of my subjects of special study was the history of the trade union movement. That, my personal contact with the effect of mass unemployment, and my desire to do good for my fellow men, led me to take an interest in organizations intended to alleviate the effects of poverty and unemployment. In this year I spent several days first with the Toc H 'Mark' in Derby and then with the Mansfield Settlement in the East End of London. In politics I regarded myself as a Liberal, not one of the National Liberals who had joined the National Government under Ramsay Macdonald in 1931, but a follower of Lloyd George. When the debating society had held its own election to coincide with the general election, I had stood as the Liberal candidate, fervently supporting Free Trade, and had come bottom of the poll with only nine votes. The other candidates and their votes were: Mitchell-Thomson (later Lord Selsdon), Conservative 72; Mancroft (later Lord Mancroft), New Party (Mosley) 41; Tancred, Independent 39; Nicholson, Communist 16; Bennett, Labour 14.

Mitchell-Thomson was to become one of my *bêtes noires*. In 1932 he was senior prefect of the house and leader of the tough, games-playing, bawdy, philistine element, with which I found myself increasingly at loggerheads. After he had left and I myself had become a prefect, Toby Low (later Lord Aldington) – not one of that group – being the senior prefect, I became a target for their dislike, an aversion that was mutual. Life, having been relaxed for about a year, became tense and unhappy again, and I was longing to escape from school, although I was beginning to view the prospect of life in the army with some apprehension.

During the Easter holidays I suffered more than I normally had from indigestion, to which I had been prone for some time, partly no doubt because I was a voracious eater. Appendicitis was diagnosed and it was decided that I should undergo the operation in a nursing home in Shrewsbury at the end of the holidays. Convalescence in those days was lengthy, and it would mean that I would only have a few weeks back at school before the army entrance examination at the end of June. This did not worry me, as I was confident that I would pass with ease and revision would be easier while convalescing than at school with all its distractions. However, the decision to operate coincided with a letter from Mr

Browne, the don who dealt with such matters, telling me that the Civil Service Commissioners had ruled that I could not take French as well as Latin and Greek, as the rules laid down that not more than two foreign languages could be taken! He advised me to take history instead. I realized with a shock that I had studied little of English history at Winchester, most of the history I had read having been that of Greece and Rome. However, Mr Browne said that a thorough reading of G. M. Trevelyan's *History of England* should get me through, and I applied myself diligently to it. He was proved right, as I achieved 72 per cent in the history paper.

I did not return to Winchester until 6 June, three weeks before the examination. Once it was over, I enjoyed the relaxed atmosphere of feeling that I had nothing more to worry about. I left Winchester with a strong dislike of public school life, but with gratitude for the education that I had received there, its academic teaching, its cultural activities and its beautiful surroundings. The largely classical education that I had received implanted in me a critical and analytical outlook. I was a devotee of Socrates in questioning everything and seeking the rational solution. I am afraid that it made me tiresomely argumentative. I believed that argument could persuade men to recognize the rational solution and to adopt it. Later experience was to disillusion me on this score, until it seemed to me that the rational solution was almost the last thing that would be adopted. The familiar or the received prejudice of the party or clique was preferred by most people, who wished to avoid the mental effort involved in thinking out problems *ab initio*. I tended to be an iconoclast. Whatever the disadvantages such an attitude might have, it made it easy for me to learn new subjects, a talent for which I was to be grateful in the years to come.

I went straight from school at the end of term to stay with the Watsons at Caythorpe in Lincolnshire. This had become an annual escape from the family. Diana Watson was the same age as myself and was the only child of Frank and Audrey Watson, who had married late in life. They were old friends of Dick Wellesley, Frank Watson being Financial Adviser to the Egyptian Government. Frank and Audrey were believed to have been engaged for 13 years because she would not leave the hunting in winter to join him in Egypt.

They spent every summer with Audrey's unmarried sisters, Nora and Hilda Reid, at Caythorpe Hall, a large Georgian country house. Holidays there consisted almost entirely of one tennis tournament after another. I greatly enjoyed being away from the family in the company of Diana and her cousins Leila and Lydia Watson, who lived nearby.

Soon after I got home, the results of the army entrance examination arrived. I had passed in eighth. I was slightly disappointed, having hoped for one of the first three places; but it was gratifying, and I qualified for a Prize Cadetship, which reduced the fees my father had to pay by £25 a year. The die was now cast, and it was with mixed feelings that I faced the future. I was keen to become independent and to set off on an active career; but I realized that army life would have much in common with all those things I had disliked most about school life, and I was doubtful if I was physically or temperamentally suited to the life of a soldier.

2

For a Soldier I Listed

For a soldier I listed, to grow great in fame,
And be shot at for sixpence a day.
                    Charles Dibdin (1745-1814), *Chanty*

My 1933 diary stopped abruptly at the end of my visit to
Caythorpe. The next, terse entry is on 1 September:

Join RMC (Royal Military College). Rather appalled: hus-
tled about like hell: everything very much the military.
Place like a prison.

There is then no further entry for three weeks, when it was
resumed. In that day's entry I wrote:

I hated it when I first came here. Grind, grind, grind, and
cursed at the end of it. I dislike it less now, but do not like
it much yet. Easier when less to clean. Trying to keep in
close touch with God, but very hard to remember all the
time; only easy when nothing to do.

A week later I wrote to Jack Parr, my housemaster at Winchester. He kept the letter and returned it to me 41 years
later, when I was a Field Marshal and Chief of the Defence
Staff. I wrote:

Life here is not exactly the acme of comfort or conveni-
ence; you probably know more or less what the life one
leads in this place is. It is of course a very great contrast

to Win. Coll. No spare time at all, and all the out-of-work
hours have to be spent cleaning equipment. As we batter
our rifles, bayonets, scabbards etc. about on the square
every morning, and they have to be polished like glass for
inspections four times a week, every little minute is taken
up. I have just about recovered from the shock of the first
two or three weeks, and can (metaphorically only) sit down
and take notice of my surroundings and companions.
They are a mixed lot, not all so stupid as one is led to
suppose, quite a number of good men, plenty of medium,
and one or two pretty nasty. For the first time really I
can begin to observe in detail the difference between the
outlook of Win. Coll. and Portsmouth Grammar. The
place overflows with chaps from Wellington, and their
outlook does not really correspond with the Wykehamist;
quite what is the radical difference I don't quite know, but
I hope to find out. There is one thing that does annoy me
rather with most of them, and that is the way in which
they regard the written and mental work in this place.
All of it, especially Map Reading, Tactics, Organization
and Administration and things like that are part of one's
job, which one has got to know. The instructors mostly
do their best to impress on us that we are no longer
at school, and are learning our job; but the majority
regard it as a lesson which one has got to do because
the officer tells one to and that is all. It is unfair, I
think, on the troops if they are put in the charge of
an officer who hasn't taken the trouble to learn his job
thoroughly – they can't refuse to serve under him and
their lives are in his hands; but I suppose the passing out
standard is sufficient knowledge for an officer. They may
know it in time, but it seems a wrong attitude to what
is after all one's life's work. The work we do is fairly
interesting, which is more than one can say about seven
hours a week on the square. I am looking forward to the
beginning of November when we pass off the square and
have a long week-end off. After that, only three hours a
week on the square. My company commander is an old
Sergeantite – Major C. Nicholson of the 16th Lancers. He
knew Mr Monro and seemed to know you too. Of course
we see very little of him. The two terrors of the place are

the Battalion Sergeant–Major and the Adjutant, a very formidable combination!

The drill was not the worst part. Well done it could be quite enjoyable. The two bugbears of life at Sandhurst were the frantic rush in which diverse activities followed each other – drill, physical training, study, equitation each demanding a different uniform with only the minimum time to change from one to the other – and woe betide anyone improperly dressed: and, worst of all, the hours spent in polishing and cleaning one's uniform and equipment. The leather had to have a surface like glass and the metalwork shine like the stars. However much hard work one put into it, the result never satisfied the under-officers, and it was immediately ruined as soon as one went on parade and bashed it all about. The rich could bribe the college servants to do their cleaning for them, being doubly rewarded by the excellence of the result and by being spared the effort needed to produce it. These injustices, the way one was shouted at and abused in foul language by the cadet NCOs and under-officers, and the general philistinism of the place made it seem like purgatory. Fortunately the four terms of the whole course only lasted for 15 months, and one lived in the expectation that life would be improving as every month went by after the rude shock of initiation.

I was fortunate in finding a few kindred spirits in my company, Number 4 Company in the Old Building, the principal one being William Collingwood. He and I shared a love of music and the arts and a contempt for the values and attitude of the crowd, in which Old Wellingtonians formed a large bloc. (He had been at Charterhouse.) Life did improve in subsequent terms, and one of the principal pleasures for me was equitation which was compulsory. Although by no means an expert horseman, I enjoyed riding. The instructors were hard-bitten cavalry sergeants, who made us start from scratch the hard way, as if we were cavalry recruits. The result was wholly beneficial, and for the first time in my life I began to feel entirely secure in the saddle, however ill-behaved and ill-tempered the horse might be, and many of them were. I found much of the military instruction interesting and enjoyed outdoor work such as map-reading

and tactical exercises, although I found rifle-shooting, at
which I was no good, extremely boring. As a candidate
for the Royal Tank Corps, I naturally studied mechanical
engineering as a voluntary subject, under the supervision
of Captain 'Pip' Crouch of the Corps. He had impressed on
me how keen was the competition to enter his Corps. The
course was really no more than elementary garage work,
but it was an occupation I enjoyed, having always been keen
on tinkering about with machines, although never expert at
it. Cross-country running remained the only sport at which
I was anything more than average, if that; but, when the
summer came round in my third term, I joined an unofficial
team of cricketers, who did not take it seriously and amused
themselves by playing against local villages. I was an erratic
bowler and a wild batsman, but enjoyed it. With more time on
my hands than in my first term, I resumed my literary activities and wrote a number of articles for the college journal,
the one over which I took most trouble being an assessment
of Prince Eugène, Marlborough's great colleague. In this I
was encouraged by Lieutenant Lytton-Milbanke of the Rifle
Brigade, later the Earl of Lytton, and himself of literary bent,
perhaps inherited from Byron.

At the end of my first year I came second in the academic
list, although in military rank I had not progressed beyond
lance-corporal. This brought me a cadet scholarship worth
£60, £20 of which my father returned to me, most, if not
all, of which I devoted to hunting in my last term. For ten
shillings one could hire one of the college horses for a day
to hunt with the Garth hounds, who, I think, charged cadets
ten shillings as a 'cap'. The previous winter I had had to
make a choice between continuing to play golf, which I had
done with enjoyment but no great skill since I was about ten,
or hunting. At home in Shropshire the latter meant hiring
a horse for about £3 a day and paying a cap of about £1.
I could not afford both golf and hunting, and, when my
brother Rodney went to sea in HMS *Frobisher*, taking some
of my golf-clubs with him, I came down firmly on the side of
hunting. Now much more confident in the saddle, I became
a keen follower.

Antony, who had been with Number 43 Squadron RAF
at Tangmere, equipped with the Gamecock fighter, since

he left Cranwell, was now posted to Number 8 Squadron in Aden. He had an A-model Ford two-seater and suggested that I should look after it for him, until he could either ship it out or sell it. Cadets (Gentleman Cadets, as they were called) at Sandhurst were not allowed to have cars, but I had a sympathetic platoon officer in Eric Bols of the Devonshire Regiment, who turned a blind eye and let me keep it in his garage. Life in my last term, when I was promoted to junior under-officer, was therefore a great improvement on all that had gone before, and I was by now reconciled to the idea of life in the army, although I did not intend to be committed to it for ever.

At the beginning of that term, however, I nearly gave it up altogether. During the summer holidays I had attended the northern equivalent of the Duke of York's camp, held in Chatsworth Park in Derbyshire. One of the organizers was a young parson, whom I had met when I had visited the Toc H Mark at Derby and who was then working with Toc H in Manchester. He had invited me to help run the camp, and, while there, told me that he was going out to New Zealand to do similar work there. He tried to persuade me to go with him and to consider the possibility of training to be a priest when I got there. He was a man for whom I had a great admiration, and I considered his proposal very carefully. I made no mention of it to my parents, but, when I returned to Sandhurst after the summer holidays, went to see the chaplain, Padre Heale, and discussed it with him, saying that I had almost made up my mind to go. Fortunately for me, as I now believe, he dissuaded me, and my thoughts never turned in that direction again.

At the end of 1934 I passed out first in the list, thus gaining the King's Gold Medal and the Anson Memorial Sword, together with the prizes for Economics, Military History and Military Law. Of more practical value was an army scholarship, worth £50 a year for five years. Although I realized that the intellectual competition I had been up against had not been very challenging, I was naturally proud of my achievement and delighted that it brought such pleasure to my parents, who had done so much for me.

I had a month's leave before I was commissioned on 31 January 1935. My father had to go to Paris and Stuttgart on business, and my mother and I went with him to Paris and stayed there. It was my first trip abroad, and it whetted my appetite for foreign travel. We went to two plays, one of which was the French version of Margaret Kennedy's *The Constant Nymph*, in which Louis Jouvet and Madeleine Ozeray took the principal parts. I was entranced. We visited the Louvre, Versailles and all the usual sights, and although January was not the best month to visit Paris I fell in love with the whole atmosphere of the city. I could read French fairly easily, but soon realized that the pronunciation learnt at school was incomprehensible to the average Frenchman.

Young officers joining the Royal Tank Corps did not go direct to one of the battalions (as they were known in those days), but to the depot at Bovington in Dorset to spend seven months learning driving and maintenance, gunnery (at Lulworth a few miles away), and tactics. The advantage of this system was that the young officer, when he reached his unit, was not totally ignorant and would be qualified to supervise his men. The disadvantage was that it was yet another bout of school and that one was not welcomed into the family life of a unit. The reverse was the case. We were treated once more as schoolboys, starting at the bottom all over again, and in no way made to feel welcome. The adjutant, Rupert Noel-Clarke, was a fussy, rather pompous man and I soon found myself in trouble. Having had our fill of drill at Sandhurst, we found ourselves on the square again under the instruction of a particularly tiresome little sergeant, who wasted a lot of time putting us through saluting drill. One day, after we had finished our drill parade, our paths crossed somewhere in the camp and he failed to salute me. I put him on a charge, but found myself hauled over the coals instead. My next misdemeanour concerned calling. We had to leave visiting cards on the wives of all the officers in the garrison. As this could only be done between three and four o'clock in the afternoon, the whole process took up a lot of afternoons. I had the bright idea of going round on the afternoon of an important football match, which we all had to watch, and I could be fairly confident that most of the wives would dutifully be doing so with their husbands. I was right and got rid of almost all my cards; but my trick was spotted and I was up before the adjutant again. My next appearance before him was for failing in my duty as officer in charge of the brigadier's daughter. Sheila Bolton was a not very exciting 16-year-old, and I had been ordered to dine with the Old Wykehamist brigadier commanding the centre, and to escort his daughter to the mess dance at the Gunnery School at Lulworth. Once there, I found more interesting company, and she was left unattended for several dances. The adjutant was not pleased when, as my appearance before him seemed to be becoming a weekly event, I suggested that he would save us both time and trouble, if he waited until the end of the month and rebuked me for all my sins of the month at one time.

On the whole I enjoyed my time there. I liked driving vehicles of all kinds, especially tanks, and was already proficient on a motor-cycle, having ridden the one that Antony owned when he was at Cranwell. Although I never found mastering the details of intricate mechanisms easy, I found it interesting, particularly the practical work. The country round about was lovely and I had acquired a car, a new Ford 8, paying for it by what is now called hire-purchase, which raised its price from £100 to £115. My pay as a 2nd Lieutenant was 9s 10d* a day. There was very little of this left over by the time I had paid my mess bill, although I limited my drinking in the mess to about a pint of beer a week. I had taken up smoking as it gave me relief from the allergy caused by riding horses but I only smoked about six cigarettes a day, cheap Cypriot ones. In addition to my pay I had my army scholarship of £50 a year, and my father gave me £100, making it clear that it could not be repeated in future years, as his job was coming to an end that year, although he was only 57. By careful managing, refusing to go pub-crawling or chasing the girls in Bournemouth, and keeping to my self-imposed limits on drinking and smoking, I managed to pay for the car and enjoy myself. When summer came, we moved to the Gunnery School at Lulworth and were able to bathe in the sea and walk along the lovely cliffs between the Cove and St Alban's Head. I had my first experience of sailing there, crewing for Basil Carey,

---

* Equivalent to 48p at the time of decimalization in 1970, although its purchasing power in 1935 was, of course, much higher

as well as of the Royal Navy and its hospitality. Rodney's ship, HMS *Neptune*, was based at Portland at the time and I have a clear memory of a very convivial evening in her gunroom. I was still at Bovington, before the move to Lulworth, when T. E. Lawrence, whose cottage, 'Clouds,' was hidden in thick rhododendrons at the back of the tank driving area, suffered the motor-cycle accident from which he died. While he lay unconscious in the small military hospital at Bovington, the friends who came to see him stayed in the officers' mess, and I had the opportunity to talk to some of them, like Colonel Newcombe. Lawrence was something of a hero to me at that time, and I had seen him on his motor-cycle once or twice, but never close-up.

We were due to join our battalions in October, and by then were keen to do so. I was posted to the 2nd Battalion at Pinehurst Barracks, Farnborough, on the edge of Aldershot. The one and only Tank Brigade had been formed on 1 April 1934 with three medium battalions, the 2nd at Farnborough, the 3rd at Lydd in Kent and the 5th at Perham Down near Tidworth on Salisbury Plain, while the 1st (Light) Battalion was formed from their light companies. The only other battalion, the 4th, was not in the brigade. It was at Catterick in Yorkshire and specialized in the support of infantry. When the medium battalions lost their light companies, they were reorganized into three mixed companies, each having a close-support section of two medium tanks, equipped with 3.7-inch howitzers for firing high-explosive and smoke, a medium section of five medium tanks, all of them the old Vickers medium Mark I or II, and a light section of seven. Owing to the recent formation of 1st (Light) Battalion, the light sections had no light tanks when I joined, and had to make do with Carden-Loyd carriers or 15-hundredweight trucks. However, the advantage from my point of view was that the officers of the light companies had also gone to the 1st Battalion and I found myself, on joining the 2nd, commanding the light section of B Company, and the only officer in it.

My company commander was the highly decorated, scatter-brained, chain-smoking, friendly but hopelessly inefficient Major Drake-Brockman. He was not of much help to a young officer desperately keen to learn his job, but he was no hindrance either. The only other officers in the company were the second-in-command, who also commanded the close-support section, Sid Bearne, a large, taciturn, sensible and helpful captain, who quietly saw to it that Drake-Brockman's idiosyncrasies did not do any harm, and Tony Lascelles, a fellow Old Wykehamist, who had come into the army through Oxford. A shy, scholarly man with an excellent brain, he was a first-class athlete and player of ball-games. My section sergeant was a tough old soldier, Sergeant Sharman, who was up to a good many tricks and, as I came to learn, needed keeping up to the mark. My soldiers were of a high standard in every respect, in intelligence, in behaviour and in their willingness to tackle anything. The soldier of the Royal Tank Corps of those days was the cream of the army. His chances of getting a job on leaving the colours were high, which was an attraction. If he did not pass the Third Class Army Certificate of Education during his recruit training, he was not accepted into the corps, and, if he wished to stay in the army, he had to join another corps. I found my soldiers friendly and helpful, and my greatest pleasure was my feeling of responsibility for them.

In 1976 I received a letter from one of them, ex-Trooper Burton, who won the Military Medal and finished his service as a Lieutenant-Quartermaster, in which he wrote: 'You drove us hard in those days, but the training you gave me stood me in good stead during the war years.'

I cannot say that I felt that I was warmly welcomed into a 'family' of officers, although received more so than at Bovington. The officers of the Royal Tank Corps were an odd mixture in those days. Some had been the pioneers of the tank in the First World War. They were of all kinds, and tended to be men of character. Some were officers who had joined since the war, because they saw the corps as the arm of the future. Some came from the disbanded Irish regiments, and they tended to be the least useful material. The younger officers tended to be more homogeneous in origin, mostly promising games players, who had an interest in motor-cars or motor-cycles, and little or no private income – very much the same material as those who joined the RAF. Most came from public schools, although few from Eton, Harrow or Winchester. One of the principal tasks of Captain

Crouch at Sandhurst was undoubtedly to recruit the best games-players, particularly rugger-players, that he could. The commanding officer, Lieutenant-Colonel 'Nini' Evans, was a pleasant, rather aloof man with an amusing French wife. I found life agreeable and was able to hunt with the Garth, riding a 'ten-bobber' hired from a cavalry regiment in Aldershot. This was an advantage of serving in a cheap regiment, which was not 'horsey'. William Collingwood, then serving with the Northumberland Fusiliers at Bordon, the other side of Aldershot, found that he could not afford to hunt, although he had a larger private income than I. This was because his regiment insisted that one had to hunt in top hat and black Melton coat and subscribe to the regimental polo fund.

At the end of 1935 Lieutenant-Colonel Evans was posted to Egypt to command the tanks there, sent out to deal with the threat from Italy, which had invaded Abyssinia. His place was taken by Douglas Pratt, a warmer character and an excellent commanding officer, who showed a keen interest in bringing on the younger officers and was deservedly popular with all ranks.

In January 1936 I went back to Bovington for six weeks for a wireless instructor's course, one that I was glad I had done. On return, another subaltern and I, with Corporal Robinson who had done a similar course in India, were faced with the task of training fifty wireless operators from scratch, as the Royal Tank Corps had just taken over from the Royal Corps of Signals responsibility for operating its own wireless sets. It was a challenging task and a rewarding one, at which we worked long hours. As the summer approached, I turned from cross-country running to training for the athletic team, in which I was the least skilful of the four hurdlers, an event I had taken up at Winchester to avoid running in the three miles, which I found boring.

Every summer the Tank Brigade concentrated in camp at Tilshead on Salisbury Plain for three months of training. Here we exercised under the eagle eye of the fierce brigade commander, the great 'Hobo', Percy Hobart. He was a merciless trainer, who drove us all hard and overlooked no detail, his intensity matched by his keen interest in all ranks under his command. He was universally respected, admired and served with enthusiasm. But the summer of 1936 was a disappointing one. The 1st (Light) Battalion had been sent to Egypt and had taken most of the wireless sets with it. The two-man Carden–Loyd carrier, its T-model Ford engine boiling over all the time, could hardly move any faster than walking-pace across country, and the 15-hundredweight truck was not much better – in wet weather worse. Once camp was over, I found myself on a course again. After a year with his battalion, every young officer in the Royal Tank Corps was sent on a six-month course at the Royal Military College of Science, then at Woolwich. It consisted of five months of elementary science, linked to military subjects, and one month's practical work in the workshops. We lived in bare rooms behind the Royal Artillery Mess, to which we had to pay only a shilling a day. Here we saw traditional army mess life at its most formal, from which we could escape to London when our finances, helped by the low mess charges, allowed. Although regretting having to leave the battalion for six months just as I was finding my feet, I enjoyed this period. I could ride one of the Royal Artillery depot horses before breakfast, accompanying the course for Ordnance Mechanical Engineers, who were forced to learn to ride before being posted to India, and my brother Rodney was doing his sub-lieutenant's course at Greenwich at the same time. I would pick him up in my car and we could go up to London together, on the way back having a pint of beer and a hot-dog in the skittle alley of the Royal Naval College. We were the same group of six young officers that had been at Bovington together, one of whom was a wild Australian called Wallace. His antics earned us a reputation for bad behaviour, and the Inspector Royal Tank Corps, Brigadier Patterson, came down from the War Office to rebuke us.

A month's leave followed the course, and I took the opportunity to indulge in some foreign travel. My grandmother, Nora Wellesley, had been compensated some years before by the State of Texas for the closure of a tiny oil well, which Courtenay had left her. This had brought her £2,000, one-sixteenth of which was distributed to each of her grandsons on their twenty-first birthday. With interest, this brought me £132, which I had decided to spend on travel.

My mother and I spent a week visiting Belgium, Luxemburg
and the valleys of the Moselle and the Rhine, travelling in
my car. We naturally visited the battlefield of Waterloo, and
found the Ardennes attractive, although the weather was far
from ideal, as we did also the Moselle valley. I was able to
practise my German and to see something of what life under
the Nazis was like, soldiers and swastikas everywhere. On the
return journey we went to a ludicrously bad performance of
Parsifal in Brussels, which put me off Wagner for life.

I was to spend the rest of my foreign travel money on a
longer trip in the autumn. A Shropshire friend, John Shaw,
was going to stay with a family in Vienna to improve his
German and to drive out there with a friend of his, Raymond
Thompson, a budding stockbroker, whose Ford V8 would
provide the transport. I was delighted to join them, and we
set off in October through France to Monte Carlo. We gave
Paris a miss, and our first real bit of sight-seeing was to be
the first of several visits in my life to the attractive little town
of Vézelay, between Auxerre and Avallon, with its lovely
Basilique de la Madeleine. I had discovered that neither of
my companions was a keen sightseer, being fonder of the
flesh-pots. We spent two days at Monte Carlo, driving round
the countryside by day and getting rid of our francs at the
Casino in the evening. From there we headed straight for
Venice, with little time to stop and see anything on the way.
In spite of rain, Venice fulfilled all my expectations. Being
the end of October, there were few tourists about and, when
the clouds lifted and the sun broke through, the palaces and
churches shone with a marvellous brilliance. I spent most
of the time admiring their interiors and the pictures they
contained, an enthusiasm my companions did not share.
The same applied to Vienna when we got there. I found it
both a beautiful and sad city. Its glories had departed, and
its cafés, with their newspapers in wooden holders, full of
old people dressed as if for a funeral, consoling themselves
with chocolate cakes, had a mournful air. One could feel
the menace of Nazi Germany, close at hand, a threat that
had been hanging over Austria since the murder of Dollfuss
three years before.

After four days in Vienna, Raymond and I set off back,
stopping at Salzburg and visiting Berchtesgaden on our way

to Munich, where I was greatly impressed by the pictures in the Alte Pinakothec and the capacity of the Germans for beer in the Hofbrau. At Rothenburg-am-Tauber, the unspoilt medieval buildings were marred by Nazi swastika flags hanging from every window. In general, we found the Germans in the countryside polite and friendly, while those in the towns tended to be grim, surly and suspicious of foreigners. We saw several signs of anti-Semitism, especially in Frankfurt, where the synagogues were boarded up, with their windows broken. The trip had been a cultural feast for me and widened my horizons, further whetting my appetite for foreign travel.

On my return to Farnborough after my first trip, I had found many changes, all for the good. Drake-Brockman had been replaced by Brevet-Lieutenant-Colonel John Crocker. After the First World War, in which he had served in the infantry, he had returned to his profession of solicitor, but disliked it and joined the Royal Tank Corps when it was officially formed in 1923. He had an excellent, clear brain and was a man of outstanding ability and absolute integrity, setting and demanding the highest standards in every respect. He spoke quietly, even when angry, and was always calm and cool-headed. His greatest asset to a young inexperienced officer was his insistence that one must make

one's own decisions. If they were wrong, he would correct them, in private and in the most constructive manner. I learnt more from him about how to command soldiers than from any other man, and was very fortunate to be in his company at that time. He was to rise to great heights in the army, finishing his career as Adjutant-General. The other very welcome change was that the Carden-Loyd carriers and 15-hundredweight trucks had been replaced by light tanks, mostly the two-man Mark III, but with a few of the faster two-man Mark IVs. I took over the light section again and was given the additional responsibility of carrying out trials on the experimental machine which Martel was favouring. It consisted of a Christie-type suspension (as had already been adopted by the Russians for the machine that was later to be developed into the famous T34), the engine being a 500-h.p. Napier aero engine, fitted transversely between the rear sprockets. Since the tank was nothing more than an open box of just sufficient strength to form the structure for the tracks and weighing only a few tons, it naturally had a remarkably lively performance, and was very exciting to drive. The only seat was the driver's, and when Colonel Crawford, the Assistant Director of Mechanization at the War Office, came down to see it show off its paces, the only thing I could give him to sit on was a wooden box. I accelerated down the road, which now forms part of Farnborough airfield, and, travelling at high speed, abruptly turned off onto the trial ground. The colonel was not prepared for this and was rather badly knocked about, which may have accounted for the fact that the trials were soon brought to an end. However, it was the basic prototype of the Nuffield Christie-type tank, later developed into the Crusader.

With John Crocker as company commander and a full section of seven light tanks, three of which were now the three-man Mark V, training on Salisbury Plain that year was a great advance, more realistic and more enjoyable. One incident had a lasting effect on me. Each company was being put through a test exercise by Hobo. After B Company's performance, I was sent for and rebuked for moving on the skyline. I attempted to argue that, although I may have appeared so from where Hobo was, I would not have been seen from where the enemy were supposed to be. I was dismissed with the words: 'Young man, you came here to learn, not to argue.' On return to camp, I was helping myself to lunch in the officers' mess tent, when Hobo came along, accompanied by Colonel Tilly, the chief instructor at Bovington. 'Hello, Carver, how are you?' said Tilly. 'Very well, thank you, Sir,' I replied. 'Yes,' said Hobo, 'very well and very insubordinate. Mark my words, Carver,' he added, 'the secret of success in the army is to be sufficiently insubordinate – and the key word is sufficiently.' Mark them I did, as he himself was to discover!

The year of 1937 was a busy one for me. In addition to my duties as section commander and wireless instructor, I was in charge of the battalion's highly successful motor-cycle trials team and was studying for a preliminary interpretership in German, which I passed towards the end of the year. At that time I also took over acting as adjutant while the latter, the well-known rugger player, 'Tinny' Dean, was on leave

for a month. It was a considerable responsibility for a 2nd
Lieutenant, and I learned much from it.

Although I was enjoying life at Farnborough I was longing
to go abroad. In those days, if an officer was posted abroad
and did not want to go, he could pay another officer to
go in his place. I had just concluded a satisfactory deal by
which I should not only achieve my aim of being posted to
an armoured car or light tank company in India, but would
receive £100 for doing so, when the posting order for the
officer whose place I was taking was unfortunately cancelled.
I was then twice posted myself, and on each occasion, to my
great disappointment, it was cancelled. Eventually a definite
posting came at the end of the year to the 1st (Light) Battalion. It had returned from Egypt towards the end of 1936, but
now was being sent out again. I was delighted at the prospect
of going there, and, after a month's embarkation leave at
home, hunting and attending hunt balls, I joined the 1st
Battalion at Perham Down at the end of January 1938, finding myself allotted the tasks of transport officer and baggage
officer for the move. Tony Lascelles had also come from the
2nd and was made adjutant. The commanding officer was a
fiery, hot-tempered, energetic and enthusiastic man, known
as 'Blood' Caunter. He could get very excited, and was said
to have been seen on an exercise in Egypt shouting into
his binoculars and beating the side of his tank with his
microphone. He certainly kept everyone on their toes.

We were due to sail in the aged troopship HMT *Nevasa* on
12 February, and only about ten days before, I was horrified
to be informed that, instead of going to Egypt with the
battalion, I was to go to Germany and join a German Panzer
Regiment in exchange for a German officer, who was to join
one of our battalions. This was an outcome of a recent visit by
Field Marshal Blomberg to the Tank Brigade. I was furious
and protested, apparently in vain. Then, fortunately for me,
relations between Germany and Austria deteriorated, Hitler
started his campaign of intimidation of Chancellor Schusch-
nigg, and the exchange was cancelled. If I had been serving
with a German Panzer Regiment in 1938 and 1939, I have no
doubt that my career would have taken a different course.

My reputation as an efficient officer was marred by
over-keenness in stowing the baggage in the railway trucks

at Tidworth. In my enthusiasm to get everything in, I had packed the trucks so full that they could only be unloaded from the side from which they had been loaded. Unfortunately, when the train was shunted on to the quay at Southampton, it was the other way round. I was not popular, when the train had to be shunted out, turned round and brought back again. We sailed on a grim, stormy day to the accompaniment of the traditional forced jollity. The *Nevasa* was an old ship, in which the troops lived in a huge hold, sleeping in hammocks. It was my fate to be orderly officer the first night, as we hit the full force of a westerly gale at the end of the Channel. Visiting the troop-decks was literally a nauseating experience, the hammocks swinging to and fro in the stuffy atmosphere, stinking of sea-sickness. The orderly sergeant and I found one of the sentries asleep, and after the sergeant had kicked him to his feet and was threatening him with dire punishment, the unfortunate man was sick over the sergeant's boots. The sergeant was promptly sick himself, and I followed suit. We felt that honours were even. I was orderly officer again after we had passed Gibraltar. The weather warmed up and the troop-decks were horribly stuffy. Canvas ventilators could be fitted, if the commanding officer recommended it to the ship's captain. I earnestly urged him to do so, but was soundly ticked off, being told that the soldiers must learn to endure the heat. Caunter believed that endurance of physical discomfort was good for one. He himself never suffered from sea-sickness and regarded it as a form of weakness, for which he had no sympathy. He was an unimaginative man, and I did not like him much. I suspect that he did not much approve of me.

On arrival in Egypt, we moved into a tented camp in the garrison of Helmieh, near Heliopolis on the eastern outskirts of Cairo, where we shared a permanent officers' mess with the 31st Field Regiment, Royal Artillery. A few offices were in huts, but everything else was in tents. This became unpleasant in April, when the *khamsin*, the hot wind from the south, blew, covering everything with sand and dust and making life utterly miserable. It would start in the east and work round through the south to the west, usually taking about 48 hours to blow itself out. Apart from this and the muggy heat of July and August, it was a pleasant life.

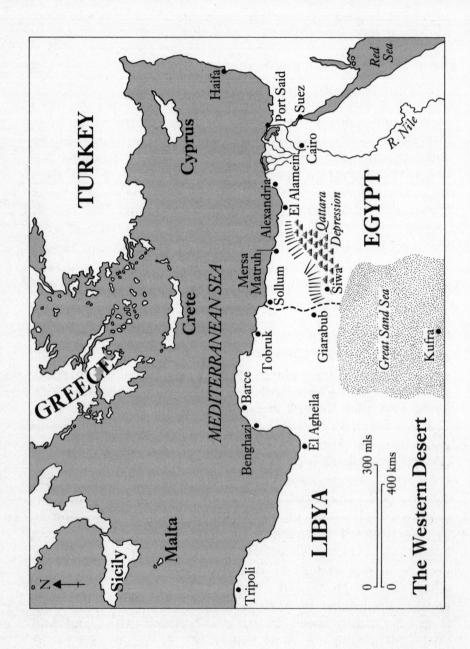

The Western Desert

I was kept busy as transport officer with about 40 vehicles of all sorts and their drivers to look after. One of them, McParland, whom I later met again as a corporal when we were both crossing the Rhine in March 1945, in a letter to me in 1973, wrote:

> Ranks and status go for nothing but human relations to me seems very important. I always remember the very efficient way you done your job. Like vehicle inspection. The average transport officer on monthly checks would just stand up in his 'Best B.D.' and ask the driver off the list: 'Lights? Horn? Prop-shaft bolts?' taking the driver's word for it. Not you. You appeared in overalls with all the necessary tools and checked each item individually. Sometimes I called you (under my breath) four-letter words, even as much as seven-letter words, but now when I recall it all you taught me much. The only way to be efficient is to be 'Efficient'. I see Dear General you are still in the Army. Now as a 'civvy' I've never forgot my army training.

One of the greatest pleasures came from trips into the desert. On the first of these, Major Donald John McLeod, a wise and charming elderly major with experience in both the Iraqi and Egyptian deserts, led a party of about 30 of us, young officers, NCOs and soldiers, to teach us how to navigate and drive in the featureless desert north-west of Cairo. The maps were almost totally blank, and, where they did mark features, they were not accurate. Our navigation was not very sophisticated, being carried out by sun-compass. It was an anxious moment when, after careful calculation, one appeared not to have succeeded in reaching the feature expected; and a satisfactory one when one had. The great empty spaces were most impressive, particularly at dawn and dusk, and at night under the brilliant canopy of stars. I was greatly attracted to desert travel and could not have enough of it.

Social life in Cairo was also pleasant. Much of it centred on the swimming pool of the Gezira Sporting Club. The Watsons lived in an attractive house on Gezira Island, which was a pleasant and valuable gateway into local society. As we received field allowance to compensate us for living in tents, as well as colonial allowance, my pay was increased from £15 to £22 a month. I had been able to get my car shipped out free by the line that shipped cotton for Carver Brothers, and occasionally I could manage the journey by the desert tarmac road to Alexandria to stay with my Uncle Herbert and his family, where bathing in the sea was a welcome change from Cairo in the summer. I did not get much riding. I would sometimes exercise polo ponies for cavalry or gunner officers who were on leave, or ride with the Spinks twins into the desert near the Pyramids at Mena, where their father, the last British Sirdar of the Egyptian Army, had a delightful house. Another old friend of my uncle, Dick Wellesley, was Tom Russell, Commandant of the Cairo Police, renowned for his activities in countering the traffic in drugs, who invited me and a gunner sub-altern, Scott-Moncrieff, to spend Christmas shooting near the Damietta mouth of the Nile. We spent several days with Tom and Dorothea Russell in a government rest house, by day walking about shooting mostly snipe, which were easier to hit than back at home, in the evenings being embarrassed listeners to the almost continuous nagging of the distinguished and charming Russell Pasha by his highly intelligent, but maddening wife.

Before that Christmas expedition, much of importance had happened. At the time of the Munich crisis of September 1938, there was anxiety about the attitude of Italy and a fear that she might take some action against Egypt from Libya. A force was hurriedly got together from the British garrison in Cairo and despatched by rail to Mersa Matruh in the Western Desert. It was based primarily on the Cairo Cavalry Brigade, which consisted of the 7th Hussars in light tanks, the 8th Hussars in Ford 15-hundredweight pick-up trucks, on which were mounted Vickers-Berthier heavy machine-guns, the 11th Hussars with their old Rolls-Royce armoured cars, and 1st Royal Tanks with light tanks. The only medium tanks in the country, the ancient Vickers medium Mark Is and IIs of 6th Royal Tanks, were left in Cairo, their role being that of internal security. Third Regiment Royal Horse Artillery, with short-range 3.7-inch howitzers, provided the only guns and 1st Battalion the King's Royal Rifle Corps (60th Rifles) the infantry. There was no anti-tank or anti-aircraft artillery and the only air support came from one squadron of Gladiator fighters and three Blenheim bombers, flown in from Habbaniya in Iraq. The Italians made no move. The most significant event was the arrival, like a *deus ex machina,* of Hobo to command the mobile forces and begin the process of converting them into a mobile division. His impact was immediate, the cavalry alarmed at what the fire-eating tank enthusiast might do to them.

The Italian threat having been allayed, the force returned to Cairo. I passed the practical part of the promotion examination from Lieutenant to Captain, having already passed the written part, and promptly went off on leave to Greece. I travelled steerage on a clean and comfortable Italian boat to Piraeus, and stayed in a hotel in Athens, seeing all the usual sights. I was immensely impressed and found that the Parthenon, Sounion and other well known classical remains far exceeded in beauty and interest the high expectations my classical education had led me to sustain. Comic relief was provided by the spectacle of the funeral procession of the Archbishop of Athens, a Gilbert and Sullivan affair in the pouring rain at which almost everything that could go wrong did.

After a week seeing the sights in and around Athens, I set off by bus to the south, visiting Daphni, Eleusis, Corinth and Acro-Corinth before reaching Mycenae. There I was almost the only guest in the simple and friendly inn, La Belle Helène, which had been the headquarters of the British School in Athens when they had excavated there. The proprietor was called Agamemnon, his wife Clytemnestra and his brother Orestes, or so I was informed by the only other guest, an elderly retired French doctor, who appeared to live on a diet consisting almost solely of raw garlic. He told me that, after his wife's death, he had decided to '*simplifier la vie*', had become a vegetarian and spent his time travelling around the world. As my guide book was the French *Guide Bleu* and he spoke no English or Greek, we formed a mutual aid society and went round the ruins of Mycenae, Tyryns and Argos together. He was an amusing and voluble companion, and I was delighted to have his company. I found that my knowledge of classical Greek was of more value than I had expected. I could read the language and understand a fair

amount of what was written, although I found it as difficult
to interpret what was said to me as it was to make myself
understood. I had a phrase book which was taken from me
by a bus conductor near Marathon, who was so amused by
the phrases it contained that he insisted on keeping it as a
way of entertaining his passengers. Τί ώρα φεύγει το
λεοφορείος; (What time does the bus leave?) soon rolled off my
tongue fluently. The reply always seemed to be πέντε και μισή
(Half-past five), although the bus seldom left when it was meant
to.

I was sorry to leave the friendly family atmosphere of the
Belle Helène, and went by train from Mycenae to Tripolis,
crammed into a third-class carriage with passengers carrying
poultry, fish and vegetables, as the train puffed slowly up
into the hills. Next day a bus took me on to Sparta. From
there I walked to Mistra and back to see the impressive and
beautiful remains of the Byzantine city. I appeared to be
the only tourist and was shown round by a policeman who
spoke French. A hair-raising journey in an overcrowded bus
on a newly built road through the mountains brought me to
Olympia, where I was able to admire the beauty of the sanctuary and all it contained almost entirely on my own. Having
spent two nights there, I returned by train to Athens, where
I was hoping to collect more money, having handed a cheque
to Thomas Cook's when I first arrived. Unfortunately it had
not been cleared, and, with practically no money, I had to
spend two days doing nothing but sit in the National Garden,
reading *The Times*.

At last my cheque was cleared, and I took the early morning bus to Delphi, where I spent the whole of the following
two days in and around the sanctuary, taking photographs
and making pencil sketches of the temples and monuments,
which I found to be an excellent way of imprinting their
detail on my memory. The bus journey back to Athens
proved to be an amusing one. I shared the back seat, which
had more leg room than the other tightly packed ones, with
a Russian woman and a Greek soldier. Although neither of
them had more than a few words of English, the three of us
and the conductor managed to carry on a conversation of
some sort all the way to Athens, while we bounced up and
down as the Jehu of a driver sped over the potholes. At one

stop the Russian persuaded me to buy three of the loaves of bread, shaped like round air cushions, on which we sat to take the place of the missing springs of the seat. They came in useful when we stopped near the pass of Thermopylae for the usual lunch of black olives and cheese, washed down with *retsina*, which I hoped acted as a disinfectant to counteract the clouds of flies which settled on everything. I paid for lunch for all four of us with the princely sum of 29 drachmae, worth 1s 1d (5½p) at that time.

The last few days of my leave were spent on a visit to the island of Mykonos, from which I went by caique to Delos. The stay of two nights at Mykonos was a delightfully peaceful interlude, giving me an insight into the simplicity and charm of life in the Greek islands. When I returned to Piraeus, I was almost out of cash again, but nobody in Athens would change me a cheque. I arrived back in Alexandria, having been away for a month, with only the equivalent of 3s 6d (17p) in my pocket and had to borrow enough money to get me back to Cairo from my Uncle Herbert. For a total expenditure of £32, £5 of which was spent on photography, I had travelled to Greece and back and enjoyed a holiday that was to remain one of the highlights of my life.

That winter I took part in a particularly interesting desert trip. Its object was twofold: to try out a number of different new vehicles to assess their 'desert-worthiness', and to see whether there were any possible direct routes between the oasis of Siwa and the Nile valley, other than the known one which crossed the salt marshes of the Qattara Depression east of the oasis of Qara and skirted the southern ends of the great sand dunes, which ran north and south across the gravel-encrusted sand desert north of the oasis of Bahariya. The distance from Cairo to Siwa across the desert was some 400 miles. The expedition was led by an officer of the Royal Army Service Corps and I was his second-in-command. On the journey to Siwa, we followed a route north of Bahariya to the eastern end of the Qattara Depression crossing, the position of which was fairly firmly established, although the maps of that area of the desert were of doubtful accuracy. One of the fascinating features of desert travel in those areas, where few had ventured before, was that the tyre marks of previous travellers, depressing the pebbles of gravel in the sand, remained a permanent memorial of their passage. In one area, which we believed had not been visited since a surveyor had travelled there in a T-model Ford in the 1920s, we came across the unmistakable narrow tyre marks of his vehicle.

At the eastern edge of the salt marsh, I was detached with a small party of vehicles to reconnoitre an alternative crossing, which, from the map, appeared possible, as the width of the salt marsh was shown as only a few miles at that point. We were to join up again with the main body on the track east of Qara. We had no wireless: every pound we could carry was devoted to water, petrol and food. Wireless sets, with their operators, batteries and charging sets, were considered an unnecessary luxury. I managed to find the narrow bit of salt marsh and to cross it without difficulty, but ran into very difficult ground on the far side, a succession of hard ridges running at right-angles to the direction in which I wished to go. Some of the vehicles were not well suited to this rough ground, and to try and hurry over it ran the risk not only of breaking them, but of damaging their loads, particularly of petrol, which was carried in very flimsy tins in equally flimsy wooden crates. The tins were in fact colloquially known as 'flimsies'. Darkness fell while I was still negotiating this difficult terrain, and there were many miles to go to the track. Navigation imposed further delays, as it involved frequent halts to check our line with a magnetic compass, before selecting a star to drive on. It was well into the night before I eventually reached what appeared to be the Qara track, inspection of which did not reveal clearly whether or not the rest of the party had already been along it. Reluctantly I decided that I must split the party yet again, leaving some of the vehicles where they were on the track and going myself along it, first in one direction to see if I could find the main body, and then, if necessary, returning and trying the other. I had not been going long before, to my great relief, I saw headlights coming in my direction and soon met the leader, who had become anxious about our fate and had guessed, correctly, that we had reached the track beyond the point at which the main body had stopped for the night.

Siwa, with its famous temple of Jupiter Ammon and its effervescent water, was a fascinating spot. I wished I had been able to spend longer there and go on to the oasis of Jiarabub on the Libyan frontier, but we had to get back. After a call on the Sheikh of Qara, where the inhabitants lived in caves on the side of the steep and imposing escarpment, we crossed the salt marsh by the standard route and set a course due east to search for a gap in the main sand dune, the Ghard el Rammak, which lay across the desert about half-way between the salt marsh and the Nile valley. The dunes built up gradually from west to east, the eastern edge forming a steep slope, driving down which required considerable skill. It would not have been possible to cross them in the opposite direction, as one could not climb up these slopes. To ensure that one did not sink in, one had to keep up a good speed while driving eastwards. In bright sunlight the undulations of the surface could not be detected by the eye, and one had the feeling that one was flying in an aircraft, subject to sudden, unforeseeable bumps. The vehicles had to move in a wide formation so that they did not drive in each other's tracks, in which they would have got stuck. Suddenly one would arrive at the steep eastern edge. A quick change into low gear, ensuring that the vehicle was headed directly down the slope, and then full throttle to ensure that it was driven firmly straight down to the gravel desert at the foot. If one got stuck half-way down or slewed sideways, one was in for a long digging operation with the danger that the vehicle would fall over sideways and be irrecoverable. Fortunately the drivers were all skilled by this time, and we had no serious mishaps.

I was proud of my navigation when I found the gap, the Fassulet el Rammak, marked on the map, but dismayed when, several miles beyond it, we came across another long, high dune barring our way, which was not marked on the map. The only thing to do was to detach a small party, which I led, to travel up and down the dune to see if there was any way through. Luckily it was not long before I found one. We met no more obstacles in the 120 miles beyond it, before, with great satisfaction, I saw the tips of the Great Pyramids appearing over the hills marking the west side of the Nile valley. When, later, I went over all my navigational calculations with the Survey department, I found out that their information on the area west of the dunes had been based on an expedition mounted from Siwa, and east of them from one coming from Cairo, and that the two had not been accurately correlated. Our expedition had not only been a fascinating experience, but it had also given me valuable training and confidence in my own judgement and decisions.

The year 1939 was to be for me, as for so many others, a decisive one. I had originally intended to go back to England on leave in the summer, driving along the North African coast to Algiers, thence shipping the car to Marseilles and back across France, returning through the Balkans to Greece, and shipping the car from there. This would have been too severe a test for my faithful Ford 8, and I exchanged it for a newer German-made Ford 10. However, by the spring it was clear that war clouds were threatening and that, if I got leave at all, the route that I had planned would not be a wise one to embark upon. I therefore sold the Ford 10 and bought for £16 a 1928 Lancia Lambda, which a gunner officer whom I knew had failed to sell before he was posted home. Antony had owned one for a short time, and I was delighted to be the proud possessor of one of these remarkable cars, which was a joy to drive. It was not in a good state, but I came to an agreement with my mechanist staff-sergeant, Bill Bailey, later to rise to the rank of lieutenant-colonel in the Royal Electrical and Mechanical Engineers, that, in return for his help in keeping it in order, he could use it when I was away in the desert, as I was that year for long periods.

The gathering war clouds had another effect on my life. Four years had passed since I had been commissioned, and I had done nothing about studying for another career. I had continued with my German and spent several boring hours a week learning it under the tuition of an elderly retired German professor in Cairo. He certainly did not make me any more enthusiastic about the language than I had been before. But my military duties had kept me very fully occupied; I found them more interesting than I had expected. I enjoyed many aspects of the life I was leading, especially my contact with and responsibility for the soldiers under my command. This fulfilled a desire to feel that I was helping others less fortunate than myself, as well as being a refreshing experience in itself. I liked my soldiers and appreciated the cheerful way in which they took life as it came. The aspect of my life which I disliked was that of the officers' mess, and the off-duty social life of officers generally. In order to escape from it, I had already applied to learn Chinese and considered a transfer to the military police as a possible channel of transfer to the Colonial Police. The clear signs that war with Germany, and probably Italy also, was almost inevitable, thrust the idea of leaving the army into the background, at any rate until the threat of war either receded or became a reality.

I was in fact kept exceptionally busy that year. Hobo's immense energy was devoted not only to developing the tactics and organization of the Mobile Division (Egypt), which was to become the famous 7th Armoured Division, but also to its logistic support, which was non-existent. Units had been expected to collect their own requirements direct from the railhead at Mersa Matruh. Little thought and no practical action had been applied to the problems of casualty evacuation and treatment, to recovery and repair of vehicles and all the other aspects of maintaining a mechanized force in an area of no natural resources several hundred miles from its base. Hobo was fortunate in acquiring the services of Major Cecil Smith as his principal administrative staff officer. 'Smuggins', as he was universally known, was an exceptionally able officer of the Royal Army Service Corps, proud of his Military Cross, gained with the infantry in the First World War, of having qualified at a Guards drill course and at the Staff College, all rarities for an officer of his corps. Like Hobo, he tolerated no slackness or inefficiency, was a master of detail and a superbly efficient staff officer; but he was more tolerant of human failings and less of a bully than Hobo, and was, as a result, although a hard taskmaster, easier to work for. It is not surprising that he rose to the rank of Major-General as head of his corps and was knighted.*

One of the requirements of a logistic system for a mobile force in the desert was to devise an organization which could control the vulnerable, but essential, 'soft-skinned' transport vehicles of the fighting units, ensure that they met the

---

* He died at the age of 91 in 1988.

divisional transport and other logistic units at a rendezvous in the desert, where their requirements could be supplied, that they were kept out of harm's way during the day, and, at the end of it, were directed to where they could deliver fuel, water, rations, stores, mail, reinforcements and all the needs of the fighting units. With no roads or landmarks, and very few wireless sets available for the use of the logistic services, this posed difficult problems. Part of the solution lay in the creation of the post of commander of the divisional 'B echelons'. He would receive his orders from the divisional logistic staff and be responsible for collecting the requirements and controlling the movements of all the unit 'B echelon', that is the transport vehicles that did not actually accompany the unit in action on the battlefield. I was selected to be this officer's adjutant, while retaining my job as unit transport officer, handing over the latter to another young officer when we took part in exercises. In addition to these responsibilities, I was given two others. The first was to carry out desert trials of the prototypes of two experimental armoured cars, one a very conventional one, a Humber, later to be accepted, the other an unconventional Morris with independent suspension and transmission to each of its four wheels. This gave it a remarkable cross-country performance, so much so that one was tempted to drive it too fast over rough ground, which I undoubtedly did. Its major fault was to overheat on soft sand. In order to find the cause of this, I insisted that a coolant temperature gauge should be fitted, which extraordinarily had not been done. This involved delays in the trials, and Hobo sent for me to berate me for the delay in reaching a decision as to the acceptability of the vehicle, saying that the experts had told him what the cause was and that it could be cured. The 'experts' were a representative of the firm and of the War Office branch that was keen that the design should be accepted. I replied that, if he wanted me to give him an answer, he must wait until I was satisfied that I had arrived at it: if not, he must get somebody else to carry out the trials. 'Get out of my office, you impudent little bugger!', he shouted, as I hastily retreated to the door. Next day I received a message to say that he was coming to inspect the vehicle. Thinking that this would probably mark the end of my army career, I viewed his visit with trepidation. 'Hello,

Mike, how are things going,' he said on arrival, and, after listening carefully to my explanation, told his staff to give me every help in getting a temperature gauge fitted as quickly as possible. As I was to learn on many future occasions, the way to gain Hobo's respect was to stand up to his bullying; but one had to be sure that one was on firm ground when one did so.

My other responsibility was one which, like my Greek holiday, was to remain one of the unforgettable experiences of my life. For nearly three months I was based at Mersa Matruh, the small port in a lovely lagoon 150 miles west of Alexandria, with which it was connected by rail and a rough track, and almost the same distance from the Libyan frontier at Sollum. I had a dual task, to train drivers in desert driving and young officers and NCOs in navigation and the arts of desert life, and to carry out a systematic 'going' reconnaissance of the desert between Mersa Matruh and the frontier as far south as the escarpment which ran from Qara to Siwa, 70 miles south of the coast at Matruh and twice that distance on the frontier. The result would be a map showing the types of surface as a guide to the suitability of the desert for the movement of vehicles and the speed at which they could be expected to cover it, also filling in details of escarpments and depressions. With a small permanent party of fitters, I would receive every fortnight a new collection of officers and soldiers to be trained. My group of five or six Morris 8-hundredweight trucks would leave the glorious lagoon beach early on Monday morning and return on Friday, having covered about 150 miles, often negotiating escarpments and other obstacles which were not marked on the map. The weekend would be spent maintaining the trucks and restocking with stores before the next trip. I had no wireless, my only communication link with Cairo being through the Egyptian army brigade commander's office. It took so long to get a telephone call through, and I was invariably away when it did, that my unit soon gave up trying to contact me. To be 350 miles from one's commanding officer, with no means of communication, not even a proper road, and to be entirely responsible for every aspect of such a fascinating task at the age of 24 was an ideal position, the best job I ever had. The commanding officer ('Booming Bill' Watkins took

over from Caunter that spring) made one attempt to visit
me. I was warned of this by the Egyptian brigadier, when
I returned one Friday. I had no wish to have my weekend
interrupted, and moved my camp to another beach outside
Matruh, making arrangements to be informed both of his
arrival and of his, very frustrated, departure, after having
been informed by the Egyptian army that, in my keenness,
I had gone straight back into the desert. I was putting into
practice Hobo's advice to be 'sufficiently insubordinate'.

In the summer of 1939 General 'Copper' Gordon-Finlay-
son, whose sons had been in the same house at Winchester
with me, handed over command of British troops in Egypt
to General 'Jumbo' Maitland Wilson. Finlayson, an old-
fashioned, traditional gunner, had never got on with Hobo
and relations between them had been tense, Finlayson, not
without justification, regarding Hobo's tactical ideas as
unrealistic. He also objected to Hobo's total disregard of
all orders from the staff of his headquarters concerning
restrictions on the use of vehicles, imposed partly for
financial reasons, partly to preserve them in case of war.
Hobo was determined to exercise all parts of his division as
thoroughly and as often as possible. In the early summer the
whole division moved up to the area near Mersa Matruh,
travelling across the desert, through which I had helped
to mark with empty petrol barrels what became known as
'the barrel track'. This long desert move by units, many of
which were not as well trained in it as we were, led to a
considerable amount of damage to vehicles and loss of stores,
further exacerbating relations between Hobo and Finlayson
and their staffs. Wilson arrived in time to watch the end of a
long series of exercises in July, and appeared impressed with
the division's achievements, although appalled by the lack
of equipment and poor state of what there was. When war
broke out in Europe in September, Hobo was recalled from
leave in England and the division hurriedly moved out again
to Mersa Matruh to face the possibility of an Italian invasion.
When that did not materialize, Hobo took the opportunity to
initiate another series of ambitious exercises, the last of which
led to a major clash between him and Wilson, leading to his
dismissal by the newly arrived Commander-in-Chief, Wavell,
in November.

By that time I had just been appointed Camp Commandant of the divisional headquarters, officially known as Mobile Division (Egypt) and Abbassia District. This meant that
I was responsible for the administration of all the personnel,
equipment and stores of the headquarters, complicated by
the fact that we were on peacetime accounting procedures
and that no official authority existed for most of the equipment and stores we had acquired. Most of the personnel
were still members of the regiments from which, like myself
and my tiny staff, they had been borrowed. First Royal
Tank Regiment (as it had been renamed in April on the
formation of the Royal Armoured Corps, which brought
the Royal Tank Corps and the cavalry together in an uneasy
alliance) lent me an illiterate, but well-meaning, sergeant
and half a dozen soldiers to help me out. I found myself
my own commanding officer, adjutant, quartermaster, chief
clerk and even typist, until I had taught one of my soldiers
to operate the machine by the same two-finger method
that I have practised ever since. I was not sorry to leave
the regiment, as 'Booming Bill' Watkins, a humourless, but
efficient and kindly man, had taken over command of the
Heavy Armoured Group, that is 1st and 6th Royal Tanks,
both having acquired some of the new A9 medium tanks, and
had been replaced by 'Moley' Molesworth, a dead-beat major
who had been passed over for promotion for years. It had
the advantage that I could live out of the mess, and I shared
a flat in Abbassia with a pernickety bachelor major, Charles
Ward, who acted as brigade-major to Watkins. We engaged
a Sudanese cook and a boy assistant, and lived a pleasant
life, welcoming my brother Antony and his wife, Elizabeth,
whom he had married in 1938. Her father had been in the
Egyptian civil service and had at one time been Governor of
the Western Desert, based at Mersa Matruh. Antony was the
RAF intelligence officer at Mosul in Iraq, having become an
Arabic expert in Aden, and had been sent to Cairo for
an attachment to the Middle East Air Force Headquarters
to carry out a special study. Their rather bohemian habits shocked Charles Ward. He was so upset to find them
sitting in their dressing-gowns, smoking, at the breakfast
table, when he returned from early Holy Communion at
the Anglican Cathedral one Sunday morning, that he could

hardly be persuaded to eat his breakfast, fond as he was of his food.

The apparently unglamorous appointment of Camp Commandant was a most valuable introduction into the intricacies of army administration and logistics, which was to stand me in good stead, not only in the appointments on the staff that were to follow, but also later as a commander. To have been initiated into the abstruse rites of quartermasters was a privilege shared by few other commanders. Almost as soon as I took over, I had my first experience of a real quartermaster's problem and how to solve it. When the headquarters had been in the desert shortly before I took over, it had been issued with, among others, a large tent called an EPIP (eepy-eyepy), or European Personnel Indian Pattern. There was no record that the tent with its 99 pins, steel, large, had ever been handed back to the Ordnance Depot. If it had been left in the desert, the bedouin would have made off with it. Ordnance were demanding their pound of flesh, which was a considerable sum. I appealed to Mr Cook, the regimental quartermaster-sergeant of 1st Royal Tanks, a highly efficient operator, who had often helped me out as transport officer, and who had the added advantage of being a prominent freemason. Hobo himself and, more significantly, several of the key civilian heads of branches of the Ordnance Depot were also of that fraternity. 'Have you any steel pins or old canvas?,' inquired Mr Cook. 'Well, I've got plenty of used light tank track pins and a torn latrine screen, but that's hessian not canvas.' 'Leave it to me: I'll see what I can do', he replied. A few days later he rang up and told me to send 99 used light tank track pins and the old latrine screen down to K branch of the Ordnance Stores with the papers he was sending me. On them I read: 'One tent EPIP and 99 pins, steel, large, unserviceable, rendered to produce.' The magic worked.

Hobo had been replaced as divisional commander by a cavalryman, Major-General Michael O'Moore-Creagh, a very different character, full of charm, a good sound officer, but lacking Hobo's intense drive and mastery of detail. The rather *ad hoc* organization began to be replaced by one better suited for war. Mobile Division (Egypt) was re-named 7th Armoured Division and separated from Abbassia District. Its subordinate formations were, first, 7th Armoured Brigade, commanded by Hugh Russell, successor of the Cairo Cavalry Brigade, which had passed through the stage of being called the Light Armoured Brigade. Its units were 1st Royal Tanks, with a mixture of medium and light tanks, and 8th Hussars, in the process of conversion to light tanks. Secondly, 4th Armoured Brigade, ex-Heavy Armoured Group, now commanded by Caunter. It contained 6th Royal Tanks and 7th Hussars, the latter with light tanks only. Eleventh Hussars, with armoured cars, became the divisional reconnaissance unit. The Pivot Group, commanded by 'Strafer' Gott, provided the infantry and artillery. 'Strafer' had arrived in Egypt in command of the 1st Battalion King's Royal Rifle Corps (60th) and had acted as GSO1, or chief of staff, of the division until handing over to Horace Birks of the Royal Tanks. He had the two motorized infantry battalions, the one he had commanded and 2nd Battalion The Rifle Brigade, and two artillery regiments, 3rd and 4th Regiments Royal Horse Artillery, the former reorganized as an anti-tank regiment and the latter equipped with 25-pounder field guns, and commanded by Jock Campbell.

3

The Desert my Dwelling Place

Oh! that the desert were my dwelling place
Lord Byron (1788-1824), *Childe Harold*

As Italy's attitude became more menacing, the division prepared for war. Eleventh Hussars and the Support Group were the first to move up to Mersa Matruh in April 1940, followed in May by the rest of the division, except for 7th Armoured Brigade which remained in Cairo. At short notice Major Ward and I had to give up the flat, our Egyptian landlady, who was the wife or widow of an Egyptian army officer, being kindness itself in absolving us of paying the balance of the rent, and arranging for the storage of our furniture. My beloved Lancia had to be sold for what I could get from the garage in Abbassia, only £10. Had I been able to keep it to this day, it would be worth thousands as a veteran.

When we moved, the full establishment of an armoured divisional headquarters was authorized and I found myself promoted to the appointment of staff captain (Q) on the divisional staff, with the acting rank of captain, just after my 25th birthday. I worked directly under 'Smuggins' at Rear Divisional Headquarters, as the only other staff officer on the 'Q' side, the DAQMG, Major 'Pip' Roberts from 6th Royal Tanks, worked at the advanced operational headquarters. In the month before war broke out against Italy I was fully occupied stocking the empty water cisterns, or 'birs', which were scattered all over the desert between Mersa Matruh and the Libyan frontier, with water, petrol and rations. The concept was that, with the shortage of transport and the threat of air attack, normal daily supply of units in the forward area would be difficult to maintain, and units could then obtain their needs from these reserves. However, when war did come, almost my first task was to remove them all. It was found possible to maintain daily supply by lorry, and the reserves in the cisterns tied up not only valuable stocks of commodities, but also supplies of water containers ('fantassies' or camel-tanks, designed to be carried two to a camel) which were essential to maintain daily supply. In addition, the reserves were a standing temptation to marauding quartermasters and others, and it was impossible to keep track of their contents.

During this period the bulk of the division, including the headquarters, was at Gerawla, on the coast just east of Matruh. Eleventh Hussars and the Support Group were at Matruh itself, the former having a squadron at Sidi Barrani with one troop forward at the frontier at Sollum. The Cairo Infantry Brigade provided the garrison of Matruh itself, the whole force, which was no more than the strength of a weak division, forming the Western Desert Force, commanded by Lieutenant-General Dick O'Connor, transferred from Palestine, where he had been commanding the 6th Division.

Warned that war with Italy was imminent, 11th Hussars and the Support Group moved up to the frontier during the night of 10/11 June, the rest of the division following next day. The Support Group assumed responsibility for the coastal area, with one of its battalions forward at Sollum and the other in reserve at Buq Buq, half-way to Sidi Barrani, which was 50 miles behind the frontier. Fourth Armoured Brigade moved up south of the main escarpment, 60 miles south of Sidi Barrani, while 11th Hussars advanced to the frontier wire as far south as Fort Maddalena, 50 miles south of Sollum. The first action of the war was their capture of the fort at Sidi Omar, the occupants of which were not aware that war had been declared. Fourth Armoured Brigade then moved up and captured Fort Capuzzo, which commanded the road from Sollum to Bardia, while 11th Hussars penetrated further to the west and intercepted traffic on the road from Bardia to Tobruk. Among their prisoners was General Lastucci, Chief Engineer of the Italian Tenth Army, a major on his staff and the latter's pregnant

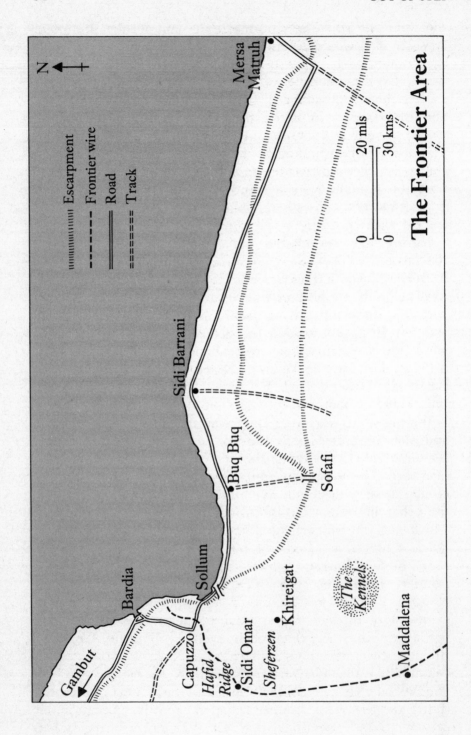

The Frontier Area

wife. The lady could not be left all alone in the desert, at the mercy of thirst and the Arabs, and therefore accompanied her husband and the general into captivity, travelling in the general's Lancia staff car. When the party eventually arrived at divisional headquarters, the staff officer, having been interrogated, was sent back to a prisoner-of-war cage. The general, having given his parole, was sent off, still in his own car, with a British soldier driver and escort and the pregnant lady, to Western Desert Force Headquarters, where he met General O'Connor, whom he had known on the Italian front in the First World War. The lady was driven on, still in the Lancia, to Alexandria, where she was admitted to hospital. The BBC gave the incident publicity as an example of the chivalry of the British, but made the mistake of saying that the lady was the general's wife. This came to the ears of his wife in Rome, who protested through the Swiss authorities. The BBC therefore made a correction, announcing that 'the pregnant lady captured with General Lastucci was not his wife.' That so infuriated the general that he went on hunger strike in his prisoner-of-war camp, until he had received an apology.

These light-hearted forays into Libya could not, however, continue for long. Hesitant as the Italians were to venture far from the coast road, nevertheless they were vastly superior in numbers and considerably so in the air also. By early July they had recaptured Fort Capuzzo, although the Support Group hung on to the top of the escarpment east of it, including the important Halfaya Pass, the only route up it near the coast other than the main road from Sollum to Capuzzo. Eleventh Hussars' armoured cars patrolled up to, but seldom beyond the frontier wire. We were operating on a shoestring in every respect, restricted by acute shortages of weapons, vehicles, wireless sets, spare parts for all of them, and of ammunition. Major Snook's two ancient 60-pounder guns, the only artillery with a range greater than the 25-pounders of 3rd and 4th Regiments Royal Horse Artillery, were limited to one round per gun per day. They were sited at Fig Tree Wells near Sollum, from which position they could shell Capuzzo itself, Snook having an observation post at Musaid on top of the escarpment. The story went round that a captured document had given the allotment

of the brothel in Bardia, Sunday afternoon being the period
reserved for the officers of the garrison of Fort Capuzzo.
The intelligence staff appreciated that, if they could be
prevented from leaving the fort at that time, their morale
would suffer sufficiently to persuade them to surrender.
Snook's weekly ration of 14 rounds was therefore reserved
for that purpose. However it was not enough to persuade
them to raise the white flag.

With units scattered over so wide an area, with the bare
minimum of vehicles to haul supplies from the railhead at
Mersa Matruh so many miles over the rough desert, and
with severe shortages of every kind, the logistic staff was
faced with a host of problems. We were expected to work
miracles, but could only juggle with the slender resources
we had. Luckily we all knew each other well and, as long
as we were seen to be personally acquainting ourselves with
the problems, and putting every possible effort into solving
them, complaints, although frequent, were good-humoured.

'Smuggins' Smith and I constituted the 'Q' staff at Rear
Divisional Headquarters, while, as has already been explained, Pip Roberts was with the operational staff at Advanced
Headquarters. I shared with 'Smuggins' a table under an
awning on one side of a three-ton lorry, the other side being
the office of a delightful Irishman, Dan Walsh, the Senior Ordnance Mechanical Engineer, responsible for recovery and repair, and Major Edward Genochio, the DAAG,
who dealt with all personnel matters. When the wind blew,
particularly if it was the dreaded *khamsin*, everything was
covered with dust and sand, the papers blew all over the
place, typewriters got clogged up and staff work was very
frustrating. But most of my time was spent on the move,
travelling over the desert to visit the field supply depots,
dumps of stores where our transport collected the division's
needs, or the replenishment area, where they handed it
over to the unit 'B echelons', or the units themselves. The
two subordinate headquarters, 4th Armoured Brigade and
the Support Group, were frequent ports of call. The Italian
Air Force was the only enemy we had to take any account
of. Fortunately their pilots were regular in their habits,
carrying out their raids in mid-morning and mid-afternoon,
thus allowing them to return to their airfield at El Adem for

regular mealtimes. Their targets were normally Sidi Barrani
and Mersa Matruh, and it was prudent to avoid those two
places at those times. Advanced Divisional Headquarters was
west of Sidi Barrani and Rear Headquarters about 15 miles
east of it, both on the edge of the sea on the Italian Air Force
route, but, luckily, not often attacked. A bathe in the lovely
clear blue sea was a welcome refresher after a long, hot and
dusty day's work, especially as the water ration did not allow
one to wash oneself all over every day. If one was prudent,
as I was, one's very small ration of washing water, after
use, was filtered through sand in an empty 'flimsy' petrol
can, and what came through was used again, probably to
wash one's socks. I worked very long hours, but enjoyed it,
especially the considerable responsibility I held and the trust
which 'Smuggins', whom I greatly admired, placed in me. He
overlooked no mistakes, but gave me every encouragement.

On a visit to one of the battalions of the Support Group
at the top of Halfaya Pass in August, I felt very ill, and,
when I called in at 'Strafer' Gott's headquarters, he made
me see his medical officer, who found that I had a very high
temperature. After a bumpy journey back to a medical post
near Sidi Barrani, I was sent on by ambulance to the main
dressing station at Mersa Matruh, the night I spent there
coinciding with an air raid. An ambulance train took me to
Cairo, where I finally came to rest, still very feverish, in the
army hospital at Helmieh, where my illness was eventually
diagnosed as glandular fever. As those who have suffered
from it know, it leaves one very weak. I must have spent
three or four weeks in hospital, followed by sick leave of,
I guess, a fortnight in Cairo. While on the latter, having
nothing better to do one day, I was watching a cricket
match at Gezira Sporting Club between the club and a
team representing General Headquarters Middle East. The
latter were short of a player, and the captain, a major in the
Military Secretary's department, asked me if I would play.
Having explained that (a) I was a very poor player, (b) I had
not got the right clothes, and (c) I was on sick leave, and not
supposed to play games, I nevertheless agreed. GHQ did not
do well, and, in desperation, the captain asked me if I could
bowl. I replied that I was an erratic bowler, but better at that
than as a batsman. I was put on, and to my astonishment took

three wickets for very few runs. When the game was over, the captain asked me my name and what my job was. When I had told him, he said: 'Would you like a job in GHQ?' 'That was a freak performance: I don't normally bowl like that,' I said, 'and, in any case, my only desire is to get back to my job in the desert as soon as I can.' An interesting sidelight on the methods of selection of staff officers in GHQ!

I was immensely grateful that my job had been kept open for me, the official procedure being that one was replaced after an absence of three weeks. While I had been away, the other two members of the 'Q' staff had left. Pip Roberts had moved to 4th Armoured Brigade as brigade major and 'Smuggins' to O'Connor's headquarters, his place having been taken by Lieutenant-Colonel Jack Napier, an officer of the Royal Tank Regiment. He lacked Smuggins's drive, grasp of detail and experience, but had great charm, a good brain and a fund of sound commonsense, and was a very pleasant man to work with. At that time Marshal Graziani, reluctantly and under great pressure from Mussolini, had pushed General Berti's lumbering Tenth Army forward over the frontier into Egypt, advancing as far as Sidi Barrani. Mussolini had insisted that, if Hitler's Operation *Sea Lion* was to land German troops in England, his forces must also stake their claim against Britain, just as he had done against France, when Germany had attacked her. However Hitler did not risk the Channel crossing, and Graziani, having reached Sidi Barrani on 16 September, decided that he had not the resources to go as far as Mersa Matruh, and settled down to consolidate his position. No serious attempt was made to do more than harass his advance. Seventh Armoured Division's tanks were nearly worn out, and neither O'Connor nor his supporting airman, Air Commodore Collishaw, had the resources to do more than that. The division was withdrawn to concentrate astride the track to Siwa, south-west of Mersa Matruh, contact with the Italians, who set about constructing a semi-circle of fortified camps running south of Sidi Barrani, being maintained by 11th Hussars and the Support Group. The latter did so by the use of 'Jock columns', named after Jock Campbell, commanding officer of 4th Regiment RHA. They consisted of a company of motor infantry, backed by a troop of 25-pounder guns, located behind the armoured car patrols, who called for their support if they came under fire or saw an attractive target. These columns covered a wide area of desert and gave the Italians the impression that we were in much greater strength than in fact we were.

Wavell's plan was to counter-attack the Italians, if they advanced further and threatened Mersa Matruh, as it was expected that they would. When I returned to the head-quarters in October, the division was poised for this event-uality; but, as the weeks passed, there was no sign of it. Then came the surprising news that Mussolini had declared war on Greece and invaded it from Albania, which he had occupied in 1938. This was the thin end of a wedge that was later to have decisive effects on the desert campaign: the tug of war between its demands and those of helping Greece. Hitherto Wavell and the Chiefs of Staff at home had thought only in defensive terms as far as the Western Desert was concerned. But the very poor showing of the Italian army, in spite of its overwhelming superiority in numbers, led Wavell, partly as a means of taking the weight off Greece, to think of a counter-offensive, even if Graziani did not stick his neck out and advance further. Wavell's resources were increasing with the arrival of Indian, Australian and New Zealand troops, and a gradual improvement in supplies of equipment. His most significant reinforcement, as far as the desert was concerned, was three regiments of tanks, 2nd Royal Tanks with the Nuffield A13 Crusader, developed from the Christie design, 7th Royal Tanks with the heavily armoured Matilda infantry support tank, and 3rd Hussars with light tanks. They had arrived in Egypt at the end of September, having sailed round the Cape. Second Royal Tanks and 3rd Hussars joined the division, one squadron of the latter joining 2nd Royal Tanks, changing places with one of the former, a regiment consisting solely of light tanks not being effective even against the Italians. With this reinforcement, and with both armoured brigades up in the desert, the division was a much more formidable force than it had been hitherto, each armoured brigade having three regi-ments of tanks and a battery of 25-pounders from 1st RHA. The Support Group had two motorized infantry battalions, carried in 15-hundredweight trucks and Bren-gun carriers (descended from the Carden-Loyd), and 4th RHA with

25-pounders. They also had a company of French colonial infantry from Syria, commanded by Capitaine Foliot, who had thrown in their lot with de Gaulle. Not surprisingly, their administration was complicated. I visited them regularly to see to their needs, and, on one occasion, did so just before they were due to make a raid on an Italian position near Bir Enba. I understood that I was to attend the Capitaine's 'order group' for the operation. It turned out to be an excellent lunch, gazelle and desert snails featuring on the menu, at the end of which the Capitaine made a long and eloquent speech, followed by the cry: 'Maintenant, mes camarades, à Bir Enba'. I asked my neighbour, one of his officers, whether or not we could expect more detailed orders. 'Wait for a few hours, until we've all sobered down, and you will get them,' was his reply!

At the beginning of November Wavell approved the plan which O'Connor had put forward to meet the former's proposal for a counter-offensive raid to cut off and capture the five Italian divisions which occupied the ten fortified camps, forming a semi-circle from Maktila on the coast, fifteen miles east of Sidi Barrani, to the Sofafi group on the escarpment, forty miles to the south-west. His plan was to pass 4th Indian and 7th Armoured Divisions through the 15-mile gap near Bir Enba between the northern and southern groups of camps, 4th Indian, supported by the Matildas of 7th Royal Tanks, attacking the northern group of camps in succession from the rear, while 7th Armoured cut them off from reinforcement and supply, moving in a wider arc to the west. Having dealt with that group, the southern would receive similar treatment.

The plan was hatched in the greatest secrecy, and know-ledge of it confined, in theory at least, to the minimum number of senior officers; but, as Wavell himself recognized in the Lees Knowles lectures he gave in Cambridge in 1939, commanders and operational staffs may draw up brilliant plans: they cannot be executed until the logistic prepara-tions for them have been made. The plan would involve an advance of nearly 100 miles by 7th Armoured Division and a further 50 by 4th Indian before they got to grips with the enemy. Motor transport was, as always, at a premium, and much of the fleet available would be needed to move the Indian infantry. The only way the plan could be made possible was to establish a field supply depot, holding several days' requirements, forward of the area where the division was concentrated, in spite of the risk that, if its existence were detected by Italian air reconnaissance, it could give away our offensive intentions. Planning the contents and layout, as well as. actual supervision of its establishment, was very much my concern, and on 11 November I began to form the depot 25 miles west of the Siwa track. I was therefore brought into the secret at an early stage. Dispersing the depot over a wide area, and taking great care to conceal it as far as possible, appears to have been successful. This task was superimposed on the normal one of seeing that every unit was made as fit for battle as it could be within the resources available. From the moment of my return, therefore, I was very busy indeed.

It was with a feeling of considerable excitement that we all moved west on 8 December 1940, continuing the move that night. The total distance covered varied between units, averaging 70 miles in the day. It would have taken too long to attempt it all by night, as driving over the desert in the dark was a slow and hazardous business. Without lights, one could not see the surface, especially when enveloped in clouds of dust. A long night move was liable to lead to loss of direction, disorganization of units, and damage to vehicles and their loads. This was particularly the case with inexperienced drivers, and many of them were new to the desert. However everything went without a hitch, and the first attack, on Nibeiwa camp, was made at dawn and was immediately successful.

The first of the many problems to face the divisional 'Q' staff was the vast haul of prisoners. Somehow they had to be collected, fed, watered and moved back all the way to railhead at Matruh. A total of 38,300 of them had to be handled in the three days the Battle of Sidi Barrani lasted. It could never have been done without making full use of their own transport units, equipped with excellent heavy Lancia lorries, the drivers of which fortunately proved very cooperative. Some of them, and some other Italian soldiers who were unofficially taken on as officers' mess waiters, became camp followers of the division for several weeks, until it was realized that their status as prisoners-of-war was being jeopardized. The next problem arose when, instead of returning to base after a five-day raid, which had been the original concept, the order was given to advance to the frontier and cut off Bardia. Just when our transport resources were stretched to breaking point, we had to reach out even further. It was only made possible by the sterling work of the divisional Royal Army Service Corps companies, driven on and inspired by their dynamic commander, Lieutenant-Colonel Pat Eassie. 'Blood' Caunter's 4th Armoured Brigade was pushed forward south of the escarpment and ran into difficulties of supply, aggravated by heavy air attacks, when it reached its old stamping ground round Capuzzo. However by 14 December they had encircled Bardia, cutting the road from Tobruk.

Logistic problems now loomed larger than ever. Water supply was an acute one. Wells near the coast were very salty and there were no other sources. Every gallon had to be transported all the way from Matruh and the ration was reduced to half a gallon of salty water per man per day for all purposes. Wavell's decision to withdraw 4th Indian Division from the desert and send it to the Sudan, replacing it with 6th Australian Division, added to the transport crisis. Attempts were made to make some use of Sollum for landing supplies, but it was only an open roadstead and was under fire from Italian medium guns in Bardia. Some water and other stores were delivered there by the Royal Navy, but its use provided only a marginal relief. Christmas was to be far from a festive season as far as food and drink were concerned. A special issue of NAAFI stores for the division was somehow 'acquired' by the rough, tough 6th Australian Division.

We were just beginning to get supplies back to normal, when the division was launched forward another 80 miles to surround Tobruk, as Bardia fell to the Australians. While the latter moved up to prepare to attack Tobruk, 11th Hussars and 7th Armoured Brigade pushed even further on towards Derna and Mechili. On 22 January the attack on Tobruk began, and next day, when success was seen to be certain, 4th Armoured Brigade was ordered to Mechili, 100 miles further west, to cut off General Babini's armoured brigade there. Unfortunately a combination of petrol supply

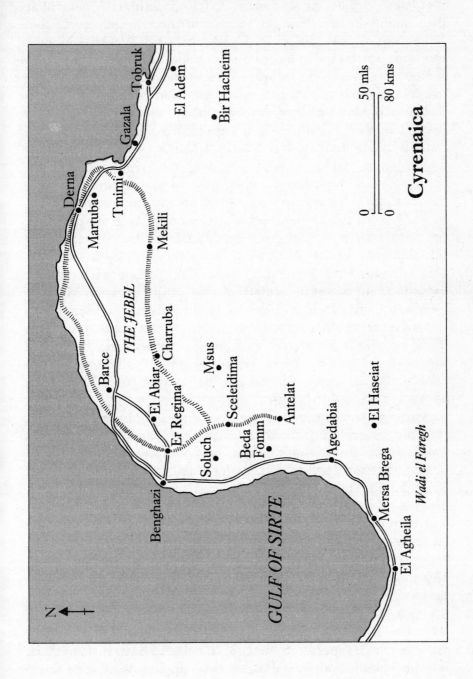

Cyrenaica

problems and inaccurate maps led to a failure to surround
the Italians before they got away into the hill country of the
Jebel Akdar, the 'bulge' of Cyrenaica; and a pause in our
headlong advance was forced on us by logistic realities.

We were now 300 miles as the crow flies, half as much
again in desert mileage, from our railhead at Matruh. Until
Tobruk could be opened up as a port, we were living on a
very slender shoestring. As a result of mechanical troubles,
the division's tank strength had fallen to only 50 cruisers
and 50 light tanks, enough for only two regiments at full
strength. One regiment in each armoured brigade was dismounted and its tanks parcelled out among the other two. In
spite of these difficulties, General O'Connor was for pressing
on. The Italians withdrew from Derna on 29 January, and
his plan was for the Australians to press them back through
the hills towards Benghazi, while 7th Armoured Division
moved 80 miles south-west through the desert from Mechili
to Msus. If the Italians held on in the Jebel or at Benghazi,
the division would continue westward to the coast road, cut
off Benghazi and attack it from the south. If, however,
the enemy appeared to be withdrawing, the division would
continue south-westward and cut the coast road at Agedabia,
another 70 miles further on.

As before the Battle of Sidi Barrani, this could not be made
possible unless we formed a field supply depot beforehand,
forward of where the division was concentrated. I found
myself therefore laying out a depot 30 miles south-west of
Mechili, protected only by armoured car patrols of the 11th
Hussars. I had discovered from them that the area beyond
was very rough, stony ground, and I sited it just short of that.
At this time I had changed places with the DAQMG who had
replaced Pip Roberts, and was based at Advanced Divisional
Headquarters. A further logistic problem, which affected me
personally, was that our winter clothing had never caught
up with us. November 1 was the normal date for the change
from the shirt and shorts of summer into something warmer, and the preparation for the Battle of Sidi Birrani had
interfered with supplies. I wore everything I had, grey flan-
nel trousers underneath my tank overalls. Fortunately my
mother had asked Audrey Watson to send me up a woollen
sweater from Cairo, for which I was very grateful.

While I was establishing the field supply depot, information was received on 2 February 1941 that the Italians had begun their withdrawal. It had originally been intended that the advance would not be resumed until 10 February at the earliest. Now it was suddenly decided that 11th Hussars would set off immediately, and that the rest of the division, less the truncated 7th Armoured Brigade, would follow next day. I had to do some frantic extra stocking of the depot and got into very hot water for hanging on to some of the lorries, which had been delivered there, in order to have a reserve on wheels. On the night of 3 February I was faced with a barrage of demands from the general staff which seemed to me impossible to meet. I could only get the answer by going to see Jack Napier at Rear Headquarters, and had a terrible drive through the desert in the middle of the night, fortunately finding the headquarters, partly by landing up with a wheel in one of its slit-trenches. The next day, 4 February, was one I will never forget. While the division was refuelling at the depot at midday, General Creagh decided to change his plan. In view of the need for speed in order to reach the coast road before the retreating enemy, he decided to form a wheeled force of all arms out of the Support Group to come under the command of Lieutenant-Colonel John Combe, commanding officer of the 11th Hussars, and to give this force priority in replenishment and movement over 4th Armoured Brigade. Caunter was furious, raised every objection and attempted to frustrate the implementation of the order. I had a very difficult time both in transmitting the orders and seeing that they were implemented. I was not totally successful, and 'Combe Force' began to run out of petrol when it neared the coast road.

I travelled in an uncomfortable 'command vehicle', a Morris armoured car without a top, which I shared with Captain Williams of the Army Education Corps, who had to struggle with his cipher books in the cramped space. It was cold and wet, and the bumpy, rocky ground for 15 miles beyond the depot flung us from side to side. I felt that it was not one of my best days; but once we were on smooth desert again and could speed up, the exhilaration of the chase became infectious, more so as we plunged on in the moonlight. A halt was made at midnight, as the leading armoured cars had

come across Italian 'thermos' bombs, small mines dropped
by aircraft. Rather than try and negotiate this hazard in the
dark, the whole division was halted for the night, Combe
Force three miles east of Msus, 4th Armoured Brigade, which
had caught them up, a few miles behind them, and divisional
headquarters behind them. The advance was resumed at
first light on 5 February towards Antelat, 30 miles further
south-west, while the Support Group, less 2nd Battalion The
Rifle Brigade, who were with Combe Force, headed due west
to descend the escarpment at Sceleidima and cut the road at
Ghemines. Seventh Armoured Brigade, which only had the
weak 1st Royal Tanks under command, was told to move
up to Msus.

Eleventh Hussars' armoured cars reached the road 20
miles west of Antelat at midday, reporting only light traffic, and Callum Renton's 2nd Battalion The Rifle Brigade
had established a position across it two hours later. Fourth
Armoured Brigade did not reach Antelat until 5 p.m. having
gingerly negotiated the thermos bombs at Msus in single file.
Air reconnaissance of the road south of Benghazi the day
before had confirmed that the Italians were streaming south.
Being out of wireless contact with O'Connor, Creagh had
decided that the tanks should follow Combe Force to Antelat.
By the time they got there, it was clear that they should
head west for Beda Fomm in order to strike the flank of
the column of vehicles, the head of which would be stopped
by Combe Force. The leading tanks attacked a large column
of all arms west of Beda Fomm before darkness fell. By this
time everyone was screaming for petrol. The Rifle Brigade's
carriers had run dry before they reached the road, Caunter
was still raging, while his energetic and resourceful DAA &
QMG*, George Webb, was scrounging it from every conceiv-
able source, which did not make my job easier. The rushed
start, the subsequent reorganization, the atrocious section of
rough 'going', the wide separation of different parts of the
division and the night move, meant that, with very indifferent wireless communication, I had little idea where further
supplies were or when they could be expected. All I knew was
that I was getting stick; but I also knew that, although I was

* Deputy Assistant Adjutant and Quartermaster-General

out of touch with them, Jack Napier and Pat Eassie would be moving heaven and earth to get supplies up to us.

The decisive day of the campaign was 6 February 1941. The battle raged all day both at Beda Fomm and at the Rifle Brigade's position west of Sidi Saleh. At divisional head-quarters we could only wait and keep our fingers crossed, the demand for tank and artillery ammunition now becoming as urgent as that for petrol. The gallant riflemen, and the anti-tank and other gunners with them, held firm, the tanks of 4th Armoured Brigade returned again and again to the attack, as more and more Italian troops, including tanks and artillery, pressed down from the north; and at last news came from Strafer Gott's Support Group that they had got across the road behind them. After one final fling first thing in the morning of 7 February, white flags went up everywhere and the surrender began of the whole Italian force of over 25,000 men, 100 tanks, 216 guns and 1500 lorries. Our first logistic problem was how to handle them with the slender resources we had at the end of our extended shoestring. By now the Australians were in Benghazi and it was a fairly easy matter to send the prisoners back there down the road in their own lorries to where there was water and food.

Seventh Armoured Division was naturally proud of its part in achieving the final victory in a lightning campaign, in which O'Connor's two divisions had destroyed ten Italian ones, capturing 130,000 prisoners, 180 medium and over 200 light tanks, and 845 guns, for a total loss to themselves of 500 men killed, 1373 wounded and 55 missing, most of this total being in the infantry divisions. We of the logistic staff certainly felt that we had made a major contribution in making possible the rapid moves over long distances. The tanks of the division had in fact done little hard fighting, 4th Armoured Brigade having fought a brief skirmish in the rear of Sidi Barrani and not getting to grips with the enemy again until the final Battle of Beda Fomm. Seventh Armoured Brigade had hardly been in action at all. The burden of the daily task had been carried by the armoured cars of 11th Hussars with additional squadrons from the King's Dragoon Guards and the Royal Air Force. Their task was reconnaissance and they seldom exchanged fire with the enemy, the Italian Air Force being the principal threat to them. The infantry divisions,

first 4th Indian, then 6th Australian, had borne the brunt of
the major battles, Sidi Barrani, Bardia and Tobruk, in which
the support of the Matildas of 7th Royal Tanks had been a
decisive factor.

Once the battlefield had been tidied up and 11th Hussars
had penetrated along the coast road as far as Marble Arch,
there was a general air of relaxation, especially when it
became known that the division, which had only 12 cruiser
and 40 light tanks fit for further service, was to return to Cairo, handing over to the newly arrived 2nd Armoured Division. Assuming that, for the moment, the war was over, the
two parts of the headquarters joined together and, throwing
all precautions to the winds, moved into one of the white
Italian Government rest houses which were spaced at intervals along the coast road. We were all at dinner one moonlit
night, when we were attacked by the German Air Force. It
was a very unpleasant experience. I lay down at the foot of
the wall of the courtyard and was almost completely covered
with earth from a bomb that landed nearby. Many of our
vehicles were destroyed and we were lucky not to have suffered more casualties than we did. When the raid was over,
we lost no time in moving out into the desert and adopting
our usual dispersed formation.

We started back on 18 February, along the road through
Benghazi and the Jebel Akdar. All I can remember of the
move was being stuck for hours in a monumental traffic jam
at the foot of the escarpment outside Derna. A huge, drunk-
en Australian soldier leaned over the door of my truck and
kept up a ceaseless flow of filthy language, trying to provoke
me into saying that I did not like Australians. There was no
possible way of getting rid of him, and I had to endure it,
until eventually the traffic began to move again.

It was an odd feeling, resuming a peacetime sort of life in
Cairo. I had lived at great intensity, with almost every minute
of the day filled with work to do, so that to have no immediate
logistic problems to solve was an anti-climax. Several of my
brother officers took advantage of our return to Cairo to
marry the girl-friends they had left behind them. I was
not tempted in that direction, quite apart from the advice
my father had given me before I left England. 'Don't get
married in Egypt, and, whatever you do, don't get married

there in wartime,' he had said. My mother had raised her eyebrows at that; but he reminded her that, although Egypt had been the cause of their meeting each other, they had not got married in Egypt or in wartime. It was sound advice, although, I must admit, there were as many happy outcomes of such marriages as there were failures. One of those who made the plunge was Tony Lascelles. Immediately after his wedding to Ethne Charles, I took the night train to Luxor, not having been able to visit the temples there before the war. Tony and Ethne turned out to have made the same choice for their honeymoon, and the three of us were almost the only guests in the hotel. I spent a pleasant few days there seeing all the sights and being suitably impressed, although I was not enthusiastic about Egyptian antiquities. I found them monotonous, and preferred the Arabic monuments, such as the mosques and tombs of Cairo, and oriental *objets d'art* of later periods than that of the Egyptian Pharaohs. One of my favourite possessions is a fifteenth-century Persian tile which I bought in the Mouski, the Cairo bazaar, after a year of bargaining, in the course of which the merchant and I became very friendly, and he reduced the price from ten pounds to two.

When I returned to Cairo, I found that I was due to accompany General Creagh on a mission to Turkey to discuss arms supplies and general military assistance. I looked forward to that as a chance to see a new country, but for some reason it was cancelled and Dickie Creagh went without me. It may have been because I had been selected to attend the next course at the Middle East Staff College, due to start in April. This was a wartime course, which compressed into four months the formal instruction in how to conduct staff work which had taken two years in peacetime at Camberley or Quetta. I was fortunate to have been chosen to attend it at the tender age of 26. The college was established in the Telsch Hotel on Mount Carmel above Haifa in Palestine. Most of the instructors had come out from England, while all the students were from the Middle East, a select group having already seen action against the Italians either in the Western Desert or on the borders of Abyssinia and Italian Somaliland. We thought we knew all the answers, and were not inclined to be deferential to our instructors, the majority of whom, if they had seen action at all, had only done so in the defeats of France and Norway. Fellow students included Australians, New Zealanders and South Africans, as well as British officers of the Indian Army. There was also a Pole, Major Kandel, a good deal older than most of us, who had escaped from Poland and made his way through the Balkans to Egypt. We assembled at Haifa on the Saturday before the course began on a Monday, and he spoke no English. I conversed with him in French and asked him how he was going to manage. 'J'apprendrai l'Anglais le dimanche,' was his reply: and he did. Soon, when one greeted him and asked him how he was, he would answer: 'Ploddy well, thank you, ploddy well.' After a time he sensed that this gave us some amusement. Drawing me aside one day, he said: 'Mike, what does this word "ploddy", that everyone uses all the time, really mean?.' I did my best to explain. Half-way through the course, he gave a lecture in English on the organization of the Polish forces in the Middle East. At the end of the course, he was asked by the Commandant, Brigadier Eric Dorman-Smith, what he had thought of it. 'Very interesting,' Kandel replied, 'but I was surprised that there was no mention of the most important principle of war.' Somewhat taken aback, Dorman-Smith asked what it was. 'The most important principle of war is to be stronger than your enemy,' was the reply. In the Middle East at that time we all supported that view.

Eric Dorman-Smith was thought by many then to be one of our most intelligent soldiers. He certainly had a very quick brain and a lively character. He was a trenchant critic, but not so good when it came to proposing a course of action. His principal motive seemed to be to suggest some startlingly novel solution, regardless of whether or not it had a hope of working. He set out to make a splash, and was too obviously concerned with the impression he himself made to endear himself to the students. He had the reputation of being a great one for the ladies, a characteristic we were not able to observe, except at the nearby Piccadilly night club.

Two friends from the desert were also on the course, Pat Turpin, who had been adjutant of the divisional Royal Army Service Corps, and Lyon Corbett-Winder, who had been adjutant of 1st Battalion The King's Royal Rifle Corps

THE DESERT MY DWELLING PLACE

(60th Rifles). We had a long weekend off for Easter, and with them I visited Nazareth, Mount Tabor, Samaria, Jerusalem and Bethlehem. Of all the sights we saw, the Dome of the Rock at Jerusalem impressed me most, with its wide open space round the elegant small mosque with its magnificent golden dome. The weather was perfect, all three of us were keen photographers and at that time Palestine was entirely peaceful. It was a very pleasant interlude.

Although Palestine was at peace and we pursued our studies in a relaxed atmosphere, enjoying all the good things that Palestine provided in the way of food, drink and entertainment, events of great moment were in train not far away. At about the time the course started, early in April 1941, Rommel had launched his counter-offensive in Libya and driven the inexperienced British 2nd Armoured and 9th Australian Infantry Divisions back to Tobruk, practically eliminating the former, capturing Generals Neame and O'Connor in the process. This was followed in May by the disastrous campaign in Greece and Crete. One of the most interesting and striking lectures was given to us by Colonel Freddie de Guingand (later to be well known as Montgomery's chief of staff). He was the army member of the Middle East Commanders-in-Chiefs' Joint Planning Staff, and was outspokenly bitter about the decision to send a British expeditionary force to Greece.

War came closer to us later in May, when Rashid Ali's revolt in Iraq led to the despatch of troops from Palestine to support the garrison of the isolated RAF station of Habbaniya, west of Baghdad. It came closer still in June, when we were half-way through the course, with the opening of the campaign against Vichy-dominated French Syria. We were not very far from the front line, and took the opportunity to see something of the fighting. Hardly surprisingly, this was not popular with the Australian participants. The reaction of an Australian commander was predictably hostile, when a party of 'Pommie' young officers, equipped with shooting-sticks, binoculars and Telsch Hotel picnic lunches – cold chicken and strawberries and cream, washed down with Palestinian white wine – arrived at the front in taxis to 'see the form'. One party ventured rather too far and was cut off by a counter-attack at Quneitra on the Golan Heights. They had to make their way back on foot, abandoning the taxi, after which taxi fares to the front were increased to a sum which, to the relief of the Australians, made such battlefield tours prohibitively expensive. The war came even nearer to us in the form of attacks by the German and Italian Air Forces on Haifa, their target being shipping in the harbour, the oil refinery having been badly damaged in a raid earlier in the year. The Telsch Hotel was on the opposite side of Mount Carmel to the harbour, and from its roof we had a grandstand view of the firework display put up by the anti-aircraft defences, which were seldom, if ever, successful. It was much more dramatic when one of the Royal Navy's cruisers was present. We were far enough from the target to feel fairly safe from attack, but, on a visit to Tel Aviv, the hotel we stayed in was in the centre of the only attack on the city during the war. It gave us an idea of what people in England were accustomed to.

June also saw the failure of Operation *Battleaxe*, the second attempt to drive Rommel back from the Libyan frontier and relieve Tobruk. Whereas I had felt no guilty conscience about enjoying the relaxed atmosphere and fleshpots of the Telsch Hotel while others were fighting the Syrian campaign, I certainly felt twinges of conscience that I was doing so while 7th Armoured Division was in difficulties in the desert.

Although I felt that my apprenticeship on the staff under 'Smuggins' had taught me more about the essentials of staff work than much of the instruction I received, there were many aspects of it which my experience in the desert had not covered. I found most of it interesting and easy to assimilate. My fellow students were a cheerful and lively lot. It had been much preferable to hanging about Cairo with no immediate task on hand; but, now that 7th Armoured Division was back in the desert, I was anxious to return and hoped that I should do so. I was therefore delighted when my posting order arrived shortly before the end of the course in August: to return to Headquarters 7th Armoured Division as DAQMG, one up from my previous job, with the acting rank of major.

When I arrived there, I found that Jack Napier had left and been succeeded by Jackie Bowring, a cavalry officer who was not of the calibre of either of his predecessors. Things were quiet, the bulk of the division having been withdrawn to the area south of Mersa Matruh and 4th Armoured Brigade to Cairo to be re-equipped. The Germans and Italians had remained in possession of Capuzzo and Halfaya Pass and were watched and harassed there by what was known as the Forward Group. This consisted of 22nd Guards Brigade, in the area of the coast between Buq Buq and Sollum, and the Support Group south of the escarpment, Strafer Gott commanding the whole group, subordinate to Headquarters 7th Armoured Division, still commanded by Creagh. Gott's Support Group Headquarters was augmented by a few officers of the divisional headquarters to help him handle the operations and logistics of the Guards Brigade as well as his own Group. I found myself responsible for the logistics, dealing directly with Strafer and exercising considerably more independent responsibility than I should have done back at Rear Divisional Headquarters.

Early in September Strafer Gott replaced Creagh in command of 7th Armoured Division, Jock Campbell taking over Support Group. At the same time Major-General Frank Messervy, with part of the headquarters of his 4th Indian Division, took over the Forward Group, and I remained with it, attached to his staff. Serving with an Indian Army formation, and one with as justifiably high a reputation as 4th Indian, added interest to my work. One improvement came in my driver, an intelligent Indian lance-naik, who replaced the pleasant, but thick-headed Private B. who had driven me since I returned. Whenever I stopped, to visit a unit or for any purpose, on my return to the staff car – a Ford V8 station wagon – the lance-naik would have made a simple sketch-map of landmarks of any kind he had seen en route, the mileage and the approximate direction between them, asking me if it was correct. This was in stark contrast to B.'s total lack of interest in such matters. One day, after we had been unsuccessfully attacked by a lone Italian aircraft – the pilot tried to drop hand grenades on me, having apparently no other ammunition, and I tried and failed to bring him down with rifle fire – I asked B. what he would have done if I had been killed. He pondered for a time and replied: 'I'd 'ave buried yer.'

In spite of constant attempts to train him, he never had any idea of the direction in which he was going or should go.

On 14 September Rommel advanced over the frontier with 21st Panzer Division, apparently under the impression that an abandoned field supply depot at Bir el Khireigat, 20 miles south of Sollum, was in use or being built up to support an offensive. I was sleeping on the ground at the headquarters, about 50 miles from the frontier, and distinctly heard the rumble of moving tanks, a sound which was inaudible when I lifted my head from the ground. Jock Campbell's orders were to withdraw, which he did skilfully, losing nothing, but harassing the enemy with artillery fire. The armoured cars covering the front were from 4th South African Armoured Car Regiment, who lost a truck containing all their orders and ciphers. This caused considerable consternation, but does not appear to have provided Rommel with information of any importance.

I moved the rear headquarters of the Forward Group back by stages along the telephone line which ran through the desert, connecting my instrument to the 'top outer pair' at every halt, which my signaller correctly told me would put me straight through to Headquarters 13 Corps, so that I could both keep them informed and arrange a readjustment of our supplies. As we withdrew, squadrons of the South African Air Force pounded away at the panzer division. Having failed to find petrol at the mythical depot, the Germans ran dry after they had advanced some 50 miles to Bir Habata, near where our headquarters had been, in the afternoon. Rommel was lucky to return alive. His command vehicle, captured from 2nd Armoured Division in April, was bombed, the driver killed and he himself had the heel blown off one of his boots. One of the tyres was punctured and went completely flat. Separated from all other vehicles and with no driver, Rommel and his staff took a long time to mend it, and only managed to get back through the frontier wire at dawn with Rommel himself at the wheel. The effect of the operation, christened appropriately by the Germans as 'Midsummer Night's Dream', was to persuade Rommel, erroneously, that the British were making no preparations for an offensive.

When it was over, 4th Indian Division took over the front with its own brigades and I returned to Headquarters 7th Armoured Division, not at all happy at the prospect of working under Jackie Bowring. I was delighted when I was told that I was to take over as GSO2 (General Staff Officer 2) at Main Headquarters from Pip Roberts, who was to go to England as an instructor at the Staff College at Camberley. Although I had found work on the 'Q' staff interesting, I was anxious not to become labelled as a 'Q' expert and keen either to return to my regiment or transfer to the 'G' staff. My immediate superior was the GSO1, Lieutenant-Colonel 'Rickie' Richards of the Royal Tank Regiment, the GSO3 being Captain Pat Hobart, Hobo's nephew, who had been adjutant of 2nd Royal Tank Regiment in the campaign against the Italians. I had only been in the job for two weeks when Strafer Gott told me that I must give it up and go to Cairo to help form an Armoured Corps Headquarters. He had been ordered to provide two staff officers, well experienced in the needs of armoured divisions. Pip Roberts had been stopped from going to England, and he and I together were to form the headquarters, which had to be ready to take the field in a month's time. I was bitterly disappointed, but had to accept Strafer's explanation, which was put in flattering terms.

4

'The Flinty and Steel Couch of War'

William Shakespeare (1546–1616) *Othello*

The Armoured Corps Headquarters, subsequently to be known as Headquarters 30 Corps, was required to command the mobile forces in the major offensive operations which General Auchinleck was planning with the ambitious aim of recapturing the whole of Cyrenaica and destroying the German and Italian armoured forces in the process, the relief of the isolated garrison of Tobruk being incidental to the plan. Ever since he had taken over from Wavell as Commander-in-Chief at the end of June, Auchinleck had been under pressure from London to mount such an offensive. He had been reluctant to do so, and, when he and Air Marshal Tedder had flown to London at the end of July to argue his case, he had maintained that he would need certainly two and preferably three complete armoured divisions to be sure of success. Although there was a total of 500 tanks of all kinds in the Middle East at that time, 7th Armoured Division was the only armoured formation, and neither of its brigades, 4th and 7th, could be fully up to strength in tanks until the end of September, by which time 4th Armoured Brigade would have been completely re-equipped with the American Stuart tank, colloquially known as the 'Honey'. Auchinleck's visit resulted in the decision to despatch 22nd Armoured Brigade, the Yeomanry brigade of 1st Armoured Division, round the Cape. It could not arrive until the end of September, and would not be ready to take the field until November, a month being little enough time to see that all its tanks were modified for desert conditions and in good mechanical order, and that the crews were trained in desert lore and tactics.

To command this operation an army headquarters was formed on 9 September, originally called 'Western Army', becoming the famous Eighth Army on 27 September 1941. The commander chosen for it was Alan Cunningham, a gunner, brother of the C-in-C of the Mediterranean Fleet, the famous A.B.C. He had commanded the forces which had swept up from East Africa to Addis Ababa, covering huge distances, but meeting little resistance, nothing like that which General Platt's forces had had to overcome at Keren in northern Abyssinia. The formation which had played the major part under Cunningham had been General Brink's 1st South African Division, and it had been moved up to Egypt to form part of Eighth Army. Having motored so many miles, and being more generously equipped with motor transport than infantry divisions of the British and Indian armies, it was thought suitable, at any rate by Cunningham, to provide the mobile infantry for the armoured corps. Eighth Army was to command two corps, 30 and 13. The latter was to contain the bulk of the infantry, commanded by Lieutenant-General Godwin-Austen, who had led the 12th African Division, consisting of troops from West and East Africa, under Cunningham in Abyssinia, the corps headquarters being the original one, formed from Headquarters Western Desert Force. The commander selected for 30 Corps was Vyvyan Pope, one of the most able officers of the Royal Tank Regiment, who was Director of Armoured Fighting Vehicles in the War Office at the time of his appointment. He arrived in Cairo on 25 September, having flown from Gibraltar in the same Catalina flying-boat as Wavell on his way to India. The aircraft was badly damaged by a large wave on take-off, adding to the many mishaps with aircraft that Wavell suffered and proving a bad omen for Pope.

I reached Cairo five days later and reported to the office in GHQ of Brigadier Hugh Russell, then 'Brigadier AFV', the Middle East equivalent of the post that Pope had held in Whitehall. He had been the charming and able commander of the Cairo Cavalry Brigade, subsequently 7th Armoured

Brigade. I therefore knew him well. Pip Roberts was already
there. We were presented with an 'establishment', that is a
detailed organization for an armoured corps headquarters
which somebody in the War Office had concocted, but told
that it was out of the question to produce either the men or
the equipment which that document specified; that General
Pope insisted that the headquarters should be as small as
possible and include the minimum of administrative and
logistic staff – no chaplain's post or anything like that; that
our principal source of manpower, including all signals,
would be 8th Division Headquarters, brought down from
Palestine, and that the headquarters had to be fully operational in the desert in a month's time. Our immediate source
of manpower was to be the Royal Armoured Corps Depot at
Abbassia, which held officers and soldiers who had arrived
as reinforcements or had been discharged from hospital and
had not been posted back to their units. Pip and I, at that
stage, were the only officers of the headquarters, apart from
General Pope, Hugh Russell, selected as the Brigadier General Staff, and Brigadier Unwin as DA & QMG, that is head
of the administrative and logistic staff. The 'establishment'
given to us as our guide provided for a lieutenant-colonel
on the 'Q' staff, but none on the 'G' side, three majors
being subordinate to the BGS, one for operations, one for
intelligence and one for 'staff duties', the last-named being
responsible for organization, movement (other than operations), and allotment of priorities for equipment. Pip, being
senior to me, became the AQMG as a lieutenant-colonel and
I the GSO2 (SD). To produce a new headquarters from
scratch and have it ready to take command in the field within
a month was an ambitious project. Fortunately some of the
officers and soldiers posted to us had already had experience
in the desert, including 'Smuggins', whom I was delighted to
welcome as the Deputy Director of Supplies and Transport,
that is head of the corps RASC. I had an awkward interview
with two senior chaplains, one Church of England, the other
Roman Catholic, who arrived expecting promotion, only to
be told that General Pope refused to have any. They had to
return in ecumenical dudgeon to console themselves at the
bar of Shepheard's Hotel, the C of E chaplain, Hughes, later
to become Montgomery's head chaplain.

Working like blacks at our task, we were horrified on 5 October to be told that the aircraft taking General Pope, his ADC and Brigadiers Russell and Unwin to a conference at Eighth Army Headquarters, had crashed shortly after taking off, killing all its occupants. I had not yet met Vyvyan Pope, but had heard very good reports of him. I felt the loss of Hugh Russell keenly. His successor was Jack Napier, under whom I was happy to serve again. Pope himself was replaced by Major-General Willoughby Norrie, who had been on his way out to the Middle East with the headquarters of 1st Armoured Division. Its 22d Armoured Brigade, which had just arrived at Suez, was to join 30 Corps for the battle, the rest of the division not being due until December.

As soon as we had assembled the personnel of the headquarters and its signals and had acquired the basic minimum of our equipment, we moved out of the barracks and set up in tents not far from the Pyramids, in order to get everyone accustomed to the routine of desert life while we were still near enough to the base installations to remedy all the hundred and one deficiencies which our move into the sand had revealed. On 21 October, only three weeks after I had reached Cairo, we moved up into the Western Desert south-west of Mersa Matruh and took over command of 7th Armoured Division, 1st South African Division and 22nd Guards Brigade.

The two principal problems immediately on my plate were the tank problems of 7th Armoured Division and the motor transport problems of the South Africans. Seventh Armoured Division was to have three armoured brigades, its original 4th and 7th and the newly-arrived 22nd. When the 4th moved up into the desert, after being re-equipped in the Nile delta, and started training, not only was it found that the range of the 'Honeys' on one fill of petrol was only 40 miles, but also that their rubber-covered tracks began to break up on the sharp stones of the desert. Both faults caused consternation. Nothing could be done about the former and, after losing odd chunks of rubber, the tracks of the Honeys remained perfectly serviceable and gave no further trouble. Seventh Brigade's problem was that they had a mixture of cruiser tanks of different marks, A10s, A13s and A15s, many of the earlier models not in their first youth and the A15s suffering from teething troubles. Twenty-second Brigade's tanks all had to be modified to make them fit to operate in the desert and, after their long voyage, many needed other forms of repair or were deficient in important equipment. Until these needs were met, they could not start the desert training they urgently required. On my shoulders lay the responsibility of trying to extract their needs from the base organization. With less than three weeks to go before the battle was due to start, it was a hectic time.

Norrie soon realized that 1st South African Division had an immense amount to learn about movement and operations in the desert, where tanks might appear at any time, a very different matter from driving from Nairobi to Addis Ababa. He urged General Brink to move away from the coast and start training actively for the role of a mobile infantry division. But Brink was short of motor transport, which was on its way from East and South Africa. He wanted the British to help him out by providing it from their stocks, which they were most unwilling to do. Norrie felt that Brink was being obstructive and not really trying, and at one stage he threatened to ask Cunningham to give him 4th Indian Division instead and let the South Africans take their place in 13 Corps.. It was a great pity that this was not done, as, with their considerable desert experience and skill, the Indians were better fitted for the mobile rôle.

The overall plan for the operation, nicknamed *Crusader*, had been finalized at the end of September. While 13 Corps, with the New Zealand and 4th Indian Divisions, supported by First Army Tank Brigade (132 Matildas and Valentines), masked the Italian Savona Division, defending the frontier area from Sidi Omar through Capuzzo to Halfaya Pass, 7th Armoured Division with 491 tanks would cross the wire further south and swing up towards Tobruk 'to find and destroy the enemy's armour', with the secondary task of protecting 13 Corps' left flank. First South African Division, echeloned on 7th Armoured's left rear, was to protect the latter's communications on the west and south-west, and later, when the enemy's armour had been defeated, was to capture the Sidi Rezegh ridge as a preliminary to a link-up with the garrison of Tobruk, which would attack southward to meet them. When 30 Corps had defeated the enemy armour, 13 Corps

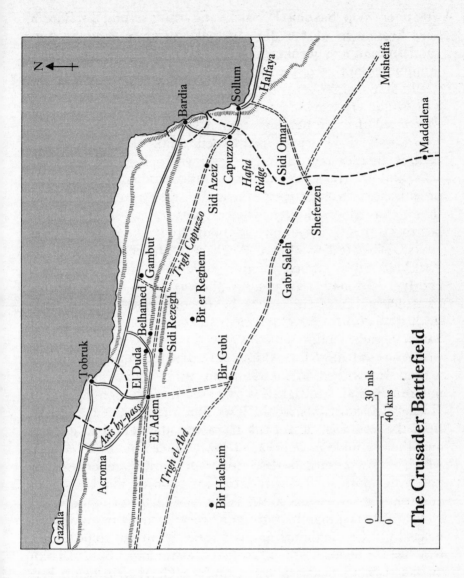

The Crusader Battlefield

would envelop Savona Division and the garrison of Bardia, and then move west to link up with 30 Corps and Scobie's 70th Division in Tobruk.

Cunningham's concept was that 7th Armoured Division would initially move as far as Gabr Saleh, 35 miles west of Sidi Omar and the same distance south of Sidi Rezegh, 4th Armoured Brigade on their right keeping close to Freyberg's New Zealand Division on the left flank of 13 Corps. By then it should have become clear where Rommel's armour was, and the presence of Norrie's tanks there should have provoked a clash between them. Norrie's nearly 500 tanks should have been able to defeat Rommel's, thought to be not more that 200 German (actually 174, not counting light tanks). The Italian Ariete Armoured Division, with about 150 M13 tanks (much inferior to any of the British), was known to be some way away to the west. The enemy armour thus defeated, Norrie would be free to move all his tanks towards Tobruk and Godwin-Austen to start moving round Savona's right flank.

Norrie did not like this restriction on his freedom of action. He wished to move all his tanks, including 4th Armoured Brigade, straight for the area Sidi Rezegh–El Adem. He believed that this would force Rommel to move his tanks from the area east of Tobruk to engage this threat to his rear and thus remove any threat of tank attack against 13 Corps, which in any case had 130 tanks of its own. Godwin-Austen, and even more so Freyberg, strongly opposed this suggestion and wanted Gatehouse's 4th Armoured Brigade to be under 13 Corps' command until the enemy armour had been defeated. Cunningham finally decided on a compromise, leaving Gatehouse under Norrie's command, but insisting on his concept being followed and on Gatehouse being kept close to the New Zealanders. I was little concerned with these discussions, being fully occupied with getting the formations ready for battle, particularly the South Africans.

The move forward to the frontier was left to the last moment. The final advance, which took us through the frontier wire, was made during the night of 17/18 November, a stormy night near the coast, which helped to conceal the move from the enemy's air force, which was attacked on the ground by our own. General Cunningham travelled with us, intent on remaining until the great decision had been made about what to do after Gott's tanks had reached Gabr Saleh. It was an exhilarating experience. The greatest force of tanks assembled by Britain since the Battle of Cambrai in 1917 swept forward through the empty desert, unopposed and apparently unseen by the enemy, unheard also, as we had observed wireless silence throughout the advance – only listening watch. Our tails were up and, certainly in 30 Corps Headquarters and in 7th Armoured Division, we were full of confidence.

Ironically, as far as Cunningham's concept was concerned, we had been too successful in the concealment of our plans and moves. By the end of the day, 18 November, good progress had been made, but there did not appear to have been any reaction from Rommel, and it was not clear where his panzer divisions were or what they were doing. The reason was that his attention was still rivetted on his planned attack on Tobruk. Norrie wanted to concentrate on advancing to Sidi Rezegh and joining hands with Tobruk, but Cunningham insisted on a more cautious plan which involved a wide dispersion of Gott's three armoured brigades. This was to have fatal consequences. While Davy's 7th Armoured Brigade and Campbell's Support Group advanced to Sidi Rezegh, Scott-Cockburn's 22nd was sent west to deal with the Italians at Bir Gubi and Gatehouse held back to guard Freyberg's flank.

Rommel at last reacted, and his 21st Panzer Division attacked Gatehouse in an inconclusive action at the end of the day. It was to be the first of a number of occasions on which we greatly overestimated the number of enemy tanks we had knocked out. The battle was resumed next day, again without any decisive result. Meanwhile Davy and Campbell had secured Sidi Rezegh airfield, and Norrie pressed Cunningham to give the order to Major-General Scobie in Tobruk to attack southward towards them, while they thrust north; but Cunningham was still concerned that Rommel's tanks had not been defeated and might turn on Freyberg. Scott-Cockburn, whose task of watching the Italians was to be handed over to the South Africans, instead of joining Davy and Campbell as Norrie had intended, was moved to join Gatehouse.

Both the South Africans and Scott-Cockburn were slow to move, and the latter did not join Gatehouse on 20 November until shortly before dusk, after he had been fighting 15th Panzer Division for two hours, his tank strength having fallen to 97 from the 165 with which he had started the operation. Gatehouse's optimistic claim about the number of tanks he had knocked out (in fact the Germans reported no losses) led Cunningham to agree that Scobie and Campbell should launch their attacks on 21 November, while Brink should send his 5th Infantry Brigade to join the latter. Gatehouse and Scott-Cockburn would prevent Cruewell's Afrika Korps from interfering. Norrie felt that things were working out well, and he was confident that the day would see the link-up with Tobruk effected and Rommel's forces east of it cut off.

However Rommel and Cruewell had at last woken up to the threat posed by Gott's forces at Sidi Rezegh. Both panzer divisions drove north away from Gatehouse and Scott-Cockburn, who were slow to follow up, and attacked Davy and Campbell while the latter was attacking northwards and meeting stiff opposition, as did Scobie in his thrust towards them. The situation became very confused, and by the end of the day Davy had lost many of his tanks and Campbell had suffered heavy casualties.

During these eventful days I had at first found myself suddenly with less work to do. My principal task was to produce the tank and gun state, that is the strength of serviceable ones, at the end of the day. For this I was entirely dependent on information provided by the divisions, who had considerable difficulty in getting accurate reports from their subordinates until long after dark. Next day's plans naturally depended to a considerable degree on the strength of the brigades, especially on 21 November. When Norrie left the main headquarters, he took Major Dick Hobson, the GSO2 (Operations), with him, forming a small tactical headquarters. This left the operations staff short-handed and I was called upon to take Hobson's place in the command vehicle, where I found that Jack Napier was clearly not in good health.

The morning of 22 November started quietly, but it was to turn out a thoroughly bad day. The Afrika Korps attacked the Sidi Rezegh area from both flanks all day, inflicting further casualties on Davy and Campbell and being little affected by the activities of Scott-Cockburn or Gatehouse. After dark 15th Panzer Division, moving to refuel, hit the latter's headquarters and one of his regiments, throwing 4th Armoured Brigade into confusion. Gatehouse himself was returning to his headquarters and was lucky to escape capture. As usual it was long after dark before we, at Headquarters 30 Corps, had anything like a clear picture of what had occurred or what the situation was, except that the general position was not as favourable as it had appeared 24 hours earlier. Nevertheless Cunningham persisted with the plan to link up, intending that the South Africans should take over the task of attacking northwards, reinforced by one of Freyberg's brigades advancing west from the frontier, while Gott's depleted armoured brigades held off Rommel's tanks. At midnight he made a major change in his plan, deciding that 13 Corps should assume responsibility for the attack, using the whole New Zealand Division as well as the South African, which would be transferred to Godwin-Austen's command. Norrie's task would be to 'continue the destruction of the enemy armoured forces' while 'helping 13 Corps in its attack and protecting its flank and rear'.

The first we knew of this change of plan was when a staff officer from Headquarters Eighth Army arrived at 9 a.m. on 23 November. As by then everybody was immersed in the day's battle, I was sent by Norrie to represent him at a meeting at Headquarters 13 Corps to discuss how to implement it with Cunningham's Brigadier General Staff, Sandy Galloway, and Godwin-Austen's, John Harding, both 20 years my senior. I had to point out all the practical difficulties, and they accepted that the existing command arrangements would have to continue until the situation could be stabilized. This was far from being the case. Cruewell, out of touch with Rommel, moved 15th Panzer Division round behind all Gott's brigades and, having joined up with the Italian Ariete Armoured Division near Bir Gubi, drove north to join 21st Panzer, attacking and overrunning 5th South African Brigade in the process, fending off with little difficulty the belated attempts of Gott's brigades to intervene. His losses in the attack, however, were heavy.

Cunningham, disturbed at the heavy reduction in Norrie's tank strength, had asked Auchinleck to come up and discuss the situation, suggesting to him that the offensive should be temporarily abandoned. Auchinleck refused, and told him to renew the attack to link up with Tobruk, the main effort in which would now have to be made by Freyberg. Our task was to reorganize ourselves and protect what was left of the South Africans – only one brigade – and 'be prepared to help the New Zealand Division in the event of a concentrated enemy attack during their advance'.

In order to discuss with Gott how best to do this, Norrie decided to visit him in the morning of 24 November, taking his tactical headquarters with him. On this occasion he took me instead of Dick Hobson, possibly just for a change, possibly because, with Jack Napier not well, he thought that the GSO2 (Operations) should be at the main headquarters, possibly because he thought that somebody who was thoroughly versed in the local jargon and in 7th Armoured Division's methods would be more helpful to him than Hobson, who was new to the desert and its ways. The other officers forming the tactical headquarters were Norrie's ADC, Captain Grant-Singer, the Brigadier Royal Artillery, David Aikenhead, and his staff officer, Captain John Gibbon*, and the GSO3 (Intelligence), Captain Antony Part†. Tony Part travelled with me in the wireless truck which kept us in touch with main headquarters and with everything that went on on the corps forward net, that is the operational frequency with which we communicated with subordinate formations. The whole party consisted of two Ford station-wagons and two 8-hundredweight trucks.

Cunningham flew up to a landing strip near main headquarters 30 Corps and was brought from there to meet Norrie at Gott's headquarters by Colonel George Clifton, the colourful New Zealander who commanded the Corps Engineers. Soon after he had arrived, the startling information came from 7th Armoured Division that a large body of German tanks was bearing down on us only a few miles away, having apparently passed through our armoured car screen without being spotted. Gott decided to move his

---

* Later General Sir John Gibbon, Master-General of the Ordnance.
† Later Sir Antony Part, a distinguished civil servant.

headquarters eastward, Norrie remaining with him and telling George Clifton to get Cunningham off to his aircraft immediately. We packed up in haste and moved about ten miles to the east, which turned out to be one of the few peaceful bits of desert.

This was the start of Rommel's dash to the frontier, which was to prove fatal to him. He was under the false impression that Norrie's forces had been eliminated and did not realize that Freyberg had moved west towards Tobruk. His plan was to link up with the Italian Savona Division in the frontier defences and cut off all of Eighth Army from its line of communications. He set off himself at the head of 15th Panzer, leaving Cruewell to follow with the 21st, when he had got them together and refuelled them, and it was the 15th that was heading straight for where we were. They continued south-east, sweeping main and rear headquarters and all the administrative transport helter-skelter before them as they did so. Fortunately they did not stop to examine the northernmost of the two field supply depots, on which all our replenishment depended, although they passed through part of it. The whole of Rommel's mobile force having penetrated our armoured car screen, it was very difficult to form a picture of what on earth was happening, especially as the operational formations, 1st South African and 4th Armoured Brigades, were hardly affected, being on the southern and northern flanks respectively of the thrust. Main headquarters was perpetually on the move. When it could get a message through, it painted a picture of utter confusion. In the afternoon we moved farther east and, as we did so, came across one of main headquarters' armoured command vehicles abandoned. Both the vehicle and the wireless sets were in perfect running order. It was merely out of fuel. We filled it up and I drove it, operating the set at the same time, while Antony Part kept the operational log. From then on, until we finally joined up again with main headquarters on 2 December, we constituted the only part of 30 Corps Headquarters through which Norrie could exercise command. Main and rear headquarters finally came to rest alongside main headquarters 13 Corps near Sidi Azeiz. Towards the end of the day a clearer picture began to emerge of what had happened. Fourth Armoured Brigade, with the weak 22nd, was intact and had not been engaged, remaining in its favourite area of Bir er Reghem, twelve miles south-east of Sidi Rezegh, as was 1st South African Brigade at Taieb el Essem, twelve miles south of them. The remnants of Davy's 7th were with Campbell's weak Support Group south of Gabr Saleh, whither both had been sent to reorganize. There they had been just south of Rommel's route, the Trigh el Abd, along which his forces were now all strung out. Gott and Norrie decided to move south during the night, through Rommel's tail, and join up with the Support Group. The move was made in a long column, the rear of which I brought up in a borrowed armoured car. We could see parties of German vehicles sending up coloured Very lights to guide their stragglers in, and we threaded our way between them. As we did so, I realized that we were being followed by a motor-cycle combination, a vehicle which only the Germans used. I passed a wireless message to Rickie Richards, the GSO1, and asked him to send one of the protective troop's tanks round to the rear of the column when we finally halted, thinking that perhaps more Germans might have tagged on behind the motor-cycle. When we did so, I shouted orders in my best German to the motor-cycle crew to dismount and inspect their vehicles, which they dutifully did, taken aback when a Crusader tank appeared out of the darkness, to the crew of which they surrendered without protest.

Not surprisingly it took quite a long time to form even an approximate picture of what the situation was. It was more favourable than might have been expected, and than we realized at the time. Rommel's dash had inflicted no damage, and had we taken more decisive action on the two following days to exploit it, Freyberg's New Zealanders could have been saved from the troubles and casualties that were to be inflicted on them a few days later. A contributory cause of our failure to do so was that a change of command was taking place at Headquarters Eighth Army, Auchinleck dismissing Cunningham and sending Neil Ritchie up from Cairo to replace him. Freyberg meanwhile had continued to fight his way forward towards Tobruk in a series of night attacks, contact with Scobie's troops being finally achieved and a narrow corridor opened between Ed Duda and Belhamed by the morning of 27 November.

By that time Rommel had at last woken up to the reality of
the situation, and he began to move back from the frontier
towards Tobruk. Gott succeeded in blocking his move, but,
as his tanks withdrew at night to refuel and replenish their
supplies, the Afrika Korps and the Italian Ariete Armoured
Division slipped past to threaten Freyberg's rear and southern flank. Neither Godwin-Austen nor Freyberg had given
much attention to that, assuming that Norrie was protecting
them from it; but they could now no longer disregard it, and
Godwin-Austen moved his headquarters into Tobruk, while
Norrie was told by Ritchie to get Pienaar's 1st South African
Brigade up to join the New Zealanders.

The next day, 29 November, was confusing, as Rommel
and Cruewell gave conflicting orders for the two panzer
divisions to attack Freyberg in the area of Sidi Rezegh.
We had with us a tactical wireless intercept truck, manned
by a middle-aged Pole, and he picked up a message which
appeared to indicate that 15th and 21st Panzer Divisions were
going to concentrate on the airfield and attack Freyberg from
the south. The only way we could warn him of this was to tell
Headquarters 13 Corps, with whom we could communicate
most rapidly on a high-power speech set. I went with Norrie
to the set and we sat there intensely frustrated while a long
discussion went on between Ritchie and Godwin-Austen,
neither of whom, quite clearly, was accustomed to speaking
on the wireless, discussing (in clear) the general state of the
New Zealand Division and of ammunition supplies both for
them and for Scobie's troops. At last the conversation came
to an end and Ritchie said: 'If you have nothing more to
say, say "OK Out", Over,' to which Godwin-Austen replied:
'I have nothing more to say. OK Out, Over.' Back again
came Ritchie with: 'I said, if you have nothing more to say,
say "OK Out", Over.' 'I said that I have nothing more to say,'
an irritated Godwin-Austen replied, 'OK OUT, OVER.' As
there seemed to be no end to this exchange, Norrie broke in
and asked Godwin-Austen to warn Freyberg, the reaction of
both Ritchie and Godwin-Austen being that it was Norrie's
task to prevent such an attack, which did not in the event
materialize.

The next two days were spent in a vain attempt to get
Pienaar to join Freyberg and do something to help him,

Norrie at one stage leading the brigade personally in order to try and speed its snail-like progress. But it was all to no avail, and Gatehouse, into whose brigade almost all of Gott's 120 tanks had been concentrated, was no more effective in helping the New Zealanders, who were heavily attacked on two successive days, until, on the night of 1/2 December, Freyberg was forced to withdraw, Ritchie accepting his decision.

The attempt to link up with Tobruk had failed. Norrie had already proposed that, instead of battering away in the Sidi Rezegh area, the main effort should be switched to that of Bir Gubi, in order to lever Rommel's forces away from Tobruk. Ritchie now accepted this plan, for which he would reinforce 30 Corps with Frank Messervy's 4th Indian Division, which had successfully reduced the Italian frontier defences, leaving only the isolated garrisons of Bardia and Halfaya, watched by Klopper's 2nd South African Division. As we prepared to implement this plan, Rommel dashed back to the frontier again to try and rescue his garrisons, causing Ritchie to order Norrie, much to his annoyance, to move Gatehouse's tanks eastward again. However the threat to Rommel's rear, posed by our move towards Bir Gubi, brought him back again and removed Ritchie's growing concern. Neither our attacks nor Cruewell's attempts to counter them on 6 and 7 December were well carried out; but by then Rommel had decided that the combination of his losses and the precariousness of his supply situation demanded a withdrawal, not just from the perimeter of Tobruk but out of Cyrenaica altogether, back to his old resting place at Mersa Brega. After a flaming row with his Italian superiors, he and they began to withdraw.

Richie now decided that he needed only one corps for operations farther west and that it should be 13 Corps, partly on the grounds that, being on the right, it was already better placed, partly because he thought that operations in the hilly country of the Jebel were better suited to a primarily infantry formation than to an armoured one. We were very disappointed, as we felt that we were much better suited in every way to command what we thought would be a very mobile pursuit operation. Norrie protested in vain, and we returned reluctantly to the frontier area to take command of

1st and 2nd South African Divisions and Bill Watkins's First Army Tank Brigade. Our task was to deal with the garrisons of Bardia and Halfaya, an anti-climax after what, in spite of its setbacks, confusion and casualties, had turned out to be a victory.

Exciting and interesting as it had been to have held a key position as Norrie's sole executive staff officer for the eight days in which we had been separated from main headquarters, it had been a considerable physical strain, glued to the wireless all day and much of the night, relieved for short periods by Tony Part or John Gibbon to snatch meals. These were prepared by the driver of our truck, except for the evening one which, if Willoughby Norrie were there, was prepared by his elderly 11th Hussar batman, and which I used to eat with him in his staff car. It was accompanied by a glass of whisky and a Burma cheroot, over which we would discuss the day's events and the plan for the morrow. I can recall my anger one evening when, after a particularly tiring day, I went over to Norrie's staff car, only to find that my place had been taken by Randolph Churchill, who had made his way up from Cairo. He had eaten my slice of bully, had drunk my whisky and was puffing at my cheroot, while asking Norrie in languid tones: 'Well, General, do you think this battle is in danger of degenerating into a stalemate?' I returned in disgust to my truck, opened a tin of bully and brewed a mug of tea. Norrie decided that I was officially to become his GSO2 (Operations), Hobson being sent back to Cairo, whence he was posted to India, my place as GSO2 (Staff Duties) being taken by Major Noel Wall, a 7th Hussar, who had been brigade major of 7th Armoured Brigade to George Davy. The latter took over as Brigadier General Staff from Jack Napier, who returned to the base in poor health. George Davy was to prove a lively, quick-witted and amusing man to work for, and the whole staff was invigorated by his personality, raising the morale of those who had been swept away with main and rear headquarters and had kicked their heels in idleness, justifiably anxious about their security.

Reduction of the German and Italian garrisons of Bardia and Halfaya was a straightforward affair, for which the South Africans had strong air support as well as naval gunfire from the cruiser HSM *Ajax* and the gunboat *Aphis*.

Bardia surrendered on 2 January and Halfaya on the 17th, the haul of prisoners totalling 13,800, of whom about one-third were German. One thousand British, who had been captured, were released.

While planning this last operation, I had an amusing experience. I had flown down to Mersa Matruh in the rear seat of an RAF army cooperation *Audax* to discuss the plan to attack Halfaya with 1st South African Division, who gave the pilot and myself a large lunch, washed down with beer. On the return flight I dozed off, until suddenly the aircraft came down, landed on a smooth bit of desert and the pilot got out. I cursed myself not only for going to sleep, and not therefore knowing where we were, but for the unforgivable sin in the desert of not having with me my compass or any reserve of food or water. 'What's up?' I asked the pilot. 'Oh, I only wanted to do a pee,' he replied. I also got out and was relieved in more ways than one when we took off again without incident.

Once these operations were over, we had little to do and I managed to fit in one of our six-monthly rations of five days leave in Cairo, staying with Tom and Dorothea Russell, the Watsons no longer being there. They had been on annual leave when the war had started. Frank and Audrey had returned to Cairo, but Diana stayed in England and trained to be a nurse. Frank died in Cairo in 1941 and Audrey then returned to England. The luxury of a hot bath, a comfortable bed, good food and entertaining talk – Dorothea Russell was a great conversationalist – was a welcome change; but being at a loose end soon palled, and I was glad to get back to work in the desert.

5

Slings and Arrows

To suffer
The slings and arrows of outrageous fortune
or to take arms against a sea of troubles,
and by opposing end them.

William Shakespeare (1564–1616) *Hamlet*

While 30 Corps had little to occupy it in the frontier area
after the surrender of the frontier garrisons, 13 Corps was
going through a difficult time farther west, which culminated in Eighth Army's withdrawal to Gazala, 70 miles west
of Tobruk. By then 'Strafer' Gott had replaced Godwin-
Austen in command of 13 Corps. He was succeeded in
command of 7th Armoured Division by Jock Campbell*,
who was almost immediately killed in a car accident, his place
being taken by Frank Messervy.

Over the next two months the front stabilized on the
Gazala line, as the forces there were built up and Tobruk
and the area immediately east of it, round Belhamed, developed as a major logistic base to support the reconquest of
Cyrenaica. Churchill was pressing Auchinleck to undertake
this as soon as possible, primarily to ease the problem of
supplying Malta. The Auk was reluctant to embark on such
an operation, until he had restored his armoured strength
and had built up sufficient logistic stocks at Tobruk, bringing
the railway and water pipeline up to there, to make Eighth
Army independent of supply by sea. The navy continued to

* He had been awarded the Victoria Cross for his exploits at Sidi Rezegh.

suffer casualties from the German air force based in Greece
and Crete, as well as in Cyrenaica.

I turned my attention to trying to improve our operational
methods in two interconnected areas: that of obtaining
more accurate and up-to-date information of the operational
situation, and, with the help of that, of obtaining support
from the Royal Air Force. There had been a marked contrast between the support which the RAF provided for the
attacks on the frontier garrisons, where the target was
fixed and easily recognizable, the positions both of the enemy
and our own forces being clearly defined, and their inability
to do much during Operation *Crusader*. In the latter the
difficulty that pilots faced in any case in knowing where
they were in the desert was compounded by the intermingling
of the two opposing sides on the ground and our own lack
of accurate, up-to-date information on where our own or the
enemy forces were. To improve the last was necessary in any
event, but was also an essential first step in improving air
support.

When I had been with Norrie's tactical headquarters,
attached to Headquarters 7th Armoured Division, I had
realized that, if I kept a wireless set tuned in to their forward
control net, I obtained all the information that they received
at the same time, and did not have to keep asking them what
was going on. When I left them, I continued, whenever
possible, to keep a set 'listening in' to their forward control.
A development of this was to provide the army liaison officer
attached to the RAF army cooperation squadron with a set
'listening in' to the 30 Corps forward control net. Owing to
the distance between him and us, he might have difficulty
in hearing all that went on, but it provided me with a direct
link, by-passing the official channels through Headquarters
Eighth Army and Desert Air Force, which proved too slow
and were complicated by niceties of protocol between army
and RAF staff responsibilities. I managed to acquire the necessary sets and operators from the sympathetic commander
of the corps signals, but we had to keep quiet about it, as the
arrangement ran counter to the official rules. In his memoirs
and elsewhere Montgomery gave the impression that, when
he assumed command of Eighth Army, there had been little
attempt to develop adequate procedures for air support. The

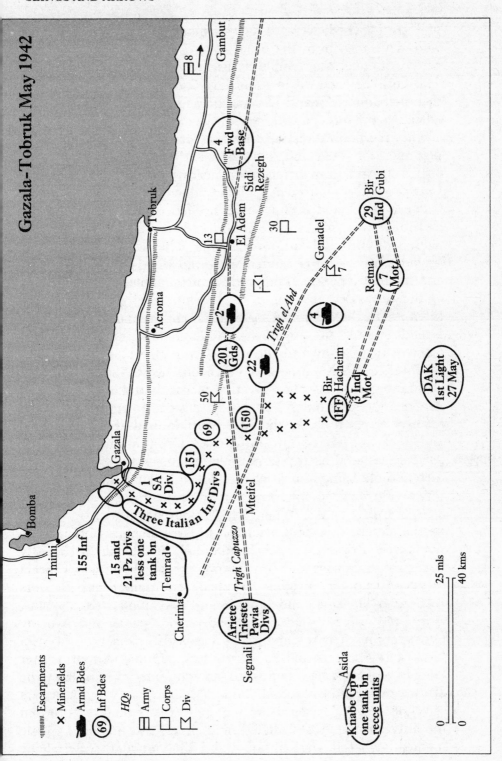

Gazala–Tobruk May 1942

Bomba

Tmimi

155 Inf

15 and
21 Pz Divs
less one
tank bn
Temrad

Cherima

Gazala

1
SA
Div

Three Italian Inf Divs

151

69

50

150

Mteifel

Segnali

Ariete
Trieste
Pavia
Divs

Trigh Capuzzo

Asida

Knabe Grp
one tank bn
recce units

Acroma

Tobruk

13

El Adem

201
Gds

2

22

Bir
IFF Hacheim

Trigh el Abd

30

1

4

Genadel

7

3 Ind
Mot

DAK
1st Light
27 May

4 Fwd
Base

Gambut

8

Sidi
Rezegh

29 Bir
Ind Gubi

Retma

7
Mot

Escarpments
✗ Minefields
Armd Bdes
69 Inf Bdes

HQs
Army
Corps
Div

25 mls
40 kms

0
0

procedures which were so successfully established in his time were developed from the base which I and others laid in this period, as was Montgomery's use of personal liaison officers who both 'listened in' to subordinate wireless nets and visited their headquarters and commanders, as a supplement to the official command channel.

The reorganization of the two armoured divisions and planning for their employment in the reconquest of Cyrenaica became my principal concern as the weeks passed. *Crusader* had convinced Auchinleck that a more even balance between tanks and infantry was needed within the armoured divisions, and that, in the infantry divisions, the artillery – field, anti-tank and anti-aircraft – should be decentralized to brigades, as the latter tended to be separated from each other and liable to operate as 'brigade groups'. The Support Group of the armoured division was therefore enlarged to include three motorized infantry battalions and renamed a 'motor brigade', and all brigades, armoured and infantry, provided with their own artillery. Two valuable additions to the equipment of the armoured divisions were the 6-pounder anti-tank guns, supplied to the motor battalions, and the American Grant tank. The latter, designed originally as an infantry support tank, like the Matilda and the Valentine, had thick frontal armour and carried a 75-mm gun of limited traverse, as well as the same 37-mm gun as the Stuart in its turret, while being almost as mobile as the latter and the Crusader. There were not, however, enough of them to replace all the cruiser tanks. When 7th Armoured Division returned to the desert in April, each of the regiments of their 4th Armoured Brigade, now commanded by Rickie Richards, had two squadrons of Grants and one of Honeys. Twenty-second Armoured Brigade rejoined its original parent, 1st Armoured Division, and both it and Raymond Briggs's 2nd Armoured Brigade had one squadron of Grants and two of Crusaders in their regiments. This gave Norrie a total of 167 Grants, 149 Stuarts and 257 Crusaders, 573 tanks in all, while Gott in 13 Corps had 276 Matildas and Valentines in his two army tank brigades, 1st and 32nd.

While we had been restoring our tank strength both in quantity and quality, so had Rommel. We did not then know in detail what it was, although ULTRA and other wireless intercept sources revealed it when operations were active. We now know that by the second half of May he had a total of 560 tanks, of which 228 were Italian. Of his 332 German, which were almost equally divided between 15th and 21st Panzer Divisions, 223 were Mark III(H) with the same short 50-mm gun they had had in *Crusader*, but almost all now with additional armour in the front. He had 19 Mark III(J), almost all in 21st Panzer, which carried the formidable new long 50-mm gun, the same as the anti-tank gun. He had 50 Mark II light tanks and 40 Mark IV with the short 75-mm gun. Four of the new Mark IV, with its long and very effective 75-mm gun, were in the field, but without any ammunition. By the end of May, therefore, Ritchie had the superiority of three to two in tanks which Auchinleck had insisted on as a prerequisite to taking the offensive.

Ritchie's plan for this, Operation *Buckshot*, was looked upon by both Norrie and Gott with considerable misgivings. While Gott's 13 Corps held the Gazala line from the coast down to Bir Hacheim with 1st South African and 50th Infantry Divisions and Koenig's 1st Free French Brigade, 30 Corps, with 1st and 7th Armoured Divisions and a number of Indian infantry brigade groups, would advance westward from Bir Hacheim, depositing an infantry brigade in a defensive 'box' every 30 miles. Ritchie's intention was that, if Rommel reacted to this, he would have to move his panzer divisions away from the main body of his army and find himself opposed by the superior number of Norrie's tanks, operating between these 'boxes' or 'cowpats', as we rudely called them. If Rommel did not so react, 30 Corps would establish itself south of Benghazi, between Msus and Sceleidima, and thus strangle Rommel's supply line.

When Norrie was given the outline of this plan, his first reaction, as usual, was to ask Strafer Gott what he thought. The latter viewed with the greatest concern a plan that would remove all the mobile forces to a considerable distance before they posed any serious threat to Rommel's rear, while leaving wide open Gott's own flank and rear, close behind which, round Belhamed, was the large static and vulnerable No. 4 Forward Base outside the defences of Tobruk. Rommel could strangle Gott long before Norrie could put the noose

round his neck. On return from his talk with Gott, Norrie
gave the plan to his new BGS, George Hatton, who had
succeeded Davy, and told him to produce his comments on it
in the form of a military 'appreciation'. Hatton saw this as his
chance to establish himself. He was a Canadian-born officer
of the Royal Engineers, who had come from India to Egypt
and had replaced Jackie Bowring as AA & QMG* of 7th
Armoured Division at the end of Operation *Crusader*. He had
had no operational experience and was not a prepossessing
personality. Hatton realized that neither Norrie nor his staff
officers, Noel Wall, Peter Hordern and myself, took kindly
to his arrival. Hatton shut himself up in his tent and produced a staff college appreciation, balancing all the factors
and elaborating how the obvious problems could be solved,
but missing the crucial issue. He had, somewhat naturally
perhaps, assumed that Norrie wanted a paper to show how
the order could be obeyed.

Norrie, having read the paper, dictated to his personal
clerk a note addressed to 'The Brains Trust, Majors Carver,
Hordern and Wall, copy to the BGS', enclosing the outline
plan and Hatton's paper, and instructing us to write our own
independent appreciation and return it direct to him, with a
copy to the BGS. We had no hesitation in condemning both
the plan and Hatton's paper. Norrie having accepted our
paper and rejected his, relations between Hatton and both
Norrie and ourselves were to remain strained, with inevitable
effects on the smooth functioning of the headquarters. If
Norrie had been a more decisive character and Hatton
had had more self-respect, they would have parted there
and then. Thereafter Operation *Buckshot* went through a
number of fundamental changes. When I attended one of
Eighth Army's planning conferences on the subject, and Jock
Whiteley, Ritchie's BGS, had finished explaining the latest
change of plan, the officer sitting next to me, who had been
getting more and more agitated as Whiteley spoke, sprang to
his feet and explained that the plan which Eighth Army now
proposed was identical with the deception plan which he, as
the officer responsible for it at GHQ, had been trying to put
over on the enemy in the preceding weeks.

* Assistant Adjutant and Quartermaster-General.

As the weeks passed, it became clear that Rommel was himself planning to attack, and, with a sigh of relief, *Buckshot* was consigned to the dustbin and Eighth Army prepared to receive Rommel's attack on 'ground of its own choosing'. Differences of opinion as to how best to do this soon proved almost as sharp as those on how to take the offensive. When the Gazala line had first been occupied in February, it had been thought of only as a covering position, while the main defensive position was built up on the frontier. Auchinleck and his fellow Commanders-in-Chief were determined not to have to face again the commitment of supplying and supporting an isolated garrison in Tobruk. But the pressure for a renewed offensive had led to its being developed as the springboard for the reconquest of Cyrenaica, behind which a major logistic base and forward airfields would be established. Now suddenly it had to be considered as a defensive layout, and for that it had several disadvantages. While it was fairly continuously defended by 1st South African and 50th Infantry Divisions, and well protected by minefields, for the 20 miles south from the coast to the Trigh Capuzzo, there was then a gap of nearly another 20 miles, covered only by a string of minefields, between 150th Brigade at Sidi Muftah and the French brigade's position at Bir Hacheim. It was soon realized that it was imperative to prevent Rommel from establishing himself in the area of El Adem–Belhamed by a rapid move, either, avoiding the minefields, by a wide outflanking movement south of Bir Hacheim, or by bursting through them on the general line of the Trigh Capuzzo.

There was much discussion as to which of these two courses he was likely to adopt. Lumsden, whose 1st Armoured Division was deployed in the area astride the Trigh Capuzzo and El Abd, believed that Rommel would come his way, while Messervy, on the left, naturally tended to look in that direction. Ritchie and Norrie wished to be equally well prepared to meet either contingency. The discussion centred on the deployment of Carr's 22nd Armoured Brigade and Messervy's 7th Armoured Division, and the tasks and command of the former. The Free French at Hacheim were stuck out on a limb, and the experience of *Crusader* made everyone reluctant to leave infantry brigades, even in well constructed defences protected by minefields, too far away from our own tanks. It was also felt that Rommel's armour must be opposed far enough away from the vulnerable El Adem–Belhamed area to ensure its security. Infantry brigade positions, or 'boxes', had also been prepared for an Indian brigade at Bir Gubi and for Renton's 7th Motor Brigade at Retma, half-way between Gubi and Hacheim. The brigade was commanding the armoured car screen and columns supporting it, keeping contact with and observing Rommel's Panzerarmee Afrika (as the Panzergruppe had been renamed when the Italian 20th Mobile Corps came under his command) near Segnali, 40 miles north-west of Bir Hacheim. When Rommel moved, the brigade was to withdraw to its 'box', as it kept contact with his advancing forces, if they came that way. The tanks of 7th Armoured Division, 4th Armoured Brigade, would be held just south of the Trigh el Abd, ten miles north of the Retma box and 16 north-east of the French. First Armoured Division's 2nd Armoured Brigade was ten miles north of the 4th, just south of the Trigh Capuzzo, five miles south-east of 201st Guards Brigade in their 'box' at Knightsbridge. They were Lumsden's Motor Brigade and had been renumbered from 22nd to avoid confusion with 22nd Armoured Brigade. The latter was three miles south of the 2nd.

Norrie's plan was that, if Rommel thrust through the minefields towards Lumsden, Messervy could move 4th Armoured Brigade the short distance north to join him. If, however, he came round Hacheim, 4th Armoured Brigade would move south to a battle position between Retma and Hacheim, being joined there by 22nd Armoured Brigade, and, if no threat farther north developed, by Lumsden as well. The latter was very reluctant to contemplate a transfer of Carr's brigade to Messervy's command in any circumstances. He had at last got his division, with its two original armoured brigades, together again: he considered a division of two armoured brigades to offer a much superior formation over which to exercise his undoubted powers of command and military skill; and he had no confidence in Messervy, who, he considered, had mishandled his division when he had taken command of it in January.

Lumsden was undoubtedly a soldier and leader of exceptional quality, tough, decisive and clear-headed. He was immensely popular with those under his command, but his intense loyalty to his own formation and his full confidence in his own judgement and ability made him a difficult subordinate or equal. He showed little regard for the interests and difficulties of others. Norrie could handle him face to face, but it was not in his nature to force matters to a clash. In discussion on the telephone or wireless Lumsden usually got his way. One of his least attractive traits was to try and browbreat staff officers of other formations, like myself, with lashes from his sharp tongue.

GHQ's sources of intelligence, which we now know to have been ULTRA, gave us a clear warning that Rommel would attack on or about 26 May 1942. When Auchinleck received confirmation of this on 20 May, he wrote to Ritchie, expressing the view that Rommel would try and break through on the line of the Trigh Capuzzo, and showing concern that Norrie's armour did not appear sufficiently concentrated to meet it. In order to free 7th Armoured Division from the need to feel obliged to remain close to the French at Bir Hacheim, he sent up 3rd Indian Motor Brigade to occupy yet another 'box' between Hacheim and Retma. Ritchie justifiably pointed out that the armour was disposed so that it could quickly concentrate to meet either threat and have a sizeable advantage in numbers over any force that Rommel could deploy. But the fact that Auchinleck had access to special sources of intelligence lent considerable weight to his prognostication that Rommel would choose the northern option.

In the afternoon of 26 May the enemy, mostly Italian, facing 1st South African Division and the northernmost brigade of 50th Division, became active, chiefly with artillery fire. Already warned by intelligence, we became even more alert, and I asked for frequent 'Tac Rs', tactical air reconnaissance sorties, over the area of Segnali. By 4 p.m. it was clear that the Panzerarmee was on the move eastward, although the poor visibility, caused by a sandstorm, made it difficult for the RAF and our armoured cars to provide accurate reports. By about 9.30 p.m., well after dark, our armoured cars were reporting enemy movement south-east from where they had halted at last light. As armoured cars were on the outer flank and relied more on what they could hear than on what they could see in the dark, it was not possible for them to judge how large a force was involved in this south-eastward move, or whether it was German or Italian. My own guess was that it was the main thrust, and I decided that I must remain awake in the operational command vehicle all night. I put a wireless set listening on 7th Armoured Division's forward control net, so that I could receive the reports Callum Renton's 7th Motor Brigade passed back from the armoured cars. As the night wore on and the stream of reports continued, I rang up Pete Pyman, who had succeeded Rickie Richards as GSO1 of 7th Armoured Division, to ask him for his assessment. By about 1 a.m. I became very concerned and spoke to Pyman suggesting that he wake up Messervy. At 2.15 a.m. I woke up Norrie and told him that I thought that Rommel's main force was on its way round Bir Hacheim. I suggested that, after discussing the situation with Messervy, he should warn Lumsden to be prepared to send 22nd Armoured Brigade to join 7th Armoured Division. I remained in Norrie's caravan while he rang Messervy, and was disappointed when Norrie said that Messervy believed that the move reported by 7th Motor Brigade could be Italian and intended to divert our attention from the main thrust by the Afrika Korps farther north. Messervy had agreed to order 4th Armoured Brigade to 'stand to' well before dawn, but not to move south to their battle position, in case in the event they had to move north. Norrie was certainly not convinced that this was the main thrust, justifying the switch of 22nd Armoured Brigade from Lumsden to Messervy. Indeed he was not even prepared to ring Lumsden at that stage. Worried at his view, which was undoubtedly influenced by Auchinleck's prognostication to Ritchie, I rang Roger Peake, GSO1 of 1st Armoured Division. He made it clear that Lumsden would oppose any switch of 22nd Armoured Brigade, unless there was positive information that the Afrika Korps had not continued its eastward move, but was involved in the south-eastward one. By about 4 a.m. I had become even more convinced that the movement reported by Renton was the main thrust, and I woke Norrie again and told him that I thought he must give Lumsden at least a warning order for 22nd Armoured Brigade to move south to join Messervy, and order the latter to ensure that 4th Armoured Brigade was in its southern

battle position by first light. Norrie rang Messervy, who
agreed, and then Lumsden, who argued at length against
any move of Carr's brigade, Norrie giving way to him to my
intense concern. I then put in a request for a Tac R sortie,
covering the area up to 20 miles south of Bir Hacheim, at
first light, 6 a.m. It was symptomatic of the state of affairs in
the headquarters that it had not crossed my mind, until then,
that I should wake the BGS, George Hatton. Peter Hordern,
the GSO2 (Intelligence), and I had been in constant touch
all through the night and had found ourselves in firm
agreement in our assessment of the situation.

At 6.45 a.m. reports from armoured cars and from the Tac
R were received that 250 to 400 tanks were in the area south
and south-east of Bir Hacheim, the nearest being only ten
miles from 4th Armoured Brigade. There could be no doubt
that this was the whole of the Afrika Korps, and possibly the
Italian mobile corps as well. Norrie rang Messervy to make
sure that he was ordering Richards to occupy his southern
battle position and immediately afterwards rang Lumsden
to order him to send Carr's 22nd Armoured Brigade south
to join Messervy. Lumsden argued strongly against this,
and, when Norrie insisted, said that they could not move
for another hour and a half, as they had not been given
a warning order. Norrie told him to get them moving as
quickly as possible, and for Lumsden to follow with 2nd
Armoured Brigade as well. While these conversations had
been going on, I had asked for a bombing attack on the
concentration reported by the Tac R.

Rommel was already on the move again. His plan was
based on a serious underestimate of Ritchie's strength. He
thought that the southern flank of 50th Division's defences
lay north of the Trigh Capuzzo, and that, south of that, the
minefields were undefended and ended altogether at the
Trigh el Abd, ten miles north of Bir Hacheim, the garrison
of which he estimated that he could polish off in an hour.
He thought that both 1st and 7th Armoured Divisions were
between the minefields and Knightsbridge, although he
placed 22nd Armoured and 201st Guards Brigade (which
he may have confused with each other, not knowing of
the latter's change of number) back in army reserve at
Gambut. He knew nothing of the presence of the brigade

'boxes' between Bir Hacheim and Gubi and thought that
Gott had only one army tank brigade. His plan was for
the whole Panzerarmee, the Afrika Korps on the right and
20th Italian Mobile Corps (Ariete and Trieste Divisions) on
the left, to sweep round what he thought was the southern
end of the minefields and turn up north behind them to
Acroma, destroying Norrie's armour round Knightsbridge
on the way. Ninetieth Light Division, accompanied by special vehicles with aero-engines mounted on them to raise
dust-clouds, giving the impression that they were tanks,
would strike north-east from Hacheim to El Adem and
Belhamed, capture headquarters and supply dumps and
prevent reserves being sent from Tobruk and east of it
against Rommel's right flank. He estimated that it would take
him only 24 hours to defeat Norrie and mop up Gott's corps,
after which he would turn his attention to Tobruk itself. At
the last moment he realized that the minefields extended all
the way south to Bir Hacheim, and he therefore ordered a
wider outflanking movement, necessitating refuelling south
of Bir Hacheim. Trieste never got the order and turned east
several miles north of Bir Hacheim.

The first formation to be hit by Rommel's forces was 3rd
Indian Motor Brigade, which had not completed preparing
its defences, had only half of its complement of 2-pounder
anti-tank guns and had not yet been joined by the squadron
of Valentine tanks which had been allotted to its support. Its
artillery opened fire on Ariete, to the latter's surprise, at 6.40
a.m. At 7.15 Ariete attacked and, assisted by 21st Panzer,
had completely overrun the brigade by 8 a.m., Ariete losing
52 tanks in the process. On receipt of the information from
his armoured cars at 6.45, Messervy had ordered Richards
to move to a battle position north of Retma, four miles
south-east of his leaguer area; but, when he heard the
news of the attack on 3rd Indian Brigade, he changed it to
a position near them. Richards did not order his regiments
to form up for the move until 7.20. While in the process of
doing so, they ran head-on into 15th Panzer, and a fierce
battle followed, in which the 8th Hussars lost almost all
their tanks and 3rd Royal Tanks 16 of their 26 Grants, both
using up almost all their ammunition. Fifteenth Panzer also
suffered heavily, but Richards ordered his brigade all the

way back to the area south of El Adem, leaving 15th Panzer free to move north. Some ten miles east of this battle, one of the German reconnaissance units, heading 90th Light Division's advance, ran into Messervy's headquarters and quickly overran it, Messervy and Pyman escaping, having removed their rank insignia. We were ten miles north-east of them and soon became concerned for our own security. We packed up and moved the headquarters further north-east, while Norrie himself, who was on his way to see Lumsden, was forced to take refuge within the El Adem 'box', where Gott had his headquarters. The overrunning of 7th Armoured Division's Headquarters and the collapse of 4th Armoured Brigade meant that we had very little idea of what was happening. Lumsden had been disgracefully slow in implementing Norrie's orders. Carr had not even begun to move when, at about 8.45 a.m., he was surprised by 21st Panzer Division, which had slipped between 3rd Indian Motor Brigade and 7th Motor Brigade at Retma, and was forced north-east. Briggs was even slower. At 9.45 a.m. he summoned his commanding officers to give them orders to move south to strike the flank of the tanks which were engaging Carr. When eventually they began to move at 11 a.m., they realized that the enemy was to the west, not the south, of them, and it was 2 p.m. before they delivered an attack which hit 15th Panzer Division's infantry regiment. The regiment was also being attacked from the west by the Matildas of 44th Royal Tanks with 50th Division's 150th Brigade, of which 18 were knocked out. This battle went on until dark, the enemy moving off to the west and Briggs returning to the area from which he had started, south-east of Knightsbridge.

In deciding what to do next day, 28 May, Norrie's problems were that he had very little idea of where the enemy had got to and what casualties had been inflicted on him, and that 7th Armoured Division was still disorganized. He had to rely solely on Lumsden both for information and for action. He was worried about the lack of information concerning the situation in the area between El Adem and Bir Hacheim, where he feared that a fair proportion of Rommel's forces might be. There was little if any clue as to the whereabouts of 21st Panzer Division, Ariete or Trieste. The general

assessment was that most of Rommel's forces were somewhere near Bir el Harmat, south of Knightsbridge, and that
he would thrust east towards El Adem to link up with 90th
Light Division, who were somewhere to the south of there.
Norrie's orders to Lumsden were defensive, designed to
meet such a thrust. Had he realized the difficulties that faced
his opponent, he would have ordered Lumsden to take a
bolder course.

Nehring's Afrika Korps had lost over one-third of its
tanks. Fifteenth Panzer, with only 29 fit tanks, was out
of fuel and almost out of ammunition on Rigel Ridge,
north-east of Knightsbridge. Twenty-first was a few miles
further west with 80 tanks. Their supply echelons were near
·Bir el Harmat, cut off from them by the battle that had raged
all afternoon in that area. With them was Nehring's headquarters, where Rommel was also, separated from his staff
and having narrowly escaped capture while trying to visit
Kleeman, commander of 90th Light. Ariete was even further
south, entangled in the eastern edge of the minefields north
of Hacheim, while Trieste was still trying to find a way
through from the west. Rommel's original underestimate
of the strength of Eighth Army and his mistaken idea of its
deployment led him to believe that he had already disposed
of almost all Norrie's forces. In spite of his own difficulties,
he ignored the threat of any attack on his right flank and
ordered the Afrika Korps to continue its northward thrust
next day in fulfilment of his original plan. This made him
even more vulnerable than he already was to a blow from the
east. In the event 15th Panzer was unable to move and only
the 21st advanced, reaching the escarpment overlooking
the coast road, after dispersing some Valentine tanks and
overrunning a South African company. As Rommel had
made no eastward move, Lumsden had done nothing all
morning, apart from readjusting his dispositions. By about
midday we were getting a clearer idea of the true situation
and the opportunities it presented. Norrie, in close contact
with Gott, ordered Lumsden to close the gap in the area of
Bir Harmat between himself and Haydon's 150th Brigade,
while O'Carroll's 44th Royal Tanks with the latter were
ordered by Gott to close it from the west. This should cut
off supplies to the Afrika Korps and make it possible to deal

with its two panzer divisions separately. But it was late in the afternoon before his orders were translated into action by Briggs's 2nd Armoured Brigade, which found that Ariete had moved into the area. Their attack, delivered in the face of the setting sun, led to the loss of almost all the Grants of the 10th Hussars at the hands of 88-mm guns, and achieved little. Rommel's position had meanwhile been greatly eased by clearance of a gap in the minefields west of Bir Harmat by Trieste. Not only did this open up to him a shorter and more secure supply route, but it meant that 150th Brigade was now almost totally encircled by his forces. The brigade had received an unexpected visitor when they shot down and captured Cruewell, who was on his way in a light aircraft to try and contact Rommel. He had been placed in command of all the static troops facing Gott.

Rommel had now realized the danger of his position and recalled 21st Panzer from the north to help 15th and Ariete to resist Briggs's attack. Norrie's orders for 29 May were for Lumsden to resume his attempt to join hands with 150th Brigade and sever Rommel's supply line. The attempt to do so led to a battle which went on all day south of Knightsbridge and resulted in heavy losses in two of the regiments of 2nd Armoured Brigade, 9th Lancers and 10th Hussars. Fourth Armoured Brigade had been withdrawn the night before back south of El Adem under the command of 7th Armoured Division, their headquarters having been resuscitated. It was not until midday that they were ordered west again to help Lumsden. Although it had been an unsatisfactory day for Norrie, it had been an anxious one for Rommel. He had been forced to use up more of his dwindling stocks of ammunition and fuel, and had not yet received any more through the gap made by Trieste. He therefore decided temporarily to pull in his horns into a defensive ring, protecting the area bounded on the north by Sidra Ridge and on the east by that of Aslagh, later to be known as 'The Cauldron', while he opened up the minefield gap and got rid of 150th Brigade, which was inconveniently close to it.

Unfortunately this move, together with intelligence from a wireless intercept about the precariousness of his logistic situation, led to over-optimism at Eighth Army and GHQ. All that was needed to finish him off, it was thought, was to continue to engage him east of the minefields, while preparing a wide enveloping movement to the south round Bir Hacheim and from the north by a southward thrust by 13 Corps. The next day, 30 May, passed in much the same way as the previous day. Lumsden renewed his attempts to advance towards 150th Brigade. Both 2nd and 22nd Armoured Brigades were involved and lost more tanks, the former reduced to only 30 by the end of the day, by which time all the tanks were concentrated in one weak regiment in each brigade, and they were no nearer to making contact with Haydon's brigade, now feeling very isolated.

Lumsden's depressing experience over the previous three days had convinced him that attacking with tanks in daylight, even when strongly supported by artillery, as his latest attacks had been, would only mean a repetition of tank losses with little gained from them. He persuaded Norrie and Ritchie that night attacks by infantry to capture the screen of anti-tank guns and clear mines (if there were any) should precede any further attempt to advance with tanks. This fitted in with Ritchie's concept. He wanted 13 Corps to attack westward from their main position towards Tmimi and Temrad, while Norrie sent mobile columns round Hacheim to threaten Rommel's supply line west of the minefields. Lumsden should build up his strength in tanks again, while covering the El Adem area against the threat of any eastward move by Rommel. Ritchie wanted to start this operation on the night of 31 May, but Gott and Norrie said it could not be organized in that time and asked for a further 24 hours. The result of this was that Rommel faced no threat of an attack from the east that day and was free to concentrate on attacking the isolated 150th Brigade, which, after a very gallant fight, was overrun by the end of 31 May, inflicting heavy casualties on the infantry of the Afrika Korps. They had received little support from the rest of Eighth Army. Although Ritchie had agreed to postpone his planned counter-offensive until 1 June, he insisted on a limited attack being made on the night of 31 May to bring some relief to Haydon.

It was now clear that Rommel was not, as had been optimistically assessed, either withdrawing through the minefields or so starved of supplies that he could not attack. Auchinleck

and Ritchie wished to turn the tables on him by a major
westward thrust by Gott, reinforced with 5th Indian Division,
while Norrie stood guard in the area of Knightsbridge. Once
Gott's thrust had led to Rommel's withdrawal, Norrie would
exploit it by a thrust to Segnali, or even further to Mechili.
The concept was admirable: its execution more difficult.
The organization of 13 Corps had been for defence. All
the transport to move its infantry and supplies would have
to be concentrated in the area east of 1st South African and
north of 50th Division's positions, only a short distance from
the Afrika Korps, now in sole possession of The Cauldron.
If Norrie's armour were moved north of Rigel Ridge to
protect this vulnerable concentration from attack, he would
uncover the direct route to El Adem. The preparations for
Gott's offensive, codenamed Operation *Limerick*, would take
several days. During that time Rommel would realize what
Ritchie intended. Nobody liked the plan, but the alternative
– a wide sweep round Hacheim, favoured by Harold Briggs,
commander of 5th Indian Division – offered even slenderer
chances of success. To move his division all that way posed
severe logistic problems; and, unless accompanied by all
Norrie's tanks, it would then be vulnerable to a rapid move
by Rommel westward through the minefields. If Norrie's
armour went also, El Adem and Belhamed, Eighth Army's
vulnerable heart, would be uncovered all the time they
were moving round. Norrie and Gott kept in close touch
and together represented their doubts to Ritchie. While
discussion was still going on, 21st Panzer, on 2 June, again
struck north, inflicting heavy casualties on 4th Armoured
Brigade.

Twenty-first Panzer's move had decided Ritchie against
Operation *Limerick*, and he came round, reluctantly, to a
renewal of the attack on The Cauldron as the only feasible
method of attempting to regain the initiative. It was christened Operation *Aberdeen* and was to take place on the night
of 4 June. The general plan was that 13 Corps would launch
an attack by Willison's 32nd Army Tank Brigade on Sidra
Ridge, while 5th Indian Division, under Norrie, supported
by 4th Royal Tanks, would attack Aslagh from the east.
Messervy, working in close cooperation with Harold Briggs,
would pass Carr's 22nd Armoured Brigade, its strength now

raised to 156 tanks, through to cover a further advance by an Indian brigade. Carr would then advance further west into the rear of the forces facing Willison's attack, after which he would turn east again and sweep the area back to Knightsbridge, there rejoining Lumsden, who would be ready to exploit the success it was hoped the South Africans would have gained in their westward advance. The action would take place on the boundary of the two corps and, as it was very largely an infantry operation, it was at first suggested that Gott should command it. He objected that this would mean that he virtually took over responsibility for all the combat forces of Eighth Army. An unsatisfactory compromise resulted, in which Norrie was given prime responsibility for the attack on The Cauldron, although he exercised no direct command of Gott's troops attacking Sidra Ridge from the north. It was a highly complex plan and he did not feel that we, at Headquarters 30 Corps, were the right staff to control the detailed and mutually interconnected actions of 5th Indian and 7th Armoured Divisions. He therefore delegated detailed planning and execution to Messervy and Briggs together, who would form a joint tactical headquarters. They knew each other well, and were happy with the arrangement, which we all felt would be more likely to result in close cooperation between the infantry brigades and the armour than a more remote control by corps headquarters. Our main task would be to keep in touch with 13 Corps and see that their attack on Sidra Ridge was closely coordinated with that of Messervy and Briggs. The disadvantage of the arrangement was that there was no firm grip of the whole operation either in planning or in execution, although Norrie personally kept in close touch with the two generals.

The attack started at 2.50 a.m. on 5 June, and, at first, all seemed to be going well. But the reason for this was either inaccurate navigation or faulty information of where the enemy on Aslagh Ridge, who turned out to be Ariete, actually were. The attack had hit empty desert, and, when Carr's tanks passed through in daylight, they ran into heavy anti-tank and artillery fire and veered off to the northeast. Willison's attack on Sidra Ridge had meanwhile failed with heavy loss. Half-way through the morning it was clear that the attack had ground to a halt. In response to an appeal from Messervy, Norrie ordered Lumsden to send 2nd Armoured Brigade, which was north of Rigel Ridge, to help 22nd west of Knightsbridge, but, owing to constant changes in where Messervy said he wanted it and a major misunderstanding of its orders, it never came into action and ended up north-east of Knightsbridge. Rommel had meanwhile been planning a counter-attack with 21st Panzer eastward along the Sidra Ridge and 15th north-east through a gap in the minefield south of Bir Harmat. This came late in the day, surprising us all and scattering the joint headquarters of Messervy and Briggs, and those of the latter's two brigades, to the four winds. As a result we had only the haziest idea at 30 Corps Headquarters of what the situation at the end of the day was, in particular of the fate of the Indian brigades.

When contact with Messervy was re-established, Norrie ordered him to restore the situation as it had been before the counter-attack, handing over both Lumsden's armoured brigades to him to add to his own. Richards was still north of Rigel Ridge, licking the wounds he had received on 2 June, and Carr, who had lost 60 tanks the day before, moved backwards and forwards and finally came to rest north-east of Knightsbridge without having engaged 21st Panzer. The latter was further south, mopping up the Indians, and was attacked late in the day by 2nd Armoured Brigade, in the teeth of protests by its commander, Raymond Briggs. None of these moves had interfered to any significant degree with Rommel's elimination of the unfortunate 9th and 10th Indian Brigades and their artillery. He took 3,000 prisoners, 96 field and 37 anti-tank guns and had reduced Norrie's tank strength from the 300, to which it had been rebuilt, to 132, having also knocked out 50 from Willison's brigade. Meanwhile Gott's attempts to get Pienaar and Ramsden to take effective offensive action on 6 June had failed to produce more than pinpricks, and, when he knew of the failure of the attacks on The Cauldron, he was not inclined to exert further pressure.

While Rommel's armoured divisions had been fighting in and around The Cauldron, his two motorized divisions, 90th

Light and Trieste, had been trying to subdue Koenig's Free
French Brigade at Bir Hacheim. He had sent them there on
2 June, the day he had ordered 21st Panzer north to cut off
13 Corps, expecting them to complete the task in one day.
When Operation *Aberdeen* finally ground to a halt at the end
of 6 June, they had still not done so; and, as activity in The
Cauldron and north of it died down, he was free to switch all
his effort and that of the Luftwaffe onto the French, whose
only support from outside, apart from the RAF, came from
columns of Renton's 7th Motor Brigade, which harassed
90th Light and escorted supply convoys in and out of the
isolated garrison. Rommel himself directed the attacks on 8
and 9 June, by which time Koenig saw no point in further
resistance and asked Norrie for permission to withdraw,
which he was given.

Rommel lost no time in exploiting the situation. Early
in the morning of 11 June he ordered 90th Light to make
for the escarpment south of El Adem, while 15th Panzer
headed for the airfield. Twenty-first Panzer and Ariete were
to 'demonstrate' eastward from The Cauldron to prevent
Norrie's armour, now concentrated round Knightsbridge,
from interfering. Refuelling problems delayed their start
until 3 p.m. and their move was not seriously interfered
with by 7th Armoured Division, whose area of responsibility
it was. Richards was ordered to move south-east to head off
15th Panzer, but, having reached one of his favourite battle
positions, he resisted orders to descend into the shallow valley up which von Vaerst was moving and merely exchanged
long-range fire with him, as the latter settled down for the
night a few miles to the south-east.

Next day saw a great opportunity missed to deal with 15th
Panzer Division while it was on its own. Norrie told Lumsden
to move his 2nd Armoured Brigade to join Richards under
Messervy's command for this purpose, while he held off the
rest of the Afrika Korps; but Messervy, on his way to argue
with Norrie about the plan, was forced to take refuge in a
'bir', a dried-up water cistern, and it was a long time before
Norrie realized that his orders were not being implemented.
He then told Lumsden to assume command of both brigades
and launch the long-delayed attack. There were inexcusable
delays in executing this order, and, before any move had

been made, Rommel surprised Lumsden by attacking with 21st Panzer and Ariete on his western flank, while 15th at last also began to move. The result was confusion and a heavy loss of tanks in all brigades, leaving Lumsden with 90, huddled round the Guards Brigade 'box' at Knightsbridge. Lumsden moved his headquarters north of the Raml escarpment and communication between his staff and ours was lost for most of the night, so that Norrie did not realize the extent of his losses nor that some of his tanks had moved north of the escarpment.

Meanwhile Auchinleck had flown up from Cairo and was conferring with Ritchie. It was clear that the position, as it had been on 27 May, could not be restored, and there was a serious danger that the large salient, formed by the defences held by 1st South African and 50th Divisions, might be cut off. However, to evacuate these immobile troops, dug in to their defences, was no simple task. The two generals had considered a withdrawal to the frontier, abandoning Tobruk, but had rejected it. Wireless intercept confirmed that Rommel was very short of German infantry and in difficulties, as ever, over supply. He could not keep on attacking without a break. Ritchie decided to hand over command of all the tanks to Lumsden, who was to come under the orders of Gott. His corps was to hold its present positions, the left flank resting on the firm points of Knightsbridge and the string of posts north of it to Acroma on the Axis by-pass. Norrie was to assume command of all the various brigades, mostly Indian, scattered about in the area south and east of Tobruk, while the RAF put all their effort into trying to destroy 90th Light, which was threatening that area.

But Rommel was to give Ritchie no respite. He ordered another pincer movement to entrap Lumsden's forces in and around Knightsbridge, while 90th Light was to capture 29th Indian Brigade's position at El Adem, although Kleeman's so-called division was now reduced to no more than 1000 men with 15 field and 40 anti-tank guns. The Afrika Korps' attacks in the morning of 13 June were not strongly pressed, and Lumsden was confident that he could hold them; but renewed attacks in a duststorm in the afternoon drove his armour off Rigel Ridge and threatened to encircle the Guards, who had not yet been directly attacked. Gott gave Lumsden permission to withdraw them during the night, and by dawn Lumsden's whole force, which now included only 70 tanks, was concentrated near Acroma, and Rommel was in possession of the whole Rigel–Raml Ridge, overlooking the area to the north of it.

There was now no doubt in anybody's mind that Gott's two divisions, 1st South African and 50th, must be withdrawn, if they were not to be cut off. There had always been a contingency plan to meet the worst case, which involved withdrawal to the Egyptian frontier, based on the Middle East Commanders-in-Chiefs' firm decision that they must not again be involved in supporting an isolated Tobruk. At 7 a.m. on 14 June Ritchie ordered Gott to put in hand their withdrawal to the frontier. He hoped that, with 2nd South African Division in Tobruk and 10th Indian Division in the area of El Adem–Belhamed, he could hold on to the western perimeter of the Tobruk defences and the El Adem–Sidi Rezegh area long enough to enable the rest of the army to reorganize on the frontier and return to the fray. But he realized that he might not succeed in achieving this and that Tobruk could be isolated before he was able to re-enter the ring. With this in mind, he rang Auchinleck at 9.30 a.m. and explained his plan, following his call with a long signal which ended with the question: 'Do you agree to me accepting the risk of investment in Tobruk?' He assumed that, if Auchinleck's answer were 'No', he would withdraw his whole force to the frontier, although this would mean abandoning or destroying very large stocks of supplies in Tobruk and No. 4 Forward Base at Belhamed.

Thus began a triangle of misunderstandings between Ritchie, Auchinleck and Churchill, the last resolutely opposing any idea of the abandonment of Tobruk. Auchinleck was torn between allegiance to the Commanders-in-Chiefs' previous decision, unwillingness to dispute the resolution of Churchill and the Chiefs of Staff, and Ritchie's realism. His answer was a compromise, backed by his customary optimism; that Ritchie must hang on to the general line Acroma–El Adem–Bir Gubi, and 'NOT allow Tobruk to be invested'. After messages had passed to and fro between

Eighth Army and GHQ, each one out of phase with one passing in the opposite direction, Ritchie persuaded himself that what he was doing was in line with Auchinleck's intentions and that there was a fair chance that he would succeed in preventing Rommel from moving east of El Adem. Neither Norrie nor Gott was so confident, although the latter believed that Tobruk itself could be organized to withstand a siege of considerable duration.

Gott's immediate problem was the practical one of how to withdraw two divisions with only the narrow bottleneck of the coast road, leading into Tobruk, by which to do so. He quickly realized that it was not possible, and ordered Ramsden to take the bold and imaginative course of breaking through the Italians facing him and making a wide sweep through the desert back to the frontier. Lumsden was to hang on to Acroma, while Pienaar pulled his division back down the coast road and through Tobruk. All this was to be accomplished during the night of 14 June. Our task in 30 Corps was to hang on to El Adem, held by 29th Indian Brigade, Belhamed–Sidi Rezegh by the 20th and Gambut by the 21st Indian and de Larminat's 2nd Free French Brigade. Seventh Armoured Division, with only 7th Motor Brigade and 4th South African Armoured Car Regiment, provided a screen of columns south-west of El Adem. Once Pienaar had withdrawn, all Lumsden's tanks were to move round the Axis by-pass to join Messervy and be concentrated in 4th Armoured Brigade in the El Adem–Sidi Rezegh–Belhamed area. Rommel did his best to disrupt these plans by attacks on Lumsden's reduced force near Acroma, but his troops were exhausted, and, although he inflicted more casualties on Lumsden's tanks and forced the evacuation of two defensive positions, he did not succeed in reaching the escarpment overlooking the coast road.

We were all very weary also, and hoped that we should be granted a short breather, in which to get the defence of the El Adem area properly organized, but it was not to be. The relentless and apparently indefatigable Rommel ordered Kleeman's 90th Light to capture El Adem on 15 June.

Twenty-ninth Indian Brigade had one battalion detached from its main position, holding the point at which the Axis by-pass crossed the escarpment five miles north-west of El

Adem. This was attacked and overrun by 21st Panzer just before last light, von Bismarck driving eastward towards Ed Duda after dark. Next day, 16 June, the post at Ed Duda was evacuated, 20th Indian Brigade, under Messervy as was also the 29th, concentrating in its two positions at Belhamed and Sidi Rezegh. We were now back in our old Crusader haunts, and Norrie was much concerned that, with his weakness in tanks, he could do nothing to prevent all these Indian infantry positions from being surrounded and attacked one by one. Messervy, himself an Indian Army officer, missed no opportunity to stress this. All the available tanks, some 90, were now concentrated in Richards's 4th Armoured Brigade under his command. They were busy sorting themselves out at 4th Armoured Brigade's old Crusader haunt at Bir er Reghem south-east of Sidi Rezegh. Norrie met Messervy at midday, and was persuaded by the latter that Reid's 'box' at El Adem should be evacuated that night, and that the only sound course was to withdraw all his forces back to the frontier. Norrie, always susceptible to the view of 'the man on the spot', undertook to seek Ritchie's permission. The latter, in spite of Auchinleck's emphasis on the need to hold El Adem, was noncommittal, and agreed that 'only the man on the spot' could decide. When Norrie passed this on to Messervy, the latter promptly told Reid to withdraw that night. With that unfortunate decision, the keystone of Auchinleck's hopes was knocked away.

Gott had meanwhile come to the conclusion that Klopper's 2nd South African Division, reinforced by 201st Guards, 11th Indian and what was left of Willison's 32nd Army Tank Brigade, could hold the defences of Tobruk, if necessary, for four or five months, and that the right strategy was to withdraw to the frontier and there build up a force capable of resuming the offensive to liberate Tobruk, as *Crusader* had done. Norrie agreed with him, as, it appeared, did Ritchie also, although he had to comply with Auchinleck's directive, as long as it seemed possible to do so. When Gott, Ritchie and Klopper conferred together in Tobruk on 16 June, Gott suggested that he himself should stay in Tobruk to command the garrison, but Ritchie did not agree and left it to Klopper, on whom he impressed the need to organize

columns to act aggressively outside the perimeter, linking up
with the activities of 30 Corps outside. However the decision
to evacuate El Adem that night made nonsense of that,
and the deterioration of the situation during 17 June even
more so. The El Adem 'box' having conveniently removed
itself, Rommel had ordered the Afrika Korps to clear up
the posts held by 20th Indian Brigade at Sidi Rezegh and
Belhamed, and then advance to Gambut and cut the road
from Tobruk to Bardia. Our attempts to prevent this were
unsuccessful, and Norrie ordered 20th and 21st Indian
Brigades to withdraw on 18 June, leaving Tobruk isolated.
We moved our headquarters, which had been uncomfortably
close to the battle, right back to the frontier wire, five
miles south of Sidi Omar. Soon after we had got there,
and when Norrie was absent, Strafer Gott turned up on
his way from Tobruk to join his own headquarters, which
was further east. Knowing me well, he let his hair down,
and we had a long talk about the situation and how it
had come about. Two points he made remained clearly
imprinted on my memory: that Ritchie's almost blind loyalty
to The Auk had led him to take an over-optimistic view of
events and reject the realities of the situation; and that there
was no reason why Tobruk should not hold out for some
time. It had more troops in it and was better equipped
in every way to meet a siege than it had been when surrounded in April 1941. He was his usual calm, balanced and
reassuring self.

Auchinleck, disturbed to discover that his policy, about
which he had sent reassuring messages to Churchill and
Smuts, had collapsed, flew up next day, 18 June, to see
Ritchie. The upshot of his discussions was that we were to
hand over all the troops in the frontier area to Gott and
move back to Mersa Matruh to take command of a reserve
there, based on the New Zealand and 10th Armoured Divisions, which would serve the dual purpose of a force to be
prepared for a counter-offensive, or, if events turned sour
again, as a backstop position. So back we went, past familiar
desert landmarks, bumping along through clouds of dust
in the heat of midsummer. We had just begun to sort
things out, when we heard the shattering news of the fall
of Tobruk on 21 June. This led to a further change of plan.

Mersa Matruh was to become the main defensive position. General Holmes's 10th Corps, newly arrived from Syria, was to assume responsibility for its defences, Gott's 13 Corps fighting a delaying action from the frontier back to the Sidi Hamza position south of Matruh. We were to move further back to El Alamein, where a series of defensive positions had been prepared by Headquarters British Troops in Egypt, Pienaar's 1st South African Division being moved back from the frontier to occupy the main position near the coast at El Alamein itself.

Back we went again, and set our minds to yet another task, expecting to have at least several weeks in which to get it properly organized. But the rot had set in. Flushed with victory and replenished with all the transport and stores he had captured in Tobruk, Rommel's eyes were on the Nile Delta. The original Axis plan had been that, after the capture of Tobruk and the clearance of Libya, the German and Italian forces would halt, while their effort was switched to the reduction of Malta, before any further advance in the desert. But neither the Italians, who would have to provide the assault force, nor the Luftwaffe, who would need to redeploy to support it, were particularly keen on Operation *Hercules*, as it was called, and both Hitler and Mussolini were happy to be swept forward on Rommel's tide of victory. On the other side, Eighth Army had lost confidence in its ability to stop him. When tanks tried, they were defeated; while infantry, even when they had laboriously entrenched themselves in the rocky ground, were surrounded and rapidly overrun. If they moved out of their defences, they were even more vulnerable as they motored round the desert in conspicuous soft-skinned lorries. However active it might be, the air force seemed to have little effect on the battle. Confidence between the leaders and the led, from the highest level downwards, was sadly lacking, as was that between infantry and armoured formations, accentuated by the heterogeneous structure of the army with its Indian, South African and British Divisions, to which, as it withdrew, New Zealand and Australian were added. In many of the Indian Army units the junior officers, ignorant of Urdu, could only communicate with their troops through the Viceroy's Commissioned Officers, and, when the latter became casualties, as they frequently did, command broke down. The succession of defeats had brought morale generally to a low level, and a long withdrawal, punctuated by frequent changes of plan and counter-orders, lowered it further. Those who had been in the thick of it since 27 May, as we had, were desperately tired. When we finally reached El Alamein, I worked out that, over the month that had passed since then, I had averaged two and a half hours' sleep in twenty-four.

6

Flooding in the Main

For while the tired waves, vainly breaking,
Seem here no painful inch to gain,
Far back through creeks and inlets making
Comes silent, flooding in, the main.
Arthur Hugh Clough (1819–1861),
Say Not the Struggle Naught Availeth

Norrie faced his task with some misgiving. The so-called El
Alamein line consisted of three partially prepared defensive
positions, one on the coast at El Alamein itself, dug and partially wired and mined, designed to hold a division, a second,
dug, but not wired or mined, at Qaret el Abd, 15 miles to the
south-west for a brigade, and a third, hardly prepared at all,
for another brigade, a further 15 miles south-west, overlooking the Qattara Depression. Without a strong armoured force
to operate between them, they could very easily be by-passed.
Norrie quickly appreciated that Ruweisat Ridge, running
west to east five miles south of the El Alamein position, was
of great tactical importance. The troops available to us were
1st South African Division, 6th New Zealand Brigade and two
Indian brigades, the 9th and the 18th. The South Africans
were in the El Alamein 'box', the New Zealanders at Qaret
el Abd and 9th Indian Brigade at the southern position,
Naqb abu Dweis. Pienaar was reluctant to be shut up in the
El Alamein defences, indeed to occupy any fixed defensive
position at all. That factor, Norrie's wish to block the area
between the defences and Ruweisat Ridge and to hold the
latter, and Auchinleck's directive about forming mobile

columns to operate between the defensive positions, led to
a revised layout. The El Alamein 'box' was held by only one
South African brigade, the other two being semi-mobile on
the edge of Ruweisat Ridge to the south, 18th Indian Brigade
preparing a defensive position at Deir el Shein, five miles
west of them and eight miles north-east of 6th New Zealand
Brigade. This layout would make a rapid encirclement of the
El Alamein 'box' difficult, but the lack of any tanks gave us
little confidence that it could be held by these troops alone. A
further unsettling influence was Auchinleck's insistence that
Eighth Army must be kept mobile and 'in no circumstances
be encircled or immobilized'. This concept, the formation
of mobile columns out of infantry brigades and the issue of
a contingency plan covering withdrawal, if necessary, to the
Nile Delta, led many to assume that this would be yet another
position to be abandoned. Norrie did not take this view, and
was determined to make it a last stand. We had hoped for
some weeks at least in which to get things properly organized,
but were not to have even one.

On 23 June Rommel crossed the frontier (with only 44
tanks, although we did not know this). Two days later he
was in contact with 13 Corps south of Matruh, the day that
Auchinleck took over personal command of Eighth Army
from Ritchie. The Auk promptly decided that he could not
hold the position. He had also become disillusioned about the
value of holding fixed defences, which the enemy by-passed,
and chose this moment to issue a directive, prompted by
Eric Dorman-Smith, who accompanied him as an additional
chief of staff, that infantry formations should be organized
into mobile brigade groups, sending back to base surplus
infantry who could not be made mobile. It was not an
auspicious time at which to attempt major changes, and it
added to the confusion and lack of confidence that the high
command knew what it was doing, and to the tendency of
odd bodies of men and vehicles to seek refuge in rearward
movement. The combination of these orders with Rommel's
energetic irruption into the area south of Matruh led to a lack
of cooperation between 10 and 13 Corps in a confused battle,
in which the New Zealanders suffered. They had joined
Gott outside, handing over the defences to 10th Indian and
50th Divisions. This was immediately followed by an almost

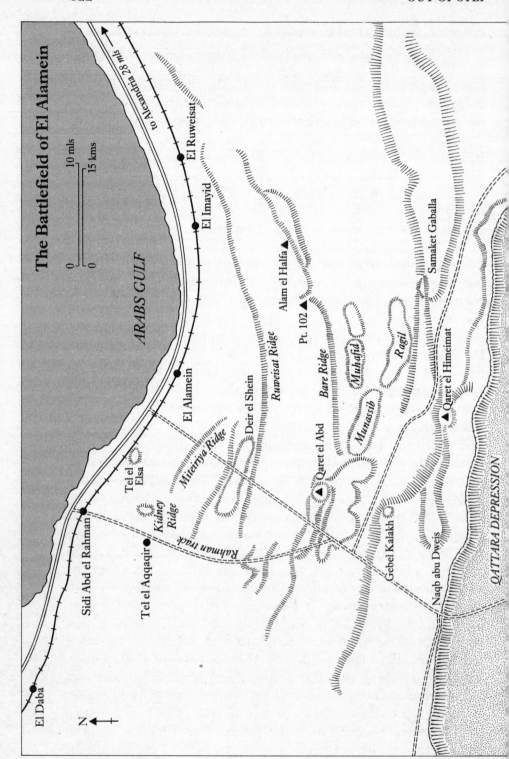

The Battlefield of El Alamein

equally confused withdrawal, in which 1st Armoured Division, which had all the remaining tanks under its command, found themselves at times mixed up with the Afrika Korps, travelling in the same direction.

By 30 June Rommel's leading troops were in contact with the western edge of the El Alamein defences, although both 4th and 22nd Armoured Brigades under Lumsden were still further west. Auchinleck's plan was that 13 Corps would come in on Norrie's left, the boundary between them being immediately south of Ruweisat Ridge, which was Lumsden's destination. The New Zealand Division, commanded by Inglis, Freyberg having been wounded for the umpteenth time, would concentrate on its 6th Brigade, with 5th Indian Division south of them, taking 9th Indian Brigade under its command. Tenth Indian and 50th Divisions had come down the coast road, and I had had a hectic time trying to direct the withdrawing troops to their destinations and sorting out the stragglers. I did it by sending officers with wireless sets to key points and giving them wide authority, referring to me only in case of doubt or dispute. On the whole it worked well, the weary and bemused retreating units being relieved to find an organization which seemed to be in control and to know what it was doing.

Characteristically Rommel gave us no respite. On 1 July he launched an attack, almost an exact repetition of that he had delivered at Mersa Matruh. Thrusting between the El Alamein 'box' and Ruweisat Ridge, 90th Light was to encircle the former, while the Afrika Korps turned south and enveloped 13 Corps from the rear. But the Africa Korps was in almost as great a muddle as 1st Armoured Division, with which it was still mixed up. The South Africans had difficulty in determining which was which, as 4th Armoured Brigade appeared from the west, moving south of the El Alamein 'box',and finally came to rest in soft sand, into which it sank, south-east of the 'box'.

The brunt of Rommel's attack was taken by the gallant 18th Indian Brigade in its first battle, to whom we had sent up nine Matilda tanks during the night. They held up Nehring's Afrika Korps all day, while 90th Light was stopped by the South African positions further east. Now that we were more static and concentrated, David Aikenhead, the

corps artillery commander, was able to concentrate the fire
of all the guns that could be brought to bear, and his staff
officer, John Gibbon, and I kept in close touch. But the
pressure on 18th Indian Brigade proved too great, and, by
the time darkness fell, they were overrun. Their sacrifice was
not in vain. It was the turning point of the whole campaign,
a tribute to Norrie's perception in choosing their position
and to their gallantry in defending it, 2nd/5th Battalion
of the Essex Regiment and 4th/11th Sikhs deserving the
highest praise. The Afrika Korps, starting the day with only
55 tanks, could muster only 37 fit for action next day,
Rommel persisting in his attack, although changing his plan.
Nehring was now to strike north-east also, on the right of
90th Light, to complete the encirclement of the El Alamein
defences. The Italian 20th Mobile Corps was to take over the
southern thrust.

Auchinleck planned a counter-thrust. While 30 Corps held
any eastward drive by Rommel, Gott, with Lumsden under
command, was to counter-attack Rommel, whose weakness
in tanks and infantry was known from intelligence, from the
south. But, as so often, his grand intention was whittled down
in execution. The outcome was a head-on clash between
Lumsden's 1st Armoured Division and Nehring's Afrika
Korps on Ruweisat Ridge in mid-afternoon with inconclusive
results. The fact that the battle lines were now firmly drawn,
and we knew more or less where our troops were, made it
possible to give the RAF a free hand. They made full use
of it, to which German accounts, including Rommel's diary,
bear witness. From then on, the latter never ceased to report
the battering they received from the air, the results of which
had a far more significant effect on their morale than it did
in terms of actual casualties to men or equipment. The only
incident of the day which caused us concern was an attack at
4.30 p.m. by 21st Panzer on 1st South African Brigade just
north of Ruweisat Ridge. The attack was beaten off without
their help, but was renewed, with 90th Light joining in, at
6 p.m. and again after dark, both the brigadier and the
brigade major being wounded. His temporary successor
demanded permission to withdraw, Pienaar supporting him,
unless Norrie could provide some tanks to come under his
command and protect their flank. Norrie refused, knowing

that Auchinleck intended to use all the available armour in a counterstroke. Pienaar insisted that the matter be referred to the C-in-C, who gave way and said that Pienaar must use his own discretion. He promptly issued orders for their withdrawal, whereupon Norrie, as he had said he would, ordered a column from 50th Division, with gunners from 7th Armoured, to take their place, which they did at dawn on 3 July, driving out troops from 90th Light, who had occupied it after the South Africans had withdrawn. The battle continued on that day also, but Rommel's troops were at the end of their tether, their morale lowered by heavy and persistent air attacks.

At last, we felt, we had brought his endless succession of victories to an end. But to stop him was not enough. Auchinleck, provided with accurate information from wireless intercept, realized that Rommel was at his weakest and that the time was ripe for a counter-attack which could rout him. His plan was for 30 Corps to continue to stop any eastward enemy move, while 13 Corps swung up from the south in Rommel's rear. Unfortunately, partly because all the available tanks, nearly 100, were left with 30 Corps in a semi-defensive rôle, this bold concept did not produce much effect in practice. We now know that the tank strength of the Afrika Korps was down to 36 on 4 July, and 15th Panzer was very anxious about its position when Rommel insisted on moving the 21st back, with the idea of thrusting further south. They were also very short of ammunition. First Armoured Division did little more than 'demonstrate' along Ruweisat Ridge on both days, and neither the New Zealand nor 5th Indian Divisions seem to have reacted very forcibly to Auchinleck's orders, passed on to them by Gott. Kippenberger's 5th New Zealand Brigade had some moderate success in a night attack on the Italian Brescia Division, but their 4th Brigade suffered a severe attack by the Luftwaffe as it was forming up to join him, both the brigadier and the brigade major being killed. No further pressure was exerted, 5th Indian Division limiting its offensive action to artillery fire, some of which was directed at the New Zealanders and our own armoured cars. We now know that a great opportunity was missed on these two days. From 6 July onwards Rommel's strength began to grow again, and he set about making his position

more secure, his hopes of a rapid advance to Alexandria and
the Nile having been dashed.

Auchinleck did not intend to leave him in peace. He also
was developing his strength, one significant reinforcement
being Morshead's 9th Australian Division. An attack by them
and the South Africans westward from the El Alamein 'box'
on 10 July was successful in securing two Tels, or mounds,
which dominated the area, the westerly one being Tel el Eisa,
where the Australians captured Rommel's tactical wireless
intercept unit. But it did not lead to a breakthrough along
the coast road, as Auchinleck had hoped. He next switched
his effort to the area of Ruweisat Ridge, then defended by
the Italian Pavia and Brescia Divisions. These attacks were
made on 14 and 15 July by the New Zealand and 5th
Indian Divisions, supported by 1st Armoured, all under 13
Corps. The action of the armoured brigades was not closely
coordinated with that of the infantry, who had attacked
under cover of darkness and found themselves vulnerable
to counter-attack by enemy tanks in daylight. Fourth and 5th
New Zealand Brigades reached their objectives on Ruweisat
Ridge, having passed through both Brescia and most of 15th
Panzer Divisions on the way. They were attacked by the latter
from the rear during 15 July, suffered heavy casualties and
were withdrawn during the night to a line running south
from where 5th Indian Brigade, in spite of severe casualties,
had secured their objective on the ridge. Relations between
the New Zealanders and 1st Armoured Division became sour
as a result of this failure.

Encouraged by intelligence reports of the low state of
the enemy's morale and strength, Auchinleck had decided
to strike again on 21 July. The whole operation was, once
more, to be under Gott, and the plan was for a direct
westward thrust along and south of Ruweisat Ridge. All the
tanks were to be under Gatehouse, replacing Lumsden who
had been wounded in an air attack. It proved to be a most
unfortunate failure, the Valentines driving straight onto a
minefield under anti-tank fire, suffering heavy losses, while
2nd Armoured Brigade, also caught in minefields, failed
to support the New Zealanders. The latter were counter-
attacked, suffered heavily and were forced to withdraw,
feeling bitter at the failure of the tanks to help them.

We were no more successful in a series of attacks further
north. Although in most cases the infantry reached the objectives of their night attacks, there was considerable confusion
about whether or not and where gaps in the minefields
had been cleared, which delayed the advance of the tanks.
Before they had begun to pass through, the enemy counter-
attacked the infantry and regained their positions. On 31
July Auchinleck reported to Churchill that it was no longer
feasible to break through or turn Rommel's flank. A counter-
offensive would have to await the arrival of reinforcements
and could not be launched before mid-September. His message, based on an appreciation drawn up by Dorman-Smith
on 27 July, sparked off the visit of both Churchill and
Alan Brooke to Cairo, which led to Auchinleck's relief by
Alexander and Montgomery's assumption of command of
Eighth Army, after Gott, first chosen for it, had been killed.

Since our arrival back in the El Alamein line and the
withdrawal from Mersa Matruh, I had seen a good deal
of Auchinleck and his *éminence grise*, Dorman-Smith. I had
found the Commander-in-Chief a warm, friendly person,
understanding and courteous, ready to listen and shrewd
in his comments. I had not always felt confident that he
understood the practical problems of moving units about,
communicating orders, seeing that tanks were full of petrol
and ammunition, and all those requirements that had to be
met before a collection of units, designated in an order,
could form an effective fighting force and translate their
orders into effective action on the battlefield. I thought
that he was too prone to think that stirring words would
by themselves produce results. I felt even less confident
that Dorman-Smith appreciated these factors. He seemed
to assume that, once he had conceived an idea and issued
orders, it was as good as done. I recall one occasion on
which he gave orders for 7th Armoured Division to carry
out a certain task. When I pointed out to him that they had
no troops under command, only their own headquarters, he
did not seem to think it made any difference. Auchinleck
seemed mesmerized by Dorman-Smith's fertile imagination
and the speed with which he could produce ideas and commit them to paper with clarity and precision. But we dis-
trusted his influence, and held him largely responsible for,

as we believed, giving formations tasks which were, at the time, beyond their resources. From what we now know (as Auchinleck and Dorman-Smith, privy to ULTRA, perhaps knew then), the resources would in fact have been adequate for the tasks set, if the formations ordered to carry them out had been better organized, and if they had been confident in the army's leadership.

By this time there had been many changes in that leadership. Messervy had been removed on 19 June, and succeeded in command of 7th Armoured Division by Renton, promoted from 7th Motor Brigade; and Richards had handed over 4th Armoured Brigade to Fisher. The change which affected me most was the departure of Norrie on 6 July. He told me that he had asked to go. If that was truly the case, he acted wisely from his own point of view. It meant that he arrived in England, where he was on friendly terms with Churchill among others, and was able to give his own version of events, before the spring-cleaning was carried out with new brooms. He asked me for a copy of the operational wireless log since 27 May, which he took with him. He was succeeded by Ramsden, who had been commanding 50th Division, a dull, earnest, pedestrian infantryman, who inspired none of us with enthusiasm and confidence. He was quickly swept away when Montgomery arrived. George Hatton, to our great relief, was succeeded at the end of July by George Walsh, a meticulously efficient but humourless gunner. Hatton had never hit it off with Norrie or with 'the Brains Trust'. After a time he gave up trying to assert himself, and was content to let the operational staff deal directly with the commander with little intervention by himself. It would have been better if he had left before the battle had started, and Norrie had had a senior adviser of greater standing and experience, nearer his own age than the three majors of the Brains Trust, all in their twenties. The fact that there was no intermediary between myself and Willoughby Norrie gave me a responsibility and an experience of the problems of high command, which were to be of the greatest value to me in the future.

I owed a great deal to Willoughby Norrie, who was always kindness itself to me. I had great admiration for his courage, calmness and resolution in adversity; for his clear,

unprejudiced mind and the tolerance, charm and persua-
siveness which he displayed in dealing with difficult characters, like Pienaar. But I came to realize that there was a
reverse side to that coin: that he was too easy-going with his
subordinates, too ready to leave the decision to them, and
not to drive them or force them against their will. He was
always ready to listen and to seek the advice of others, but
he lacked the confidence in his own judgement to stand up,
either to superiors or to subordinates, and fight for his own
decision. He would combine with Strafer Gott to face up to
Ritchie, but did not like to do it alone.

How much of the failure of all these battles was his fault,
my fault, the fault of all of us in 30 Corps and Eighth Army? I
have given my views on this in my books *Tobruk* and *Dilemmas
of the Desert War*.* They were arrived at after a careful study
of the records of both sides, in particular of the technical
details and numbers of tanks and anti-tank guns actually in
use against each other and the tactics employed. My general
conclusions were that there were faults all round, at every
level of command, from top to bottom; that there were no
strictly technical or theoretical reasons for Eighth Army's
defeat at Gazala; but that there were inherent deficiencies in
organization, training and command, which meant that the
army's full power was never developed.

At the time I accepted the general view that our defeat
was primarily due to the technical superiority of German
tanks – that we were out-gunned and out-armoured, except
in the case of the Grants, and, as far as armour only was concerned, the Matildas and the Valentines. That the principal
enemy was the German anti-tank gun, and the aggressive
way it was handled, was not so clear to us at the time. The
other stock view, which I accepted from Norrie, was that
our troubles during the Gazala battles had stemmed from
Ritchie's unwavering loyalty to The Auk, who constantly
'breathed down his neck' the optimistic and unrealistic view
taken by GHQ. In the light of studying the campaign after
the war, and of my service under Ritchie in North West
Europe, I would not lay as much stress on this as we did at
the time, although there is undoubtedly a strong element of

---

* Published by Batsford in 1964 and 1986 respectively.

truth in it. But GHQ had sound reasons, based on accurate intelligence, for its optimism, and the team of Norrie and Gott could have done more to help Ritchie in his relations with Auchinleck. But persistence in the clearly unsound plan for Operation *Buckshot* undermined their trust in Ritchie's judgement, as The Auk's mistaken prediction of Rommel's most likely avenue of attack on 27 May undermined their trust in him, not that it was ever particularly high in either case. How I came to revise my ideas about the causes of our failure is described in chapter 10.

At the beginning of August I was not looking forward to the future with great enthusiasm. The roles of 30 and 13 Corps seemed to have been reversed, as had positions in the desert. Neither the new commander nor the new BGS seemed to be a very sympathetic character, the latter making it clear that he thought we had made a mess of things, and that in future our staff work was to be conducted in the strictest staff college manner. One by-product of 23rd Armoured Brigade's disastrous experience on 21 July was to have interesting consequences. A few days after the battle I met Lieutenant-Colonel 'Nobby' Clarke, commanding 46th Royal Tanks, and we discussed the apparently insoluble problem of how to deal with minefields. He said that in England he had seen experiments with a rotating drum fitted in front of a tank, equipped with chains which 'flailed' the ground, exploding the mines. He understood that the idea had originated in Egypt and that the first model of such a drum had been made in the Middle East. I followed this up by asking all the staff departments and services of Headquarters 30 Corps to ask their opposite numbers in GHQ and the base if they knew of or could find any trace of such a drum. Within a few days one had come to light in a depot in Alexandria, and the originator of the idea, a South African engineer, Major du Toit, had been traced. Fortunately our Chief Engineer was also a South African, and he took up the project with enthusiasm, fitting the original drum and some copies to 3-ton lorries, driven from the engine. This did not provide enough power, and the lorries were apt to get stuck. However we thought we had proved the soundness of the concept, and enlisted the support of Brigadier Kisch, the Chief Engineer of Eighth Army. If

we wanted to get high-level support for going ahead, we
should, he advised, organize a demonstration, which must,
at all costs, be successful. If we took precautions to see that it
was, he would turn a blind eye to a certain insurance policy.
We therefore arranged to detonate the mines electrically, if
the flail did not do so as it passed over them. This would
be necessary in any case to prevent damage to the vehicle.
The demonstration was a genuine success and resulted in 24
Matildas being converted to the mine-clearing rôle, with an
auxiliary engine mounted externally to drive the rotor. They
were manned by 42nd and 44th Royal Tanks and took part
in the Battle of El Alamein three months later; they were the
forerunners of the successful 'Crab', the Sherman tank used
in this rôle in Normandy in 1944.

Meanwhile momentous discussions were taking place in
Cairo, where Churchill and General Sir Alan Brooke, the
CIGS, had arrived on 3 August. The latter's first talks with
Auchinleck led to the suggestion that Montgomery should
come out from England to take over Eighth Army, and
that Strafer Gott, who Brooke realized was badly in need
of a rest, should replace 'Jumbo' Wilson as Commander
of British Troops in Egypt, that is in the base. Corbett,
Auchinleck's useless Chief of Staff at GHQ ('Well known as
the stupidest officer in the Indian Army,' Strafer said to me
once, 'and that's saying some.') was to go. But both he and
Churchill soon came round to the view that Auchinleck must
also go, and the revised plan was for Alexander to relieve
him, Montgomery replacing the latter as commander of First
Army, designated to serve under Eisenhower in Operation
Torch, the Anglo-American invasion of French North Africa,
then being prepared. Gott was to have Eighth Army, and on
6 August was summoned to Cairo. Shortly before he left, I
had a long talk with him. We discussed the problem of how
to break through what, by mid-September, was likely to be
a continuous front, covered by minefields. He did not relish
the idea of a direct attempt at a penetration. It savoured too
much of the battles of the First World War, which he was
determined should not be repeated. He knew that I had
crossed the salt marshes of the Qattara Depression and knew
the route to Siwa, and suggested that a wide out-flanking
movement deep into the enemy's rear by that route would be

the answer. I pointed out the problems of logistic supply, of the capacity of the sandy desert and the salt marshes to bear the traffic, the vulnerability to air attack and the vast distance to be covered, before reaching any objective which would seriously threaten the enemy: all, in my view, ruled it out. We must steel ourselves to find a solution to getting our tanks right through the defences and their minefields by night. There was no way to do it on the cheap. He made it clear that he would not be prepared to conduct such a battle. 'It's time they got some fresh people in with new ideas, Mike,' he said. It was uncharacteristic of him to give up. On his way to Cairo, the aircraft in which he was flying was attacked by German fighters, forced to land in the desert and set on fire. Most of its passengers, including Gott, were trapped inside and killed. The news came as a great shock to us. I felt his death keenly, as I had a great admiration and affection for him. Almost all who served under him worshipped him: for his serenity, good humour and courage whatever the situation; but above all because whenever others were uncertain as to what to do, he was prepared to propose a positive solution, which, at the time, seemed wise. But the deeper I delved into the record after the war, the more I understood why, from Gazala back to El Alamein, some of the Commonwealth commanders, Australian, New Zealand and South African, and their historians, have cast doubt on his judgement and exercise of command in that period, at the end of which he was undoubtedly exhausted. Tragic as it was for him, and all who loved and respected him, it was fortunate for Eighth Army that he did not assume command.

7

A Day's March Nearer Home

Yet nightly pitch my moving tent
A day's march nearer home.
James Montgomery (1771–1854),
At Home in Heaven

While my spirits were depressed by the news of Strafer's death, they were raised again by a signal from Eighth Army ordering me to take over from Pete Pyman as GSO1 of 7th Armoured Division, Pete having been selected to command 3rd Royal Tanks, reorganizing at the base. To be chosen for this plum job in my old division, which meant promotion to the rank of lieutenant-colonel at the age of 27 was a tremendous boost to my morale, and I handed over as GSO2 (Ops) at Headquarters 30 Corps without regret to Victor FitzGeorge Balfour, little knowing that we were to see so much of each other in future years.

Seventh Armoured Division was at the extreme southern end of the El Alamein line, and I drove down there to take over my new job on 15 August 1942. An hour's talk with Pete sufficed as handover, his main theme being to warn me that the divisional commander, Major-General Callum Renton, was in a very tricky frame of mind and disliked the Commander Royal Artillery, Brigadier Vaughan-Hughes. I discovered that the result of this was that Renton refused to make use of the 'General's Mess', and insisted on having his meals brought to him either in his staff car-cum-bivouac or in the command vehicle. Fortunately I knew him well and soon persuaded him to adopt a more normal life-style. The fact that all the reports his brigade had made of Rommel's thrust round the south of Bir Hacheim on the night of 26 May had been brushed aside by Pete Pyman and Messervy rankled in his mind, and had soured relations between him and Pete. He spent much time attempting to discover what had actually gone on in the headquarters on that fateful night, but Pete was able to maintain that all records had been destroyed when the operational command vehicle had been knocked out during the German attack on the headquarters. Neither knew that the divisional signals had kept a duplicate log. Henry Crawford, the signals commander, who had been the first adjutant of the divisional signals, kept it under lock and key. When he left, he entrusted it to me, on the understanding that it was not to be made use of, unless a serious inquiry into the events of that night were instituted. When I handed over as GSO1 of the division to Pat Hobart in April 1943, I entrusted it to him, and he decided to destroy it.

Two days before I had taken over my new job, Montgomery, contrary to Auchinleck's orders, had assumed command of Eighth Army from Ramsden, who was acting as army commander. It must have been very soon after that that Monty visited the division, all officers of the rank of lieutenant-colonel and above being paraded to meet him. We were not particularly impressed with this self-assured white-kneed export from Britain. He was needlessly offensive to some of the older officers and infuriated one or two in particular.

At this time 7th Armoured Division contained all the tanks of Eighth Army, except the infantry support tanks, mostly Valentines, which were all in 23rd Armoured Brigade supporting 30 Corps in the north. Most of our tanks were in 22nd Armoured Brigade, now commanded by Pip Roberts. Fourth Armoured Brigade, commanded by Bill Carr (who had previously commanded the 22nd) was organized as a light brigade with one regiment of Stuarts (the temporarily amalgamated 4th and 8th Hussars), a squadron of Crusaders of 3rd County of London Yeomanry, two armoured car regiments, 11th Hussars and 12th Lancers, with 1st KRRC as its motor battalion and 3rd RHA as its gunners. Renton's old 7th Motor Brigade, now commanded by Jimmy Bosvile, had three battalions of the Rifle Brigade (2nd, 7th and 9th),

2nd KRRC, and a regiment of Crusader tanks, made up of a squadron each from the regiments that had formed 2nd Armoured Brigade (The Bays, 9th Lancers and 10th Hussars). We were responsible for the extreme southern end of the line, south of the New Zealand Division on Bare Ridge, both divisions being under 13 Corps, its new commander, flown out from England, being Brian Horrocks. We had 20 miles of front to look after, the southern limit of which was the escarpment marking the edge of the Qattara Depression. The dominating feature was the hill, Qaret el Himeimat, which had been an important landmark on the desert route from Cairo to Mersa Matruh. North of it the ground was hard: south of it, sandy slope led down to the escarpment. Bosvile's brigade held the line from the New Zealanders down to Himeimat, and was engaged in laying two parallel minefields across the front, known as January and February, between which they held a thinly defended line of posts. A third minefield covered their reserve position five miles further back. Fourth Armoured Brigade had Christopher Consett's 1st KRRC (60th Rifles) round Himeimat, backed up by 4th/8th Hussars' Stuarts. The Crusaders of 3rd County of London Yeomanry (The Sharpshooters) were back at Samaket Gaballa, a prominent hill 15 miles east of Himeimat. Pip Roberts's 22nd Armoured Brigade was in reserve north of them.

If Rommel attacked, the plan was for us to delay him for as long as possible, gradually withdrawing east and then north-east to a ridge called Alam el Halfa, which was an extension of Bare Ridge, held by the New Zealanders, and 20 miles east of them. This would have meant that Eighth Army was executing a manoeuvre known as 'refusing the left flank'. Monty's first act significantly strengthened this plan. He had 44th Division, an inexperienced London Territorial infantry division, sent up from the base to occupy the Alam el Halfa ridge. As the August days passed and no attack came, the whole position became stronger. Not only did we complete the minefields, but a fresh armoured division, the 10th, commanded by Alec Gatehouse, was organized and brought up from the base to the area south-east of Alam el Halfa. Twenty-second Armoured Brigade, to our annoyance, was removed from our command and placed immediately west

of the 44th Division under Horrocks's direct command, partially filling the gap between the 44th and the New Zealand
Divisions. This left us very weak in tanks. Our rôle remained
that of a delaying force: to entice Rommel into a trap, where
he could be held and pounded from the air. When he had
thus been pulverized, our task would be to dash westward,
and cut his supply lines by thrusting north to the coast.

We received accurate intelligence that Rommel was building up his forces opposite us and planning to attack at the
time of the full moon, which fell on 26 August. However he
was having great difficulties over petrol supply, due to the
activities of the Royal Navy, and we were as frustrated as he
must have been, when he postponed his attack from day to
day. We could not complain, as every day that passed made
us stronger. At last, on the night of 31 August, he moved, and
his first shock came from an attack by RAF heavy bombers,
Wellingtons, on his concentration area. The moon rose 20
minutes before midnight by the time we were keeping. I
soon began to receive reports from 7th Motor Brigade that
the enemy were shelling the gaps in the minefields, which
we had been using to let our armoured cars patrol forward.
My first reaction was to pass on a request for air attack on
the area west of the minefields, which was met by RAF
Wellingtons and naval Albacores, the latter dropping flares
to illuminate Rommel's concentration of vehicles. This also
helped us by silhouetting the leading tanks for the benefit
of Bosvile's anti-tank gunners. German attacks on our thinly
held front were continuous, and by 4.30 a.m. they had made
a breach in the first minefield, passing 60 tanks through
before it got light. A second breach was made soon after,
and Bosvile was forced to withdraw his troops to the second
minefield, which he had succeeded in doing by 7.30. By that
time 4th Armoured Brigade had been forced off Himeimat,
and Carr withdrew his motor battalion to Samaket Gaballa,
4th/8th Hussars being ordered to harry the enemy from
the escarpment between the two hills.

By now it was clear that Rommel's attack was taking
the form of three thrusts, all in our area, the northern
one just south of the New Zealanders on Bare Ridge, the
centre through the depression of Deir el Munassib, and the
southern one north of Himeimat. In the next few hours it

became evident that the last was the main one with at least 100 tanks. It was in fact the two panzer divisions, 15th and 21st, of the Afrika Korps, the centre thrust being 90th Light and the northern one the Italian 20th Mobile Corps. We were taking the full brunt of Rommel's attack; little else was happening on the whole of the rest of Eighth Army's front. As the Afrika Korps pushed eastward, they began to outflank Bosvile's brigade, at the same time pushing 4th/8th Hussars back on their right flank. About 9 a.m. Bosvile asked Renton for permission to withdraw further to his reserve position north of the eastern end of the Ragil depression, where he would be more or less in line with 22nd Armoured Brigade, five miles to the north, and Carr's position at Samaket Gaballa, rather further away to the south. Renton agreed; but, when Horrocks heard about it, he was very angry. I had an acrimonious conversation with him, in which he complained that we were not imposing enough delay and were too concerned with preserving our forces. He insisted that Bosvile's troops should return to the second minefield. I said that this was impracticable, and to order it would only cause confusion. I summoned Renton to the radio to speak to him, and, after a further acrimonious exchange, Renton was forced to order Bosvile to send the Crusader squadron of 10th Hussars that was with him to move west again. At midday they moved north-west and made contact with the New Zealanders, at about the same time as 23rd Armoured Brigade, now commanded by Rickie Richards, moved south from 30 Corps to fill the gap between the New Zealand Division and 22nd Armoured Brigade.

A severe duststorm blew up in the middle of the day, preventing either air or armoured car reconnaissance from seeing where the enemy were; but we were fairly certain that they could not have slipped through us. In fact they were in considerable difficulties. The progress of all their thrusts had been much slower than they had planned. They had expected a rapid move eastward to the area of Alam el Halfa, where they would turn north and make for the coast, encircling all Montgomery's forces, a repetition of Rommel's plan for Gazala. But the Afrika Korps had penetrated only ten miles and the thrusts on its left even less. Its commander, Nehring, had been wounded and 21st Panzer's, von Bismarck, killed. The slow going had made them use more petrol than expected, and they were desperately short of it. We did not, of course, know all this, and wondered why they were not thrusting eastward more strongly. In the early afternoon they came into contact with Carr's position at Samaket Gaballa and pushed him off it. By 3.30 p.m. they were pressing against Bosvile's reserve position. It was now clear that the Afrika Korps had turned north-east, crossing the Ragil depression. We lost touch with them for a time, but the position was clarified again when, at 5.30 p.m., with only an hour's daylight to go, Pip Roberts's 22nd Armoured Brigade reported 120 German tanks to the south of them. A fierce battle followed, in which Roberts's position held firm, knocking out some 30 enemy tanks for the loss of 20 of their own. The Afrika Korps withdrew into Ragil, where they were subjected to intense air attack almost all night. We claimed to have knocked out a further 38 tanks during the day, but the German accounts only listed a total of 22 out of action. However it was the decisive day of the campaign, the furthest east that Rommel reached – the end of his hopes of reaching the Nile.

Battered from the air all night, Rommel made a half-hearted and unsuccessful attempt to renew his advance next day. After another night of continuous air bombardment, he decided to withdraw. Montgomery planned to cut him off by a counter-attack south from Bare Ridge, reinforcing the New Zealanders with an infantry brigade from 44th Division and tanks from 23rd Armoured Brigade for the operation. But it was successfully resisted by the Italians on Rommel's left flank, and he withdrew without further loss to our previous forward positions, from which, especially from Himeimat, he could overlook the whole area south of Bare Ridge, complicating our preparations for the subsequent Battle of El Alamein.

Our attention was immediately switched to these preparations, one of the first tasks being to lay new minefields across our front to give us the security behind which they could be made. A wholesale reorganization of Eighth Army now took place. The most significant change as far as I was concerned was in our commander. Horrocks had been very dissatisfied with Renton, whom he thought too infected with anxiety about keeping his forces 'in being'. Callum Renton was not a good divisional commander: he was too subject to moods, and was undoubtedly over-sensitive about casualties – he had seen too many men killed, wounded or taken prisoner, particularly the latter, to no purpose. Nevertheless it was his tragedy that the occasions which led to clashes between him and his superiors were almost invariably ones in which he was in the right, as he had been in the Battle of Alam Halfa. His successor was John Harding, and there could have been no better choice. I have described him, and explained my admiration for him, fully in his biography,* and I will not repeat it here. Suffice it to say that he infused the whole division with his own energy, enthusiasm and commonsense. The division would have resented the arrival of one of Montgomery's favourites from England, but we knew John Harding as one who had been through the vicissitudes of the desert war as we had.

He arrived on 17 September, and I had to explain to him the problems that faced us. We had to lay three belts of minefields across our front to ensure that with the few troops we had available, Rommel did not interfere with our preparations or force us to keep troops in the forward area who should be re-equipping or training. We would then have to plan to advance west through both these minefields and our old ones, now occupied by Rommel's forces, which he would no doubt develop into a formidable obstacle. All our activities would take place in full view of the dominating height of Himeimat. In the reorganization of Eighth Army that was to take place, we were the Cinderella. Seventh Motor Brigade left us on 23 September to join 1st Armoured Division, and we were left without any infantry formation until Koenig's Free French Brigade joined us on 18 October. Pip Roberts' 22nd Armoured Brigade returned to us, but was to be kept in reserve while it was reorganized, partially re-equipped and trained for the future battle. Fourth Light Armoured Brigade, with only one regiment of tanks, The Royal Scots Greys, two armoured car regiments, its motor battalion, 1st KRRC, and its gunners, had to look after the whole front, which was however narrowed by 44th Division

* *Harding of Petherton.* Weidenfeld & Nicolson, 1978.

taking over the northern part of it, when they relieved the New Zealanders on Bare Ridge. Mark Roddick took over command of the brigade from Bill Carr, and there were many changes also at divisional headquarters, almost all the senior officers being replaced.

Although Horrocks's 13 Corps in the south had only a subsidiary role in the Battle of El Alamein, that of exerting sufficient pressure in the south to force Rommel to hold a significant proportion of his forces, especially of his armour, there, our task was to try and break through the minefields and, if possible, turn his southern flank. The chief problems lay in three fields. First, that, because we were overlooked by Himeimat, we had to keep our main force well back from the minefields until the last minute. This meant a long approach march in the dark. Second, that we were very short of infantry: although the Free French Brigade had four battalions, only the two Foreign Legion ones could be used for offensive operations; the Senegalese and Pacific Islands battalions could only be used for guard duties. Koenig also insisted that his brigade must be used on its own and be given a special task. Finally, we faced the complicated task of clearing gaps under fire in both our own and the enemy minefields, a total of five, perhaps six, marking the gaps, and then passing through: the approach to and the passage through at least the first of the enemy's minefields would have to be completed in one night, leaving Roberts's tanks to face enemy tanks and anti-tank guns in daylight. The French were to attack and capture Himeimat, so that we were then not immediately overlooked, although we should still be observed at a greater distance from the escarpment to the west of it. It soon became clear that we just did not have enough troops of the right kind to do all this. We were therefore given 44th Division's reconnaissance regiment, commanded by Lyon Corbett-Winder, who had been adjutant of 1st KRRC at the beginning of the war and a fellow student at Haifa. It was to form the minefield task force, exercising coordination over the engineers, military police, armoured cars and other troops involved in clearing and marking the minefield gaps and the routes leading to them.

There was a great deal to be done, and the five weeks from Harding's arrival to the October full moon period seemed all too short. There was much discussion about the details of how our task was to be tackled and about the respective responsibilities of everyone in all its stages. Producing clear orders to ensure that everything was coordinated and everyone knew exactly what they had to do was not easy, and was my main concern. After the final meeting to tie everything up, I asked John Harding if he would like to see the operation order before I signed it and sent it out. 'No,' he said, 'you're clear about what I want. It's your job to write the orders. I have no more to do now. I don't want to be disturbed by anyone for the next 48 hours, not even the corps commander. Have you got a good book for me to read?' The only ones I had, which I carried with me throughout the war, were two anthologies of prose and verse, *The Knapsack*, edited by Herbert Read, and the *Daily Telegraph Second Miscellany*, edited by Budge Firth, and Tolstoy's *Anna Karenina* and *War and Peace*. John Harding had not read either of Tolstoy's famous novels, and I lent him *Anna Karenina*.

It was with a sense of considerable excitement, and a feeling that it was a moment of destiny, that the day of battle dawned. Benzedrine pills had been issued to help one to keep awake, but, having got on all right without such artificial aids hitherto, and having all too often experienced last-minute postponements, I refused to take any. The battle started, as far as we were concerned, soon after dark on 23 October, when 22nd Armoured Brigade began its ten-mile approach march to the first minefield, in which the first gap had been cleared by half past midnight, nearly three hours after the start of the artillery bombardment. Heavy casualties to the infantry and sappers in the minefield task force prevented us from even reaching the second minefield before dawn, which found Pip Roberts's tanks crowded into a constricted area astride the first minefield, overlooked from Himeimat, which the French had failed to capture.

Horrocks conferred with Harding, and it was agreed that an attempt to get through the second minefield should be made on the following night, 131st Brigade of 44th Division being placed under our command for the purpose. The infantry attack succeeded in getting beyond the minefield, and gaps were cleared by 2.30 a.m. on 25 October, but they were under accurate enemy fire and several tanks strayed out of the cleared lanes and were blown up. There was argument about whether the gaps were clear of mines, and Harding drove his jeep to the area and personally directed operations to get things going, his ADC being killed beside him. In spite of the drive and determination exerted by him and Roberts, it was not found possible to get the tanks beyond the second minefield, and Horrocks, having consulted Montgomery, agreed that no further attempts should be made, in order to preserve the division's strength to take part in the break-out which was expected to take place in the northern sector. I had been tied to the operational command vehicle almost without a break, while Robin Hastings, the GSO2, accompanied John Harding on his prolonged visits to the scene of action. Glad to see the end of that frustrating phase of the battle, we moved north on 28 October into reserve near El Alamein station, leaving 4th Light Armoured Brigade behind and taking with us 'Bolo' Whistler's 131st Brigade, made mobile in three-ton lorries, which was to remain with the division as its Lorried Infantry Brigade for the rest of the war.

On the night of 2/3 November we moved forward under command of Herbert Lumsden's 10 Corps, expecting to exploit the breakthrough which was anticipated at any moment near Tel el Aqqaqir. Lumsden's plan was that we should lead the break-out south-westward, keeping clear of where 51st Highland Division was attacking. We would then head west, followed by 1st and 10th Armoured Divisions. Unfortunately Montgomery had other ideas. He wanted the New Zealand Division, to whose command 4th Light Armoured Brigade had been transferred, to lead the way, still under the command of 30 Corps, and to block the enemy's withdrawal at Fuka, while Lumsden swung all three of his armoured divisions round in a wide arc to press the enemy up against the coast in the 40-mile-wide area between Fuka and the former front line. Lumsden did not receive Montgomery's new plan until well after dark, and it was midnight before we had our orders changed.

It was both an exhilarating and a frustrating night. We were all desperately eager to get going and be the first to break out into the open desert, but the congestion on the dimly marked tracks through the minefields, ploughed deep in dust, the changes of plan and the uncertainty about what was going on led to endless delays. John Harding could hardly contain his impatience. Herbert Lumsden was justifiably incensed by Monty's interference by remote control, suspecting, not without reason, that it stemmed partly from his desire to favour Freyberg over Lumsden and his armoured divisions. I found myself acting as a buffer between Harding and Lumsden, as we ground our way through dark and dust. At last, at half past eight, well after dawn, we were through, and Harding urged Pip Roberts to hasten on behind the ever faithful 11th Hussars. He soon came upon a large column of enemy, which Harding told him to thrust aside or get round. But, as Pip leapfrogged his regiments round its southern flank, they kept on coming up against opposition. It was in fact the Italian Ariete Armoured Division, and they fought back hard and well, until they had been totally surrounded and destroyed.

Next day saw further changes of plan as Montgomery realized that Freyberg was not going to block Rommel's retreat. We became increasingly frustrated, John Harding seeing clearly that a succession of short hooks to the coast was going to miss the boat, and that the right answer was to send a force westward through the desert to overtake Rommel's forces struggling back down the coast road. He urged Lumsden not to use us as one of these hooks, but to give us priority in petrol supplies and let us, who knew this part of the desert like the backs of our hands, drive west, until we could be certain that we had overtaken Rommel's withdrawal, then cut up north to block him, probably between Sollum and Bardia. But two influences were against us. First was the pressure on Montgomery from the RAF and his own staff to open up the coast road as soon as possible in order to move airfields further west and to ease the problems of logistic supply; and, secondly, Lumsden's desire to give his own old division, 1st Armoured, a leading rôle in the pursuit. If John Harding's plea had met with a favourable response, I have little doubt that we might well have succeeded in cutting off Rommel's remaining armour and putting even more of his forces into 'the bag'.

So we swung up north and, by the time that Pip Roberts had reached our objective south of Daba, it was clear that our

presence there was superfluous. John Harding was not prepared to sit there and do nothing, and, without any orders,
he set the division off on a south-westward course. We were
on the move when Lumsden's orders were received at 1.40
p.m. We were to capture the area of the airfields between
Fuka and Mersa Matruh, moving round behind the New
Zealanders, who were making for the airfields and the coast
road near Fuka. The need to deviate round the tail of the
stationary New Zealand Division delayed us for three hours
and added to our fuel consumption, so that we were forced
to halt after dark, 20 miles short of our objective.

Rommel had intended to stand at Fuka, but realized that
he was being outflanked and gave orders that night, 5/6
November, for a withdrawal to Matruh, while Briggs, who
had been delayed by petrol supply and other troubles, had
got no further than 20 miles west of us by dawn. At that time
Pip, accompanied by John Harding, set off north-west, and
by 10.30 a.m. his brigade was in action against German tanks
and armoured cars, while the 11th Hussars further east had
reached the landing grounds and found them unoccupied.
They reported enemy moving west along the coast road to
the north of them. Roberts was now very short of fuel, but
the B echelons caught up and, after refuelling, he resumed
his advance, coming up against German tanks, hull-down on
the edge of the escarpment, in the early afternoon. It was
in fact 21st Panzer Division, almost out of fuel, although we
did not know it. John Harding told Pip to try and get round
them to the west, but he had not succeeded in doing this
before dark, by which time the heavens had opened, the rain
poured down and the desert turned into a bog, although the
German tanks managed to get away during the night.

We had already been told to move as soon as we could
on a wide outflanking sweep of 170 miles through desert,
almost every stone of which was familiar to us, to catch the
enemy as he climbed to the top of the escarpment on the
frontier at Sollum and Halfaya; but the night's rain made it
almost impossible to move wheeled vehicles and slow going
even for the tanks, most of which were nearly worn out,
as we had been low on the priority list for re-equipment.
Twenty-second Armoured Brigade was reduced to only 47
Grants and Shermans, 15 Stuarts and 30 Crusaders. At the

time, and in his book *El Alamein to the Sangro*, Montgomery blamed the rain for his failure to cut Rommel off; but he had already failed to do so, and the rain merely forced us to follow him up more slowly.

We crossed the frontier three days later, on 9 November, and on 13 November our armoured cars entered Tobruk. Pip Roberts's tanks were now totally worn out and Roddick's 4th Light Armoured Brigade rejoined us, their armoured cars driving forward both along the road through the Jebel and, once again, through the desert from Mechili to Msus and Agedabia, Benghazi being reached on 20 November, when contact was also made with Rommel's rearguard at Agedabia. When divisional headquarters reached Msus on 15 November I was feeling ill and running a high temperature. At first the medical officer thought it was a bout of 'flu, and I asked him not to evacuate me as a casualty, at least for a few days, as I had just completed three months in the temporary rank of lieutenant-colonel, which gave me the war substantive rank of major. That meant that I would not have to revert to that of captain, if I went sick or lost my job for any other reason. I hung on for a day or two, but by then it was clear that I was suffering from the disease which was sweeping through Eighth Army at that time, jaundice or 'infective hepatitis'. This meant that I would have to go to hospital, and I was flown to Tobruk in a Dakota transport aircraft that had brought up ammunition. It was not until some time later that I discovered that the date on which I had officially taken over from Pete Pyman was 21 August, six days after I had actually done so, because he had had five days leave before joining 3rd Royal Tanks. I therefore reverted to the rank of captain.

Feeling pretty miserable, I was delivered to a tented South African Hospital, set on an escarpment inside the perimeter of Tobruk. It was disgracefully badly run, the patients, in the cold wet weather which prevailed, being largely left to look after themselves. After about a week there, we were visited by the senior medical officer of 30 Corps, which had just taken over command in the forward area from 10 Corps. He was none other than 'Q' Wallace, whom I knew well, as he had been the senior medical officer of 7th Armoured Division and then of 30 Corps, when both were formed. I told him what I thought of the place, and within 24 hours I was put on board a hospital ship in Tobruk harbour, which seemed like heaven: nurses, clean sheets, food that a jaundiced patient could swallow, the greatest possible contrast to the previous week. I felt so much better by the time that we reached Alexandria that I was able to get up and walk off the ship. However I was listed as a lying case, and a medical orderly insisted that I lie down on a stretcher to be lifted into the hospital train which took us to Cairo, where I was sent to bed again in 64th General Hospital at Helmieh. There I learned that John Harding was keeping my job open for me and had sent my staff car and driver back to Cairo to bring me back to the headquarters as soon as I was fit to return.

Just as I was hoping, within a few days, to be allowed out of hospital and take a week's sick leave in Cairo, the order went out that the Cairo hospitals were to be prepared to receive more casualties from an expected battle south of Benghazi, and those patients fit to be moved were to be sent to hospitals in Palestine and the Lebanon. I protested in vain and found myself a lying patient again in a hospital train to Sidon. When I got there, I realized that I would not in fact have been fit to return to the desert, the after-effects of jaundice being much more debilitating than I had expected.

The local garrison commander turned out to be Jackie Bowring, who was kindness itself to me, heaping coals of fire on my head. When I was allowed out and granted sick leave late in December, he had me to stay for a few days in Beirut and then gave me a local taxi with a 'work-ticket' of unlimited mileage to allow me to visit Baalbek and other sights on my way to Damascus, from which I would take the train back to Cairo after a week's leave. I could not persuade the taxi-driver to take me up the rough road to see the Krak des Chevaliers. He said that the tyres he had would have to last him the war, and he would not leave the tarmac. I was greatly disappointed. After spending Christmas Day in Damascus, I left by a very slow train and reached Cairo a few days later. I found that my driver and car were still there, although I had sent a message telling him to return to the headquarters, when I had been sent to Sidon. Although I had been away for over a month, John Harding, to my delight, was still keeping my job open for me and I was back in the saddle on 5 January 1943.

While I had been away the division had taken part in a battle at El Agheila, which had driven Rommel further back to Buerat, half-way between El Agheila and Tripoli. Montgomery was not taking any risks in trying to bounce him out of that position, but ordered a pause while he built up his army's strength to make it possible to drive straight through to Tripoli, some 170 miles further on, which involved passage across some difficult hilly country. His original plan had been to attack the position with four divisions under 30 Corps, from north to south 50th, 51st (Highland), the New Zealanders and ourselves, while 10 Corps would be brought up behind, ready to take over the advance beyond Tripoli. But a severe storm, which hit Benghazi just at the time I returned, caused chaos in the harbour. Ships loaded with stores and ammunition broke loose, four being sunk, the breakwater was breached and the capacity of the port reduced from 3000 to 1000 tons a day. However there were signs that Rommel was thinning out, and Montgomery decided to go ahead on 15 January with the Highland Division, supported by the Valentines of Richards's 23rd Armoured Brigade on the coast road, ourselves, with 4th Light, 8th Armoured and 131st Lorried Infantry Brigades, and, on our left, Freyberg's New Zealanders, driving through the hilly desert to reach the escarpment south of Tripoli, ourselves at Tarhuna and the New Zealanders between there and Gharian. Pip Roberts's 22nd Armoured Brigade, re-equipped at the expense of 10 Corps, was in army reserve in the centre.

We were full of confidence and anxious to get going, when we set off by night on 14 January. Next morning Custance's tanks were in action against German tanks and anti-tank guns, including the new 75-mm, the same gun as that carried by the German Mark IV Special tank. Progress was slow, and 4th Light Armoured, commanded by Brigadier Roscoe Harvey, Roddick having been wounded, was sent round to the west of the New Zealanders to forge ahead on the division's main axis. The leading armoured cars were soon reporting that the 'going' was atrociously bad, rocky and intersected by a succession of *wadis*. Although the enemy withdrew during the night, progress was frustratingly slow, as we struggled across the grain of the country. The armoured cars, bouncing over the rocky outcrops, had to find routes down into and then up out of a succession of deep *wadis*. It was quite the worst going we had ever encountered, much worse than the stretch between Mechili and Msus, which at least had been flat. At last we struggled through, and by last light on 18 January Custance's leading tanks were in action against German tanks and guns ten miles south of Tarhuna, guarding the pass down the steep, high escarpment which led over the plain 50 miles to Tripoli. By now we were almost out of range of our own aircraft, but close to Italian and German airfields, and our leading troops, especially the armoured cars, were often subjected to air attack.

John Harding's patience was wearing thin, and he told Neville Custance to press on vigorously next day and prevent the enemy from establishing himself in a strong position guarding the pass. Roscoe Harvey was told to try and find a way down the escarpment further west, although none was marked on the map before Gharian, to which the Free French from Chad were making their way under Brigadier-General Leclerc. If Harvey was successful, Freyberg would move his division down that way. Custance set off again at dawn on 19 January, but made little progress. What happened then is described in my biography of John Harding:[*]

Determined to inject some vigour into his (Custance's) brigade, Harding went to join him, travelling in his command tank which he parked next to Custance's. Finding that his radio was being jammed by Custance's, he moved his own tank away and climbed up on top of Custance's. The enemy artillery was active and Harding was standing up on top of the tank, trying through his binoculars to spot the flash of the guns in order to pass the target to his own artillery, when a shell landed in front of the tank, its fragments killing one of the crew who was standing there and hitting Harding right across his body from his left arm to his right leg, at the same time knocking him off the high

[*] *Harding of Petherton*, p. 110.

Grant tank. His first reaction was to crawl under the tank, from which he was brought out when the shelling stopped and quickly placed in the hands of the nearest doctor. Harding's only memory of what then happened to him was his anger at the doctor cutting up his new pair of cavalry twill trousers.

As soon as I heard what had happened, I got on the radio to 30 Corps and asked to speak to the commander, Oliver Leese. I told him all I knew and stressed that it was important that a replacement be provided urgently. Custance would be hopeless; Whistler at that stage had little experience of armour; Harvey had only very recently been promoted from commanding his regiment, the 10th Hussars. I cannot recall whether or not I suggested Pip Roberts: I think I may have done. Whether or not I did, Montgomery, as soon as he received the news, appointed him, and he set off on the difficult journey to join us.

I quote again from my biography of John Harding to describe what happened next:

The doctors now reported that Harding was very unlikely to survive a journey by ambulance back across the atrocious going over which the division had passed. The author therefore got on to Leese and asked for an ambulance aircraft to be sent up next day, by which time a landing strip would somehow or other be created in the forward area. Ambulance aircraft were not normally allowed so far forward, but Coningham, the Desert Air Force commander, gave special permission for an aircraft, escorted by fighters to the extreme limit of their range, to do so. The RAF landing ground reconnaissance and construction party attached to the division, supported by a whole infantry battalion, worked all night and by the morning had a strip ready. It was essential that there should be no delay in loading the aircraft, as the fighters could only stay in the area for less than ten minutes. Harding was brought by ambulance to the strip, loaded into the aircraft and away again in less than that time, while the fighters engaged the Luftwaffe and shot down two of their fighters.

Little progress was made next day, but on 21 January 4th Light Armoured found a route down the escarpment which the New Zealanders could use, and the enemy withdrew from the Tarhuna pass just as Whistler's 131st Brigade was preparing to attack it. By this time the Highlanders were making good progress along the coast road, and it became a keen race between all three divisions as to who was going to earn the laurels of entering Tripoli first. We won, the 11th Hussars, followed by tactical divisional headquarters, driving into the town unopposed at dawn on 23 January, four hours ahead of the Valentines of 23rd Armoured Brigade, carrying the Highlanders of 51st Division, three months to a day after the start of the Battle of El Alamein.

While others prepared to enjoy the meagre fleshpots Tripoli offered, we immediately had our attention turned to the pursuit westwards, one of our pleasant tasks being to greet General Leclerc and his Free French from Chad, who ran out of petrol as they reached Gharian, further frustrated by finding the road down the escarpment there demolished. Pip Roberts now handed over his temporary command of the division to Bobbie Erskine, who had been BGS of 13 Corps ever since Strafer Gott had assumed command of it. In the previous few weeks he had been acting as an operational chief of staff to Monty, who had been exercising direct command over the Highland Division and 22nd Armoured Brigade, leaving Oliver Leese's 30 Corps to command us and Freyberg. Pip was due to go back to England, but was diverted to command 26th Armoured Brigade in First Army in Algeria, who were badly in need of commanders with battle experience. Erskine, like Strafer, was a 60th Rifleman. He knew the form, was a cheerful, extrovert character, full of enthusiasm; but, like Strafer, with no illusions, not prone to thinking that exhortations alone would produce results. We immediately established a rapport, which was to endure.

While Montgomery summoned generals from all over the world to hear how he had won his battles, and was visited by Churchill and Alan Brooke, we struggled westward, frustrated both by the difficult going to the south, where there were few, if any, roads leading west, sand dunes blocking the way below the great escarpment, up which there were few routes, and also by the skilful rearguard actions, accompanied by demolitions, mines and booby-traps, fought by Rommel's retreating force. Heavy rain made it difficult, in some areas impossible, to move off the single road. Fourth Light Armoured Brigade, now commanded by the South African Brigadier Newton-King, who had commanded their 4th Armoured Car Regiment, were the first to cross the frontier into Tunisia on 2 February, just north of the escarpment. Roscoe Harvey had taken over 8th Armoured Brigade from Custance, whose 'stickiness' had at last led to his relief.

We felt both proud and smugly superior that we carried the burden of pressing the whole front back, while others disported themselves in Tripoli or languished on the long lines of communication, a lot which Horrocks in particular felt intensely frustrating. If we had a complaint, it was that this unglamorous task, with its daily trickle of casualties from mines, booby-traps, shellfire and a very occasional air attack, did not receive the same publicity as the major set-piece battles which only occurred at rare intervals. By 15 February the whole division had entered Tunisia, Whistler's Queens Brigade capturing the small town of Ben Gardane. The area between the high escarpment and the coast was now narrowing, and movement across country was impeded by areas of soft sand and salt-marsh. One area of the latter caused considerable delay on the approach to Ben Gardane, until the divisional engineers, scraping together every bit of wood they could find from all over Tripolitania, built a causeway and 'corduroy' road across it. Eighth Armoured Brigade's tank strength had fallen to only twelve, and they were replaced in the division by 22nd, now commanded by Brigadier Robert (Loony) Hinde. He was new to the desert, but soon became at home in it, although never good at knowing where he was. He was an unconventional cavalryman of great courage, an original character whom we all soon came both to like and to admire.

This change-over and problems of supply imposed a delay of a few days before the advance could be resumed towards the important road-junction of Medenine, 40 miles on and only 15 miles east of the old French positions of the Mareth Line, designed to defend Tunisia against attack from Italian Libya. The only forces that could go forward were armoured car patrols. Our maps of the area were very inaccurate,

but they showed that there was an important group of
hills between Medenine and the Mareth Line and that the
area was intersected by *wadis*. Information that could be
gleaned from the French was vague and contradictory. It was
important to have a clear picture of the ground in order to
plan the capture of Medenine and the hills beyond as soon as
the division was able to advance again. I decided to supplement the reports of armoured cars with a series of personal
reconnaissances by jeep, which I carried out over the next
few days. Finding no enemy about, I penetrated beyond
our armoured car patrols, almost up to the Mareth Line
itself, and was able to recommend to Loony Hinde the best
route for his tanks to follow when they resumed the advance
on the night of 18 February. Mist next morning made
direction keeping difficult, but, led by 5th Royal Tanks,
commanded by that expert in desert navigation, Jim Hutton,
the brigade rapidly outflanked Medenine and captured the
hills beyond, while Whistler's infantry occupied the town.
The area between it and the Mareth Line was thickly strewn
with mines and booby-traps, with which we were by now
very familiar. Further south 4th Light Armoured Brigade
penetrated up into the hills, beyond which they joined hands
with Leclerc's Free French, who had made their way along
south of the escarpment.

While we had been closing up to the Mareth Line, the
Germans had been delivering a series of sharp blows against
the Americans in Anderson's First Army as they advanced
from Algeria into Tunisia, the severest of which was at the
Kasserine Pass on 19 February. Having made the Americans
reel back, Rommel quickly switched the Afrika Korps south
in the hope of giving Montgomery a bloody nose also. His
intention became clear from intelligence in the first days
of March, and we were hurriedly reinforced with Julian
Gascoigne's 201st Guards Brigade, as well as 8th Armoured,
while 51st Highland Division came up on our right and
Freyberg's New Zealanders on our left, the latter taking over
Medenine, having some of the new 17-pounder anti-tank
guns with them. Oliver Leese's 30 Corps was in command of
the whole front. A tremendous effort was put into making
the best use of the ground to meet the expected attack
and into making detailed contingency plans to concentrate

tanks and artillery on threatened sectors, particular attention being paid to coordinating the siting of all anti-tank guns with widespread laying of minefields. By 6 March we were keyed up and ready for the attack. We had been kept well informed of the enemy's approach, and were not surprised when daylight revealed two main thrusts, the southerly by 10th Panzer Division with 35 tanks against the New Zealand Division and, in the centre down the line of the road from Toujane to Metameur, by 15th and 21st Panzer with 106 tanks straight at us, while 90th Light and the Italian Spezia Division delivered half-hearted attacks against the Highlanders. Twenty-first Panzer launched an unconvincing attack on the Guards, who turned them north to where 15th Panzer was attacking the Queens Brigade more effectively. With the help of two troops of 1st Royal Tanks from 22nd Armoured Brigade the Queens beat off all attacks, knocking out a large number of enemy tanks. After a pause to reorganize in the early afternoon, the panzer divisions attacked again at 4 p.m. and were met by the same effective resistance and heavy concentrations of artillery. Air attacks had been limited by the weather. During the night sounds of tank movement could be heard, in response to which I arranged a series of heavy artillery concentrations on areas where I expected them to form up, but no attack came, and by dawn it was clear that they had withdrawn. They had lost about 50 tanks, and not a single one had penetrated our defences. We had not lost one: in fact we had suffered hardly any casualties of any kind, and had not had to move more than two troops of tanks to support the fixed defences. The flexible use of concentrated artillery on predetermined target areas, organized by our Commander Royal Artillery, Roy Mews, had been a notable feature of the battle. Bobbie Erskine was delighted at the success of the first major battle the division had fought under his command, known as the Battle of Medenine.

I remember this period as a very pleasant one, although the weather was often wet and windy. We were in great spirits, no longer feeling that we were the Cinderella of Eighth Army, as we had before El Alamein. Although the area was desert, it was full of wild flowers, and there was more bird and animal life than in the more arid desert we had known. However we did not have much leisure in which to enjoy this.

Preparations for the next major battle to turn the enemy out
of the Mareth Line and take the pressure off First Army took
up the next two weeks. More divisions were brought up and,
as a preliminary, the Guards Brigade was ordered to secure
some important high ground, held by part of 90th Light
Division, which overlooked the area in which the artillery to
support the main attack was to be deployed. The approach
to it, over two *wadis*, was difficult, had not been thoroughly
reconnoitred, and was mined. In spite of very gallant attacks
by 6th Grenadiers and 3rd Coldstream Guards, they failed
to dislodge the enemy and suffered heavy casualties. When
we were told by Oliver Leese that Monty's plan was for a
full-scale assault on the northern end of the Mareth Line,
facing many of the same difficulties as had the Guards
Brigade, and that he was not planning more than a diversionary move through the hills to the south, Erskine and I
pressed Leese to try and persuade Montgomery to change
his plan: to make the northern attack a diversionary one,
and to send a major mobile force widely to the south, where
4th Light Armoured Brigade, the Free French and the
Long Range Desert Group had found possible routes. To
Erskine's chagrin, we were not successful and when, on the
third day of the Battle of Mareth, Montgomery abandoned
his main thrust in the north and switched his main effort to
the southern outflanking threat posed by the New Zealand
Division, we were annoyed that it was 1st Armoured Division
and not we ourselves who were sent to join Freyberg. We
were left to carry out subsidiary operations in the centre, and
took no major part in that battle or that on the Wadi Akarit
beyond Gabes on 6 April, which opened the gateway into
the Tunisian plain. As soon as the gate was open, we led the
pursuit inland, while the Highland Division moved along the
coast road, our objective being Sfax, 80 miles on. We generally had no roads to help us, but had to follow tracks or move
directly across country. It was sandy, but lightly cultivated,
one of the features being groves of olives and fruit trees:
inhabited, but thinly populated. The New Zealand Division,
led by 8th Armoured Brigade, came up on our left, between
us and the Americans further west in the hills. Opposition
consisted only of rearguards until we neared Sfax, when
22nd Armoured Brigade had a brisk action with 15th Panzer

Division at Agareb, 15 miles west of the town, on 9 April.
Early next morning the 11th Hussars entered Sfax just ahead
of the Valentines of 23rd Armoured Brigade, carrying the
first Highlanders. The advance to Sousse was now taken over
from 30 Corps by 10 Corps, and we were told that we should
not move for a fortnight. About this time I was surprised to
receive a long signal which appeared to be from the naval
C-in-C Mediterranean to the army C-in-C Middle East. It
went on to read: 'From Carver HMS *Formidable* to Carver
HQ 7th Armoured Division. Carver Landing Craft X lost his
false tooth on landing at Arzeu longitude 0°20' West latitude
35°50' North (just east of Oran). Have failed to locate it from
the air. When you have cleared coast of North Africa please
recover it.' This was the first I knew that Paul had taken
part in the North African landings, although I think I knew
that Rodney was flying from HMS *Formidable* and was in the
Mediterranean.

A major reorganization of the army now took place, Eighth
Army tending to stand back and let First Army finish off the
campaign, while Montgomery turned his attention to taking
on responsibility for planning and preparing for the invasion
of Sicily. For this purpose he recalled to his staff David
Belchem, who had only left it to command 1st Royal Tanks
in 22nd Armoured Brigade since the capture of Tripoli. I
was delighted and excited to be told that I was to take over
command from him on 14 April, handing over as GSO1 to
Pat Hobart. Although I was sad to leave Headquarters 7th
Armoured Division, which I had almost come to regard as
home, I was thrilled at the prospect of escaping from the
staff to active fighting in tanks, and especially in command of
my own regiment. I realized that I faced a major challenge.
I had not served with the regiment nor fought in tanks since
the war started. I had seen others fail when they faced the
same test, and my feelings were mixed: confidence that the
experience I had had would serve me and the regiment
well, with uncertainty about what both the regiment's and
my own reaction would be when I faced my first test of
command in battle.

8

Command of Every Part

And hast command of every part
To live and die . . .
                        Robert Herrick (1591–1674),
                    To Anthea, Who May Command Him
                                        Anything

David Belchem had left before I arrived, taking with him
the commanding officer's staff car and batman, neither of
which he showed any sign of intending to return. I was
therefore left with nowhere to put my belongings, other
than my tank. I was surprised and disturbed to detect a
certain air of unease. Everyone seemed to be reserved and
a trifle embarrassed in their approach. Fortunately I had
an old friend in Gus Holliman, who was commanding A
Squadron, the Crusader or light squadron, and I asked him
whether he thought my feeling was correct, and what was its
cause. He told me that David Belchem had rubbed everyone
up the wrong way, particularly in the last week or two. He
had had a disagreement with the adjutant, David Murison,
about the accuracy of a report on the action on the outskirts
of Sfax, in which Belchem had written up the part of the
regiment in exaggerated terms. Murison had, as a result,
been replaced as adjutant by the intelligence officer, John
Rogers. Murison had been a popular and respected adjutant,
and the general feeling throughout the regiment was that
Belchem's action was unfair. Gus advised me to reinstate
Murison, and forecast accurately that this would remove the
feeling of disquiet and would help me personally. I was glad

to take his advice, which proved sound. Confirmation from a lower level that we had judged aright came many years later in the war memoirs of Peter Roach, who was then the driver and wireless operator of the commanding officer's scout car. He wrote:

> Our colonel left, having successfully carried out his duties, and was borne away by a faithful (batman) in a rather battered staff car. He was replaced by a young, serious and very professional soldier, devoid of messes and batmen ... This involved me in many journeys with Col. C, because he had to know the terrain over which we might have to act. I enjoyed moving about and I liked him in spite of a seemingly stern exterior. My only difficulty was that he had a slight stammer, and when driving on tracks and cross country, I was sometimes past a turning before he had told me which way to go. I did my bit from then on by looking for a nod or shake of the head and we made our way around amicably.
>
> In the few minor skirmishes which we fought under him, he was quiet and very much in control, and a great confidence grew. He was a great stickler for orders being obeyed, particularly punctuality. The time of march was the time at which we would move and not some vague assessment, and once or twice when he was kept waiting at brigade conferences his brow was dark, and at times he apologized to the whole regiment, waiting on parade for briefing, for the delay.*

Two days after I had assumed command we moved forward to the area south-west of Enfidaville, which 10 Corps was planning to attack with the New Zealand Division, 4th Indian Division pushing into the hills on their left, and 7th Armoured Division probing forward between them and the French 19 Corps under First Army in the hills to the west. It was ideal as a breaking-in period for me. We were engaged in active operations, but not very intensively. I was able to pick up the wireless procedures and general habits of the

---

* Peter Roach, *The 8.15 to War*, Leo Cooper/Secker and Warburg, London, 1982, pp. 93–4.

regiment, accustom myself to the way in which it went about life, and get to know all and sundry, while they could take stock of me. I knew a number of the senior non-commissioned officers who had served with the regiment ever since we had arrived in Egypt. The only officers from that time were Gus Holliman and the second-in-command, James Pink. I found, as I had expected, that the general level of efficiency was high. Things were done quickly, efficiently and with the minimum of fuss. I soon found myself at home presiding over the 'regimental net', the wireless frequency to which all the tanks of the regiment were tuned in. Sergeant Brown, the commanding officer's operator, ruled it with a rod of iron, and he confided in me his pleasure that I wasted no time or words on it, in contrast to my predecessor. The New Zealanders and 4th Indian had a tough fight to capture Enfidaville and the hills to the west. My twenty-eighth birthday passed as we felt our way gingerly towards the foothills on the left of the Indians. Eighth Army's next objective was Hammamet, 20 miles further up the coast, and it was clear that some stiff fighting confronted us in much more difficult country than that which we had faced hitherto.

We were therefore relieved when, on 30 April, we were suddenly told to move back, load onto transporters, and be switched to join First Army, which had now captured the key town of Medjez el Bab, only 40 miles south-west of Tunis. Both 7th Armoured and 4th Indian Divisions were to join 9 Corps, to command which Horrocks had been transferred from 10 Corps, its commander, my old company commander John Crocker, having been wounded at a demonstration of a new infantry anti-tank weapon, the PIAT (Projector Infantry Anti-Tank). We set off on a 300-mile journey, starting on the night of 30 April and finishing at Le Krib on 2 May. From there I went forward with my squadron commanders to have a look at the ground east of Medjez el Bab, while we received a few more Sherman tanks from First Army sources and my resourceful technical adjutant, Captain Bailey (who as Staff-Sergeant Bailey had helped me look after my beloved Lancia in Cairo before the war) drove to the Kasserine Pass with his flame-cutter, opened up the American Army Shermans abandoned on the minefield there, and acquired an invaluable supply of spare parts,

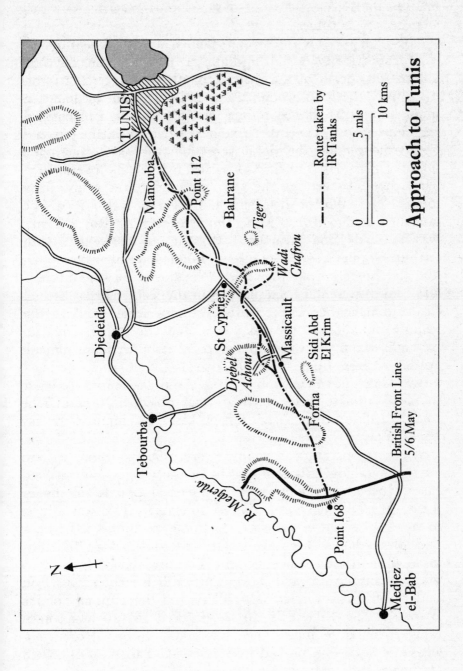

Approach to Tunis

Route taken by
IR Tanks

5 mls
10 kms

TUNIS

Manouba

Point 112

Bahrane

Tiger

Wadi Chafrou

St Cyprien

Massicault

Sidi Abd El Krim

Djedeida

Djebel Achour

Forna

Tebourba

British Front Line
5/6 May

R. Medjerda

Point 168

Medjez el-Bab

N

notably the injectors for our diesel-engined Shermans, which were as rare as rubies.

The plan was for 9 Corps to launch an attack astride the road from Medjez el Bab to Tunis, with 4th Indian Division on the left, north of the road, and 4th British on the right, to capture the high ground a few miles beyond the line, ten miles beyond Medjez el Bab, which 5 Corps had reached at the end of April. Seventh Armoured Division on the left and 6th Armoured on the right were then to pass through the infantry divisions and drive forward to the hills overlooking Tunis itself, preventing the Germans under von Arnim from forming yet another defensive line. The attack was to be launched at dawn on 6 May. Jim Hutton's 5th Royal Tanks was to lead 22nd Armoured Brigade in the centre, with Arthur Cranley's 4th County of London Yeomanry on the left and ourselves on the right. We moved forward at 5.15 a.m., my regimental headquarters in the lead. I had attached the reconnaissance troop (three Daimler scout cars) to the leading battalion of the brigade of the 4th Indian Division through whom we were due to pass. As the Indians made good progress from one objective to another, we moved forward behind them, and at 11 a.m. we were ordered to pass through them on their final objective. Apart from some shelling, this posed no problem as there were no mines about.

We were operating in country very different from the desert, open rolling hills reminiscent of the fringes of Salisbury Plain. Instead of following a geometrical pattern of movement, we could move from feature to feature. This was a help to me, as everyone else was as new to the conditions as I was. I had always had a 'keen eye for ground' and had no difficulty in giving my squadrons definite objectives and devising a plan combining fire and movement, with the squadrons, the battery of 5th Royal Horse Artillery and the company of 1st Battalion The Rifle Brigade so disposed that I had something in hand to meet the unexpected. As Gus Holliman's Crusader squadron probed its way forward to the ridge west of Furna and then on towards the village of Massicault, I could see that Pip Roberts's 26th Armoured Brigade of 6th Armoured Division on our right was both lagging behind and veering away to the east, opening up a gap between us which would leave the high ground south of the road (Sidi Abd el Krim) untouched. If the enemy held it, our right flank would be very vulnerable as we advanced. I therefore ordered Norman Crouch's C Squadron to move south of the main road and occupy it. As they did so, an 88-mm anti-tank gun fired on them and hit Major Crouch's tank, seriously wounding him. His second-in-command, Colin Sproull, quickly brought effective fire to bear on the gun, which was knocked out; the high ground was occupied and the advance resumed. It was my first experience of a friend being seriously wounded as a direct result of an order I had given, an unpleasant feeling. Nevertheless I had no doubt that my order had been correct.

We spent the night in a 'leaguer' a few miles beyond Massicault. I sent C Company of 1st Rifle Brigade and the troop of the Royal Engineers, attached to us, forward to the bridge over the Wadi Chafrou a few miles further on to make certain that the enemy did not destroy it during the night. Apart from anxiety about Norman Crouch, I was pleased with the day's operation, and I felt that we had done well. My main concern was that Gus Holliman's Crusaders were showing signs of their age. His numbers had fallen from eleven to seven in one day, all due to mechanical faults. 'Pedro' Pedraza's B Squadron had twelve Shermans and Colin Sproull's C Squadron 14. At 4.45 a.m. we started off again and, as I expected, found that the enemy was covering the Wadi Chafrou and an irrigation ditch which ran parallel to it, with fire from tanks and anti-tank guns supported by artillery. The tactics I had employed the previous day proved effective, the deliberate fire of tanks and our own supporting guns methodically eliminating the opposition or forcing it to move, while Holliman's Crusaders worked round the western flank near St Cyprien. Two incidents enlivened the morning. In order to get a better view of the area beyond the wadi, I moved my tank up to the side of a small farmhouse, where I hoped to be unobserved. However, just as I drew up beside the back door, an anti-tank gun fired at us, the shot fortunately bouncing off the front plate. I saw where it had fired from, and instantly ordered '75-mm/HE action'. My tank was a Grant, in which the 75-mm gun was in a sponson. It was almost unheard of for the commanding officer's tank to fire its main armament, and the sponson had become the home of a white rabbit, called Tripoli, which the crew had acquired there. They had intended to eat it when they arrived at Tunis, but by now it had become a well-loved pet. After a pause, instead of the expected reply '75-mm loaded', the plaintive voice of the gunner came over the internal communication system 'What about Tripoli?' My retort was sharp and showed no concern for the rabbit's nerves. The gun having fired, I ordered the driver to reverse, only to find myself, with my head outside the turret, entangled in the washing-line, watched by the terrified farmer's wife from the kitchen window. Not long after this we were alarmed to find ourselves being attacked from the rear by infantry, supported by mortars and machine-guns. I soon realized the cause of this. About an hour previously B Squadron had been troubled by snipers firing at tank commanders from farm buildings on their right. A company of the Welsh Guards from 26th Armoured Brigade was near us at the time, apparently doing nothing, and I had asked their commander if he could send some of his men into the buildings to flush the snipers out. When he told me that it would take him three-quarters of an hour to organize, I told him to forget it. However he must have misunderstood me, and set about organizing a formal attack in the best School of Infantry style. Unfortunately we were by then on the objective, and I told Colin Sproull to threaten them with a counter-attack if they did not desist immediately. The only casualty to us was one officer slightly wounded in the back. It was not the first time that we had been attacked by our own side. We had been heavily bombed by three squadrons of our own bombers the previous day. It had produced a lot of noise and had made us very angry, but the only damage inflicted was to the impedimenta we carried outside the tanks, bedding rolls, cooking equipment and the like.

As soon as we were across the wadi, we came under fire from a Tiger tank, the first we had encountered, and one or two 88-mm anti-tank guns, and we could see enemy tanks and anti-tank guns out of range. The ground south of the road was flat and open, although farm buildings and orchards provided cover. North of the road there was more incidence in the ground, and I decided to make use of it to advance by bounds and thus outflank the enemy straight ahead of us. In leading his Crusaders in this direction, Gus Holliman's tank was knocked out by the Tiger, he and his crew fortunately escaping without injury, as the shot had hit the engine compartment. Our tactics were successful and culminated in a shoot by B Squadron against a company of enemy tanks engaged in refuelling near the crest of the ridge, beyond which the ground fell away towards Tunis, only five miles away. We pressed on down the road to the village of Manouba, three miles from the outskirts of the city itself. German vehicles kept appearing from every direction, and we soon had a large and varied collection of prisoners, including a paymaster with a copious supply of cash. Armoured cars of the 11th Hussars advanced towards the city, and I sent the motor company and a troop of tanks to help them, when they met opposition on the outskirts. These were later relieved by The Queens of 131st Brigade.

We were not to enter Tunis itself. Our task for 8 May was to secure the high ground about six miles away on the road to Bizerta, in order to prevent the enemy, pressed back by the Americans north of the River Medjerda, from entering Tunis from that direction. We were now in much closer country than any we had yet experienced, and could no longer move in our extended formation across country. For the first time in the war, we had to move in line or double-line ahead, following roads or tracks. We met no opposition, although continuing to collect large numbers of prisoners. At 8 a.m. we were ordered to advance and capture the bridge over the River Medjerda at Protville, six miles further on. This was protected by a ridge of high ground, overlooking a flat plain intersected by irrigation ditches and a wadi, a marshy area to the east and the river to the west preventing us from outflanking it. I asked, without success, for air support, and while we were methodically attempting to suppress the enemy fire, which included an 88-mm, there was a large explosion, clearly the demolition of the bridge, and we were able to get forward to the ridge ourselves. From it we could see the enemy on the far side of the river withdrawing towards Porto Farina, but they were out of range of our tank guns. CC Battery 5th RHA enjoyed themselves, while the reconnaissance troop searched for a

way to cross the river. I decided to join them and went
forward in my scout car in the thick corn, going down to
the river bank on foot with Corporal Roach when the scout
car could get no further. It was clear to me that we could
not get tanks across. On our way back to the scout car we
were fired on with a machine-gun by one of my own tanks.
Fortunately the bullets went over our heads and the firing
did not last long; but James Pink got the rough edge of my
tongue when we reached the wireless set in the scout car.
We stayed there until the following morning, 9 May, when
we could see American troops advancing on the far side of
the river and were ourselves relieved by 1st/5th Queens of
131st Brigade. We had fired our last shot in anger in Africa
after three years of desert fighting, little realizing how much
more there was still to do in Italy and North-west Europe.

I soon realized that my principal problem would be to
counter a sense of anti-climax. We were the only one of the
tank regiments that had started the war in Egypt present at
the end, but the temptations of Tunis were not to be ours:
they were reserved for others, principally the Americans,
some of whom we were amused to see chased out of the city
by the Gurkhas of our old and valued friends, 4th Indian
Division. We were moved back to Bou Arada, 50 miles to
the south-west, until our future was decided. I was told that
David Belchem had promised the regiment that, once Tunis
had been captured, it would be sent back to England and that
everyone would be awarded a special medal in addition to the
Africa Star. There was no basis for this promise, which I had
to discount. I also faced another potential morale problem.
On the way from Tripoli to Tunis the regiment had acquired
a large number of stray dogs. My medical officer, 'Doc' Wells,
and I were concerned that every one of them was a potential
source of rabies, and we agreed that they must be destroyed
before we moved elsewhere. The regimental sergeant-major
warned me that it would cause considerable resentment. I
summoned the whole regiment, there being no risk of air
attack, and included the announcement in a general talk. I
got the doctor to describe the symptoms of rabies and I told
the soldiers of the series of very unpleasant injections in the
stomach which Dan Walsh, our original Ordnance Mechanical Engineer, had had to undergo when he had been bitten

by a dog in Cairo. There was no trouble when the armourer
and the butcher together began their grisly task.

After a mercifully short stay at Bou Arada, the whole
division moved back to Libya and encamped on the coast at
Homs, 60 miles east of Tripoli. Our tents were set on the sea
shore, some of them among the palm trees between the road
and the sea, bathing in which was our principal and much
appreciated leisure activity. The divisional staff did their best
to provide other forms of entertainment, their provision of
an ex-Italian army brothel however being disapproved of by
higher authority. The ladies had to be returned to Tripoli,
where they were available to those who spent short periods
of leave there. Vivien Leigh and Leslie Henson came with
an ENSA party and played by moonlight to a packed house
in the ancient Roman theatre of Leptis Magna. We were
gradually re-equipped with new Sherman tanks, which had
to come by transporter the 1500 miles from Cairo. It was
with no regrets that we said goodbye to the Crusaders. All
three squadrons received diesel-engined Shermans, and the
reconnaissance troop was re-equipped with Daimler scout
cars and Bren-carriers. Gus Holliman went back to England
as part of a scheme to provide regiments at home with
battle-experienced commanders, his place being taken by
Barry O'Sullivan. He had been captured with 3rd Royal
Tanks at Calais in 1940 and had later made a gallant escape
from his prisoner-of-war camp, making his way to Switzerland. He seemed to have difficulty in adapting himself to
our procedures and understanding the basis of our tactics;
but he had a high reputation for courage and enthusiasm,
and I hoped that, once he got into action, he would prove
his worth. We did not know where we should be going next
– Sicily, Sardinia, Italy or the Balkans. Wherever it might be,
we would have left the desert behind us and would have to
fight in totally different conditions. We applied our minds to
this, and I held frequent TEWTs (Tactical Exercises Without
Troops) in suitable areas in the hilly country between Homs
and Tripoli. In retrospect it is clear that we should have
made a more basic change in our organization, mixing tanks
and infantry more closely together, instead of keeping the
armoured and lorried infantry brigades separate. During
this period Eighth Army was visited by King George VI. We

lined both sides of the road beyond Tripoli, the King driving along in Montgomery's open staff car, stopping to speak to the brigade commanders. He was suffering from stomach trouble and was not in an easy humour. When introduced to Loony Hinde, he asked if they had ever met before. 'I don't think so,' said Loony, drawing the royal response: 'You b-b-b-bloody well ought to know!'

When the invasion of Sicily took place in July, it was clear that we were not going to be involved. That we were to participate in an amphibious landing elsewhere, however, was soon evident, as training in driving tanks on and off landing-craft began. Our seaside holiday had been a pleasant interlude, and we had been kept fairly fully occupied getting our vehicles fit for battle and training for a new type of warfare, but the long hot summer was beginning to pall and we were keen to get into action again, if only to get on with the war and see it finished. Eventually we were told that the division was to form part of 10 Corps, now commanded by Lieutenant-General Dick McCreery, a 12th Lancer, who had been Alexander's chief of staff and had taken over from Horrocks when the latter had been wounded in an air-raid on Bizerta. The corps was to be the British contribution to General Mark Clark's Fifth US Army, and included the 46th and 56th Infantry Divisions as well as 7th Armoured. The infantry divisions were to assault on the northern sector of the landing area south of Salerno, and we were then to pass through, turning north for Vesuvius and Naples. The distance from Tripoli and the other ports of embarkation to Salerno limited the speed with which the force could be built up. We had to wait for the landing-ships to return from putting the infantry ashore before we could embark. It was not therefore until almost a week after the initial landings on 9 September that we embarked at Tripoli in four LSTs (Landing Ships Tank). We were to sail at midnight and were all safely on board and correctly loaded well in time. Shortly before we were due to sail, a naval captain, his cap set at a jaunty Beatty-like angle, came rather unsteadily down the quay and embarked on the LST next to mine, on which James Pink and the battery commander, Brian Wyldbore-Smith, were travelling. Shortly afterwards I was summoned to speak to James Pink across the taffrail. He explained that

the figure, Captain Jackie Sutton RN (retired), who was
commodore of the flotilla of LSTs, complained that there
were too many vehicles on the top deck and insisted that
the ship be reloaded. I stepped across and found Sutton,
clearly the worse for drink, in the cabin of the ship's captain.
I asked the latter if he were satisfied with the loading, which
had been carried out as planned and with the full approval
of the embarkation staff officer. He said he was. I therefore
told Captain Sutton that I refused to reload the ship, which
would delay our sailing, due in a quarter of an hour. He saw
he was getting nowhere and gave in.

After an uneventful voyage, we arrived off shore in
Salerno Bay shortly before dark. In our first run in, the ships
grounded on a sand bank, and, having pulled off astern with
the help of a kedge anchor, and pumped out surplus water
and fuel, we got further ashore, but not quite far enough for
us to disembark. By this time it was dark and an air-raid was
in progress. Captain Sutton, next to us, shouted through a
loud-hailer at the bulldozer, which was pulling the LSTs the
final few feet necessary for vehicles to disembark, that, if his
LST were not the next to be pulled in, he would switch his
searchlight on. A rude retort was made, in response to which
he carried out his threat, only to have the searchlight shot
out by a light anti-aircraft gun on the shore. As we started
our disembarkation, I was called to the side by James Pink
and Brian Wyldbore-Smith. They told me that Sutton was
refusing to let them disembark, accusing their soldiers of
having stolen some parts from a jeep which he had somehow
acquired and which was on board. I told them to arrest him at
pistol point and lock him up in his cabin until all the vehicles
had disembarked. This they did, and, as soon as I had time
to do so after we had got ashore, I wrote a report to Loony
Hinde, explaining what had happened and relying on the
ruling of the Duke of Wellington, quoted in the Manual of
Military Law, that a subordinate was entitled to arrest his
superior if the latter was drunk or otherwise incapacitated. I
heard no more, but was to encounter Captain Sutton again.
By that time I had discovered that he was a notorious naval
character, who had had to retire as a result of an incident in
which he had killed the proprietor of a café in Cyprus, when
he had knocked him down a flight of stairs in the course of

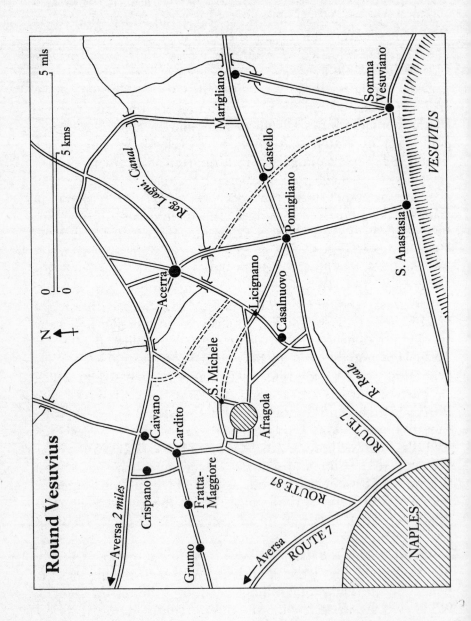

Round Vesuvius

an argument over the bill. In the curious way in which the
naval reserve of officers was organized, he was automatically
promoted on the reserve as time passed.

The crisis of the Salerno beachhead had just passed by
the time we landed, but the enemy shelling was still heavy
and we were crowded into a small, intensely cultivated area,
which made it unpleasant. After we had pressed forward
towards Battipaglia, the enemy withdrew, and we prepared
to switch to our main task of pushing towards Naples. On
28 September 7th Armoured Division passed through 46th
Division, when the latter had captured the pass between
Vietri and Nocera beyond Salerno. 131st Lorried Infantry
Brigade, with 5th Royal Tanks under command, was in the
lead and we followed behind, grinding slowly along the one
road in single file. It was impossible to get off the road, and
all we could do at the halt was to pull into the side, at night
sleeping as best one could either on the pavement, if there
was one, or in one's tank if it rained, which it did. By the end
of 1 October Whistler's brigade had worked their way round
the north side of Vesuvius, capturing the village of Somma
Vesuviana. Twenty-second Armoured Brigade was to take
over the running next day, heading for Capua, while 23rd
Armoured Brigade, also under the division's command,
pushed south of Vesuvius to Naples. We were to lead the
22nd and, delighted to be active at last, passed through the
infantry at 5 a.m. My problem was to decide what route to
take. I had been given a firm route to be cleared as the
divisional axis, but it was not necessarily the best one to
advance along in the first instance, being the obvious one,
although fairly tortuous. The armoured cars of the 11th
Hussars were trying out various routes. I could wait until
I heard their reports, but that might mean sitting still and
doing nothing for some time. On the other hand, if I committed the whole regiment to a route on which either enemy
opposition was strong or there were obstacles, which would
call for considerable work by the sappers before I could use
it, the delay might be even greater. The answer lay in a judi-
cious balance between thrusting on and not committing too
much. It paid off. I kept a balanced force of reconnaissance
troops, tanks, guns and infantry far enough back to be able
to switch them to another route, if I found that the one the

leading squadron was following seemed unpromising. I soon realized that the key to progress lay in judging this correctly, and we made a steady advance, in spite of opposition and every sort of obstacle, including fallen tram-wires. It rained heavily, the area was both densely populated and intensively cultivated, with vines strung up on wires at the level of the tank turrets, so that one's field of vision was extremely limited and it was seldom possible to move off the roads or the indifferent tracks between them. There could not have been a greater contrast to the desert. We struggled forward, blown bridges and muddy vineyards causing more delay than opposition from the enemy. Towards the end of the day we had reached the large village of Afragola, whose inhabitants told us that the Germans had just left and moved to the villages of Cardito and Caivano, a few miles to the north. As Pedraza's B Squadron moved round the north side of the village to the main road from Naples to Caserta, they came under fire from a self-propelled 75-mm anti-tank gun. Some enterprising reconnaissance on foot by Lieutenant Canham of the reconnaissance troop and Bobbie Gillespie of B Squadron led to the destruction of the gun, but further progress was prevented by anti-tank mines, the tanks of both Pedraza and his second-in-command having their tracks broken. As it was getting dark and pouring with rain, and the vineyards and orchards were exceptionally thick, I decided that I must get the regiment together for the night. We leaguered with the tanks nose to tail on either side of the road north of Afragola. Every movement or noise brought down a burst of enemy artillery or mortar fire on us. It was one of the most unpleasant nights I experienced in the whole war. My tank had slid into a ditch and I had jumped into a manure heap getting off it. It was impossible to bed down: the only place to sleep was inside a tank, and mine was already overcrowded with a relief wireless operator and spare batteries. I did eventually try and get some sleep, perched on the commander's seat. At intervals the gas cape, which I had draped over the turret hatch (the flaps of which had been removed, so that I could not close it) filled with water and collapsed, cascading a gallon or two on top of me. The enemy could get right up to the leaguer unobserved, and I had every reason to expect that they might attack us during the night. Nobody had much sleep that night and I have seldom been so glad to welcome the dawn.

Next day we were at first told to wait for the rest of the brigade to progress further before resuming our advance; but, when Loony Hinde came to see me, he told me to get going towards Caserta. The first attempt by tanks alone proved that we needed to combine their action with infantry. Desmond Pritty's C Company of 1st Battalion The Rifle Brigade was unfortunately heavily shelled while forming up, and we had to start again, reinforced by I Company on a plan concocted with Victor Paley, their commanding officer, and Peter Gregson, CO of 5th RHA, who was able to use the whole of his regiment and a battery of 69th Medium. A Squadron was to lead the advance either side of the road to Cardito, with Pedraza's B on its left and Colin Sproull's C on the right, hoping to occupy the enemy's attention on a wide front and exploit any gap found. A Squadron met with more trouble than the infantry, two of their tanks being knocked out and two ditched, while one troop, having misunderstood its orders, moved to the wrong place. Barry O'Sullivan was clearly unable to cope with these problems, and I had to tell him on the wireless to hand over to his second-in-command, Brian Smethurst. Unfortunately, his wireless operator, Sergeant Burton, thinking that he was speaking to the rest of the crew on the internal communication set, broadcast to the whole regiment his approval of the decision. C Squadron, having also run into opposition and lost two tanks, I switched B Squadron to support the infantry up to the village and in their clearance of it, which was completed in the late afternoon.

I was told not to attempt to push on further, but to make certain of the ground we had captured. We were still being heavily shelled at intervals, and had to repel several attempts by the enemy to return to Cardito. However, during the night he withdrew and, when we resumed the advance, the only opposition we met was from snipers and shelling. The former was usually dealt with by firing a round of 75-mm HE with delay fuse into the building from which the fire came. Demolitions, mines, the rain-sodden tracks and other obstacles were the principal causes of delay. While the engineers of 4th Field Squadron, a troop of which was attached to us, worked hard to help us forward, we did all we could to help ourselves by trying every possible road and track, the reconnaissance troop making a tremendous effort and taking great risks as they did so. As a result we maintained steady progress, managed to effect a crossing over the Regi Lagni canal, and, by the end of 5 October, were on the outskirts of Capua. One-hundred-and-thirty-first Brigade now came up and took over responsibility for that area, while we turned west to clear the more open ground between the Regi Lagni canal and the River Volturno, the far side of which was defended by our old opponents 15th Panzer Division. Air photographs showed a bridge at Grazzanise, and we were told to see if the bridge was intact and if there were enemy still in the village on the near side. Lieutenant Bob Stedman of C Squadron, accompanied by his lap-gunner, left his tank and followed the southern bank on foot right up to the bridge, passing through the edge of the village, which was occupied by the enemy, under accurate fire from mortars, machine-guns and a self-propelled gun on the far bank. He returned with the information, supplemented by a sketch, that it was a wooden bridge, blown at both ends, but crossable on foot. For this gallant exploit he was awarded the Military Cross. He was a Canadian, who, after training at their military college at Kingston, joined the British army as a regular. He had commanded the troop of tanks at Headquarters 7th Armoured Division, and, when I left, had begged me to get him transferred to a more active command in 1st Royal Tanks, which I was delighted to be able to do. He left the army after the war and had a highly successful business career in Canada.

We could get no further, and were due to be relieved that night. There would clearly have to be a pause in operations before a crossing of the Volturno could be launched. The rest of the afternoon was spent in the open fields being shelled by the enemy artillery and answering in kind. Knowing that we could not move for some hours, it was possible to cook a better meal than usual behind the shelter of a wall. I had bought a tinned steak and kidney pie from the NAAFI before we left Homs for just such an occasion. Brian Wyldbore-Smith had been less provident, but had his eye on some succulent piglets rooting in the field. In attempting to catch one and put it in a sandbag, his crew chased them beyond the shelter of the wall, bringing down enemy artillery fire, fortunately without casualties, although the pigs got away unscathed by the action of the gunners of either side.

The next three weeks were spent in fighting to cross the Volturno, in which we were not involved. It was during this time that I was summoned by my B echelon commander to deal with 'Doc' Wells. An Italian Air Force pilot had crashed near them and broken his legs. 'Doc' Wells had been summoned to deal with the casualty, and was lost in admiration and envy for the pilot's fleece-lined flying boots. Rather than cut them to enable him to treat the pilot's legs, he was proposing to amputate the legs themselves. Only I, it was thought, could make him alter his decision, which I did. The American 1st Armoured Division began to arrive in the area during this period, and its fiery commander, Major-General Ernie Harmon, asked Bobbie Erskine to send an officer from 7th Armoured Division to describe to his officers what tank fighting in Italy was like and what lessons we had learned. I was chosen, and duly reported to Harmon's G3, equivalent to our GSO1, in his 'pup' tent in a very wet orchard. He told me that we would dine with the general and all his staff in the mess tent that evening, and that, after an interview with the general in the morning, I was to address all officers of the division of the rank of lieutenant-colonel and above. He warned me that Harmon was a fierce, fiery character, his bite being almost as bad as his bark. I soon discovered this when, over dinner, he interrogated each of his staff about what he had done that day and castigated most of them for failure to do more, threatening to sack several. It was therefore with some trepidation that I entered the general's little bivouac tent next morning. Pulling a bottle of whisky from under his camp bed, he opened the conversation by passing it to me with the words: 'Have a bourbon, colonel.' I protested that it was much too early in the day, to which he retorted in his gravelly voice: 'A good tank man never refuses a drop of liquor.' I was forced to give way, and we got on like a house on fire, which was what I felt like when I went out to address a very gloomy lot of officers, the rain dripping off the steel helmets they were never allowed to remove. After a fiery exhortation from Ernie Harmon about how they were going to 'kick the god-damned bastards up that god-damned Liri valley', I was introduced as the man who would tell them how to do it. I could never afterwards remember what I had said, but it clearly impressed Ernie Harmon, who told Bobbie Erskine that I 'sure was a fighting type'.

At the end of the month 7th Armoured Division switched from the centre to the left of 10 Corps, its orders being to try and get across the canal beyond the Volturno, if it could, without involving a major assault. A sapper reconnaissance had found a possible site for tanks to ford, but, when an officer patrol from A Squadron penetrated beyond it on foot, they found that a bog prevented tanks that had crossed the ford from turning inland from the coast. A study of air photographs persuaded me that the bog came to an end near the forward posts the Rifle Brigade had established on the far side of the canal. Accompanied by the reconnaissance troop commander and one from A Squadron, I crossed over the canal by a footbridge and found that my interpretation was correct. We then reconnoitred a route back to the ford which tanks could follow, stripped off our clothes and swam about in the cold water until we could locate the best place for tanks to ford, my navel being exactly the fording depth of a Sherman tank. While we were doing this, a burst of machine-gun fire was heard nearby, and we feared that we might be faced with the embarrassing and very cold experience of having to make our way back naked to the regiment, abandoning our clothes on the north bank. Fortunately, if it was the enemy, they came no closer to us.

We crossed by this ford on the night of 29 October, but ran into some trouble with mines when we turned inland from the shore. They had clearly been laid as part of the coast defences and, although the sappers had swept the route I had reconnoitred, the tanks churned up the sand and hit mines which had sunk below the level at which the mine-detectors reacted to them. Having negotiated the mines, we found ourselves struggling on very soft ground, intersected by ditches, being engaged by enemy infantry and the odd anti-tank gun at short range, while shelled at long range by a very heavy gun. The whole area was overlooked by Monte Massico, half-way between the rivers Volturno and Garigliano. Our objective, the small town of Mondragone, lay at its foot. We were shelled also by the guns of 46th Division on our right, which caused us more annoyance than damage. Loony Hinde visited me at 2 p.m. and agreed that further advance would necessitate a more formal infantry and tank operation. By that time our tank strength had fallen to twenty-four, fifteen having been bogged, four disabled by mines, one knocked out and one broken down. We therefore stayed where we were, prepared to resume the advance next day under command of 131st Brigade. Loony also gave me the unwelcome order that I was to go back next day to fly to Algiers to attend a conference at GHQ to discuss the lessons learned in armoured operations since landing in Sicily. I reluctantly handed over to James Pink, made my way back to an airfield near Naples and thence, in a series of flights in US Air Force Dakotas, sitting among the freight, to Sicily, Tunis and finally Algiers. I do not remember much about the conference, apart from the fact that I resented being summoned all that way back to attend it. I managed to obtain a more direct return flight and was back with the regiment a few days later, just before the whole division was withdrawn from the forward area and told that it was going to be shipped to the United Kingdom – 'return' would not be correct, as it had been formed in Egypt.

We handed over all our equipment to the 5th Canadian Armoured Division, who looked disdainfully at some of our ancient transport vehicles, and moved into an empty macaroni factory at Castellamare near Pompeii. There we celebrated Cambrai Day, 20 November, anniversary of the first great tank battle, the soldiers drinking mugfuls of Marsala, of which a plentiful supply had been discovered nearby, since beer was not obtainable in large enough quantity. The regimental band had somehow caught up with us for the occasion. The bandmaster did not endear himself to us by trying to insist that he should be accommodated in an hotel, not liking the comparatively comfortable conditions we were enjoying on the floor of the factory on which the macaroni was dried. We did not know when we should sail, and, as the weeks passed, it became clear that we should not be home for Christmas. It was difficult to keep the soldiers occupied and amused, although the divisional staff did their best with week-end trips to commandeered hotels at Amalfi and other resorts on the Sorrento peninsula, visits to Naples and, if the navy were cooperative, to Capri. The interlude gave me the opportunity to think about and to record the operations we had been engaged in, and to consider the lessons to be learned. I concluded that the right organization for the regiment was to have three identical squadrons, each of three troops of four tanks, no longer regarding one of them as a reconnaissance squadron. Four tanks in a troop (instead of four troops of three tanks, as was laid down) meant that one did not have to change the organization as soon as a few tanks fell out, for whatever reason. Linked to this was the need for a vehicle of much better cross-country performance for the reconnaissance troop. There were many lessons to be learned about cooperation between all arms. In that close country, the need for it had been even greater than in the desert. Whereas I found that my lack of previous direct personal experience of tank-versus-tank fighting in the desert was no handicap to me, it was clear that the greater knowledge I had of the characteristics of other arms, derived from my experience on divisional and corps staffs, stood me, my regiment and my supporting infantry, gunners and sappers in good stead. I now felt fully confident in my exercise of command.

At last the date of embarkation was fixed for 20 December. As the regiment filed off to the docks at Naples, I flew with the advance party via Algiers to Marrakesh in Morocco. From there we were flown by night in a US Air Force Liberator non-stop to Prestwick in Scotland, where I arrived early in the morning of 23 December 1943, nearly six years since I had set sail for Egypt from Southampton. Having discovered when I could catch a train to London, and one from there to Minehead in Somerset, I rang up my parents, who had no idea that I was returning. They were staying at Wootton Courtenay, and had been on their way there by train from Shropshire about a month before when my father had suffered a heart attack, of which I had been informed. He had recovered, but they decided to stay on there in the house of a friend rather than return immediately to Ticklerton. My father answered the telephone, and did not at first understand who it was. When I repeated my name and added, 'Your second son, Michael', his only response was: 'I expect you want to talk to your mother!' She arranged to meet me at Dunster, instead of Minehead, the last station on the line, which would have been more sensible in the black-out. I could not remember all the stations between Taunton and Minehead; the names were blacked out, and the strong Somerset accents of the stationmasters made them all sound alike. However, I got out at Dunster late in the evening and was welcomed with great emotion by my mother. It was wonderful to be back for Christmas, joined by my brother Antony, with Elizabeth and their son Nicolas, then almost two years old. Antony was then commanding a bomber operational training unit at Honeybourne in Gloucestershire. Rodney was an instructor at the naval air station at Henstridge in Dorset. I went there to see him, and Antony flew me on New Year's Day from Henstridge to Honeybourne, where I spent a few days with him and Elizabeth. He then flew me to Norfolk, where 7th Armoured Division was to be stationed. Twenty-second Armoured Brigade was quartered round Brandon, near Thetford, and 1st Royal Tanks were to be accommodated in Nissen huts under pine trees on either side of the drive of Didlington Hall, which was to house divisional headquarters. The ships bringing the division docked in the Clyde on 7 January, and the huts of Didlington Hall in the wet, wintry weather of East Anglia did not seem to offer much improvement on the vineyards of Italy, certainly not as comfortable as the macaroni factory. Having checked in, everyone went on leave for several weeks, equipped with ration cards, clothing coupons and other essential impedimenta of British wartime life, familiar to most, but strange to us. I returned to Wootton Courtenay and found it difficult to adjust myself to doing nothing and to the uneventful life my parents led. One of our favourite cousins, Elizabeth Montagu-Pollock, came to stay, and I was delighted to see her again. She was a most attractive and sympathetic character, and in the next six months was to be a wonderful source of sympathy and help to me in readjusting myself to an entirely different life from that I had lived since the war had started. Her flat in London was to become a real refuge, in which I could be sure of a warm welcome and an understanding sympathy. We were not lovers – her affections were engaged elsewhere – but she was a confidante, to whom I could pour out the feelings which, as a commanding officer, prepared to face battle again soon, I had to keep bottled up inside me. She had a great influence on my mother, and came with me to help when Rodney brought his fiancée, Anne Edward-Collins, for a week-end at Ticklerton, to which my parents returned in the spring. My mother objected on principle to anybody her sons appeared likely to wish to marry, and we anticipated trouble. Anne was serving as a Wren officer at Henstridge, and came of a well known Cornish family, her father being in the Indian army and one of her uncles an admiral. My mother was not welcoming, but was prevented by Elizabeth from behaving too badly. I was unable to attend their wedding, as by then we were nearing the date for the invasion of Normandy.

The intervening months had not initially been easy. Several senior non-commissioned officers who had splendid records of gallantry and devotion to duty as tank commanders, applied to transfer to units less likely to be in the front line again. They were undoubtedly influenced by their wives, from whom they had been separated for several years and who resented their husbands going into the heat of battle again, when so many others had been in Britain all that time and not risked their lives in action. I managed to persuade some to change their minds: others I thought it better to let go. This difficult period came to an end after Montgomery had visited us on 17 February. He gathered everyone round a jeep and told us that, now that he had been appointed to command 21st Army Group, the formation which would carry out the invasion of the Continent, he had recast all the plans and would guarantee their success: we had served under him before and knew that he would not send us into battle on a plan that would fail or needlessly risk our lives. It was a remarkable performance and it transformed the regiment's morale. He was followed a week later by King George VI. We provided a guard of honour at Brandon station, and I travelled with him in his car to Didlington Hall, where he was to visit divisional headquarters. My soldiers lined the drive on both sides, and I persuaded him to stop and talk to some of them. One was Sergeant Hall, who had recently joined us, having served previously with the cavalry, 19 years in all, as I told the monarch. 'G-g-g-Good G-g-g-God,' he remarked, 'N-n-n-nineteen years in the army. How awful!' I suppose I should have expected it as the typical reaction of a naval officer, but it was hardly the response that Sergeant Hall expected from his sovereign! He must have been in mischievous mood that day, as, reminded by Bobbie Erskine of his previous encounter with Loony Hinde, who sat next to him at lunch, he pulled the latter's leg unmercifully.

Morale was also raised as new tanks began to arrive. Most were the British Cromwell, with a British 75-mm gun, which was new to us and which we liked, being less conspicuous and more lively than the Sherman; but we were glad to have one of the latter in each troop, armed with the powerful British 17-pounder anti-tank gun, which had an armour-piercing performance much superior to that of the 75-mm. There was much argument about whether we should put them all in one troop in each squadron or distribute them one to each troop. I was firmly in favour of the latter and was undoubtedly proved right when we went into action. The reconnaissance troop was equipped with a new model of the American Stuart light tank, from which it was decided to remove the turret. We trained on the Swaffham and Stanford training areas and fired our guns on the ranges there and, in the case of the 17-pounder, on the coast. There I met Hobo again, now commanding 79th Armoured Division, the organization which included all the specialized forms of tank and armoured vehicle designed to deal with coast defences. These included flame-throwers, amphibious tanks, special 'armoured vehicles Royal Engineers', bridge-laying tanks and Crab mine-clearing flail tanks, developed from the Scorpion we had used at El Alamein. Hobo was his old intolerant, entertaining and enthusiastic self.

There were not many changes with the regiment, the chief being an influx of young subalterns of high quality, anxious to win their spurs in battle. I was delighted to welcome back as second-in-command Gus Holliman, recently married to his old flame Peggie, but was later to lose him again when he was sent, shortly before we moved to our embarkation camps, to command 5th Royal Tanks, whose recently appointed commanding officer had been found wanting. He was replaced by 'Stump' Gibbon, who had been captured at Tobruk, when serving with 44th Royal Tanks, and had escaped when being transferred by train from a prisoner-of-war camp in Italy to one in Germany. He was senior to me in service, with a calm slow manner, which belied his stalwart, robust character. Barry O'Sullivan's place in command of A Squadron was taken by the South African cricketer Bob Crisp, who had a high and well-deserved reputation for bravery with 3rd Royal Tanks in Greece and in the desert, where he had been severely wounded. He and I never hit it off, being very different in character and outlook. One departure, which I much regretted, was that of my tank driver, Corporal Tom Tasker. His father, who ran a butcher's business in Grimsby, had died, and Tom's presence was apparently essential if the inhabitants of that town were to get their ration of meat. He was to have a distinguished career both as a butcher and as a farmer, in 1963 becoming President of the National Federation of Meat Traders' Associations and a member of the government's Meat and Livestock Commission, sadly dying in 1979 at the age of 63 of a combination of sclerosis and cancer.

During this period there was much discussion as to whether, as a result of the lessons we had learned in Italy, the organization of the division should be changed to one which gave a more even balance of infantry and tanks than the official one of an armoured brigade of three tank regiments and one motor infantry battalion, and an infantry brigade of three infantry battalions, carried in three-ton lorries, and no tanks. Under terms of great secrecy, within the confines of a Cambridge college, we were initiated into Montgomery's plan which forecast that, after a short period of battle in the close 'bocage' country of Normandy, we should break out into the open country of Northern France, ideal for tank action. It was therefore generally accepted that we should stick to the official organization of the division, although it was clear that one of the tank regiments, initially at least, would have to be allotted to the lorried infantry brigade.

Early in May we left Brandon and moved to a camp in Orwell Park, between Ipswich and Felixstowe, where we were to embark, the leading squadrons in LCTs (Landing Craft Tank) and the rest of us in LSTs. We were at last told the divisional plan, including where we were to land, and were kept incommunicado from the rest of the country, while rehearsing the drill for loading and unloading the

landing craft. My main concern was whether, after weeks
of inactivity, our wireless sets would function properly when
we landed. At last, on 4 June, we drove to Felixstowe. To my
dismay I found that the American LSTs on which we were to
embark had more anti-aircraft guns on the upper deck than
the loading plans allowed for. The US Navy officers who
had brought them across the Atlantic were complete novices
and knew nothing of the problems of loading. Fortunately I
found a tough old chief petty officer, who was prepared to
take decisions; he, the embarkation staff officer and I had
to improvise revised loading plans against a tight time-scale
dictated by the tide. While we were doing this a naval
officer, his cap set at a jaunty Beatty angle, came strutting
down the hard, leading a bull-terrier. He seemed familiar.
As he approached, I could not believe my eyes. It could not
be Jackie Sutton; but it was. I went up to him and asked him
what his job was. He was apparently the harbourmaster. 'You
may not remember me,' I said, 'but I remember you'; and,
having reminded him of what had happened at Salerno,
I said: 'If you attempt to interfere in any way with the
loading of the LSTs, I will have you locked up again, as I
did at Salerno.' Without a word, he turned round, and we
never saw him again. After loading we pulled away from the
shore and anchored, with masses of other craft, in the mouth
of the Orwell between Felixstowe and Harwich. I was much
concerned at the inexperience of the ships' officers. My anxiety was removed when a completely new set arrived from the
Mediterranean where they had taken part in all the landings.
The captain of the LST on which I was, was a highly efficient
American of Norwegian origin. One of his first acts was to
tell the cook to serve my soldiers the American rations, held
for the ship's crew, instead of the 'compo' which had been
put on board for them. Although well-intentioned, it was not
entirely popular with my soldiers, as they peered at strange
concoctions of peanut butter and other American delicacies
ladled into their mess tins. At least there was no attempt to
make them change from tea to coffee.

The landing craft, with A Squadron on board, left on
5 June, and we in the LSTs sailed in the afternoon of 6
June, D Day. We rounded the North Foreland shortly before
dusk, and ships in the convoy behind us, which carried our

B echelon and 1st Rifle Brigade, were shelled by the German
coast defence guns at Cap Gris Nez, fortunately without loss.
We were off the invasion beaches at Arromanches at dawn on
7 June, D + 1. It was an astonishing sight: flotillas of ships
and craft of every description, some engaged in bombarding
the shore. Every now and then enemy aircraft would appear
and the American anti-aircraft gunners, mostly coloured
men, would cram their steel helmets down on their heads
and fire, apparently blindly, in the general direction of the
aircraft, often almost straight at the ship next door. I was
glad when we approached the shore and had to go below
into our tanks. It seemed safer there. The tide was running
out and our LST grounded just short of a large hole in the
beach, probably a bomb crater. There was much argument
about whether we could or should disembark into this; but
there was no alternative, as the ship was firmly stuck there
until the next high tide. Keeping our fingers crossed, we
drove out and were relieved to find that the hole was not as
deep as we had feared. For the first few days after landing,
we found ourselves helping 50th Division to push forward
towards Tilly against increasing opposition. It was just like
Italy all over again, except that the weather was better.
The 'bocage' of Normandy consisted of apple orchards and
small fields, separated by banks, on top of which grew thick
hedges. These banks formed ideal defensive positions, and
tanks were particularly vulnerable when they attempted to
surmount them. An enterprising US Army engineer developed a three-pronged attachment, made from the German
beach obstacles, which we fitted to the front of our tanks
and which removed a slice of the bank; but at this stage we
did not have that useful tool. While we were supporting 50th
Division, in the course of which we were subjected to quite
heavy shelling, I was infuriated when my tanks were shot at
by tanks on our left, which were quite clearly our own. They
were from Erroll Prior-Palmer's 8th Armoured Brigade,
who apparently had not seen Cromwell tanks before.

As progress towards Tilly slowed down, 1st US Infantry
Division on our right had made better progress, having
reached Caumont, and it appeared that a breakthrough
could be achieved in that area. The division was therefore

extricated, and on 12 June switched to the right, aimed
at the town of Villers Bocage. Twenty-second Armoured
Brigade led, followed by 131st Lorried Infantry Brigade,
under whose command we were placed. 'Bolo' Whistler had
been promoted to command the 3rd Infantry Division, and
it was now in the hands of Brigadier Ekins, not a patch on
his predecessor. One of his battalions, 1st/7th Queens,
was under Loony Hinde's command and one, 1st/5th,
in the process of landing. His brigade therefore consisted
of Michael Forrester's 1st/6th Queens and my regiment.
Good progress was made on 12 June, and in the morning
of 13 June 22nd Armoured Brigade reached Villers-Bocage,
their leading regiment, Arthur Cranley's 4th County of
London Yeomanry, and most of 1st Rifle Brigade passing
through the town to the high ground on the far side. Just as
they had done so and while part of the regiment was still in
the town, the German 2nd Panzer Division counter-attacked.
Most of both 4th CLY and 1st Rifle Brigade were cut off,
and many of them were taken prisoner. Hinde reorganized
the rest of his brigade on high ground west of the town,
between it and Amaye, and Bobbie Erskine sent up 1st/5th
Queens, who had now arrived, to join him, Brigadier Ekins
going up with them to discuss their task with Hinde. When
he tried to return, he found the enemy across the road west
of Amaye, and Erskine told me to assume command of
131st Brigade, which consisted only of Michael Forrester's
1st/6th Queens and ourselves, with supporting anti-tank
and field artillery and a squadron of 11th Hussars. My orders
were to make sure that the village of Briquessard and the
two cross-roads north of it were securely held. Briquessard
was where the minor road, by which we had moved south,
joined the main road from Caumont to Villers-Bocage. I
sent 1st/6th Queens to Briquessard and looked after the
other cross-roads myself, sending the reconnaissance troop
to make contact with the Americans on our right. We were
all well established by the end of the day. I was then told
that my task for the following day, 14 June, was to open
up the road to 22nd Armoured Brigade at first light and
keep it open. My plan was for 1st/6th Queens to stay in
Briquessard with A Squadron under command: B squadron,
picking up one company of 1st/6th Queens on their way,

was to advance through Briquessard to the high ground west
of Amaye, followed by myself and then C Squadron and the
reconnaissance troop, whose job of liaising with the Americans had been taken over by the 11th Hussars. B Squadron
set off at first light, meeting only a few parties of enemy, who
were quickly dealt with, and soon reached their objective.
Enemy tanks had been reported on the high ground south
of the road between me and Amaye. I therefore moved C
Squadron through B onto this high ground, leaving the
reconnaissance troop to cover the road behind us back to
the 1st/6th Queens, and moved up behind C Squadron
myself. They were soon engaged with enemy tanks half a
mile south of the road where they quickly knocked out
two Panthers, a Tiger and several Mark IVs, and drove the
enemy over the crest into some very thick orchards. I then
rearranged the two squadrons and assumed a semi-circular
battle position facing south, one troop of each squadron
watching the northern flank.

Guns were firing at us from all directions, and we had several casualties. I had established contact with the 8th Hussars
in Amaye and could therefore report that the first part of my
task had been completed. I was told that we were to hold our
positions indefinitely, as it was hoped that 'friends on our
right and left' would soon be able to advance and straighten
out the line. The 8th Hussars were being worried by enemy
infantry who were in some orchards on the southern edge of
the Amaye. I therefore laid on an attack with the company of
the Queens, supported by B Squadron, to clear this area. It
stirred up a hornets' nest: in fact, I think it coincided with a
renewed enemy attack. Several enemy tanks appeared, there
was a lot of shelling and it was some time before it all died
down. It was now about midday, and the centre of interest
suddenly shifted to the west. From where we were, we could
see some enemy tanks and self-propelled guns across the
valley to our right. One of them selected my tank as its target,
which necessitated a hurried dive through a hedge and over
a six-foot drop, in the course of which I lost my lunch off
the top of my tank. Being on the top of a hill with enemy
all round, it was extremely difficult to find positions from
which one could oneself get a view, and yet remain concealed
from the enemy. This activity was the prelude to an attack

on Briquessard and the road south-east of it. A Squadron, with 1st/6th Queens and the reconnaissance troop, were soon heavily engaged, helped by artillery support from the Americans and our own field and medium guns. I was a bit anxious about the area of the bridge over the stream between us and them, as I appreciated that the enemy might make a strong bid to cut the road there: the reconnaissance troop only had light tanks, from which the turrets had been removed, their largest gun being a 0.50-in machine-gun, and I told B Squadron to send a troop back down the road to help them. I need not have worried, as they did splendid work, rushing up and down everywhere, firing off their guns like mad, and completely defeated the attack in that area. By about half past four this attack had died down, and I felt confident that we could hold the position, extended though we were, against all comers, although I should not have liked a simultaneous attack from north and south.

Shortly after this, Loony Hinde came to see me. Fiftieth Division had not got any further forward in the direction of Tilly, where they were opposed by the German Panzer Lehr Division, and we were still very much out on a limb. It had ʰ ᵉen decided that 22nd Armoured Brigade was to withdraw that night, and the front was to be stabilized in the area of Briquessard. I was disappointed, as I thought that we had seen off the enemy. My task was to hold the road open during the night and follow the rest of the brigade back, my tail to reach Briquessard by first light. While Loony was giving me these orders in an orchard a hundred yards behind my tank, he suddenly stopped and said: 'Anybody got a matchbox? I must get that caterpillar. It's a very rare one.' 'For God's sake, Brigadier,' I said, 'we can't waste time on caterpillars: I've got a battle on my hands.' 'Don't be a bloody fool, Mike,' was his reply; 'you have a battle every day of your life: you don't see a caterpillar like that once in 15 years!' Fortunately somebody had a matchbox and, having secured the caterpillar, we were able to get on with the orders. Before I had finished talking to him, the enemy launched another attack, well supported by artillery, towards Amaye from the south. This was a much more severe attack than any he had launched before, and we were soon all hard at it from every direction. I pushed B and C Squadrons well forward onto the crest of the hill to strike at the flank of the attack and to get all available tanks into action. We came in for a lot of fire from some very large guns, and were soon engaged with enemy tanks of all kinds and infantry scurrying up the hedgerows. We did a great deal of damage with little loss to ourselves, and, after about an hour, the enemy withdrew and became very quiet, allowing us to have a 'brew' and refill with ammunition.

I could not keep my tanks strung out all over the place once it became dark, and I appreciated that the bridge might be the danger area at night. I therefore ordered the company of the Queens with the reconnaissance troop and one troop of B Squadron to take up a position for the night covering the approaches to the bridge from all directions. The rest of the regiment was to form a close leaguer in two lines, parallel to and just south of the road west of Amaye. It was open ground and 200 yards from the nearest place which enemy infantry could reach unobserved, so that I was confident that we could protect ourselves and the road from an infantry attack. I was certain that enemy tanks could not get through the 'bocage' at night, certainly not without making a fiendish din, and that if they tried to cut the road, they would choose this area. The real difficulty would be to keep awake. I personally had had little sleep the night before, and we had all been hard at it all day since four o'clock in the morning. As it grew dark, we moved slowly and as silently as we could into leaguer, and it was not long before the first vehicles of 22nd Armoured Brigade began to come past down the road. At midnight we heard the hum of aircraft, and soon the sky was lit up by the multi-coloured firework display provided by the Pathfinders. This was followed by the deep roar of the bombers, the thud of bombs and the vibration of the earth, as Bomber Command attacked Villers-Bocage, reducing it to a heap of rubble. The raid lasted for half an hour. Whether it was this attack or the punishment that we had inflicted on them during the day which kept them quiet, at any rate the Germans made no attempt to attack us or the road during the night. In fact, as we discovered later, they withdrew to lick their wounds. By 2 a.m. 22nd Armoured Brigade were all clear. I allowed another half hour in case of stragglers, and then set off down the road. The only incident was provided by two ammunition lorries, one of which had driven into the ditch; the second had driven into it and lay across most of the road. Both were on fire and the ammunition was exploding. I closed down and charged the edge of the second lorry at 30 miles an hour, which succeeded in pushing it into the side of the road and scattering the ammunition. We were all in by first light, disappointed at not having been able to exploit our success, but glad that we had at least given 2nd Panzer Division 'a bloody nose' in its first action in Normandy. It did not, however, prevent them from attacking Briquessard next day, but they were beaten off by 131st Brigade, who had now assumed responsibility for the front. Twenty-second Armoured Brigade, which I had rejoined, moved into reserve a few miles behind the front line, which was subsequently withdrawn further to make it easier to hold between the Americans on our right and 50th Division on our left. Montgomery had abandoned the idea of trying to break out near Caumont, and had switched his main effort to the area west of Caen, 7th Armoured Division undertaking no major operation for the next three weeks.

On the morning of 27 June I was holding a conference of my squadron commanders and others to discuss the lessons of recent operations, when I was called to the telephone to speak to Loony. He told me that I was to take over command of 4th Armoured Brigade in place of John Currie, who had been killed. The brigade was in 8 Corps somewhere west of Caen. I was to hand over to Stump Gibbon and leave in half an hour, calling in on him on the way to see Bobbie Erskine, who would give me further directions, as well as lunch. I protested that half an hour was not enough time in which to bid farewell to the regiment I had commanded for 15 months. I would not be able to visit the B echelon and say goodbye to them. I was allowed a further half hour. I hated the idea of leaving this splendid body of men, for whose lives and well-being I felt a keen responsibility. But to be chosen to command an armoured brigade, and one with such close links with 7th Armoured Division, at the age of 29 was a great honour and an even greater responsibility. Fifteen months was a long time to be left in command of a regiment in war, and I had realized that I was likely to be moved soon. I was delighted it was not back to the staff. Saying my farewells with a talk to each squadron in turn, a heavy lump in my throat,I set off in my scout car, followed by my Humber staff car carrying all my belongings. The reaction to my departure from one of my soldiers has been recorded: 'We were all on parade one day for the colonel to address us,' he wrote. 'He was leaving to become a brigadier and hadn't wanted this, but these were orders. There was considerable emotion on both sides. Obviously he was desperately proud of his regiment, in which there was a great store of admiration and infinite trust in return. However, this had to be.'

The same soldier, Peter Roach, who had been my scout car driver when I had taken over command, but had graduated to being a tank commander in the reconnaissance troop, had also written of our time in Italy: 'The real work was done quietly and without fuss by the tanks, all of us acutely sure that we were directed by a man who knew what he was doing and really cared for us.'* To read that 39 years after the event was a reward in itself.

* Roach, pp. 140 and 116.

9

High is the Rank

High is the rank we now possess;
But higher we shall rise,
Though what we shall hereafter be
Is hid from mortal eyes.
                    Scottish Paraphrase of I John, 3.2.

Fourth Armoured Brigade had landed in Normandy as an independent armoured brigade group, supporting 51st Highland Division. Its three tank regiments, all equipped with Shermans, were The Royal Scots Greys, 3rd County of London Yeomanry, known as The Sharpshooters, and 44th Royal Tanks, one of the territorial regiments of the Royal Tank Regiment, converted from infantry in 1939. They had been the 6th Battalion of The Gloucesters and came from Bristol. Second KRRC was the motor infantry battalion and 4th Regiment Royal Horse Artillery had been attached to the brigade since the landing. Bobbie Erskine told me that the brigade was taking part in 8 Corps' attack west of Caen, and that I should report to corps headquarters to find out where they were and get my orders. I reported to Harry Floyd, the BGS, and, while I was there, met the corps commander, Dick O'Connor, whom I had not seen since the early desert days. He seemed to have lost some of his sparkle as a result of his time as a prisoner-of-war in Italy. I was told that the brigade had been placed under command of Pip Roberts's 11th Armoured Division, which was in the process of fighting its way forward across the River Odon, eight miles west of Caen, having passed through 15th Scottish Division, who

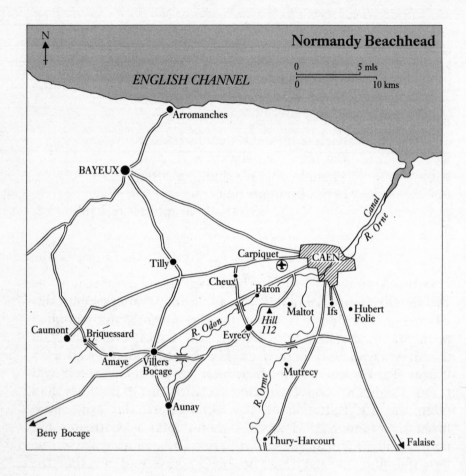

Normandy Beachhead

had captured the ground north of the river the previous day. I drove on to the divisional headquarters, where Pip and his GSO1, Brian Wyldbore-Smith, explained that 159th Lorried Infantry Brigade had secured the river crossings and that 29th Armoured Brigade was in the process of passing through them to capture the high ground beyond, of which Hills 112 and 113 were the dominant features. They hoped to thrust through to Evrecy and then on to the River Orne, two miles further on. The Germans were fighting fiercely, counter-attacking the flanks of the salient this thrust had created. My brigade's task was to help secure these flanks as 29th Armoured Brigade advanced. The Sharpshooters were helping 15th Scottish Division to do this on the left flank, while The Greys watched the right. The 44th had been ordered across the Odon to come under 29th Brigade and push out on the right flank on the far side. They gave me a map reference for the main brigade headquarters, where I would get an up-to-date location for the tactical head-quarters. At the former I found the DAA & QMG was Evie Hambro, a wartime 15th/19th Hussar, who had been at St Peter's Court with me. I also found there an elderly cavalry colonel, whose name I have forgotten, filling the honorary position of second-in-command of the brigade. Operational command was being exercised by Lieutenant-Colonel Sandy Cameron, commanding officer of The Sharpshooters, at tactical headquarters, to find which I was given a map reference near the village of Cheux. Leaving my staff car at main headquarters, I set off in my scout car, and, threading my way through gaps in what had been enemy minefields, I saw two Sherman tanks side by side near where I expected to find the headquarters. They carried the right sign, the black Jerboa, and, having dismounted from my scout car, I climbed up on top and found the two commanders glued to their wireless earphones. Having waited in vain to be asked my business, I tapped the major, whom I assumed to be the brigade major, on the shoulder, and was waved away. I insisted, until he angrily took off his earphones and said: 'Can't you see I'm busy? What do you want?' 'I want to take over command of the brigade,' I replied. Crestfallen, his attitude changed.

I found the situation somewhat confused, and it remained so over the next few days, as 53rd Welsh Division took over from 15th Scottish on the right. There were several German counter-attacks, some of their infantry infiltrating among our own, and the latter becoming very excited, not only about what they called snipers, but also whenever they heard what they thought were enemy tanks moving about. I gave orders that, in my brigade, 'snipers' were to be referred to as 'isolated enemy riflemen'! The Welsh were particularly jittery and I had to organize several sweeps of tanks and my own motor infantry through their area. As had been the case when I took over command of 1st Royal Tanks, I was fortunate to be given a period of not too intensive action in which to establish confidence in my exercise of command. I quickly realized that the brigade major, Major Pat Robertson of the Grenadier Guards, was not up to the job. Norman Gwatkin, who had been adjutant of Sandhurst when I was there, was commanding a brigade in the Guards Armoured Division not far away. When our activity died down, I went to see him, and through him I arranged that Robertson should be transferred to a staff job at their divisional headquarters, where unfortunately he was wounded, not very badly. I was fortunate in obtaining as his successor Dick Ward, who had gained a high reputation as a squadron commander in 5th Royal Tanks in the desert. Hambro also left for the staff college, and I was delighted to acquire Jim Stanton as my DAA & QMG. He had been a pillar of the administrative staff of 7th Armoured Division. I also took the opportunity to rid myself of the encumbrance of my second-in-command, who served no useful purpose. Although he was a personal friend of the army commander, General Miles Dempsey, no difficulties were raised, and he was transferred to be second-in-command to Nigel Duncan's brigade of 'Scorpions' in 79th Armoured Division. He was not replaced, and I never felt the need for the appointment.

My first visit to 2nd KRRC had left me uneasy. There was a general air of slackness, and I thought that Bill Heathcote-Amory, who had commanded them with distinction in the desert, had lost his grip. For a very young, newly arrived tank brigadier to sack a highly respected infantry officer, who had commanded his battalion for a long time, could be greatly resented. I sent a letter to Bobbie Erskine, himself an officer of the KRRC, asking if he could pay them a visit, although I was not under his command, and let me know if he thought I would be right to have Amory removed. He came, was as shocked as I had been, and strongly supported my proposal to do so. He was replaced by Lieutenant-Colonel Littledale.

Eleventh Armoured Division had not been able to advance beyond Hills 112 and 113, and 44th Royal Tanks had lost a considerable number of tanks trying to extend the bridge-head westwards. On 3 July we were switched to the command of 53rd Welsh Division, while 11th Armoured Division was withdrawn. I was not impressed with the Welsh nor with their commander, Major-General Willie Ross. He was the type of commander whose 'order groups' tended to be like councils of war, rather than occasions when clear and defi-nite orders reflected the grip of the commander on the situation. A few days later 43rd (Wessex) Division took over the eastern sector of the front, linking up with the Canadians on their left, and we came under them. Their commander, Major-General G. I. Thomas, was a very different character from Ross. A small, fiery, very determined and grim gunner, without a spark of humour, he would bite the head off anyone who attempted to disagree with him or question his orders, as I was soon to find out. A further attempt was now to be made to capture Hills 112 and 113 and advance to and over the River Orne beyond, with 43rd Division on the left and 15th Scottish on the right. Thomas's plan was for two brigades of his division to capture the ridge, of which Hill 112 was the highest point on the right, the third then advancing a mile beyond on the left to capture the village of Maltot. Fourth Armoured Brigade was then to thrust through six miles to the Orne and try to capture a bridge over it. It looked like Balaclava all over again. However, after fighting for and securing assurances of ample artillery support (Thomas having tried to fob me off with smoke screens), the only stipulation I insisted on was that, before launching my leading regiment over the crest of Hill 112, the square wood on its reverse slope must be firmly in our hands. If it were not, my tanks would be shot up from the rear as they went forward. After further heated argument and objections from the infantry, it was agreed. My plan was for The Greys to lead the advance, as they had had the easiest time in the previous operation.

The infantry attack was launched during the night of 9/10 June, the Churchills of a squadron of 9th Royal Tanks supporting the final phase of the attack being almost all knocked out by anti-tank fire from this wood, which the infantry had not cleared. Having confirmed this myself when I took my tactical headquarters forward, I reported it by wireless to Tiger Urquhart, the splendid sapper who was GSO1 of 43rd Division, saying that I would not order my leading regiment over the crest towards the River Orne until the wood had been cleared of enemy, as had been agreed. He referred this to G. I. Thomas, who came on the set himself and said that his information from his infantry brigades was that all the objectives had been secured, and that therefore I must start my forward thrust. I said that I was on the spot, as his infantry brigadiers were not, and that, if he did not believe me, he could come and see for himself. This, not surprisingly, did not please him. He insisted that I should order my tanks to advance over the crest. I said that, if I did, I expected that the leading regiment would suffer at least 75 per cent casualties, as a result of which they would not be able to reach their objective. He asked me which regiment I proposed to send. I told him it was The Greys. 'Couldn't you send a less well-known regiment?' he replied, at which I blew up. Finally he accepted my arguments, but relations between us, poor to start with, were permanently soured.

A fresh attack was made in the early hours of the next day, the infantry being joined in the wood by a squadron of The Greys at first light; enemy artillery fire was so heavy that the infantry were withdrawn, and, as it was no place to leave tanks on their own, The Greys came with them. The Germans also counter-attacked elsewhere and Thirty-first Army Tank Brigade lost many of the Churchill tanks in its three regiments. Thomas was now resigned to the failure of his operation, and The Greys and 3rd CLY spent the day repelling German counter-attacks designed to throw us off the ridge. We stayed in this unpleasant area for the next ten days, switching to support 53rd Division, but not taking part in any major operation. It was here that the news reached us that 3rd CLY was to be amalgamated with 4th CLY from 7th Armoured Division. It had originally been intended to build up the latter again after its losses at Villers-Bocage, and a new commanding officer, Bill Rankin of the 15th/19th Hussars, had been appointed. However the casualties among officers and senior NCOs in both regiments led to the decision to replace 4th CLY in 7th Armoured Division by the 5th Inniskilling Dragoon Guards and to incorporate 4th CLY into the 3rd. It was naturally assumed by the latter that Sandy Cameron, who had served for four years in the 4th before commanding the 3rd, and had such an outstanding record as a Territorial Army officer, would remain in command.

That decision had not been finally made, when we moved round to join 2nd Canadian Corps south of Caen at the end of the month. Before that we had been held in readiness to reinforce 8 Corps Operation *Goodwood*, in which 7th and 11th Armoured Divisions tried to break out of the bridgehead east of Caen. This had failed, the situation stabilizing after an advance of a few miles in the open plain. The Canadians pushed southwards out of the ruins of Caen to the west of this thrust, and we were placed under their command, expecting to take part in a further attempt to break out towards Falaise. The area was subjected sporadically to some heavy shelling, and one bout of this was in progress when I happened to be visiting The Sharpshooters. I was shocked to observe that Sandy Cameron had clearly lost his nerve. I said nothing at the time, but, when I got back to my headquarters, thought carefully about the implications of removing a Yeomanry commanding officer with such a magnificent record, two MCs and two DSOs. I realized that, for his own sake and for that of his regiment, he must go. Fortunately the fact that no final decision had been made about Bill Rankin made it possible to use the amalgamation as a valid reason for the change, combined with the argument that Sandy Cameron's experience would be invaluable in the training organization at home. Having obtained the agreement of Rickie Richards, the Major-General Royal Armoured Corps at Twenty-first Army Group, who was anxious to find Rankin a command, I went to see Sandy next day and told him of the decision. He protested violently and demanded to raise it to a higher level, until I had to indicate to him that I had no doubt that he was suffering from nervous strain and that, on that account alone, I should insist on his replacement. He greatly resented the decision, but 20 years later wrote me a charming letter admitting that I had been right.

Before the Canadians had started on their attack, we were switched to the opposite end of the British Second Army's sector to support 'Bolo' Whistler's 3rd Division, forming part of 8 Corps, which, it was hoped, would break through towards Vire, alongside the Americans who were making steady progress southwards. I was delighted to be under Bolo's inspiring command, although his orders were for me to parcel out my three tank regiments one to each brigade. The area was one of very thick bocage, and we were to advance across the grain of the country. There was no doubt therefore that it had to be an infantry slogging match, the tanks moving closely with them. One of the brigades was commanded by Eric Bols, who had been so kind to me at Sandhurst and whom I was delighted to see again. An attempt the week before by 30 Corps to break out near Mont Pincon had failed, and I now heard about the repercussions. The corps commander, Gerry Bucknall, had been replaced by Horrocks and a wholesale sacking of senior officers in 7th Armoured Division had taken place. Bobbie Erskine, Loony Hinde and Roy Mews, the Commander Royal Artillery, had all been replaced, as had 'Stump' Gibbon in command of 1st Royal Tanks, Pat Hobart taking his place. 'There, but for the Grace of God, went I,' I thought. One early morning in that area stands out in my memory. It was a lovely summer's day and, just as it was getting light, I was travelling along a small lane, sitting on top of my scout car, on my way to visit some of the tanks in the front line. I was not absolutely certain exactly where the forward posts were, which lent an air of excitement to the beauty of the morning. I remember wondering what life after the war would be like. Would I miss the intensity of an active life, lived to the full close to nature, as life on the battlefield, for all its fears and frightfulness at times, undoubtedly was? I was afraid I might.

After a week, 3rd Division had outflanked Vire and cross-ed the River Allière, Gerry Hopkinson's 44th Royal Tanks playing a leading part in the final stages. We were then relieved by the Churchills of 6th Guards Tank Brigade and switched back to Neil Ritchie's 12 Corps near Evrecy, close to Hill 112. There we joined 53rd Welsh Division

again, moving across the Odon and pushing south-eastwards
against moderate opposition, as the Canadians on our left
attacked towards Falaise. At first Ross wanted to advance
in a series of 'set-piece' infantry attacks, leapfrogging one
infantry brigade through another. Not only would this be
a very slow process, but he also spent hours in discussing
his plans and issuing his orders. It was clear to me that the
whole front was breaking up and that we could and should
thrust forward more boldly. Exasperated by his ponderous
methods, I said something like: 'If you will let my brigade
lead and give me one of your infantry brigades as well, we
can forget all these divisional plans and get moving.' Hardly
surprisingly perhaps, he took offence; but in practice adopted my proposal. We started off on 14 August and, by last
light on the 15th, 44th Royal Tanks had cut the road leading
to Falaise from the west. The Greys then took over the lead
with 1st Highland Light Infantry, and made good progress
until they reached the road running south from Falaise to
Argentan on 18 August, 44th Royal Tanks pushing forward
to the right of them and The Sharpshooters further to the
right again, all three being then on the edge of wooded high
ground, overlooking and forming the northern lip of the
valley of the Orne.

The general situation was that von Kluge's German Army
Group B, which had launched its unsuccessful counter-
attack towards Mortain on 7 August, was in full retreat
and in danger of being cut off by Patton's Third US Army,
which had swung round their right flank up to Argentan by
13 August and was pressing north from there, and by Guy
Simonds's 2nd Canadian Corps, which was thrusting south
from Falaise. Under his command, the Polish Armoured
Division had closed the gap between the two, although it
was not strong enough on the ground to prevent the Germans from escaping through them, especially at night. Our
advance was forming the northern arm of a pincer inside
the ring held by the Poles. On 19 August all three regiments,
but particularly The Greys on the main road, had an exciting
day, firing large quantities of ammunition, knocking out a
great many vehicles of all kinds and taking many prisoners,
as the Germans tried to escape by every possible route. On
20 August I was told that we were to come under the

command of the Canadians. With some difficulty I found
their headquarters during the night, and was immediately
impressed by Guy Simonds, who was roused from bed in his
caravan and, dressed in blue pyjamas, gave me my orders.
He was quick to appreciate what I told him and gave me
clear and decisive orders to move into the gap between us
and the Americans and clear it up. This we did next day,
44th Royal Tanks and 2nd KRRC leading the way and taking
3000 prisoners, while I had great difficulty in stopping both
the Polish and the American artillery from continuing to fire
into the area. The situation could only be described as car-
nage. Not only were there German corpses everywhere and
masses of abandoned and destroyed equipment, but dead
German army horses and dead French cows littered every
lane and field. The sight was terrible, the stench appalling.
The French farmers and villagers were at their wits' end, the
task of burying all the dead, human and animal, being the
most urgent.

We had been switched to the support of 'Tiny' Barber's
15th Scottish Division, but told that, as there was no route
forward available that could take tanks, we must wait until
formations with higher priority had moved east to the Seine
before we could do so. I was desperately keen to get moving,
and equally anxious to get away from the fearful sights and
smells that surrounded us. Fifteenth Scottish Division had
been told that they were to cross the Seine near Louviers.
I worked out a route following by-roads, which would keep
us clear of the routes allotted to the division and to others,
and sent a squadron of the Royal Dragoons' armoured cars,
which had been temporarily given to me, to see if the bridges
were intact and would take tanks. They reported favourably
on the former, being more doubtful about the latter. I
decided to risk it and told The Greys to lead the brigade
along it, Aidan Sprot's reconnaissance troop reporting on
the bridges as they advanced. I accompanied them in my
scout car, both my driver, Sergeant Stan Simmons, and I
disliking having to drive over the half-squashed corpses of
German soldiers and horses that littered the narrow lanes
for the first several miles. It was with immense relief that we
broke out into country clear of the debris of war, in which we
were enthusiastically welcomed by the French. I had several

anxious moments over bridges. I stopped to watch doubtful ones, keeping my fingers crossed as the edges crumbled away when more and more tanks drove over them. Fortunately my plan worked, and we reached Ailly, just south of the Seine near Louviers, on 28 August. We crossed next day at St Pierre du Vauvray into the bridgehead formed by 15th Scottish, and on 30 August, under command of 53rd Division again, led the advance north-east towards Gournay, The Sharpshooters leading, with 44th Royal Tanks on the right and The Greys on the left. During the day we came under the command of 7th Armoured Division, who were passing through the 53rd. Verney, the new commander, summoned me to his headquarters to receive orders. This would have meant an absence of hours, while I struggled back across the Seine and forward again through all the traffic congestion. I therefore said that I was too involved in the battle and that, as Jim Stanton, with my main headquarters, was close to 7th Armoured Division and was actually on his way there, Verney could give him any orders for me that could not be passed by wireless. Ereld Cardiff, his AA & QMG, told Stanton that Verney was annoyed and had said that I had 'made a bad start with 7th Armoured Division!'

The division's eventual objective was Ghent, our route being through St Pol and Lille. Eleventh Armoured Division, under 30 Corps on our right, was heading for Antwerp, their route including Amiens. We therefore had to cross the Somme west of that town. Opposition was likely to come from the German Fifteenth Army, which had been defending the coast north of the Seine and was trying to withdraw across the path of our advance. As we thrust forward, we kept on coming across parties of German troops on our left flank, often behind our forward tanks. I therefore had to keep a careful watch in that direction. We made good progress during that day and the next, taking 1500 prisoners and a large collection of vehicles of all kinds. By dusk on 31 August the leading tanks were six miles beyond Poix, 60 miles beyond the Seine and only ten from the Somme. Verney had come to see me at my tactical headquarters, which was in the village of Bazancourt, when he arrived. While we were talking, some German troops appeared from the west, and my tanks went into action to deal with them.

Verney appeared concerned, and I took the line that this was a very normal occurrence, laying it on a bit thick. The Germans, about a company in strength, surrendered, and I handed them over to the local French resistance to march them back. Verney seemed relieved to be able to return to his headquarters.

Our task was to find and secure a crossing over the Somme west of Amiens. I directed 44th Royal Tanks on the right to the bridge at Picquigny, seven miles west of Amiens, and The Greys to that at Longpré, a further seven miles downstream. The Sharpshooters followed The Greys, guarding the left flank and making contact with the 4th Canadian Armoured Division, which was coming up on our left. Each had a company of 2nd KRRC with them. The enemy was met soon after our advance began, but they were soon brushed aside. The RAF reported the Picquigny bridge blown and the 44th were redirected to Ailly on the outskirts of Amiens, where the bridge was blown as they approached it. The Greys had an interesting and successful battle at Longpré, where the main bridge was blown, but they managed to capture a smaller bridge nearby before the enemy demolished it, Roly Gibbs's company of 2nd KRRC playing an important part in securing it. Unfortunately the bridge was damaged during the attack and could not be used by any more tanks after Aidan Sprot's reconnaissance troop and two troops of Shermans had crossed. The enemy were still holding out in some villages on our left flank, and, unfortunately, the commanding officer of 2nd KRRC, Littledale, was killed when he drove into Airaines, not realizing that it was still in enemy hands. He was succeeded by Robin Hastings, who had commanded a battalion in 50th Division in the landings, which had suffered such severe casualties in the subsequent fighting that it was disbanded. Forty-fourth Royal Tanks found another bridge on the outskirts of Amiens, which was over the corps boundary, but which 11th Armoured Division was not using. We were ordered to cross the river by it and thrust out to the north, the 44th leading and my tactical headquarters following. We drove on in the moonlight to some high ground twelve miles beyond, before halting for the night.

For the next few days, directly under the command of 12 Corps, we defended the corps left flank, advancing to St

Pol through an area pitted with huge bomb craters, caused by air attacks on the German V-1 launching sites. On 5 September we returned to 7th Armoured Division and moved behind 22nd Armoured Brigade south of Lille, crossing the frontier into Belgium at Estambourg, where we received an enthusiastic welcome from its inhabitants. When we reached Audenarde, scene of Marlborough's famous battle, we were told to halt, while 131st Lorried Infantry Brigade passed through to join 22nd Armoured Brigade in the capture of Ghent. I was given no operational task, but, as we had a completely open left flank, facing the area where a large part of the German army was being pressed back by the Canadian and Polish troops of First Canadian Army, I asked for and obtained permission to face west next day, 6 September, and protect the corps' left flank. It was as well that I did. At first light the brigade took up battle positions on a front of 15 miles on the high ground between the River Escaut (called the Scheldt in its lower reaches) and the Lys canal. Each regiment, with its company of 2nd KRRC, covered the approaches to a bridge over the river, The Sharpshooters Audenarde, 44th Royal Tanks Kerkhove and The Greys Avelgem. It was not long before my suspicions were proved correct and a stream of Germans began moving east, heading for the Escaut along the whole brigade front. With only one motor company with each regiment, it was impossible to prevent infiltration through the villages and hedgerows. In spite of heavy losses the Germans continued to try and break through. All through the afternoon the tanks were sweeping their areas over and over again. It was clear to me that we could not hold them at night on such a broad front. Luckily there was a road running east of the river, which could be used as an alternative axis, provided that we held the bridge at Avelgem and kept the Germans from crossing the river anywhere. After warning Verney of the situation and securing his agreement, regiments were pulled back at last light to the immediate vicinity of the bridges and I moved my headquarters and all the transport east of the river. During the night the German 712th Division tried several times to reach the bridges, but got no further than the main road between the villages. At first light on 7 September each regiment counter-attacked and drove the disorganized

enemy back to the high ground, capturing a large number
of prisoners and inflicting heavy casualties. The enemy made
no further attempt to break out to the east, and, the second
battle of Oudenarde (or Audenarde as it is now called) being
over, we handed over the area to 15th Scottish Division.

During the next ten days we were involved in operations
north of the Scheldt and west of Antwerp, which had been
captured by Pip Roberts's 11th Armoured Division. We had
crossed the river at Termonde by a wooden bridge, built to
replace one destroyed in 1940, which the Royal Engineers
classified, after we had crossed it, as capable of taking only a
load of nine tons after repair. It *had* seemed to sway a bit as
we drove our 33-ton tanks over it. Forty-fourth Royal Tanks
enjoyed a memorable liberation of the town of St Nicolas, the
celebrations being brought to an abrupt halt when a German counter-attack was threatened. I had already become
cautious about premature liberation of places which I could
not be certain of securing permanently. One faced an acute
dilemma. One wanted to push forward one's reconnaissance
to discover where the enemy was, and one was naturally
anxious to liberate the population from their yoke as soon
as possible; but, unless one could be certain that the enemy
could not return, one's presence put the population at risk.
Fortunately for St Nicolas The Greys and the 44th between
them beat off the counter-attack.

Montgomery was now planning Operation *Market Garden*,
the airborne operation to drive north into Holland through
Eindhoven and Nijmegen to Arnhem. We handed over our
area to the Polish Armoured Division and moved round to
join 8 Corps in the north-east corner of Belgium, 44th Royal
Tanks joining 30 Corps, their task being to link up with
the US 101st Airborne Division when they landed between
Eindhoven and Nijmegen. I was directly under command
of 8 Corps with the task of pushing the Germans back
towards the River Maas (as the Meuse is called in Holland),
having the Belgian Brigade also under my command. It
had been formed from Belgians who had made their way
to Britain and was commanded by Brigadier Piron, who
was to become head of the Belgian Army after the war.
He was rather a 'sticky' commander, and, when he seemed
reluctant to obey my orders and take some positive action,

I threatened to have him removed. Having cleared the area up to the Willemsvaart canal, we could get no further and spent the rest of the month round Weert, engaged in a sparring match with aggressive German parachute troops on the far side. During this period I took a few days leave in Brussels, staying with Bobbie Erskine, who had been appointed Military Governor of Belgium. We lunched with one rich Belgian family, who did not seem to have suffered in any way from the war. We had a huge and splendid meal, served on gold plate.

At the beginning of October we handed over our area to the US 7th Armoured Division and moved up to Nijmegen to join 30 Corps. There we took over an area between the Waal and the Lower Rhine, south-west of Arnhem, from which by then 1st Airborne Division had been withdrawn. Here the Royal Netherlands Brigade, the Dutch equivalent of Piron's brigade, was placed under my command, as were also the armoured cars of The Royals. My headquarters was not far from Horrocks's and Pete Pyman, his BGS, asked me to come over and dine in the officers' mess. I said that Horrocks and I did not get on, and it would be better if I did not come, but Pete insisted. I sat next to Horrocks, and over dinner he started making derogatory remarks about the armoured corps in general, and then specifically about 7th Armoured Division and the Royal Tank Regiment. I lost my temper and replied by saying that, if he was going to make remarks about the armoured corps, I would give him my views of the infantry. I said that, if I were given a choice of which infantry to fight alongside, I would choose in order of priority: New Zealand, Australian, Indian, Highland, Rifle regiments, north country regiments, Light Infantry, and, bottom equal, Welsh and Home Counties. Horrocks, whose regiment was the Middlesex, then lost his temper and ordered me to leave the mess, which I said I was only too pleased to do. Pete Pyman hurried out after me and begged me to return and apologize. I said that I would do nothing of the sort, and drove off.

I was not surprised when, within a few days, we were replaced in 30 Corps by Erroll Prior-Palmer's 8th Armoured Brigade and moved back to join 12 Corps west of Eindhoven, where, with the Netherlands Brigade still under command,

I took over responsibility for a front of 20 miles, and then
supported 15th Scottish Division's successful attack to capture Tilburg. It was while I was there that I was called upon
by my Roman Catholic chaplain to marry a Dutch couple.
Apparently by Dutch law, as it then was, a young lady could
not marry under the age of 30 without the consent of her
parents, unless she received permission from a bishop and a
judge. This lady was far gone in pregnancy, but her parents,
and the bishop and judge who had jurisdiction, were all
behind the German lines. As the occupying army in time of
war, I had the power to execute a valid marriage, which my
chaplain had not. It was clear that they very much wanted
to get married and that there was no time to lose, so, with
the guidance of my chaplain, I performed the ceremony in
my caravan. I hope they were happy ever after! It was also
in this area that I was visited by Montgomery, the first time
I had seen him since he had come to talk to 1st Royal Tanks
in Norfolk. He asked about the brigade and discussed the
command of 2nd KRRC. Robin Hastings was to go to the
staff. He said that Christopher Consett was available, but
that he did not have a high opinion of him. I knew that
that dated from Christopher's clash with him when they met
near Himeimat soon after Monty had arrived to command
Eighth Army. I said that I knew Christopher's faults, but
also his great qualities as a fighting soldier and leader, and
that I could handle him. Monty acquiesced and left in a
cheerful, friendly mood, handing over a large consignment
of cigarettes for the soldiers.

Next day I was told to meet Neil Ritchie at a cross-roads
near Eindhoven. When I got there and was sitting in his
car, he said that he had some stern words to say to me.
Monty, he said, was very displeased with me. He had heard
that I had been very rude to several senior officers and had
ordered that I should be warned that, unless I ceased this
habit, I was likely to lose my command. Ritchie spoke in
the friendliest and most understanding way, but I could not
refrain from telling him that Monty had visited me the day
before and had given no hint of any displeasure. I said that
I realized that I had behaved badly with Horrocks, but had
been greatly provoked: that I had also had a row with G. I.
Thomas and had often been impatient with Ross, as well as

with Verney, in my view with justification. I promised that I
would do my best to restrain myself in future. Ritchie was his
usual straightforward, direct and honest self. It was a model
'ticking off'.

At the end of October we were suddenly rushed back to
our old stamping ground near Weert to meet a threatened
counter-attack, coming under command of 7th US Armoured Division in 8 Corps. I was present when Dick O'Connor
came to General Sylvester's headquarters to give him his
orders, which were to hold the line of the canal firmly
and not to get involved in attempts to counter-attack by
crossing it. When I received written orders from divisional
headquarters, and had deciphered their strange verbiage
and format, which included a crudely drawn 'trace' which
seemed to fit no map that I had, I realized that they were
for an attack to cross the canal. The plan would entail tanks
driving in single line ahead on roads raised above the marshy
area on either side. Hardly able to believe this, I went to divisional headquarters to see the G3 (chief operations officer).
He confirmed that this was the plan. When I said that it
was not what O'Connor had ordered, he replied: 'Yeah, I
know; but the general wants to hit the bastards hard.' I
returned to my headquarters, rang up O'Connor's BGS and
told him what was afoot. As a result O'Connor came down
to see Sylvester and ordered him not to put his plan into
execution. He must then have got on to General Dempsey,
and the latter to Monty. Next day General Omar Bradley
arrived and relieved Sylvester of his command. I discovered
this when I went to his headquarters to find out what was
happening. When told that the general had been sacked,
I expressed some not very convincing sort of condolence.
'Oh,' said the G3, 'he was an old-time tank man. We knew
he wouldn't last long!'* Fifty-third Division then took over
the area and we came under them, supporting them when,
on 13 November, they attacked across the canal. Five days
later, we switched to the command of 'Bubbles' Barker's 49th
Division, supporting their attack towards Venlo on the Maas.
The ground was flat and very wet, and the opposition tough.

---

* In fact, Montgomery had instigated his dismissal after he had first met him
on 13 October.

The regiments were parcelled out to support each brigade in a series of hard-fought set-piece infantry attacks, so that there was not much for me to do personally. On my way up to visit 44th Royal Tanks in my scout car, I was forced onto the muddy verge by guns coming in the opposite direction. Although there were signs saying 'Verges cleared of mines', there was a loud explosion and the scout car stopped abruptly while I was talking to Dick Ward on the wireless. The front right-hand wheel had been blown off and Sergeant Simmons was moaning, saying that his foot had gone. I dropped the microphone and started to try and lift him out of the driving seat, but he cried out with pain and I saw that I could not get him out until I had removed the steering-wheel. I opened the first-aid kit and gave him an injection of morphia. With considerable difficulty I removed the steering-wheel. By this time the passing gunners had produced an ambulance jeep with a stretcher, to which we transferred him and they told me that there was a dressing station a few miles away, near where the 44th were, to which they would take him. When that was over, I returned to the wireless set in the scout car, told Dick Ward what had happened and where I was, and ordered the 44th to send a jeep to collect me. I sensed both surprise and a certain hesitation in Dick Ward's reply and Gerry Hopkinson's acknowledgement. I discovered later that, as I had suddenly gone 'off the air' to the background noise of an explosion, Dick had assumed that something had happened to me, and had told Gerry, as the senior commanding officer, to assume temporary command of the brigade. When I arrived at his headquarters, everyone made a great fuss, offering me cups of tea. It was not until I looked in a mirror that I realized I was covered from head to foot with mud. I went to the dressing station to find out how Sergeant Simmons was. The doctor said that I should not have given him morphia, as it had prevented him from doing so. He confirmed that he had lost his foot. Eventually he had to have his leg amputated, but became an expert player of both bowls and golf. When the scout car was recovered, it was found that the front wheel had passed over two mines before detonating the third and that the rear offside wheel, just below where I was sitting, was resting on one which had not exploded. It was a lucky escape for me.

We spent the rest of the year and the first six weeks of 1945 in that general area under the command of 11th Armoured Division, while their 29th Armoured Brigade was being re-equipped with the new British tank, the Comet. For most of the time we were responsible for a stretch of the River Maas, and carried on a war of patrols and harassing fire against Germans on the far side. On one occasion I was reconnoitring the near bank on foot when I met a German officer face to face round the corner of a hedge. I had left my tommy-gun on my scout car and had no pistol with me. All I could do was to turn and run round the corner of the hedge. As I did so, I could see that the German officer was doing the same!

In the middle of January I took my 'Python' leave. Under the 'Python' scheme, anyone who had spent a total of three and a half years overseas was entitled to be posted to a job in Britain. This would have played havoc with most of the units which had served previously in the Middle East. As an alternative, those who were entitled to benefit were offered six weeks leave and a guarantee of a return to their unit. Fortunately most took leave instead of the posting, I myself restricting mine to three weeks. On arrival in England, I rang up Elizabeth Pollock, to be told by the friend with whom she shared her flat that she had died of a combination of measles and meningitis, while staying with her aunt in Scotland a week or two before. It was a severe shock which cast a cloud of gloom over my leave. During it, I was able to see Paul, visiting the light aircraft-carrier, HMS *Vengeance*, in which he was a flight direction officer. She was a new ship and was tied up in the Clyde, about to start her working-up period. I had not seen Paul for seven years and was glad to be able to spend two days on board with him.

On my return to 4th Armoured Brigade I received the sad news that, while I had been away, Gus Holliman had been killed by a shell which hit his scout car as he arrived at regimental headquarters of 1st Royal Tanks for a conference. His death came just after his son, Jeremy, had been born, and I felt it more keenly than that of any other of my wartime friends and brothers in arms. Twenty-ninth Armoured Brigade's re-equipment had been delayed by its involvement in dealing with the German counter-offensive

in the Ardennes, and we therefore continued to take its place
in 11th Armoured Division. Tim Readman, the outstanding commanding officer of The Greys, had, much against
his will and mine, left to be the principal staff officer to
Rickie Richards, Montgomery's armoured corps adviser. I
had wanted Duggie Stewart to replace him. He had commanded their A Squadron with great skill and courage for
a long time before going to the Staff College; but Tim
persuaded me reluctantly to agree that Frank Bowlby, his
second-in-command, should take over. I thought Frank to
be too old and slow, but Tim assured me that he would be a
brave, respected and original commanding officer. If I had
had my way, there would have been another change, that
of command of 4th RHA. Len Livingstone-Learmonth was
a splendid fighting gunner, but, when nothing active was
going on, he was idle and totally neglected the administration
of his regiment. The last straw came when, in spite of a
wireless message that I was on my way to his headquarters,
I found him and key members of his staff asleep at ten in
the morning. My adverse report, against which he protested
violently, was approved by the Commander Royal Artillery
of the division and his superior, Bill Heath, at 12 Corps.
However the head gunner at Second Army, Brigadier Jack
Parham, had resented the fact that 4th RHA had become
a permanent member of the brigade and wore its sign. He
regarded the regiment as his, to be sent wherever he wished.
He refused to agree, and I was faced with the embarrassing
situation of having told Len that he was sacked, and then
having to accept that he was not. The period of coolness
in our relations lasted only until the next battle, which was
soon upon us. During this period also Dick Ward went
off to take command of 22nd (Westminster) Dragoons, a
Yeomanry regiment in 79th Armoured Division, which had
had particularly close links with the Royal Tank Regiment,
his place as brigade major being taken by 'Pedro' Pedraza,
fresh from the Staff College. As we knew each other so well,
he quickly settled in.

Montgomery's aim was now to clear the area between the
Maas and the Rhine, preparatory to forcing a crossing over
the latter. Crerar's First Canadian Army was to drive south-
east from Nijmegen, while Collins's Ninth US Army pushed

north-east from the River Roer, and Dempsey's Second British Army was out of the battle, planning the Rhine crossing. Eleventh Armoured Division came under command of 2nd Canadian Corps and was to take over the advance, when the infantry divisions had cleared the thick Reichswald forest south of Cleve. This would involve forcing its way through the Siegfried and Schlieffen lines in country which included many large woods. Once we were unleashed, we were to keep the pressure up night and day. Pip Roberts's plan was to leapfrog his brigades, Jack Churchill's 159th Lorried Infantry and my own, through each other. I handed The Sharpshooters over to Jack and received Max Robinson's 4th King's Shropshire Light Infantry in return, so that we could each form two battle-groups, each of an armoured regiment and an infantry battalion. We were to lead off when 3rd Canadian Division had captured Udem on our left. After I had carried out a reconnaissance of the front line on 24 February, I summoned my commanding officers and Pedraza to meet me at a cross-tracks behind it. Bill Rankin arrived first, and while he and I were studying my map side by side, a shell landed nearby and wounded Bill all up the left side of his body. Fortunately there was an aid post nearby and we were able to get him there quickly. Having given my orders, I went to see Pip to discuss future plans. He had his senior medical officer with him, who asked if I was all right. I told him that luckily I was. 'I think I had better have a look at you,' he said, 'as you've got a large tear in the back of your battle-dress.' A shell fragment had in fact cut a hole in it and my jersey and shirt, but had not even scratched my back.

We had expected to start, with The Greys and 4th KSLI leading, in the morning of 26 February; but it was not until 6 p.m. that we were finally released. I had remained at my main headquarters in telephone contact with Pip, until shortly before dark. I then had to move my tactical headquarters as quickly as possible to its battle site and had given orders to keep the track between the two clear of other traffic. To my fury I found that transport of another formation was making use of it at a crucial junction. The only way to get forward was to knock down a house and then drive over two of their lorries. I ordered the soldiers in the house and those in the offending lorries to get out of the way. At first they would not believe that I meant what I said, but they moved quickly when my tank began to drive at the house.

The battle that followed, which lasted until 4 March, was the toughest we had fought since Normandy. The Germans had recovered from the débâcle in France and were now in their own country, fighting fiercely for every village and wood. Shelling was heavy, the ground was very wet and the weather bitterly cold. It was an exhausting time, as operations went on night and day, and to make matters worse I started a feverish cold. Pip was a first-class commander, keeping up the pressure without nagging, and ready with helpful suggestions as to how to overcome difficulties. The Greys and 4th KSLI, making use of a road over the boundary which the Canadians were not using, outflanked the enemy and made their way onto the ridge south of the Balberger Wald, beyond which the ground fell away to Xanten in the Rhine valley. Our task was complete on 4 March, and three days later we left 11th Armoured Division and moved back over the Maas to join Ritchie's 12 Corps to prepare for the Rhine crossing.

We were to be under command of 'Tiny' Barber's 15th Scottish Division, one of the best in Second Army, and one of my regiments, 44th Royal Tanks, was to be equipped with the amphibious DD (Duplex Drive) tank. This was a waterproofed Sherman equipped with a propellor which gave it a maximum speed of five knots in the water. The tank itself was below the water, screens erected by inflation providing flotation. Gerry Hopkinson only had ten days in which, with the help of instructors from Hobo's 79th Armoured Division, to train his regiment on the Maas how to operate their tanks in a fast-running river. He and I went to look at the sector of the Rhine which he was to cross below Wesel. By timing flotsam in the stream, we estimated that it was flowing at five knots, which meant that his tanks would need to get out on the far bank about a thousand yards below where they had entered the water. We also decided that, with only ten days in which to train, it was out of the question to attempt a night crossing, and Tiny Barber agreed. But Hobo threw a spanner in the works. He had told Twenty-first Army Group that he must have an additional brigade headquarters placed under his command to supervise the DD training for the crossing, which involved the Staffordshire Yeomanry, who were with 51st Highland Division on the left of 15th Scottish, as well as the 44th Royal Tanks. Ritchie explained to me that, although everybody thought this unnecessary, to pacify Hobo it had been agreed that I should be under his command for this purpose. The Staffordshire Yeomanry had used DD tanks for the D-Day landings and knew all about them. I therefore agreed with their commanding officer that I would not in any way interfere with his training. If 79th Armoured Division issued any orders on the subject, I would merely pass them on to him. They were going to attempt a night crossing, and 79th Armoured Division had developed a complicated method of navigating across the river to make this possible. I received orders that 44th Royal Tanks were to send all their tank commanders up to Nijmegen to be trained in this. I refused, saying that it was unnecessary, as it had been agreed that they would not attempt a night crossing. Alan Brown, Hobo's chief of staff, rang me up and said that Hobo insisted. I said that time was so short for their training that to send them to Nijmegen for two days would prejudice their chances of being successful in daylight, and that the operational plan did not call for a night crossing. I thus would not send them. I was thereupon summoned to see Hobo that evening. After a hazardous drive on icy roads in the dark, I was kept waiting for a long time. Hobo then faced me in a grim mood, accusing me, correctly, of direct disobedience of his orders. I said that I served two masters and had to give priority to the operational one. He threatened to have me sacked, to which I replied that I had no alternative but to refer the whole matter to the corps commander. Breathing fire and slaughter, he dismissed me, his staff officer, Joe Lever, sympathetically seeing me out. As soon as I got back to my headquarters, I rang Neil Ritchie and explained the whole matter. 'Oh dear, Mike,' he said, 'can't you settle it somehow?' I assured him that there was no give on either side. He promised to discuss it with Tiny Barber and Headquarters Second Army. When he rang back next day, he confirmed that he supported the line I had taken, but said that a compromise had been agreed. If I sent a few non-commissioned officers from the 44th, Hobo would be satisfied. I agreed that I would, but warned him that they would not be the tank commanders. Gerry Hopkinson managed to produce a sergeant and two corporals, and Alan Brown confirmed that Hobo would accept that. I considered that I had acted correctly on Hobo's original advice to me to be 'sufficiently insubordinate', although he would not have relished being reminded of it.

We moved back to the area between Udem and Sonsbeck on 16 March, joined six days later by the 44th, who moved into a specially camouflaged area near Xanten. I planned to cross with them in a Weasel, a very small two-man un-armoured tracked amphibious vehicle, which, when carrying a wireless set and batteries and the minimum of personal kit, gave us four inches of freeboard. Fifteenth Scottish Division's infantry started crossing in tracked amphibians, called Buffalos, in the early hours of 24 March. Forty-fourth Royal Tanks arrived at 5 a.m. in their assembly area by the river's edge, where they inflated their screens. Reconnaissance parties to inspect and mark the exits on the far bank had crossed with the infantry. There was some sporadic enemy shelling and two tanks had their screens pierced. At first light, 6.15 a.m., they started to enter the water on a two-squadron front. I saw the tanks of the left-hand squadron trying to get out at a place different from that which Gerry and I had agreed on, and getting stuck. I asked him on the wireless why they were doing this, and he referred to a visit by some officer on the previous day. I did not understand this, and drove over to talk to him. He told me that an intelligence officer from 79th Armoured Division had visited him and produced air photographs purporting to show that the exits we had chosen were mined. He had assumed that he had been to my headquarters en route and that I had agreed a change. I was very angry, all the more so when I discovered later that the officer had never called at my headquarters either before or after visiting the 44th. It increased my resentment at Hobo's action.

By switching all crossings to the right-hand squadron's area, Gerry had 55 of his tanks over by 8.15, three being hit by shellfire and sinking in midstream, their crews rescued by Buffalos, and five getting bogged down on the far bank. Soon after this, our artillery fire suddenly stopped and the roar of hundreds of aircraft was heard, as 6th Airborne

Division passed low overhead and dropped by parachute and glider beyond 15th Scottish Division's objectives. Enemy resistance slackened after this, and by the end of the day the 44th had helped 44th Infantry Brigade to reach their objectives and link up with 227th Brigade on their left. Next day they made contact with 6th Airborne and placed a squadron under their command, I having agreed this with the divisional commander, Eric Bols, to whose headquarters I had made my way in my Weasel, having crossed the river without incident. Eric had had an exciting landing in his glider and swore that in future he would choose a parachute. Fourth RHA crossed by raft that day, but the rest of the brigade had to wait until they could use a bridge on the night of 26/27 March. I was glad to see my tactical headquarters again, life based on a Weasel proving very Spartan.

For the next few days we helped 15th Scottish and 6th Airborne Divisions expand the bridgehead, and then passed to the command of 53rd Welsh Division to thrust northwards just east of the Dutch border, 7th Armoured Division moving parallel on our left. I received an infantry battalion from the Welsh and gave The Sharpshooters to their leading infantry brigade, so that I could form two armoured/infantry battle groups, as I had for the Udem–Sonsbeck battle, The Greys and 2nd KRRC forming one, 44th Royal Tanks and the infantry battalion the other. Progress was slow, partly because the enemy was plentifully supplied with 'Bazookas' or Panzerfausts, the light anti-tank weapon fired from the shoulder. In this country of woods, farms and villages, in which the boggy ground often restricted tanks to movement on roads and tracks, they were effective weapons. On one day The Greys and 2nd KRRC seemed to be particularly sluggish. I had decided to give them a little more time to get going before personally visiting them to urge them on, when Ritchie announced that he was on his way to see me. I had to wait for him, and he then asked me why I had not personally been to see why they were being so slow. He insisted on going himself, which queered my pitch even further. He was rightly annoyed at the slow progress and urged me to take drastic action. After I had myself visited them, I decided that both commanding officers would have to go. Both, Frank Bowlby and Christopher Consett, had

shown up poorly in the Udem–Sonsbeck battle, although
their units had done well. Frank had clearly become quickly worn out by the physical strain and Christopher never
seemed to be at the right place at the right time, lacking
his old fire and grip. I decided to visit them after dark. I
did not visit Christopher, as he drove over a mine in his
scout car, burst his ear-drum and had to be evacuated as
a casualty. I had a difficult and rather anxious drive in my
scout car through woods, from which I was not certain that
the enemy had been totally cleared, to find Frank Bowlby's
headquarters. On my arrival he told me that he had decided
to sack the squadron commander, Major Chassels, who had
been in the lead at the time when Ritchie had appeared. I
agreed, but then added that he himself would also have to
go. He protested violently. I tried to persuade him that he
was not really fit and that it was not fair on the regiment or
on himself that he should remain in command. He refused to
accept this. I then said that my mind was made up and that I
proposed to say that I knew that he suffered from recurrent
malaria and that this affected his physical capacity to exercise
command. The alternative was an adverse report. He was to
hand over to Hugh Brassey straight away and leave next day.
I then saw Hugh and said that I would immediately set in
hand arrangements to extract Duggie Stewart from the Staff
College to take Frank's place. It was the most difficult and
unpleasant interview that I ever had to face, and I believe
that Frank never forgave me.

We were now squeezed out by the progress of formations
on both sides and the lack of a road leading in the right
direction, but a few days later we were in the van again, heading for Ochtrup. I was following behind the reconnaissance
troop of The Greys, or thought I was until I came up against
a road block and was told by a helpful German that enemy
soldiers were just beyond it. James Hanbury had led his
troop up the wrong road and I was not pleased to be left to
lead the advance myself. We reached Ochtrup on 3 April and
were switched to the command of 52nd Lowland Division to
turn east for Rheine and cross the Dortmund–Ems canal,
continuing the advance beyond over the flat, wet country
north of the Teutoburger Wald and the Mittelland canal.
It was an unsatisfactory period, as 52nd Division was not

an easy formation to work with. They had been trained as a mountain division, and had seen no action until being used to assault the Dutch island of Walcheren, ironically below sea level. Their commander, Major–General Hakewill-Smith, was elderly, 49 years old, as were his brigadiers, and their methods were even more pedestrian than 53rd Division's. Hakewill-Smith's 'order groups' were like Kutuzov's councils of war, as described by Tolstoy in *War and Peace*, and were dominated by his Commander Royal Artillery. Our principal difficulties arose from the combination of being largely restricted to using roads and the enemy's plentiful supply of Panzerfausts, manned both by his soldiers and the equivalent of the Home Guard.

We were therefore pleased to leave that area and make a long move of 100 miles to join 53rd Division on the River Weser 20 miles south of Bremen. We rested there for a few days, devoted to maintenance of the tanks which were fast wearing out, before moving forward to cross the River Aller at Rethem. While the rest of the division, supported by The Sharpshooters, turned north down the valley heading for Verden, we were to move wider to outflank it. I had been given Frankie Brooke's 6th Royal Welch Fusiliers, so that I could form my two battle groups. The Fusiliers were carried in 'Kangaroos', armoured personnel carriers which were Sherman tanks without turrets. They had not used them before and had little time in which to organize themselves and train with them. I teamed them up with The Greys on the right, 44th Royal Tanks and 2nd KRRC being on the left. Our opponents were the German 2nd Marine Division, who fought hard and skilfully, using villages, woods and farmhouses as strong points. Both regimental groups made good progress, leapfrogging quadron/company groups in outflanking moves, while dealing with these defended areas. The country was sandy and tanks could move freely, except where there were boggy streams. Several bold moves were made by night and day through thick woods, liberally spraying machine-gun fire to discourage the Panzerfausts. The climax came when The Greys broke through to the north-east of Verden on the night of 17 April, helped by artificial moonlight – searchlights shining into the clouds. They approached the enemy from the rear and cut the road north of the town. It had been a most successful battle, a model of its kind, in which we had been able to combine mobility and firepower more effectively than at any time since we had crossed the Somme. It convinced me that the organization of the brigade into two battle-groups, each of an armoured regiment and a mobile infantry battalion, was the best one for an armoured brigade, certainly for the majority of operations. What we clearly needed was an armoured personnel carrier specifically designed for the task.

Our next main task was to support 52nd Division in the attack on Bremen from the east. The Greys and 44th Royal Tanks both had some tough fighting on the outskirts, but on 24 April, my thirtieth birthday, enemy resistance was cracking. I had managed to bring my whole headquarters forward into a village on the north bank of the Weser between Verden and Bremen, which had escaped the ravages of war, and had asked Jim Stanton to see that the officers' mess provided a specially good dinner that evening. As I was on my way back in my scout car from visiting the two regiments, I received a message from Pedro that I was required to go and see Hakewill-Smith at his headquarters in the outskirts of Verden. He had tried, but failed, to get me out of it. I was not in the best of tempers, as earlier in the day I had been visited by Horrocks, under whose command the division was. He had seemed little interested in the progress of the battle, but had asked me how many tank casualties the brigade had suffered since we had crossed the Rhine. I happened to know, as I had been going through the figures with Jim Stanton the evening before. When I told him, he said: 'That's not much. Erroll Prior-Palmer's 8th Armoured Brigade has had many more. You can't be trying.' To which I replied: 'Sir, I reckon my success by the casualties we inflict on the enemy, not by those he inflicts on us.' One more nail in the coffin of our relations!

We spent a few more days clearing up the area between Bremen and Rotenburg, and were then switched to 12 Corps for the crossing of the River Elbe above Hamburg. There were movement timing problems, but I selected a cross-country route which seemed from the map to be free of obstacles. It took us across Luneburg Heath, and I noted it down as a suitable training area for tanks once the war was over, as it clearly soon would be. At Winsen, between Luneburg and Hamburg, we rejoined 53rd Welsh Division, except for The Greys, who joined 6th Airborne Division in 8 Corps on our right. On 1 May one squadron of The Greys crossed by floating bridge at Lauenburg, but the rest of the regiment was stuck behind 11th Armoured Division, who had priority. However, by concealing their identity, they managed to infiltrate themselves across during the night, and on 2 May the regiment led 6th Airborne Division north-east to Wismar, 70 miles away on the Baltic coast. They sped along, reconnaissance troop leading, against a constant flow of German soldiers fleeing from the Russians and only too anxious to surrender. Some did not seem to realize that the tanks were British. At one stage level crossing gates came down as The Greys approached, while a train-load of German tanks and their crews passed, neither side taking any action. Almost the only hostile act took place in Wismar, which The Greys reached at 1 p.m., when a German soldier threw a hand-grenade at Duggie Stewart, who shot him dead with his pistol. At 9 p.m. the first Russians arrived, and, after some handshaking and vodka drinking, the Iron Curtain descended, later to be moved 40 miles further west to accord with the Yalta agreement.

On 3 May The Sharpshooters crossed the Lauenburg bridge to support 158th Brigade, entering Hamburg un-opposed the following morning, while the rest of the brigade, including my headquarters, also crossed and moved into Bergdorf on the eastern outskirts of the city. By then the surrender negotiations were in train and four days later, 8 May, the news was flashed that the war was over. It had been a long trek from Mersa Matruh.

10

Nimmukwallah

I am *nimmukwallah,* as we say in the East; that is, I have ate of the King's salt, and, therefore, I conceive it to be my duty to serve with unhesitating zeal and cheerfulness, when and wherever the King or his government may think proper to employ me.
Arthur, First Duke of Wellington, 1769–1852, on being posted to command a brigade at Hastings on his return from India, 1806.

Our celebration of VE night was enlivened by the presence of some New Zealand aircrew, who had escaped from their prisoner-of-war camp. We had our own tame New Zealander in Harry Hart, who ran the YMCA canteen which had joined the brigade when it served with the New Zealand Division after El Alamein, and had stayed with us ever since. Maori songs and dances went on well into the night, while fusillades of tracer bullets lit up the sky. It was no night to venture out of doors. Within a few days we moved to the other side of Hamburg, passing through the rubble which was all that was left of the centre of the city. We should have felt sorry for the inhabitants, emerging from their cellars, like rabbits from their burrows, in search of a meagre ration of food, but I am afraid that few of us were so charitable. The general feeling was that they deserved their fate and had brought it on themselves. Celebrations of victory tended to continue indefinitely. I therefore issued an edict that they must cease, and that a cocktail party at my headquarters, which was installed in a house belonging to a rich ex-Nazi in Blankenese, would be the final party to end all parties. It was a prolonged, noisy and riotous occasion, attended by all the officers of the brigade. My medical officer and I were the only ones to put in an appearance at a reasonable hour for breakfast next morning. I asked why he looked so worried. 'You remember that fight which took place between officers of 4th RHA on the balcony and The Greys, who climbed up to attack it,' he replied. 'Well, one of The Greys had a stone urn dropped on his head, which took a bit of his ear off. I had to sew it on again, and I have a nasty feeling that I sewed it on the wrong way round.' 'What are you going to do about it?' I said. 'Oh, I'll just have to wait a few days until I take the bandage off.' When he returned from visiting The Greys a few days later, he was his usual cheerful self. It was the right way round.

We soon moved again, to Ascheberg on the shore of the Plöner See in Schleswig-Holstein, where the officers lived in a country house by the lakeside. Our main task was to exercise control over the large number of German soldiers and airmen, as well as some sailors, who had surrendered, most of them having been driven west by the Russians. It was a satisfactory experience to have two very senior German generals under my command and to give them stern orders. On the whole they were only too eager to comply, their troops being concentrated in enclaves on the coast until the process of demobilization could be put in hand. Each of my units was responsible for supervising one or more of these enclaves. Life soon assumed a pleasant, relaxed character. A German remount depot at Neumunster produced a horse for me, a barrel-shaped, dock-tailed animal which I christened Marshal. Although nothing to look at, he would have made an excellent hunter, always game to tackle a tricky obstacle, of which there were plenty, the fields of Holstein being bounded by banks, like those in Ireland. I also acquired a second, very different animal, which I named Julius: a large, good-looking horse, over sixteen hands, tubed and highly strung. I had seen a sergeant of 44th Royal Tanks trying to ride him in a jumping competition, and grossly maltreating him when he refused a jump. I therefore told Gerry Hopkinson that he was not fit to ride him, and took him in hand myself. Corporal Job, one of my drivers who was an expert groom, and I took four months to calm Julius down, and another two before I could take him into the show ring. By that time horse-shows were well established, as were hunter trials, run in pairs and timed. I usually rode Julius in the former and Marshal in the latter. Horse racing was not allowed, as going too far when most of the Germans were on a near-starvation diet.

While enjoying this free and easy life, much of it spent in outdoor sporting activities, I had to think about what the future held for me. Peter Scott, my intelligence staff officer, suggested that I should join him in the Provincial Insurance Company, the chairmanship of which he would inherit from his father. I considered the offer carefully. If I were to stick to my original intention of regarding service in the army as merely temporary, here was a chance to start a new career. But I did not feel that an office life, spent in playing with money, and particularly one which was closely connected with Manchester, was what I wanted to do. I also felt a strong sense of obligation to the army. By chance I had come through the war unscathed, having achieved a rank and acquired a comprehensive experience of military matters well beyond the normal for my age. I considered that I had a duty to the army and to the nation to see that what I had to offer was not wasted. I recalled the words of the Iron Duke, quoted at the head of this chapter, and decided to soldier on, fully realizing that I should soon have to come down in rank, although, I hoped, not by too many steps. A gloomy deputy military secretary gave all the officers a talk, explaining that the army would soon have to start this process. 'You wouldn't like to spend the next ten years as a brigadier, would you?' he said to me. He seemed surprised when I replied: 'Well, I'd rather spend them as a brigadier than as a major!' In fact I was left in command of the brigade for longer than any other commander, as the Territorial Army units were run down and the army began to be based on regular units only, although the junior officers and soldiers were very largely national servicemen. In the course of this transformation, we were moved round, taking over areas which had previously been the responsibility of divisions; first to Flensburg, then to

Münster in Westphalia, to Walsrode in Hanover and finally to Lüneburg.

Midsummer's eve of 1945 in Copenhagen was a memorable occasion. Soon after the end of the war 2nd KRRC had been sent to Aarhus in Denmark to guard a German cruiser, tied up there. They quickly established very friendly (one could with truth say intimate) relations with the Danes, and managed to arrange for one of their companies to provide the guard on the Royal Palace in Copenhagen on this great celebration of liberation. Christopher Consett (who had returned a fortnight before VE Day) asked my permission to send a lorry to Rheims to collect champagne for the dance they intended to give at Wivex's restaurant. This was against all the rules, and I refused. Christopher sent it all the same, and invited 'Bubbles' Barker, now commanding 8 Corps at Plön, and myself. It was a splendid occasion, which I disgraced by tripping up and falling over when waltzing with Princess Anne of Bourbon-Parma (later wife of ex-King Michael of Romania), then a lance-corporal in the French PFAT – *personnel feminine de l'armée de terre*. In September 1946 I took leave and spent two weeks of it with Antony and Elizabeth in Spain. He was the air attaché and we travelled round in his staff car, visiting Toledo, Granada, Ronda, Seville, Salamanca and Avila, most of the trip being combined with his official visit to Gibraltar. It was a cultural feast after the deprivation of the war years, and I lapped it up. I had always admired the great Spanish painters, El Greco especially, and his 'Burial of the Count of Orgaz' in the church of Santo Tomé at Toledo impressed me as his supreme masterpiece. Entering Gibraltar from the vast open spaces of Spain gave me an instant feeling of claustrophobia, accentuated by our reception at the Rock Hotel. We had stopped to bathe on our way from Ronda, and arrived at the hotel looking very untidy, just as many correctly dressed officers and their wives entered for a cocktail party. They had assumed that the staff car must hold some senior officer, and looked down their noses at us with disdain. I pitied my grandfather for having had to spend his life there, but revised my opinion when we dined with the delightful Spanish diplomat who lived in the house, Monte de la Torre, between Gibraltar and Algeciras, where Ernesto Larios, who married my father's sister Emmie, had lived. Her daughter, Sylvia, who had stayed with us at Ticklerton before the war, was living in a flat in the stables, and we were delighted to see her again.

The winter of 1946–7 was a very severe one. The Elbe was frozen over and our main sporting activity at Lüneburg was shooting, including wild boar which were roaming the area in considerable numbers. In an attempt to get the army back to pre-war standards of efficient administration from the easy-going habits into which we had drifted, I instituted strict and thorough administrative inspections of all my units, almost all of which had their comic side, when some horror was discovered, like the dead hare hanging in a barrack-room cupboard of 2nd Royal Tanks. 'What's that?' was my unimaginative comment. 'It's a ha- ha- ha-' stuttered Tony Lascelles, their commanding officer, as we all collapsed into laughter. A disastrous inspection of the 7th Hussars, culminating in the basin in which I was washing my hands before lunch emptying the water all over my trousers, and one of the 1st Rifle Brigade, commanded by Vic Turner, VC of El Alamein fame, in which the fog was so thick that, from the inspecting officer's dais, I could see nothing at all of the parade, were other instances.

But all good things come to an end, and, early in the New Year, I was told that I was to hand over the brigade to a cavalryman, Rex de Winton, and take up a lieutenant-colonel's job in the Fighting Vehicle Directorate of the Ministry of Supply in London. It was with no little emotion that, on 14 February 1947, two weeks after I had reached by time promotion the permanent rank of major, I left the brigade that I had commanded for over two and a half years, The Greys and 4th RHA being the only units that remained of the ones over which I had assumed command in Normandy. London in February 1947 was a cold, grim place, all the colder as the country was in the grip of a fuel crisis. My first problem was where to live. After a few weeks in my club, the United Service or Senior, feeling rather depressed and lonely, I took a service flat in Knightsbridge, which I shared with my brother Paul. His ship had formed part of the fleet which the Royal Navy contributed to finishing the war with Japan. He had returned via Australia to his pre-war job with Barclay Perkins's brewery in Southwark, and had been living in Chelsea as a paying guest with a spinster cousin of my mother's, Anne Dalby. From that Knightsbridge base I had to create some sort of social life for myself, starting from scratch, the few months I had spent in England in the previous nine years having revolved round Elizabeth Pollock. Female company in Germany had been limited to officers of the ATS, later to be known as the WRAC, one of whom had caught my fancy for a time. I had sentimental memories of dancing far into the night in Madrid with Consuelo Linares-Rivas, and I still corresponded with Anne of Bourbon-Parma, but none of those attachments could be regarded as serious. A fellow paying guest of Anne Dalby's, when Paul was there, had been Elizabeth Lowry-Corry. Paul had been invited to her home for a dance in Suffolk and had mentioned to me that, if I got an invitation there, I should not miss it.

One day in April Paul was out and I was in my bath when the telephone rang. It was Anne Dalby. She said that Elizabeth Lowry-Corry and her sister Edith were looking for a partner to go with them to a debs' dance. Was I free? Debs' dances seemed to be rather out of my line and I had actually undertaken to take someone else to the cinema that evening, but, mindful of Paul's advice and not being madly keen on the cinema companion, I accepted. It was to prove the most momentous decision of my life. I duly presented myself in white tie and tails at the door of the flat in Quebec Mews which the two sisters shared. Elizabeth opened the door and ushered me into a narrow dark passage, leading to a steep flight of stairs. At the head of them was the loveliest girl I had ever seen. It was love at first sight with a vengeance. After dinner in the flat, Martin Renner making up the party, we went off to the dance given by Victor Goodman for his daughter at Hurlingham. Edith turned out to be all I had hoped, and she naturally did not take it seriously when I proposed to her as we parted on her doorstep. From then on I paid assiduous court, while she kept me on tenterhooks, first going off on a holiday to Switzerland and then taking a job as a housing manager in Lancaster. By the summer I was becoming impatient, but was encouraged by being asked to spend the August bank holiday weekend at her home at

Edwardstone. There, in the corner of one of her father's fields, the 14-acre, she finally said, 'Yes', and my cup of happiness was filled, to be constantly replenished, even to overflowing, in all the years since then.

My mother was not pleased. I cannot imagine why, except that she had her own fantasies about the paragons she hoped her sons would marry. A lunch I gave at Quaglino's for parents and parents-in-law to meet was a sticky affair, as I suspect most such encounters are. My parents had left Ticklerton and were living as paying guests with my mother's cousin, Archie Bell and his wife May, at Pendell Court, from which they all moved to Uvedale Lambert's house, South Park, the other side of Bletchingley, while Uvedale and Melanie were in America. Fortunately my father gave Edith a warm welcome, as did May and Archie. Their son, Willie, had become engaged to Belinda Dawson shortly before us, and I had bought Belinda's car from her when they married, a rather battered open Ford 10. Our wedding was fixed for November at Edwardstone, and my next concern was to find somewhere for us to live after that. That was no easy matter in London in those days, especially if one had little capital. Although my pay during the war, and until I left 4th Armoured Brigade, had been good for somebody of my age, and I had had little to spend it on, I had handed over most of my savings to my parents, my father having practically no income once he had given up his Home Guard job. I suppose I had amassed about £2000 for myself. I found that, by the time one had paid 'key money', that did not go far, and I began to wonder if I should ever find a flat fit to start our married life in. Eventually I found a maisonette above a wholesale grocer's shop at 268 Brompton Road. It was immediately above where the Circle and District Line underground breaks out into South Kensington station, the whole place trembling as the trains passed underneath every two minutes. The entrance was part of the shop and often blocked with goods and dustbins. Below us, and above the shop, was another flat, occupied by two cheerful working men and their female companion, perhaps the wife of one of them, who seemed to spend much of their time repairing motor-cycles in the flat. I had to pay £1500 for the 'key' and the contents, the bare minimum of furnishings; but the rent was very low and therefore 'controlled'. Edith approved, and I moved in about a month before the wedding, cooking some curious concoctions for myself.

It was a blustery, rainy day on 22 November 1947 when I waited, with Paul as my best man, for Edith to arrive on her father's arm, having only a few hundred yards to travel to St Mary's church from Edwardstone Hall, her home, where the reception was held, our health being proposed by my father-in-law's senior tenant farmer, Mr Younger. We had originally intended to spend our honeymoon in Spain, but currency for foreign travel had been cancelled, and we went instead to a small country hotel in Devon. It was not a success. The hotel was full of old people; there was not much food and nothing to do. I had a day's hunting on Dartmoor, but that was no fun for Edith. After trying another hotel near Torquay, which was even worse, we decided to cut the honeymoon short and get into our own flat in London, heaving a sigh of relief as we settled in there.

This exciting time, from a personal point of view, was superimposed on a very frustrating experience in the Ministry of Supply. My predecessor, 'Fay' Compton, had left before I arrived, and I found it very difficult to discover what I was meant to do. The Fighting Vehicle Directorate was the department of the Ministry which coordinated the research into, and the development and production of all vehicles for all three services, but principally, of course, for the army. In those days of post-war controls and rationing, it was also the government department that 'controlled' and generally sponsored the motor and associated industries. It was a huge, unwieldy bureaucracy, which had mushroomed during the war, and had absorbed the Ministry of Aircraft Production, which, as the air side, remained virtually independent. I had been given to understand that I had been posted there so that my experience as a 'user' could contribute to the design and development of future tanks; but I found that it was in the War Office, in the Armoured Corps Directorate, of which Pip Roberts was then the head, that 'user opinion' was crystallized. My branch, the coordinating branch of the Fighting Vehicle Directorate, was no more than a post office between the War Office, the Fighting Vehicle Development Establishment at Chobham and the production branches, each of those three elements doing their best to deal directly with each other rather than through me, which was, in most cases, the more efficient way of doing business. My immediate boss, Brigadier Willie Blagden, was of little help to me. He was a technical expert on wheeled vehicles, devoting almost all his attention to them, and a good deal of it to trying to convince people that they could do all that tracked vehicles could do and more. He was responsible for the basic design of the future Saladin armoured car with its derivatives, including the Saracen armoured personnel carrier. But he moved in his own circle, never letting me know what he was doing and not caring what I did, as long as it did not interfere with his activities. I often got the impression that he would have preferred me to do nothing. The head of the directorate was Major-General Charles Dunphie, a very able and charming cavalryman, who had started his service career as a cadet in the Royal Navy, transferring to Woolwich to become a gunner, before moving on to the cavalry. He also moved in his own circle, dealing at major-general level with the Director of Weapon Development and the arms directors in the War Office. The former was Frankie Festing, an incongruous appointment. There seemed to be no system by which people knew what others at different levels were proposing or doing. In theory my branch was supposed to provide that service, but every other branch at every level was determined to withhold information for fear that somebody else would interfere, and stop them doing what they wanted to do. The load of paperwork was huge, most of it technical, which I was totally unqualified to understand. Unlike clerks in the army, the civil service ones took not the slightest interest in the contents of the files: they were merely manipulators of paper. I had to read vast piles of paper to discover what, if anything, was relevant, instead of having it neatly 'flagged' for me, as it would have been by my chief clerk on a military staff. Things improved in some ways when 'Fish' Fisher, who had commanded 2nd Armoured Brigade at El Alamein, succeeded Blagden when the latter went to head the wheeled vehicle department at Chobham. The improvement, however, was counter-balanced by the replacement of Charles Dunphie, who went to join Vickers, of which he was later to become chairman, by Major-General

Clayton. The latter was a dull, characterless gunner, who had been promoted all the way on the technical staff, but knew nothing about fighting vehicles. He was a dead loss.

Frustrating as it all was, it was good for me. I had not used my brain in an analytical way, tackling a heavy load of paper, for a long time. I had to learn to understand the technical subjects I was dealing with, the short prewar course at the Military College of Science, plucked from the recesses of my memory, proving useful. I had to concentrate on extracting the relevant from a mass of material, and then analyse it. In the course of doing so, I came to question many of the assumptions that I and others had made about the relative quality of our own and the German tanks, and the causes of the inferiority of which we had complained. It had generally been assumed that we had been badly let down by our techni-cal experts, both in design and in production, particularly on the gun side. I discovered, however, that generally speaking gun design had been ahead of the demands of the 'user', of the ability of tanks to accept them, and of the willingness of all concerned to risk a break in production to introduce a new gun. In addition 'user opinion' had fluctuated between demand for high armour-piercing performance and high-explosive. capacity, the latter predominating whenever the concept was prevalent that it was not the task of the tank to fight other tanks. The fundamental fault, which bedevilled British tank design and production throughout the war, had been the prewar concept that two different types of tank were needed: one type in which mobility was the prime requirement, the other where protection was paramount. The right answer would have been one tank, in which fire-power was given priority over both those characteristics. The pressing needs of production to replace losses and to supply Russia were a strong factor working against any major change in basic design, the ridiculous position being reached in 1943 that 75 per cent of all British tanks pro-duced were obsolete and never used as tanks in action, our forces having to be equipped principally with the American Sherman instead.

My analytical studies were greatly assisted by editing a paper on fighting vehicles for the Commonwealth Advisory Committee on Defence Science. When the committee called

for this, Eddie Masters, Chief Engineer of the Development
Establishment at Chobham, said that all his staff were far too
busy to produce such a paper. Under pressure he agreed that
I could produce it as a result of discussions with the heads
of all the design branches concerned, provided that they
approved of what I had written about their speciality and
that he approved the complete paper. It was an invaluable
experience. I would interview and question the branch head,
and then go away and write a section, which I would submit
to him. In that way I greatly added to my own knowledge
and clarified my ideas (as well, I like to think, as clarifying
his). The final paper was well received, and it gave me great
pleasure, on a visit to Chobham as Chief of the General Staff
in 1972, when the then Chief Engineer, David Cardwell, laid
the paper on the table. These and other studies, including
an important one on how much fuel and ammunition a tank
would normally consume during an average battlefield day,
should really have been undertaken by the 'user' branch, the
Royal Armoured Corps Directorate, where Harry Arkwright
had succeeded Pip Roberts, who, to our general dismay, had
retired at the age of only 43 and joined a firm of biscuit
manufacturers. But the classic method of arriving at 'user
opinion' within the army was to circulate the question down
the chain of command to all units, the result of which was
to accept the majority view. The latter almost invariably represented the generally accepted assumptions, the validity of
which had not been seriously analysed or challenged. In this
work I had naturally referred back to events in the desert.
Now that the full technical details of the tanks and anti-tank
guns of both sides were available, and I had access to the trials
carried out at the weapon proving ground at Shoeburyness,
which had tested both the guns and the armour, I realized
that the cry that we had always been outgunned and out-
armoured, and that that had been the main cause of our
defeats, was not altogether true, certainly not during the
Crusader battles of 1941. This led me to re-examine the
course of those battles from all the material I could gather,
which I brought together in a series of articles in the *Royal
Armoured Corps Journal* under the title of 'Desert Dilemmas'.
They caught the eye of the editors of the South African
Official History, Messrs Agar-Hamilton and Turner. As a

result we entered into a voluminous correspondence about
the battles of 1941 and 1942, in which the South Africans had
taken part. They had access to the captured war diaries of the
Panzerarmee Afrika, and both their and my understanding
of those battles was significantly enhanced by our exchange
of views. Their work resulted in two excellent books, *The Sidi
Rezegh Battles 1941* and *Crisis in the Desert.**

My regular contribution to the *Royal Armoured Corps Journal*
nearly brought me a court martial. In those days book reviews
were anonymous but, for some unknown reason, the editor, a noted naval historian, Lieutenant-Commander Peter
Kemp, appended my initials to a review of Monty's book *El
Alamein to the Sangro.* This had been largely written by David
Belchem, Monty having added a touch and his characteristic
punctuation here and there. It had been printed by the army
printing service and circulated by them when Monty was still
in Germany in January 1946, when he had given me a copy.
Now, when he was Chief of the Imperial General Staff, it
was published by Hutchinsons at a high price. I commented
that it was very much an official account from the point of
view of the commander, and that, considering that it had
been officially produced a few years before, it was a high
price to pay for a short book. Brian Wyldbore-Smith was
Monty's military assistant at the time and showed the review
to his master. Monty took offence and wrote a minute to the
Director of Military Intelligence, asking him if, in accordance
with King's Regulations (which said that an officer must get
permission to publish anything he wrote arising out of his
official duty), I had submitted the review for approval; and,
if I had, why it had been approved. The DMI, to his relief,
found that I had not – I would not have thought of submitting
a book review, which in any case I expected to be anonymous
– and passed the file to the Vice Adjutant General, saying that
it was a breach of King's Regulations. The latter passed the
file back to the CIGS's office, confirming this and saying that
it was a clear case for court martial. By that time Monty had
calmed down, as well as no doubt realizing that he would not
come well out of a decision to court-martial me. He passed
the file to the Director Royal Armoured Corps with a minute

* Oxford University Press, 1957 and 1952.

saying: 'You will interview Lieutenant-Colonel Carver (whose real rank I believe to be Captain) and tell him that a junior officer is not allowed to criticize the head of the army. If either he or I retires he can write what he likes. I intend to write a good deal!' Harry Arkwright sent for me and showed me the minute, both of us having a good laugh over it.

Articles and book reviews for the *Royal Armoured Corps Journal* were not my only literary activity. The Greys had commissioned a retired major of the Royal Tank Regiment, Eric Sheppard, to write their regimental history from the end of the First to the end of the Second World War, but were dissatisfied with the draft of the first chapter and had cancelled the commission. Tim Readman, now their Colonel, asked me if I would take it on. I was glad to help them and to have something other than my rather frustrating office work to occupy me. I soon discovered that the material available was very thin, the regiment's records and war diary having been dilatorily compiled. The fact that I had been with them, both in 7th Armoured Division and 4th Armoured Brigade, throughout almost the whole of their active service in the war was a great help. I completed it in 1950 and it was published privately by the regiment, printed by McCorquodales of Glasgow in 1954 and entitled *Second to None*, their regimental motto. I enjoyed the experience of writing my first book, which was well received.

A further study which I initiated in the Ministry of Supply was of some significance. The War Office's policy for its future vehicle fleet seemed to me, and to many in the production branches, to be totally unrealistic. Impressed by the difficulties caused to the repair and spares organizations by the large number of different types of vehicle with different engines, by the problems of special modifications required for different climatic conditions, and by the problem of waterproofing before an amphibious operation, the War Office had specified a specially designed range of vehicles with all-wheel drive, equipped with a standard range of Rolls-Royce-designed engines, varying from a 4-cylinder version for the Nuffield 'Champ', which was to replace the Jeep, to an 8-cylinder for the 10-ton truck. All these vehicles were to be capable of operation at all heights from sea level to over 10,000 feet in climates from Arctic to tropical. They would have no, or only very limited, commercial application. As the War Office at that time was planning for a large wartime army, the wartime requirement would far exceed the peacetime one. Not only would the government pay the full costs of development, but they would meet the capital cost of production equipment and of providing shadow factories for wartime production. The cost of re-equipping the army with these vehicles would be astronomical. I sympathized with the view of the motor industry that, unless the services accepted militarized versions of commercial vehicles for their transport fleet, there was no hope of producing them at an acceptable cost, nor of producing them at all in war. The War Office's policy had already led them to turn down Rover's offer of the Landrover at £450 per vehicle with no development costs and no contribution to capital costs of production. After driving in one, Festing was firm in declaring that it was not acceptable as a military vehicle, as it was too difficult to get in and out of. The Austin 'Champ' was preferred. This conflict of views led me to study how the army's needs had been met during the war. I discovered that a large proportion of our wheeled vehicles had been made in Canada and the USA, fortunately ordered before the need to expand their armies had arisen, and that, if the great bulk of our and their armies had not been inactive until late in 1943, some time after wartime production had started, they could never have been equipped to an adequate scale at all. Finding the War Office adamantly resistant to my arguments, I gave a short paper to John Cowley, ex-AA & QMG of 7th Armoured Division, who was then on the Defence Research Policy Staff under Professor Sir Henry Tizard. Not long after this the War Office was forced to see sense by the demands of the Korean War. In a matter of months, Vauxhalls, Rootes Brothers and Nuffields had produced militarized versions of their commercial vehicles as the general army work horse, the 3-ton lorry. These were run against each other in a prolonged test on the cross-country track at Chobham. Vauxhall's Bedford truck won the contest and served the army well for very many years thereafter.

In February 1949 I paid my first visit to America to participate in an Anglo-American-Canadian standardization conference. The Ministry of Supply party crossed first-class

in the Cunard Line's *Queen Mary*. It was very rough and I
was foolish enough to attend early communion service on
Sunday morning, the day after we sailed. I was prostrated
with sea-sickness, from which a kindly steward rescued me
by introducing me to Kwells sea-sickness pills. The skyline
of New York, as we approached, did not disappoint my
expectations, and I was fascinated by the skill of the captain
as he turned the huge ship in the stream of the Hudson
River and brought her alongside without the help of tugs, the
crews of which were on strike. We took the train to Ottawa,
where we held discussions with the Canadians and visited
their armoured centre at Camp Bordon, before taking the
sleeper from Toronto to Washington, where we joined up
with the War Office team, led by Frankie Festing, for the
preliminary conference. From there we flew to Norfolk,
Virginia, the main conference being held across the James
River at Fort Monroe, the headquarters of General Devers,
Commanding General of their Continental Command, to
which Jim Hutton was the British Liaison Officer. Jim Alger,
who had been the US Liaison Officer at Chobham, was also
there. I had been commissioned by Edith to get her such
things as nylon underclothes, nightdresses and lipsticks,
which were unobtainable in Britain, and Stella Hutton and
Consuelo Alger gave me much useful advice on that subject,
with which I was as yet unfamiliar.

We did not find the Americans cooperative. They had
prepared their positions with voluminous briefs, from which
they were not authorized to depart. Their idea of standardization was that we should accept their position, although,
if we did that, they were not in many causes prepared to
be bound by an agreement. One example typical of that
attitude was the question of which side of the gun in the
tank the gunner should be. We had changed from the left
to the right during the war to standardize with them. We
considered that there were good reasons for sticking to that,
but, if they wanted to change, we were prepared to accept it,
provided that it would be binding on us both. They refused
to commit themselves. The Canadian attitude was that they
would accept anything that the British and Americans could
agree to, and they became very frustrated when we could
not. One of the hard-liners was Colonel Joe Colby of the US

Ordnance Tank Arsenal at Detroit. Over a bottle of Bourbon in my hotel bedroom, I asked him why he was being so difficult. 'At this stage, when we are in the very earliest phase of considering new designs,' he replied, 'I would be mad to agree to anything which tied my hands.' After that, there did not seem to be much point in trying. The armoured vehicle part of the conference (artillery was also being considered) was presided over by my old acquaintance Major-General Ernie Harmon, called back from retirement on his farm in Maryland for the purpose. Proceedings were suspended for a day while his most precious cow was calving, and we went off to visit Jamestown, Williamsburg and the battlefield of Yorktown. We also flew to the US Armored Center at Fort Knox for a weekend. Eventually agreement was reached that we would each produce a light, a medium and a heavy tank up to agreed maximum weights, equipped respectively with 76-, 90- and 120-mm guns; we never produced the light tank (at least not until the Scorpion much later), both produced a small number of the heavy type and then abandoned them, and our Centurion, already then in production, never carried a 90-mm gun, its 20-pounder having a calibre of 83mm, and later being replaced by a 105-mm, which the Americans adopted. Our Chieftain did eventually have a 120-mm, but Americans showed no sign of taking that. My experience at that conference made me treat attempts to standardize with the Americans with considerable cynicism.

Before embarking on the *Queen Elizabeth* at New York, I visited the US Military Academy at West Point. The Superintendent handed me over to a 'plebe', a cadet in his first year, to tell me all about the place and what life for a cadet was like. Spartan, in every sense of the word, was the right description. It consisted of an application to the nth degree of the Prussian discipline to which army recruits, in varying degrees, are subjected. I found repugnant, as I have always done, the concept that the man's individuality has to be completely obliterated before he can be rebuilt into a soldier who will never question anything, allied to an intense and prolonged system of ritual initiation. The return voyage was also rough, but, protected by Kwells, I suffered no qualms. Most of the passengers, among whom was Randolph Churchill, kept to their beds. One afternoon I was sitting in the lounge, three Greek priests and one Frenchman being the only other occupants. I thought I saw a mouse, my suspicion confirmed by the excitement of the other four. We rang for the steward, who said it was impossible. We told him which chair it had gone under, and when he tipped it up, we all saw it again. Horrorstruck, he summoned the chief steward, who offered us all a free drink if we would keep quiet about it. He explained that there was to be a dance that evening, and if the ladies knew there was a mouse in the room, they would refuse to attend, and the ship's reputation would be ruined. I asked him how he proposed to get rid of it. He said that, when everyone had gone to bed, he would track it down and then surround it with rolled-up wet towels, which a mouse would not cross, and summon the ship's cat. We accepted the drinks and swore to secrecy.

Although most of my work in the Ministry of Supply, especially the routine element, was very frustrating, and I hated working in an office in London, the three and a half years I spent there were happy ones personally, marred only by the death of my father in March 1948. Life in recent years could not have been very happy for him, although he never complained. He had always enjoyed physical activity, but this had been limited to walking, and that not far or fast. Although May and Archie Bell could not have been more considerate, it must have affected his self-respect to be a permanent lodger with no home of his own. Sad as it was, it may have been a happy release. My mother bought a cottage, converted from a stable, at Hever in Kent, where Paul joined her. About this time he left Barclay Perkins and joined the small family firm of J. T. Davies and Son, which managed pubs and had off-licences in London and the South of England.

Edith and I spent a holiday in the spring in Ireland, visiting her cousin Claud Proby, whose wife Patricia was a distant cousin of mine, her grandmother, Rowena Pearce, being one of the daughters of William and Cara Bell,* a sister of Archie. From them we went on to stay with Edith's uncle Jocelyn Proby at Arklow, undertaking a marathon ride on ancient Irish bicycles to visit Glendalough from there. In

* see p.3

the summer we spent a short holiday at Chartres, Edith's mobility being limited by her pregnancy. We fell in love with the cathedral and came to know intimately its lovely windows and striking statuary. In December Susanna was born in Bury St Edmunds hospital and christened at Edwardstone, where we were always welcome, when we wished to escape from London. My parents-in-law were wrapped up in all their activities in the county: unlike my mother, they were not possessive, although always affectionate and welcoming. It was a great boon to have a refuge in the countryside and one to which I could feel that, through Edith, I belonged in a secure and permanent way. My father-in-law, Henry Lowry-Corry, a grandson of the third Earl of Belmore, had been a regular gunner officer, retiring as a major and then commanding the local territorial gunner regiment. He had been captured at the fall of Tobruk in 1942, and had walked out of his prisoner-of-war camp near Piacenza in Italy at the time of the Italian armistice. He spent the winter of 1943–4 sheltered by the Italian resistance in the Northern Appenines. After two abortive attempts to rendezvous with a boat, sent from Corsica, he walked, guided by the resistance, through the German lines to the 92nd (Negro) Division US Army south of Spezia. It had involved an eight-day march of 60 miles as the crow flies, much longer in fact as it was all through mountains, a remarkable feat for a man of 57, lame from a wound in the First World War. My father-in-law was a modest, highly conventional and typical retired army officer and country gentleman. Both he and his wife, Betty, great-granddaughter of the first Marquess of Abercorn, whose intellectual interests were broader, were pillars of county life; of the church, the Conservative Party, the County Council, the Territorial Army and the like, all that my parents would have liked to have been, but never were.

In 1950 I was told that in September I would leave the Ministry and attend the six-month course at the Joint Services Staff College at Latimer. In anticipation of this, I took over from Freddie Mellor a furnished house in Amersham in April. Edith was pregnant again, and it was pleasant to escape from the cramped conditions of 268 Brompton Road and have a garden to look after and sit about in. Andrew was born there in September. The course was interesting and the company agreeable. I bicycled to work, finding that there were remarkably few days in the winter when the weather made it out of the question. Half-way through the course, the Military Secretary's branch asked us all what we would like to do next. My answer was a job connected with the training side of the army, to which I felt that my experience could contribute, but anything rather than a return to office life in London. About a month before the end of the course, I was told that I had been posted to a lieutenant-colonel's staff job in the secretariat of the Western Union Chiefs of Staff in London. This was a blow: the most urgent matter was to find somewhere to live. Edith's father had settled a modest sum of capital on her and the trust allowed us to spend up to half of it on a house. We were therefore limited to something in the region of £4,000, and found one, which we thought just acceptable, near Twyford in Berkshire. Before we made a firm offer, I checked with the man I was taking over from, who had told me that there was doubt about whether the job would continue, NATO being in the process of absorbing the Western Union Chiefs of Staff organization. An anxious week followed, in which the War Office firmly insisted that the job would remain and the Western Union secretariat said it might, but perhaps be transferred to Paris or Washington; but finally they agreed that it would not. Plans to buy the house were scrapped, and we went off with the two children to Edwardstone until my fate was decided. I occupied my time by removing the ivy from the church and repairing the drive. At last, in May, I was posted as AQMG (Plans) to the NATO Headquarters Allied Land Forces Central Europe, which had replaced the Western Union Headquarters that Montgomery had set up at Fontainebleau. I had mixed feelings about returning to 'Q' staff work, but we both liked the idea of living in France.

The headquarters was in the Cour Henri IV of the palace of Fontainebleau, and had previously been the French army *École d'application d'artillerie*. Under Western Union, Montgomery had been the Chairman of the Commanders-in-Chiefs' Committee, with Marshal de Lattre de Tassigny as the army C-in-C, Air Marshall Brook the air force one, and the French Admiral Lemonnier the naval C-in-C, although the fleets at sea were not his responsibility. The Land Force headquarters was organized on French lines, inter-service matters being dealt with by a typically British committee system, which mystified the French. When I arrived, it had officially been transformed into a NATO headquarters, subordinate to Supreme Headquarters Allied Powers Europe (SHAPE), which Eisenhower, as Supreme Commander, had established at Rocquencourt near Versailles, and to which Montgomery had transferred as his deputy. Our Commander-in-Chief in theory was Marshal Juin, but he was still in Morocco, and General Guillaume acted for him. The Americans had not yet joined us, and life in the Headquarters went on much as it had under Monty. We wore plain clothes, the idea being that a sudden influx of foreign officers in uniform might provoke communist protests. Hours of work were leisurely. This suited the French officers, as most of them lived in or near Paris, and the British also, as they found it difficult to take the work seriously. The chief of staff was a delightful, old-fashioned French Major-General de Lassus de St Génie with exquisite manners. Both verbal and written communications were much more formal than on a British staff, and it took me some time to accustom myself to the form of French staff papers, which had few, if any, numbered paragraphs and were therefore very difficult to refer to. I was *chef de section* (plans) in the *Quatrième Bureau*, that is logistics. The section consisted of a French lieutenant-colonel, Robert Le Lièvre, who understood very little English and was a charming, sensible and knowledgeable man, but no ball of fire, and a Belgian major, Marcel Rousseau, fluent in English, amusing, lively and able, who eventually became Quartermaster-General of the Belgian Army and a great personal friend. My superior, head of the *Quatrième Bureau*, was Colonel Cazenave, a highly efficient logistic staff officer, very sensitive to any suggestion that the British or Americans knew more about logistics than he and the French Army did. He never spoke or wrote English, although he understood it fairly well, and all my dealings with him had to be in French. All papers in the headquarters had to be translated into French and English. A few weeks after I had arrived, the Americans appeared on the scene, headed by a burly Major-General

Walter J. Muller, who became deputy chief of staff (personnel and logistics), responsible therefore for the first and
fourth Bureaux, the British Major-General Jim Martin, an
ex-Indian cavalryman, becoming his opposite number for
Operations and Intelligence, the third and second Bureaux.
American habits of work were soon imposed on us. We had
to wear uniform, start work earlier and curtail the long,
leisurely lunch hour at the officers' mess, which was so
dear to the French and Belgians, and to which the British
took no exception. Cazenave and Muller were soon at cross-
purposes. The latter had been Patton's 'G4' and conceived it
as his mission to impose standard American Army methods
on the alliance. He neither understood French as a language
nor appreciated their point of view in any respect. Instead of
using an official interpreter, Cazenave would take me along
when he went to see Muller, and I would then find myself the
go-between, while each harangued the other or, more often,
told me to tell the other something which was designed to
enrage him.
    Although I threw myself into the cause of the alliance with
enthusiasm, and enjoyed the challenge of doing most of my
work in French and collaborating with my French and Belgian and some of my American colleagues, I found the work
often very frustrating. Apart from the Muller–Cazenave
problem, there was none of the satisfaction, that 'Q' staff
work normally provides, of actually supplying the army's
needs. Our work consisted of devising logistic plans to meet
the operational plans of the 3rd Bureau. As logistic support
was in principle a national responsibility, our plans were even
more theoretical, if that were possible, than the operational
ones. We were much concerned with procedures and with
trying to organize the lines of communication so that the
different allied logistic systems were soundly aligned and did
not interfere with each other, and that the resources of the
continental countries, such as railways, ports and airfields,
were fitted into the allied plans. We had no power to insist
on anything. If national armies or ministries did not wish
to comply with our proposals, there was nothing we could
do about it.
    While getting a grip on my job, I had to find somewhere
to live. After a long search, I found a house, La Roseraie, in

the village of Féricy seven miles out of Fontainebleau on the other side of the Seine. It had been the village smithy, was sparsely furnished and had no indoor lavatory. However, Monsieur Normand, the farmer-owner, agreed to reduce the rent to cover the cost of installation, which was carried out efficiently with remarkable speed by the local builder. Once this was done, I moved in under the eagle eye of Madame Avezard, the butcher's wife across the road, and received a friendly welcome from my neighbours, who included two old half-English widows, Madame Mack and Madame Walker. Edith and the family arrived in July, and I was relieved that she liked the house, where we were to be very happy. We were then the only foreigners in the village and soon found ourselves very much at home in it. Brigadier John Hunt,* who later led the first successful Everest expedition, lived at Héricy, the next-door village. He was entitled to a staff car, which I was not, and gave me a lift daily to and from the office. Picnics in the forest of Fontainebleau and visits to local sights, like the chateaux of Vaux-le-Vicomte, Farcheville and Provins, provided pleasant weekend activities, and I was kept busy in the garden, which had been neglected for some time. The *Centre National du Sport Equestre*, run by the French army, was established in the stables of the palace of Fontainebleau and kindly let British officers ride some of their horses, the commandant paying us the compliment of saying that '*Les officiers britanniques n'ont jamais abimé un cheval.*' This made it possible for me to hunt on Saturdays in the winter, when various hunts came to Fontainebleau to chase their particular quarry, deer or wild boar, in the forest. It was a different sport from hunting in England. There was never anything to jump, unless one was lucky enough to find a fallen tree, and a kill meant the end of hunting for that day, being followed by an extended ceremony, called the 'curée', at which the kill was reenacted, while champagne was drunk and compliments paid to the courage of the rich or aristocratic ladies, dressed in their tricornes and gold lace. It was very much a snob, social affair, but provided an opportunity for galloping along the rides of the beautiful forest.

---

* Later Lord Hunt.

I was in my office one Saturday morning, dressed for the chase, when I was summoned to a meeting with some US Air Force officers, who had come from their headquarters at Wiesbaden to discuss possible enemy logistic targets to be attacked in war, for which my advice was required. They were in uniform and greeted my entry with looks of astonishment and alarm. 'It's all right,' said a Belgian colleague, 'he is the representative of the Luxemburg air force!'

In April 1952 we attended Paul's wedding in London to Penelope Bleaker, after which we left the children with a nurse at Edwardstone and set off by car on a holiday to Italy, visiting Avignon on the way. Our journey took us to Pisa, Florence and Siena on the way to Rome, returning by Assisi, Perugia, Bologna, Parma and Asti before crossing back into France by the Mont Cenis pass, which was just open. It was a gargantuan feast of art galleries, churches and general sight-seeing, which we devoured with great enjoyment and no feeling of indigestion. The general atmosphere of Italy in spring added to our appreciation of its beauty. After Paul's marriage my mother stayed in her cottage at Hever for a few years, and then moved to one in Chilmark in Wiltshire, close to Tisbury, where we had lived in 1917, for the countryside of which she had retained a great affection.

In 1952 I crossed swords again with George Hatton, who was then the Major-General in charge of Administration at the headquarters of the British Army of the Rhine, of which John Harding was the Commander-in-Chief. Until NATO was established, both the American and the British armies in Germany had been organized purely as occupation troops, the former supplied through Bremen, the latter through Hamburg. At this time they were being reorganized into operational formations, prepared to face the threat of a Russian invasion of West Germany. The Americans were in the process of establishing a land line of communication from their occupation area in Southern Germany back to the French ports of Rochefort and La Rochelle, but the British had no such plans, which made no operational sense. The French wanted us to create a supply line forward from Le Havre. The use of any port east of that made them suspect that we would abandon the continent before the threat reached France. Cazenave was particularly adamant that

nothing east of Le Havre would fit allied plans. Hatton
resisted all arguments, partly on the ground of cost, partly
that, logistics being recognized as a national responsibility,
it was no business of the alliance. This was completely unrealistic. To stay tied to Hamburg, or any German port, was
absurd in military terms, and any alternative had to be coordinated with the authorities of the 'host country', whether it
were Holland, Belgium or France. Hatton wished to keep
the choice and all negotiations purely in British hands and
refused even to discuss the matter with our headquarters. He
thought that my job was to press his view at Fontainebleau,
and was infuriated that, on the contrary, I was a strong
supporter of the alliance attitude. He complained to the
War Office that I was opposing their policy and demanded
that I should therefore be removed. I was summoned to see
the Quartermaster-General, Maurice Chilton. He was polite
and understanding. He told me that serious consideration
was being given to basing a supply line on Antwerp, but that
this was subject to obtaining the necessary finance, and that
the War Office was not yet in a position to start preliminary
negotiations with the Belgian government. I took the line
that coming clean with NATO about his intentions could
only help, but, as in so many other fields at that time,
Whitehall was intensely reluctant to admit that the alliance
could exert any form of influence or authority. In spite of
Chilton's understanding attitude, Hatton got his way. When
Montgomery at SHAPE was informed about the situation, I
am told that he said: 'Certainly, Carver should be removed.
I will have him on my own staff and promote him!' That is
what happened. In October 1952 I left Fontainebleau to take
over from George Cole as head of Montgomery's exercise
planning staff, being promoted to the temporary rank of
colonel. In many ways I was sorry to leave Fontainebleau.
It had been a very agreeable life, particularly off duty. We
had made many friends, three of whom we were to maintain contact with for many years thereafter: Tom Jones, an
American cavalry ex-Rhodes scholar, Marcel Rousseau and
Jacques Cavard, whose final appointment as a lieutenant-
general was to be the French military representative to the
NATO military committee. However the job had become
more and more frustrating, as the possibility of achieving

any concrete progress appeared to recede into the mists, and the prospect of working directly for Monty naturally seemed full of promise. We managed to take over, from an officer leaving SHAPE, the lease of the Villa Chantoiseau at L'Etang-la-Ville, near St Germain. It had been built as a summer week-end villa for Madame Spitzer, who lived in Paris, and it was perched on a steep hillside looking across the valley to St Germain. The rent was considerably more than that of La Roseraie – half paid in cash under the counter – but the allowances at SHAPE catered for that. Putting red tabs on my uniform again made me feel that the tide of my military career had turned.

11

Towards Great Persons

Towards great persons use respective boldness.
George Herbert (1593–1633),
The Temple: The Church Porch

The job at SHAPE, which I was to take over from George
Cole, was head of Montgomery's exercise planning staff. It
involved planning and running his annual study period for
the senior officers of NATO of which the first had been
held in 1952. The staff consisted of an American naval
aviator captain and a naval commander, an American air
force colonel, a French army lieutenant-colonel, two Belgian
majors and one British major. In addition to working up
the study period, misleadingly called a CPX (Command Post
Exercise), I was used by Monty as a sounding-board for his
ideas and for those that were fed to him by other people. I
had my first taste of this before I joined him. He was due to
have a discussion with Général de Brigade André Beaufre,
the brilliant Frenchman who headed the Interallied Tactical
Study Group, on the subject of what should be the tactical
doctrine for the allied armies. I was summoned to attend
it and to draft a talk, based on it, which Monty was due
to give to some military audience. He was pleased with the
result, which helped me to start on a good footing. The next
study period was due to take place in March 1953, and in
December George Cole and I accompanied Monty on a visit
to Portugal, where the Portuguese government put at his
disposal a fort at the mouth of the Tagus below Lisbon,
used as a VIP guest house. Lieutenant-Colonel Luis Pina,

then Portuguese military attaché in London and later head
of their armed forces, flew with us in the Dakota which the
RAF provided for Monty's exclusive use. On the flight Monty
quizzed him about the Portuguese armed forces. 'How do
they choose their generals?' he asked Pina. 'The brigadiers
go on a course, and those who come out top are made
generals,' he replied. 'Very curious method!' said Monty:
'Who teaches them?' 'Well, I was an instructor there myself,'
said Pina. 'You!' retorted Monty: 'You, a lieutenant-colonel,
taught brigadiers how to become generals! What did you
teach?' 'I taught strategy and the principles of war.' 'What
do you, a lieutenant-colonel, know about that?' Without a
moment's hesitation Pina replied: 'One thing I know about
strategy and the principles of war is that you don't discuss
them with Field Marshals,' to which the Field Marshal could
find no reply, the only time I knew him at a loss for one.

We shut ourselves up in the fortress, going through the
whole programme for the exercise, agreeing the theme,
selecting the speakers, or, in the case of some of the presen-
tations, the actors, and discussing all aspects. Our discussion
was interrupted by a lunch at which Monty unmercifully
bullied the Portuguese Minister of Defence, trying to force
him to lower the age of senior officers and to accept British officers as instructors at their staff and senior officers'
colleges. We spent one afternoon on the lines of Torres
Vedras and attended an embarrassing dinner at the British
Embassy, where Monty bullied the ambassador, a typical
Old Wykehamist bachelor, as unmercifully as he had the
Minister. As we drove away, he said: 'That man's useless. I
shall get on to Anthony (Eden, then Foreign Secretary) and
tell him he must be sacked.' George Cole and I pleaded that
he was just the sort of ambassador to suit Portugal, which
hardly justified a high-flyer; but Monty appeared relentless.
However he did not succeed in having him removed.

George and I went to the casino at Estoril one evening
and found the fortress locked on our return. However, we
managed to gain entry somehow, tip-toeing past Monty's
open window. Although brutally rude to the Portuguese, he
was cheerful, relaxed and friendly to us, and I learned much
from George about how to handle him. It was fatal to disagree
with him directly; but, provided that one could somehow

suggest that a different view from that which he had first put forward was one that he had suggested himself, he was quick to see the point and change his mind, if he had not already committed himself to another view before a wider audience. He gave clear decisions and instructions, and then left one completely free to get on with the business, referring to him only if one came up against solid opposition which no amount of pressure or persuasion through other channels had been able to remove. His position at SHAPE was an odd one. He took no part in the normal executive work of the staff, but acted as a sort of Inspector-General of the armed forces of the nations other than Britain and America. He paid visits to them, voicing his criticisms in his most direct fashion to their political and military leaders, who often greatly resented it. On his return to SHAPE, his recommendations would be circulated to the staff in a report, the main points being made by him personally to the Supreme Commander, who had to spend some of his time in calming those who had come under Monty's lash.

George Cole handed over to me after the visit to Portugal, and I was left on my own to prepare for the exercise. This involved keeping very senior officers up to scratch in submitting the texts of their talks in time to get them translated, rehearsing them in 'playlets', in which only the British senior officers were prepared to act, and finalizing all the administrative preparations required to deal with over 200 officers of three-star rank and above of twelve different nations. Running the exercise itself was a challenging experience. I sat at a table with Monty and had to keep a note of everything said in discussion, reminding him, as appropriate, of the points he wanted raised and by whom. This was fairly firmly stage-managed. In the intervals I dictated to my French or Danish secretary a summary of the main points of the session; and at the end of the day, I sent a summary to Monty who slept in his office at SHAPE during the exercise. He was still living in the Château de Courances near Fontainebleau over 40 miles away. The climax of the exercise was Monty's concluding talk, the only item on the last day. He had outlined the form of this in our discussions in Portugal in December, and I had produced a draft of it before the exercise had started. I had to submit the final draft on the

last evening, and it needed little change. It then became the
basis of almost all his lectures and speeches for the next
twelve months. The main theme of the exercise was the effect
of the use of atomic weapons on the operations of all three
services, and the need to revise our tactics as a result. The
general conclusion was that they made the old-fashioned
set-piece battle, both in the attack and the defence, out of
date, and that new organizations and methods to exploit the
weapon were required. Although lip-service was paid to the
effect of its use by the enemy, the overall consequences, both
to the armed forces and to the population of the countries
under attack, were undoubtedly underestimated by us all,
although considerable emphasis was laid on the problem of
handling refugees.

Before Monty had gone off on his annual skiing holiday at
the end of January, he had compiled my annual confidential
report. This is what he wrote:

I consider that this officer is outstanding for his rank.
In the late war I gave him command of an Armoured
Brigade when he was very young; I think he was under 30.
I must take the blame if it gave him a swollen head, which
I believe it did.

He is very ambitious and there is no harm in this so long
as it is kept within bounds. But before he can rise to heights
to which his gifts entitle him, he has much to learn.

He is widely read and has developed his military knowledge. But this alone is not sufficient; he must also develop human qualities, which at present he lacks. He must
broaden his outlook. And he must quite definitely be less
critical of other people, and must cultivate tact, tolerance
and discretion.

It is important for him to understand that the higher
the mountain the more fiercely blow the storms about it;
as he gains in rank he will need the support and sympathy
of others if he is to weather the storms. He will not get
that support unless he can learn to be less critical in his
general outlook.

This is a friendly hint to a very good officer. I took
Colonel Carver on my staff with full knowledge of his
make-up, and hoping that I could help him to navigate

some rough seas. I have the highest opinion of his ability. He has an attractive personality and I like him.

If he can take advantage of the hint he should do well in the Army and should rise to the highest ranks. He has had a good start and *could* be a future CIGS.

If he cannot benefit from the hint, but merely regards me as one of the many 'bloody fools' who stand in the way of his quick promotion to high rank, he will never succeed in his ambitions; he will without doubt run into trouble and will crash badly.

When he leaves my staff, it is my view that he should go direct to command a Regular Armoured Regiment for at least two years; he has to add to his experience the training of a unit in peacetime. I would then like to see him get command of a Regular Infantry Brigade for three years.

He should then go to the IDC, after which he should be given command of an Armoured Division.

I recommend that his future career in the Army is organized on these general lines.

I have given Colonel Carver a copy of these remarks as otherwise he might not see what I have said about him. I want him to read my remarks, and accept the hint!

The plan that the next step in my career should be to command a regiment again was accepted by me and, at that time, by everyone else, including John Harding who was now CIGS. I had mixed feelings at the prospect. I was longing to get my teeth into a real, rather than a theoretical, job again and welcomed the prospect of command and contact with soldiers once more; but reversion in rank for a second time and return to the social side of a regimental officer's life held no attractions, the latter very much the reverse.

Initial planning for the 1954 study period, CPX THREE, started immediately CPX TWO was over. Monty had been persuaded by the Commandant of the US Marine Corps that one of the main features should be the conduct of a major amphibious assault. I thought this totally inappropriate. Not only did I consider that, if the enemy had atomic weapons, it was out of the question to launch such an assault, but I could see no application of it within NATO, unless Europe, or an important part of it, had been overrun. However Monty had committed himself. I could not devise any scenario which did not have unacceptable political implications, and was therefore forced to invent an imaginary one. I took a section of the coast of East Germany and reversed it; but my troubles did not end there. The US Navy and the US Marines insisted that land-based aircraft had no part to play; but the US Air Force, backed by the RAF, refused to accept that. The scenario soon became a hotly contested US inter-service battle, the US Marines being prepared to fight all comers, including the US Navy, to preserve the pure essence of their doctrine. By inserting an island, the geography and distance from the shore of which determined the number of aircraft sorties that could be delivered from it, I made it possible to ensure that the number of sorties over the operational area was equally divided between carrier-based and land-based aircraft, the marines still insisting that the ratio should be one marine, one navy, one air force sortie. After that had been settled, Monty was due to go to Canada to open the Toronto trade fair, and the US Marine Commandant had unfortunately got Monty to agree that he could come to Canada to discuss aspects of the exercise, which he said could only be tied up at a high level. I warned Monty of the snags and begged him not to discuss anything if I were not there. He therefore decided that he would take me with him rather than his military assistant, Dick Keith-Jones, who had recently taken over from Dickie Sharples and had not yet established himself in Monty's confidence. However he was persuaded to change his mind by his chief of staff, Major-General Wansbrough-Jones. I warned him that the US Marine Corps would try and persuade him to alter the exercise setting to conform to their doctrine, and entreated him not to commit himself to any change as we should find ourselves in trouble with the other American services. My fears were justified. When the marines had photographed our model, they had taken an oblique picture, which made the crucial island appear further from the coast than it was intended to be. They tried to persuade Monty that I had therefore made an error in estimating the time which land-based aircraft could spend over the beaches, thus calling into question the value of air support that was not carrier-based. When Monty returned, he told me that I appeared to have made a miscalculation. It was not until we had a further conference with the marines that I detected the trick they had played. They gave in, when I threatened to sink one of the carriers by submarine attack if they did not work from the true model. This incident brought home to me the extreme sensitivity of inter-service relationships in the US armed forces. It seemed to determine their policies more than any other factor.

When I arrived at SHAPE General Ridgway had succeeded Eisenhower as the Supreme Commander. He was a grim, inflexible man, and Monty made little effort to maintain good relations with him, but was on excellent terms with General Laurie Norstad, the air deputy, and with Al Gruenther, the chief of staff, who succeeded Ridgway as SACEUR in July 1953. These two knew just how to handle Monty by a nicely judged balance of flattery and by-passing. Norstad, aided by Basil Embry, who had succeeded him as the air C-in-C at Fontainebleau, succeeded in converting Monty into being an advocate of centralized control of air forces. This alarmed the British Chiefs of Staff, particularly John Harding. After a lunch with Embry, Monty told me to write a paper supporting these views, which he proposed to send to the Chiefs of Staff. I also thought that Monty had gone too far, and, in drafting it, significantly altered the sense in the direction of preservation of tactical air forces to support army groups. Monty returned it to me with a note saying: 'You seem to have misunderstood me: I have therefore revised your draft.' When I read it through, I saw that, although he had altered the wording and the punctuation here and there, he had in fact climbed down and accepted the essence of the paper, but changes always had to appear to stem from himself.

Work on preparation for the exercise kept me very busy, but I was able to snatch some leave when Monty went to England for several weeks to brush up his equitation under the instruction of the Household Cavalry in preparation for Queen Elizabeth's Coronation. Edith and I took the children by car to Tamariu on the Costa Brava, recommended to us by Antony, driving through the Massif Central and seeing the sights on the way, including Puy de Dôme, Albi and Carcassonne. There were few other tourists and we had the small beach almost to ourselves. We listened to the radio commentary on the Coronation in French, beautifully done, while sitting in the hotel kitchen. Unfortunately it was the wettest June in Spain for a hundred years, and we left before the road leading down to the village collapsed.

While we were at SHAPE we were fortunate in making several good friends and finding some old ones. Among the former were Stuart and Anne Chant* and Ben and Harriet Harrell, both of whom also lived in L'Étang-la-Ville. Ben was to finish his career in the US Army as the NATO commander in South East Europe. Among the old friends were Ereld Cardiff, who was head of public relations, and Bernard Fergusson,† who was in the intelligence branch. Bernard and I shared the use of a tennis court in the grounds of a home in Versailles for children with weak hearts with Don Cook, Paris correspondent of the *New York Herald Tribune*. The sight of Bernard on the court in a very short pair of Palestinian shorts, a yachting cap and his eye-glass was enough to give any child a weak heart. Don and his wife Cherry were to remain good personal friends ever after. I had been introduced to him by Chester Wilmot, the Australian correspondent and author, whom I had known since he arrived in the desert in 1940 as the Australian Broadcasting Corporation's war correspondent with the 6th Australian Division. In January 1954 he was tragically killed, when one of the first Comet aircraft in commercial service broke up in mid-air off Italy.

Monty held his annual cocktail party for the staff of SHAPE at Courances in July, and I was somewhat taken aback when, arriving with Edith, he greeted us with the words, 'Oh, I didn't realize you were married.' This was a total contrast to his reaction when, in January 1954, I went to see him just before he went off on his annual skiing holiday. I had been approached by John Borthwick with the proposition that I might join his family meat business, Thomas Borthwick and Sons, in a job in New Zealand, with the prospect of being the head of it in that country. I had first met John when he had been on Hobo's staff in 79th Armoured

---

* Later Lady Sempill.
† Later Lord Ballanilae.

Division, and we had renewed our acquaintance when I had been in London. I was in two minds as to whether or not to consider the offer seriously, and was due to meet the chairman shortly. I might have to make my decision while Monty was away, and wished to warn him of this. Expecting a fairly sharp reaction, I was surprised when, for the first time in my knowledge of him, the protective shield which he always appeared to hold between himself and personal feelings fell. We sat down together at the table in his office, and the first thing he said was that I must think about it carefully from a family point of view. He described movingly the problems he had faced when he married Betty Carver (Hobo's sister) and, with nothing but his pay, assumed responsibility for her two boys. He then went on to say that I was not very popular in the army, but was highly regarded by those at the top, like himself, John Harding and John Crocker. These 'protectors' of mine would soon retire. I would then be on my own and others might have their knives out for me. If I were fully satisfied that I wanted the job and that it was in the interests of my family to take it, I might be well advised to do so. There would no doubt be protests from the War Office, but I could rely on him to deal with those. After that the shield went up. The only times I saw it lowered thereafter were when I took my leave of him at SHAPE and when he was bed-ridden in his old age. His implication that I could only survive with the help of 'protectors' immediately inclined me to stay in the army to prove him wrong. I made that decision in any case after I had met the chairman and sensed that the prospects of the job would not outweigh the disadvantages of exile to New Zealand. I never regretted it.

My time at Fontainebleau and SHAPE coincided with the start of a correspondence with Hobo that lasted until his death in 1957. After our row over the Rhine crossing, no communication had passed between us until, one day after the war, he turned up at my headquarters near Plön. He was open, friendly and welcoming, and made no reference to the row, but talked at length of how his career had suffered as a result of his intolerance and insubordination. He hoped that I would learn from his mistakes and watch my step. I was delighted to be able to bury for good and all my resentment at the way he had behaved. When Edith and I were in

London, he was Lieutenant-Governor of Chelsea Hospital,
where we were frequent visitors, falling in love, as everybody
did, with his delightful wife Dorrie. Hobo and I would have
long discussions about armoured warfare and other matters,
his lively and unorthodox mind posing a constant challenge
to one's assumptions. Our correspondence covered every
subject under the sun, from current political and military
affairs to the French and their literature, the Americans and
their crude habits, art and architecture, religion, dreams,
ghosts, and the failure of senior officers of the Royal Tank
Regiment to father sons. Fortunately for me, he kept all
my letters as I kept his, and Dorrie sent them to me after
his death, so that I have the complete correspondence.* In
spite of being a revolutionary in military matters, his views
on all other subjects were conservative. He despised the
Labour Party, poured scorn on modern art, architecture and
literature, and favoured ancient lineage and the inherited
privilege and sometimes wealth that went with it. His ideas
were not often original, but were provocatively put. He
enjoyed argument, as I did. My attitude to politics and
inherited privilege was more left of centre, but I sympathized
with his views on art and literature. Some of our exchange of
letters was concerned with the regimental history that Basil
Liddell Hart had been commissioned to write. This led to
correspondence between Liddell Hart and myself, and to
a triangular exchange in which each of us commented on
what the others had written. The issues which were the
subject of keenest discussion were the European Army,
the best organization for our forces on the continent, and
how they should fight. American pressure for the rearma-
ment of Germany had prompted the French Prime Minister,
Réné Pleven, to propose the European Defence Community.
Under it, an army was planned in which there would be no
national formation above the level of battalion. No sensible
soldier of any nation thought this a militarily sound solution
but, in default of any other proposal for rearming Germany
acceptable to the French, the USA and Britain supported it,
although we refused to join. Few of the members (France,
West Germany, Italy, Belgium, Holland and Luxemburg)

* It has now been deposited at the Tank Museum, Bovington.

showed any great enthusiasm for the project and all were dragging their feet, while the United States became more and more impatient, as the possibility of German troops contributing to the defence of Western Europe grew no nearer. Nobody had been more scornful of the project than Monty, and everyone was astonished when he told a group of British MPs on a visit to SHAPE that lack of progress was all Britain's fault for refusing to join. Chester Wilmot told me the sequel, the truth of which Monty confirmed to me many years later. He was sent for by Churchill, then Prime Minister, to see him at Chartwell. Winston castigated him for embarrassing the British Government by his apparent volte-face. Monty protested that he was an international soldier, not subject to the British Government. 'But we pay you, and I could sack you,' growled Churchill. 'If you sack me, I shall write my memoirs, and I'll say a good deal about you,' replied Monty. Churchill grunted and said no more. As soon as Monty had left, he telephoned Field Marshal Alexander, then Minister of Defence, told him what had occurred, and said: 'Which would be worse: to leave Monty where he is and risk a repetition of such incidents, or sack him and let him write his memoirs?' 'Oh, much worse to let him write his memoirs,' was Alex's immediate reply. In August 1954 the French parliament refused to ratify the EDC treaty, and Eden solved the problem by obtaining French agreement that Germany, through joining the Brussels Treaty, should become a full member of NATO, the condition being that Britain should maintain a force of four divisions and a tactical air force on the continent.

My views on how the army should be organized had been developing ever since I arrived at Fontainebleau, and had been refined as a result of several discussions with André Beaufre. He and Liddell Hart were inclined to favour a highly dispersed formation, organized on a basis of fives: five battalion-sized units in a small division, and five divisions in a small corps. Their arguments rested on the vulnerability to atomic attack of large concentrations; the effectiveness of the delaying tactics which the Germans had employed in the later stages of the war, when they had held up much superior forces with battle groups using offensive/defensive tactics on a wide front; and the desire to economize in headquarters. I considered that such formations would neither be effective in action, nor be adequately controlled, if every commander had five major subordinates. Both Hobo and Liddell Hart disliked the fact that NATO based its plan on defending the Rhine. They deprecated reliance on a river obstacle, encouraging a linear concept of defence, and cited as proof the ease with which Guderian had crossed the Meuse at Sedan in 1940, and the expertise of the Russians in such operations. Monty said that he agreed with my concept, which was that the river line should be used as a delaying line, manned by soldiers of the country through which it ran. Immediately behind that should be an empty area in which atomic weapons could be used against forces that had succeeded in crossing. In reserve behind that would be armoured divisions, which would-counter attack immediately after atomic weapons had been used. The divisions would consist of two brigades, each of two tank and two mechanized infantry battalions and one of artillery. Additional infantry brigades would be held as reserves on the scale of one per division. I am afraid that we gave little consideration to the fate of the unfortunate inhabitants of this atomic 'killing ground', other than to regard refugees as a serious hindrance to military operations. All of us were opposed to army organization being based primarily on the standard infantry division, as all NATO armies were, several additional such divisions being planned to be mobilized on the outbreak of war. Hobo, Liddell Hart and I were even more strongly opposed to the organization which the British army began to adopt a few years later, which abolished armoured divisions and distributed most of the tanks to all the infantry brigades.

My friendly relations with Liddell Hart, which had been cemented by a dinner in Paris at which General Siegfried Westphal, Rommel's former chief of staff, was also present, came under a cloud as a result of an article I wrote for the *Royal Armoured Corps Journal*, reviewing the Rommel Papers, which Basil edited. He took offence at a remark about 'his attempt to prove that the German generals, Rommel among them, owed their successes to his teaching', although it was intended to counter the accusation that he had devoted too much space to this. It was some time before I realized that his objection centred on my use of the words 'attempt to prove'. He insisted that it cast doubt on what was indisputable, and had been acknowledged by German generals themselves. Through the good offices of Hobo, the misunderstanding was cleared up and we resumed our normal friendly relations, which were to last all his life. As a footnote, it is of interest that the passage in the English edition of Guderian's *Panzer Leader*, in which he acknowledges his debt to Liddell Hart, does not occur in the original German text. The episode was typical of Basil's prima donna-ish sensitivity to any suggestion that his teaching or predictions on warfare had not always been correct.

January 1954 saw the return of the annual confidential report season. Before that, John Crocker, retiring as Adjutant-General, had opposed my reversion in rank to command a regiment. He argued that it would create a poor impression in the army to see someone, who had commanded a regiment successfully in war and then a brigade for nearly three years, revert in rank for the second time to command a regiment ten years after having first done so. John Harding had agreed with him, and they had told the Military Secretary to put my name before the selection board again. Meanwhile, after a lunch with General Richard Gale, then C-in-C in Germany, Monty had agreed with the latter that I should join his staff as Brigadier General Staff, and had so informed me. He then wrote my report, which he told Dick Keith-Jones to give me to read before he signed it, with orders that I should not initial it until he had done so. The Military Secretary, General Euan Miller, was coming to see him within a few days, and Monty was not going to commit himself finally until after that visit. This is what he wrote:

Last year I said that Colonel Carver would probably have to navigate some rough seas in his Army career and I gave him some friendly advice. He has now worked another year with me as head of the SHAPE Exercise Planning Staff, which job gives full scope to his fertile brain and imagination. I am more than ever confirmed in the view I expressed a year ago that Colonel Carver is a very brilliant officer. He has settled down well and has proved that he can hold in subjection certain faults that I outlined in my last report.

His work on my Exercise Staff has been beyond all praise. I like him and would take him on my staff at any time in a senior appointment. He has already shown that he is a first-class C.O. and Bde Comd in war.

Last year I recommended he should go to command an Armoured Regiment when he leaves SHAPE in May 1954. But he is 39 in April and I now cancel that recommendation. He should go from SHAPE direct to a Brigadier appointment. I recommend that this very gifted officer should go as BGS Operations and Training to a C-in-C, and for preference to Northern Army Group in Europe.

In the paragraph recommending my next appointment he wrote: 'BGS Ops & Trg in a C-in-C's command'. When he told the Military Secretary what he had agreed with Gale, Miller said that it was out of the question that I should go to a brigadier's appointment. The selection board had chosen me to go as deputy chief of staff to Bobbie Erskine, C-in-C East Africa, in the rank of colonel, and this had been approved by John Harding. Monty had to climb down, but, not to be defeated and forgetting that I had already seen the report, he inserted the words 'or deputy chief of staff' after 'Trg' and 'overseas' after 'command'. I was amused when I saw this, when the report was returned to me to initial. He had already informed me of the result of Miller's visit. At first I felt disappointed. In a letter to Hobo, I wrote:

I feel a bit insulted at having to deal with AQ of a force of a brigade or two after dabbling in intercontinental atomic strategy. At first I felt like fighting it, although I couldn't, of course, till I'd cleared up point 1 (John Borthwick's offer). However on reflection I see there are some compensations. I can take the family. I know and like Bobbie Erskine: Loony Hinde and Harry Thurlow, two other principals, are also old friends. I suppose that few other Colonel's jobs in the army are likely to carry a similar degree of independent responsibility. There is something active going on. It will give me experience of this colonial half-war, half-policing business.

Two events in my personal life coincided with this change in plans for the future, the most important of which was the birth of our second daughter, Alice, on 11 February in a clinic in Neuilly. She was born at breakfast-time, and by lunch-time Edith had received a magnificent bouquet, with a handwritten personal note from Al Gruenther. He never missed a trick, and was a delightful and impressive man to deal with. The other event was Antony's posting to the Allied Air Force Headquarters at Fontainebleau. He and Elizabeth moved into a house at Barbizon. Alice was christened in the Anglican chapel in Versailles, where Bernard Fergusson played the harmonium.

CPX THREE was held at the end of April and was voted a success. Monty was in his best form and everybody seemed to enjoy it, even the French, who generally showed little enthusiasm for such exercises and disapproved of any attempt to introduce a humorous touch. They considered that the defence of Europe was too serious a matter to be the subject of any levity. One must remember that they were facing grave problems in Indo-China, Dien Bien Phu being under attack at that time. There were two amusing incidents during the exercise. One of the problems under study was in the Mediterranean, and the floor of the hall was covered by a model of it. Monty was standing on it, blowing his whistle and ringing his bell to get everyone back to their seats. As Marshal Juin, dressed in old-fashioned uniform with breeches and field boots, passed him, Juin said in French in a low voice: 'What do you think you're doing there, standing on the sea? There's only one man who could do that and not sink, and you're not him!' Monty understood French better than he would admit. He turned to me and asked what Juin had said, and I told him. 'Tell him,' he said, 'that, although I may not be Jesus Christ, he's certainly the devil!' Needless to say, I did not. The other incident concerned a talk by General 'Nuts' McAuliffe, then commanding Seventh US Army. I tried to persuade him to delete a typical American joke from it, on the ground that jokes did not translate well, but he refused. My Turkish translator came to me and asked me what it meant. I explained that it was intended to be a joke. 'I can't make it funny in Turkish,' he said. 'Well, you'll have to make your generals laugh somehow,' I replied, and thought no more about it. McAuliffe spoke after lunch, and his talk was not one to keep his audience awake. He paused when he came to his joke, and the audience was roused from its somnolence by loud, well regulated laughter from eight Turkish generals. At the end McAuliffe said to me: 'See, you were wrong. Those Turks sure have a fine sense of humour!' I asked my translator what he had done. 'Quite easy,' he replied, 'I wrote into the Turkish interpreter's text: "Get slightly ahead of the speaker, and then say: Will all Turkish generals now please laugh." Being well disciplined men, they did!'

John Jervis-Read was to succeed me and had been present for the exercise and several weeks beforehand. I handed over to him immediately after it was over and said good-bye to Monty. The shield came down for a minute. He gave me the telephone number of his home at Isington Mill, and said that, if I ever needed his help, I was not to hesitate to call on him. He wished me good luck, shook my hand and up went the shield again. A few days later we packed the whole family into the car and crossed the Channel on our way to Edwardstone. I spent a month's leave based there, during which I spent a night aboard HMS *Centaur* of which Rodney was Commander Flying. He had been struck down by polio in 1950, but, by remarkable personal determination, had resumed flying on and off carriers again.

At the end of my leave, I flew on a trooping charter flight to Nairobi, Edith and the family to follow by sea, accompanied by the French governess we had engaged before we left France. Susanna had started lessons with a retired schoolmistress in L'Etang-la-Ville, and we thought it was a good idea that she should continue to be taught in French. Bobbie Erskine had invited me to stay with him when I first arrived, and had offered me the official General's house at Karen. He did not use it as it was considered too far out of the city and too near a small forest which could harbour Mau-Mau to be suitable for him. Lady Erskine had not accompanied him, and he was in a rented house near the Muthaiga Club. I arrived at 9 a.m. on the Queen's official birthday, having had little sleep on the flight, and found myself whisked off to watch the parade at Government House, followed by a sherry party there. To prevent me going to sleep after lunch, Bobbie insisted that we should play golf, which I had not done for 17 years. Needless to say, my play was erratic, one drive landing in the middle of a hard tennis court to the surprise of the players. On several occasions, venturing gingerly, for fear of snakes, into the long grass in search of my ball, I was met by a small boy offering to sell me one, an offer I accepted more than once. Having had a look at Flagstaff House at Karen, a pleasant house with an attractive garden and a glorious view of the Ngong Hills, I had no hesitation in deciding to live there, and set about engaging servants with the invaluable help of my personal assistant, Sue Lane, whose parents lived in Kenya and who therefore spoke Swahili fluently.

The command set-up in Kenya was curious. When the emergency was declared in October 1952, Colonel Geoffrey Rimbault, from whom I was taking over, had been chief of staff to Lieutenant-General Sir Alexander Cameron, General Officer Commanding East Africa Command. The command was subordinate to GHQ Middle East in the Suez Canal zone, and was responsible for military affairs in the colonies of Kenya, Uganda, Tanganyika, Mauritius, Seychelles, Northern Rhodesia and Nyasaland, the forces in the last two being handed over to the Central Africa Federation when it was formed in 1953. In 1952 there had been no army units from Britain in the command, only infantry battalions of the King's African Rifles and similarly recruited supporting units with African soldiers. One British infantry battalion had been flown to Nairobi from the Suez Canal zone when the emergency was declared. Cameron had then taken the lofty view that his wide responsibilities precluded him from concentrating on the affairs of Kenya, where, as in all colonies, the Governor was titular Commander-in-Chief. Evelyn Baring had only held that position for three weeks when he declared a state of emergency, his predecessor having left three months before. His appeal to London for a major-general to act as Director of Operations was answered by the despatch of Loony Hinde, although at first the War Office would only agree to him being called chief of staff to the Governor. He had considerable difficulty in asserting his authority and in getting the different departments of

the Kenya Government administration to act with vigour
and in harmony. John Harding, then CIGS, visited the
colony in February 1953 and realized that something more
on the lines of Templer's administration in Malaya was
needed. The result was the appointment of Erskine, from
Eastern Command in England, as Commander-in-Chief with
authority over all three services (the navy consisting of HM
East African Ship *Rosalind,* a coal-burning minesweeper,
at Mombasa) and a rather vague coordinating authority
over police engaged in security operations against the Mau-
Mau in Kenya. As a result of pressure from Baring, Hinde
remained as Director of Operations. Major-General 'Slim'
(so called because he was fat) Heyman was appointed chief
of staff to Erskine, Geoffrey Rimbault being relegated to the
position of deputy chief of staff, his responsibilities being
confined to all 'AQ' affairs, that is personnel and logistic,
for the whole command, as well as general staff matters in
colonies other than Kenya, and ones within Kenya which
were not connected with the emergency. Cameron stayed on
as deputy to Erskine concerned with these matters. This had
proved confusing and embarrassing. Cameron had been the
occupant of Flagstaff House at Karen and had left at the end
of 1953, which is why it was available for me.

I soon found that all was not plain sailing. The division
of responsibility between Erskine and Hinde was ill-defined
and caused some embarrassment to both and much confusion to the staff. A second visit by Harding with the Colonial
Secretary, Oliver Lyttelton, in February 1954 had led to the
establishment of the War Council, which had significantly
improved the overall direction of the emergency. Its formal
membership was limited to Baring, his deputy Frederick
Crawford (who had acted for him while he had been away
on three months sick leave, from which he had only just
returned when I arrived), Erskine and Michael Blundell,
representing the European elected members of the Legislative Council. Blundell's initiative had led to the formation of
the War Council. Richard Turnbull, Minister for Defence,
and Edward Windley, Minister for African Affairs, both
officials, almost always attended, and the highly effective
secretary was George Mallaby, who had come from the
Cabinet Office in London.

A major operation, known as *Anvil*, to clear up the 'passive wing' of Mau-Mau in Nairobi, had taken place at the end of April. It proved to be the turning point of the campaign, although that was not immediately apparent. The process of 'screening' the Kikuyu population of the city (and the associated Embu and Meru tribes) and imposing restrictions on those allowed to remain (45,000 out of the 65,000 there before the operation) took longer than expected, and meant that no other major operation was carried out in that year. The troops available to Erskine consisted of two British infantry brigades and one large East African one. The British were the 39th, commanded by Harry Thurlow* and the 49th, which only had two battalions, commanded by George Taylor. Seventieth East African Brigade was commanded by John Orr and consisted of four Kenya battalions of the KAR and one each from Tanganyika and Uganda, as well as an African armoured reconnaisaance squadron and a gunner battery. This amounted to a total of 10,000 British and African soldiers, in addition to 21,000 police, almost all African, and 25,000 Kikuyu Home Guard. The security forces therefore outnumbered the European population which, excluding the British forces and their dependents, totalled 45,000.

My involvement with operational matters was limited. The 'Q' side of my job did not take up much of my time. The logistic needs of the army were not difficult to meet and I had an efficient, although extremely irritating, AQMG as a subordinate. The main problem was the supply of patrols operating in the forests of the Aberdare Mountains and Mount Kenya. This was solved by a combination of air-drop and animal transport. The former consisted both of free-drop from light aircraft, piloted by the Kenya Police Reserve Air Wing, and parachute drop by RAF Dakota. I took part as an air-despatcher in one operation over the top of the Aberdares, and found pushing heavy loads out of the door at 12,000 feet without oxygen an exhausting experience. The most difficult and sensitive aspect of my job was the disciplinary side. Shortly before I arrived, Arthur Young of the City of London Police, who had acquired a high reputation

---

* Lord Thurlow, formerly Cumming-Bruce.

as Gerald Templer's Police Commissioner in Malaya, had
taken over the Kenya Colony Police. He soon found himself
in league with the Attorney-General, the Irish John Whyatt.
Whyatt had been the official 'Minister for Law and Order'
before the emergency, and his preference for law over order
had been one of the principal reasons for delay in dealing
with the subversive movement among the Kikuyu. Young
found that, as Police Commissioner, he had no authority
over the Tribal Police in the native reserves, who acted
under the authority of the administration, that is the district
and provincial commissioners. They were in theory under
the authority of the Minister for African Affairs (previously
known as the Chief Native Commissioner), Edward Windley;
the provincial commissioners, however, were accustomed to
act very much as their own masters. Young and Whyatt took
the line that, until the law was clearly seen to be paramount
and the policeman regarded as a friend of the people rather
than as a tool of government, there was no hope of winning
the hearts and minds of the Kikuyu to the government's
side. There was no problem with all the other tribes, as they
were only too happy to support the government against the
Kikuyu, who exerted such a strong influence both because
of their central geographical position and also on account
of their greater dynamism. Young and Whyatt insisted that
any illegal action, particularly one involving any form of
brutality, committed by anyone in authority, whether he
be a British soldier, a Kikuyu chief or a Kenyan European,
should be subject to the most rigorous investigation; if it
appeared that there was a case to answer, the suspect should
be brought to trial. Their demand that certain Kikuyu chiefs
should be charged with murder led to a clash between them
and the administration, the latter being supported by Baring.
They both resigned, Arthur Young being replaced by Dick
Catling, whom he had already brought in from Malaya, and
John Whyatt being succeeded by Eric Griffith-Jones, also
from Malaya. Both were able, energetic and much easier
to work with than their predecessors, and were to make
significant contributions to Kenya over a long period.

Bobbie Erskine was determined that the army should not
be infected either by the methods employed by the Mau-Mau
or by the lenient attitude, traditionally taken in the colony,

towards offences committed by Europeans against Africans. Shortly before my arrival a British officer, serving in the KAR, had been convicted by court-martial of disgraceful conduct and causing grievous bodily harm to two Kikuyu forestry workers suspected of being terrorists, having been acquitted of their murder by a previous court martial. He was sentenced to five years imprisonment and cashiered. After my arrival some soldiers were convicted by court martial for rape of a Kikuyu woman and given a heavy sentence. These sentences had shocked the reactionary element – the great majority – of the European population, who saw them as undermining their position. No European in the history of the colony had ever been convicted for killing an African, although, before I left Kenya, one had been sentenced to death for that offence. Killing other Europeans was taken fairly lightly also, especially if it could be called a *crime passionel*. Erskine had no sympathy for this reactionary element. It was no secret that he referred to them as the White Mau-Mau, which was one of the reasons for his unpopularity with much of the settler and business community. The liberal views of a distant cousin of his, Derek Erskine, reinforced their suspicions. Derek, as an impecunious cavalry officer, had eloped with his commanding officer's daughter and had started a grocer's business in Nairobi. It was considered below the dignity of a European to participate in the retail trade, which was dominated by Asians, with whom Derek found it necessary to establish good relations if he was to survive. The influx of troops and their camp followers to East Africa in the Second World War and the isolation of the colony offered opportunities to Derek, from which he prospered. In 1954 he was one of the richest men in the colony and a keen promoter of better relations between all the races. Neither his success nor his political and social attitudes endeared him to his fellow Europeans, who tarred Bobbie with the same brush.

I shared Bobbie Erskine's distaste for the dyed-in-the-wool reactionary attitude of the majority of whites. It often made conversation on social occasions an awkward ordeal, as one was expected to join a chorus of disapproval of any 'concession' to the Africans, which would only undermine the position of the 'loyal' ones, and of the tendency of the Asians to sit on the fence, while they exploited white and black alike. One incident was a shocking revelation to me of such attitudes. I acted as a supernumerary churchwarden at the little church at Karen, services at which were taken by a curate from the cathedral in Nairobi, where Bishop Leonard Beecher was an inspiring influence for good. The church was full for the early communion service on Easter Day 1955, but there was no sign of the parson. I knew that in a back pew was an African bishop from another colony, who was staying with the local secretary of the Church Missionary Society. I asked him if he would officiate. He had doubts about whether this would be acceptable, but was persuaded. I told the congregation that the Bishop of X, who was in the congregation, had kindly agreed to take the service. They seemed pleased, but, when they saw he was black, nearly half of them got up and left. A year later it was considered perfectly normal for an African curate to take services regularly in that church. I had been prepared to face such attitudes by my friendship with Oliver Woods, then the highly respected colonial correspondent of *The Times*. He had commanded a squadron in 3rd County of London Yeomanry in 4th Armoured Brigade, and we had seen each other again on a number of occasions when I was in London. He knew the colonial scene intimately and was admired by officials, settlers and nationalist leaders alike. He was to remain one of my greatest friends until his death at a sadly early age, when he was engaged in writing a history of *The Times*, from which he had retired, having been deputy editor-in-chief of Times Newspapers.

I escaped from my office, in the group of wooden huts that constituted command headquarters, as often as I could, two or three times a week on average. Most of my visits to units up-country were made by light aircraft, either chartered or more often in Piper Pacers or Cessnas of the Kenya Police Reserve Air Wing, run by Wing Commander Francombe. They were often exciting flights, especially in the rainy season, when clouds hung low over the hills. One could fly through a gap over one of the ridges of the Aberdares only to find that there was no gap over the next ridge, and that perhaps the gap behind one had closed. Being already at a height above sea level of eight or nine thousand feet, there was no chance of breaking out above the clouds, and one's only hope was to get out down the valley. Some of the KPR pilots were superb, but they took risks in an unorthodox way, and some paid for it with their lives. Some of the landing strips were very primitive, and I often kept my fingers crossed, both when landing and when taking off. Ant-bear holes were one of the hazards, cattle on the strip and birds were others, the latter particularly when hordes of locusts were followed by flocks of storks and other large birds. I enjoyed flying both for its excitement and for the wonderful views it gave one of the country, as I did the trips by Landrover and on foot through the reserves and the forests, into which Mike Prynne's 39th Corps Engineer Regiment were building rough roads. I was amused to find that the Landrover was universally preferred to the Austin Champ, which the War Office had originally chosen. The latter not only got stuck more often on wet jungle tracks and was very heavy to extricate, but it needed constant changes of carburettor jet at different altitudes, if its engine was to operate properly. The Landrover suffered from neither of those faults, it and the Bedford three-ton lorry doing sterling work in the roughest conditions from sea-level up to 10,000 feet.

By the time that Bobbie Erskine left in April 1955, it was clear that we were well on the way to victory. Some 5,500 Mau-Mau had been accounted for since Operation *Anvil*, the total of active terrorists, operating in gangs, having been reduced from about 12,000 to 5,000. This success was due to the combination of three factors: first, restrictions imposed on the whole community, particularly very severe ones on the Kikuyu including concentration into protected villages, which brought with it a revolution in agriculture by concentrating holdings and terracing; second, development of more sophisticated military operations, based on specialized organizations and more skilful patrol techniques; finally, a great improvement in intelligence, provided by a fully integrated military/police intelligence organization, headed by John Prendergast. The last two owed much to the development of 'pseudo-gangs'. These were teams of ex-Mau-Mau terrorists, converted to acting against their former associates, usually led by young European members of the Kenya Regiment, disguised as Africans. The activities of the latter, whether in that role or as interrogators, were recognized by the Mau-Mau as one of the major threats to them, and allegations of torture and other malpractices were frequent. I found myself at the centre of the controversies these aroused. Guy Campbell, the buccaneering ex-KRRC commanding officer of the Kenya Regiment, regarded any inclination to give credence to allegations against his men as acceptance of Mau-Mau propaganda, playing into their hands and undermining the morale of his men and the whole security apparatus. But, unless those allegations that appeared to have some foundation in fact were investigated, they could not be denied, apart altogether from the requirements of justice and of the pressure from political and other sources, like the churches, that they should be. The Church of Scotland, led by David Steel's father, was particularly critical, and, however divided on religious issues, on this one all the churches were united. In one particularly disgusting case, involving unofficial interrogation of a Kikuyu woman, some members of the Kenya Regiment were brought to trial by court martial. Over this issue Dick Catling and Eric Griffith-Jones maintained a well-judged balance between the needs of justice and those of prosecuting the emergency.

Erskine was succeeded by General Gerald Lathbury, whom I hardly knew. A light infantryman, he had commanded an airborne brigade at Arnhem, and after the war 16th Airborne Division in Palestine, before being commandant of the Staff College. I found him a difficult man to get to know and with whom to establish good relations. He was moody and sometimes very bad-tempered: seldom open and straightforward. His temper varied with the time of day, being particularly bad first thing in the morning or just after he had returned from an aircraft flight. I discovered that the latter gave him severe headaches: as he spent a great deal of time flying all over the colony, this no doubt accounted for his moods. His arrival raised two uncertainties as far as I personally was concerned: whether, as Lathbury was bringing his family, we should be turned out of Flagstaff House, and what the future of my job would be. Uncertainty about the former was, to our great relief, soon settled. Lathbury, strongly so advised by Erskine, thought it too far out, and turned Heyman out of his house, the latter persuading the Kenya Government to spend a large sum in finding him another. It was some months before my future was decided. The requirement for British troops had clearly been reduced, particularly as Lathbury decided to go much further than Erskine had in employing small specialized forces, rather than regular formations, to pursue the dwindling numbers of Mau-Mau gangs. The top-heavy command organization, with one general and two major-generals, was to be slimmed, Loony Hinde leaving without replacement and Heyman's place as chief of staff being taken by myself in the rank of brigadier. This came about in October 1955. Thirty-ninth Brigade was sent home, leaving 49th, then commanded by Charles Harington, who lived with us until his family arrived. I had known him first as GSO1 of 53rd Welsh Division in the war and we had both been at SHAPE together. He was a refreshing contrast to his predecessor. John Birkbeck had by then replaced John Orr in command of 70th East African Brigade.

Once I had become chief of staff, I found it easier to establish a smooth working relationship with Lathbury, especially if I arranged for others to see him in the first hour after he had arrived in the office. His great interest was bird-watching, and he rose before dawn every day (about 7 a.m. all the year round) to indulge in it. He was always punctual in arrival at his office and expected everything to be fully organized for him, but objected if staff came in earlier than he did to make it possible.

The end of the emergency was now clearly only a matter of time, and the eyes of all in East Africa were turned more and more to the future. The Templer report on colonial forces had stressed the need for the British Government to hand over responsibility for them to the colonies, and to make them more capable of standing on their own, particularly where there was a likelihood or a possibility of the colony becoming independent. The future of the East African forces, and of the security forces generally in the command, as well as that of any British element that might be stationed in the area, became one of my principal concerns. The only one of the colonies in the command about which there was any talk of independence at that time was Uganda, where the Governor, Andrew Cohen, was in favour of pressing ahead. The possible path to independence was complicated by the existence of the East African High Commission, which operated common services, such as railways, docks, harbours, post, telecommunications and civil aviation, for Kenya, Tanganyika, Uganda and Zanzibar. Many, including the Commonwealth Relations Office and some of the Colonial Office, expected the Commission to develop into a Federation, similar to the Central African Federation, obtaining independence as such rather than as separate independent countries. The Governors constantly complained that the War Office charged them too much for the cost of their locally raised forces, maintaining either that they did not need them for the defence of their own territories, or that the War Office equipped, organized and trained them to a standard that was not necessary for purely local purposes. It was the case that there were some very unrealistic ideas floated at that time for forming a great African reserve of units to serve anywhere within the Commonwealth. But, when faced with proposals that they should assume total responsibility for their forces, either independently or on an East African basis, they were none too keen to do so. Some of their officials questioned the need to maintain military forces at all and considered that the money would be better spent on police, including a mobile para-military element. The latter was eventually adopted as the solution for Mauritius, where a company of the 6th (Tanganyika) Battalion KAR had previously been stationed.

I found the organization for dealing with these matters practically non-existent. A body called the East African Defence Committee met twice a year, consisting of the C-in-C, the Air Officer Commanding the RAF in Aden, to whom the RAF at Nairobi were subordinate, and the three Governors, Evelyn Baring for Kenya, Andrew Cohen for Uganda and Edward Twining for Tanganyika, three very different men. Baring, son of the great nineteenth-century proconsul in Egypt, Lord Cromer (62 when Evelyn was born), a suave, diplomatic Old Wykehamist, who would never approach the kernel of the subject directly, preferring to weave his way round it, but with a hard core of determination and principle from which nothing would deflect him: Cohen, avant-garde, left-wing intellectual with a quick, active brain; energetic, impatient and with little small talk; always anxious to get on with the business and be done with it as quickly as possible: Twining, an old colonial hand in the best tradition of the paternal district officer who had risen through provincial commissioner to Government House: shrewd, humorous, with no illusions about his fellow men, white, brown or black, and not expecting too much of them: in no hurry. Almost every question came round to money. Tanganyika recognized the need, although its own security requirements were not great, but pleaded poverty. Uganda questioned the need, and, although richer than Tanganyika, saw no need to pay more. Both expected Kenya, whose needs and riches were greatest, to meet the lion's share of the bill. Kenya was determined that she should not carry an unfair burden, and considered that her efforts were of benefit to the other two. Baring always hoped that what could not be billed to the British Government, should be shared in the proportion 3:2:1 to Kenya:Uganda:Tanganyika; while Cohen fought for 4:1:1. Baring and Twining were prepared to haggle at length, but Cohen's patience invariably deserted him, and the solution was usually either 3:2:1 or 4:2:1, with Twining getting his way with the minimum of intervention.

This bargaining against the clock, with no previous discussion, did not produce good answers, and I was instrumental in establishing a committee of the officials from the three territories who dealt with these matters, which met every quarter in each capital in turn and produced a coordinated view for the meetings of the full committee. One of the difficult problems we faced was the provision of African officers, of whom at that time there were none. In the very early days of locally raised forces, based in Uganda on those of Emin Pasha, there had been some who were given the title of *effendi*. One of them still lived in Nairobi, and I used to visit him at Christmas, when he would dress up in his old uniform, complete with his effendi's sword, to receive me. We decided to resurrect this rank for promoted warrant officers, on the lines of the Viceroy's Commissioned Officers in the old Indian Army, and one of the first was Sergeant-Major Idi Amin in the 4th (Uganda) KAR. But we were also concerned to encourage better-educated Africans to train as officers and to devise ways and means to bring this about, although old KAR hands viewed it with deep misgiving.

When it came to planning the administrative and logistic foundations for the future forces, I found myself sympathizing with the officials in their view that to impose the British army's pattern would be unnecessarily expensive. As an example, I proved that it was totally unnecessary for the army to provide any system for the storage and distribution of petrol. Its needs were minute in relation to the total needs of the territories, and any crisis affecting its supply would affect daily life of the country far more acutely. I also proved that the army was wasting a vast amount of money in overhauling and repairing old vehicles in its own workshops. It would be much cheaper to place a regular order for new ones, based on an estimate of wastage due to accidents and wear. These conclusions were very unpopular with the War Office, which placed considerable emphasis on the need to maintain the potential for a logistic base in East Africa in a major war. At that time the project to station a British brigade in Kenya after the emergency had not been mooted, and the previous plan to create a major base at Mackinnon Road near Mombasa to replace that in the Suez Canal zone, on which a start had been made before the emergency, had been dropped. If any British troops were to remain in Kenya at all after the campaign, it was not expected to be more than a battalion.

One external event added interest to our lives in March 1956, the exile of Archbishop Makarios from Cyprus to the Seychelles. He was flown from Cyprus by the RAF, and we had to accommodate him and his three companions in a military camp at Mombasa until the Royal Navy could provide a ship to transport them to the Seychelles, which in those days had no airfield. We did our best at very short notice to provide suitable facilities, including drink at NAAFI prices. Makarios was in good humour, thanked us for our hospitality and said that his only objection to taking a holiday at Her Majesty's expense was having to do so in the company of the Bishop of Kyrenia. We charged the cost to the Kenya Government, who passed it on to the Cyprus Government, adding on the duty on the drink, as they maintained that Makarios should not have been supplied with duty-free alcohol, not being a member of the armed forces! The Cyprus Government jibbed at this and a long correspondence ensued about the trifling sum. Makarios's presence in 'restricted residence' in the Seychelles disturbed the placid routine of the Governor. When it was rumoured that Greek tankers were in the habit of anchoring not far from the island on which Makarios was living, the Governor suspected an attempt to rescue him. The only security force was a handful of unarmed police, and the Governor appealed for help. We had no wish to maroon any soldiers there, but sent a guard dog, with an instructor to train the police in handling it, and, as a security adviser, a lieutenant-colonel who had proved a failure as GSO1 (intelligence) and for whom I could find no other useful employment. The normal way of travelling to and from the Seychelles was by ship which plied once a month from Mombasa to Bombay, returning the following month. The only other means was to use HM East African Ship *Rosalind*. To make the voyage there and back she had to be loaded with coal in every available space, including the decks. When they reached Victoria, the capital, the immigration authorities refused to allow the dog to land, until the Governor had declared the police station to be a quarantine station. On the colonel's advice, the shrubbery surrounding Makarios's house was cut back and the dog attached by a running lead to a wire to limit its range. Makarios immediately complained to the Colonial Secretary that he was being treated as a dangerous criminal and the Governor was forced to remove the dog which we had taken so much trouble to send there. In later years when I had dealings with Makarios we used to laugh about these incidents. He liked the Seychelles so much that he bought a plot of land there on which to build a house, but had not done so when he died in 1977.

The other external event of 1956 which had some repercussions in Kenya was the Suez affair. The only way it affected us directly was that reinforcements for Aden were flown out via Kenya. I had viewed with dismay the growing signs that Eden's government intended to use force to restore British control of the canal. In a letter to Hobo, dated 25 September, I wrote:

We have had one or two visitors here breathing Eden-like fire and slaughter about Suez. I do not understand (a) how it is proposed we should use force; (b) for what purpose; (c) on what excuse; (d) what we would propose to do afterwards. Surely once we had left the Suez canal zone, we must have realized this might happen. Before we left, we should have insisted on *international* negotiations to ensure the future. The fault seems to lie once again at the door of those who, in the face of facts, like to go on pretending that England can go it alone. The one area left where they thought they could continue to wag the flag alone was the Middle East – and now that has been proved a fallacy. A pretty mess it's made.

When, just over a month later, Operation *Musketeer* was finally launched, I happened to be seeing Evelyn Baring on business, and he asked me what I thought about it. I told him what I felt, and said that it seemed to me to show a complete blindness to the likely after-effects. I could not conceive what position Eden thought he would be able to hold, if he had occupied the whole canal. We could not return to permanent occupation. Baring's reply was: 'I think that you and I are probably the only people in this colony who think like that.' I had conceived a strong liking and admiration for him. Both Erskine and Lathbury, particularly the latter, had been irritated by what they thought was his tendency to prevaricate, his reluctance to come to a decision, and had much preferred his more straightforward deputy, Frederick Crawford. I had come to appreciate that this was Evelyn's way of trying to preserve what he conceived, usually correctly, as the long-term interests of the colony against pressure for short-term measures designed to hasten the end of the emergency. It was always pleasant to accept an invitation to Government House, Herbert Baker's creation for an intended Governor-General of East Africa, whether it was informal, to play tennis, for a meal with the family, or for major official occasions. On both, Lady Mary was a perfect hostess who made all and sundry welcome.

In June 1956 we had been two years in Kenya. In the first year the restrictions on movement had imposed limits on where we could go and what we could do as a family. We

had visited the game parks of Nairobi and Amboseli and had
spent a seaside holiday in a house on the coast at Diani, which
we shared with the Montgomery-Campbells, who lived near
us at Karen. Archie was a retired officer of my regiment who
worked for the prisons department. The French governess
had not been a success and had left us after six months. We
had thought that her previous experience of Africa would
have been a help, but she hated Africans and had been
disappointed because glamorous English gentlemen did not
gallop up to admire her. We were glad to see her go, as we
had never been happy to leave the children alone with her.
Susanna and Andrew went to a local private school, Susanna
being faced with a major problem in changing over from
French to English methods. Sue Lane came to live with us
instead, keeping an eye on the children when neither of
us was there.

Neither of my jobs had brought me into close contact with
the settlers up-country, as a more operational one might have
done, and our circle of friends, outside that of the army and
government officials, was not a wide one. One lasting friendship was that formed with Clare and Tony Dorman, who was
then in charge of the government veterinary laboratory at
Kabete, to whom we were introduced by a remote connection
of Edith's, John Bagenal, who was a district officer. In the
summer of 1956 we had enjoyed another seaside holiday
at the army leave camp at Nyali, and at the beginning of
September Edith and I went on a long 'safari' to what was
then the Belgian Congo, visiting the Murchison Falls and
Queen Elizabeth game parks in Uganda on the way. Our
Ford Consul, which we had bought when we went to France
in 1951, did not let us down, although some of the roads
were very rough. We had hoped to enter the Congo by
the Ruwenzori mountains (the mountains of the moon) and
travel down from there to Lake Kivu within the Congo, but
the Belgian customs said that I had not got the right papers.
The friendly Goan at the Uganda frontier post advised me to
try the next post to the south. It took us all day to get there, by
which time it was dark, raining and the frontier was closed.
We had been told that there was a hotel and were appalled
to find only what appeared to be a collection of 'rondavels' or
native huts. It proved however to be very comfortable. After

a glorious bath, the water heated up by a wood fire under
an old oil-drum outside the hut, we had an excellent dinner
in the company of the proprietor, a German who had spent
his last penny after the war in making his way there. Acting
on his advice, we were humbly polite to the Belgian customs
official next morning, and, to our immense relief, having
promised to return by the same route, he let us through.
We spent several days in an excellent hotel on Lake Kivu,
reminiscent of the Italian lakes, crossing into Ruanda Urundi
to see the Watuzi dancing. On our way back we picked up
my delightful driver, Sergeant Opondo, at a cross-roads
near his home village in the middle of nowhere, just inside
Kenya from the Uganda border. It had been a wonderful
experience and we had seen every sort of game.

The campaign against the Mau-Mau was clearly nearing
its end, and I had in any case been told that I should leave
in November to attend the course at the Imperial Defence
College in London which started in the new year, on which
Charles Harington was also to be a student. Much as we had
enjoyed Kenya, we had had our fill of it, missing so much
of the company and culture of Europe. Visits from friends,
like Don Cook, who had stayed with us for a few days,
brought home to us the narrowness of life in East Africa.
Operations against the terrorists tended increasingly to be
carried out by pseudo-gangs and specialized teams, and it
became quite difficult to find useful things for the majority
of soldiers, white and black, to do. We had had an anxious
week-end when all the normal security forces were cleared
out of the whole of the Aberdares and a large number of
pseudo-gangs let loose, the only form of control by Europeans being reporting points, under the overall supervision
of Ian Henderson of the police special branch. When, after
the first 48 hours, there had been no report, we began
to get cold feet, fearing that the pseudo-gangsters might
have deserted with their arms to the side of their former
comrades; but then the reports began to come in, one after
another announcing successes, and we breathed again. The
knowledge of what we were doing had been kept to a small
number. There would have been a major political row with
the European population, as well as great resentment in the
army, if things had gone wrong. Final success came on

17 October when Dedan Kimathi, the principal gang leader, wounded in a clash with a pseudo-gang, was found by a Tribal policeman at the forest edge. It was Sunday, and Baring, Lathbury and Catling were all attending morning service at the cathedral in the middle of a visit by Princess Margaret, when the news was passed to them. A month later, on the day that the army was withdrawn from operations, we returned to England on one of the Britannia aircraft that the RAF had taken over before they had been delivered to the British Overseas Airways Corporation. Almost all the passengers were soldiers who had been sent as reinforcements to Aden for the Suez operation, which had come to an inglorious end on 7 November. There had been a last-minute hitch when it was feared that Andrew had contracted German measles and that he and Edith would have to stay behind. Fortunately he was cleared. There was nearly another when we were told, as we approached Heathrow, that the weather was closing in and we would probably be diverted to Prestwick. All our plans were based on being able to go directly to Edwardstone, which, in the end, we did.

12

Sitting in the Centre

He that has light within his own clear breast
May sit i' th' centre and enjoy bright day.
John Milton (1608–1674), *Comus*

Before we began to look for somewhere to live, we had to
decide whether to look for a house in the suburbs, perhaps
an army quarter, if we could get one, or for a flat in the
centre. The former would make a car essential, but the
higher cost of the latter could be offset by doing without
one. Having been out of the country for over five years, we
wanted to revive our social life and chose the latter. Just as
I was beginning to think that we should never find anything
suitable which we could afford, I found an unfurnished
'mansion' flat in Upper Montagu Street, near Marylebone
Town Hall, which had three and a half years of a seven-year
lease to run, which I calculated that, with the key money,
we could just afford. It had pleasant large rooms in which
the small stock of furniture we had stored since we left 268
Brompton Road provided the bare minimum to start off
with. Regent's Park nearby was a suitable place to take the
children, and, when I was feeling energetic, I would walk
through the park and Primrose Hill to Hampstead Heath
and Golders Green Park, returning by bus. We had moved
in by the time that the IDC course started in January 1957.

I enjoyed the course, which provided me with an opportunity to reconsider my views about all aspects of defence
in the light of discussions with my fellow students and
the excellent lectures by distinguished and authoritative

speakers. The commandant, the delightful Admiral Sir Guy Russell, was well supported by a senior officer from each service – Major-General Roddy McLeod for the army, and Evelyn Shuckburgh from the diplomatic service. We did not work long hours and I decided to spend two evenings a week at art classes. I had experimented with oils in Kenya without much success, and signed up for adult evening classes at St Martin's School of Art, where I attempted still life on Tuesdays and life on Fridays. I was more successful with the former than the latter and was pleased to have two pictures accepted for the annual Army Art Exhibition in the autumn. One of the features of the IDC course was the summer foreign tour in August, and I chose to join the group visiting North America. Feeling rather poor at the time, I decided to take the opportunity to give up smoking. I had never smoked much, generally not until the afternoon, and had given up cigarettes soon after we had married, partly in the hope of alleviating Edith's chronic catarrh. When I set off for North America, I left my pipe behind and never smoked again. The first part of the tour covered Canada and was fairly gruelling. In Quebec, after a large lunch given us by a timber company, I followed Wolfe's footsteps up the Heights of Abraham and was disappointed to find the climb not a strenuous one. We flew from one place to another in a Royal Canadian Air Force North Star, which was unpressurized and fiendishly noisy. Flying west against the clock, we arrived exhausted, deaf and longing to sleep, while our hosts were at their peak and bursting with enthusiasm for a party to last far into the night. Visits to military and industrial establishments were accompanied by overwhelming hospitality and alleviated by some opportunities for recreation, riding cowboy-style at Calgary and fishing near the frontier with Alaska, to which we were flown from White Horse, Yukon. After this, our reception in the USA was more conventional. Fortunately we had a weekend free in Washington, and I was able to spend Sunday with Ben and Harriet Harrell.

On my return from this trip I was told that, after the course, I was to take over from Denis FitzGerald as Director of Plans in the War Office. This was good news. It was the plum job for a brigadier, at the very centre of affairs, and meant that we did not have to move. After Christmas, spent at Edwardstone, I took up my new duties, having the privilege as a director (the only one below the rank of major-general) of being allowed to enter the War Office by the front door in Whitehall. The Director of Plans held a unique position. Within the War Office I had no staff of my own, other than a female secretary. I was subordinate to the Director of Military Operations, Major-General Jack Hamilton, from the branches of whose staff I received advice, which they distilled from that which they received from all other branches of the staff. Over in the small Ministry of Defence in Storey's Gate I headed the army element of the Joint Planning Staff which served the Chiefs of Staff Committee, chaired by Marshal of the Royal Air Force Sir William (Dickie) Dickson, who had recently had the title of his appointment changed from Chairman of the Chiefs of Staff to Chief of the Defence Staff, an outward and visible, if not very effective, sign of the determination of Harold Macmillan, Prime Minister and ex-Minister of Defence, to give more authority to a central direction of defence under the forceful drive of the Minister, Duncan Sandys.

I found myself the prisoner of a highly developed ritual, hallowed by the success it was supposed to have achieved in the Second World War. The concept was democratic, designed to ensure that nobody near the top could exert influence in the early stages of planning, and that an objective view was arrived at, taking account of all the factors bearing on the plan, and that all the possible problems affecting it had been hammered out before it reached the stage of a recommendation to the Chiefs of Staff. The Directors of Plans of the three services had failed in their task if agreement between them had not been reached before it was laid before the Chiefs. Unlike them, we had no chairman, each of us taking it in turn to chair our meetings. The ritual began with 'terms of reference' for a study, stemming from a meeting of the Chiefs of Staff, the wording of which was agreed between our secretary, a bluff sailor, Captain 'Harpy' Lloyd, and the powerful secretary of the Chiefs of Staff, then George Cole, who, having been in the Chiefs of Staff secretariat in the war, was a passionate devotee of the system. At that time the Chief of the Defence Staff could not himself initiate a study by us, although, when Roddy

My father, Harold Carver, in
1918

My mother with myself, Rodney and Antony in
1917

Myself, aged about 5

My parents with brothers Paul on Haricot and Rodney on Flash, with dogs Uncle, Judy and Jim at Ticklerton in 1933 RIGHT With my father and Uncle at Ticklerton in 1932, when I was 17

The 1935 entry of young officers of the Royal Tank Corps: 2nd Lieutenants Saunders, Carver, Simonds, Wallace, Campbell, Scrafton and Macnamara

Officers of HQ 7th Armoured Division, November 1940. Pip Roberts is on the extreme right

t Haifa Staff College in
alestine, 1941
ABOVE RIGHT General
uchinleck being driven by
Major General Jock Campbell,
ortly before the latter's death
February 1942. Brigadier
atehouse is in the back

RIGHT General Ritchie with (*left*
right) Brigadier Erskine,
eneral Norrie, General Gott
nd Captain Grant Singer, May
942

Smuggins' Smith (*left*) and Pat
assie in the desert, 1942

Major General John Harding talking to an RAF officer in the pursuit after El Alamein, November 1942

Brigadier 'Loony' Hinde introducing commanding officers of 22nd Armoured Brigade to General Montgomery, Norfolk, February, 1944. I am fourth from left

With Commanding Officers and staff of 4th Armoured Brigade soon after VE Day, 1945. *Standing*: Christopher Consett, Gerry Hopkinson, myself, 'Wac' Anderson, Len Livingstone-Learmonth. *Seated*: Tommy Thomson and Jim Stanton

Myself as Brigadier,
Commander 4th Armoured
Brigade in 1945, aged 30

Edith Lowry-Corry, 1947

With 'Hobo', Major General Sir Percy Hobart, 1948, at a regimental dinner in London

BELOW With Field Marshal Montgomery and CPX2 staff at SHAPE in 1953

General Erskine talking to soldiers in Kenya, 1954

RIGHT Outside Buckingham Palace with Andrew, Susann and Edith in 1957 having be invested with the CB

FAR RIGHT At the Münster gokart meeting in 1960

LEFT With General Lathbury and Provincial Commissioners, Nairobi, 1956

BELOW With family and staff of Flagstaff House, Karen. In front are Susanna, Alice and Andrew

With General Westphal and
Frau Rommel laying a wreath
at the Afrika Korps reunion,
Münster, 1961

BELOW Major-General,
Commander 3rd Division, in
1963. Portrait by Andrew
Freeth, RA

ABOVE RIGHT With General
Gyani, Archbishop Makarios
and Colonel Waern, United
Nations Force, Nicosia 1964

Susanna, Andrew and Alice at
Saalbach, 1966

McLeod was appointed to the new post of Vice-Chief of the Defence Staff, he fought hard for this to be agreed; it was frowned on by the true believers. Once the Directors of Plans had accepted the terms of reference, the study was passed to the appropriate joint service team, of which there were three, one dealing with NATO and Europe, on which my representative was Major Roly Gibbs, ex-company commander of 2nd KRRC in 4th Armoured Brigade and future Chief of the General Staff, one with everywhere else in the world, and one with general policy and miscellaneous matters, such as the nuclear deterrent. These three teams did all the work which in later years the 'central staffs' in the Ministry of Defence undertook under the direction of the Chief of the Defence Staff, who, at that time, had virtually no staff of his own.

Once the terms of reference had been agreed and referred to a team, the members of it consulted their own departments (the MO branch of the War Office in the army's case) and, having met together, compiled a first draft reconciling the three service points of view. This would go back to the departments for comment and, revised in the light of them, would return for consideration by the Assistant Directors of Plans, my representative being a colonel. Their product would return again for comment and I would be briefed by the appropriate MO branch before it was taken by the Directors. Our product would become a formal Joint Planning Staff Paper for consideration by the Chiefs of Staff Committee, and, if approved or amended, was sanctified as a Chiefs of Staff Paper. Before the CIGS, Gerald Templer, attended the meeting, DMO would prepare a written brief, and he and I and the VCIGS, Lieutenant-General Bill Stratton, would brief him verbally. This system tended to produce answers which were a compromise between the interests, points of view or prejudices of the three separate service departments. It was very difficult to inject my own ideas or views at any stage, particularly if they ran counter to those of official War Office thinking. It was of course designed to insure against individual opinions affecting decisions. It worked best in the production of joint service contingency operational plans, in which it was essential to ensure that the plan took account of the real capabilities of all three services. It worked least well on matters of general policy, where a compromise between three different entrenched positions was seldom the best answer.

Contingency plans took up most of our time, and were concerned mostly with the colonies and the Middle East. Harold Macmillan had not yet felt the full force of the wind of change and there had been little withdrawal from the colonial empire, except in West Africa. In the backwash from Suez the Middle East was a particularly sensitive area, and became a crisis centre in July 1958. Hussein in Jordan was faced with a rebellion, instigated by Palestinians, and on 14 July King Feisal of Iraq and his Prime Minister, the pro-British elder statesman, Nuri es Said, were killed. On 17 July, at Hussein's request, 16th Parachute Brigade, overflying Israel with its concurrence, was deployed round the airfield at Amman, US Marines having landed at Beirut in Lebanon two days before.

Having successfully implemented the parachute brigade operation, the joint planners were faced with an extraordinary demand from the Chiefs of Staff, prompted by Duncan Sandys. This was for an invasion of Iraq, culminating in the occupation of Baghdad, one prong advancing east from the footholds established in Lebanon and Jordan, the other north from the Persian Gulf. My colleagues, Captain Dick Smeeton, Royal Navy and Air Commodore Fred Rosier, RAF, were as astounded at this fantastic concept as I was. Smeeton informed us that his Chief, Lord Mountbatten, had told him that he hoped we would prove it to be impossible, so that he would not find himself having to oppose it in committee against Gerald Templer and Dermot Boyle, the Chief of the Air Staff, both of whom, he believed, favoured it. It seemed to us that those who supported it had learned nothing from Suez. It was not difficult to demonstrate that it made no sense. It would have taken well over six months, perhaps much longer, to build up the resources needed to support even the minimum force, and difficult to see what operations could succeed in restoring the *status quo ante* in Iraq. Preparations could not be concealed and the political reactions to them in the Middle East and elsewhere would clearly be highly adverse. The Foreign Office representatives, who advised our team and attended our meetings,

made no bones about that. When Jack Hamilton and I
were briefing a disappointed Gerald Templer for the Chiefs'
meeting on our paper, and he had just accepted that the
operation was out of the question, we were interrupted by
Julian Amery, then Parliamentary Under-Secretary of State
for War. 'I'm sorry to interrupt you, CIGS,' he said, 'but I
believe that some lily-livered planners are trying to prevent
us dealing properly with Iraq. I hope we can rely on you to
be firm and override their objections.' To my astonishment
and concern the CIGS replied: 'Yes, US of S, you certainly
can.' In the event, to my relief, he made no attempt to pursue the madcap scheme in face of the unpalatable military
and political realities. The plan was whittled down to one
for introducing a larger Anglo–American force than that
already in the Lebanon, in case Syria, supported by Iraq,
threatened Lebanon and Jordan.

One Friday, after I had returned to the flat, I was rung
up by Roddy McLeod and warned that I was to fly that night
to Cyprus to obtain the views of the Commanders-in-Chief
Middle East on the revised plan. Having been briefed by
him at Storey's Gate and collected the top secret Chiefs of
Staff papers, I was driven to the RAF station at Benson,
near Abingdon. There I was told that I should be flying
by Canberra bomber in the early hours of the morning,
refuelling at Malta. The officers' mess was holding a guest
night and I was given a room and advised to get some sleep,
being warned that I would be woken up early to be fitted
out with flying-kit, examined by the medical officer, partly
to see if my measurements would enable me to eject without
cutting my legs off, and instructed in emergency drills. When
the time came, the medical officer was not available, having
indulged too heavily at the guest night, which was just as well
as it transpired later that, my legs being exceptionally long
from hip to knee, I should not have passed the test for the
seat I was to occupy, that of the radio operator. It was a dull
flight, as I could not see out and nobody told me that there
was a small lever which would have allowed me to ease my
body slightly from the totally rigid position into which I was
strapped. Fortunately I had brought a book in my briefcase.
My bottom was totally numb by the time we reached Malta,
where we had a typical RAF Officers' Mess breakfast, massive

but deadly dull and swamped in baked beans. We reached the RAF station at Akrotiri in Cyprus at about 10 a.m. on Saturday morning, and nobody seemed to know or be interested in why I had come. My request for official transport to take me to Middle East Headquarters at Episkopi was met by the suggestion that I should take a taxi. I got on my high horse and said that I was carrying top secret Chiefs of Staff papers for a meeting of the Commanders-in-Chief, and that, if the station commander refused to produce transport, I would ring up the army C-in-C, Lieutenant-General Sir Roger Bower. With ill grace a RAF Landrover was produced and I set off.

After a helpful meeting with the joint staffs of the 'British Defence Coordinating Committee Middle East', it was decided that the great men themselves should meet that Saturday afternoon, an unprecedented interference with their weekend relaxation. They – Bower, Air Marshal Sir Sidney Bufton (whom I had known as AOC Aden on the East Africa Defence Committee) and Rear-Admiral 'Crap' Miers, a famous submariner VC – were in no mood to take a snap decision and decided that I must have further discussions with their staffs before another meeting. I had planned to fly back on the Sunday, but Bufton tried to persuade me to postpone my return until Monday afternoon, when a RAF Comet would in any case be available, which would be much more comfortable than the Canberra. John and Irene Borthwick had invited us to Covent Garden on the Monday evening to hear Verdi's *Don Carlos*, and I was determined not to miss that. I explained to Bufton that it was essential for me to be back in London by Sunday night so that the staffs could get to work on the Cs-in-C's recommendations on the Monday morning. Very reluctantly they agreed to meet again on the Sunday morning. The result was to add a list of cautious provisos to the plan, Admiral Miers remaining uncharacteristically silent. In spite of being lunch-time when we finished, he insisted on taking me in his official car to Akrotiri where the Canberra was standing by to take off, spending the time explaining that he totally disagreed with the views of his colleagues. The Canberra and its crew were ready, but my flying kit was locked up in a hut to which nobody had the key. 'Break in and get it,' said the admiral.

I demurred and suggested that we go to the guardroom and find someone who knew where the key was. 'Well, if you won't, I will,' said the admiral, and proceeded to force an entry through the window. As he was doing so, the station duty officer appeared, and, unpopular already for taking off at Sunday lunch-time, I left the admiral to bear the brunt of his anger, which he seemed to enjoy doing.

The lack of positive action in the Middle East was not to Gerald Templer's liking, and he told Jack Hamilton to write a paper for him to put to his colleagues, favouring a more robust and interventionist policy. Jack passed his draft to me for comment. I wrote a fairly long and forceful reply, beginning with the words: 'I find myself in fundamental disagreement with this paper.' Having read it, Jack sent for me to discuss it. I was taken aback when he said that he had sent it with his paper to the CIGS. When I protested that it had been intended for him only, he said: 'I don't agree with your point of view, but it is one held by a large number of people and I thought that the CIGS should see both points of view.' Fortunately I was due to go on my summer holiday immediately afterwards, and fully expected to be told of my dismissal during it. When I returned I was summoned to see Templer. Looking over his glasses, but in a less menacing manner than usual, he said: 'I find myself in fundamental disagreement with my Director of Plans. What am I going to do about that?' 'You can always get another one,' I replied. 'I'm not going to do that,' he said, and we entered on a friendly discussion of the whole subject. It was one of his most endearing characteristics that, although he could be terrifyingly severe at times, one had confidence that, if one stuck up for one's point of view in a straightforward and direct manner, he respected one, and, although he might not accept what one said, he took account of it. In spite of his progressive attitude in Malaya, he was an ardent imperialist like many other senior officers. He was much more interested in the security of the Commonwealth that he was in the defence of Europe. I had been shocked when I went for the first time to brief him on NATO's annual defence planning review. As I entered his office, he peered over his spectacles and said: 'I hate NATO.' Before he was succeeded by Frankie Festing in September 1958, he strolled casually into my office to say good-bye. 'Young man, I know you think most of my ideas are out of date,' he said; 'You're probably right and lots of things should be changed; but I was damned if they were going to be changed in my time.'

Gerald Templer's departure coincided with Field Marshal Montgomery's retirement (or to be strictly accurate, reversion to half-pay) at the age of 71, his place as DSACEUR at SHAPE being taken by Richard Gale. He had invited me to his last CPX – CPX EIGHT – in April, a great privilege as nobody under the rank of Lieutenant-General normally had a seat. His memoirs were published in November, his criticism of Eisenhower, then in his second term as President of the United States, causing considerable international embarrassment.

I have said that the joint planning organization was less effective in dealing with matters of general policy. An example of this was our inability to reach an agreed position about the future of the strategic nuclear deterrent force. Although the V-bombers, carrying British-made hydrogen bombs, were only just coming into service, it was clear that their ability to penetrate Russian air defences would be difficult to maintain for long. To insure against that, the RAF proposed to develop a ballistic missile, Blue Streak, while also spending large sums on trying to keep the V-bombers effective. The army did not believe in the need for an independent strategic force and the navy resisted the RAF's plans to develop missiles as well as bombers. The air staff took the view that devoting much effort to conventional forces implied a lack of confidence in the deterrent value of nuclear weapons and detracted from their credibility, and they did not accept the naval staff's belief in the possibility of what was called a 'broken-back' war, that is the continuation of operations, particularly at sea, after a nuclear exchange. The army subscribed to neither of these views. There was no compromise that we could agree on. I tried a personal draft, but my colleagues could not accept any dilution of their entrenched positions. Against all precedent we were forced to submit three different papers, which did not please our Chiefs.

Frankie Festing brought a more relaxed atmosphere to the CIGS's office, so relaxed that I often wondered if he took affairs in Whitehall seriously at all. His briefings were invariably postponed until the last possible minute and he often took little trouble to absorb them. On one occasion we were briefing him for an important meeting in 10 Downing Street about nuclear warfare. We started very late and he seemed to pay little attention. At one stage he said: 'Well, I don't know what nuclear war will be like, but, when it's all over, you'll find me, dressed in sheepskins, striding over the Cheviots!' His military assistant, 'Monkey' Blacker, finally insisted that he must leave, or he would be late. Cramming the papers into his brief-case and picking up his dilapidated umbrella and terrible bowler hat, he turned and said: 'Gentlemen, if I thought anything was going to be decided at this meeting, I'd be as depressed as you are,' and strode out.

The next crisis arose in November over Berlin, when Khruschev demanded the withdrawal of all occupation forces and started a campaign of harassing allied traffic to the city, threatening to hand over control of entry to the East Germans. Tension was high by the end of the year, and I was taking Christmas leave at Edwardstone when I was summoned urgently to London. Accompanied by Air Commodore Pete Wykeham from the Air Ministry, I was to fly to Washington to take part in discussions with the Americans about plans for action, if access to Berlin by road, rail or air was interfered with. Briefed by the War Office, the Chiefs of Staff Secretariat and the Foreign Office, clasping a diplomatic bag full of top-secret papers and equipped with an imposing document appointing me an official courier, I was booked on an evening flight from Heathrow in a BOAC Britannia. As we taxied out to take off, sparks were seen coming from our brakes, and we returned for a long wait before finally taking off hours late. In mid-Atlantic I was half asleep when I realized that we were turning round. The stewards at first denied, but then admitted it, and after breakfast we were back at Heathrow. The urgency of our mission got us transferred to a Comet – as much a luxury then as Concorde became later – and, after refuelling in Iceland, we reached New York late in the day. Transferring by helicopter to La Guardia airport, we had a long wait, during which we watched Charles Laughton as the Hunchback of Notre Dame on television, before catching a flight to Washington, my luggage having got lost on the way. We had had no sleep for 48 hours, but had to go straight into a meeting with officials of our embassy in the house of Admiral Michael Denny, the head of the British Military Mission, where I was staying, as our meeting with the Americans was fixed for 9 a.m. next day.

The meeting was held in the State Department and was chaired by Robert Murphy, both our ambassador, Harold Caccia, and his French colleague, Hervé Alphand, being present. Murphy was abominably rude, accusing us of being chicken-hearted, and maintaining that our failure to be prepared to force our way up the autobahn in the 1948 Berlin crisis, having to resort to the airlift, had led to the Korean War. This was followed by a meeting with the staff of the US Joint Chiefs of Staff in the Pentagon. The atmosphere was extremely hawkish, the US Air Force taking the line that this was the last chance of having a showdown with the Russians while they could not attack the USA directly. I pointed out how easily the Russians and East Germans could put us in a position in which we would be forced to escalate or accept frustration. After the meeting I produced a sort of critical path analysis, in the form of 20 questions. The Americans showed no sign of having another meeting to answer them, and we discovered that they had sent them to General Norstad, who had taken over from Al Gruenther as the Supreme Allied Commander at SHAPE. They were not prepared to carry on the discussion until they had received his answers, and days went by without any sign of a meeting. I had nothing to do and was getting anxious about whether I should miss *The Sleeping Beauty* at Covent Garden, for which I had seats for the whole family. I persuaded Michael Denny to signal the Chiefs of Staff, urging that I should return to London to put them in the picture, provided that I returned to Washington as soon as the Americans were prepared to talk. A grudging agreement having been received, off I went.

I was met at Heathrow and driven straight to a meeting of the Chiefs of Staff, reading the joint planning paper and munching sandwiches on the way. 'Dickie' Dickson, introducing the item on the agenda, said that he welcomed

Colonel Carver, who had come from Germany to give the
views of the Cs-in-C there. Roddy McLeod intervened to
point out that Brigadier Carver, whom the CDS knew as
Director of Army Plans, had come from Washington, where
he had been representing the Joint Planners, to report on
what had been going on there. 'We know all about what's
been going on there,' retorted Dickson, 'we've had plenty of
perfectly clear signals.' Only after McLeod had insisted, was
I allowed to say a word.

I was reunited with the family at Covent Garden that
evening and our seats in the stalls circle overlooked those in
the stalls of Don and Cherry Cook and several members of
their large family. The *Daily Telegraph* had that day run a story
reporting that the Americans were being difficult over Berlin
and that a representative of the British Chiefs of Staff had
been left kicking his heels for days on end in Washington.
In the interval Don, who we had been delighted to find on
our return from Kenya had been transferred from Paris to
London, expressed surprise at my presence, assuming that I
was in Washington. I fobbed him off with some unconvincing
explanation, knowing that I was to return to Washington
next day, the Americans having at last said that they wished
to resume discussion. Norstad had brought common sense
to bear and had suggested that contingency planning for
interference with traffic to Berlin should be transferred
from Washington and London to his headquarters. This
was agreed, and a special Anglo-American–French staff,
codenamed Live Oak, headed by a British major-general,
was set up to advise Norstad in his capacity as US C-in-C
Europe, Berlin not being a NATO responsibility. The Live
Oak staff became a permanent establishment.

In 1959 Lord Mountbatten succeeded Dickson as Chief of
the Defence Staff, Admiral Caspar John, son of the painter
Augustus, taking his place as First Sea Lord and Chief of
the Naval Staff. Mountbatten soon made his influence felt,
his technique being to try and reach agreement between the
Chiefs of Staff by private lobbying, so that, if possible, their
meetings in committee merely gave their formal stamp of
approval. He was determined to strengthen the very weak
authority both of the Minister and of the CDS. One of the
steps towards this, which he proposed, was the appointment

of a chairman of the Directors of Plans, who would act as his representative on our committee, his choice for the first incumbent being Fred Rosier. Festing sent for me to discuss this. I said that I thought it was an inevitable step in the development of a more effective central defence machinery, that Rosier was an excellent choice, and that he should agree. 'My colleagues are very suspicious,' replied Frankie: 'You see, the trouble with Dickie (Mountbatten) is that, if the front door were wide open, he'd still come down through the chimney!' Even if he did undermine or by-pass the system at times, Mountbatten was a refreshing contrast to his predecessor. Business was much more efficiently conducted and we were kept very much on our toes.

A variation from our usual tasks was the establishment by Harold Macmillan of the Future Policy Study Group. A general election would be due by 1960 at the latest. Macmillan decided that whatever administration resulted from it should have available the result of a study, answering the questions: 'What will the world be like in ten years' time? What will Britain's position in it be? What should be done about it?' The body charged with the duty of providing the answers should be drawn from the principal ministries, but not subject to direction from them. Pat Dean, then head of the Foreign Office defence department, was the chairman, the members being deputy under-secretaries from the Foreign, Commonwealth Relations and Colonial Offices, the Treasury, and the Ministries of Defence and Fuel and Power. The Directors of Plans were also members. The Prime Minister did not entirely get his way over absence of direction. There was no doubt that some of it was applied, although I personally resisted it, and the report was to be subject to the scrutiny of a steering committee, consisting of the Chiefs of Staff and the permanent under-secretaries of the ministries involved, chaired by the Secretary to the Cabinet, Sir Norman Brook. The report was not completed until after I had left, and was, I believe, significantly watered down by the steering committee. The study group soon split into two general factions, almost classical Whigs and Tories. All were agreed on the importance of remaining on good terms with the USA and of the latter's continued involvement in the defence of Europe. The split occurred on how our influence with the USA should be maintained. The Tories gave priority to our maintaining an active world-wide presence and influence, supported by armed forces; the Whigs wished to give greater emphasis to our being good Europeans and involving ourselves more closely with our neighbours by joining the European Economic Community, pulling in our horns in the Middle and Far East. I supported the Whig school (although the War Office generally did not), as did the Foreign Office, the Treasury and half the Colonial Office, the half that was in favour of rapid advancement of colonies to independence. The others were generally ranged on the Tory side. One of the most interesting aspects of our study was our attempt to draw up a balance-sheet between the cost of armed forces stationed in various areas and the value to Britain of what they were supposed to be defending. The forces based in Aden, designed to deploy to the Persian Gulf, were the best value for money: they cost little and made an important contribution to our participation in the world oil business. The least cost-effective were the much larger forces in the Far East. They cost much more, and it was doubtful if they were necessary to secure our important commercial interests in Malaya. Hong Kong could not be defended against a deliberate Chinese attack.

While I was concerned with these long-term issues, other branches of the War Office were much more interested in the short-term issue of the future manpower strength of the army. Before the Suez operation it had been about 400,000. One of Macmillan's first decisions after becoming Prime Minister in 1957 was to abolish conscription altogether by 1960. The army had based its plan for a future all-regular army on a strength of 200,000. Duncan Sandys's civil service advisers in the Ministry of Defence estimated that regular recruiting could not maintain a strength of over 165,000. Fierce arguments went on between them and the War Office, where Christopher Soames was Secretary of State for War, the latter eventually obtaining agreement on 182,000. These figures did not include soldiers recruited overseas, such as the Gurkhas. I became involved in these

---

* Australia, New Zealand, Malaya.
† South East Asia Treaty Organization.

arguments when future joint service plans, such as those in
support of ANZAM* and SEATO† in the Far East, were used
as the basis of formulating future requirements. The brunt
of the argument about future organization was borne by the
Deputy-CIGS, Pete Pyman, but the Vice-Chief, Bill Stratton,
was also involved. I attended a meeting at which both of them
discussed with Festing the problem of finding the manpower
for two new elements of the army, armoured personnel carriers and light aircraft, including, it was hoped, helicopters.
It could only be found at the expense of existing units. 'I see
no problem,' said Festing: 'Turn the worst cavalry regiments
into APC regiments and the best infantry into aircrew. If you
don't know who they are, I'll tell you!' Pyman and Stratton,
both serious men, seemed shocked and uncertain whether
Frankie meant it seriously. By this time Jack Hamilton had
been replaced as DMO by Dick Craddock, and his deputy,
David Mullen, by Tony Lascelles. I got on as well with the
new team as I had with the old. Dick Craddock had a less
lively and open mind than Jack Hamilton, but his dead-pan
manner and dry wit concealed a shrewd and perceptive
mind, anchored to a rock of common sense.

A distraction from my official business came with an
approach on 29 May 1959 from Batsfords, the publishers,
suggesting that I should write a book on the Battle of El
Alamein for their British Battles series. My name had been
suggested to them by Peter Kemp, who had been editor of
the *Royal Armoured Corps Journal*. After discussing it over
lunch with their executive director, Sam Carr, I agreed, provided that I could obtain access to official material. Brigadier
Harry Latham (ex-commander of 2nd Armoured Division's
Support Group and a friend of my father-in-law) was head
of the War Office Historical Branch. He told me that he held
what was called 'the official narrative', a very full account
made up from the war diaries of both sides for the benefit
of the official historians in the Cabinet Office. He could
only let me have access to it, if he was given permission
by higher authority within the War Office. I was not likely
to be granted this, unless I could persuade the authorities
that my book would be of military value. The authorities
whom one was supposed to approach were the Director of
Public Relations and a civilian branch called C2. I suspected

that they would turn my request down, and asked Harry Latham if the authority of the CIGS would suffice. He said it would. I therefore wrote a minute on 15 June to the CIGS, on which he wrote: 'I'm delighted you should write this book. The authority you require will be given.' Monkey Blacker informed the appropriate branches, who did not react immediately. According to the strict rules of King's Regulations, I should not have signed the contract with the publishers until the text of the book had received War Office approval, an impossible rule to comply with. I decided that the sooner I could complete the book the better, so that, if the civil servants raised objections in principle, I could face them with the script to counter their objections. These were likely to be that it would cause controversy (e.g. between Montgomery and others, such as Auchinleck, Dorman-Smith and Gatehouse) or upset the official historians, who were not yet ready to publish their version, or other authors or potential ones, who had not been granted access to the official narrative.

I devoted almost every lunch-hour (which ran from 12.45 to 2.30 as a rule) to working on the narrative in the basement where the Historical Branch was housed, taking a thermos of coffee and a packet of sandwiches with me. I did much of the actual writing on my summer holiday, which we spent at Edwardstone, and delivered the completed script, typed half by myself and half by my secretary, to Batsfords on 30 October. I was delighted to receive a letter from Sam Carr on 4 November, starting with the words: 'What an admirable book you have written!' On 17 November I submitted it to the Director of Public Relations, requesting official permission to publish. On 17 December I received the reply that permission could not be given 'at present', but that the position would be reviewed after the volume of the official history covering that period had been published, probably in about two years' time. Neither the support of Frankie Festing and Harry Latham nor the personal sympathy of the Permanent Under-Secretary, Sir Edward Playfair, could prevail. The principal reason appeared to be that Alec Gatehouse had applied for permission to consult the historical record in order to refute some of the things which Monty had said about him in his recently published memoirs, and had been refused. Batsfords, who were well aware that this could happen, were understanding and patient.

A further reason for completing the book as quickly as possible was that, soon after I had begun work on it, I was told that I should leave the War Office at the end of the year and take over command of 6th Infantry Brigade Group at Münster in Germany from John Worsley, who would be going to the IDC as a student in January 1960. This was good news. Although I had hoped to command an armoured brigade again, it would be both a valuable and an interesting experience to command an infantry brigade group, which included its own armoured regiment. Financially I expected to be better off in Germany, where, occupying an official house, we should have domestic help provided. The problem arose over schools for the children. Andrew, who had attended an excellent old-fashioned private day school, Wagner's in Queen's Gate, was now boarding at Cheam School near Newbury. Susanna and Alice had attended Mrs Hampshire's (mother of the actress Susan Hampshire) school in the church hall of St Saviour's Walton Street, behind Harrods. We had hoped to avoid having to send our daughters to a boarding school, Edith having greatly disliked the snob one to which she and her sister had been sent; but we discovered that the girls' secondary school, serving the forces in Munster, would not be able to take Susanna for another year, and that in any case it would involve weekly boarding. Having made no other arrangements, we had to rush round to find a place in a school in England, Moira House at Eastbourne, where Antony's daughter Sabrina had been, accepting her.

The year at the IDC and two years as Director of Plans had clarified my ideas about the central issues of defence and about the future needs of the army. The development of my views also owed much to an almost continuous correspondence with Basil Liddell Hart, punctuated by occasional meetings. He tried out on me many of the papers he was writing at that time, which were brought together in his book *Deterrent or Defence*, published in 1960. Some of our correspondence was concerned with the argument about the relative quality of British and German tanks in the desert. The views I had formed, when in the Ministry of Supply, and published in the 'Desert Dilemmas' articles in the *RAC Journal*, were being challenged, and Basil was determined to get at the truth for his history of 'The Tanks'. After a long exchange of letters, he agreed that my figures were the most reliable and convincing.

But most of our discussion centred on nuclear weapons, their general place in strategy and their effect on the battle-field. Linked to that subject was that of the right organization for NATO armies in general and ours in particular. We were at one in our views about Britain insisting on having her own independent strategic nuclear strike force. We could see no 'vital interest' of ours, threatened by Russia or China, in the defence of which we should not be supported by the USA and would be justified in using nuclear weapons. Keeping the force capable of penetrating Russian air defences all on its own would lead us into increasing expenditure at the expense of conventional forces, which were both more generally useful to meet all types of threat and also essential to prevent hostilities leading to nuclear war. Liddell Hart had come to recognize two truths about nuclear war: first, that to engage in one would be to frustrate the object of going to war at all. If the result was to spread fearful destruction over Europe, including Britain, it could not be called defence: it was a negation of Clausewitz's dictum that war was a continuation of policy by other means. Sec-ondly, that, in any case, one could not fight a nuclear war: controlled operations were just not feasible when both sides used nuclear weapons in quantity, which by then they were presumed to have available. He regretted that the Americans had ever introduced tactical nuclear weapons into NATO's armoury and that NATO had come to base its strategy and tactics on the assumption of their use, under the false impression that this made it possible to erect an adequate defence with the smaller conventional forces which were all that the governments were prepared to provide. He believed that nuclear weapons, far from helping the defending side, were of greater value to the attacker. He had come round to the view that reliance on nuclear weapons to deter a conventional attack had ceased to be credible. All that it did was to deter both sides from using them at all. Tactical weapons were not only unnecessary for this, but positively dangerous, because, if deterrence did fail, their use would mean the destruction of Europe. The best insurance against this was the provision of adequate mobile conventional forces at a high state of readiness, able to seal off any invasion and bring it to a halt before either side had been tempted to use nuclear weapons. Regular forces would provide such troops more effectively than conscript ones. Raising large numbers of infantry divisions by mobilisation of reserves was an out-of-date concept. Reserves should take the form of locally recruited home guard or resistance-type forces, designed to operate on their own area with man-portable anti-tank weapons.

I agreed with a good deal of his analysis. At the IDC I had come round to disbelief in the value of Britain trying to maintain an independent strategic nuclear strike force, and my involvement in discussion of the subject as Director of Plans strongly confirmed me in these views, particularly when I saw the way in which those who tried to justify it constantly shifted their ground. I had also realized that talk of fighting a nuclear war made no sense. Even if one could limit it in some way, which I doubted, it would cause such destruction that its effects would be far worse than those of refusing to fight. I differed from Liddell Hart in continuing to believe that there was some value in NATO continuing to keep tactical nuclear weapons in its armoury as a deterrent. In a letter to Basil of 16 November 1957, commenting on a lecture which he gave in Germany in September of that year, entitled 'Basic Problems of European Defence', I wrote:

> If you have the capability to use them and the enemy know it, you pose him with two problems:
>
> (a) Dare he risk a 'conventional' attack, which may be very vulnerable to the use of atomic weapons?
> (b) Dare he risk an attack at all, in case it may lead to something much larger and more serious than he intended?
>
> If he *knows* that you cannot employ them against him he can afford to take either risk and therefore is less 'deterred'. It is here that I part company with Kissinger and agree with you. I think that there is a great advantage in ambiguity, created by the knowledge that we *can* do

various things. The argument that ambiguity led to the two World Wars does not hold water: it was the knowledge that we could NOT resist any immediate action effectively which led the Germans to think in 1914 and 1939 that they could repeat 1870. Kissinger advocates making the rules certain in advance, because the whole aim of his strategy was to find some way in which the USA could use her great military power in a limited war to enforce her wishes without incurring nuclear global war. He produced very flimsy reasons for supposing that the US would *win* any such wars. What we want is to *prevent* wars, not to invite the USSR to have some nice limited ones!

My basic reasoning is this. The other side, generally speaking, want change and we do not. They are not such fools as to think that a global thermo-nuclear war is a price worth paying for the changes they would like. They will seek change without force if possible: if they are frustrated in this, they will seek to use force by any means short of global war. If we make it clear that there are certain means of their doing this which would not run a serious risk of global war, they will take them. If we did not have the ability to use tactical atomic weapons, the Russians, playing on the reluctance of the West to unleash global nuclear war, would I believe be tempted to use force to solve the German problem, either by an attack with present forces, supported by a few tactical atomic weapons, or by a force rapidly reinforced, which they would hope could achieve its limited objectives without the use of atomic weapons at all. I believe that we must have the ability to bring any Communist land attack over the Iron Curtain to an immediate halt *without* using atomic weapons and face them with a choice between the following courses:

(a) To stop, negotiate, investigate etc.
(b) To persist with *limited* action, in which case it is clear that we *shall* use tactical atomic weapons and can defeat them if we do so.
(c) To enlarge the scale and scope of the war, in which case they will run a very severe risk that it will quickly lead to the global nuclear exchange (in the case of China to at least strategic attack on her cities);

(d) Deliberately to embark on the global nuclear exchange.

This leads me to practically exactly the same conclusions as yourself.

In 1959, under the influence of the American general Jim Gavin, then responsible for 'combat development' in the US Army, Basil appeared to modify his views about tactical nuclear weapons to the extent of being prepared to agree that it was less unacceptable to contemplate the use of warheads of much reduced yield, often called 'mini-nukes'; but by the time he came to write *Deterrent or Defence* he had rejected them. In the chapter 'Are small atomic weapons the answer?', he wrote:

In theory, these small-yield weapons offer a better chance of confining nuclear action to the battle-zone, and thus limiting its scale and scope of destructiveness – to the benefit of humanity and the preservation of civilization. But once any kind of nuclear weapon is actually used, it could all too easily spread by rapid degrees, and lead to all-out nuclear war. The lessons of experience about the emotional impulses of men at war are much less comforting than the theory – the tactical theory which has led to the development of these weapons.

The whole question of reliance on nuclear weapons, and of contemplating conducting a war with them, became the subject of lively discussion as a result of a lecture which John Cowley, then a lieutenant-general and the senior army officer in the Ministry of Supply, gave in 1959 at the Royal United Service Institution. He had sent me a draft beforehand and I had strongly supported the line he took in condemning the irrationality of such a policy. It caused an uproar, and Christopher Soames faced an embarrassing situation in admitting that it had been submitted in advance to him and that he had raised no objection.

I was in emphatic agreement with Liddell Hart that we, and other NATO armies in Central Europe, needed mobile armoured divisions as a 'sealing off' force, and not static infantry divisions, occupying defensive positions in a long line extended across Germany. I did not like the proposed organization of what he called his 'New Model Division', based on fives, but preferred it to the standard infantry division. We were also at one in wishing to see the organization of the British army as a whole orientated less to attempting to maintain the security of a far-flung empire and more to the needs of European defence. The War Office clung passionately to the assumption that we must plan to conduct a limited conventional war with two divisions for a period of at least six months in the Middle or Far East, justifying its demand for 200,000 regulars and a considerable establishment of reserves, including part of the Territorial Army and most of the Army Emergency Reserve. My experience as Director of Plans had led me to regard this as wholly unrealistic both on political and on military grounds. It seemed to me essential that Britain should face up both to its changed position in the world and to the demands of dependent territories, whether still colonies or 'protected', like the sheikhdoms of the Persian Gulf, to conduct their own affairs and, if necessary, defend themselves. If the ideas which Liddell Hart and I held in common were accepted, the army would be smaller, more professional, more modernly equipped and better organized to face the demands of the future. Our attitude was unpopular in much of the army, partly because of the obsession with the old empire and partly because any reduction in size involved disbandment or amalgamation of regiments. Defence of the existing organization was naturally strongest in the infantry, both regular and territorial, on whom such a policy would impose the greatest reductions. These were the ideas which formed the background of my views on defence and of the future needs of the army, when I set off with Susanna and Andrew, in the Morris Oxford we had bought 'on export', to cross on the ferry from Harwich to the Hook of Holland on a cold night early in January 1960, Edith and Alice following the same route by train a few days later. Our destination was the pleasant house, Cambrai House, outside Münster, which was the official residence of the brigade commander, who also commanded Münster garrison, the latter including some units belonging to 5th Brigade as well as a number of administrative ones.

The brigade group consisted of one armoured regiment, the 10th Hussars, three infantry battalions (recently equipped with wheeled personnel carriers known as 'pigs'), the Leicesters, the Loyals and the Seaforth Highlanders, 40th Regiment Royal Artillery, 4th Field Squadron Royal Engineers and the usual supporting units. All, except the gunners, were to change during my time in command. I was lucky to find David Alexander-Sinclair of the Rifle Brigade as my brigade-major and Erroll Daniell, an ex-Ceylon tea-planter and wartime colonel, as the liaison officer with the German authorities. The brigade formed part of 2nd Infantry Division, then commanded by William Stirling, a friend of my father-in-law, being both a neighbour in Suffolk and an ex-horse-gunner. He was succeeded by Alec Williams, who had handed over to 'Tubby' Butler by the time I left. The 'emergency defence plan', which we had to be prepared to implement at short notice and to which our training was directed, assumed the use of tactical nuclear weapons by both sides at an early stage, and certainly if the enemy succeeded in crossing the River Weser, which formed the main line of defence. In fact the plan, and the tactics to implement it, bore a close resemblance to the concept which I had favoured when with Monty at SHAPE, German insistence on 'forward defence' having substituted the Weser for the Rhine. But, as I have described, my views had changed and I found myself in the position of having to train my brigade for operations in which I did not believe. I gave at least equal emphasis to training for conventional operations. In a talk I gave to new units when they joined the brigade, I explained our purpose in these words:

> The first task of the NATO shield forces is to *deter* the Russians, the East Germans and any other satellites from *any* military action across the Iron Curtain. To do this they must:
>
> (a) be ready for *immediate* action;
> (b) be clearly capable of fighting with and against nuclear weapons.
>
> If these two conditions are fulfilled, any venture by the enemy poses the risk of triggering off a chain reaction, the end of which is the global nuclear exchange (this is

usually known as escalation). It also makes the risk of
a massive conventional non-nuclear attack unacceptable.
The second task only comes into play, if the first, that of
deterrence, has failed. It is immediately to oppose, to seal
off and to halt enemy action, while every possible step is
taken to prevent it leading to a global exchange. This is
known as 'forcing the pause'.

I then went on to quote Norstad's own description of what
'forcing the pause' entailed.

At the level of the unit, there was little realistic training
that could be done for nuclear war. It was natural and right
therefore to concentrate on the skills and tactics needed to
make best use of the weapons which the units themselves
manned. I laid particular emphasis on all those elements
of basic military training, such as fieldcraft, which I knew
to be of such importance to all arms in active operations,
to cooperation between all arms and to the ability to operate
at night. I naturally took a close interest in cooperation
between tanks and infantry, and the latter soon found that
I was prepared to walk or march as far and fast as they
did (although not to carry as much!). I was particularly
impressed with the imaginative training and high standards
imposed by Bill Cheyne, who had taken over command of
the Seaforth just before I arrived. He was a lively, intelligent
man, overflowing with energy, longing to make up for the
war years he had spent in captivity, from which he made
several daring escapes, none of them leading to freedom.
We became great friends and remained in close touch until
his tragic and untimely final illness and death in 1970. In
1960 his regiment, which was also that of the C-in-C, Jim
Cassels, was amalgamated with the Cameron Highlanders to
form the Queen's Own Highlanders, the Seaforth's farewell
ball being a splendid affair. Bill, being junior to the Cameron
commanding officer, went to command 4th KAR in Uganda.
I missed both him and his regiment, but was pleased to
welcome in their place the King's Shropshire Light Infantry,
commanded by Dick Evans, less of a thruster than Bill, but a
good commanding officer and trainer of infantry.

One of the first tasks that faced me was an unusual one:
to form the British element of an Anglo–German umpire

force for a major exercise in Schleswig–Holstein, organized
by the NATO Northern Europe Command. German and
Danish forces were being exercised with British as enemy, the
parachute brigade against the Danes and Desmond Gordon's
4th Division, which included the Canadian brigade, facing
the Germans. The chief umpire was the German General
Hax, whose headquarters was in Koblenz, and Colonel
Ernst Ferber's 32nd Panzer Grenadier Brigade, stationed
near Bremen, was to form the umpire force with my
brigade. Hax left all the detail to Ferber and myself to work
out together. David Alexander-Sinclair, normally intolerant
towards anybody outside his own organization, showed
remarkable imagination, ingenuity and tact in dealing with
his German equivalent. By the time I arrived, he had already
achieved agreement that the two brigades would be totally
integrated for the task, every umpire at every level being two
persons in one, a German and a Briton working together as
one umpire or staff officer. Ernst Ferber and I struck up
a lasting friendship, of value to us both when we became
heads of our respective armies at the same time, and, after
that, when he was the NATO C-in-C Central Europe and I
was Chief of the Defence Staff. The closeness of our relations
stood us in good stead during the exercise, when a number of
highly contentious issues arose, some with potential political
implications. One cause of them was the unscrupulous and
tactless way in which, instigated by Desmond Gordon's GSO1,
Arthur Campbell, the British enemy cheated and attempted
to frustrate the control of the exercise by the umpires.
Among the methods they employed were sending officers'
wives in civilian cars to spy on the other side and cutting the
very expensive telephone cables by which the German army
was linked to the civilian telephone system. I was so angry
at the way they behaved that, at first, I refused to go to the
buffet lunch which Desmond Gordon gave after the exercise.
David persuaded me to go, but, when we got there and I saw
the straw effigy of an umpire hanging from a tree, I left after
the barest of civilities.

I enjoyed training exercises which took us out into the
countryside, and never ceased to be surprised by the way in
which German farmers accepted as a matter of course that
we drove our tanks over their fields, parked our vehicles in

their farmyards and settled down for the night, or for longer, in their houses. They even appeared to welcome us. British farmers and landowners would have been aghast at having to accept such an invasion.

One of the advantages of being stationed in Germany was the ease with which one could drive to other parts of Europe. Roger St John, who was commanding 11th Brigade at Minden, had persuaded me that the best way of taking a holiday with children was to camp. I therefore invested in camping equipment and a second-hand trailer to take it. In the spring Edith and I took a fortnight's holiday in Northern Italy, including Venice and the lakes, with an eye to camping on the shore of one of them in the summer. We found a camp site on Lake Iseo, to which we went in August, camping also on the way there and back. A night in a thunderstorm at a site near St Moritz was an awesome experience, the rain pouring down while peals of thunder rolled round the mountains, lit up by streaks of lightning. It proved a pleasant and successful holiday, bathing in the lake, living on pasta, peaches and gorgonzola, washed down by Bardolino. We soon became expert at camp-site tactics. I would get up early to see if any other camper, in a better situation near the shore, was packing up, and would quickly stake my claim.

I was also keen that we should take advantage of being in Germany to learn to ski. Immediately after Christmas we went to Lermoos in Austria, just over the frontier from Garmisch–Partenkirchen, where we all started learning together. I could only spend one week and was surprised to find that, in that time, I could learn enough to enjoy myself on my own. In 1961 we followed the same pattern, affected by the fact that Edith was pregnant. After the Easter holidays, she and I and my mother drove to Provence to stay with Antony and Elizabeth. Antony had retired from the RAF in 1957 and worked for a time for a British management consultancy firm in Paris, until the firm closed its office there. He had by then acquired a very primitive house in the picturesque village of Bonnieux, built up against the side of the hill, and he and Elizabeth went to live there, while gradually improving it. Leaving my mother with them, we toured Provence and the Auvergne, returning by the Rhineland. Edith expected her baby in August, and, in the summer holidays, I took the children on two short camping holidays to the Dutch coast – first to the island of Ameland, where it poured with rain most of the time and then to Callantsoog, south of Den Helder, where the wind blew and the sea was as cold as in Suffolk. John was born in the military hospital at Münster at lunch-time on Sunday 13 August, and we were delighted to complete a well-balanced family. When General 'Splosh' Jones, the corps commander, rang up to congratulate us, I could not forbear to point out that I had always been a protagonist of the evenly balanced armoured brigade.

1961 saw another amalgamation in the brigade, the 7th Hussars, who had replaced the 10th, joining with the 3rd to form the Queen's Own Hussars, Marcus Fox later succeeding Hugh Davies in command. Princess Margaret, their Colonel-in-Chief, presented them with a grey drum-horse, Crusader. He was a large and lively animal, much too full of spirit to be really suitable as a drum-horse, which needs to be calm and sleepy. Hugh Davies, although he only had one useful arm, having been wounded in the war, bravely rode him in hunter trials. I was glad to be able to exercise him occasionally and found him quite a handful for two good arms. As well as learning to ski, I was keen that we should also learn to sail. I had very occasionally crewed for others, but never had the slightest idea what to do, my first experience in a dinghy having been with my Uncle Herbert's brother-in-law, George Eeman, on the Nile at Cairo in 1938. The nearest place was the Dummer See, 60 miles away, which had the advantage of being shallow, but I could not get anyone to give us consistent instruction.

Another sport which I took up was go-karting, which had become popular, parade-grounds providing perfect arenas on which to lay out courses. My brigade electrical and mechanical engineer, Major John Law, one of his lance-corporals and myself shared a kart, driving it in turn in races which I did all I could to encourage. My personal victory was to win a marathon race of 40 laps, every other kart having broken down before the end. I enjoyed the sensation of speed, the disadvantages being that, after a long race, my arms ached from the vibration and my face was so encrusted with oil and dirt that it took days before I looked respectable again. My support of go-karting got me into trouble. After I had arranged a major go-karting meeting at Münster, we were told by Headquarters British Army of the Rhine that, as it was not recognized as an army sport, everyone taking part must take out a personal accident insurance, as the War Office would not compensate them for injury. I protested that few soldiers would be prepared or able to do this. I was given to understand that it was the Ministry of Pensions and National Insurance that was at the bottom of it, and wrote to Willie Vane,* MP for Westmorland, whose wife Mary was Edith's first cousin, and who was Parliamentary Under-Secretary of State of that Ministry, to ask if he could help. He found that it was not his ministry, but the War Office which objected, and referred it to James Ramsden, his opposite number there. This infuriated the Adjutant-General's department. I had got over the problem by forming a Münster garrison go-kart club and taking out an overall insurance, based on making certain that no two races took place in the garrison at the same time. Just as the meeting was about to begin, my DAA & QMG, John Daniel, warned me that a very unpleasant message was on its way from Headquarters BAOR. I told him to ensure that I did not receive it until after the meeting was over. It said that I had very nearly incurred the official displeasure of the Army Council and laid down a host of strict conditions for go-kart meetings. What annoyed me about all this was that equestrian sports, which involved much greater risks, were officially recognized as army sports and not subject to such conditions: indeed they were granted exceptional privileges, certainly in Germany, and they were primarily, although not exclusively, officers' sports.

My tenure at command of 6th Brigade coincided with the phasing out of National Service. The last conscripts were called up on 17 November 1960 and should have left two years later; but the Government took powers to retain them for up to six months beyond the date on which they should have been released, and the last left on 16 May 1963. The principal reason for this was the tension over access to Berlin, following the erection of the wall dividing West

* Later Lord Inglewood.

from East Berlin on 13 August 1961. Almost all the national
servicemen had made good soldiers, but their presence and
their reluctance to admit that they could actually be enjoying
their service, affected the attitude of the regulars and the
prospects of recruiting them. Only when the last conscript
had left could the latter openly take a pride in having joined
the army and admit that he enjoyed the life.

In July 1961 I wrote to Major-General Dick Fyffe, the
new Director of Public Relations at the War Office, to ask
if he could help to break the deadlock over permission to
publish my book on El Alamein. He had been at the same
house at Winchester, and I hoped might be sympathetic.
One of the original objections to publication had been that,
as Director of Plans, I had been in a 'central and influential
position'. I had reason to believe that my next job would be
back in the War Office as a major-general, and feared that
the same objection might be raised again if I were there
in that rank. His answer, clearly dictated by a civil servant,
was very disappointing. Not only did he say that there was
'virtually no hope' of permission being given before the
official history of the period had been published, but that
a review was taking place within the War Office designed
to impose even tighter restrictions on writing by serving
officers, and 'in view of this, I think it is only fair to say that
you should not assume any guarantee that, even though you
submit the manuscript, permission to publish the book will
be approved'. I sent a stinging reply, which opened a chink
of light. The new Permanent Under-Secretary, Sam Way,
agreed that I could resubmit the script 'as early as you like
in 1962', although there was little sign of the official history
appearing – it was not published until 1966. Soon after that
Tony Lascelles, with whom I had left a copy of the script,
and who travelled daily to the War Office on the same train
as his fellow Old Wykehamist, Dick Fyffe, persuaded him to
read it. He was impressed and wrote to me: 'I see clearly
that it is a purely factual account with no innuendos about
anybody. I wonder whether you would allow me to let PUS
read it. I think it might influence his outlook on this business
of publication by serving officers.' I was only too glad to do
so, and the first intimation I received that it had broken the
logjam was a letter from Harry Latham in January 1962

saying, 'The War Office has recently been reconsidering the publication of your book' and suggesting that I come to London and discuss the amendments he would like to see made. I managed to get over at the end of February and reach agreement on a list of amendments, the only one of substance being what I wrote about the state of Eighth Army at the time of Monty's arrival. All of them could easily have been agreed 18 months before. Some further amendments were demanded a month later and I got the final go-ahead on 11 April. Publication was to be on 3 September, and at the end of July I received advance copies, one of which I sent to Monty. I had deliberately not consulted him for fear that he would insist on imposing restrictions on what I wished to say. Although, on the whole, I had come down on his side on the controversial issues, I had been critical of his failure to cut Rommel off at the Battle of Alam Halfa and in the pursuit after El Alamein. I was therefore delighted to get a letter from him in August, saying: 'I have read it with interest and reckon it is very good. A critical analysis of a battle some years afterwards is always of value, and I often wonder what the various writers would have done themselves in the conditions at the time. It is the conditions as known to the commander at the time which dictate his decision. As I look back now, I don't consider I would have acted in any way differently.'

The delay had one advantage, in that publication took place just before the twentieth anniversary of the battle, beating to the post another book on the battle by Brigadier Lucas-Philips, who was to make a much greater success with his book *The Small Garden*. Oliver Woods contributed a 'turn-over' article in *The Times* to reviewing my book, and reviews generally were favourable. I was particularly pleased by that in the *Observer*, which described it as 'a highly accomplished piece of work . . . Carver manages to convey with rare effect the confusion of war without in any way sacrificing the pattern of either thought or action . . . a very good piece of military history. It is also in its quiet way something of a literary feat.' Basil Liddell Hart wrote: 'I congratulate you warmly on producing what is much the fullest and best account of the battle yet published.' I had seldom felt such satisfaction in something that I had accomplished on my own. It proved to be a successful book, running into two hardback editions, totalling 11,500, and a third new one being published in 1979. A paperback edition was produced by Fontana in 1973 and reached a third impression in 1976. French, Italian, Spanish and Israeli versions were published and a pirated edition produced in East Germany.

Publication coincided with our return to England. Earlier in 1962 I had been told that I would succeed John Mogg as Director of Combat Development in the War Office, a major-general's post, in the new year. This posed the problem of where we should live. We had renewed the lease of the London flat for another seven years, but at a higher rent, and had let it furnished. We calculated that we could not afford to live in it ourselves, nor could we any longer park ourselves on Edith's parents while we searched for an alternative. Her father had demolished Edwardstone Hall and moved into the Lodge Farm. There was not room for us all there, and, in any case, they were too old to be able to cope with such an invasion for any length of time. We had not solved that problem when, in June, I was told that, instead, I was to take over command of the 3rd Division on Salisbury Plain in September. Its commander, Vivian Street, had suffered a severe heart attack and had had to give up command. He had to retire and died of another heart attack in 1970. This ill wind for him blew good for me. I was delighted to be given command of this very special division, commanding the troops of the strategic reserve, and to be on Salisbury Plain instead of in London again. It also solved our housing problem, as a quarter was provided, Clive House at Tidworth, built in the 1920s for the commander of the Tidworth cavalry brigade. We drove from Münster to Ostend, crossed the Channel by night, breakfasted at Winchester and were installed in Clive House before lunch on 4 September, Edith having altered the badges of rank on my uniform on the journey. I was a fully-fledged major-general at the age of 47, having never achieved the permanent rank of brigadier, although I had spent over ten years in that rank. Such were the mysterious ways of the army's system of promotion.

13

The Arts of War and Peace

The isles of Greece, the isles of Greece!
Where burning Sappho loved and sung,
Where grew the arts of war and peace
                    Lord Byron(1788–1824), *Don Juan*

Third Division was the only regular division in the United Kingdom and commanded most of the regular troops which formed the strategic reserve. Since 1959 the emphasis had been on airportability, and most of its training and thought was devoted to movement by air to its destination, as well as to movement, supply and fire support by air on arrival. Although much had been achieved under the leadership of Charles Harington, who commanded the division from 1959 to October 1961, there was still a large gap between realities and the requirement, not least in the availability of aircraft, particularly helicopters. In 1960 38 Group Royal Air Force had been resuscitated to command the tactical air forces, both strike and transport, to support the division, RAF Transport Command producing the strategic lift. The Flag Officer Amphibious Forces provided a link with the Royal Navy. The division, the headquarters of which was at Bulford, a few miles from Tidworth, was under Southern Command at Wilton, the C-in-C being Bobbie Bray, an infantryman who had a reputation for rudeness and quick temper, neither of which he displayed towards me. The formations of the division were 19th Infantry Brigade at Colchester, 2nd Brigade at Plymouth, 51st (Gurkha) Brigade at Tidworth and also at Tidworth the armour, commanded by Jack Greenwood, who had been a fellow subaltern with me in 2nd Battalion Royal Tank Corps at Farnborough. It did not include 16th Parachute Brigade, except for C Squadron 2nd Royal Tanks, equipped with the new Malkara wire-guided anti-tank missile, mounted in trucks, who were trained as parachutists. I was fortunate to find Dick Worsley as my GSO1, a lively and able officer, whom I had known as a subaltern with Vic Turner's 1st Battalion The Rifle Brigade in Germany just after the war, and John Tomes of the Warwickshire Regiment as my AA & QMG. Dick went to command The Royals in July 1963 and was succeeded by another very able officer, John Archer, who had been in one of the MO branches in the War Office when I was Director of Plans. Both were later to reach high positions in the army. With few exceptions the staff of the headquarters was of a high standard. It was pleasant to be near my mother, who had bought a cottage at Chilmark on the other side of Salisbury Plain when Paul had married. I was also delighted to find that Rodney was commanding the Royal Naval Air Station at Yeovilton, which gave me an exceptional opportunity to establish close links with the Fleet Air Arm. We helped each other out in unconventional ways. When Admiral Percy Gick, the Flag Officer Aircraft Carriers, laid on an exercise to test the station's security, I provided Rodney with some troops who foiled Gick's attempts to penetrate its defences. Less fortunate was the help I gave him in the exceptionally severe winter when the runways were covered in frozen snow. My Royal Engineers constructed a sledge on which a jet engine was fixed to melt it and blow it away. Unfortunately it also melted the bonding between the concrete slabs which formed the runway, which got Rodney into trouble.

The first major event was an exercise in November for Bunny Short's 51st Brigade, of which the headquarters, the administrative units and one battalion, 1st/6th Gurkha Rifles, were all Gurkha. They were flown by RAF Andover and Beverley aircraft to the disused airfield at Nutt's Corner near Belfast and ferried forward from there to the mountains of Mourne by helicopter. It was a successful exercise, marred only by exceptionally cold weather for Northern Ireland, as a result of which several Gurkha soldiers were affected by frost-bite. Quick work by John Tomes and all

concerned extracted 500 parkas, left over from the Korean
War, from an ordnance depot in England, and delivered
them to the soldiers in the field within 48 hours of the
first request. After a study period held jointly with Air
Vice-Marshal Tim Piper's 36 Group RAF and Rear-Admiral
James Walwyn's naval staff in January, our attention was
concentrated on preparations for a major exercise to be held
in September for Denis Beckett's 19th Brigade, called *Triplex
West*. The brigade, and the aircraft to support it, were to be
flown to El Adem in Libya, still a RAF station, and then to
carry out an exercise westward towards Mechili, an area of
desert of nostalgic interest to me. The squadron of Centurion tanks in preservation at El Adem was to be manned by
my one and only armoured regiment, the 5th Inniskilling
Dragoon Guards, the rest of its tanks being shipped to
Tobruk by a chartered 'heavy-lift' ship. An aircraft-carrier
and various other ships in the Mediterranean would cooperate. All this was made possible by the training rights we still
enjoyed in Libya.

In January 1963 Edith and I had taken the children to ski
at St Moritz, leaving John and Irmtraut, who had come with
us from Germany to look after him, at Edwardstone. The
snow in England was so bad that the drive to Edwardstone
and back was a hazardous one. It was also very cold at St
Moritz. The children and I made progress in our skiing, two
occasions, when one of them fell off the 'meat-hook' on the
way up, leading to nerve-racking anxieties about our ability
to get back again. The return journey by train was grim. The
heating did not work, so that the water was frozen and I had
to fight and pay through the nose to get a bottle of mineral
water. When we reached Calais, the boat could not sail and
we had to spend the night on board in harbour, before
starting on a rough crossing next day, obtaining food and
drink again involving a fierce struggle. It was so cold that
the sea at Calais was partially frozen. In the summer holidays
we all went to Brittany in the car, flying it from Hurn to
Cherbourg, and camped on the beach at Loctudy behind the
house of Hervé and Anna Coatalen, whom we had known
from L'Étang-la-Ville days. We were lucky with the weather,
but the sea went out so far at low tide that the water was very
shallow most of the time.

Exercise *Triplex West* started at the end of September and lasted for two weeks. It tested all the practical problems and procedures of deploying a force of that size over a long distance and of engaging immediately in operations on arrival. It was a success in spite of a number of contretemps between the army and the air force. The station commander at El Adem did not welcome so large an invasion, and Piper and his chief of staff, Micky Martin, were determined to see that we did not depart from any of the rubric concerned with the control of aircraft, particularly the helicopters. Our relations were temporarily soured when they accused the army post office of failing to deliver in time a bet to their bookmaker which would have won them a profitable double. When we returned to England, we were fortunately able to pinpoint the fatal delay on the RAF at Lyneham. It was very nostalgic to be in the desert again and to fly low over it in a Beaver light aircraft. I took a party of soldiers out into the open desert away from tents to spend the night under the stars in order to give them an impression of what it was really like. My visit to the aircraft-carrier taking part in the exercise gave me my first experience of landing on and being catapulted off in a fixed-wing aircraft, a Gannet. We fired the Malkara successfully and ended up by lunching with senior officers of the Libyan Arab Force, directly descended from the force we had raised during the war under Victor Paley's command. A discussion about the lessons of the exercise was held in Malta, where Harry Thurlow was the army commander. Many useful lessons emerged, although I found it difficult to envisage where we were likely to implement them. One scenario was an appeal from Libya, then still ruled by the aged Sayed el Idris, to help her defend herself against Egypt.

As soon as we returned, I paid a visit to Germany to discuss the role of the division if it deployed there, and then concentrated on plans for an exercise for 51st Brigade in the Scottish Highlands in the spring. Headquarters Scottish Command, although pleased to see us exercise there, was not prepared to act as our agent in trying to persuade all the landowners concerned to give us permission to exercise over their moors. Some of the most difficult were those who lived in England, fearful of damage to sheep, grouse, deer, trees and almost everything they could think of. However we did

TOP With Vietnamese Prime Minister, Air Vice-Marshal Ky, in Saigon, 1966
ABOVE LEFT With ADC Edward Hardman and Royal Marines, Borneo, 1966
ABOVE RIGHT Commander-in-Chief Far East, 1967

RIGHT At Jungle Warfare
School, Malaya, 1968

Receiving a whale's tooth from
the Fiji Armed Forces Rugby
team, Singapore, 1968

LEFT Five Power Talks in Kuala Lumpur, June 1968. *Left to right* Sir Michael Walker, George Thomson, Denis Healey, Sam Elworthy, myself. *Behind from right*: Sam Falle and Duncan Watson

BELOW Visiting HMS *Hermes*, Far East, 1969

With family and staff at Command House, Singapore, 1969

TOP With Edith, Lee Kuan Yew, Arthur de la Mare and Kwa Geok Choo at a farewell dinner given by Lee Kuan Yew in Singapore, February, 1969

ABOVE LEFT On the flight back from Singapore, March 1969. 'I read fast and write fast, but type slowly'

ABOVE RIGHT With Field Marshal Auchinleck, aged 85, at the Royal College of Defence Studies, London, 1969

LEFT As GOC-in-C Southern Command, aged 55, greeting Her Majesty at the School of Infantry, Warminster, 1970

TOP The Chiefs of Staff on the 50th anniversary of the establishment of the Chiefs of Staff Committee, 1973. *Left to right*: Admiral Sir Michael Pollock, Air Chief Marshal Sir Denis Spotswood, Admiral of the Fleet Sir Peter Hill-Norton and myself

BOTTOM Taking the passing-out parade at the Royal Naval College, Dartmouth, 1974

Before a flight in a dual-control
Lightning at RAF Leuchars,
1975

BELOW Presiding over NATO
Military Committee, Brussels
1975, with Admiral of the Fleet
Sir Peter Hill-Norton, the
Chairman

CHAIRMAN   SECRETAR

RIGHT Edith visiting the British
Military Hospital, Hong Kong,
1975

LEFT My farewell as Chief of the Defence Staff, 22 October 1976. *Left to right*: Admiral Sir Edward Ashmore, General Sir Roland Gibbs, Air Chief Marshal Sir Neil Cameron, Air Chief Marshal Sir Ruthven Wade, General Sir John Gibbon and Mr Victor Macklen

BELOW Five Field Marshals at the unveiling of a memorial window to FM The Duke of Gloucester, Sandhurst, 1977. *Left to right*: Hull, Baker, Harding, Templer and Carver

LEFT With my brother Antony at the wedding of Paul Strutt in 1977

ABOVE Arriving controversially
in uniform at Salisbury,
Rhodesia, 2 November 1977.
Extreme left, Colonel Reilly.
Extreme right Major Willie Rous

LEFT As Resident Commissioner
Designate for Rhodesia with
Mervyn Brown on a visit to
Julius Nyerere, Dar-es-Salaam,
1 November, 1977

LEFT BELOW With Robert
Mugabe, General Prem Chand
and Joshua Nkomo, Dar-es-
Salaam, November, 1977

succeed in persuading enough of them to grant permission to make it possible to arrange a satisfactory exercise, using the RAF station at Kinloss as our forward air base. It was unfortunate that, after all our efforts, other events intervened to prevent the exercise from taking place.

Our skiing holiday that year was taken at Saalbach, not far from Kitzbuhel in Austria, recommended to me by one of the young army skiers, David Freeth. It was an excellent choice. I gave up taking lessons, having got bored waiting for giggling German girls to practise their turns, and having come to the conclusion that I would not succeed in improving mine much more. Saalbach and its next-door resort, Hinterglemm, provided a number of fairly long runs which were not too difficult for me, and, being a small village, it was not very expensive. At St Moritz we had not dared to go outside our hotel, except to ski, for fear of running out of money. The children's skiing improved considerably, John having been left at Edwardstone again.

I had come to the conclusion that, although the soldiers in the fighting units were physically fit, the same could not be said about all of them, whatever their rank, in my headquarters. Although Wednesday afternoon was hallowed as set apart for sport, most of them took no part in it. With the enthusiastic support of John Archer, each branch of the staff and services was allotted an afternoon on which they all had to participate in organized physical activity of some sort, the most concentrated kind being 'circuit training' in the gymnasium. I had had the ambitious idea that the whole headquarters should walk from Bulford, at the east end of Salisbury Plain, to the School of Infantry at Warminster at the west end, a distance as the crow flies of 20 miles. However I was defeated by the practicalities. If we set off in line, all starting at the same time, all the ranges on the Plain would have to be closed for at least one whole day. If we walked in line ahead, skirting the edge of the ranges, it would take at least two days, and a night in between, from the time that the first man started until the last arrived at Warminster. Ironically I twisted my knee very badly when out for a walk, trying to head off a rabbit being chased by Jedda, the black labrador belonging to the Dormans, who was lodging with us while they were in Kenya.

In addition to all these activities, I had time to spare for literary ones. In November 1962 Michael Howard, then professor of the department of war studies at King's College, London, had asked me to write a chapter on training and doctrine in the British Army since 1945 for a *Festschrift* that he was editing as a tribute to Basil Liddell Hart on his seventieth birthday, which would fall in 1965. At the same time Sam Carr asked me if I would write another book for Batsford's Battles series, suggesting the Ardennes offensive, the final stages of the campaign in North West Europe or the siege of Tobruk in 1941. In reply I said that I could not afford the time to research the material for the first two; and that the siege of Tobruk alone would not merit a complete new book, having already been fully covered by Chester Wilmot in his book *Tobruk 1941*, published in 1945. I therefore suggested one covering the period from the opening of the *Crusader* operation in November 1941 to the fall of Tobruk in June 1942, for which I had all the material resulting from my correspondence with the South African official historians, both of whose books, as well as the British and New Zealand official histories of the period, had been published. Carr agreed. This time I applied in advance for official permission to undertake these two projects, which I was granted, with the reminder that they must not be controversial. I submitted my contribution to the *Festschrift* in February 1963. It was not until the end of July that Gilbert Monckton, the Director of Public Relations, informed me that permission had been refused, as it was clearly controversial. I could not dispute that, as its theme was the contrast between Liddell Hart's views and the training and doctrine of the army over the period. As I had been on the whole in agreement with Basil and opposed to official policy, as the previous chapter explained, and made this quite clear, it is hardly surprising that it was turned down. Basil and Michael Howard were disappointed, but not surprised. Alun Gwynne-Jones,* who had recently left the South Wales Borderers to succeed John Grant as defence correspondent of *The Times*, undertook to write the chapter instead, assisted by having my script, of which he strongly approved, as a guide.

* Later Lord Chalfont.

I finished what started as *The Battles for Tobruk*, and was then whittled down to *Tobruk*, in October, having been careful on this occasion not to get involved in access to sources, other than my own, which had not been made public. The complexity of the operations, extending over a longer time span, made it a more difficult task than *El Alamein,* particularly from the aspect of making it easy for the general reader, but both Sam Carr and I were pleased with the result. Harry Latham's successor, Lieutenant-Colonel Ben Neave-Hill, came down to Tidworth early in February and discussed the amendments which the War Office Historical Section wished to see made, and I had no difficulty in agreeing them. However, as it passed round the other branches, further amendments, none of great substance, were demanded, and I did not receive final permission until April 1964. The book was published on 1 October and was a moderate success. The hardback edition of 6500 was sold out by 1972, in which year Pan Books produced a paperback. It was translated into French, Italian and Hebrew.

A number of changes in command took place around the turn of the year, Ken Darling succeeding Bobbie Bray at Southern Command, David Fraser taking over 19th Brigade and Harry Tuzo 51st. The headquarters and supporting units of the latter left the country on 1 February for Brunei, Walter Walker having asked for an additional brigade headquarters for the vast front of the Borneo campaign.

By that time my attention was focused on Cyprus. On 21 December 1963 serious fighting had broken out between Greek and Turkish Cypriots, principally in Nicosia. The origin of it lay in the different interpretation they put on the constitution under which Cyprus had become independent in 1960. The Greek Cypriots saw it as confirming the island as a unitary state in which the Turkish Cypriots were fortunate to be granted a representation in all organs of government well in excess of the proportion they formed of the population, which was 18 per cent. The Turkish Cypriots, and more significantly the government and armed forces of Turkey itself, emphasized all the safeguards the constitution gave them to preserve the Turkish Cypriot community as a separate entity within the island, and as a brake on any steps which could lead to *enosis* with Greece and to a weakening of Turkey's ability to influence what went on in the island, so close to her southern coast. The demands of the Turkish Cypriot leaders to run their own affairs and their ability to block any measure at governmental or local level, of which they disapproved, led Makarios early in 1963 to propose 13 amendments to the constitution which would have weakened or eliminated their power of veto. He later claimed that he had been led to believe that the British Government would not object to them. The Turkish Cypriot leaders, headed by Dr Kutchuk, the Vice-President of Cyprus, on orders from Ankara, refused even to discuss them, and both sides began to prepare to support their respective sides with armed force. It is not clear whether Makarios and Kutchuk respectively approved of that development, but in November Makarios announced that he would go ahead and implement the amendments in January 1964. It is fairly certain that he saw this as a first step and did not mean to bring matters to a head until June. The Turks may have decided to strike before he was ready by withdrawing from all participation in the government, administration and police and effecting a form of partition. At any rate, before they had done so, Greek Cypriot extremists, among whom Nicos Sampson was prominent, decided to pre-empt them and occupy a number of strategic points threatening the principal areas in which the Turkish community lived.

The fighting which took place in the last week of 1963 was a threat to British service and other families in Nicosia and Larnaca. If it spread, not only would the 15,000 service dependants, who lived outside the Sovereign Base areas of Dhekelia, between Larnaca and Famagusta, and Episkopi, near Limassol, be at risk, but so also would be the military installations within and outside the bases, such as the airfield at Nicosia, still then a RAF station, and the supply of labour to the bases. Both Greece and Turkey might be tempted to intervene – as Guarantor Powers they each had troops on the island; NATO could become involved, as might also Russia. The British Government persuaded both sides to accept the intervention of the small British force, stationed in the Sovereign Base areas, to separate the fighters and restore peace, while the politicians sorted it out. Duncan Sandys, then Secretary of State for Commonwealth Relations, flew out in the first week of January. A joint Anglo–Greek–Turkish Truce Force was established under the command of Major-General Peter Young, the army commander on the island, himself under the command of Air Marshal Sir Denis Barnett. Young's small force was reinforced by Roly Gibbs's 16th Parachute Brigade with one of his own battalions and two from 19th Brigade. The Greek and Turkish battalions in Nicosia were also nominally placed under his command. The line which Sandys drew on Young's map with the latter's green chinagraph pencil, to delineate where the troops would remain to separate the two sides in Nicosia, was to become The Green Line, a *de facto* frontier which has lasted ever since then.

At the same time I was warned that my headquarters might be required to take over from Peter Young, who had few resources through which to exercise command away from his administrative headquarters at Dhekelia. When Sandys returned to London, the British Government sought ways of spreading the burden of responsibility and proposed an international force drawn from NATO countries. On 30 January I was ordered to place my headquarters at 72 hours notice to move to command such a force. On 1 February, after a briefing in the War Office, I flew by RAF Comet to Nicosia and spent the next day discussing matters with Denis Barnett, Peter Young and Cyril Pickard, the acting High Commissioner, returning that evening and attending a meeting of the Chiefs of Staff on 4 February, which approved a directive to the force, drafted by me and based on that which Young had issued. We were kept at twelve hours notice to move, which caused a number of practical difficulties, until 1 a.m. on 14 February. Exactly twelve hours later the first aircraft, a RAF Britannia, in which I travelled myself, took off from Lyneham and arrived at Nicosia six and a half hours later, which was half past nine in the evening. We were put up in the RAF Officers' Mess, which was holding a Valentine's Day dance, our arrival in combat kit, with pistols strapped to our waists, striking an incongruous note.

The situation at this time was extremely tense. An attack by Greeks on the Turks had taken place in Limassol the previous day, and, when troops had been hurriedly transferred from Ktima and Polis to help deal with it, fighting had broken out in both those places and the Turks in Polis had been driven into the school. The first decision I had to take was where my headquarters was to be. On my visit on 2 February it had been agreed that it should be in some empty huts on the edge of the airfield; but, as the concept of a NATO force had faded away, partly owing to the opposition of Makarios, and I was to command a reinforced British force, as well as, nominally, the Greek and Turkish battalions, pressure was put on me to replace Young's ad hoc headquarters in a hotel near the British High Commission. I decided to stick firmly to the previous plan. The hotel was too small and almost on the border between the Turkish and Greek communities. A headquarters there would get involved in local incidents, breathing down the neck of Roly Gibbs's headquarters a few hundred yards away in the golf club. The next problem was how I was to exercise command. Young had done so through 16th Parachute Brigade for the area round Nicosia and through his own two headquarters in Dhekelia and Episkopi for the eastern and western parts of the island respectively. I clearly could not do that. The division of responsibility between him and me was a delicate problem in any case. Barnett, Young and I agreed without difficulty that I would exercise operational command of all army combat units both for peace-keeping and to protect the base areas. I would ask for my own Commander Royal Artillery to be flown out with his headquarters to take over the west, but would exercise command of the east through Young's brigadier at Dhekelia. I myself came under Barnett's command. My next problem was to produce a neater lay-out of forces, moving the units from the Sovereign Bases back to areas near their barracks, and, as far as possible, giving battalions areas which coincided with an administrative district of local government. I had hoped for a lull in which to achieve this, as the United Nations Security Council was due to consider the Cyprus problem on 18 February. I actually took over command from Peter Young on the 19th, the force consisting of three squadrons of armoured cars, six infantry battalions and a gunner regiment employed as infantry, two engineer squadrons, two squadrons of the RAF Regiment, six army and six RAF helicopters and six army light aircraft. Within the next few days another infantry battalion and a fourth armoured car squadron arrived. This reinforcement coincided with increasing signs of anti-British feeling, which was developing in the press and being shown not only by the local population, especially Greek Cypriot irregulars, but also by the Regular Police. They were particularly sensitive to patrols which attempted to observe the movements of armed men or armoured bulldozers. There were also a number of instances of encroachment by Greek Cypriot fighters into areas of the Green Line hitherto only occupied by the truce force.

The comparative calm which reigned while the Security Council was discussing the island's problem was disturbed by two abductions of Turks by Greeks, which involved me in bringing pressure to bear on the leaders of both sides to prevent the incidents escalating and to obtain the release of the hostages, of whom both sides by then held a significant number. Cyril Pickard realised that little progress was likely to be made in reconciliation as long as this was so, and bent all his efforts to trying to arrange a mutual release, efforts which were later to have some success.

On 4 March the Security Council passed a resolution which recommended the establishment of an United Nations Peace-keeping Force in Cyprus for a period of three months and also the appointment of a Mediator for the purpose of promoting a peaceful solution and an agreed settlement. The first paragraph called on member states to refrain from action or threat of action to worsen the situation or to endanger international peace. This was clearly aimed at Turkey, but could also operate against intervention by Britain from the base areas. The second paragraph asked the Government of Cyprus 'which has the responsibility for the maintenance and restoration of law and order' to take all additional measures necessary to stop violence and bloodshed. As London had foreseen, the recognition given in this paragraph to the *de facto* government and its responsibility for law and order was taken as proof by the Greek Cypriots that they were primarily responsible for law and order in the whole island, while the UN Force, the creation of which was recommended by paragraph four, was merely to contribute to the maintenance and restoration of law and order and a return to normal conditions, as well as using its best efforts to prevent a recurrence of fighting 'in the interest of preserving international peace and security'. Both the Greek and the Turkish Cypriots appeared to welcome the resolution, although I could not understand why the Turks should have done so. The Greeks took it as a green light for them to get on with the job of suppressing 'the Turkish rebels', and they were keen to complete this process as far as possible before the UN Force was officially established. They foresaw, with some reason, that their case might well be prejudiced if the Mediator started his work from the basis of the *de facto* partition, which the freezing of the situation since the December troubles had brought about. They wished to see the authority of the Government re-established as far as possible in all areas before discussions took place about the final solution. The Turkish Cypriots on the other hand were naturally anxious that nothing should be done to prejudice their hopes of achieving a separatist solution, and did not really seem any more interested than the Greek Cypriots in returning to the *status quo ante* 21 December 1963, however much they might harp upon their desire to return to constitutional government.

On the very day the resolution was passed, there were attacks by the Greek Cypriots on two Turkish villages near Kyrenia and on the Turkish quarter of Ktima in the south-west of the island. The fighting near Kyrenia spread to the town and came close to Bellapais. It was several days before it died down, British troops having intervened, opening fire for the first time when the Life Guards, escorting some Greek Cypriot schoolchildren, were threatened by Turkish fighters. The excited Turkish ambassador tried to force me to send Turkish troops to protect their villages in the area. He suffered from ear trouble and spoke little English. I had a heated argument with him in French on a field telephone from the headquarters of the Turkish battalion. What with his bad hearing and the language difficulty, this was a means of communication which offered unlimited scope for misunderstanding.

On the morning of 7 March serious fighting started in the market at Ktima, which it took Drew Bethell and his 26th Medium Regiment Royal Artillery several hours to bring to an end, by which time six Greek and one Turkish Cypriot were dead, 23 of the former and seven of the latter were injured and about 300 Greeks held hostage by the Turks, the Greeks retaliating by seizing 40 Turks, including women and children, in a nearby village. A temporary truce held until I flew down there next day with General Gyani and Polykarpos Georgadjis, the Minister of Defence and Interior, while one of my helicopters took Dr Kutchuk's representative, Umit Suleiman, to talk to the local Turkish leader, Mr Altay. After hours of haggling, we reached an agreement that the release of the hostages, the dismantling of armed posts occupied during the previous day, and the clearance of livestock and goods from the market place should start at 9 a.m. next day. In spite of this, the Greeks put in a full-scale attack on the Turkish quarter at 6 a.m., Makarios later admitting that his Council of Ministers had decided on it while we had been at Ktima the day before. Bethell acted quickly and managed to get some of his men, including scout cars, between them, but they were unable to do more than obstruct the Greek action, which by midday had forced the Turks to surrender. While this had been going on, an attack had also been launched on the Turkish village of Mallia, close to Episkopi, where the Gloucesters opened fire while trying to protect Turkish women and children near the school. This made Peter Young very concerned for the safety of British families on the outskirts of Limassol, and he wanted to withdraw them into the base area. I had spent much of the day at the Archbishop's office, formerly the British Governor's residence, trying to get him to stop the fighting. While I spoke to my commanding officers on the wireless set in my Landrover outside, he would be put straight through on the telephone to the leader of the Greek Cypriot fighters on the spot. There were wide differences between the two versions of what was going on, but I managed to get Makarios to order that attacks should cease and agree the conditions on which they should do so. These allowed the Turks to keep their arms, but also authorized armed Greek Cypriot police to patrol the village. They were rejected by Kutchuk, who demanded that, rather than accept them, the whole Turkish population should move to his wretched refugee camp north of Nicosia. Before we got any further, the Greeks attacked again next morning and disarmed the Turks. This Turkish

attitude was repeated on a larger scale at Ktima. Kutchuk
insisted that, unless the Greek Cypriot armed posts facing the
Turkish quarter were all removed within a week, the whole
community should be moved to Nicosia. If he had had his
way, this would have been applied all over the island with
the dual purpose of being able to represent to international
opinion that the Turkish Cypriots had been driven from
their homes by the Greeks, and justifying the establishment
of a separate Turkish administration in the north of the
island. The sufferers would have been, as they eventually
were, the unfortunate Turkish Cypriots themselves. This
cynical sacrifice of the real interests of the Turkish Cypriots
to the bigoted nationalism and out-dated military fears of the
mainland Turks disgusted me. I sympathized with the Greek
Cypriot view that the island was basically Greek and should
be ruled as a unitary state, but I was revolted by the cruelty
and chicanery of the methods by which the Greek Cypriots,
at any rate the extremists, set about trying to implement
it, apparently condoned by Makarios's government. At the
same time I had abundant evidence that, left to themselves,
the great mass of Greek and Turkish Cypriots could live
happily together and wished to. Among the worst offenders
were the schoolmasters on both sides. When Britain took the
island over as a colony in 1922, she unfortunately accepted
that schoolmasters from Greece and Turkey, both bursting
with nationalism at the time, should be admitted to teach
in the separate schools for each community. They became
instigators of Greek and Turkish nationalism and, when I
was there, were almost invariably the leaders of the local
fighters of their community.

Haggling over terms at Ktima proved a prolonged and
difficult negotiation, transferred to a high level at Nicosia. I
had produced a formula, which was only finally accepted by
the Turks under threat from Glafkos Clerides of a renewed
attack. I regret to say that, when I left the island three months
later, the Greeks had still not implemented one important
condition it contained.

On several occasions Pickard and I had gone together
to see the Archbishop. On one of them we had complained
about the virulent attacks made by the Greek Cypriot press
on the British peacekeeping troops. As he had accepted

the presence of the force, he and his ministers should do something to counteract this. 'Well, it's very difficult,' said Makarios, 'when your soldiers don't behave very well.' I protested at this and asked him to give examples. 'My people are devoted to education in those things that we have in common with you – Christianity, democracy and the heritage of Greece – and, when your troops occupy schools on the so-called Green Line, and, as they pass, our young people see that your soldiers have drawn caricatures of me on the blackboard, they are naturally upset. Of course I understand that your soldiers mean no malice, but I am the Ethnarch and leader of my people.' 'Your Beatitude,' I replied, 'you know perfectly well that that is not the real reason for this press campaign. It is because those schools overlook the Turkish quarter and your fighters want to occupy them.' 'Well, what's wrong with that?' retorted Makarios. Pickard and I very nearly burst out laughing. That the head of a Commonwealth country, of a member of the United Nations and of an autocephalous branch of the Christian church could be as frank as that was at least evidence of his honesty. Although he was almost always devious and non-committal, he was occasionally surprisingly frank and open. When he was, one tended to surmise that he must have some devious reason for being so. On the few occasions on which he promised personal action, I found he was as good as his word.

Pickard's efforts to get hostages freed were partly successful when, on the day of the market place incident in Ktima, Makarios announced the unconditional release of 49 Turkish Cypriots. Sir Arthur Clark had returned on 5 March and Pickard, greatly to my regret, left on 10 March. Clark was a sick man and lacked Pickard's firmness and energy. The events at Ktima and Mallia had aroused fears of a Turkish invasion and Barnett and I had had a teleprinter conference with Duncan Sandys about pressure to evacuate British families. We resisted it, and U Thant, the UN Secretary-General, appealed to both sides to keep calm and peaceful, sending Signor Pier Spinelli as his special representative to the island.

The first of the UN troops arrived on 14 March, in the form of the advance party of the Canadian contingent. As General Gyani had gone to India on leave at this crucial period, the Brazilian General Piave Chaves, who had replaced

Gyani as Commander of the UN Expeditionary Force at
Gaza, came over to the island in order that there should
be an official UN Commander from whom they could take
orders. I had already been appointed Deputy Commander
(designate) and Gyani had suggested that I could act in his
place until he returned, but this was clearly not politically
advisable. Until the UN Force was officially established and
ready to go into action, I remained the Commander of
the British Peacekeeping Force, responsible to Commander
British Forces Cyprus, acting on the advice of the British
High Commissioner. I had given some thought to the awkward questions which would have to be answered if a clear
directive were to be given to the UN Force, and produced a
document, which by chance gained some notoriety as 'The
20 Questions', when a journalist at a cocktail party, at which
I was not present, learned of its existence. It was entitled
'Points to be cleared before the UN Force can be given its
orders and deployed for its duties'. It raised the question of
the future of the Greek and Turkish battalions in the island;
the interpretation of the phrase in the Security Council
resolution 'the Government of Cyprus, which has the responsibility for law and order' and all that flowed from that, in
particular the attitude of the United Nations to the police
and armed men of both sides; the general attitude to be
adopted towards the *de facto* situation of the existence of two
separate communities; the arrangements for dealing with
them both, and the question of whether or not agreements
made before the UN Force was established would remain
valid and accepted by both sides. I gave this list of points to
Barnett and Clark, and the former gave a copy to Spinelli,
suggesting that it might be informally transmitted to the UN
Secretariat in order to assist them in drawing up the directive
to the Force. It was easier to ask these questions than to provide the answers, and the next problem to be faced was the
organization of the Force and its deployment. Until national
contingents, their strength and organization, were known, it
was difficult to make any firm plan; but at least it was clear
that the Canadians were going to provide a battalion which
would be available from about the end of the month.

Meanwhile anti-British feeling was growing every day, as
we attempted to frustrate the plans of the Greek Cypriots to

improve their situation before the UN Force was established. Great pressure was being brought to bear on us to open the Kyrenia road. It was clear to me that there would be the greatest possible difficulty over this, and that it would need very delicate handling. To achieve it would entail taking drastic action in the teeth of Turkish Cypriot opposition and possibly of the Turkish battalion; to do nothing about it would increase the hostility of the Greek Cypriots and possibly place us in the position of attempting to stop them from opening it themselves. The only other course was to stand aside and let them come up against the Turkish battalion, a course of action which would have the most serious repercussions in every field. It seemed to me essential to deploy the Canadian contingent, as soon as it arrived, in the area at that time occupied by 1st Battalion The Parachute Regiment, which covered the suburbs of Nicosia and the whole Kyrenia road up to Kyrenia itself. This was not just a matter of getting another nation to do our dirty work, but because I believed that both sides would pay more attention to the first genuine UN troops, and therefore restrain themselves from resorting to violence.

As soon as General Gyani returned on 23 March, we had to get down to detail about the organization of the Force. We resisted proposals from New York to establish several international brigade headquarters, and satisfied the claims of the different national contingents for senior posts, and to have specific areas allotted to them, by handing over the Western Area to the Swedes under Colonel Waern, and persuading the Canadians to provide a brigade headquarters to replace 16th Parachute Brigade, responsible for Nicosia and Kyrenia districts, and the Danes and Finns, as well as one of my units, to serve under them. We gave the Irish and each of the two British infantry battalions their own districts, Famagusta, Larnaca and Limassol respectively, directly responsible to UN Force Headquarters. The latter was formed by my own headquarters, into which officers from other nations were introduced. The only internationally integrated unit was the military police company, commanded by a Finnish major. Units from the Sovereign Base areas returned there, and I ceased to be responsible for the security of the bases and the many 'retained sites' outside them. The British army base at

Dhekelia provided the logistic support of the whole force. It
was some time before this transformation was completed, as
the last units, the Finns and the Irish, did not arrive until
early May, although the Force was officially established on
27 March, when the first non-British unit, the Canadian
Vingt-Douze Regiment, was deployed.

Gyani had expected that the presence of a UN Force in
place of a British one would transform the situation, both
sides respecting the light blue beret; he was depressed when,
if anything, matters seemed to get worse. He was an idealistic
man, very pleasant to work with and very appreciative of all
the help and support we gave him. He tended to get worried,
to give way under pressure and to try and find some temporary compromise. He lacked a basic toughness. Makarios is
said to have described him thus: 'I don't understand Gyani.
I have known many generals, admittedly mostly British, and
they tend to be tough, rough and rude. Gyani isn't like that.
I think he should be a poet, not a general!'

While Gyani was away, there was a crisis at Ghaziveran,
a Turkish village just off the main road from Morphou to
Lefka. The Turks had set up a road-block on it and, in spite
of urgent warnings from me that, if they did not remove
it, I could not stop the Greeks from attacking them, they
persisted. The usual crisis procedure was applied, myself
contacting Georgadjis; Spinelli and I flying with him by
helicopter to the spot; negotiations for cease-fires; conditions
demanded and refused; and so on. One useful innovation
on this occasion was my use of the press corps, who lived
in the Ledra Palace Hotel and were equipped with hired
sports cars. As soon as I heard, very early in the morning,
of the attack, I told Maurice Howe, my public relations
officer, to alert them and get them moving. Their presence
en masse, trying to get action shots of the fighting, was
much more effective in stopping the shooting than that of
troops. I warmed to Spinelli. A Sicilian by origin, he had
no illusions about anything, and was both a wise counsellor
and a superb negotiator. 'No diplomat worth the name,' he
said, 'wastes his time cultivating his country's friends. What
you need to do is to get on good terms with your enemies.'
I was very sorry to see him go when Gyani returned, political advice reverting to the hands of Alessandro Flores,

a Chilean, who had worked in the International Labour Office and who looked and behaved like the dormouse at the Mad Hatter's tea party. The UN officials who came to the island were of varying quality. The Mediator, a Finn called Tuomioja, achieved nothing. He was an enigmatic, secretive diplomat, both these characteristics perhaps adopted because he was accompanied by a very indiscreet wife. Far more effective was the Secretary-General's Special Representative, the Ecuadorean Galo Plaza, who was a very different character. Rich, influential in his own country, independent-minded and outspoken, he was a breath of fresh air and fun. I respected him and enjoyed his company, in spite of the fact that he was given to making statements to the press, usually after meeting with Makarios, without consulting or warning the UN Force. Among the best were the Mexican head of public relations and the legal adviser from Sri Lanka, Neville Kanakaratne. Neville was a tiny Cambridge graduate, a bachelor with a quick mind and a great sense of humour. As his superior at the UN Secretariat in New York was a Greek, he thought it both unwise and unnecessary to refer anything to him. He was the only UN representative, other than Galo Plaza, from whom I could obtain an instant decision, and he and I became great allies.

Crisis seemed to follow crisis, and I had to deal with a number of incidents in which British servicemen, in two cases members of the UN Force, another an RAF aircraftsman and his wife from Episkopi, were accused of helping Turkish Cypriot fighters. The RAF couple were carrying a machine-gun in the boot of their car. April saw two major areas of fighting. One was Tillyria, the western part of the north coast between Lefka, where the copper mines, origin of the name Cyprus, had been worked since Roman times, and the western tip of the island, where Aphrodite is supposed to have risen from the sea. The other was the area round the castle of Hilarion, overlooking the pass in the northern mountain range, known as Pentadactylon (five fingers), between Nicosia and Kyrenia. On the Tillyrian coast Turkish and Greek villages alternated with each other, and it was an area in which Turks produced strawberries, and later other fruit and vegetables, for the British early market. The Greeks, both the unofficial fighters and the police, did all they could to impose delays, principally checking vehicles to ensure that they did not carry arms and ammunition, so that the Turks missed the flights from Nicosia airfield which would get their produce to London. Later on it was the orange crop, for shipment from Famagusta, which offered endless opportunities for delay, huge lorries full of oranges being emptied onto the road on several occasions on their journey to see if arms were concealed in the bottom. Even if any of the oranges were fit to be loaded at Famagusta, further frustrations could be imposed there. The Greeks suspected, not without reason, that Turkish villages on the Tillyrian coast were supplied with arms, ammunition and fighters by sea from mainland Turkey by night. A very tense situation developed round the Turkish village of Kokkina, which it took Roly Gibbs's brigade several days to calm down. As usual it involved me in negotiating a cease-fire agreement with representatives of Makarios and Kutchuk, which neither side regarded as satisfactory and which involved the deployment of more troops on the ground. A week later the Swedish contingent took over the area, while the Canadians assumed responsibility for Nicosia and Kyrenia.

Almost as soon as they had done so, the latter found themselves with trouble on their hands, first at Dhikomo, near the Hilarion pass, and then in Nicosia itself, where both sides began to erect new fortifications near the Ledra Palace Hotel. Once more we found ourselves arguing endlessly with both sides about the interpretation of previous agreements not to erect new defences and to allow freedom of move-ment. Gyani had made ambitious proposals for the latter, which I had warned him that neither side would accept. In a prolonged meeting in Makarios's office, at which both UN officials and Greek Cypriot representatives were becoming more and more unrealistic over proposals which there was no hope that the Turks would accept, Makarios caught my eye and we exchanged glances, agreeing that we were getting nowhere. He gently tapped the table with his pencil to bring the arguments to an end and said: 'Gentlemen, I don't think we shall reach a conclusion here. I suggest that General Carver pursues the matter with Mr Georgadjis and comes to an agreement with him.'

I had realized early on that, however much I might dislike
it, I could achieve little unless I maintained close and, as far
as possible, friendly relations with Georgadjis. A repulsively
ugly little man, he had been a notorious EOKA terrorist
who had made two dramatic escapes from prison during
Harding's campaign against them. He owed his importance
not only to his official position, which included authority
over the police, but also because he wielded more power than
anyone else over the Greek Cypriot fighters, particularly the
extreme faction in Limassol. In crisis times he was sometimes
difficult to contact, and nobody would say where he was. If
I could not contact him during the day, I would drive up to
his house in the suburbs of Nicosia after dark. Armed men
would rise up from behind the bushes in the garden as I
walked up to the door. If his staff said that he was not there,
I would say that I would wait until they had found him, and
I did not often have to wait long. Every few weeks we would
dine together in a small restaurant near his house, in an area
supposed to be out of bounds to UN and British servicemen.
On one such occasion Jimmy Hereford, my ADC, who was
in the Landrover with a radio set outside in contact with my
headquarters, brought me a message saying that a British
soldier had been shot and wounded near the main police
headquarters at Athalassa, which was in a Greek Cypriot
area. I showed it to Georgadjis, who said we must both go
straight to police headquarters. We drove there together in
my car and met the duty minister and Antoniou, the head
of the gendarmerie. We found that the British soldier was
escort to the mail from the Episkopi base area, and had been
shot in the leg when near a Greek Cypriot village a few miles
down the road, and was not very badly hurt. Georgadjis,
Antoniou and I drove straight to the village and pulled up
by a small modern house, outside which were several armed
men. They seemed surprised to see us, and were even more
taken aback when Georgadjis paraded them inside, interrogated them, and made Antoniou inspect their weapons to
see if they had recently been fired. Having satisfied himself
that they had not, he invited me to do so. The fighters were
naturally astonished to find a British general in uniform,
wearing the UN light blue beret, invited to inspect their
weapons. It was later discovered to have been a Turkish

Cypriot who had mistaken the British army Landrover for a Greek Cypriot police one.

My most dramatic meeting with Georgadjis came soon after the UN Force had taken over, and was the result of Pickard's efforts to obtain the release of hostages. The Turks still held six Greek Cypriot fighters who had been caught 'mouseholing' into the Turkish quarter through a building on the Green Line, soon after it had been established. 'Mouseholing' was the technique of knocking holes through successive walls, so that a patrol could progress from building to building without being seen in the street. Makarios's unconditional release of 49 Turks had been on the understanding that Pickard would get the Turks to release these six. One afternoon my liaison officer with Kutchuk, Major Macey, told me that these men would be handed over to me personally by the so-called head of the Turkish Cypriot police at a rendezvous in the Turkish quarter that evening. Gyani and I immediately went to see the Swiss representative of the International Red Cross, who agreed to accompany me in order to be a witness to their physical state. At the appointed hour, he, Macey and I, with a wheeled armoured personnel carrier, were at the rendezvous. We had been there for over half an hour and were beginning to fear that there was a last-minute hitch, when two old taxis drove up and the six men, two of whom were bandaged, were brought out. Macey confirmed to me that they were the men they were supposed to be. I radioed to John Archer the codeword, which signified that we had the men and that he should ring Georgadjis and say that it was extremely urgent that he should go straight to police headquarters, to which I was on my way. Leaving the men and their escort in the APC in the courtyard at Athalassa, the Red Cross representative, Macey and I went straight up to the office of Hassapis, the unpleasant head of the police. Georgadjis was there. I told him that I had brought six men whom he had wanted to see for a long time. He did not realize what I meant, until I told him their names, at which he and Hassapis became very excited. I said that, before I handed them over, I wanted two copies of a receipt, witnessed by the Red Cross, stating that they were in a good physical state. Georgadjis told Hassapis to have them typed out and himself picked up the telephone. I knew enough Greek to realize that he was talking to the Cyprus Broadcasting Corporation, announcing the release of the men. When Hassapis returned with the certificates, he and the Red Cross representative signed them. Georgadjis gave them to me and, turning on a portable rádio, said: 'Listen to this.' We then heard the announcement. When it was over, I said: 'Perhaps you would like to see them.' I was astonished that so sharp an operator had made no attempt to check whether the men really were the ones I had said they were, or what their condition was. I sent Macey down to bring them up, and, when they appeared, Georgadjis and others threw their arms round them in a scene of great emotion, while the Red Cross representative and I quietly left, the former with one copy of the certificate. Next morning Hassapis rang me up and demanded the certificates back, as he said that the men had been maltreated by the Turks, and were in a poor physical state as a result. I refused, saying that one was with the Red Cross and that I had already sent the other to UN Headquarters in New York, which was not strictly true. Two of the men had been injured when they had originally been captured, but had been treated perfectly adequately and had seemed to be in good health.

Gyani's pious hope that, as contingents of other nations replaced British units, respect for the United Nations would grow and observance of agreements would be more widespread, was not borne out by events. The Irish found themselves involved in trouble as they were taking over from their compatriots, the Inniskilling Fusiliers, at Famagusta. The two units had reached agreement not to recognize deserters in the ranks of the other, an Inniskilling company commander having found himself face to face with a sergeant-major in the Irish battalion, who had been one of his corporals. Percy Blake's Inniskillings were in the thick of a shooting match in the mixed village of Ayios Theodoros, between Larnaca and Limassol, on St George's Day, the trouble spreading to the nearby village of Kophinou, where the road to Larnaca diverged from the main Limassol–Nicosia road. Peace was restored as a result of a meeting I held with Georgadjis, Antoniou, Percy Blake and the Greek Cypriot District Officer at Larnaca.

Meanwhile the centre of excitement had shifted to the fairy-tale castle of St Hilarion above Kyrenia. On 25 April a large body of Greek Cypriot fighters surprised a Turkish fighters' camp nearby. Georgadjis himself was seen there next day, and on the 27th they attacked the castle, using a mortar. Gyani was furious, as, following an incident at Dhikomo, he was engaged in trying to persuade both sides that they should evacuate the area of the pass, including the castle, and that the Canadian UN contingent should take it over. The latter were slow to intervene in the fighting, not having kept in close touch with the fighters of either side. Tension rose to a high level, with threats both from the Turkish battalion, which was encamped in the north-western outskirts of Nicosia, and from Turkey itself to intervene, if the UN Force did not. The UN Secretariat in New York became very excited, and accused us of failing to do our job in not observing the movement of the Greek Cypriot fighters to the area or 'interposing' a force between the two sides. It appeared to almost everyone that this was a deliberate breach of the Security Council resolution by the Greek Cypriots, and it was represented as a dastardly attack made by the government themselves against the innocent Turks. The fact that the Turks had no particular right to occupy that area with armed men and to deny access to it to all Greek Cypriots was seldom represented. Turkey made the most of the fuss she had created paradoxically by her own failure to be on the alert, and from this moment onwards United Nations opinion and influence, which had on the whole been in favour of the government, swung pointedly towards a more pro-Turkish line. This encouraged the Turks to take a more stubborn attitude on all matters, and there was a noticeable increase from then on of direct influence from the mainland of Turkey on the activities of the TMT and the Turkish resistance movement generally. Henceforth there was little talk of a return to normal living conditions with the Greeks, either by compromise or as a result of pressure. The official line was constantly repeated that they could never live peacefully together again, and that therefore partition or some variation of it was the only solution. On the Greek Cypriot side, the strength of the reaction to their moderately success-ful action surprised and annoyed them. In this area there was no question of danger to women and children, and they felt that the incident had been exploited against them by Turkey and her British and American friends. Unwilling to blame the United Nations directly, they vented their frustration on the British contingent of the UN Force and British influence generally. As at this time the British contingent was still by far the largest in the Force, this was not difficult. Gyani had obtained assurances from both Makarios and Kutchuk that, in spite of recent events, they still intended to achieve a peaceful solution by peaceful means, and he published a statement to that effect. It was used as an assurance that the truce in the Hilarion area would be kept. Apart from periodical exchanges of fire, it did in fact bring operations in that area to an end.

These events highlighted two of the handicaps under which the UN Force laboured, its lack of information, or intelligence, and the limitation on what it could do. A UN Force could not have an intelligence organization. Any attempt to find out what the fighters of both sides were up to, whether overt or covert, was regarded by them as spying, and produced strong, sometimes violent, reactions and protests, the Greeks taking the line that all we were meant to do was to monitor specific agreements and get the Turks to comply with them, while the latter regarded our job as being to protect them against Greek Cypriot attacks and force the latter also to implement agreements. Before the UN Force was formed, my own intelligence staff, which, after we arrived in the island, was headed by Frank Kitson, was integrated with the other British intelligence agencies under the able direction of Denis Speares from the Foreign Office, who operated from the British High Commission. When we became part of the UN Force, Frank and his staff moved into the High Commission, where I would go daily to be briefed by them. I was allowed to pass on to Gyani any item of significant importance which it was thought he should know. In general I had fairly good information about the contacts of both sides with Ankara, Athens and their representatives elsewhere outside the island, but scanty or unreliable information about what was intended within the fighting organizations in Cyprus.

We were constantly under pressure from the UN Secretariat in New York, and also from other quarters, including London and the British press, to place our troops between the two sides and use force to stop them fighting. Although this had been accepted from the start on the Green Line in Nicosia, in spite of the fact that it rested on no legal basis, I was opposed to applying it generally, unless there was no other method of keeping the peace. It antagonized both sides and in the eyes of the Greeks, it was justifiably seen as merely providing a reinforcement for the Turks. A better method was for the peacekeeping force to keep in the closest possible contact with the influential people, including the leaders of the fighters of both sides, very often the local schoolmasters, in order to detect when tension was imminent, prevent clashes and quickly douse them when they did occur. The Canadian, Swedish and Irish contingents, who had had previous experience in the UN Force in the Congo, were slow to accept that this was preferable and more effective than displays of military virility. In a tough situation the Finns were often the most effective. They never argued, as some of the contingents did, either on political or military grounds, over what they were told to do. Few spoke any English, so that arguments by Greek or Turkish Cypriots about the rights and wrongs of the situation fell on deaf ears. A tough Finnish soldier, pointing a sub-machine gun, clearly loaded and with the safety-catch off, saying the one word he knew, 'Stop!', was generally effective.

But in the last resort it was the political influence that the United Nations could bring to bear which determined what we could achieve, not the amount of force we could use, which, in the last resort, was very much less than either side could deploy, especially if Turkey chose to intervene from the mainland. In a report to the UN Security Council at the end of April, the Secretary-General described the task of the force as 'to use its best efforts' to prevent a recurrence of fighting, to contribute to the maintenance and restoration of law and order, and to a return to normal conditions. He elaborated this by emphasis on restoring freedom of movement all over the island, and specifically in Nicosia, and between it and Kyrenia; on the removal of all 'defensive works'; on reintegration of the Greek and Turkish

Cypriot elements of the police, and on the disarmament of everyone else.

A period of comparative calm ensued, while both sides argued about the interpretation of these proposals. It was shattered on 11 May when a car containing some Greeks, in plain clothes but armed, entered the walled city of Famagusta, inhabited by Turks. It was stopped as it was about to leave, and the occupants ordered out. Firing broke out, leaving three of the occupants dead and the other wounded. The dead proved to be the son of the chief of police in Nicosia, a friend of Nicos Sampson and himself a policeman in the 'information' branch, and two mainland Greek army officers, as was also the survivor. The Greeks retaliated by abducting twelve Turkish Cypriot workers on their way back to Famagusta from the British base at Dhekelia. Tension was high and Gyani asked me to fly down at dawn next day to see how the Irish were handling it. To my dismay I found that they were manning the ramparts of the old city with Vickers machine-guns, pointing into the Greek area. I asked their colonel what his plan was. 'If there's any trouble down there,' he said, as he pointed to the wide road below us, 'I'll just lay down a line of fire between them.' As tactfully as I could, I suggested that it would be better to get some of his men off the ramparts down on the street, and to present less of an appearance of bringing machine-gun support to the Turks.

The rest of the month was notable more for incidents of shooting against UN troops than for anything else, Hilarion and the Kyrenia pass remaining the main area of activity, much of our effort being devoted to trying to ensure that the harvest was gathered in areas where Turkish and Greek fields were close to each other. This comparatively quiet period was broken by one of tension at the beginning of June. On 4 June an unauthorized radio station, which we eventually tracked down to the St Hilarion castle area, interfered with the Nicosia air traffic control radio. This and other indications pointed to the possibility of a Turkish decision to intervene, in spite of the fact that the situation in the island did not appear to provoke it at this particular time. On 6 June there were definite indications that such an intervention was imminent, and it appeared that only the pressure of the United States on the Turkish government prevented it. Consideration was once more given to the evacuation of British families, and the British forces in the Sovereign Bases with their families with them and those within the Republic were ordered to stay at home. The reason for this was difficult to explain publicly, and was said to be on account of anti-British feeling.

The most serious result of this feeling was the disappearance on 7 June of Major Macey and Driver Platt. Their absence was not noticed until the following day and every possible measure was taken to try and trace them. Macey had done invaluable work as liaison officer with the Turkish Cypriot leaders from the start. He was a fluent Greek and Turkish speaker, whose normal appointment was adjutant of the ordnance depot at Famagusta. He had a great many contacts among the fighters of both sides and was confident that his close acquaintance and friendship with them would preserve him from acts of revenge. There had been a number of threats to his safety, and, on one occasion, much against his will, I had sent him back to the ordnance depot until the rumours died down. Coordination of the search for him and his driver was put into the hands of the UN Force civilian police, in particular the Australian contingent at Famagusta. They pursued the matter with great vigour and soon found themselves up against a stone wall on the part of the Greek police. I myself in two successive weeks attended conferences on the subject with the UN and Greek police at Famagusta, neither of which produced any significant clues. When I had spoken to Georgadjis on 13 June, he hinted that it might be laid at the door of Nicos Sampson or of Paphotis, an extreme right-wing opponent of Makarios, who came from a village near where Macey and Platt had last been seen on the afternoon of 7 June. The nearest the UN police got to an explanation of their fate was a strong rumour that they were stopped on the main road between the Turkish village of Galatia in the Panhandle and Famagusta, shot at and probably killed. Their bodies and the remains of their Landrover were then somehow disposed of. In interviews both with Georgadjis and Makarios, they professed ignorance, and said that nobody would speak for fear of retribution. I had little doubt that some of the police knew what had happened, even if they were not privy to it beforehand, and that those who did know were intimidated into concealing the truth. The incident embittered relationships between the British UN contingent and Greek Cypriots and a number of incidents resulted from it.

A great deal of the activity of this month was devoted to discussions of the future of the UN Force and of the British contingent. The original mandate was due to finish on 27 June, and the Security Council did not meet again to consider what was to be done until shortly before that date. Everyone was agreed that the British element should be further reduced, the War Office being anxious to extricate my headquarters and its signals. It was generally accepted that the British contingent should be commanded by a brigadier, who, as I had, would also act as chief of staff to the UN commander. Reductions in the British force took place when the Security Council renewed the mandate for a further three months on 27 June, partly compensated for by an increase in the Irish contingent. Gyani and Galo Plaza were both to leave at the beginning of July, the former to be replaced by his compatriot, General Thimmaya, while I was to hand over to Brigadier Yeo later in the month.

While all these discussions and arrangements were in progress, both sides were busy turning their forces more and more into what appeared to be regular armies. We soon had direct evidence that arms, ammunition and men were being imported by the Turks into Tillyria. Tension rose in that area and culminated in a series of incidents on 17 and 18 June, in the second of which the Turks fired on the isolated Greek village of Mospileri. This caused great excitement, and there were all the signs of a repetition of fighting in this area. The familiar procedures were followed by Colonel Waern, the Swedish commander. At first he demanded a much clearer directive from Gyani than the latter could possibly give. The difficulties were constantly referred to the Secretary-General for guidance; but, when it was received, it was of little help, as might well be expected in view of the intractability of the political and military problems involved. The Cyprus government was pressing the UN Force to disarm the Turks and prevent the import of arms. Gyani tried to persuade the Turks to allow the UN Force to inspect all boats and any other means by which arms might be landed;

not surprisingly, this was refused. Turkey was doing her best to exaggerate every incident in the area, with the possible aim of providing justification for her intervention; there were many days when rumours of landings ran round the island. It was made all the more difficult to take any action to restrict these activities on the part of the Turks, when the Cyprus government was bringing in large quantities of weapons and military stores, which were landed at night in Limassol, driven into the mountains and either held there or delivered to Nicosia. Not only were stores brought in in this way, but in the latter half of June a considerable number of what were said to be Greek Cypriot students, returning to Cyprus from their studies, most of whom were in fact Greek army instructors for the Greek Cypriot 'National Guard', as the fighters were to be called, had come ashore in this way. On 23 June rumours that General Grivas had also arrived were officially confirmed.

About a week before his presence was admitted, Georgadjis had asked me to spend a Sunday with him, driving up to have lunch at the top of Mount Troodos. I accepted on condition that we went in my car, flying the UN flag, accompanied by my faithful radio Landrover crew. The object of the trip was to warn me that Grivas was coming and to explain that it was with Makarios's full approval. Grivas was expected to impose a stricter control over all the Greek Cypriot fighters, a measure for which Gyani had been constantly pressing. Georgadjis asked me to persuade the British not to object. In the light of subsequent events, and of Georgadjis's ultimate fate,* I have doubts about whether the Archbishop had approved of the arrival of Grivas. I believed it then, and passed Georgadjis's warning on to the High Commission and to Denis Barnett, as well as to Gyani. On our way back to Nicosia, we stopped at a village where Georgadjis was greeted with fervour, after initial

* Georgadjis was murdered eight days after the abortive attempt on Makarios's life in March 1970. Many people assumed that Makarios had proof that Georgadjis had been behind the plot and had given orders for him to be killed. He certainly expressed no regret. However it is more likely that the Greek colonels planned both, and that they got rid of Georgadjis both because he knew they were involved in the plot against Makarios and so that he could be blamed for it.

astonishment at his being in the company of a British general had worn off.

On 4 July we briefed Thimmaya. He was a very different character from Gyani, tough and realistic. 'Well, they don't seem to have killed many of each other', was his first reaction. I agreed that, since the initial attacks in December 1963, casualties on both sides, in spite of the expenditure of a lot of ammunition, had been low.

'It's nothing to what happened in my country,' replied Thimmaya. 'Why don't we just let them have a go at each other?' I explained that, although I was inclined to take that view myself at times, it would not be acceptable in New York – we were after all a peacekeeping force – and that it would inevitably provoke a Turkish invasion with all its consequences and implications, quite apart from humanitarian considerations. 'Timmy' seemed disappointed. It was refreshing to have such a realistic, amusing rock of commonsense among us.

In order to introduce my successor to the complexities of the Cyprus scene, I entertained him to dinner on 9 July at the excellent Greek Cypriot restaurant, The Gourmet, the other guests being the Greek, French and Egyptian ambassadors and the Italian chargé d'affaires. The American ambassador and several members of the British press were at an adjoining table and looked with interest at this rather unexpected grouping. Their ears pricked up when they heard the Greek ambassador say to me in a loud voice: 'My dear,, do not imagine for one moment that my country wishes to be saddled with the responsibility for this lunatic island!'

I left on 17 July, and, in the five months I had been on the island, not only had no progress towards a political solution been achieved, but the attitudes of both sides had hardened: the Greek Cypriots resolved to run their own affairs without obstruction from the Turks: the latter were more intent than ever on a solution which separated them completely from the Greeks, who were still divided between those who sought *enosis* with mainland Greece and those, including Makarios, who preferred self-determination *(autodiathesis)*. It was not easy to judge what the majority of Turkish Cypriots really felt. Ankara, influenced perhaps by the absent Raouf Denktash, called the tune, enforced in Cyprus by the TMT. I believed that, as many Greeks claimed, a large number would have accepted submission to the Greek Cypriot demands in order to escape from the oppressive siege conditions in which they lived. 'A return to normality' was one of the aims of the United Nations operation; but what was normality? Neither side wanted a return to the *status quo ante*, and the Turks never made any proposals which made administrative, economic or political sense.

The actions of the peacekeeping force had tended to sterilize the situation, preventing the real sources of power from influencing events. The Force was bound to resist pressure for change from either side, and, as most of the pressure came from the Greek Cypriots, it was driven into a position, willy-nilly, of adding to the weight of the Turkish Cypriots in the balance, although logic, history and democratic principles favoured the Greeks. The unfortunate United Nations soldier was perched on the sharp horns of this dilemma. Both sides made heart-rending appeals for his sympathy, which they exploited without compunction, and brutally insulted him if the appeal failed. He came to distrust both.

Although the Force did not seem to have achieved much of the United Nations' aim of 'helping towards a return to normal conditions' or to the creation of a favourable climate in which a political solution could be agreed, it had at least contributed significantly to ensuring that the conflict did not spread beyond Cyprus itself, and had been of great value to the British Government in almost completely removing the threat to the British bases and retained sites and to the large number of British service and civilian families who lived outside them. The odium of being the arbiter between the two sides had been adroitly diverted from British to UN shoulders, the fact that the British formed a sizeable part of the United Nations Force, and exercised a strong influence within it, being conveniently camouflaged by our light blue berets and clear enthusiasm for the UN cause.

One of the lessons I learned, and tried to pass on to others who would, or might, face a similar situation, was that every operation, even the most trivial, of a peacekeeping force has a political implication, on the local and on the international scene and on the domestic one of the nation of the contingent involved. Even such an apparently innocuous act as taking an invalid or wounded man to hospital, giving him first aid, or taking letters to the post office for those who say they dare not go there, had political repercussions. The command of the force had therefore to be closely linked to its political direction. Ideally the two functions should be concentrated in one individual. General Gyani certainly found the strain of that more than he wished to bear.

14

Somewheres East of Suez

Ship me somewheres east of Suez, where the best is like
the worst,
Where there aren't no ten Commandments an' a man can
raise a thirst.

Rudyard Kipling(1865–1936), Mandalay

I had been given short notice of my departure from Cyprus,
but was glad to return home and rejoin the family, free
from the strain imposed by never being off duty and always
aware that any incident, unless brought quickly under control, could blow up into a serious crisis with international
implications. I looked forward to picking up the reins of the
division again and to a summer holiday with the family. It
came therefore as a shock to be told that, within a few weeks
of my return, I was to hand over command of the division to
'Monkey' Blacker and myself take over from George Cole as
Director of Army Staff Duties in the newly created Ministry
of Defence in October. Not only did this hardly give me
time to get round the division and say farewell, but it would
leave us homeless at the beginning of the summer holidays.
Attempts to have the date of handover postponed met with
no response. We were saved by Monkey Blacker himself. He
was commanding 39th Brigade in Northern Ireland, where
he rented a house, from which he did not wish to move his
family until after the holidays, and considerately let us stay
in Clive House at Tidworth until the end of September. Our
house hunting having hitherto been fruitless, I accepted the
offer of an army quarter in Woking, into which we moved

on 3 October, two days before I started work in the Ministry. By then, however, our search for a house had borne fruit. At the end of August we had found a late-nineteeth-century old rectory at Shackleford, near Godalming, of no great architectural merit and with no view, but a well built, comfortable and convenient family house. We gained possession in October and moved in shortly before Christmas, very pleased with it as the first house of our own. It was to serve us well.

Director of Army Staff Duties was a misleading title for my job: it should have been called Director of Army Organization. It was the key post at major-general level in what had been the War Office and had just become the Army Department of the Ministry of Defence, under the reorganization carried out by Peter Thorneycroft as Defence Secretary and Mountbatten as Chief of the Defence Staff. I was responsible for the organization of the army, both in general and in the minutest detail. My department laid down the 'establishment' and 'equipment table' of every unit in the army; that is, the number of men, their ranks and trades, and the weapons, vehicles, radio sets etc., with which they were equipped. I was responsible for the overall control of manpower, for the size and shape of the army, and for deciding which units went where to meet the requirements of the Director of Military Operations and the Director of Quartering. Although I was responsible and called a director, I had little power of decision or direction on major matters. These were subject to discussion in a series of committees, of which I was chairman, and our recommendations were submitted to the Army Board, as the old Army Council was now called. It was a long, laborious affair to get a decision, except where operations were concerned; and the 'arms directors', the heads of the different arms and branches of the service, lobbied ceaselessly for the interests of their particular arm or branch. I was subordinate to the Deputy Chief of the Imperial (still) General Staff, Shan Hackett, who was not always an easy man to work for. In matters on which we were agreed, there was no problem, as he was quick on the uptake and decisive; but he often disagreed for the sake of exerting his authority, and in some matters the divergence in our views was fundamental. The real trouble was that his job was unnecessary, as was proved when it was abolished. The CIGS was Jim Cassels, who had been C-in-C in Germany when I commanded 6th Brigade, and was a good friend of mine. He hated Whitehall and, having been Adjutant-General before becoming CIGS, was worn out by it. The real power behind the throne was the Vice-CIGS, George Baker, Shan Hackett's rival to succeed Cassels. Coordination at my level was most effectively ensured by an informal meeting over drinks before lunch every Friday morning between Victor Balfour (Director of Military Operations), Ian Freeland (Vice-Adjutant-General), Tony Read (Vice-Quartermaster-General) and myself, held in turn in our offices. We were all personal friends and managed to sort out many of the problems of which our superiors, jockeying for position and influence, were inclined to make issues.

I took over from George Cole on the eve of the General Election which brought Harold Wilson to power by a narrow majority over Alec Douglas-Home, Denis Healey replacing Peter Thorneycroft as Secretary of State for Defence and Fred Mulley taking over as Army Minister. The major problems which confronted me were the reorganization of the Territorial Army, the fact that in future we had to rely entirely on regular recruiting, the provision of manpower for the introduction both of helicopters generally in the army and for armoured personnel carriers for infantry in Germany, the modernization of signal communications, and the ever-increasing manpower demands of the Corps of Royal Electrical and Mechanical Engineers (REME), which was responsible for the maintenance and repair of all the army's equipment. The advent of a Labour government to power, and the arrival of the forceful Denis Healey as Defence Secretary, meant that everything was questioned, overseas garrisons in particular, although the operational requirements of the campaign in Borneo and the needs of Aden, where trouble was brewing, were not seriously challenged.

Although the organizational and manpower problems of the regular army were of higher priority and absorbed more of my attention, the reorganization of the volunteer reserves, the Territorial Army and the Army Emergency Reserve, received more publicity. It was long overdue. The existing plan was to raise a number of additional infantry divisions and other units on mobilization. Ever since I had served at Fontainebleau and SHAPE, I had regarded as bogus the various national plans to produce what were called 'Post M-Day' divisions. They could not be equipped, trained or logistically supported in time to be of any value, and to accept them as a contribution to NATO's war plans encouraged nations to default on the need to produce formations ready to take the field at short notice. Territorial Army divisions fell into this category. The TA's theoretical organization was far larger than was needed, could be recruited or could be equipped, trained or even clothed. It had been kept going on equipment and stores left over from the Second World War. The overheads of its administration by a plethora of county associations, with drill halls scattered all over the countryside, wasted the little money that could be spared. In contrast, the Army Emergency Reserve, which provided individual reinforcements and units, based on the skill the volunteer derived from his civilian employment, was economical and filled an important gap between the regular army's peace-time and wartime organization. All this had been recognized, and plans to reform the reserves initiated, before I took over from George Cole and the Labour administration assumed the reins of government. Very soon after I had arrived, Lieutenant-Colonel Hugh Beach, the highly intelligent Old Wykehamist sapper who headed SD5, the branch of my directorate responsible for the reserves, presented to me his plan for a fundamental reorganization, which would merge the TA and the AER, greatly reduce the size of the former, and transform both into an organization designed, not to produce a separate volunteer army, as the TA traditionally had sought to be, but to bring the regular army from a peace to a war footing. It was a rational, sensible proposal. To signify that it was a radical reform, and to come into line with the other services (the Royal Naval Volunteer Reserve, the Royal Marine Volunteer Reserve, the Royal Air Force Volunteer Reserve), and also try and overcome the distant relations which undoubtedly existed between the TA and the AER, I proposed that the reorganized force should be named the Army Volunteer Reserve.

The proposals, which were approved by the Army Board, ran into strong opposition from the TA, supported by the

Conservative Party in opposition. They were represented as a politically inspired blow at the traditional basis of Britain's defence, and I became one of the principal targets of the lobby, fuelled by the County TA Associations, brought together at the top in the TA Council, whose chairman was the ultra-traditional Duke of Norfolk. The keenest lobbiers were the secretaries of the County TA Associations, almost all retired regular officers, usually of the rank of colonel, whose jobs were threatened. Personal contact with TA units persuaded me that the majority of their officers favoured the reorganization. They would much prefer to have a viable unit, recruited to near its full numbers, well equipped and clothed, and given good opportunities for training, even if it meant travelling long distances for the last, than the existing situation, in which a handful of men turned up in the drill hall to train with Second World War equipment, and the unit was supposed to be brought up to strength on mobilization by ex-national servicemen, whom they had never seen. I felt that my superiors in the Army Department were pusillanimous in failing to fight harder for the reorganization and letting the odium for it be deflected on to Healey and Mulley, and, to a considerable degree, on myself. I was not prepared, as some of them were, to apologize for the proposals. I believed them to be right, for the regular army, for the TA itself and for the country, and, in later years was rewarded by the admission, from some of those who had fought hardest against the reorganization, that the reforms had been right and necessary, and had reinvigorated the volunteer reserves. To my regret the Army Department and the Government gave way to pressure over the name and settled on the unsatisfactory compromise title of the Territorial and Army Volunteer Reserve (T&AVR), which, when a Conservative administration returned to power, reverted to the Territorial Army, the AER having been forgotten. The Blimps at least won that battle.

The organizational problems of the regular army received less publicity, but were more important and more intractable. When national service had been phased out, the War Office had fought first for 200,000, and then for 182,000, as its future strength of men recruited in the United Kingdom, against the figure of 165,000 which Duncan Sandys, acting on the advice of his civil servants, had proposed on the grounds that this was all that could be sustained in the long term by voluntary recruiting. A total of 180,000 had been accepted and the army's organization based on that. But recruiting trends were casting doubt on whether it was a realistic figure. The army's actual 'adult male' strength, excluding women, boys and soldiers recruited overseas, such as the Gurkhas, was 172,000. It was hoped to increase that, and, in fact, by 1966 it had risen to 177,000, still short of the target which by then had been increased to 181,000. If manpower was to be found to meet new demands, such as helicopters and their upkeep, other units would have to go or be slimmed down. The organization of the infantry was a major issue, with its high overheads in maintaining a large number of individual regiments and training depots, for which recruiting was extremely variable. The army was devoted to its system of seniority. The older the regiment, the greater its claim to preservation, although population trends had totally changed. Proposals to amalgamate or disband old-established regiments, especially in the Household Brigade, the cavalry and the infantry, aroused passionate opposition, and Royal connections, as Colonel-in-Chief, were unscrupulously played upon. Every proposal for change, which might involve a disbandment or amalgamation, was liable to be represented as a dastardly attempt by a Labour government to strike at precious traditions, which were vital to the army's morale. I had little sympathy with such reaction and wished the Army Board to adopt a more robust and less conciliatory attitude towards it. None of the suggestions being considered at that time was implemented until the major defence review in 1967, after the campaign in Borneo had ended.

As light relief to these problems, I took a week's leave in the Easter holiday of 1965, in which Susanna, Andrew, Alice and I attended a dinghy sailing course at Emsworth in Chichester harbour, run by a retired group captain RAF, 'Crab' Searl, an old desert hand. It was an excellent course, at the end of which all of us felt confident to handle a 'Wayfarer' in winds up to Force 6 in tidal waters. It was one of the best things I ever did and provided the foundation for a great deal of enjoyment in subsequent years. In July I paid a

visit to the Far East. I flew first to Hong Kong to discuss the
never-ending arguments about the strength of the garrison,
the financial contribution of the Hong Kong government
(which Whitehall regarded as grossly inadequate), and the
linked question of land occupied by the army and future
building needs. From there I flew to Borneo to learn at first
hand of the needs of George Lea, who had taken over in
March from Walter Walker command of the 'confrontation'
campaign against Indonesia. Unfortunately my suitcase, with
all my uniform except for hat and shoes, was taken off the
Cathay Pacific aircraft by mistake at Manila, and I toured
the operational area in borrowed plumage. I was delighted to
see Harry Tuzo's 51st Gurkha Brigade operating effectively
in Brunei and to be escorted round the key area of Sarawak
by Bill Cheyne, commanding 99th Brigade, which included
two-thirds of George Lea's troops. I travelled everywhere
by light aircraft or helicopter, and found the descent into
tiny airstrips or into holes in the jungle canopy a fascinating experience, somewhat reminiscent of Kenya days.
Bill Cheyne was in tremendous form and obviously highly
regarded by superiors and subordinates alike. Little did any
of us think that, tragically, he had only five years to live.
I flew on to Singapore to discuss his problems with Alan
Jolly, Commander Far East Land Forces, an officer of my
own regiment whom I had never known well. I had no idea
that a year later I would be his successor. I stayed with my old
friend and fellow officer, Tony Lascelles, who was his chief
of staff and whose wedding to Ethne I had attended in Cairo
in 1941. Everybody expected me to be exhausted by the long
flights, the very full programme and the heat; but, as I was to
find on every subsequent trip of that kind, I was exhilarated
by the activity, the novelty of the scene and dealing with
new problems and fresh faces. The backlash would come on
return to Whitehall.

Fortunately that was mitigated by a period of leave for
the summer holidays. A fortnight of this was spent in East
Anglia, the first week on a motor cruiser on the Norfolk
Broads, followed by camping by the sea at Walberswick. In
November I paid a visit to Aden, where unrest was increasing
and to which 24th Infantry Brigade had been moved from
Kenya earlier in the year to occupy the new cantonment at

Little Aden. It must have been about the end of the year that I was informed in strict confidence that I was to succeed Alan Jolly as Commander Far East Land Forces in July 1966, and that, after only six months in that appointment, I would take over from Air Chief Marshal Sir John Grandy, a fellow student at the Imperial Defence College in 1957, as the joint service Commander-in-Chief Far East, a tremendous boost to my morale, although I did not realize initially that the second appointment would mean promotion in rank from the first. I realized later that I owed this sudden stroke of luck to the need for Jim Cassels, the CIGS, to make his 'long-term plot'. At that time Field Marshal Dick Hull was the first army Chief of the Defence Staff, having taken over from Mountbatten in July 1965. On the assumption that the job rotated in succession among the three services and that its occupants served for about three years or retired at the age of 60, it would be the army's turn again in 1973. The army's choice would have to be Chief of the General Staff (Imperial had recently been dropped from the title) for about three years beforehand. The natural candidates, by virtue of age and appropriate experience, were John Mogg and myself, but Mogg was two years older than I and would be 60 in 1973. In any case it would not be possible to groom him through the system in that time and his experience was more limited than mine, although, to a large proportion of the army, particularly the more traditional part, he would be more popular as CGS. I have no doubt also that Healey insisted that a future CDS must, if possible, have held a senior joint service command. The result was that, after marking time for so long as being too young for my rank, I had suddenly to be forced through the system as quickly as possible in order to be young enough to reach the top jobs before retiring age!

Elated by the prospect of escaping from Whitehall, of serving in the Far East, and of occupying such important and interesting posts, we set off for a fortnight's ski holiday after Christmas, once more to Saalbach. On my return I was approached by 'Atco', Major General Leonard Atkinson, the Director of REME, with the request that I should succeed Shan Hackett as their non-REME Colonel Commandant. I had known Atco since Woolwich in 1936, when I had been on my Royal Tank Corps young officers' course and he on the Ordnance Mechanical Engineers' course. As DASD I had been fighting their case to be allotted the manpower they needed to maintain and repair the army's increasing inventory of equipment against the prejudices of those who did not appreciate the need, and thought that the 'tail' should always be sacrificed to the 'teeth', particularly in the traditional units. I had known many of REME's senior officers from wartime service with them, and was glad to accept the invitation. A pleasant by-product was to be received in audience by Princess Marina, their Colonel-in-Chief.

In May 1966 I managed to pay another visit to Singapore, much of it naturally taken up in discussing with Alan Jolly and John Grandy the problems I was likely to face when I took over from them. In March the Indonesian army had carried out a successful coup against Sukarno and the pro-communist elements which supported him. At about the time I was there a team of Indonesian army officers visited Kuala Lumpur to initiate peace moves with Malaysia. 'Confrontation', which had died down to almost nothing since March, would clearly soon come to an end, and much of my visit was devoted to discussion of the effects of that on the army in the Far East.

On 8 June I handed over my job as DASD to 'Monkey' Blacker and, in the same week, received a KCB in the Birthday Honours. It was normal for lieutenant-generals to receive that honour, but rare to be knighted while still a major-general, even though it was in anticipation of immediate promotion. I was surprised to be summoned to an investiture to be dubbed before I left for Singapore, and had to hire the appropriate uniform, as my own had already been sent off by sea. One of Messrs Moss Bros's buttons, to which my braces, holding up the tight 'overall' trousers, were attached, came off as I drove my ageing Morris Oxford with Edith and my mother into the courtyard of Buckingham Palace. I remained acutely anxious that the remaining button on that side would go when I knelt to be dubbed; fortunately, it held.

Some time before, John Grandy, on a visit to London, had warned me that Mountbatten would be visiting Singapore and had invited himself to stay just at the time when he would he handing over to me. Grandy had told him this, and suggested that I should contact Mountbatten and discuss the matter, ringing off before I could ask any questions. When I contacted him, Mountbatten suggested that we had lunch together, either in London or at Broadlands. I was about to start leave, during which Edith and I, with Susanna, then seventeen and John, nearly five, were planning to stay with the Dormans in Dorset. I suggested that we stopped for lunch at Broadlands on the way, requesting that Susanna and John should picnic in the park while we did so. 'You must all come to lunch,' replied Mountbatten: 'If your wife will guarantee to look after your son, I will look after your daughter!' On arrival he explained that, while a subsidiary motive for the trip was a visit to the Life Guards, of which he was Colonel, who were stationed partly in Malaya and partly in Singapore, the principal object was the production of a television series covering his life. He had told his children that he could either leave them Broadlands or capital, but not both. His son-in-law, Lord Brabourne, had protested that, in the cellars of Broadlands, he had the solution to the dilemma. He had kept film clips of every major news item in which he had featured. A television series, based partly on these and partly on 'on the spot' interviews with him, would provide the necessary cash to make both possible. Mountbatten had accepted the suggestion and the visit to Singapore was to produce an 'on the spot' recording of his acceptance of the Japanese surrender there in 1945. Two aspects of the lunch remain vivid in my memory. Mountbatten had an electrical black box which, when one offered a sixpence to it, trembled and then stuck out a hand to receive it. He explained that contributions went towards the Mountbatten family fund, to which the TV series was devoted, and he offered it a sixpenny bit to display its function to John, who was fascinated – so much so that Mountbatten suggested that I should offer it another, which I was extremely reluctant to do, feeling no compassion for the poverty of his family! The other aspect was the sight of John, sitting on a Chippendale chair in the impressive dining room, eating with perfect aplomb the strawberries and cream handed to him by a footman, who looked like Oscar Wilde in blue battledress. We all flew together to Singapore at the end of July, the elder children flying back to school at the end of the holidays.

A fortnight after my arrival peace was signed between Malaysia and Indonesia, bringing 'confrontation' in Borneo to an end. I was immediately faced with the practical problems of withdrawing the British army from Sarawak, Brunei and Sabah, handing over responsibility in fact, as it already was in theory, to the Malaysians, and adjusting the army's presence in the Far East to the new situation, which had been anticipated in the government's Defence White Paper, published in February 1966. This had stated:

It is in the Far East and Southern Asia that the greatest dangers to peace may lie in the next decade, and some of our partners in the Commonwealth may be directly threatened. We believe it is right that Britain should continue to maintain a military presence in this area. Its effectiveness will turn largely on the arrangements we can make with our Commonwealth partners and allies in the coming years. As soon as conditions permit, we shall make some reductions in the forces which we keep in the area. We have important military facilities in Malaysia and Singapore, as have our Australian and New Zealand partners. These we plan to retain for as long as the Governments of Malaysia and Singapore agree that we should do so on acceptable conditions. Against the day when it may no longer be possible for us to use these facilities freely, we have begun to discuss with the Government of Australia the practical possibilities of our having military facilities in that country if necessary.

Grandy had been told by the Chiefs of Staff to assume that 'confrontation' would end by 1 January 1967, and that withdrawal of British forces from East Malaysia (i.e. Sabah and Sarawak) would be complete within six months of ratification of a peace treaty, leaving an infantry battalion and an engineer squadron in Brunei, preferably Gurkha. The total of British army and Royal Marine units to remain in Singapore and Malaysia thereafter would be seven and one-third. This would limit them to the British contribution to the Commonwealth Infantry Brigade at Terendak, to which the Australians and New Zealanders each contributed one-third of the combat units, and the Royal Marine Commando Brigade in Singapore, both of which were under my command. To reach that level would involve the withdrawal from the theatre of 8000 men. It was also proposed to revert to the plan, which had been made before 'confrontation' had started and which Walter Walker had so strongly opposed, to reduce the Brigade of Gurkhas from the 15,000 at which it stood at the end of the Malayan emergency, to the 10,000 which had been the strength agreed with Nepal and India, when the latter became independent. Alan Jolly had counselled caution in running down the army in Borneo too quickly and had advised that a longer period would be required to effect the adjustment. A visit to Borneo to discuss the subject with George Lea and his brigade commanders, including Bill Cheyne in Sarawak, convinced me that, for many different reasons, part military, such as the morale of the soldiers, and part political, to satisfy Malaysian amour-propre, the quicker the process could be completed the better. The logistic problems in doing so were much less than Jolly had represented.

The reduction in the size of the Brigade of Gurkhas was a more delicate and different matter. A rapid rundown would create serious morale problems as well as, possibly, cases of genuine hardship. It had therefore been agreed that it would not start until the financial terms to be granted to Gurkhas finishing their service prematurely had been approved, and an approach had been made to the King and Government of Nepal, a process which was likely to take a year; and that the rate of rundown should not exceed a total of 2000 soldiers a year, including those retiring at the normal end of their engagement. This sensitive problem occupied much of my attention, and I was fortunate to have the advice of Major-General Pat Patterson, commander of the 17th (Gurkha) Division and Major-General Brigade of Gurkhas. Not only was he a highly professional soldier, but he was also a temperate, reasonable and tactful personality, who aroused none of the antagonism that Walter Walker had done, while equally determined to protect the interests of his beloved Gurkhas. One of the problems was that the Gurkha soldier enlisted for three years at a time, although most expected to serve for at least twelve. It was difficult to persuade the

Treasury that they should be compensated, if their term of service was limited to less than they might have expected, particularly because they feared that the Malaysian and Singapore trade unions would claim that, if it were accepted for the Gurkhas, the same compensation for loss of expectations should be applied also to the considerable number of civilian employees who would also face redundancy. In these complicated financial matters I was also fortunate in having as my financial adviser and 'Command Secretary' Cyril Starling, whose wisdom, patience and humour bore fruit in the satisfactory results which were finally achieved. The end of 'confrontation' also raised the question of the future of the garrison of Hong Kong, which had contributed a battalion to operations in Borneo, the old argument about the respective financial responsibilities of the British and Hong Kong governments being revived. As the colony had been able to spare a battalion for Borneo, the British government, overruling the advice of the Chiefs of Staff, decided that it could be permanently reduced by that amount.

One of my main concerns was to give a clear lead to the army in the Far East as to what it should train for. It did not seem likely that it would be involved again, either in Malaya or in Borneo, in an anti-communist guerrilla campaign in the jungle, nor that it would participate in the Vietnam war, then at its height. The only firm operational commitment was that of the Commonwealth Brigade to SEATO plans. These envisaged a conventional war in Thailand against an invasion by China, North Vietnam or both. Neither the scenarios nor the plans were, in my opinion, realistic, but they had provided the official *raison d'être* for the presence of British forces in the area, since the support of Australia, New Zealand and Malaysia for the very vague ANZAM agreement was lukewarm, and the two former were not parties to the Anglo-Malaysian Defence Agreement, drawn up on Malaya's independence. ANZAM dated from 1949 and had been intended to coordinate Australian, New Zealand and British defence planning for the area of Malaya and Singapore, the threat being conceived of as a Second World War type advance of Chinese forces, supported by Russia, through South East Asia. Its principal use was as an authority under which British commanders of all three services in Malaysia and Singapore exercised command over Australian and New Zealand units. Its operational plans pre-dated the formation of SEATO and had ceased to have any validity.

I decided that the Commonwealth Brigade should give priority to its SEATO role, but recognize that its tasks were likely to have to include operations against guerrilla bands and also larger formed bodies, as had been the case to a limited extent in Borneo, but to a much greater degree in Indo-China, both in the French war and in the one in which the Americans were then engaged in Vietnam. The Royal Marine Commando Brigade also had a rather vague commitment to SEATO plans, but Patterson's Gurkhas did not. Nevertheless, without implying that we would be involved again in operations in Malaysia, it was possible to provide a purposeful directive which kept alive and developed the techniques and procedures that had been used successfully in Borneo, while adding to them those which would be needed if a more concentrated form of opposition had to be faced. I personally thought it was unlikely, but no harm could come from concentrating minds and bodies in that direction, and it would be particularly helpful to Australians and New Zealanders, who were providing contingents to fight with the Americans in Vietnam.

Events there were naturally followed with great interest throughout the command, and in November I paid a visit there, staying with our ambassador in Saigon, Peter Wilkinson. Although technically a guest of the Government and armed forces of the Republic of Vietnam, I was in practice largely in the hands of the Americans. Flying round in our air attaché's light aircraft in none too good weather conditions was at times an alarming experience, so crowded was the airspace. I visited the Vietnamese division and the US Marines at Da Nang, the former receiving me with a guard of honour and band, whose rendering both of our national anthem and of my regimental march I fortunately managed, not without difficulty, to recognize. I also visited the US airmobile cavalry division in the Central Highlands and the Australians and New Zealanders at Vung Tau. Before I left I dined alone with General Westmorland in his house in Saigon, when he discussed his many problems with complete frankness. My visit had made me realize that they were of

far greater difficulty and on an altogether larger scale than
anything we had faced in Malaya or Borneo, and that it was
misleading to suggest, as many did, that a mere application of
the methods we had employed there would guarantee success
in Vietnam. His greatest problems arose from the long open
flank along the border with Laos and Cambodia, and the fact
that the Americans were not the government of the country
and had little control over it. He clearly led a lonely life under
much strain, and I offered him the use of an army quarter
at Penang, where his wife, Kitsy, who was in the Philippines,
could join him for a period of 'R and R' (Rest and Recreation)
at Christmas time. He gladly accepted, but nearer the time
events in Vietnam prevented him from making use of it.

On 1 February 1967 I took over from John Grandy
as Commander-in-Chief, being succeeded myself by Tom
Pearson, a Rifle Brigade officer I had known since desert
days. My other subordinates were Admiral Sir Frank Twiss,
Air Marshal Sir Rochford Hughes and, in Hong Kong,
Lieutenant-General Sir John Worsley, my predecessor in
command of 6th Brigade. The peculiarities of the army's
system of promotion and seniority meant that, although
I assumed the rank of General, I was not paid as such
for another year, and remained junior in seniority as a
lieutenant-general to both John Worsley and Tom Pearson,
although the latter had been promoted to the rank six months
later than I! On 4 February we moved into Command House,
the C-in-C's official residence, originally built for the army
commander, welcoming Mountbatten as our guest as we did
so. When I had discovered that Chinese New Year would be
celebrated on 9–11 February, during which nobody would
work and there would be no escape from the noise of Chinese
crackers, I had tried to persuade him to postpone his visit;
he would not, and was then annoyed to find that little could
be done during those days. He was a much easier guest than
I had feared, provided that one did not mind hearing the
same stories several times and pretending that one had not.
Two incidents could have caused difficulty. The first arose
from the news that the filming done in Burma on his way to
us had been a failure. Jungle scenes, illustrating his wartime
campaign there, would have to be filmed again, and there
was no possibility of a return to Burma. Mountbatten wanted

me to arrange for his team to go to the jungle warfare school
in Malaya and film him there. I said that I could send him
there as Colonel of the Life Guards, but that permission
for his filming team to go there would have to be sought
from the Malaysian government. This would inevitably take
time and could meet with difficulties. I suggested that they
should film in Singapore instead. 'But there's no jungle
here,' retorted Mountbatten, refusing to believe me when
I said that there was a perfectly good bit between the two
main golf courses. It could easily be reached by road. He
reluctantly agreed to let me take his team there. They were
delighted with it and won him over. I never saw the film,
but I believe that, when Mountbatten was explaining how
the soldiers under his command fought their way through
this jungle, one could hear an occasional 'tok'. This was
caused by golfers driving off the nearby tee, but explained
away as the noise of the Tok-tok bird, the Malayan name
for the long-tailed nightjar! The other event was a charity
film première in aid of the Commonwealth ex-Servicemen's
Association, which Mountbatten, its President, had ordered
without any reference to me. It was not popular with the
services, mainly because, by Singapore law, all money raised
for charity within the island had to be spent within it. This
caused misgivings over the Poppy Appeal on Remembrance
Day, and to impose another appeal, which could only be
spent in aid of the limited number of Commonwealth
ex-Servicemen living in Singapore, was distinctly unpopular,
not alleviated by the film selected. The only one which Run
Me Shaw could produce was Raquel Welch in *A Million Years
BC*, which was certainly quite the worst film I ever saw. The
day chosen turned out to be one of torrential rain, coinciding
with a very high tide, which caused the worst floods I saw the
whole time I was there. I had difficulty in getting back to
Command House from my office, but eventually did so just
in time to set off with Edith and Mountbatten, the two of them
leading the way in a Singapore Police car, which promptly got
stuck in the flood. I had told my driver, Sergeant Boulter,
not to enter the water until we saw them out. Having made
Mountbatten's secretary and ex-Chief Petty Officer Writer,
John Barrett, very reluctantly wade through the water to
help push them out, we drove slowly through, picked up

Edith and Mountbatten, and, with five of us crammed into the car, drove to the cinema by a roundabout route. Whether the cause was the weather or the lack of enthusiasm for the event, the result was that there was practically no audience apart from the official reception party. I therefore suggested that the auditorium should remain in darkness throughout the time that Mountbatten was present, and was relieved that my advice was taken.

He left on 20 February, and his place was taken two days later by Dick Hull, paying his farewell visit to the Far East as Chief of the Defence Staff. He warned me that, in the unfavourable economic climate, it was likely that further reductions, or a faster rundown than planned, might be demanded. The Defence White Paper published that month stated:

Our aim is that Britain should not again have to undertake operations on this scale (that of the Borneo campaign) outside Europe. The purpose of our diplomacy is to foster developments which will enable the local peoples to live at peace without the presence of external forces. But, provided that they are needed and welcome, the continuing presence of British forces can help in the meantime to create the environment, in which local governments are able to establish the political and economic basis for peace and stability. There can also be no certainty – so long as threats to stability remain – that those forces will not be required to give help to friendly Governments, or to play a part in a United Nations peacekeeping force, as they have done in recent years.

We are continuing our discussions with the Australian Government about the possibility of having new facilities in Australia. We are also examining what benefits we should get from a new staging airfield in the British Indian Ocean Territory. These arrangements would offer us greater flexibility in our future defence planning, particularly in relation to the Far East.

Under the heading of the Middle East, a laconic statement was made which was to have a considerable effect on my command during the year. It was: 'In 1968 South Arabia will be independent. When independence comes, we shall withdraw all our forces.' A month later I was told that further reductions were planned and that Denis Healey would be visiting the area in April to discuss the matter with me and with the governments of Singapore and Malaysia. The new Chief of the Defence Staff, Marshal of the Royal Air Force Sir Charles (Sam) Elworthy, warned me that what Healey had in mind was that we should leave the mainland of South East Asia by 1975–6, having by then established a base, limited to naval and air forces, in Australia, and that we should have run down the strength of the forces, and the civilians they employed, to half our current levels by 1970–1. Before I and my single service commanders had been able to study the implications of this drastic change in policy in detail, I had to leave for a SEATO meeting in Washington. The Americans were intent on taking advantage of the fact that it was held there to emphasize the involvement of SEATO members in the Vietnam war, and the need for them to become more involved. There had been difficulties about the proposed presence of the Vietnamese foreign minister, Tran Van Do, at the Council meeting, and the fact that the foreign secretary, George Brown, was planning to arrive at the very last moment before the meeting and wished to have private and separate talks with Dean Rusk, the American secretary of state, Keith Holyoake, the New Zealand prime minister, and Paul Hasluck, the Australian minister for external affairs, as soon as possible after arrival, alerted everybody to the fact that something was afoot. Fog at New York further delayed his arrival and the dramatic manner both of his entry into the scene and of his own personality accentuated the impact of the news which he brought. The reaction of the Americans, Australians and New Zealanders was understandably sharp. From that moment, right up to the publication of the British government's supplementary statement on defence policy in July, their efforts were concentrated on attempting to persuade Britain to set no fixed time limit to our eventual withdrawal from Malaysia and Singapore. Nobody seriously contested the decision to reduce our forces based there by half, but there was the greatest reluctance to accept any announcement that we would definitely leave the mainland altogether, certainly as long as the Vietnam war continued.

As was to be expected in Washington, it was not long before inspired leaks on what had passed between George Brown and his SEATO colleagues appeared in the press.

Instead of returning to Singapore, I flew on to England, landing at Lyneham early on the morning of 21 April, spending the day in the Ministry of Defence and leaving for Singapore in the afternoon with Denis Healey on board. Discussions in London had centred on the possibility of preserving the Commonwealth Brigade in some form, either by incorporating Gurkhas in it or at the expense of the Royal Marine Commando Brigade. On arrival in Singapore, Healey had a preliminary private talk with Lee Kuan Yew, who expressed his concern at the blow to confidence in Singapore which would be caused by any announcement of long-term plans for total withdrawal. Although worried at the thought of any severe increase in current unemployment, this was to him a minor consideration in comparison. In Kuala Lumpur the Tunku and Tun Razak took much the same view, the former giving the impression that he had not appreciated to the full all the implications for Malaysia, the latter being more serious and concerned. In his discussion with my service commanders and myself, Healey disclosed that he had three aims: first, to accelerate the reductions planned for the current financial year, so that a reduction of 10,000 could be achieved within it, in addition to the 10,000 reported in the Defence White Paper as having been achieved since the end of 'confrontation': second, to consider the options available for the composition of the force which would result from the 50 per cent reduction, which he expected to achieve by 1 April 1970, an interpretation of 'by 1970–1' which came as a further shock to us; and finally to obtain an idea of the factors affecting withdrawals in order to minimize the effect on both the economies and the security of Singapore and Malaysia. The principal difficulties in achieving Healey's aims lay with the navy and the army. For the air force it was largely a matter of cancelling the proposed re-equipment programme for the Far East Air Force. It was clearly sensible to leave the amphibious force until the last, in case there were difficulties over the final departure. Withdrawal of the aircraft-carrier group was more likely to be dependent on events in Aden and the Persian Gulf than on those in the Far East. The rundown of the Gurkhas could not be accelerated without breaking pledges. The only possible area for reduction therefore was our contribution to the Commonwealth Brigade and its logistic support. Without it, we could no longer contribute to SEATO's military plans, nor would it be possible to reinforce quickly Hong Kong, the garrison of which should not therefore be reduced.

I was due to pay my first visit as C-in-C to Australia and New Zealand in May, and received permission to discuss the implications of this with my colleagues there. I could tell them that we should withdraw our contribution to the Commonwealth Brigade in 1969, but had to leave open what our intention might be about what had been described in the official statement as 'a continuing capability for use in the Far East after the mid-1970s'. It was only to be expected that Australian and New Zealand Chiefs of Staff and ministers should have expressed considerable concern to me at the implications of the proposed change of policy. It was clear that both countries attached great importance to the continued existence of what was known as the Commonwealth Strategic Reserve and they hoped that some way could be found of maintaining the Commonwealth Brigade. Concern was also naturally expressed at the effect on SEATO and their own capability to contribute to it. However their greatest concern was the effect on the stability of the area generally of any announcement that we intended to withdraw altogether. There was a markedly cool reception in Australia to the idea of developing defence facilities in their country for use by us, if we voluntarily withdrew from Malaysia and Singapore, where both countries wanted us to stay, at least as long as Australian and New Zealand forces were engaged in Vietnam. On my return to Singapore, after a visit to Fiji, at the end of May, I found that Australian opposition to the break-up of the Commonwealth Brigade had hardened. Various proposals were made for its continuation in some form within the reduced force levels to which we had to work, but none made military sense and all would have resulted in the preservation of a political symbol at the expense of military effectiveness. It was eventually accepted that there was no alternative to the hard decision to withdraw our contribution in 1969.

In New Zealand we stayed with the Governor-General, my old friend Bernard Fergusson. He was very frank about his disapproval of the reductions. Even with him I found the protocol of pretending that the Governor-General was the Queen somewhat farcical. Particularly with Governors of States in Australia, it was stiffer and more pompous than royal circles in Britain. At the start of our Australian trip, John Borthwick had kindly arranged that we should spend 24 hours on one of Borthwicks' remote ranches in northern Queensland. The head of Borthwicks in Australia (it was one of the biggest firms in the country) lived in Melbourne, and the Governor's private secretary, a retired British colonel, whom I knew, had asked if there was any particular guest I would like to be asked to dine when I was staying there. I had replied that I would be grateful if the head of Borthwicks could be invited. When I arrived, the private secretary apologized that it had not been possible to comply with my request, as he had never signed the Governor's book!

While I had been involved in these weighty matters, trouble had broken out in Hong Kong, where John Worsley had recently assumed the mantle of a joint service commander, subordinate to me in that capacity, while also remaining, as army commander, subordinate in purely army matters to Tom Pearson. The influence of the Red Guard cultural revolution in China spread first to Macao, where the Portuguese authorities bowed to it, and then to Hong Kong, where serious riots took place during May, as a result of which I sent 40th Royal Marine Commando in HMS *Bulwark* to reinforce the colony. In June the trouble switched to the frontier, culminating in an attack on the police station at Sha Tau Kok on 24 June, the day before the Governor, Sir David Trench, departed on long leave. The commando had by then returned to Singapore, and I sent a further Gurkha battalion to reinforce the garrison at the end of the month. On 8 July there was another, more serious, attack on the police post at Sha Tau Kok, which had to be relieved by the army. I visited the colony a week later and had long discussions with John Worsley, who took a gloomy view and wanted further reinforcements, and the acting Governor, Mr Gass, who was more sanguine and did not. After a thorough review of the situation, I recommended to the Chiefs of Staff that a contingency plan to meet the worst case should be prepared, but that, unless the situation deteriorated, further reinforcements should not be sent. In August there were further incidents, as a result of which the frontier fence was strengthened and realigned, a back-up fence behind the frontier erected and police posts re-sited and protected. The army virtually took over responsibility for the frontier and, in September, six RAF troop-carrying helicopters were sent to the colony. When I went there again in October, visiting the Philippines on the way back, the situation was calmer, the Chinese army exercising a tighter control on their side of the frontier. One result of the excitement was that the plan to reduce the garrison was shelved, the additional battalion remaining as a reinforcement.

While keeping an eye in the direction of Hong Kong, I had to turn my attention in the opposite direction. On 1 May I had assumed responsibility from Michael Le Fanu's Middle East Command for the whole of the Indian Ocean area east of Africa, except for the Persian Gulf and Aden itself, and two weeks later had been told by Sam Elworthy that the government was planning provisionally on South Arabia becoming independent on 1 January 1968. For six months thereafter, I might have to provide air support from an aircraft-carrier to the Federal forces and maintain a Royal Marine commando afloat off Aden to rescue British residents, if necessary. The date might be deferred for three months, and an announcement was to be made in June. Before I had had time to study the implications of this in detail, I was warned, on 26 May, of the possibility of an operation with the USA and other nations to assert the right of free passage for all ships through the Straits of Tiran and the Gulf of Aqaba. Next day I was told that it would be a small probing force, operating under cover of a powerful international deterrent air strike force in the eastern Mediterranean, and that consideration was also being given to a covering force at the southern end of the Red Sea, including a British aircraft-carrier and a guided missile destroyer. HMS *Hermes*, which was at that time off Aden and due to return to Singapore, was held there and other ships sailed to join her to form our contribution to the covering force. I readily agreed to Michael Le Fanu's suggestion that,

although he had recently handed over responsibility for the
sea areas, including that of the Red Sea, he should retain
operational control of these ships. We heard no more for
some time and, as Admiral Bill O'Brien and I were increasingly concerned about what was intended to be the function
of the covering force, particularly if it were suggested that
the carrier should sail further north up the Red Sea, I asked
on 5 June for more information about its purpose. The
Arab–Israeli Six-Day War started next day, and no more
was heard of the probing force. The presence of the carrier
off Aden then became involved in the accusation by King
Hussein that US and British carrier aircraft had intervened
in the war.

Meanwhile planning for the withdrawal from Aden was
resumed. On 13 June it was decided to add a medium
bomber force, based on Masirah, to the offer of future air
support to the Federal forces, and on 19 June the Foreign
Secretary announced these decisions to Parliament. On 8
August Le Fanu warned me that the High Commissioner
to the Federation had recommended to the Foreign Office
that independence should be brought forward to December.
Three days later the ill-fated United Nations mission arrived
in Aden, and by the 24th Le Fanu was reporting a general
deterioration in the situation, with administrative control
lost in the western states. He had instructed his planners
to concentrate on completing the withdrawal as soon as
possible after handing over responsibility for Aden Crater,
due on 3 November, in which case the whole force would
be withdrawn by late that month or early December. They
were also preparing a plan for an emergency withdrawal,
to be completed within 28 days of the order being given.
A team of planners from my own staff and that of my Fleet
Commander were in Aden at the time, and able to help with
the preliminary consideration of some of the implications.
If the withdrawal were to be before 1 December, these were
considerable, and signals flashed to and fro between Le
Fanu's staff, mine and the Ministry of Defence. There was
then a lull until 6 October, when we were told that the Chiefs
of Staff had approved his plans; that there was no firm date
for withdrawal; and that a decision was unlikely before 20
October. Meanwhile the task force from my fleet, known

as Task Force 318, commanded by Rear-Admiral Edward Ashmore, was due to arrive off Aden on 12 October, HMS *Bulwark* having delivered 42nd Royal Marine Commando on 10 October, before sailing home on relief by HMS *Albion*. The commando joined the forces ashore and became responsible for Khormaksar airfield. At this stage one of the principal functions of the task force was to help in ferrying men, equipment and stores from Aden to the Gulf, a task for which the assault ship, HMS *Fearless*, and the army 'landing ships logistic' (LSL) were particularly well suited.

On 25 October Le Fanu warned me that his best guess for final withdrawal was a day or two after 20 November, but that his planning would remain flexible to enable him to withdraw at any date thereafter, basing it on handing over responsibility for the Crater three days beforehand. Two days later the Chief of the Defence Staff told me that it had been decided that independence and final withdrawal would be on 22 November, but that until 13 November the option to extend this to 30 December would be kept open. The Joint Task Force for subsequent support of the South Arabian Government was cancelled, but the naval task force, including the commando carrier with a marine commando embarked, would remain off Aden, primarily for the evacuation of British and friendly nationals, for, it was hoped, not more than two months after withdrawal. On Ashmore's advice, I requested that the aircraft-carrier and the assault ship should also remain, if the evacuation had to face the possibility of opposition: if it did not, the force would presumably not be needed. After the withdrawal, the task force would cease to be under my command and come directly under the orders of the Chief of the Defence Staff, although in fact my Fleet Commander exercised command over it for everything other than support of an evacuation. On 13 November negotiations were opened with the National Liberation Front, who were now supported by the South Arabian Army: the Federal government had virtually ceased to exist. The British government agreed that negotiations should start in Geneva on 20 November and final withdrawal was fixed for the last day of the month. It took place without incident, but the contingency plan for the naval task force was not finally cancelled until the end of May 1968.

The government had produced a supplementary Defence White Paper in July, which stated that 'by the early 1970s' the forces stationed in Malaysia and Singapore would consist 'largely of naval and air forces' and that there would still be 'some Gurkhas' in Malaysia. It went on to announce:

> We cannot plan the period beyond 1970–71 in the same detail. The reductions over the next few years will be considerable: we are determined that they will take place in an orderly manner, which will enable our Commonwealth partners to adjust their plans, and will allow Singapore and Malaysia to make the necessary economic transition as smoothly as possible. We plan to withdraw altogether from our bases in Singapore and Malaysia in the middle 1970s; the precise timing of our eventual withdrawal will depend on progress made in achieving a new basis for stability in South East Asia and in resolving other problems in the Far East.

In the debate on the paper in the House of Commons the Prime Minister, Harold Wilson, said that the final withdrawal might be as early as 1973 or as late as 1977. It was on that basis that I had to make the detailed plan. Taking into account that the paper also announced that the navy's four aircraft-carriers would be phased out, *Ark Royal* and *Eagle* 'continuing in service until the middle 1970s', the pattern that emerged was of an almost total withdrawal from Malaysia by 1970–1, the remaining forces being concentrated thereafter in the northern half of Singapore island, freeing the army's area in the south-west for commercial development. An outline plan, based on these assumptions, was evolved and forwarded to the Chiefs of Staff on 26 September. I myself went to London to attend the meeting on 24 October at which it was approved by them. I drew attention to the importance of ensuring the transfer of the naval dockyard in Singapore to commercial use; to the need to provide for the continued operation of the radar facilities connected with Butterworth airfield, near Penang; to the need to increase the garrison of Hong Kong to seven and two-thirds army units, when it was no longer possible to provide reinforcements from within the theatre; and to the need to retain our ability to reinforce Mauritius after its independence and to use its airfield for that purpose, as long as we needed to keep our naval signal station there.

Before my visit to London, I had attended the SEATO Military Advisers' Conference, held in Bangkok on 12 and 13 September, after the opening of the new SEATO Headquarters building there. I took the opportunity to make a previously approved statement, enlarging on that of the July White Paper, about the alteration in our force declarations to SEATO plans. I was also able to discuss with my Australian and New Zealand colleagues, John Wilton, Chairman of the Australian Chiefs of Staff, and Bill Thornton, an old friend of desert days, Chief of the New Zealand Defence Staff, the problems facing them as a result of Britain's defence decisions. They both made clear their personal hope that their countries would be able to continue to station forces in Malaysia, but that a radical review of their plans and policies was needed, and that it would not have been completed before the next SEATO meeting in the spring of 1968. On the weekend between the opening of the SEATO Headquarters and the Military Advisers' meeting, Edith and I took the three elder children and her sister, Elizabeth, who was staying with us, to Chieng Mai in northern Thailand, a delightful place with several entrancing temples. At one of them a Buddhist monk, who spoke English, discovered who we were and insisted that we should meet the Abbot. Searching for an appropriate mode of address, my experience in Cyprus came to my aid, and I addressed him as 'Your Beatitude', which clearly went down very well in Thai.

Ten days after my return from London, I set off, accompanied by Edith and Susanna, on a visit to India, staying in Delhi with our High Commissioner, John Freeman, whom I had last seen when he had been 'Loony' Hinde's DAA & QMG in 22nd Armoured Brigade in wartime days. I was delighted to see Gyani again. In his idealistic way, he had bought a farm and tried to set an example to his neighbours of farming in a more modern and productive way, but he despaired both of their apparently ineradicable conservatism and of the almost insuperable obstruction of the government's bureaucracy that was meant to help them. 'While I have been struggling to improve productivity in

this limited area,' he complained, 'millions have been added
to the population of India.' The grinding poverty and the
fatalistic attitude of despair towards it was the principal
impression which this, my first visit to India, made on me.
It was much worse than anything I had seen in Africa or
elsewhere in Asia. Accompanied by our defence attaché,
Major-General James Lunt, we visited Agra, Fatehpur Sikri,
Jaipur and the Ajunta caves before flying on to Nepal.

After paying official calls on the governmental hierarchy
in Katmandu, visiting the local sights and inspecting the new
road which the Chinese had built from the Tibetan border in
the east, we flew west to Pokhara. There we took to our feet,
and set off on a trek to the village of Gandruk, 9,000 feet up
below the great peak of Annapurna. Our party consisted of
six Europeans, eight Nepalese porters, a Nepalese cook and
the retired Gurkha major who ran the pension paying post
at Pokhara and came from Gandruk himself. Although we
had had no time to break ourselves in, I found no difficulty
in climbing up the sides of the ridges we crossed, but the steep
descents played havoc with my calf muscles, which slowed
me down on the return journey. I was full of admiration
for Edith's stamina and determination, as she rarely took
any strenuous physical exercise. The weather was perfect for
almost all the trek, which lasted for five days, during which
we covered some 70 miles. Our routine was to wake early in
the dark, setting off after a cup of tea, while the cook and
some of the porters went ahead to select a breakfast site and
the rest packed up the tents and followed on. The site, two
or three hours walk ahead, would be on a stream, where we
would perform our ablutions, ladies upstream, gentlemen
down, and then tuck in to a splendid breakfast. The walk
would be resumed until halting for a light lunch, the porters
then going ahead to set up camp for the night, which we
would reach about 4.30 p.m. After our evening meal, we
would generally be so sleepy that we would go straight to bed,
but at Gandruk, where we slept in the school, we sat round
a bonfire, entertained by the villagers and the local gypsy
band, which played us away in the morning. Annapurna
looked magnificent, towering above us in the moonlight. The
whole trip was an unforgettable experience. After visiting
the Gurkha depot at Dahran in eastern Nepal, I was due

to visit Calcutta, where my fellow student at Latimer, Sam Manekshaw, was the General in charge of India's Eastern Command. There had been serious riots in the city, and the Gurkha signallers at Dahran were kept busy all night on an exchange of messages with Delhi about the desirability of my doing more than refuel there. Sam insisted that there was no problem; but, when we had made our farewells at the local airfield, the batteries on my RAF Andover were too weak to start it, having been run down by their constant use for that purpose over the previous week. Urgent action by every possible source of help, including the military hospital at Dahran, got them charged up again in 24 hours, and we heaved a sigh of relief when the first engine sprang into life next day.

While I had been in Nepal, the pound was devalued, but the Nepalese rupee did not follow it, and I had sent an urgent message to Singapore, asking for reassurance that the real value of the redundancy terms which had been agreed for the Gurkhas would be maintained. Their pensions were normally linked to the Indian rupee. I received a satisfactory answer, but my visit was closely followed by one by Gerry Reynolds, the Minister of State for Defence Administration, who broke the news to the Nepalese Government that the Gurkha rundown would continue beyond the 10,000 level, of which they had already been informed, to 6,000 by 1971, but that this would not, for the time being, be publicly announced: recruiting would continue at the rate of 300 men a year.

On 22 December I received a warning from Sam Elworthy that further cuts in defence expenditure were under consideration and that the aim of the Chiefs of Staff was to ensure that we were not left with commitments without the means to meet them: that, if cuts were to be made in force structures and military capabilities, it should only be as a result of the removal of commitments. I was assured that no firm decisions had been made. It was not long before the removal of commitments was proposed. On 29 December I learnt that the Secretary of State for Commonwealth Affairs, George Thomson*, was to visit Kuala Lumpur, Singapore, Wellington and Canberra, arriving in Kuala Lumpur on 7 January,

* Later Lord Thomson of Monifieth.

to discuss Britain's proposals with the four governments. On 3 January I received a warning from Sam Elworthy of what they were likely to be. They were drastic: withdrawal altogether from our bases in Singapore and Malaysia by 31 March 1972, to be announced in the third week of January, after consultations with our Commonwealth partners, by the Commonwealth Secretary on his tour, and with the USA by the Foreign Secretary: to withdraw wholly from the Persian Gulf by the same date, but not to announce it, giving up 'at very early date' the commitment to Kuwait: to examine the possibility of shedding responsibility for military protection and evacuation of British nationals in the Middle East and Africa, the commitment for the defence and security of Mauritius, our obligations to Brunei, the commitment to reinforce Fiji with a brigade, and the Beira patrol, as well as other commitments outside my command area. This was removal of commitments with a vengeance.

The paper proposed that we should retain our obligation under the Anglo-Malaysian Defence Agreement, but not maintain any specific forces to meet it, and we should retain our membership of SEATO, but commit no forces, except to its Plan 4, that for a major war. I was told that Healey believed that the retention of these obligations was inconsistent with the reductions in defence expenditure expected, and that the Anglo–Malaysian Defence Agreement should be renegotiated and our obligations under SEATO Plan 4 terminated. I was also told that decisions would probably be taken at a Cabinet meeting on 16 January and that I was to attend George Thomson's consultations in Kuala Lumpur and Singapore. I had therefore three days in which, with my service commanders, to consider the implications, if the proposals in the paper were approved by Ministers. In essence it removed the need to plan for a level of forces which could be maintained from 1971 to 1977, and made it necessary to plan an orderly rundown to a fixed date one year earlier than that hitherto envisaged. This presented no great difficulties as far as our own planning was concerned, provided that the balance of Gurkhas remaining could be absorbed by Hong Kong, which they could, if an increase in the garrison by one battalion was approved. It would clearly not now make sense to deploy new types of strike and reconnaissance aircaft into the Far East Air Force nor to redeploy establishments within Singapore in the process of running down. Our plans for the rundown in Malaysia would hardly be affected, as by March 1972 we had in any case planned to remove almost all our forces stationed there, concentrating the remainder in Singapore. The effect on Singapore would be critical. Under our previous plan there would have been some 35,000 service and civilian personnel remaining in Singapore after March 1971, possibly until 1977, of whom some 14,200 were locally enlisted men or employed civilians. These would now all have to be discharged by March 1972. Even though it was recognized that economic aid would have to be increased to mitigate the effect of this, it was unlikely that alternative employment could be provided by that time. We were approaching finality in complicated negotiations about the terminal benefits to be paid to our local civilian employees, and we feared that this change might shatter the provisional support we had just managed, after a year's bargaining, to obtain from the governments and trade unions in both Malaysia and Singapore.

The most important implications lay beyond the date of withdrawal. Our Commonwealth partners had been able to look forward to the continuing presence of our forces, at least in Singapore, possibly up to 1977, and to assume that thereafter we should maintain forces in the area to support our obligations under the Anglo–Malaysian Defence Agreement and SEATO. It was by no means clear how we could now do this, and our rundown would have to be designed to dovetail into whatever residual capability we were to maintain to meet our obligations. In order that this should be credible to Malaysia and Singapore, and therefore act as a deterrent to anybody who wished them ill, we would have to be seen to be maintaining facilities for re-entry and for some Commonwealth military organization, capable of exercising command, to be retained. SEATO was less of a problem. Provided that a delay of up to four months in deployment of SEATO Plan 4 forces was accepted, the forces could be declared from the strategic reserve in the United Kingdom. My service commanders and I viewed with dismay the possibility of the wholesale shedding of minor national commitments foreshadowed in the paper: if however they were to be made, it was illogical to retain even more minor ones, such as the reinforcement of the Seychelles and our Western Pacific dependencies. Hong Kong would feel very isolated, and it became more urgent than before to increase its garrison and to make clear that this would take place.

These were the views that I had arrived at in discussion with my service commanders and my political adviser, Duncan Watson, before I flew up to Kuala Lumpur to meet George Thomson on 7 January. In the preliminary discussion into which we entered immediately, before meeting Malaysian ministers, I was taken aback to learn that the British Government had gone even further in two respects than the paper, of which I had been warned, had recommended. It had been decided to bring the date of final withdrawal both from the Far East and from the Gulf forward by one further year to 31 March 1971, and that Britain would make no contribution to the retention of facilities in Malaysia and Singapore, needed to make a rapid reinforcement to support them against an external threat possible and therefore credible. I stressed that the earlier date would accentuate all the problems, particularly those affecting Singapore, and drew attention to the effect on Hong Kong. I put forward the view that, if our ability and intention to deploy any part of what became known as our 'general capability' in support of our obligation to Malaysia or Singapore were to be believed, it was essential to maintain certain minimum facilities, and I urged that the solution of this problem should be sought on a five-power basis. It was after this meeting that George Thomson asked me to accompany him also to Wellington and Canberra.

After he had had a private meeting with the Tunku, we met in a formal session with Tun Razak, the Deputy Prime Minister, and Tan Siew Sin, the Finance Minister. The Commonwealth Secretary gave a sombre description of Britain's financial position and the need to take drastic measures to effect a permanent cure. He then announced that the date for final withdrawal would be 31 March 1971, and went on to say that it would no longer be possible for us to maintain a 'special capability' for use in the Far East; we should however keep a 'general capability' in Europe, which would be available for use elsewhere 'if in our judgement it is right to do so'. He made it clear that naval and amphibious forces would no longer be kept in the Far East, and stated that, if the Malaysian government wished, Britain was prepared to work out with them a reinterpretation of the Defence Agreement 'to bring it into conformity with the new circumstances'. He held out the prospect of economic aid, to discuss which Sir Alan Dudley of the Ministry of Overseas Development would pay a visit in February. The prospect of a wholesale shedding of our responsibilities for dependent territories was dispelled by a clear statement that we should 'of course continue to retain our defence responsibilities for them' and had no intention of withdrawing or weakening the garrison of Hong Kong. He said that we should continue our joint planning arrangements with Australia and New Zealand in AZAM, and finished by saying that he would convey their views to the Prime Minister and his Cabinet colleagues, but that it was intended to make a comprehensive announcement of the economy measures on 17 or 18 January; to carry conviction, this must include what was intended on the defence front. The reaction was considerably sharper than it apparently had been from the Tunku. Tan Siew Sin took the lead in emphasizing that Malaysia would never have assumed responsibility for East Malaysia, if they had not been assured of our support both in the defence and the economic fields. Both he and Tun Razak urged the importance of preserving effective air and naval deterrents to an external threat, particularly the former, and expressed the view that a 'general capability' no nearer than Europe with no firm commitment was of no value.

The reaction from Singapore was even harsher, the atmosphere having been clouded by an outspoken and derogatory statement made to the press by Lee Kuan Yew before Thomson's arrival on 8 January, and the postponement of his meeting until the afternoon of the 9th, leaving the minimum of time to get to the airfield to fly on to Australia. Both Lee Kuan Yew and Goh Keng Swee were thoroughly aggressive, and it was with some difficulty that the Commonwealth Secretary managed to get an opening in which to make the same statement as he had in Kuala Lumpur; he rebuffed the more extreme and tactless aspersions with a dignified Scottish combination of firmness and tact. Somewhat to my surprise, it was not the economic but the defence problems, caused by the accelerated withdrawal and the lack of any commitment thereafter, to which Lee Kuan Yew gave prominence both at the meeting and at the subsequent press conference, at which he appeared in much better humour than he had been behind closed doors. He maintained that public knowledge that, after April 1971, Singapore would not be capable of ensuring its own defence would have a drastic effect on confidence in the island, on which its economic viability entirely depended. He vacillated between the concept that defence must be approached on a five-power basis and emphasis that Singapore must be capable of standing on its own. Before the meeting had started, he had demanded to represent his case direct to the Prime Minister in London, stating that he had been given assurances by Harold Wilson at the recent funeral of the Australian Prime Minister, Mr Holt, who had been drowned bathing, which were not being met. His demand was reluctantly agreed to. By the time this stormy meeting and the subsequent press conference were over, there was only just enough time to get to the airport and catch the BOAC aircraft which would take us via Perth to Sydney en route to Wellington, our journey to the airport being made more hazardous by extensive flooding which resulted from a tropical storm which had provided an apt accompaniment to the fireworks in City Hall.

We went to New Zealand before meeting the Australians in order to give the latter more time to adjust to Mr Holt's death. We flew on to Wellington in an Australian VIP aircraft put at our disposal. The Prime Minister, Keith Holyoake, was on his summer holiday on his farm near Lake Taupo, to which we flew next day with Bill Thornton in a RNZAF Dakota, which gave us a bumpy ride. Mr Holyoake was accompanied by David Thomson, his Defence Minister. We met in a hut in the grounds of the Wairaki Hotel, after a private meeting between George Thomson and the Prime Minister. The perfect summer weather, the holiday background and the relaxed and friendly New Zealand atmosphere, with no visible security arrangements apart from one policeman wandering round the hotel garden, did much to soften the gravity of the occasion. Nevertheless it could not disguise their deep concern, not so much at the acceleration of our withdrawal, as at the apparent decision to withdraw into Europe. Holyoake stressed in homely but effective terms the historic fact that New Zealand considered herself closer to Britain than to Asia or Australia, even though separated by 12,000 miles of sea. He was principally concerned that whatever announcement was made should stress that we could and would maintain both the intention and the capability to return, if need be, to help them in their forward strategy of meeting trouble in South East Asia before it spread further south. David Thomson was more concerned that concrete evidence should remain to give credibility to such an assurance. He stressed that New Zealand forces could not remain there without the facilities provided by a major military power, either ourselves or the USA. It was clear that this blow came at a particularly awkward time, when New Zealand, in economic difficulties and having herself devalued, was trying to achieve considerable reductions in her own defence spending, while faced with the need for re-equipment, which had to be met by overseas expenditure, as did the maintenance of her forces in Vietnam and Malaysia.

We flew on to Canberra that afternoon, arriving there in the evening of 11 January, only a few days after Mr Gorton had taken office as the new Prime Minister. After preliminary meetings with our High Commissioner, Charles Johnston, a formal meeting with the Australian Cabinet was held in the morning of 12 January in the Cabinet Room of the Parliament Building. Here there was no relaxed holiday atmosphere, but one of grim, dignified seriousness. At the start the Prime Minister made it clear that it was an historic occasion in the relations between Britain and Australia. He left most of the talking, in reply to George Thomson's statement, to his colleagues, and in an impressive display of tough, firm and realistic unanimity, they made abundantly clear that they viewed with dismay decisions which, in their eyes, meant that we were abandoning interest outside Europe: that our withdrawal would create a dangerous vacuum in a sensitive area, which could not be filled by Australia, New Zealand and the local countries themselves, and in which the USA was most unlikely to replace us. They dismissed almost contemptuously assurances of help if they were directly threatened, and pointed out that it was not the security of their own interests so much as those of the world generally with which they were concerned, stressing the importance of Eastern Asia in this respect. They pressed strongly for a postponement of the date of withdrawal in order to give everybody, including themselves, time to adjust to a policy which was basically different from that announced only six months before; for flexibility in its application, particularly in regard to the preservation of defence facilities which they, New Zealand, Malaysia and Singapore could use; and suggested that defence economies were preferable in Europe, where the danger of conflict was less. In the afternoon I had a valuable meeting with John Wilton, who expressed his hope that Australian forces would remain after our withdrawal and stressed the importance of early discussion on a five-power basis of the defence organization which would take the place of that of the Commonwealth Strategic Reserve, based fundamentally on a United Kingdom command and supporting organization. He did not think that any firm decisions would be forthcoming for some time.

George Thomson and his party set off back to London next day, Friday 13 January, I myself dropping off that evening at Singapore. By the time he reached London Lee Kuan Yew was already there and had pressed his case on British television, enlisting a considerable degree of sympathy. His fluent advocacy, combined with Australian pressure, gained a nine-month reprieve, and on 16 January I received a signal from Healey, giving details of the announcement which the Prime Minister was to make that afternoon in the House of Commons and which was subsequently incorporated in the 1968 Defence White Paper. Apart from the alteration of the date of withdrawal from 31 March to 31 December 1971, it followed the lines of the statement which George Thomson had made on his whistle-stop tour. It included announcements that withdrawal from the Persian Gulf would take place by the same date, and that the Gurkha rundown would be continued to reach a level of 6000 by 1971. The signal stated that the Hong Kong garrison would 'remain at its present strength'. The Prime Minister stated that 'there is no question of reducing the strength or effectiveness of the Hong Kong garrison'; but the White Paper was more cautious and read: 'We shall honour our commitments to our dependencies and maintain a garrison in Hong Kong sufficient to fulfil our responsibilities there.'

My first concern on return from this trip was to revise our plans for reductions and withdrawal, the three critical areas being the need to keep a viable fleet in being as long as we retained a commitment to the Persian Gulf and South Arabia, with which was linked the future of the naval dockyard in Singapore; the future arrangements for the air defence of Malaysia and Singapore; and ensuring that the revised total strength of the Gurkhas could be fitted into the garrisons of Hong Kong and Brunei. I had to make assumptions on these and other matters without advice from the Chiefs of Staff, but had fortunately guessed right, and they approved my plan when I went to London in March to attend their meeting to discuss it.

When Lee Kuan Yew had been in London, he had received assurances about the transfer to him of air defence equipment and facilities to enable him to establish a Singapore Air Force. I was concerned that we should not get too far committed in this field before the interests and intentions of others concerned had been considered, principally those of Malaysia and Australia. I was also concerned that Singapore's ambitious ideas in this field did not lead to a Malaysian–Singapore arms race and that, before Malaysia became too far committed to a type of defence expenditure which she could ill afford and should not be her first priority, she should be able to judge how far she could expect to continue to rely on the presence of Australian fighter squadrons as the first line of her defence. From this time on I found myself in continuous opposition to Whitehall pressure to exploit the situation to improve the prospect of British arms sales to both Malaysia and Singapore. Before I went to Kuala Lumpur on 23 January to discuss the effect of the latest plan with Malaysia, I sent a signal to Sam Elworthy, saying that I proposed to set up an air defence advisory working group, under the chairmanship of the commander of 224 Group RAF, Air Vice-Marshal Brian Eaton, an officer of the Royal Australian Air Force, inviting as members the defence liaison officers of the Australian and New Zealand High Commissions in Singapore and Kuala Lumpur and representatives

of the Malaysian and Singapore armed forces, asking for
authority to discuss this with the governments and high
commissions concerned. I received this, and the Malaysians welcomed the proposal. Singapore, Australia and New
Zealand were more cautious, all fearing that we were trying
to commit them at too early a stage. Fortunately the Australian Minister of External Affairs, Paul Hasluck, happened
to be passing through Singapore the following week and
gave his approval, making it clear that his government's
cooperation was dependent on any arrangements we arrived
at being based on full cooperation between the Malaysian
and Singapore armed forces. Shortly after this, I succeeded
in obtaining agreement that similar groups should be set up
to study naval and army matters. However only Malaysia and
New Zealand showed much enthusiasm for my initiative, and
they did so for different reasons. Malaysia saw it both as a
means of continuing the commitment of Britain, Australia
and New Zealand to her defence, while at the same time
seeing that Singapore could not act independently. New
Zealand supported it as a means of forcing decisions by
Britain and Australia, without which she could not make
her own. The British government wished to avoid any form
of commitment beyond our withdrawal, and was reluctant
to discuss at that stage the future of the Anglo–Malaysian
Defence Agreement or the form which the possible deployment of any part of our 'general capability' might take.
The Australians were equally reluctant to commit themselves until they had had more time to consider their policy.
Singapore was determined to preserve its freedom of action.
Lee Kuan Yew had little faith in the continuing stability of
Malaysia after a total withdrawal of our presence. He feared
that, once the Tunku had left the helm, it could be taken over
by Pan-Malay extremists. He also feared that, in an unstable
Malaysia, Johore, on which he was dependent for his water
supply and which had never been altogether reconciled
to being governed from Kuala Lumpur, might get out of
control. His attitude to his future defence requirements was
undoubtedly influenced by the Israeli mission which was
training his armed forces. They saw Singapore's situation,
surrounded by the Islamic Malay countries of Malaysia and
Indonesia, as very similar to their own. While making ritual

obeisance, therefore, to my proposals for close cooperation between the armed forces of Malaysia and Singapore, each primarily regarded them as designed to fight each other, in the case of Singapore particularly to secure her water supply, if things went wrong in Johore. Lee Kuan Yew described his defence policy as that of 'a poisonous shrimp'. It could not directly attack you, but could cause you a lot of trouble if you tried to swallow it. In the background of all these discussions was the continuous battle between Britain and the rest about the disposal of all our very valuable assets, fixed and mobile. The British government, led by the Treasury, wished to obtain the highest possible price for anything we handed over, while the others thought that, as a *quid pro quo* for our withdrawal, they should get what they wanted for as little as possible, preferably for nothing. As far as land was concerned, we were bound by the terms of the Anglo–Malaysian Defence Agreement (which also applied to Singapore) to hand it over, with all fixed assets on it, for nothing.

In March Malaysia proposed that five-power talks to discuss all aspects of the withdrawal plan should be held in Kuala Lumpur in June. The others had agreed without much enthusiasm. When I had been in London in that month to discuss my plan with the Chiefs of Staff, I had attended a meeting in the Commonwealth Relations Office to discuss what the government's line in the talks was to be. It had dawned on them that the reports of the five-power working groups that I had set up would provide a ready-made agenda, and that it would be useful to try and coordinate ideas on an Australian–New Zealand–United Kingdom basis before the talks. The SEATO Council meeting in Wellington at the end of the month would provide a suitable opportunity for this. My working groups suddenly came to be regarded as an essential foundation for the talks, and there was a danger of too much being expected of them.

At this meeting in the CRO the problem of Brunei had also come up for discussion. The Sultan had abdicated in October 1967 in favour of his son, apparently in protest at what he considered to be the cavalier fashion in which the previous Commonwealth Secretary had announced the departure (long overdue for several reasons) of the High

Commissioner, Mr Webber, and the appointment of his
successor. The lease from the Brunei Shell Company of the
camp at Seria, in which the Gurkha garrison was housed,
fell due in 1968 and, before any promise of the continued
presence of Gurkha troops in Brunei was made, it was hoped
to bring the ex-Sultan round to a more reasonable frame of
mind and eventual acceptance of a revision of the agreement
by which Britain was responsible for the security and external affairs of the Sultanate. To this end George Thomson
was to visit Brunei on his way to the SEATO meeting, at
which he would be representing Britain. In his talks the
outstanding problems were not discussed, but were left over
to be dealt with when the new Sultan and his father were
to be invited to London later in the year after the former's
coronation. They had been persuaded to accept a new high
commissioner, the way to a more reasonable compromise
having been smoothed by a visit by that expert pourer of oil
on troubled waters, Malcolm Macdonald.

The statement that I, at the SEATO Military Advisers'
meeting, and George Thomson, at the subsequent Council
meeting, made about our rundown, involving cancelling all
our force declarations to SEATO plans after 1971, was
received surprisingly calmly, although the Commonwealth
Secretary had to face some embarrassing criticism of the
government's decision to withdraw, when all the other members of SEATO were being pressed to increase their effort
in Vietnam, and while a solution to the problems of the area
seemed as far away as ever. He met it with his customary
courtesy and firm, straightforward honesty. The informal
meeting of British, Australian and New Zealand officials,
which Duncan Watson and I attended, was disappointingly
unproductive. The Australians would not commit themselves about anything, until they had a clearer idea of how
far we were prepared to commit ourselves in the area after
our withdrawal and they had assessed the degree to which
Malaysia and Singapore would cooperate, while the New
Zealanders took the understandable line that they could not
decide anything until they knew what Australia intended.
The attitude of both to accepting the working group reports
as the basis for the June talks was ambivalent. They would
not accept them as having any official standing, while saying

that they could not determine their own position until they had studied their results.

Soon after I had arrived in Wellington, I had received a telegram from Antony telling me that my mother had suffered a stroke and was seriously ill in hospital. Before I left I received the news that she had had a second stroke from which she had died. It was sad that, being so far away and involved in such serious affairs, I could not have reached her bedside. She was 81 and had retained both her mental and physical faculties to the full. The first stroke had left her almost totally paralysed and she would have had to be transferred to some sort of home, which she would have hated. The second stroke came therefore as a merciful release. Her ashes were buried beside my father's in the churchyard at Culmington in Shropshire, in the countryside which she had come to love when we had lived at Ticklerton.

On my way back to Singapore I visited the New Hebrides and the Solomon Islands, for the reinforcement of both of which, in case of trouble, I was responsible. I found the Anglo–French condominium arrangement in the New Hebrides worthy of Gilbert and Sullivan. This was illustrated by the hurricane warning received on the Sunday we were there. We were planning a beach picnic, while the wife of the British Resident (actually a New Zealander) was due to enter hospital for her confinement. At breakfast the anxious French Resident rang up to ask what his British colleague was doing about the warning. My host protested that he had received no warning and had some difficulty in contacting the meteorological officer (who was British), while my aircrew rushed to the airfield to secure my Andover or, if the hurricane was likely to reach the island, to fly off before it did so. The met officer, when eventually aroused, said that the hurricane would come nowhere near the island. The reason for the French Resident's anxiety was that the French police were subordinate to the French colony of New Caledonia, three hundred miles away, which was in the probable path. The chief of police there had issued a general warning to all his subordinates, regardless of where they were. While the French battened down, we went ahead with our picnic.

On my return to Singapore in mid-April my main concern was to try and see that the reports of the army and navy working groups were completed in time to be studied before the June talks. The air defence group had already reported. Many of the matters they discussed were highly contentious and agreement was not easy to obtain, but I was able to forward them to all the participants, under no authority but my own, at the end of May. The talks were held on 10 and 11 June, Britain being represented by Denis Healey, accompanied by Sam Elworthy, and George Thomson, with Joe Garner, his Permanent Under-Secretary. Paul Hasluck represented Australia, Keith Holyoake New Zealand (as Prime Minister he also held the external affairs portfolio), Tun Razak Malaysia, and Lim Kim San and Goh Keng Swee Singapore. I was called upon to describe the reports of the working groups and drew attention to the comments I had made in forwarding them. Singapore was the only delegation prepared to state its unreserved acceptance of their recommendations. New Zealand regarded them as 'generally acceptable', although stressing that they had not yet made the necessary decisions, and that the work of the groups, which had been of great value, should continue. Healey made the point that further progress was dependent on political decisions, and attempted to extract from the Australian and Malaysian representatives their intentions regarding the Malaysian end of the combined air defence system, recommended by the air defence group, particularly in relation to the airfield at Butterworth, where the RAAF was stationed, and the radar on top of the nearby island of Penang, then manned by the RAF. Most of the discussion centred on this issue, to which the presence of Australian fighters at Butterworth and the handover by the RAF of the radars at Penang and in Singapore, and their Bloodhound surface-to-air missiles at the latter, were essential components. Singapore made clear her determination to form her own air force, equipped initially with Hunters.

The conference agreed without much difficulty to a communiqué reaffirming the continued interest of all five countries in the peace and stability of the area and welcoming the statement by Singapore and Malaysia that their defence was indivisible and required close and continuing cooperation between them. One paragraph each was devoted to the subjects covered by the working groups, that on air defence stating that 'the conference recognized that an integrated air defence system covering both Malaysia and Singapore was required and agreed that the air defence working group should study the form of the integrated control and management of such a system.' It recorded Singapore's decision to form her own air force, Australian willingness to keep the RAAF at Butterworth until 1971, with no firm commitment thereafter, and our readiness to maintain the RAF elements of the system up to the time of our withdrawal, and to 'make available' the 'ground environment' thereafter, as well as our willingness to help in training others to man it. The naval paragraph noted *inter alia* the agreement of Singapore to the continuation of the Malaysian naval base at Woodlands on Singapore island, and the agreement of the two governments to make arrangements for the control of the naval base waters. For the army it was agreed in principle that there should be a jungle warfare training school and a joint exercise planning machinery 'on a multi-national basis'; and that all five countries would take part in a major exercise in 1970, involving major reinforcement from Britain, noting her intention to continue training in the area after 1971.

The communiqué said no more about the Anglo–Malaysian Defence Agreement than that a new understanding about it would be necessary in due course. It recorded that, in the light of the commitments and contributions of other governments, the Malaysians would be prepared to consider additional contributions over and above the current strength of their armed forces, and Australia and New Zealand undertook to take the proceedings into account in formulating their long-term plans: meanwhile they would continue to maintain forces in the area and help Malaysia and Singapore to develop their own forces.

This all sounded good, and everybody seemed pleased with the result, but, when I tried to get things moving again in all three service fields, I ran up against considerable obstruction, particularly from the Australians, led by the Permanent Secretary of their Defence Department, Sir Henry Bland. He wanted to get matters out of my hands and into those of civilian officials like himself in all five countries. As a result I was not allowed to reconvene the working groups, based on the agreements reached in the June talks, the official record of which was long delayed, and there was no progress in any field before October.

Two other issues had occupied my attention during that time. In January trouble had broken out in Mauritius, inter-communal riots having marred the approach to independ-ence, the problems arising out of which I had discussed with the Governor, Sir John Rennie, when I visited the island three months before. As soon as the Governor had requested reinforcements, I had ordered my air commander to fly the 1st Battalion King's Shropshire Light Infantry, stationed at Terendak, from Singapore via Gan to the island, informing Sam Elworthy that I had done so. If London disapproved, I could turn them back en route. Fortunately London approved and congratulated me on the speed with which the battalion got there, the first aircraft landing in Mauritius 27¾ hours after the Governor had initiated his request. After their arrival, tension was gradually reduced. Independence was set for 12 March and considerable dis-cussion took place between the Governor and London both about his request for more troops to cover the independence period and also about what was to happen after it. Whitehall finally and reluctantly agreed to keep the troops there after Seewoosagur Ramgoolam had taken over as prime minister, although they insisted that they should leave before he held post-independence elections in December, which they did.

The other development was the deterioriation in the rela-tions between Malaysia and the Philippines. They had ap-peared cordial when President Marcos had paid a ceremonial visit to Kuala Lumpur in January at the time that George Thomson started his tour there, announcing the British government's withdrawal plan. Nobody suggested then that strained relations between the two countries, fellow members of the Association of South East Asia Nations (ASEAN), would be a major factor in Malaysian thinking throughout the year and complicate the development of a smooth re-evaluation of our defence relations with Malaysia and our commitment under the Anglo–Malaysian Defence Agree-ment. The spark that lit the fire was the revelation in March of a scandal in a so-called Special Forces training camp on the island of Corregidor at the entrance to Manila Bay. A mutiny was said to have taken place among trainees, a large number of whom were alleged to have been shot out of hand. They were Muslims from the Sulu archipelago and it was alleged that they were being trained for subversive operations in Sabah, to which the Philippines laid claim, based on the historic suzerainty of the Sultan of Sulu. This rang all the alarm bells, and from then on everybody was convinced that the whole affair was being exploited by, if it had not indeed originated with, Marcos himself as an election issue to confound his opponents and assure him a second term as president in the elections due in 1969. The argument lay between those who assessed it as no more than this, and those, certainly including the Tunku himself, who genuinely expected, if not an invasion, at least infiltration and subversion of Sabah with the real intention of detaching it from Malaysia.

On 1 April the Tunku had sent a message to Harold Wilson saying that this threat was serious enough to warrant asking for British help to build up the defence of the area. I was told to discuss with him what we could do to help, but not to agree to send anyone to Sabah. Accompanied by our High Commissioner in Kuala Lumpur, Michael Walker, who was keen that we should assist in any way possible, I had a difficult interview at which the Tunku made a number of wholly unrealistic suggestions, while I temporized as tactfully as I could. The Tunku's real aim was to try and force Britain into a commitment to support him with armed force, if necessary, in keeping Sabah and Sarawak within Malaysia. Eventually I managed to whittle our contribution down to help in training a light anti-aircraft unit, which he proposed to deploy to Sabah; an exchange of intelligence, which I hoped would enable us to refute some of the wilder rumours flying around; and visits to Sabah by some naval minesweepers. The last involved a complication in that we normally notified the Philippines of the movement of naval ships through the Sulu Sea, the waters between Sabah and the Philippines, although we did not accept their claim to them as territorial waters. I was also concerned with the position of the Royal Navy officers serving as commanding officers of ships of the Malaysian Navy. Although at an ASEAN meeting in Djakarta on 7 August, Tun Razak and Mr Ramos, the Philippine foreign minister, had agreed to a six-month 'cooling-off' period and to meet thereafter to discuss reconciliation, the period

proved to be short. Towards the end of the month a bill
was tabled in the Philippine Congress, the aim of which was
said to be to correct certain technical errors in a document
deposited with the United Nations in 1962, delineating the
Philippine claim to territorial waters. In fact it included the
bulk of Sabah and a small part of Indonesian Borneo in
the territory claimed. It was further amended in its passage
through the Philippine constitutional machine to exclude the
possible offence to Indonesia. As seen by Malaysia, it claimed
the territorial waters of all but a small western part of Sabah
as Philippine territorial waters. They immediately objected
and considered breaking off diplomatic relations, delivering
an official note on 4 September.

On 6 September I had another meeting with the Tunku.
Michael Walker was most anxious that I should be able to
offer some concrete help in order to avoid the possibility that
the Tunku might ask officially for help under the Defence
Agreement. Having resisted pressure to deploy ships and
aircraft to Sabah, I explained that major units of the Far East
Fleet would be sailing through the Sulu Sea, on their way to
an exercise off Australia, on 23 and 24 September, when he
was himself due to visit Sabah, and that I would discuss with
Admiral O'Brien the possibility of a fly-past over the capital,
Jesselton, by aircraft from HMS *Hermes*, while he was there.
Meanwhile I stressed the need to maintain silence about the
proposal. On the same day I reported to Sam Elworthy that
the fly-past could be arranged and that I recommended the
earliest possible notification to the Philippine Government,
in order to avoid the danger of misinterpretation, if the
Malaysians did not keep silent about our intentions. I also
mentioned that six RAF Hunters would be staging through
Labuan (an island off Brunei, but belonging to Sabah) on
19 September on their way back from Hong Kong, and
that they could stay at Labuan on 20 and 21 September
and carry out flights over Jesselton (or Kota Kinabalu as it
had been renamed) in addition to the proposed fly-past by
aircraft from HMS *Hermes* on the 23rd, an addition insisted
on by Rochford Hughes, who disliked being upstaged by the
navy. The answer from the Chiefs of Staff was that the fleet
should stick to its plan to sail through the Sulu Sea, notifying
the Philippines in advance as usual. They did not like the

idea of the naval fly-past, but could see no objection to the
alternative proposal about the RAF Hunters, although they
would have to refuel at the US Air Force base at Clark Field
in the Philippines on the way. A decision would be given by
Ministers on the morning of 18 September. This left little
time as the Hunters would have to take off from Hong Kong
at 8 a.m. local time on the 19th, which was midnight 18/19
September in London. Both Hughes and I would then be in
Hong Kong, he celebrating the fiftieth anniversary of the
formation of the Royal Air Force and Battle of Britain Day,
and I on a routine visit to see Basil Eugster, who had recently
taken over from John Worsley, and also the Governor, David
Trench, who was due to go on leave again in October. At
10 p.m. local time, when I was dining with Basil Eugster, I
received a signal from Sam Elworthy, giving the go-ahead for
the RAF flight and stating that Michael Walker would explain
to the Tunku why it would not coincide with his visit. John
Addis, our Ambassador in Manila, would inform Marcos
both of the flight and of the forthcoming fleet movement.

None of us knew that by this time Marcos had signed the
offending bill. This was announced on the news next morning, and I realized that, at the routine press conference which
I was due to give before leaving Hong Kong that afternoon,
I should be faced with questions. It was inevitable that the
Malaysians would exploit the overflight of Kota Kinabalu
by some public statement. It would clearly be important to
make clear that it was not a reaction to the signature of the
bill, but at the same time not to appear to disown completely
whatever the Malaysians might say. I knew that, by the time
of my press conference, the overflight would have taken
place and, if all had gone according to plan, the aircraft
would be in Singapore. Unfortunately, by the time I faced
the press, I had not seen the instructions sent to Michael
Walker and John Addis, which had not been repeated to
Hong Kong, nor did I know what the Malaysian reaction
had been. I was asked a number of awkward questions, which
I managed without difficulty, playing down any suggestion
of a danger of military operations which might entangle us
on the side of Malaysia and the USA on the side of the
Philippines. The Reuter correspondent then asked me to
comment on a report from Kuala Lumpur that Malaysian

officials had said that RAF Hunters from Hong Kong had been to the Philippines and then 'landed at the airbase at Sabah', and that this was a demonstration of 'Britain's strong commitment to Malaysia over Sabah'. I pointed out that they had flown on a routine flight, as planned, and that there was no reason to change the route, admitting that it was as a result of a Malaysian request that they had deviated slightly from the normal pattern to overfly Kota Kinabalu itself. I was able to deny clearly that it was a reaction to Marcos's signature of the bill. The difficulty came from the same correspondent's question: 'Assuming that the Malaysians did say something like what was reported, is there any basis in fact and is it in Britain's interest for British Far East Forces to make a demonstration of support?' To say 'No' would clearly have been greatly resented in Kuala Lumpur: to say 'Yes' would have had the same effect in Manila, as well as in London. I fell back on the political guidance I had been given, emphasizing that we had had every right to transfer sovereignty over Sabah to Malaysia, and that since then the people of Sabah had twice confirmed their desire to remain part of Malaysia: we therefore fully supported the case that Sabah was part of Malaysia. It was not until I got to Bangkok next day that I knew that I had been misreported by United Press International as having said that all my 'troops, ships and planes stand behind Malaysia in this growing crisis'. This naturally caused excitement, not least in Manila, where it clouded Addis's notification on 20 September that the fleet would be passing through the Sulu Sea a few days later.

All this added fuel to the fire and was followed by a series of exchanges, in the course of which I was exonerated by London of their initial suggestion that I had spoken out of turn: indeed I was congratulated on my choice of words, and John Addis was told to give Marcos an accurate report of what I had said. The Hunter flight went without incident, but on 26 September a RAF aircraft on a direct flight from Hong Kong to Labuan was diverted by Manila air traffic control and buzzed by two fighters, one with Philippine and the other with US Air Force markings, and on the same day Marcos made an inflammatory speech, identifying Britain as the real opponent of Philippine claims to Sabah. On the following day a crowd of demonstrators attacked and did some damage to Addis's residence. They had burnt effigies of President Johnson and the Tunku outside the US and Malaysian embassies. They attempted to do the same to an effigy of me, but by then it was raining and I refused to burn (I resented the imputation that I was 'too wet to burn'), and it was apparently their frustration at this that provoked the attack, for which the Philippine government later apologized. Matters were complicated both by the fact that there were still six more Hunters in Hong Kong due to fly to Singapore, and that, on the fleet's return from Australia, *Hermes* and the guided-missile destroyer, HMS *Glasgow*, were due to carry out exercises with the US Navy in the Subic Bay training area, the latter being revealed by an Australian journalist. At the last moment the Philippines allowed five Hunters to refuel at Clark Field on 31 October, the sixth flying direct to Labuan, and the ships were diverted to exercise elsewhere, while attempts were made by all concerned to calm things down without prejudicing our attitude to right of passage through the Sulu Sea. The Malaysians accused us of having let them down and having failed to honour the Anglo–Malaysian Defence Agreement, threatening to refer the matter to the International Court of Justice. The echoes of the affair continued to resound until the end of my time in the Far East in February 1969, and undermined the cooperative attitude that Malaysia had originally adopted over various aspects of the withdrawal plan. It was instrumental in influencing the Tunku to turn to France to equip his air force with Mirage aircraft and his army with Panhard armoured cars.

The exercise, to which the fleet had sailed, was a major joint service exercise which I had planned with the primary purpose of providing an opportunity for 3rd Commando Brigade Royal Marines, whose units had been engaged almost exclusively in land-based operations since 1963, to get back to training in amphibious operations, especially as the new assault ships (LPD), HMS *Fearless* and *Intrepid*, were coming into service, as were the army's landing ships logistic (LSL), *Sir Lancelot, Sir Galahad* and *Sir Bedevere*. It had also been decided to station a small hovercraft squadron of the Royal Corps of Transport in the command. I therefore decided in the middle of 1967 to plan for a major amphibious

exercise in the autumn of 1968. Shoalwater Bay, off the
Australian training area near Rockhampton in Queensland,
would not only provide a new and welcome change of
scene, with all the advantages deriving from unfamiliarity,
but would make it possible for the Fleet to combine the
amphibious exercise with their annual exercise with the
Royal Australian Navy. I had made my first approach to the
Australians in October 1967 and, although I had obtained
agreement in principle, I had considerable difficulty in getting them to accept that it was not just a naval exercise. As
it would take place in Australia, they rightly insisted that
they must control it, but they had no machinery to control
a joint service exercise, and cooperation between their three
services left a lot to be desired. In the end satisfactory
arrangements were evolved by which the Australian admiral
controlled the purely naval phases, while Admiral Griffin,
who had succeeded Ashmore as second-in-command of the
Far East Fleet, controlled the amphibious phase, the land
aspects being controlled by Pat Patterson from one of the
LSLs. One of his Gurkha battalions had been flown to the
area to oppose the Marines. The air force arrangements
were less satisfactory. The best solution would have been
for Brian Eaton, commanding 224 Group RAF, to be in
control, but, although he was an RAAF officer, this was not
acceptable to them. It was an ambitious, and on the whole,
highly successful, exercise, which provided a fitting climax
to the joint service machinery for training and operations
developed within Far East Command, based on cooperation
between the Flag Officer Second-in-Command of the Fleet,
assisted by Commodore Amphibious Forces, the General
Commanding 17th (Gurkha) Division and the Air Officer
Commanding 224 Group RAF. This valuable structure was
soon to be broken up.

The exercise also provided an opportunity for a valuable informal meeting to discuss withdrawal plans, presided
over by Henry Bland, and attended by the Australian navy
minister, all the Australian Chiefs of Staff, Bill Thornton
and myself. Bland announced that Australia had decided
to keep two of her Mirage squadrons at Butterworth, but
that they were not committed to keeping any of their army
in Malaysia after our withdrawal from the Commonwealth

Brigade in 1969. Their decision, and that of New Zealand, about that would depend on assessment of the options and their cost. They wished to send teams from all three services to Singapore and Malaysia to examine the problems in detail with us and with the two governments. By mid-November, when I went to London to discuss the development of our plans with the Chiefs of Staff, the air force team had confirmed the decision about Butterworth, recommending that a detachment of RAAF Mirages should rotate from there to Tengah airfield in Singapore, which would be the base of the Singapore Air Force. The army team had recommended that they could retain the army element they had contributed to the Commonwealth Brigade, but only if it were based in Singapore, a move to which New Zealand reluctantly agreed. These conclusions having been reached, I was allowed to set my five-power groups to work again, the naval group doing so after we handed over the naval dockyard to a specially formed company, owned by the Singapore Government, for whom Swan Hunter were the managing agents. Some 3,000 of its local employees were transferred to the company's books, a major contribution to mitigating the effect on the economy and people of Singapore of our decision to withdraw. The groups had made good progress by the time that I handed over, on 4 March 1969, to my successor, Admiral Sir Peter Hill-Norton. The manner of that handover had its lighter side. Peter felt that he ought to arrive by sea, although he was not prepared to spend the time travelling by that means all round the Cape. He flew in a RAF Britannia to Gan, where he embarked on a Royal Fleet Auxiliary supply ship, the aircraft, with all his baggage, preceding him to Singapore. This suited me well, as the Britannia was available to take me and the family, with all our baggage, back to England, and I could depart before he arrived. I asked Brigadier Frank Clarkson, my chief signal officer, if a RAF Britannia could communicate direct with a Royal Fleet Auxiliary. After considerable discussion in the joint signal staff, I was told that it could be arranged, and I said that, when we passed overhead, as we should do some 100 miles west of the northern tip of Sumatra on our way to Gan to refuel, I would send Peter a message. As we neared the point, the captain of the aircraft reported that he had picked up what he thought was the RFA, and I sent a message saying that we would descend to 1500 feet and circle the ship, at which time I would hand over Far East Command to him. I received the reply: 'Your signal received. I shall be on the port side of the bridge, waving a red handkerchief,' to which I replied: 'I will be on the starboard side of the flight deck, waving a white handkerchief!' I saw his red-spotted handkerchief, but I doubt if he saw mine.

I was sorry to leave the command and would have been happy to stay in Singapore for longer, but it was the navy's turn, and it was, no doubt, thought important for Hill-Norton to hold a senior joint service command, even for a short period, before he took over from Le Fanu as First Sea Lord, as he expected to do in 1970, when Le Fanu was due to succeed Sam Elworthy as Chief of the Defence Staff.* I had been told that, unless something untoward happened, I could expect to succeed George Baker as Chief of the General Staff in 1971, when he would have completed three years in the job. The Military Secretary had told me that there were two possible jobs I might do before that: either Master-General of the Ordnance, if Charles Richardson retired early, which he might (but actually did not) do, or Southern Command. The latter, with headquarters at Hounslow, was normally held by a lieutenant-general, currently David Peel-Yates, and would be responsible for command of all troops, other than combat units, in what had previously been Southern and Eastern Commands. Combat units in the whole of the United Kingdom would then be under Strategic Command at Wilton, of which John Mogg would assume command at the time I was due to leave the Far East. I preferred and received Southern Command, even though the responsibilities would be much less than those I had been exercising. MGO before CGS (and thereafter presumably CDS) would mean a long continuous spell in Whitehall: Southern Command would give me an opportunity to gain first-hand experience of the whole training and administrative machinery of the army in the United Kingdom, with its local links, which would be valuable to me as CGS; and it

* Le Fanu did not in the event do so. He was found to be suffering from leukemia, from which he died shortly afterwards. Elworthy stayed on for another year, and was then succeeded by Hill-Norton.

would be conveniently placed for Shackleford, schools for John and places where the other children were likely to be.

My job in Singapore had been of great interest: there had been plenty to occupy me, but the pressure of work had not been by any means excessive. When I had been in Singapore, I had played tennis four days a week, if I could; sailed a GP14 dinghy twice a week in the races held by the Army yacht club; competed in regattas which all the service yacht clubs held in January, and the passage races between them, learned to water-ski and generally enjoyed myself. Sundays had normally been devoted to launch picnics. We would take *Uriah Heep*, an old army motor fishing vessel, crewed by Malay soldiers of the Royal Corps of Transport, and anchor in a suitable place to bathe and goggle. If there was enough wind, I would sail the dinghy out to join the family and our guests there. It was one of the most agreeable aspects of Singapore life. In addition to official visits to the places which I have already mentioned, we also went to Japan in October 1968 to attend the celebrations marking the centenary of the Imperial Meiji regime, the first time that the Japanese had publicly paid tribute to the Emperor and his family since 1945. There was some sucking of teeth in the diplomatic circle in which I was seated, when the Japanese Prime Minister, at the end of his speech of congratulations, shouted 'Banzai', and it was taken up throughout the huge auditorium. I had had a private audience with the Emperor. Having been told that I had written a history of The Royal Scots Greys, he spent most of the time asking about the part they had played at the Battle of Waterloo, an easier subject for me than marine biology, which was his speciality. Susanna and John had been with us in Singapore throughout, the latter starting school at the excellent army infant and junior schools there, the former taking an extramural course in nineteenth- and twentieth-century art at Singapore University. Andrew and Alice had flown out for summer and Christmas holidays. In the former we had taken *Uriah Heep* to islands off the east coast of Malaya, in 1967 camping on Pulau Tioman, in 1968 basing ourselves on the Malaysian government rest house in the Perhentian islands, where the bathing and goggling was superb. Immediately after Christmas 1967 we had taken all the family, except John, on a tour of the fabulous collection of temples at Angkor Wat in Cambodia. They are undoubtedly to be ranked among the Wonders of the World, and it is tragic to think that, at the time of writing, they must be disappearing again into the jungle in which the French missionary, Charles Bouillevaux, found them in 1850. Our visit to them and the trek in Nepal were the highlights of our Far Eastern experience. We had had a very busy social life, entertaining and being entertained, a never-ending stream of visitors passing through Command House, especially in the winter. Most were welcome, none more so than Alice's American godfather, Tom Jones, on 'R & R' from Vietnam. As a result, we met many interesting people of a great many different nationalities, and formed friendships, some of them long lasting, with inhabitants of Singapore and Malaysia and with members of the diplomatic corps in both countries, our closest contacts naturally being with the British, Australian and New Zealand High Commissioners and their staffs, as well as with my military colleagues, including successive US Cs-in-C Pacific.

My dealings with Whitehall had a lighter side, when I received an order to give full cooperation to a film company producing a version of Leslie Thomas's *The Virgin Soldiers*. I happened to have read it, having been lent it by Colonel Harry Posner, the lively head of Army Psychiatry in the Far East, who took a wry professional interest in the sexual habits of soldiers. My reply to the Ministry of Defence was short: 'Have you read the book?' I got no answer, but a series of staff signals followed, instructing us to make every facility available to the company, to which we consistently returned the same answer. When the arrival of the filming team was imminent, I agreed with my service commanders that we would forbid service men or women from acting as extras and would do the minimum to meet the Ministry of Defence's orders. The team would be in Singapore in the summer holidays, and there was nothing we could do, apart from parental guidance, to stop teenage children of service families from participating (the son of the American ambassador, Frank Galbraith, on vacation from high school in the USA, acted as a British soldier and found it very hard work). I signalled Whitehall, reporting our decisions and strongly recommending that on no account should the

Ministry of Defence, and certainly not the Commander-in-Chief Far East, appear on the credits as having cooperated. I ended the signal by a reference to all my previous ones and the question: 'Has ANYBODY repeat ANYBODY in the Ministry yet read the book?' The response was electric. Major-General Pat Man, the ultra-conservative Director of Army Personal Services, had at last been persuaded to read it and was horrified. Panic signals followed, telling us to do the absolute minimum.

I had appreciated the good relations I enjoyed with Lee Kuan Yew. He and I dined alone together every six months, alternating in our respective official residences, a privilege our High Commissioner did not enjoy. After his over-reaction to the announcement of our withdrawal, I had admired the resolute and pragmatic way in which he and his colleagues, notably Goh Keng Swee, set about turning the situation to Singapore's advantage. Before we left, he gave a dinner party for us and presented me with a locally executed scroll, depicting a large and a small rock in a river. The translation of the Chinese inscription ran:

General Sir Michael Carver took over as Commander-in-Chief, British Far East Command, two years ago at a time when Singapore's defences were most vulnerable. His contribution towards Singapore's security will always be remembered with gratitude. Now that he has completed his tour of duty and is about to leave for a higher appointment, I am presenting him with this scroll of painting which depicts: 'THE INDOMITABLE SOLITARY ROCK IN A TURBULENT STREAM' as a token of our goodwill and friendship.

LEE KUAN YEW (Seal)

I found the people of the region, Malay, Dayak, Chinese, or Thai in origin, each in their different way, charming, sensible and easy to deal with. I was immensely grateful for the good fortune that had come my way in being appointed to such an interesting and rewarding post, which I had enjoyed more than any other in a career which had included many that could be so described.

15

The Patriot's Boast

Such is the patriot's boast, where'er we roam,
His first, best country ever is, at home.

Oliver Goldsmith (1728–1774),
The Traveller

The first question of importance I had to face was the proposal that all the army commands in the United Kingdom should be merged into one Headquarters United Kingdom Land Forces at Wilton, to which both the 3rd Division, commanding the strategic reserve units, and army districts, commanding all the others, would be directly subordinate. It was hoped that this would make considerable economies in manpower, both uniformed and civilian. Victor Balfour, the Vice-CGS, asked me for my opinion on the subject while I was still on leave before I had taken over my new command. He warned me that my predecessor, Peel-Yates, as well as Napier Crookenden at Western and Bill Jackson at Northern Command were opposed to it. I told him that my provisional view, based on my experience as Director of Army Staff Duties, was that, although I doubted if it would result in manpower economies as great as assumed, I was inclined to favour it, as leading both to greater efficiency and to increasing the standing and local value of the district commanders at major-general level. It did not take me long, after I had assumed command, to confirm this view. The introduction of computers had made a greater centralization of such things as store-keeping and distribution both desirable and more efficient. All that command headquarters, many of the

routine jobs in which were held by retired officers, appeared
to do was to act as an unnecessary buffer between district
headquarters and the Ministry of Defence, disagreeing with
one or the other just for the sake of expressing a separate
opinion. Concentration into one headquarters should make
it possible to decentralize more decision-making from the
Ministry. When the proposal was implemented soon after I
had left Southern Command, it proved to be a great success.

As well as being concerned with the affairs of Southern Command, I was *ex-officio* C-in-C (designate) United
Kingdom Land Forces in war, and, as such, a member of
the Cs-in-C (UK) Committee, which was responsible to the
Chiefs of Staff for planning for and training all three services
in Home Defence. This covered both guarding key points
and cooperation with the Home Office Regional Emergency and Civil Defence Organization and the Police. My
colleagues were the C-in-C Navy (Home) and the AOC-in-C
RAF Support Command. We met every three months and
held an annual study period, attended by almost all Chief
Constables and senior Home Office officials. This aspect of
my duties had the advantage of giving me a valid reason
for visiting all the army district headquarters in the United
Kingdom, including Scotland and Northern Ireland, as well
as my colleagues at Western and Northern Commands.

I spent most of my time away from the office at Hounslow,
which I was happy to leave in the capable hands of my chief
of staff, for most of the time Rex Whitworth, and, for
a short period at the end, Bill Scotter, who had served
under me both when I was Director of Plans and also when
DASD. I was very well served by both of them. I was lucky
also to have Cyril Starling again as my Command Secretary.
The workload was not heavy, and the office was unbearably
noisy, being immediately under the flight path of aircraft
using the southern runway at Heathrow. I sailed, chiefly
with REME, both as a crew member in their dinghy team
and at their annual regatta in the Mermaids of the Seaview
Yacht Club on the Isle of Wight, delightful boats to sail. It
was an event in which I was to sail for many years thereafter.
I also played tennis for the headquarters team. My Director
of Ordnance Services, Alan Parnaby, and I were the third
pair, and were delighted when, our combined ages adding

up to 105, we thrashed the third pair of the Irish Guards, totalling 43! It was in that year that I was asked to assume two honorary posts, Admiral of the Army Sailing Association and President of the Army Lawn Tennis Association. I did not feel qualified for either, but realized that both associations wanted influence in high places, and was delighted to accept, if I could help, which I did in subsequent years by lending all the support I could to the establishment of the Army Dinghy Sail Training Centre and Sailing Club at Netley, in the grounds of the old Royal Victoria Hospital on Southampton Water, and the indoor tennis courts at Aldershot. They made significant contributions to army sailing and tennis respectively.

That summer saw the first (apart from the Norfolk Broads) of the holidays we were to spend on canals. It was on the Canal du Nivernais, joining the Yonne at Auxerre with the Loire at Nevers. The canal passed through the depths of rural France, and we had perfect weather for the week we spent on it with the whole family. On our way there we had a splendid picnic with Don and Cherry Cook and some of their huge family near Chartres. We drove off on the wrong side of the road, wondering why they waved at us so frantically, and later camped on the banks of the Loire. From the canal we went on to see Antony and his family at Bonnieux, camping on our way back through the Massif Central to the beach at Arromanches on which I had landed on 7 June 1944. On our return, Andrew went up to Cambridge, having gained a place at Clare College, where my uncle, Dick Wellesley, had been and to which I had wished to go. He began by reading philosophy and logic, but later switched to economics, which became his profession. In the Christmas holidays we all went to Saalbach again to ski, John, now aged eight, being introduced to the sport. The snow was thin and it turned out to be our least successful ski holiday.

1970 had a number of highlights: a lecture in Winchester Prison: ADC General to The Queen: Iris Portal starting the life of the Marquess Wellesley: John going to Horris Hill School: the Kermit Roosevelt lectures: the Conservative victory at the general election in June; and a tour of Germany as representative Colonel Commandant both of the Royal Tank Regiment and of REME. These should perhaps be taken in turn. Geoff Hodges, who had been the headmaster's secretary and in charge of physical training when I had been at Winchester, in his retirement was education officer at Winchester prison. He asked me to lecture to the prisoners, and, to my surprise, said that they would be interested in the desert war. I took considerable trouble to prepare my lecture and had a generally attentive audience, including, somewhat to my concern, a 'trusty' who had been my transport sergeant at Münster, and the son of a brother officer, the latter having served with me when he was a corporal. It made me realize that, in the hackneyed phrase, it was a small world. I had often seen the grim Victorian exterior of the prison, and was not surprised to find it equally forbidding inside.

In February I was honoured by being appointed one of the Aides-de-Camp General to The Queen, the principal advantage being that of the grant of a private audience on appointment. I had been received in one immediately after my return from the Far East, and was on four subsequent occasions to enjoy the quarter of an hour of relaxed conversation which intervened between her reception of newly appointed ambassadors and her lunchtime. 'You will not find the duties arduous,' she remarked, which was correct, the most pleasant being attendance at one of the State Openings of Parliament.

In the same month Iris Portal, sister of R.A.B. Butler,* and an authoress under the name of Iris Butler, came to stay to discuss the project of writing a biography of my great-great-great-grandfather, The Marquess Wellesley, Governor-General of India and elder brother of Wellington. I had inherited from my uncle, Dick Wellesley, a trunkful of his papers and others relating to him, the principal ones being the correspondence between him and his wife when he was in India.† My cousin, Hugh Farmar, who was intensely keen on his Wellesley ancestry, had urged me to lend my support to a biography, the only previous one, a mediocre effort by W. McCullogh Torrens, having been published in 1880. He had first approached Carola Oman, who had suggested Iris. It was a happy choice. With her great interest in

---

* Lord Butler of Saffron Waldon.
† See page 2.

the history of India, with which her family had been closely connected, and her sensitivity to all the human facets of the story, she became absorbed in the task, which culminated in her excellent book *The Eldest Brother*. When it was published (by Hodder and Stoughton) in 1973, I gave a cocktail party for her, at which were assembled almost all of the Marquess's living descendants.

In March Edith and I went to Germany, I in my dual capacity as representative Colonel Commandant both of my own regiment and of REME. I had become one of the three Colonels Commandant of the Royal Tank Regiment when in the Far East, and had taken over as the 'representative' from Alan Jolly, when he retired towards the end of 1969. The representative Colonel Commandant was the one who undertook the duties, ceremonial and executive, on behalf of the others, and it was clearly sensible that I should do so for both the RTR and REME while at Southern Command. I was well placed to do so and could spare the time, and it would not have been suitable for me to be spokesman of a particular interest when I became CGS. It was an exhausting tour, as it involved talking to an endless succession of soldiers, and their families, every day and all day for a week. Finding anything new to say was impossible. I paid a more relaxed visit to 1st Royal Tanks in September, when they were training, not very seriously, in Bavaria.

In April John had started at his first boarding school, Horris Hill near Newbury, the headmasters of which were the Stow brothers, Jimmy and Sandy. Jimmy had been one of the liaison officers, provided by 2nd KRRC, at 4th Armoured Brigade Headquarters in the last year of the war. On our return from Singapore John had attended a day preparatory school at Weybridge, but now, at eight and a half, was happy to be among his contemporaries at boarding school, and it would not have been easy to keep him at home in term-time when I became CGS. There was a question mark over that when the Conservatives won the election in June. To have been chosen by Healey might not be a recommendation, and I had reason to believe that certain Conservative circles, influential with Heath, had their knife into me over the reorganization of the Territorial Army and also thought that I had acquiesced too readily in the rundown in the

Far East – not that I had had any choice. However, after a lunch with Peter Carrington at the Turf Club in October, and also one with Robin Balniel, his Minister of State, all doubt was removed.

Before the election I had given the Kermit Roosevelt lectures in the United States. A descendant of President Theodore, Kermit had died serving as an officer in the British army in the Second World War. His mother had established a trust fund in his memory for a senior British army officer to lecture annually to American army audiences, and for a senior American officer to do the same in Britain. By this time the money had run out, but the two armies funded the lectures' continuation. One lectured to the military academy at West Point, the national defense college in Washington, the joint service staff college at Norfolk, Virginia, the army command and staff college at Fort Leavenworth, near Kansas City, and the army war college at Carlisle, near Baltimore. After that, one was invited to give a lecture at the Canadian National Defence College at Kingston, Ontario. I had prepared two lectures, one for the lower level audiences on 'The Problems of Peacekeeping', the other on 'The History of British Military Involvement East of Suez'. Starting at West Point, I had to lecture at 6.30 p.m. in a darkened hall to cadets who had been on the go at an intense pace since dawn. At the height of the Vietnam war and at that time of day, they could not have been less interested in the subject, and I suspect that almost all of them slept through it. I did not give that lecture again. 'East of Suez' however proved an apter choice. The day I delivered it in Washington to the equivalent of our own Imperial Defence College (later renamed the Royal College of Defence Studies), with a large number of senior serving and retired officers also in the audience, was the day the Americans extended their operations from Vietnam into Cambodia, although the news of it was not announced until the evening. I had traced the whole history of our involvement from Elizabethan times, displacing the Portuguese, Dutch and French maritime empires, up to our recent decision to pull in our horns. I concluded with these words:

That, Gentlemen, is the story. It is a long one, an active
one and one which has done as much as anything else to
shape the form and traditions of our army, of our navy
and of our air force too. Of what value to you is this long
historical survey? I believe, that there are some lessons to
be learnt from history. The principal one, I believe is the
danger of not thinking out where you are going when you
first embark on some foreign adventure, especially a war-
like one. Each step brings further commitments – extends
you further – unless you apply a ruthless self-questioning
of your aim; and see that what you attempt does not go
imprudently far beyond your resources. Of course one
must take risks. Where should any of us be if we hadn't?
But there is a difference between a bold step taken in
spite of the dangers fully realized, and an unthinking
advance from one situation to another until is impossible
to draw back. Such ruthless self-questioning is rare: and
acting on it rarer still. Not many soldiers like doing it; few
politicians, and even fewer diplomats. We had one soldier
in our history who was a master of it, the famous Duke of
Wellington, who, as Colonel and Major-General Wellesley,
contributed much to this story.

My story began with the sailor and the soldier following
trade with their flags. I hope that their departure from
this very important part of the world will not see the end
of our trade in it. After all, we have continued to trade in
this great country of yours, although our flag left it a long
time ago – nearly 200 years, I believe.

We were staying with George Lea, head of our military
mission, who gave a dinner party to which many distinguished guests were invited. It was disrupted by our breaking
off to watch Nixon on television justifying the invasion of
Cambodia, after which I found myself in an acrimonious
argument with the well-known columnist, Joseph Alsop, who
was strongly in favour, while I expressed doubts about where
it would lead. Next day was a Saturday, and I had arranged
to play tennis with Westmorland, then Chief of the Army
Staff, at Fort Myer, where the senior army officers lived.
On my way there in a US Army car, the driver of which
was tactfully in civilian clothes, several carloads of young

Americans, on their way to the protest demonstration round the White House, yelled at me: 'Get out of Cambodia!', to which, dressed in my tennis clothes, I replied in my plummiest English accent: 'I'm afraid I'm not there!' I partnered Westy against his deputy, Richard Stilwell, with whom I had played in Bangkok, when he was head of the US Army Advisory Group there, and the famous General Maxwell D. Taylor, then aged 68. He had commanded 101st US Airborne Division during the Second World War, and I had supplied his division with a rum ration when Gerry Hopkinson's 44th Royal Tanks had supported them in the advance to Arnhem. He had been Chief of the Army Staff, Chairman of the Joint Chiefs, Special Adviser on security matters to President Kennedy and Ambassador in Vietnam. Shortly after that, he had visited Singapore, where his son Jack, who often played tennis with me, was in the American Embassy, and I had then admired his skill on the tennis court. He had played for the US Army between the wars. It was a very hot afternoon, and between every game Dick Stilwell would consult the soldier manning a radio set at the side of the court for news of how the demonstration round the White House was shaping. 'It's all right, General, there's no rioting yet,' came the reassuring reply, and on we went, the first set going to our opponents at 14–12, after which Max Taylor handed over to a younger general.

Before leaving for Canada, Westy presented me officially with a sporting rifle, the first of several presents of firearms which were distinctly embarrassing. The RAF refused to take it back on their scheduled flight until I had obtained a firearms certificate for it in England. It eventually went to Antony's Elizabeth's nephew, Paul Strutt. When Westy came on an official visit to me as CGS, he presented me with an American officer's pistol and 36 rounds of ammunition in the middle of Heathrow airport. My French colleague, General de Boissieu, gave me an 1873 French officer's revolver, and the Romanian General Ion Georghe, a 0.22 pistol and 54 rounds (in addition to the Romanian Navy's presents of a stuffed heron and a fearful picture of a sailing ship sinking in a storm in the Black Sea, inspired by the public relations handout, listing my interests as bird-watching and sailing). I had the pistols made incapable of firing and presented them to the Surrey Police. When I was CDS, my Swedish colleague produced another sporting rifle in my office, which he had not declared on entering the country. That was handed over to the Metropolitan Police for use in their firearms bureau. The whole problem of official exchanges of presents was fraught with difficulties and embarrassments, and I fervently wished for an international agreement to ban them all.

I was to take over from George Baker on the significant date of 1 April 1971, and handed over Southern Command to Basil Eugster on 19 February. It was clear to me that my principal concern was going to be Northern Ireland, where the situation had seriously deteriorated since the army had been called in in August 1969. We had spent our summer holiday in 1970 in the Republic, accompanied by Alice, John and Tom Holmer, son of Paul, who had been Deputy and Acting High Commissioner in Singapore when we were there. The holiday was spent partly camping, partly in a so-called farmhouse at Newport on the west coast, actually the rectory in which the author Canon George Birmingham had lived, and finishing our tour with Edith's uncle, Jocelyn Proby, at Arklow. It was interesting to get a view of events from the other side of the fence. On 4 February 1971 Lieutenant-General Sir Ian Freeland had handed over the command in Northern Ireland, which he had held since shortly before the troubles broke out, to Vernon Erskine-Crum, an up-and-coming guardsman, one of the army's bright boys, of whom great things were expected.

On 17 February I was making a farewell visit to Salisbury Plain and had motored from Taunton, where I had spent the night, to the headquarters of Salisbury Plain Area at Bulford. On arrival I was told that I was urgently required to ring up the Military Secretary, Tom Pearson. When I did so, he told me that Erskine-Crum had died of a sudden heart attack, and that George Baker wished to consult me before recommending a successor to the Defence Secretary, Lord Carrington. He read out a list of eight names, of whom four I thought were possibles, and two front runners. Weighing the pros and cons of the two, I firmly recommended Major-General Harry Tuzo, then Director of the Royal Artillery. In the intense competition of the time, he had not looked like getting further promotion. He seemed to me to have

the right qualities of toughness, resilience, breadth of outlook and rapidity of mind. Although a gunner, he had
commanded an infantry brigade in Borneo, and therefore
had some of the right experience. The other possible choice
was Major-General Pat Patterson, then Director of Army
Training, and also unlikely, largely because of age, to obtain
further promotion. He was extremely experienced in anti-
subversive operations in the Far East and a splendid soldier.
However I doubted his ability to handle the non-military
aspects, particularly the politicians, the press and others.

Harry Tuzo was appointed, and on 1 April, my first day in
office as CGS, we found ourselves together in a meeting in
Number 10 Downing Street, at which Brian Faulkner, who
had recently succeeded Chichester-Clark* as Prime Minister
of Northern Ireland, faced Ted Heath, Alec Douglas-Home,
Reggie Maudling and Peter Carrington, Prime Minister,
Foreign Secretary, Home Secretary and Defence Secretary
respectively. The background to this meeting was the mounting provocative activity of the IRA. This had been particularly offensive at the funerals of IRA men, killed in clashes
with the security forces (as the army and the Royal Ulster
Constabulary, the RUC, were called) or by Protestants. These
funerals were staged as military affairs, with participants in
uniform and shots fired over the grave. There had been
constant pressure on the army from the Northern Ireland
government at Stormont to take stronger action against this
flagrant flouting of the law. Other forms of IRA activity consisted of attacks on police stations, murders of Special Branch
police and ambushes of individual members or patrols of the
security forces. On 10 March a particularly brutal murder
took place of three young soldiers of the Royal Highland
Fusiliers. This increased activity led to mounting pressure
on the army both to take a tougher line and also to guard
police stations and escort the police, none of which it was
anxious to do, given the legal difficulties and the likelihood
that stronger action would not only lead to stronger reaction
from the Catholics, but also not in itself be effective. Whitehall had added its own pressure on the army in order to try
and keep Chichester-Clark and his Stormont government in

* Later Lord Moyola.

power. The prospect of direct rule was very unpopular in Westminster at this time. But on 23 March Faulkner, who had been one of the members of the Northern Ireland Joint Security Committee pressing hardest for strong action, succeeded Chichester-Clark as Prime Minister. This meeting in No. 10 was therefore his first meeting as Prime Minister with the senior ministers of HMG, as it was also for myself and Tuzo. Faulkner pressed for tougher and more resolute action against the IRA, and there was a good deal of not very realistic discussion about ways and means of controlling movement across the border. One remark of Faulkner's stuck in my memory. When asked what had made it possible to bring IRA terrorist activity to an end on a previous occasion, he replied that the decisive factor had been that the Dublin Government had then also taken tough measures against them, including the use of internment. This did not prevent him and some of our own senior ministers from suggesting action that would inevitably have aroused the anger of the Republic.

April turned out to be a fairly quiet month, but IRA activity increased in May and continued to do so in June as the season of Orange Order marches got into its stride. The flash-point came in Londonderry, when two men, Cusack and Beattie, were shot by the army when seen to be about to fire weapons. Republicans claimed that they were innocent, and the incident was exploited to the full by Bernadette Devlin and the SDLP. There was a spate of rioting in Londonderry and continual attacks on the police and army post at the Bligh's Lane factory under the Creggan, overlooking the Bogside. This put an end to hopes both of capturing the 'hearts and minds' of the Catholics of Londonderry and that leaving the Bogside and Creggan alone would result in their calming down. When Tuzo had taken over, he had listed his priorities as: first, to bring to justice all subversive elements; second, to reassert the rule of law; and third, the capture of arms, ammunition and explosives. He had stressed that intelligence and cooperation with the RUC were the keys to success in achieving these goals. Arising out of the 1 April meeting, there had been considerable discussion about the security of the border and a detailed examination of the value of trying to close it, the inevitable result of which was to conclude that, even if one devoted very large resources of manpower to it, it would not be very effective. Pressure was also applied to trying to get the RUC into better shape, accompanied by arguments about the need to guard police stations and who should do it. The RUC maintained that the army should: the army naturally regarded it as an unprofitable use of manpower. It was not popular either with the UDR, who were not in any case normally available in the daytime. This led to demands for full-time UDR units. The use of the T & AVR was also considered, but rejected for good political reasons.

By mid-July the situation in Belfast and Londonderry had clearly deteriorated. Rioting was frequent, petrol and nail bombs being increasingly used. Incidents of shooting and bomb explosions had also increased. There was mounting criticism from the Protestants and in Great Britain that the army was not doing enough, although it was constantly accused by Republicans of atrocities, harassment and over-reaction. Tuzo proposed a plan to arrest up to 100 suspects, but nobody could solve the problem of what to do with them after arrest. Protestant pressure for internment was growing. The main aim of Tuzo's proposal was to reduce this pressure, subsidiary aims being to gain some information from interrogation and to frighten the IRA by making them realize that we had our fingers on them and were ready to pounce, if internment were decided upon.

This plan was discussed in London on 19 July, the idea being that it should be put into effect after 12 August, the date of the annual Apprentice Boys' March in Londonderry. Pressure from Faulkner to implement it earlier, in order to fend off pressure from Ian Paisley, who was demanding internment, led to the decision to implement it on 23 July. Unfortunately, in announcing it, the Home Secretary, Maudling, hoping to gain the maximum political value from it, overemphasized the significance. He said: 'The army's operation in Northern Ireland this morning marks the beginning of a new phase in the battle against the IRA . . . Its significance is the stress it lays on the fact that the function of the security forces is not merely to contain disorder and violence, but to search out the men and the organization responsible. This will be pursued. In this new phase the security forces will act with the utmost vigour.'

The reality fell far short of that. In the early hours of 23 July the army and the RUC together visited 100 houses in Belfast and a further 27 in the next four days. The operation led to the prosecution of only 20 men and the discovery of one or two weapons and some documents. It caused considerable annoyance to the Catholics, being greeted with dustbin-lid banging and leading to rioting in which nail bombs were thrown and shots fired at the security forces. It came as an anti-climax and made both Protestants and Catholics feel that security force action was ineffective, almost ridiculous. At the same time it gave the latter the mistaken impression that the reaction to internment might be no more severe. Between 23 July and 3 August there were 90 riots and attacks on military posts with petrol bombs, as well as a considerable increase in explosions to a rate of three or four a day, as well as incidents of arson. The atmosphere became particularly tense in Londonderry as the date of the Apprentice Boys' March approached. The possibility of banning the march was naturally considered. Paisley and the hard-line Protestants insisted that it must go forward, and that to give way to threats of Republican violence against it was unacceptable. As the arguments for and against banning or restricting the march developed, it became clear that Faulkner would not agree to a ban, unless he got internment in exchange.

The possibility and the problems of introducing internment had been discussed in Whitehall for a considerable time, and contingency plans had been prepared. The RUC estimated that the numbers to be interned would be about 450, of whom 150 were hard-core, who must form the first simultaneous pick-up. They would give no details of how they arrived at these figures. The construction of a hutted camp on the disused airfield of Long Kesh to accommodate this number was delayed by argument about who should pay for it, and HMS *Maidstone*, an old submarine depot ship, tied up in Belfast harbour and used to house troops, would also initially have to be used. By the beginning of June, the possibility of introducing internment was being frequently discussed, and Faulkner said publicly that he would introduce it only on the advice of the GOC* and the Chief Constable and in consultation with the government at Westminster.

On 11 June I visited Northern Ireland and discussed with Tuzo the linked subjects of banning marches and internment. Faulkner's line at that time was that one could not be accepted without the other. Tuzo and I agreed that marches should not be banned and that internment should not be recommended. On 19 July, with the Belfast marches of 12 July behind us, in which the deployment of large numbers of soldiers along the march routes had prevented any serious violence, Tuzo and I had a meeting in London with Lord Carrington to consider what should be done about the 12 August Apprentice Boys' March in Londonderry. We stuck to the line that, with some changes from its traditional route, it should be allowed to go ahead: that internment should not be introduced, but that 'disruptive operations' should be carried out, with the primary aim of reducing the pressure on Faulkner to take positive action against the IRA.

While Faulkner represented the situation as deteriorating, I recommended to Ministers on 3 August that internment should only be introduced as a last resort, and that we should 'ride it out' in the face of threats from both sides. After some discussion, my view was accepted. Next day Tuzo reported that Faulkner had said that he had received so many appeals from both Catholics and Protestants to ban the march, because of the likelihood of bloodshed, that he could not morally resist them. He was therefore pressing for the 'double act'. Tuzo reiterated that we would not recommend it on military grounds, but asked that he should immediately initiate the planning for his reinforcement in case the 'double act' was agreed. If it were, he recommended that it should take place on 10 August and reported that the RUC had increased their estimate of the number to be interned to 500, 300 to be in the initial pick-up.

On the following day, 5 November, Faulkner decided, in spite of Tuzo's advice and almost certainly for political reasons, to ask for the 'double act', and came over to London to present his case, accompanied by Tuzo and Howard-Smith,

* General Officer Commanding, i.e. Tuzo.

the foreign service officer who was the government's representative with the Northern Ireland government. Faulkner, with his Permanent Secretary, Kenneth Bloomfield, met Heath, Douglas-Home, Maudling and Carrington in Number 10 at 6 p.m. When Tuzo and I were called in, we were given no indication of what had passed, but were asked to give our assessment of the security situation. This was naturally Tuzo's task. He skilfully walked the tightrope of describing the difficulties facing the security forces, when they could take little, if any, direct action against the instigators of the trouble, while not giving a handle to Faulkner to grasp as a justification for internment. I repeated my previous advice that we should not ban the Apprentice Boys' March, but impose restrictions on it and guard the route. After prolonged discussion, at which we were not present, Ministers finally gave way to Faulkner's demand. As a *quid pro quo* they tried to extract from him a permanent ban on all marches and the disbandment of rifle clubs. He agreed to a six-month ban, but evaded the rifle club issue. The final formula agreed was that the introduction of internment was 'a decision of the Stormont Government, after considering all the factors, and having consulted the British Government'. Next day, Tuzo rang me from Northern Ireland to say that, for fear of a leak, he wished to bring the date and time for the pick-up forward to 4 a.m. on Monday 9 August. Ministerial approval was quickly obtained, anxiety being expressed that none of the suspects should escape the net as a result either of a warning or of the net not being cast widely enough.

In retrospect, I believe that my advice to ride out the Apprentice Boys' March without the 'double act' was sound. I have no doubt that internment would have been necessary later on in the year, but the haste with which it was decided upon and implemented was undoubtedly largely responsible for the intense emotion it aroused and the criticism it received. If it had been introduced after due warning and careful and thorough consideration of all the aspects, especially as to who was to be picked up, it could have aroused less opposition, although it would have run the risk that the worst offenders would disappear, either by slipping over the border or by going into hiding in the North. Ideally those to have been picked up should have been limited to the really dangerous individuals, that is to say the leaders and instigators of violence and the worst thugs, the tops and the bottom ends of the scale, and a selection of those whose interrogation might pay dividends. The list was undoubtedly larger than necessary and included some who should never have been on it at all, leading to widespread criticism and opposition. Some of this can be excused on the grounds of the short notice given, but there was also a suspicion that Faulkner encouraged the RUC to recommend a large pick-up for the sake of its political impact on the Protestants. The 'harassing' operation of 23 July had led to some slender improvement in the accuracy of the RUC's list and lulled the IRA into a false sense of security. Tuzo's demand to bring the operation forward to 9 August was motivated by the fear of a leak by the RUC which would give the most wanted suspects warning and time to escape over the border. Commanding officers of army units were told at 6 p.m. on 6 August, their intelligence officers on the 7th, company commanders on the 8th and the soldiers themselves given their orders that evening. The province was reinforced by three additional battalions, which arrived on the 9th, 10th and 11th as the operation was proceeding, bringing the total in Northern Ireland to 14 battalions.

Last-minute detailed planning took place in a feverish atmosphere, when the final list of 520 names was eventually received from the RUC. Of these 326 were actually arrested, little or no force being required to persuade them to go along with their captors. They were removed to three assembly centres, the barracks at Girdwood in East Belfast and, at Ballykinler in County Down, and the camp at Magilligan at the eastern mouth of Lough Foyle. A special interrogation centre had been set up some time before in the barracks at Ballykelly, a former RAF station north-east of Londonderry. Once the pick-up had been made, it was necessary to redeploy the troops quickly to deal with the threat of rioting and any other reaction. By 12 August Belfast was quiet after some rioting and burning, thanks to the energetic action of Frank Kitson, the brigade commander there. The reaction from the Catholic area of Londonderry was severe, and got progressively worse over the eight days following the operation. Barricades were erected throughout the Bogside

and Creggan, and on 19 August an operation was mounted
to clear them. By last light there were still some in the
Creggan which had not been removed. During the day
Tuzo and Howard-Smith had met with 30 prominent local
Catholics. They were persuaded to allow the latter to use
their influence to get the inhabitants to remove the remaining barricades themselves. They were unsuccessful, and by
the beginning of September the barricades were still there.
This well-meaning attempt to restrict the use of force in
Londonderry proved unfortunately to be the thin edge of
the wedge that led to the establishment of the 'no-go' area,
which was to prove so troublesome later.

When I returned from leave, which I had taken with the
family in Scotland, I found that the most urgent problem was
concern about 'deep interrogation' that had been carried out
on eleven of those who had been picked up for internment.
The full story is covered by the Compton and Parker reports,
which were published in November 1971 and March 1972
respectively. The story went back to the anxiety expressed
by my predecessor, George Baker, at the lack of expertise or
capacity in the RUC for obtaining information generally, and
specifically for interrogation. After considerable discuson in
Whitehall about how this could be remedied, it was decided
that the Interrogation Wing of the Joint Service Intelligence
School would do so. I had been aware that, as a result of this,
it had been decided to prepare a special interrogation centre
in Northern Ireland; that a plan had been prepared and
agreed with the RUC, who would carry out interrogation;
and that a team from the Intelligence School would be sent
over to help them set it up and run it. I understood that this
had the approval of the Director General of Intelligence in
the Ministry of Defence, who was not responsible to me as
CGS, and of the Secretary of State. I was not aware of,
and had not inquired into, the details of the methods to
be employed.

In fact the methods used owed their origin to the experience of the Korean War, when British servicemen who
had been captured had been subjected to prolonged and
sophisticated methods of interrogation. As a result, training
in resistance to this type of interrogation had been instituted
in the Services generally, and specifically for those most likely

to fall into enemy hands. Turning this experience inside out, the methods used for training had been employed for actual interrogation with considerable success in Malaya, Kenya, Borneo and Aden. In the last-named, they had given rise to allegations of torture, and, as a result of the Bowen report (November 1966), the rules governing their use had been revised and specifically endorsed by the Defence Secretary at the time, Denis Healey. When, on my return from leave, I inquired more deeply into what the details of the methods had been, who had carried them out and the extent to which this had been explained to and authorized by Ministers, I received evasive answers. With some difficulty I obtained a description of the methods – wall-standing, hooding, noise, and bread and water diet – later given in detail in the Compton report. My immediate reaction was surprise that Ministers should have authorised these: I personally would not have done. I was told that they had been explained to the Prime Minister and the Home and Defence Secretaries. When I probed deeper, I discovered that they had not been given a description of the details, but had been shown the rules approved by Healey in 1967 and told that the methods conformed with them, which they did, provided that the rule 'subjects are to be treated humanely' was given a fairly generous interpretation. I insisted that Carrington should be told the full details of what had in fact been done. As a result of this, it was agreed that the responsibility for ensuring that the Secretary of State was informed about intelligence matters concerning Northern Ireland was transferred to me as CGS, and not left, as it had been vaguely before, to DGI, the Deputy Chief of Defence Staff (Intelligence) or the CGS or VCGS. I continued to feel that Carrington, Maudling and Heath had been misled in this affair, as I felt I had myself, but blamed myself for not inquiring more deeply earlier on, and felt extremely grateful to them for the robust line which they maintained throughout all the subsequent controversy and the embarrassment that it caused. I later discovered that Tuzo had not himself been aware of the detailed methods it had been planned to employ, and I very much doubt if either the Chief Constable of the RUC, Graham Shillington, or Brian Faulkner was either.

The combination of internment and interrogation, and the allegations to which they both gave rise, greatly antagonized the Catholic population of Northern Ireland and the Government and public opinion of the Republic. It was a far cry from the days of August 1969, when the army had been welcomed in the Catholic areas as an alternative to the RUC and the B Specials. We were now Enemy Number One.

HMG's next aim was to reduce violence and terrorism, while forcing Faulkner to introduce reforms in order to give better representation to the Catholics. HMG felt that they had done their bit by agreeing to the 'double act' and providing forces to implement it. It was now up to Faulkner to deliver his side of the bargain. However violence escalated. Between August and December 1971 there were 723 explosions, and a further 299 devices were neutralized before they went off; this compared with 252 and 130 in the previous five months. There were more armed robberies of banks, post offices and shops. The Official IRA tended to concentrate on attacking the army, while the Provisionals went in for spectacular acts of terrorism likely to gain publicity. The scale of incidents went up from an average of 60 a month to 124 in November and 98 in December. In spite of the escalation of incidents, progress was made in terms of captures of weapons and ammunition and of arrests – 400 men on the 'wanted list' were picked up and 112 'routine arrests' made in November and December. Before this, in October, Major-General Robert Ford had succeeded Tony Farrar-Hockley as Commander Land Forces, that is deputy to Tuzo. After the internment operation the number of battalions, which had been raised to 17, was reduced to 13, but had to be raised again in October to 16, and armoured reconnaissance increased to the equivalent of two regiments.

On 4 October I prepared an appreciation of the situation for a meeting between the Prime Minister and Faulkner, based on one provided for me by Tuzo. I suggested that there were three options. The first was to continue to maintain operations at low intensity. This would cost less in terms of troops involved: it was less likely to provoke a Catholic uprising or the permanent alienation of Catholic opinion both north and south of the border; it would do nothing to appease the Unionists, could weaken Faulkner's position, and therefore lead to direct rule. The second option was to abandon hope of political progress and pursue a tough policy. It could bring short-term benefits, but it would need more troops and was unlikely to contribute to any long-term solution. It would harden the attitude of the Catholics, north and south, in support of the IRA, and was likely to swing international and some elements of British opinion behind them. The third was to step up the intensity of operations with the three extra battalions recently sent over; to remove some of the constraints imposed on military action by the desire to help 'political initiatives', including the restriction on 'humping' and closing the roads which crossed the border; to intensify border operations, and to carry out an operation in Londonderry to eliminate the 'no-go' area. However, I stressed that military action alone would not provide a solution. If we succeeded in improving the security situation, it would have to be exploited by political action, and there might be only a short 'window in time' in which the situation would remain favourable for such exploitation. Unless the political action had been decided upon and prepared for, a favourable opportunity in the security situation might be missed.

By November I had come to believe that the most likely time for such a 'window' to appear would be February or March 1972, but I felt that it would be fleeting. At a Ministerial meeting at the end of November I put this view forward. I said that, if things went well, by February the IRA might be seen to be ineffective. There might then be a short period before the Protestants would begin to feel that the threat had been removed and that they need not therefore give anything away. If, however, by that time there had been little progress, the Prime Minister might feel that the only answer would be a major operation 'to finish it off once and for all', as he had suggested to me at Chequers on the eve of the visit of Mr Lynch, the Prime Minister of the Republic, in June. I said that I did not believe that this was possible to achieve without concurrent political action. Either of the situations that I had postulated could involve direct rule.

A visit to Northern Ireland in mid-December led me to feel that the 'window' was imminent. I therefore suggested to Carrington that, unless the right moment for action appeared earlier, we should aim to take the political initiative in mid-February. I said that I thought that any proposal would have to be acceptable to the RUC, to Faulkner personally, although not necessarily to his party, to the Catholic hierarchy, to Gerald Fitt, the SDLP leader, and to Lynch. I went on to suggest that the elements of such a proposal could be: first, that responsibility for law and order should be transferred to Westminster, with the GOC being responsible for all security operations, army and police: secondly, that as many as possible of those areas of public administration in which inter-sectarian problems loomed large should be made the responsibility of public boards on which the minority community should be fully represented; they should be responsible to the Government of Northern Ireland: finally, that the method of representation and election to Stormont should be revised by a commission in the light of the establishment of these boards. If it proved impossible to negotiate such a proposal, the Government should announce publicly that they intended to implement it as soon as it could be agreed.

I went on to say that action was urgently needed to improve matters in three areas. The first was the leadership of the RUC. I suggested that a non-Irish deputy should be introduced as heir-apparent to Graham Shillington, who ought to retire soon. The second was the need for an impartial civil affairs organization to help the population of the Catholic areas to obtain their rights and dues from the bureaucracy. I suggested that there should be an official charged with this responsibility for each police division in Belfast. Finally there was a need for an Inspector or Director of Internment to deal with and coordinate all aspects of internment and the problems arising out of it. For Londonderry I suggested a lowering of provocative activity by the security forces to a level which maintained the morale of the Protestants without provoking the Catholics to an extent which caused us severe casualties, further antagonized them and brought no dividends.

I put these ideas forward at a Ministerial meeting early in January 1972. No decision was taken, perhaps because Ministers were preoccupied with a miners' strike at the time, but there was agreement that the comparatively quiet situation in

Belfast emphasized the importance of a search for a political solution. Questioned as to what would be involved if it were decided to carry out an operation to clear the 'no-go' area of Londonderry, where the barricades were still up, I estimated that it would need seven battalions to clear it and four would have to remain to keep it clear. Such an operation was likely to involve a considerable number of civilian casualties and would therefore harden the Catholic attitude against the security forces. It was agreed that it might eventually have to be done, but that it should be avoided while hope of a political initiative was being pursued.

In the second half of January there was an upsurge in terrorist activity in the form of bombing, shooting and attacks on the police, more in the rural districts and in Londonderry than in Belfast. The ban on marches had been renewed for a further six months, and the reaction to it was to march. The security forces were faced with a particularly difficult problem in dispersing illegal gatherings, mostly to protest against internment, without this leading to confrontations and casualties which could be exploited for their propaganda value. But they were illegal and therefore had to be stopped, quite apart from the need to avoid the inter-sectarian clashes to which they gave rise. The news media invariably exaggerated the numbers involved and the confrontation and disturbance they caused.

NICRA* planned marches on 29 January from Dungannon to Coalisland, and on Sunday 30 January in Londonderry. The Joint Security Committee, that is Faulkner, a few of his Ministers, Tuzo and Shillington, decided to stifle the first at source. This would not be possible in the case of Londonderry, except for the group due to start from the Shantallow. Although the Creggan and Bogside were not altogether 'no-go' areas, it would have caused a major confrontation to attempt to stifle the marches at source in that area and was not considered a prudent course to take. Instead Tuzo decided to halt the march at William Street, the edge of the Catholic area, and prevent it from proceeding to its destination at the Guildhall, well inside the Protestant area. One of the major problems of Londonderry at this

* The Northern Ireland Civil Rights Association.

time was the unruly and obstreperous hooligan element who
threw bottles, stones, bricks, petrol bombs and other missiles
at the security forces. They could seldom be arrested, and,
even when they were, received light sentences. William Street
was their favourite area and they had reduced it almost to
rubble. There was mounting pressure from the Protestants
for their arrest and punishment.

In evolving the plan to deal with the NICRA march in
Londonderry, it was decided not to attempt to arrest any of
the ringleaders, which would cause a major riot, but to arrest
a number of hooligans and arrange for a special court to sit
on the 31st. The number of marchers expected was estimated at anything between five and twenty-five thousand.
The RUC Chief Superintendent in Londonderry, Frank
Lagan, himself a Catholic, was opposed to trying to stop
the march at all. He advised merely photographing the
ringleaders and prosecuting them afterwards. This advice
was rejected by the Joint Security Committee which decided
that the march must be contained within the Bogside and
Creggan. Twenty-six barriers were to be set up, knife-rests
of dannert wire secured by concrete blocks, each manned by
a platoon of soldiers with an RUC constable present. The
normal garrison of Londonderry was to be reinforced by two
battalions and two companies, one of the battalions being 1st
Battalion, The Parachute Regiment, normally the resident
reserve battalion in Belfast. The order issued were that the
march was to be handled in a low key: there was to be no challenge within the Bogside or Creggan, no action against the
marchers, unless they tried to break through the barriers or
used violence against the security forces. CS gas was only to
be used in the last resort, if water cannon and baton rounds
proved ineffective. It was foreseen that NICRA would not
be able to control the hooligans. An arrest force was to be
held centrally, provided by the Parachute Regiment, and its
operation order described its task as to maintain a brigade
arrest force to conduct a 'scoop-up' operation of as many
hooligans and rioters as possible. It was only to be launched,
in whole or in part, on the orders of the brigade commander.
It was to be held at immediate notice in Foyle College car
park, and was likely to be launched on two axes, one towards
hooligans rioting in the area of William Street and Little

Diamond, the other towards the area of William and Little James Streets. The order stated that it was expected that the arrest operation would be conducted on foot.

This order was issued on 27 January, the very day that Heath, Maudling and Faulkner met at No. 10 Downing Street to discuss what appeared to be a rapidly approaching opportunity for a political initiative, which, if the trend continued, was likely to occur at the end of February or early March. The implementation of the order, when it was put into effect three days later on Sunday 30 January, to be christened 'Bloody Sunday' as a result, was to frustrate those hopes for many months to come.

This is not the place to record those events in detail. The report of the Widgery Tribunal* went into great detail about the events of that day which, up to the moment of launching the 'scoop-up' operation, went very much as expected. It is worth recalling the main points of Lord Widgery's summary of his conclusions. First, that there would have been no deaths† in Londonderry on 30 January, if those who organized the illegal march had not created a highly dangerous situation in which a clash between demonstrators and the security forces was almost inevitable; that the decision to contain the march within the Bogside and Creggan had been opposed by the Chief Superintendent of Police in Londonderry, but was fully justified by events and was successfully carried out; that if the army had persisted in its low key attitude and had not launched a large-scale operation to arrest hooligans, the day might have passed off without serious incident; that the intention of the senior army officers to use the Parachute Regiment as an arrest force and for other purposes was sincere, but that the brigade commander 'may have underestimated' the hazard to civilians in doing this in circumstances in which the troops were liable to come under fire; that there was no reason to suppose that the soldiers would have opened fire if they had not been fired on first; that soldiers who identified armed gunmen fired on them

---

* HL 101. HC220, published by HMSO, 18 April 1972.
† There were 13 dead and 13 injured, none of them from the security forces.

in accordance with the standing orders in the Yellow Card.* Each soldier was his own judge of whether he had identified a gunman. Their training made them aggressive and quick in decision, and some showed more restraint in opening fire than others. At one end of the scale some soldiers showed a high degree of responsibility: at the other, notably in Glenfadon Park, firing bordered on the reckless. These distinctions reflected, said Lord Widgery, differences in the character and temperament of the soldiers concerned.

His penultimate conclusion included a sharp sting in the tail. It was that none of the deceased or wounded was proved to have been shot whilst handling a firearm or bomb. Some were wholly acquitted of complicity in such action, but there was a strong suspicion that some others had been firing weapons or handling bombs in the course of the afternoon, and that others had been closely supporting them. But he went on to conclude that there was no general breakdown in discipline, and that for the most part the soldiers acted as they did because they thought their orders required it. He commented that no order and no training can ensure that a soldier will always act wisely as well as bravely and with initiative, and went on to express the view that the individual soldier ought not to have to bear the burden of deciding whether to open fire in confusion such as prevailed on that day, but that, in the conditions prevailing in Northern Ireland, it was often inescapable.

We were fortunate to have, in Lord Widgery, a President of the Tribunal who understood soldiers well and sympathized with them in the difficult situation in which they were placed. In the immediate aftermath it was not, of course, all as clear as that. The first that I personally knew about what had happened was when I was rung up at Shackleford by Major-General Coaker, the Director of Military Operations in the Ministry of Defence. He gave me the bare outlines and told me that a fairly hostile description of events, making accusations of firing without being fired on, had been given on the BBC TV news. Such detail as had been received from Headquarters Northern Ireland had been passed to Lord

---

* A card given to every soldier, advising him of the conditions under which he should open fire.

Carrington and to the Prime Minister. My first reaction was gravely to underestimate the furore it would all arouse. Bearing in mind the rather lurid picture that had been painted beforehand of what might happen, thirteen dead (and I am not sure that at that stage this figure had been clearly established) did not seem out of line with the sort of casualties that a head-on confrontation between troops and the IRA in the Bogside could have been expected to lead to. As far as I can recall, I rang up Carrington and confirmed that he had received the news and discussed it with Heath. His reaction was, if I remember aright, his normal, phlegmatic and resigned one.

By Monday morning I was left in no doubt that the public and political reaction to the events of the previous day was extremely sharp and critical of the way in which the operation had been executed. As always, it was difficult to get at the truth of what had happened, and I found myself, on the information provided by Tuzo's headquarters, trying to explain it in detail to the Prime Minister and other Ministers, defending, as I had to, the action of all those involved. As the days went by, doubts began to arise in my mind, which were eventually supported by the Widgery report when it was made public. What was abundantly clear was that we had forfeited all the progress we had made in trying to swing Catholic opinion away from the IRA; it also made Ministers realize that it would not be tolerable for much longer to continue with a situation in which, in theory and to a certain extent in fact, Stormont made the decisions about policy for enforcing law and order in Northern Ireland, while Westminster had to bear the ultimate responsibility if things went wrong.

The next hurdle facing us was the march that NICRA planned for the following Sunday, 6 February, at Newry. Ministers were naturally extremely anxious that there should be no repetition of the events at Londonderry. Fortunately the problem was simpler in that the area from which the march was to start was the edge of the town, which was in any case smaller and more compact than Londonderry. I flew over it myself in a helicopter and discussed with Tuzo his plans to deal with the situation. These included an outer ring of vehicle control points, designed to hold

up traffic travelling towards Newry on the day, and a close
inner ring of more efficient road blocks than had been used
in Londonderry. These would stop all movement into the
centre of Newry which could lead to inter-sectarian strife,
and were made strong enough to require considerable force
to move them. The RUC were to be in front, and the soldiers
were given strict orders that they were not to open fire just
to prevent a road block from being overrun, and were to
stick strictly to the orders about opening fire given in the
Yellow Card. I confirmed this personally in writing as an
order to Tuzo.

In the event it all passed off without incident and the era
of NICRA marches came to an end, while the front of the
stage was taken by bombing, especially in Belfast. Not only
there, however, for in February, as an act of revenge for
Bloody Sunday, a bomb was set off in the Parachute Brigade Officers' Mess in Aldershot, killing five women civilian
workers, an old gardener and Father Weston, their Roman
Catholic chaplain. This gave a shock to public opinion and
did much to restore sympathy for the army in Northern
Ireland and to discredit the IRA. At this stage we still had 17
battalions, 6 armoured car squadrons and 4 Royal Engineer
squadrons in Ulster.

In spite of the setback, the search for a political solution
continued, and the pressure mounted for Westminster to
remove the responsibility for law and order from Stormont
and for HMG to assume it. The decision was finally taken
to do so, and, if Faulkner was not prepared to accept it, to
assume direct rule from Westminster over the whole field.
There was little surprise when he refused to accept and
came over to face Ministers to argue against it. He returned
empty-handed to Belfast and, after a few days devoted to
consultation with his colleagues, his Government resigned
as a body. On 24 March 1972 Heath made the historic
announcement which brought the 50 years of Stormont
rule to an end.

The instrument of direct rule was to be a Secretary of State
for Northern Ireland, for whom an office and civil service
structure had to be conjured up out of the air, or at least
from the fifth rib of the Home Office, and Willie Whitelaw

was appointed as the first incumbent. He was to prove an excellent choice, made all the easier for me both because I knew him personally, and also because he was such a close friend and confidant of both Carrington and the Prime Minister, apart also from being an ex-soldier. I had already given thought to the problem of the relationship between the GOC and the Secretary of State for Northern Ireland for the activities of the armed forces there. I therefore drew up a new directive for Tuzo. This stated that he would exercise command of all land forces and operational control of naval and air forces stationed or employed in Northern Ireland, and would coordinate the tasking of the RUC for security operations with other security forces. He was responsible to me as CGS, acting on behalf of CDS, and through me to the Secretary of State for Defence for the conduct of operations by the armed forces in Northern Ireland. The directive went on to say that the Secretary of State for Northern Ireland was responsible for law and order, and that the GOC, as Director of Operations, would advise him, or his senior representative in Northern Ireland, on the military aspects of his responsibilities for law and order, would consult him on all policy matters concerning operations, and act in agreement with him on such matters. If there were any disagreement between them, he was to refer the matter to me, and I would in turn refer it, if necessary, to the CDS and the Defence Secretary before a final decision was taken.

The new broom required a revision by Tuzo of his directive to the troops. It stated that the general aim was to reduce the army profile as far as possible in areas where a military presence was likely to cause provocation or reaction; to continue operations elsewhere (and to step them up where appropriate) in order to increase public confidence; to form reserves to deal with the unforeseen; and to pursue the closest cooperation with the RUC and its Special Branch. Nevertheless it was essential to defeat campaigns of violence from any quarter; armed attacks were to be defeated by resolute armed action in conformity with the Yellow Card; all other forms of violence were to be met with vigorous follow-up action appropriate to the need to maintain security. This directive was based on the government's general policy to exploit the introduction of direct rule in the hope

of creating a better 'hearts and minds' climate among the
Catholics without thereby provoking Protestant reaction.

The attitude taken by Lynch's government in Dublin was
fairly favourable, but a 48-hour strike called by the Ulster
Defence Association and Vanguard* on 27 and 28 March
boded ill for Protestant reactions. However a lull did ensue
and Easter passed off fairly quietly. In the weeks following,
however, a pattern began to emerge of direct attacks on the
security forces, who viewed with some misgiving Whitelaw's
introduction of release of detainees as part of the 'hearts and
minds' campaign. The significant statistics for the months
following the introduction of direct rule were:

	March	April	May	June	July
Shooting incidents	399	724	1223	1215	2778
Internees released	–	119	207	130	1
Weapons captured	78	74	52	58	101
Arrests by security forces	375	229	199	233	364

This deterioriation in the situation appeared to the army
to result from the low profile which they had been told to
adopt. As a protest against the continued existence of 'no-go'
Catholic areas in Londonderry, the Protestants attempted to
establish some 'no-go' areas of their own in Belfast. Preven-
tion of this posed many difficult problems to the army and
led to some tense situations. If the Protestants were invei-
gled by peaceful persuasion into removing obstructions and
abandoning their attempts to control entry into their areas,
Republican sympathizers accused the army of collusion with
the Protestant extremists; but a direct armed clash between
the army and the UDA, when the former was already facing
the IRA, was not a situation that anybody wished to provoke.
Two favourable developments in this period were signs
of better cooperation from the Gardai, the police of the
Republic, and the declaration of an indefinite ceasefire by
the Official IRA on 29 May, when the number of their
supporters interned had been reduced to 29. A month later
the Provisional IRA followed suit. By this time the total

---

* Protestant extremist organizations.

number of Provisionals interned had been reduced from 739 in March to 283, and those detained from 184 to 90. This hopeful sign was counterbalanced by the UDA declaring 'no-go' areas in Belfast, ringed by 180 barriers, leading to a tense clash with the army south of the Shankill Road, where the UDA threatened a Catholic area.

The Provisional ceasefire led to an immediate power struggle within the movement. Seamus Twomey, the Belfast Provisional brigade commander, did not approve of the order to maintain it that he had received from the Provisional Army Council in Dublin, and engineered an incident on 9 July in the Lenadoon estate on the outskirts of Belfast, where the Catholics tried to squat in houses vacated by Protestants. On the pretext that the army had broken the ceasefire, he resumed operations, having embarrassed Whitelaw by revealing that the latter had been having secret contacts with the IRA leaders. This period was marked by the difficulty of balancing the political and military factors. The Government achieved some success in detaching support from the IRA both in the Republic and in Northern Ireland, but at the cost of building up a Protestant reaction, indirectly encouraging the formation of Protestant armed bodies, on the excuse that the army was neither protecting the Protestants nor pursuing the IRA vigorously enough, and also at the expense of some loss of control over and suppression of the activities of the IRA. In the week ending 19 July there were 572 shooting incidents in Belfast alone, and on Friday 21 July 20 bombs were exploded simultaneously by the IRA, killing 10 and injuring 130, mostly in the main bus station.

The events of that day, quickly christened 'Bloody Friday' as counter-propaganda to 'Bloody Sunday', created a general feeling of revulsion, which made it possible for the Government to take sterner measures, particularly to deal with the 'no-go' areas, than they had hitherto been prepared to contemplate. Ever since 'Bloody Sunday', and indeed long before, discussion had continued over what to do about 'no-go' areas, in particular the Bogside and Creggan in Londonderry. Their existence was a constant irritant to the Protestants and a convenient stick with which they could belabour the security forces and the Westminster government, now responsible for law and order. Pressure

from them, combined with the growing concern of the
army at the deteriorating security situation resulting, or so
it appeared to them, from the low profile attitude imposed
by the Government's policy, which also included release of
detainees, made it essential to review the situation.

In early July Tuzo forwarded to me his appreciation. He
suggested that the choice lay between a return to the level
of operations that had preceded the 'political initiative' and
a major offensive. The former was likely to be prolonged
and to involve a high level of casualties but low prospects of
success. It would do little if anything to appease Protestant
anger and frustration, and could finally lead to a situation
of virtual civil war. A major offensive would produce quicker
results and there would be less time for reactions to build
up either on the Catholic or on the Protestant side, but it
would involve a considerable increase in the forces available.
He would require a total of 25 battalions in the infantry
role (an increase of eight, or nearly 50 per cent), and 9
armoured reconnaissance squadrons: he would need to call
up 56 companies of the UDR for three weeks, and would
want more wheeled armoured personnel carriers, as well
as tracked ones, and armoured vehicles Royal Engineers,
the latter indistinguishable in public view from tanks. In
forwarding my own views, I said that there were three
options. The first was to confine operations to retaliation
against the IRA; the second was to take the offensive with
a general invasion of the Catholic areas, leading to their
subsequent domination by the army; the third was to opt
out, and to try and hand the problem over to the United
Nations. I said that, if the situation was allowed to continue
unchanged, we should be faced with the choice between
fighting the UDA directly, in order to prevent them from
fighting the IRA, or taking the general offensive against
the IRA as an indirect method of preventing the UDA from
fighting them. If we did neither, we should be failing to
prevent inter-sectarian strife and to show that violence did
not pay. There would be repercussions outside Northern
Ireland; the authority of government, and respect for the
forces of law and order would be gravely undermined.
We should be prepared to declare a state of grave emergency in Northern Ireland and resort to the same sort of

measures that a government would be prepared to take in war.

It was while this review of the situation was being considered that the bombing outrage of 'Bloody Friday' took place on 21 July. Carrington flew over to Belfast to attend a meeting of the Joint Security Council that evening, at which it was decided that certain operations would be carried out in Belfast and that the level of army activity in Londonderry would be increased. It was clear that 'Bloody Friday' had made it much easier to contemplate a departure from the low profile and a major operation to deal with the 'no-go' areas. The issue was faced at a meeting on 24 July, at which I was present and proposed a major operation to clear the 'no-go' areas both of Belfast and of Londonderry. In the face of some opposition from the Northern Ireland Office, it was agreed that, if the political situation permitted or suggested an intensification of military operations, the restoration of a military presence in the Bogside and Creggan would be the prime objective. If operations were decided upon, reinforcements should be sent. I was authorized to discuss this with Tuzo later that day. I flew to Belfast and discussed plans with the GOC, while the additional troops required were brought to appropriate states of readiness. We agreed a target date for the operation of 31 July, and met Whitelaw and his PUS, Sir William Nield, at Stormont to discuss the draft of a paper to put to Ministers on 27 July. We all agreed that 'Bloody Friday' had created a climate suitable for a major operation. Tuzo and I argued that it should be simultaneous in Belfast and Londonderry. To act in Londonderry alone, when the bomb outrage had taken place in Belfast, would not only look like an act of revenge on Londonderry, but would also miss an opportunity to improve the situation in Belfast. Whitelaw had reservations about a major operation in the latter and was opposed to the use anywhere of AVREs*, which we considered necessary to clear the larger barricades, probably booby-trapped and covered by fire. Although I had agreed to Tuzo's bill for reinforcements to bring his total of battalions to 27, I warned him that he must expect this to be reduced to 18 by the beginning of October, as I could not contemplate

* Armoured Vehicles Royal Engineers.

the strain on the army as a whole of maintaining such a high strength for long.

On 27 July Ministers agreed to the plan to mount a major operation both in Londonderry and in Belfast. There was considerable discussion of the legal aspects, particularly concerning possible extension of the circumstances in which troops could open fire. It was expected that fierce fighting would take place. The reinforcements would raise the number of troops in Northern Ireland to 21,000 and 9000 UDR would be called up. The movement of reinforcements involved 114 aircraft sorties from both Germany and Great Britain and two sailings each by two Landing Ships Logistic, all movement being completed between 6 p.m. on 28 July and 2 p.m. on the 30th. My directive for the operation, which had been given the codename *Motorman*, stated that its aim was to restore law and order throughout the province by making sure that there was no area where the security forces did not operate freely. The first step was to introduce a strong military presence in areas recently dominated by the IRA, to see that as far as possible there were no obstacles to free movement of any kind in the province, other than those needed by the security forces for the purposes of security. A further aim was to track down and pick up arms, ammunition and explosives, and the active terrorists themselves. 'It must,' I said, 'be made clear to all that they should avoid antagonizing those who are not directly supporting the IRA, in order to isolate the latter.' I realized that this was not easy. They must not depart from the overriding principle of minimum force; they must be seen to be in support of law and order and must minimize the risk to the innocent. I concluded by saying that the Defence Secretary was confident that they would conduct themselves with discipline, restraint, courage and skill.

Ministers, haunted by fears of something worse than 'Bloody Sunday', were much concerned at the possibility of casualties among other than active terrorists. This raised the very difficult question of whether a warning should be given of what was contemplated, and, if so, how and when. No warning involved clear risks to the public, while the more precise and the longer the warning, the greater the risks to the soldiers and possibly indirectly also to the population.

Whitelaw gave a general warning on a television programme on 28 July that barricades must come down, and that, if they were not removed, the security forces would have to do it. H-hour for the operation was decided on as 4 a.m. 31 July. At 9.30 p.m. on Sunday 30 July Whitelaw issued a warning that during the night 'there would be substantial activity by the security forces' and advised everybody to stay indoors. At 6.50 a.m. on 31 July, nearly three hours after the operation had started and when he had had first reports which indicated practically no resistance, he broadcast again, saying: 'The barricades are coming down; any that are not will be moved.' There were immense sighs of relief that the gloomiest prognostications had not been fulfilled. In spite of the risks involved, there is little doubt that the warnings served their purpose. It was a highly successful operation, but it did not result in any significant attrition of the IRA, as they went to ground over the border into the Republic, nor was there any significant increase in the acquisition of intelligence. After the long build-up and fears of fierce battles, there was a slight feeling of anti-climax.

I myself went over to Northern Ireland a week later and began to set the scene for a rundown from the high level of forces. I told Tuzo to plan provisionally on a reduction to 22 battalions by 1 October, 21 by 11 October and 18 by 1 December. By mid-September Robert Ford, the Commander Land Forces, was contesting this, maintaining that less than 22 battalions would prevent domination of the 'hard' areas.

Operation *Motorman*, it was felt, had again created a climate which could be exploited in aid of a further political initiative. The first step was the publication of the Northern Ireland Office's Green Paper, a significant document which used for the first time the expression 'The Irish Dimension' to describe the affinity between the parts of Ireland. The army was again faced with the difficulty caused by Whitelaw's desire to release detainees and the effect of such releases both on the security situation and on the mood of the Protestants. The desire to show impartiality was greatly resented by the Protestants, who intensely disliked being equated with the IRA whom they regarded as rebels. Towards the end of September Whitelaw assembled the Darlington Conference, a meeting representing all branches of political opinion in

Northern Ireland, to discuss the Green Paper in a country hotel near Darlington. It was thought to be a considerable success, and it reinforced the Government's intention to go ahead with the Green Paper's proposals for a Northern Ireland Executive, formed from an Assembly, but based on representation of all political parties – the first step in the process of 'power sharing'. The second step, which in the end proved fatal to the first, was to try and make progress in 'The Irish Dimension'.

October saw an increase in clashes between the security forces and various extreme Protestant bodies, the Ulster Volunteer Force, a more extreme and sinister breakaway body from the UDA, and the Tartan Gangs, the junior version. There were accusations from various quarters that the army dealt more leniently with these than with the IRA, accusations that were denied, although Tuzo made it clear that he was reluctant to find himself fighting two different wars at the same time. After much discussion of this issue, a policy document was agreed between him and Whitelaw, defining what the relation between the security forces and the UDA should be. A more difficult problem was the relationship between the UDR and the UDA, and the question as to whether a man should be dismissed from the former, if he were found or suspected to be a member of the latter.

By 1 December Operation *Motorman* was over, and I told Tuzo to concentrate on preventing inter-sectarian clashes, 'while making the greatest possible inroads against the Provisional IRA'. The level of violence had been significantly reduced and a number of political moves was set in hand. January would see a Border Poll, February a White Paper on constitutional proposals, and local government elections would be held between March and May. In the Orange Order marching season of July, legislation to give effect to the White Paper would be introduced, leading to a new local authority structure in October and implementation of a new constitution at the end of the year. In the light of this programme, I planned to keep the force level at 18 battalions throughout the year. Although this would place a considerable strain on the army, I considered it essential to run no security risks while this delicate political programme was in progress. However, I made it clear both to Tuzo and to my political masters that it would have to be reduced thereafter.

Operation *Motorman* had not removed all the frustrations, problems and difficulties which faced the security forces. Although there had been some improvements both in the organization of intelligence and in the law and its administration, in neither of those fields could the situation be regarded as satisfactory. Intelligence was still poor. A new Director and Coordinator of Intelligence, responsible to the Northern Ireland Secretary, had been appointed and given wide powers. This had drawn political and security intelligence more closely together, but at the expense of a separation between Lisburn, the military headquarters, and Stormont, as well as of the close links which had been established with the Special Branch of the RUC. This set back the army's hopes for the badly needed improvement of the latter. The morale of the branch had been severely affected by the Compton and Parker Reports on the deep interrogation practised at the time of the introduction of internment. As a result they were reluctant to engage in any interrogation at all, which had its effect not only on intelligence generally, but also on the possibility of obtaining convictions in the courts of those who were arrested. The report of the commission headed by Lord Justice Diplock, and the subsequent legislation giving effect to most of his recommendations, eventually improved matters in the legal field to a significant degree. The army's frustration in both these fields led to gradual and increasing pressure that it should rely less on Special Branch and do more to obtain its own intelligence, a tendency I was initially reluctant to accept, all experience in colonial fields having been against this and in favour of total integration of police and military intelligence. However the inefficiency of the RUC Special Branch, its reluctance to burn its fingers again, and the suspicion, more than once proved, that some of its members had close links with Protestant extremists, led me finally to the conclusion that there was no alternative. In fact, for some time various surveillance operations by soldiers in plain clothes had been in train, initiated by Frank Kitson when he commanded the brigade in Belfast, some of them exploiting ex-members or supporters of the IRA, of which I was aware and for which I had obtained Ministerial approval.

On 1 February 1973 Tuzo, who had carried a very heavy burden with notable success, was succeeded by Lieutenant-General Sir Frank King. Towards the end of his time, Tuzo's patience was nearly exhausted, which was not surprising, and from time to time this led to clashes between him and Whitelaw and his staff. Frank King was a very different character, tough, taciturn and unmoved by any excitement, looking very much the Berkshire farmer that his father had been, in contrast to the lively, extrovert, ebullient and sometimes emotional Tuzo. The principal features of the situation at this time were a serious increase in intimidation on both sides, intensifying the polarization of the two communities: an increase in Protestant militancy, involving *inter alia* a growth in private armies: a greater degree of sophistication in the tactics, equipment and methods employed by the IRA, particularly in the use of snipers, with carefully planned get-aways: a greater degree of cooperation from the Gardai south of the border, but a continued weakness in the RUC under their respected, pleasant but ineffectual Chief Constable, Graham Shillington: the need for constant imaginative effort to gain and retain the support of the public, in Northern Ireland, the rest of the United Kingdom and internationally, to which the army's 'information policy' cell, headed by Colonel Maurice Tugwell, made a significant contribution. On the credit side also was the deteriioration in the quality of both the leadership and the rank and file of the IRA, as the security forces inflicted casualties on or arrested them. Considerable thought was given to technical methods by which both snipers and bombers would be countered, and to non-lethal methods of dispersing crowds.

The border plebiscite, planned for January, was postponed until 8 March, which led to much discussion as to whether the White Paper with its constitutional proposals should precede or follow it. The latter was decided upon, and there was further discussion as to whether reinforcements were needed in case either led to trouble. I was very reluctant to commit more than the minimum. King wanted ten extra battalions to be available. I finally agreed to recommend to Ministers that two or three should be sent for the plebiscite, and remain there for the publication of the White Paper; the balance of the ten asked for were to be put at notice, but not sent unless needed. Ministers agreed to send two and to place six more at notice when the publication date of the White Paper was announced. I was given delegated authority to despatch two of these, if requested by the GOC and if the Northern Ireland Secretary agreed. Ministerial agreement would be needed to send more. In the event the border plebiscite on 8 March and the publication of the White Paper on 20 March passed quietly, the latter provoking only a statement on 22 March from the Provisional IRA condemning it.

On 9 April Major-General Peter Leng succeeded Robert Ford as Commander Land Forces and promptly issued his concept of operations. He stated that, in the light of public opinion and the trend towards a solution sought by democratic means, the army should be seen to act firmly and effectively against organizations resorting to violence, particularly the IRA. The main weight of operational effort was to be devoted to neutralizing IRA strongholds in Belfast, while maintaining the *status quo*, or, if possible, improving the security situation, elsewhere. The army should attempt to reduce intimidation and ensure that no inter-sectarian incident was allowed to escalate and thus neutralize all other efforts to achieve the overall aim.

On 30 May local government elections were held successfully in a calm atmosphere. They showed significant support in the Catholic areas for the SDLP and little for the extreme Republican groups. The elections on 28 June for the Northern Ireland Assembly also passed quietly. Of the 78 seats, Faulkner's Official Unionists won 23, West's Unofficial Unionists 10, Paisley and Craig's Loyalist Coalition 17, the SDLP, led by Fitt, 19, Alliance, led by Cooper, 9; Bleakley was the sole representative of the Northern Ireland Labour Party. From this somewhat ill-assorted mixture the Executive of eleven was formed, Faulkner being the leader with five of his own supporters, four SDLP and one Alliance member. This significant political step appeared to create a favourable atmosphere, encouraging greater cooperation from the Republic, as well as seeing a withering away of the activities of the Northern Civil Rights Association. May had however seen the rise of a 'Bring the Boys Home' campaign, initiated by the mother of an army cook (who was himself much embarrassed by it), and exploited by left-wing organizations of various sorts, as well as by the IRA.

On 9 July I made my last report before handing over as CGS to General Sir Peter Hunt ten days later. I said that the basic problem was how to force or persuade a small number of really hard-core terrorists to stop shooting and bombing. They were little influenced by progress on the political front. Their total failure to find any political support in the recent elections could even reinforce their resolution to continue terrorist activity. A new and definite course should, I suggested, be set for the following six months, the elements of which I foresaw as, first, a reduction in force levels by stages, provided that the security situation allowed, to 16 major units by October/November 1973, 14 by Christmas and 12 by April 1974. Secondly, more urgency should be applied to the reinvigoration and reorganization of the RUC, for which a new Chief Constable of the right personality was essential. Finally, the risk of premature release of really hard-core men from internment or detention in Long Kesh could not be afforded. There should be no abnormal acceleration of releases, until it had been clearly established that the IRA and the Protestant extremists had abandoned bombing, mining and shooting. I was encouraged to put forward these views at a Ministerial meeting on 12 July, when they met with general agreement, although the proposed reduction of force levels was only accepted provisionally, and was not to be discussed openly.

And so my intimate connection with the Northern Ireland scene came to an end. It had been a great responsibility, but a most interesting one, which had at the same time brought me into close touch with senior ministers of the government and with almost the whole of the army. I had made a regular practice of visiting Northern Ireland approximately every six weeks, alternating between one-day visits, restricted generally to the headquarters, and two-or three-day visits which included seeing a large number of units. As, apart from units of the resident garrison, they changed over every four months, I had seen a very large proportion of the army as it passed through service in the province. To meet the soldiers, cheerful and professional in spite of the difficulties of their task and the hardship and discomfort of the conditions in which they served, was an inspiring experience which made me proud to be their professional head. After I had left, most of the year was taken up in working towards the implementation of the White Paper. The Sunningdale Conference on 6 December attempted to take a step forward within 'The Irish Dimension', a step which proved fatal to the whole delicately constructed edifice when the General Election in February of 1974 followed so soon after the devolution of power to the Northern Ireland Executive and Assembly on New Year's Eve.

Although Northern Ireland had taken up most of my time and attention, all the other problems and affairs of the army and of the Chiefs of Staff had to be attended to. The army, in common with its sister services, was still in the process of readjusting to the reductions resulting from the decisions taken by the Labour government in 1968. Its need was for as much stability as could be achieved, given the disturbance caused by having to send a succession of units, partly from Great Britain, partly from Germany, on four-month tours of duty in Northern Ireland. The length of the tour was constantly reviewed. Longer ones would mean less disruption to the army as a whole, but both a greater strain on morale and more disruption to training. Money and manpower, as ever, were at the root of all our problems. The cost both of equipment and of keeping men and women in the service was constantly increasing, not just in relation to general inflation, but in real terms. Although we were planning (unrealistically, as subsequent events were to prove) on the basis of the proportion of the gross national product spent on defence remaining at its current rate of 5.2 per cent, on the assumption that the GNP would grow at an annual rate of 3.25 per cent, and that the army would continue to receive about 36 per cent of the defence budget, we were still faced with problems in maintaining the army at its current size and shape. The problems were not immediate, but they were imminent, and I did my best to prepare the army to meet them. There were always arguments about new equipment, the principal ones being over collaboration with the Germans over the tank to succeed Chieftain, the choice of an anti-tank guided weapon to fire from the army's helicopters, a new armoured personnel carrier, and, as always, new communication equipment to exploit the fantastic advances in electronics.

I was fortunate in my colleagues on the Army Board. John Mogg was a tower of strength as Adjutant-General, concerned with all personnel problems, and Tony Read as Quartermaster-General, with stores. Monkey Blacker, and later David Fraser, served me well as Vice-CGS, making it possible for me, once I was firmly in the saddle, to get away on visits overseas, both to see the army outside the United Kingdom and also to accept invitations to visit foreign armies. Old memories were stirred by the amalgamation parade in July 1971 of the Greys and the Carabiniers to form the Royal Scots Dragoon Guards. The Queen took the parade in Holyrood Park in Edinburgh, Arthur's Seat providing a splendid backdrop, and many old friends of wartime days were present. Towards the end of the year I visited Cyprus and the Far East. The spring of 1972 brought visits to the United States and Japan, and in the autumn a visit to Turkey and a circuit of the world, starting in Muscat, where we were helping the Sultan to deal with the rebellion in the Dhofar. We continued east, I representing Peter Hill-Norton at a SEATO meeting in Bangkok, followed, after a weekend in Bali, by short visits to Australia and New Zealand. Staging through Western Samoa and Honolulu, where my old SHAPE comrade, Bill Rosson, C-in-C of the US Army in the Pacific, looked after us, I visited the training area we had established at Suffield near Calgary in Canada. This was proving a great success, making it possible for complete armoured battle groups from the army in Germany to train realistically on its wide open spaces. A visit to Ottawa followed, the whole trip having lasted only a fortnight. Before the end of the year I paid a visit to the German army, of which Ernst Ferber, my colleague of the 1960 exercise in Schleswig-Holstein, was then the chief.

1973 provided three exceptionally interesting foreign visits, the first, in February, to India. Sam Manekshaw, who had become the first Indian Field Marshal, had invited me before he had handed over to General Bewoor. The highlights were visits to Ladakh and Sikkim. We flew up to Leh in an Indian Air Force AN12, the Russian equivalent of a Hercules. From there I went by Alouette III helicopter over an 18,000-foot

pass to Tankse in the Shyok valley, where I watched the final
of the divisional ice-hockey played at 14,000 feet above sea
level, not far from the disputed border with China. It was
astonishing to be back in Delhi the same evening, although
we thought we might not be, as the AN12's engines were very
reluctant to start at Leh. They normally kept them running
all the time they were there. After a cultural weekend on our
own in Orissa, visiting the famous temples at Bhubaneswar,
Kanakra and Puri, we spent a day in Sikkim. Having paid
our respects to the ruler in Gangtok, I went higher up, first
by helicopter and then by jeep to the 14,500-foot Chola Pass,
where we were face to face with the Chinese. The return
to Gangtok was enlivened, first by difficulty in getting the
jeep to start, and then by a hazardous flight through holes
in the clouds sweeping up the mountainside. After a night
in Calcutta, we went on to Singapore, where I visited the
Commonwealth Brigade, the existence of which had been
preserved by the Conservative government deciding to leave
one British battalion in Singapore and to continue to contribute to the headquarters and other units. In many respects I
found the Indian Army resembled our own army at the time
I had joined it. We received the warmest of welcomes and
felt very much at home. Sam Manekshaw paid a return visit
to London in April, although he was no longer CGS. In May
we went to Sweden, returning a visit to Britain by General
Almgren. One object of it was to see the unconventional Swedish 'S' tank, which had no turret, and I found the way they
faced their very different military problems of much interest.
Eating fresh fish, grilled over a wood fire in a small hut on
the banks of the River Torne, which forms their frontier with
Finland, was a memorable experience. That was immediately
followed by another return visit, this one to Romania, General Ion Georghe having been my guest the previous year. We
were also very warmly welcomed there, the highlights being
a visit to their Mountain Division in the Carpathians, who
laid on not only an impressive demonstration of their skills,
but also a splendid open-air lunch, and the subsequent trip
to see the famous painted churches of Moldavia, cared for
by charming nuns.

It had been an eventful time also for the family. Alice had
gone up to Durham University in October 1972, to the new

Collingwood College, immediately after she and Andrew had accompanied us on our trip to Turkey. Susanna was working in London and John at school at Horris Hill. We lived in the official CGS's flat in Kingston House, of which we were the first occupants, the lease of the previous one having expired. It was conveniently near Knightsbridge Barracks, from which I rode a Life Guards horse round Hyde Park every morning before breakfast. Holidays and weekends were spent at Shackleford, our neighbours there, Robin and Betty Pilkington, kindly lending us their charming wooden house at Glenmorven on the north side of the Sound of Mull in Scotland for a fortnight in August.

I was to take over as Chief of the Defence Staff from Peter Hill-Norton in October 1973 and handed over CGS to Peter Hunt on 19 July. Three weeks before that, immediately after his graduation, Andrew married Anne Stewart, daughter of Brian, who had been 'Our Man' in Hanoi when I had been in Singapore. She also was at Cambridge, and the wedding took place on a glorious summer's day in Clare College chapel, Edith's brother Armar officiating, the reception being held in the college's lovely garden across the river.

I had greatly enjoyed my time as CGS, in spite of the strain of wondering every day what horror was going to occur in Northern Ireland. Although the CGS is only *primus inter pares* on the Army Board – significantly less regarded as the boss than the First Sea Lord in the navy and the Chief of the Air Staff in the RAF – I always knew that I had a highly efficient, responsive and loyal body of men and women behind me, to be the chief of whom was a source not only of great pleasure but of immense pride. Although I looked forward keenly to becoming Chief of the Defence Staff, I knew that I should miss that strong bond and source of support, as I did.

16

The Heights

The heights by great men reached and kept
Were not attained by sudden flight.
> Henry Wadsworth Longfellow (1807–1882),
> *The Ladder of St Augustine*

The three months which passed between handing over the post of CGS to Peter Hunt and taking over as CDS from Peter Hill-Norton included the summer holidays and passed quietly and pleasantly. In July I took part in a concentrated salmon fishing expedition in Labrador, organized annually by the Canadian armed forces on the Eagle River. To get there and back I travelled in the well of a RAF Vulcan bomber on a training flight to Goose Bay, not a very comfortable four and a half hours' flying, but an interesting experience. On arrival we were kept hard at the fishing from dawn to dusk. As a complete novice I was not in the end ashamed of my catch, but I came to the conclusion that it was not a sport for which I would make great sacrifices. It was however a valuable way of getting to know some of my NATO colleagues. Admiral Tom Moorer, Chairman of the US Joint Chiefs of Staff, was there, as was his eventual successor, General George Brown of the US Air Force. My Canadian colleague, the highly strung, outspoken and abrasive General Jim Dextraze, was our host.

Having time to spare and no longer being tied to the United Kingdom by the affairs of Northern Ireland, we had planned a summer holiday in France, and I had promised Edith that, instead of camping, we would take a villa. We had found one on the Atlantic coast of France on the Île d'Oléron, west of Rochefort and La Rochelle, a part of France hitherto unknown to me. Not being pressed for time, we spent a night on the way with Don and Cherry Cook in L'Étang-la-Ville, where we ourselves had lived when I was at SHAPE, and did some sightseeing on the way south. The family, except for Andrew, was with us, and we were delighted to discover glorious beaches, which were not crowded. I hired a dinghy, which John and I sailed from Le Château when the tide was suitable.

Hill-Norton wished to finish his stint at the Ministry of Defence on Trafalgar Day, to which I was agreeable, it being a Saturday, so that I came into the office on the anniversary of the Battle of El Alamein, 23 October. It was an interesting first day, beginning with an intelligence briefing on the Israeli–Arab Yom Kippur war, which had broken out on 6 October. The Israelis, after their initial reverses, had turned the tables on the Egyptians, penetrated west of the Suez canal and all but surrounded the Egyptian Third Army at the southern end of the canal. A precarious ceasefire was in train, and the Russians had been threatening to intervene alone, if the Americans would not do so with them, in order to force the Israelis to withdraw. In response to a stern Russian message and indications that they had placed air transport forces and airborne divisions on alert, the Americans, in the early hours of the morning, had brought their forces world-wide to a higher than normal state of readiness without consulting their allies. They took steps soon afterwards to notify them, but this was not done until after we in London had learned of it indirectly, and there were muddles in Brussels over the official US notification to NATO, which led to a good deal of ill-feeling within NATO towards the USA. This aggravated the frustration and annoyance of the Americans towards their European allies, already at a high level as a result of denial or reluctance to grant them overflying and staging facilities for their arms lift to Israel, and the marked tendency of the Europeans to wish to avoid confrontation with the Arab countries for fear of its effect on their oil supplies. Our own government consistently took the line that we had raised no objection to the US alert, nor to the manner of notification, despite some misgivings; but it was a long time before the after-effects of the ill-will created on both sides of the Atlantic died down within NATO, and it coloured attitudes and the conduct of business in the alliance for at least a year afterwards.

At the time I took over, the Conservative administration was still in power. Peter Carrington was Defence Secretary and I was delighted to be able to continue the same easy relationship with him that I had enjoyed for the previous three years as CGS over the affairs of Northern Ireland. He was a stimulating and pleasant man to work for, direct and straightforward, challenging in his demands, but appreciative, understanding and realistic. A Conservative administration was naturally favourably inclined towards defence, and during the years I had been CGS we had received strong support, especially in anything related to Northern Ireland. Since coming into office, they had made a few cosmetic changes to the measures introduced at the time that Denis Healey had been Defence Secretary, such as leaving a small garrison in Singapore and running on the sole remaining aircraft-carrier, HMS *Ark Royal*, beyond the dates when both were due to phase out, misguided changes in my view, but of no fundamental import. However the relentless Treasury pressure to reduce defence expenditure continued, and had reached a climax in the summer over the annual PESC* discussion on public expenditure for the next four years. The Chancellor of the Exchequer, Anthony Barber, had demanded that the proportion of our Gross National Product spent on defence should be reduced from its current 5.5 per cent to 4.5 per cent. Carrington had firmly resisted this, and indeed to attempt it in so short a term would have caused chaos in defence. In a final round at Chequers, with Heath refereeing between them, Carrington had won, but only on the undertaking that an interdepartmental working group would be established from officials of the Ministry of Defence, the Treasury, Foreign and Commonwealth Office, the Central Policy Review Staff and the Cabinet Office, which would examine the implications of reducing the defence budget to 4.5 per cent of GNP, and present to Ministers collectively both those implications

* Public Expenditure Scrutiny Committee.

and various options by which it could be achieved. This body, known as the Defence Studies Working Party, had been established, and had got as far as defining the studies to be undertaken and preparing the background, when, largely as a result of the direct confrontation with the miners over wage demands, the Government resigned, and, after the General Election in February 1974, was replaced by a Labour administration.

The Labour Party manifesto had committed them to seeking to reduce the proportion of GNP spent on defence to the equivalent of that spent by our major European allies, that is about 4 per cent, but had avoided the more extreme demands, made at the party conference in the previous year, that it should be reduced by one thousand million pounds a year, that is by one-quarter. Sir John Hunt, the fairly recently appointed Secretary to the Cabinet, fortunately suggested to Harold Wilson, the Prime Minister, at a very early stage, that advantage should be taken of the body already established to conduct the review of defence expenditure, which he assumed the Government would wish to undertake, and that it should not be rushed. Wilson accepted this advice, as did the new Defence Secretary, Roy Mason, whom I had met briefly before when he was the minister concerned with equipment at the time when Denis Healey was Defence Secretary. He was a very different type from Peter Carrington. A sturdy, tough Yorkshire miner, a no-nonsense patriot, who was confident that he could win our battles for us by the same methods of negotiation and influence by which he had established himself in the National Union of Mineworkers and in the Labour Party. Intellectually was not in the same class as Carrington, but he took great trouble to master his briefs, writing extensive notes in his own hand from which he spoke. He disliked free-ranging discussion and exchange of views, preferring to determine his position before a meeting from a study of his briefs. This could lead to difficulties, as he was very reluctant to shift his position as a result of discussion. He seldom, certainly in the earlier stages of our working together, seriously questioned the advice he was given. This naturally made life easy for the Chiefs of Staff and myself in particular, but it had its disadvantages. One was that, in dealing with my colleagues,

I lacked the pressure which would have come from a knowledge that the Defence Secretary was questioning or probing positions adopted by the single service staffs: my colleagues could take the view that, if I were not being pressed or questioned by the Defence Secretary, I should not press or question them. Another disadvantage was that the arguments against a proposal, and the counters to them, might not have been thrashed out within the Ministry of Defence at the level of the Secretary of State before he had to face the opposition of the Chancellor of the Exchequer, Denis Healey, in the Defence and Overseas Policy Committee of the Cabinet.

Two major bones of contention affecting NATO had been left on my plate by my predecessor. The first arose from the desire of the air staff to associate RAF Strike Command with NATO more directly and more fully than it already was in the limited role of command of the UK Air Defence Region. The objections to this came partly from the naval staff, and partly from NATO naval circles, that is from the Supreme Allied Commander Atlantic (SACLANT), who was also C-in-C of the US Atlantic Fleet. They stemmed from the difficulty in obtaining agreement over how to define the relationship of C-in-C Strike Command and his subordinate groups both to SACEUR* and to SACLANT, as a number of RAF squadrons, not restricted to the specialized long-range maritime patrol squadrons, were assigned to support SACLANT. More would be so assigned, when eventually naval squadrons were transferred to the RAF from HMS *Ark Royal* when she was paid off in a few years' time. RAF tanker squadrons also supported aircraft operating under both NATO commanders. It also raised the contentious and time-honoured argument about whether the RAF, operating in support of the navy, should be under their command, as the navy wished, or 'in support' as the RAF demanded. My predecessor had been unable to resolve the deadlock, but I found a wording acceptable to all, and without too much delay NATO agreed that the C-in-C of RAF Strike Command should become a major subordinate commander to SACEUR with the title of C-in-C UK Air.

* Supreme Allied Commander Europe.

The second problem caused more difficulty. The Americans had been pressing for more efficient and flexible arrangements to provide operational command of the allied air forces in NATO's Central Region – the second Allied Tactical Air Force, composed of the RAF in Germany, the Dutch and Belgian Air Forces, and some of the German; and the fourth ATAF, the remainder of the German Air Force and those squadrons of the US Air Force assigned to the tactical role in support of the US Army in Germany. The Germans complained that the two different allied tactical air forces used different methods and procedures, which caused them difficulties, having squadrons in both forces. The Americans made the same complaint, as well as complaining of the lack of any central means of exercising command of air forces at Headquarters Allied Forces Central Europe, a situation which had persisted since the move of the headquarters to Holland, when France left the military structure. At that time the three headquarters which had existed at Fontainebleau, HQ Allied Forces Central Europe, HQ Land Forces and HQ Air Forces, had been combined into one, the commander being a German army general with a British air marshal as his deputy. However the headquarters lacked the means, the staff and communications to exercise operational command over the tactical air forces. The problem was not just one of finding the resources. It was bedevilled by a doctrinal argument which had national and industrial implications. In general the German and American air forces tended to agree, while the RAF and their Belgian and Dutch colleagues found themselves on the opposite side of the debate. The US Air Force was much influenced by its experience in Vietnam, where it had come to mistrust low flying techniques, had gained a healthy respect for surface-to-air missiles (SAM), learnt to appreciate the need to devote as high, if not a higher proportion of air effort to suppressing them and their electronic systems, as to attack on other targets, and had developed a highly centralized computer-based system for the direction and control of their air effort. In doing so they had had to take into account the limited training of their pilots. In Vietnam they had only stayed in the country for a short period. In the USA they tended to train under strict control, many of their wartime pilots being reserve air force officers. They wished to introduce these methods into the NATO European air forces, certainly in the Central Region. We tended to oppose this for a number of reasons, partly interconnected. We mistrusted the concept as leading to too highly centralized a system, which would not respond to the demands of support of the land battle. It would involve flying at medium level, which we believed greatly increased the vulnerability of aircraft to SAM and other air defences. We believed in, and had put all our money into, very low flying techniques, relying more on the pilot's initiative than on intimate control. Even if it were sound operationally, which the RAF doubted, a change would mean abandoning practically all our future equipment programme for the RAF, and force us to buy American both for aircraft and for the very expensive control system.

The German Air Force supported the USAF for a number of reasons. They disliked the strong hold of the allied tactical air forces, one commanded by a USAF and the other by a RAF officer. They wished to unify their air force as far as possible under national control and to free it as much as they could from its close links with their army. Several German Air Force senior officers were of the view that, had such links not been so close in the Second World War, it would have been more successful. They had already established national tactical control centres, which could work direct to a centralized Headquarters Allied Air Forces Central Europe, thus by-passing and perhaps eventually eliminating the control exercised by the Allied Tactical Air Force Headquarters. Our Chief of the Air Staff, Denis Spotswood, felt strongly about this. The Americans thought that we were the nigger in the woodpile, and their Defence Secretary, James Schlesinger, brought strong pressure to bear on us in NATO. He quoted lack of progress as evidence of obstruction and resistance to American desire to reinforce and support Europe, threatening that failure to support their view would lead to strong congressional pressure to withdraw forces from Europe.

I was invited by my American colleague, Admiral Moorer, to pay an official visit to the USA in March 1974, and, in preparation for this, agreed with Spotswood the limits to which we could go in agreement over the proposals being made for the new head-quarters and its powers. In a tête-à-tête discussion with Moorer in his office in the Pentagon, I put our views to him and suggested a formula for agreement, which, if he were to accept, I undertook to recommend to my Belgian, Dutch and German colleagues. To my surprise, he did so. Fearing that he had misunderstood, I questioned him, but he maintained his agreement and confirmed it that evening at a dinner given by the head of our defence mission, Admiral Ian Easton, having discussed it meanwhile with George Brown, the Chief of Staff of the US Air Force. I felt that my visit had been worthwhile. I also spent half an hour in discussion with the formidable Jim Schlesinger and tried to put over to him the European view within NATO, particularly in respect of our desire to maintain a defence industrial potential, viable in the long term, in Europe, and the fact that European governments, like others, were more prepared to spend money on defence if a significant part of it benefited their own industry, an argument he was never inclined to accept. I found him a stimulating opponent in discussion, although the bad manners he had displayed at the NATO Nuclear Planning Group meeting at the Hague in November 1973, the first time I had met him, prejudiced me against him. They had infuriated Peter Carrington.

My visit to the USA had included a visit to Colorado Springs, which gave me the opportunity to see the house, Briarhurst, and the church at Manitou, which had been built by my great-uncle, William Bell, a nineteenth-century American railway pioneer, and to find in the church register not only the entry of my cousin Rowena Bell's marriage to Harold Pearce, at which my maternal grandfather, William Bell's brother-in-law, had been a witness, but also that of the christening of my uncle Richard Wellesley. Two books I was given by enthusiasts in local history confirmed many of the family stories, relating to that period in their lives, which I had been told by my mother and members of her family.

On my return, I hastened to clinch the deal which I thought I had secured with Tom Moorer. In the course of one day I flew to Brussels and saw General Crekillie, and to the Hague to see General Wijting, both airmen, and obtained their agreement. A few days later I went to Bonn to see Admiral Zimmerman, my German colleague, who also agreed. However, over lunch, General Limberg, shortly to take over as Chief of Staff of the German Air Force, told me that he would not agree. When I taxed Armin Zimmerman with this afterwards, he said that it was he that made the decision, not the German Air Force. However, I had formed the impression, which was later to be confirmed, that Zimmerman was determined to steer a middle course between the German Air Force and the German Army, who sided with us on this issue, and to remain sitting on his naval fence. At the next meeting at which NATO discussed this matter, Moorer went back on his agreement with me, and maintained that there had been a misunderstanding, an object lesson in not discussing such contentious matters without both participants having a staff officer present to record it. Not until two years had passed, after many difficult meetings, did the essence of what had been agreed come about, all participants in the struggle having by that time conceded some of their hardest defended positions. To both issues I felt that I had made a significant personal contribution.

Important as these issues were to NATO and to ourselves, they weighed little in the scales compared with our Defence Review. At an early stage the problem had to be faced of how the review should be conducted and its terms of reference. Fortunately it was decided to make use of the Defence Studies Working Party, already established, and to insert between it and Ministers a committee of senior officials, chaired by the Secretary to the Cabinet, John Hunt, on which I served. My fellow Chiefs of Staff were suspicious of this machinery, which appeared to them to undermine the staunchly defended position of the Chiefs of Staff and their right to give their collective advice, untainted by political considerations, to the prime minister and the Cabinet. By assuring them that the Ministry of Defence input would originate with the Defence Policy Staff and would always be cleared through the Chiefs of Staff Committee at every stage, they gradually accepted what was proposed, although they remained suspicious. At the very beginning I realized that, unless the Chiefs of Staff proposed priorities on which the Review could be conducted, they would either be established by somebody else or none would be established at all, and we should be faced with the usual 'shopping list' of how to effect economies to meet a financial target set by the Treasury. At a meeting of the Chiefs of Staff Committee, having failed to get the established system to come up with any clear priorities, I proposed them myself. To my surprise and relief, they were remarkably easily accepted by my colleagues, and eventually by Ministers. They were in essence to put lowest priority on all our ex-imperial commitments outside the NATO area; even if all of them were to be given up, which was hardly realistic, their abandonment and the force reductions that could result would not provide economies of at all the sort of scale that were being sought. The next area to seek for these that I suggested was the Mediterranean, in which Cyprus was the most significant in political, military and financial terms. I had never myself been much impressed by the argument that RAF squadrons based in Cyprus were an important politico-military asset in the Near East, and recent events arising out of the Arab–Israeli war had demonstrated that we exerted practically no influence in that area in spite of their presence. Our peacetime naval presence in the Mediterranean was minimal – usually two ships based on Malta – and the wartime naval reinforcement was fairly unreal, consisting as it did of assuming that all those ships which would normally be scattered round the oceans, for example in the Indian Ocean or the South Atlantic, could be gathered in and despatched to the Mediterranean. The economies to be achieved by the abandonment of these far-flung commitments would have to include these ships. Finally there were a number of somewhat unrealistic plans for the employment of Royal Marine Commandos in assault landing ships and of airborne and airportable army formations, with RAF support, to a series of alternative plans both in the Mediterranean and also in Scandinavia. Those in the Mediterranean were particularly unrealistic. In general they had originated in 1968, when these forces and the air transport to carry them became available as a result of our withdrawal from the Far East at the time of the previous Labour administration. Just as the Chiefs of Staff had been searching for a new role for these forces to avoid their disbandment, the Russian invasion of Czechoslovakia had taken place, and Denis Healey had been able to offer them to NATO as part of the alliance's reaction to that event. They could certainly no longer be said to have a high strategic priority. This left us, as the areas of high priority, our contribution to NATO's Central and Northern Regions, both army and air force, and naval and air force, to the eastern Atlantic and the Channel: the defence of the United Kingdom itself, and our strategic nuclear deterrent, the ballistic missile submarines. No attempt was made to differentiate between these in priority. The only objections to these priorities came from the Foreign Office, who were not prepared to accept either that we could abandon some of our non-NATO commitments or the claims of the higher priority areas to the exclusion of others; their view was not pressed by the Foreign Secretary himself, James Callaghan, when the priorities were agreed by Ministers. I had realized that some of the assumptions we had made were unlikely to be achieved in practice, but to propose them and get them accepted put the onus of defending the retention of these commitments on the Foreign Office, creating the impression that the Chiefs of Staff were realistic men who were prepared to define priorities for defence policy, and were not sentimentally attached to hanging on to the remnants of Empire.

On these assumptions then, the laborious machinery of the Defence Review was set in motion. It absorbed most of my attention throughout 1974. Great credit is due to my assistant Chief of Defence Staff (Policy), Rear-Admiral Tony Morton, who had been the naval planner when I had been C-in-C Far East in Singapore. He not only handled the inevitable inter-service disputes with tact and skill, but also managed to persuade his Treasury, Cabinet and Foreign Office colleagues on the Defence Studies Working Party to accept the rationale for forces and their equipment, which initially they were disinclined to do. Every now and then he would come up against obstacles which he could not overcome, and would have to appeal to me. My method was then to hold a private meeting of my fellow Chiefs of Staff, at which we would thrash out the differences and agree on guidance to the defence policy staff, in order to allow them to progress to the stage at which they submitted their report to us formally. It was an effective method and no objection was taken to it, although it transgressed the pure doctrine of Chiefs of Staff Committee procedure, by which a paper was intended to work its way up from the bottom without interference or influence from the top.

The Treasury had tried to impose on us a series of arbitrary reductions of the percentage of GNP to be allotted to defence over a ten-year period, on the assumption that the GNP itself would increase by 3 per cent per annum. At this time the defence budget ran at about 5.5 per cent of GNP, and the plans for the future on which we had been working assumed that we should continue to receive this, leading to a constant rise in defence expenditure in real terms. The Treasury's proposal, accepted by Ministers for the terms of reference, was that the Defence Review should examine the implications of reducing in four different ways: to 4.5 per cent by gradual decrease over ten years: to 4.5 per cent by 1978/9 and then staying level: to 4 per cent over ten years; and finally to 4 per cent by 1979 and then level.

When we began work on this basis, we soon realized that even the first of these would involve reductions in our forces which would not be acceptable. We also appreciated, from experience of previous exercises of this kind, that this approach would prove highly unsatisfactory. It would lead to 'shopping lists' of reductions, and the mere fact that items were listed at all would qualify them in other people's eyes for reduction. The end result would then probably be, as happened in most negotiations with the Treasury, a bargain between the best and the worst figure. It was impossible to make military sense by this approach. The Chiefs of Staff therefore decided at a fairly early stage to establish what we described as the 'critical level of forces', defining it as the level below which the resultant reduction in our contribution to NATO would call into question our support of the alliance, and thus put at risk the cohesion of the alliance itself. We arrived at this largely by following logically the priorities we had already established. The forces which we considered must remain intact were those assigned to the direct defence of the United Kingdom, the ballistic missile submarine force, to the Eastern Atlantic part of SACLANT's command, to C-in-C Channel, and to the Central Region of SACEUR's command, although in the

last case we assumed that we should be able to reduce
the army in Germany by 5,000 men as part of the second
phase of the Mutual and Balanced Force Reductions being
negotiated with the Warsaw Pact in Vienna, an assumption
that proved optimistic. It meant in general a reduction in
the navy of all those ships, mostly destroyers and frigates,
which could not be justified by the needs of anti-submarine
warfare, including the virtual phasing out of our amphibious assault capability. The army was in any case worried
about its ability to recruit and maintain in service enough
men to meet its hitherto assumed future order of battle,
especially as four units, reduced to company status, had
recently been restored as full battalions to help meet the
Northern Ireland commitment. They had already set in
hand an extensive manpower economy study to see what
they could do about it. Their aim was therefore to see
that any reductions that might be forced on them as part
of the Defence Review fitted in with their plans to adjust
manpower to meet what appeared to be the realities of
life. However, as they had not yet come to very clear conclusions as to what those were, their attitude throughout
the Defence Review was secretive, enigmatic and difficult
to explain or justify. I found it infuriating and frustrating.
On the other hand I had the greatest sympathy with the
army's fundamental dilemma. As long as Northern Ireland
remained even a potential commitment on anything like
its current scale, the army was fully justified in recruiting
every man it could, and employing as many as possible in
units which could be made available for service there. But
manpower was expensive, and when it came to balancing
its reduced budget, the only source of saving left other
than continued economies in the general support of the
soldier and his family, which were liable to be reflected
in lower rates of recruiting and re-engagement, was the
army's equipment programme. Here it was not easy to make
economies, partly because the army had recently completed
a major re-equipment programme, and partly because it
formed a significantly smaller proportion of its budget than
was the case with the navy and the air force. To the outside and uninstructed observer, it appeared that the RAF
was to take the brunt of the reductions. The application

of our priorities logically resulted in a major reduction in the air transport force, built up after the Suez affair to support east of Suez commitments by air transported forces, rather than by maintaining large garrisons overseas. There were no plans to replace the ageing Comets and Britannias, although these still had a useful time to run, if their use could be justified. The size of the tactical transport force was determined largely by the already reduced parachute drop capability, a valid reason for which was difficult to concoct. It was therefore inevitable, and indeed overdue, that the air transport force should be reduced, particularly as the largest single item of defence expenditure in the coming decade was the replacement of the RAF's aged and out-of-date Vulcans, Canberras and Lightnings, as well as eventually also the Phantoms and Buccaneers, by the new multi-role combat aircraft, jointly developed with Germany and Italy, to be known as the Tornado. It had never been realistic for the air force to plan to keep in being its large and increasingly irrelevant transport force, while facing a major and expensive re-equipment programme. In reality, therefore, although of course it could not be admitted publicly, the Defence Review made it possible for all three services to carry out a reorganization designed to face up to future realities, while laying the blame for the reductions involved on other shoulders.

After one or two difficult meetings with my colleagues, in which I persuaded them to face realities and not to support a line which would not stand up to questioning outside the Ministry, we arrived at an agreement on the 'critical level', and the arguments to support it, as well as on the less detailed and rather sketchy implications of being forced below it to the various financial levels we had been told to examine. In persuading my colleagues to accept what to them was often unpalatable, I made use of the remark made to me at an early stage of the review by the PUS, Michael Cary. He had said that Roy Mason had hinted to him that the Chiefs of Staff would never be able to come up with the right answers, and that therefore some other machinery within the Ministry should be charged with the responsibility of formulating the Ministry's input to the interdepartmental working party. He, Michael Cary, was of the same opinion

and apparently thought that I would agree. I hotly disputed
this and said that I took full responsibility for seeing that
the Chiefs of Staff and the machinery through which they
worked would produce the goods, and that, although the
defence secretariat had their full part to play in this, I
would not agree to any other body giving military advice
to the Secretary of State and the Defence Council. I was
vindicated when we presented the result of our work in
that august but little used and not very useful body. In my
time as a Chief of Staff, it had never met except to have its
photograph taken! Roy Mason decided that the Ministry of
Defence input for the Defence Review should be discussed
by and have the approval of the Council. However, when
it came to the day, there was very little discussion and
he did not encourage it, sensibly realizing that to do so
would open up the possibility of inter-service disagreements
which had already been faced and sorted out by the Chiefs
of Staff in their committee. To our relief and somewhat
to my surprise, he questioned nothing and accepted our
'critical level', and the justifications for it, almost without
discussion.

As was to be expected, things did not go so smoothly
when we moved outside the Ministry. At the working level,
Tony Morton and Arthur Hockaday, the excellent Deputy Under-Secretary (Policy), had a tough time with their
Treasury colleague, Leo Pliatsky, in getting the concept of
the 'critical level' accepted and in avoiding deeper probings
into detailed assessment of different options by which the
lower financial targets might be reached. In the course of
their discussions all the well-recognized 'sacred cows' were
trotted out and dusted over, the ballistic missile submarine
force, the future tank, the multi-role combat aircraft, the
maritime Harrier and the anti-submarine warfare cruiser, as
the future mini-aircraft-carrier had come to be called. The
fact that all these and many other aspects of defence were
called into question and examined in detail was valuable
in educating the other departments, whose representatives
came to take a much more understanding and appreciative view as a result, although, as I was to learn in the
Steering Committee, it did not necessarily extend to their
superiors.

The Working Party produced a voluminous report. The most important aspect of it was the support it gave, with Treasury reservations, to our concept of the 'critical level'. There were also Foreign and Commonwealth Office reservations, understandably, to the sweeping nature of the assumptions we had made about adandonment of non-NATO commitments, such as Hong Kong, Cyprus, Gibraltar and the Caribbean. These reservations were strongly pressed when the Steering Committee began its consideration of the report in a number of meetings skilfully chaired by John Hunt, who was a strong supporter of the defence case. The unknown quantity was the head of the Central Policy Review Staff, Victor Rothschild. He began by asking very awkward and probing questions on a number of sensitive issues. However, as I appeared to be able to provide satisfactory answers, he swung to our side and in the end asked equally difficult questions of the Treasury. As the need to present our recommendations to Ministers in a form short and clear enough for them to read became imminent, positions were more clearly defined. The great victory was to secure approval of the concept of the 'critical level', although, at Treasury insistence, carefully qualified by the explanation that this level was the judgement of the Chiefs of Staff and not necessarily endorsed by the Steering Committee itself or by the departments involved.

The next hurdle was consideration by Ministers, due to take place on 18 July. In preparation for this, it was arranged that I should give a presentation to Ministers to explain in more detail just what the 'critical level' would consist of, what reductions it would involve, and how our forces did and would, if reduced to the 'critical level', compare with those of our allies. This was preceded by a presentation of the threat from the Warsaw Pact by the Director General of Intelligence, Admiral Sir Louis le Bailly. These were very valuable opportunities to get our point of view across, and appeared to have a marked effect on Wilson in persuading him in general to support our case.

The next meeting was held on 18 September and was the decisive one. The Treasury was largely isolated, and the argument, which won the day, was that in our precarious economic situation we could not afford to antagonize the

Germans and Americans. The 'critical level' therefore was that which those two countries would see as critical, and the majority of Ministers was prepared to accept the judgement of the Chiefs of Staff on this. However, as was to be expected, we did not get away with everything. It was agreed that we should plan on the basis of the level of forces we had assessed as critical; that we would withdraw altogether from Cyprus; that we should assume that the Government of Hong Kong would contribute not less than 75 per cent of the cost of the garrison, which would itself be reduced; that we would make the minimum provision for the defence of those two awkward relics of Empire, the Falkland Islands and Belize; and that officials would examine how to fit all the rest of the commitments, from which we were unable to disengage, within the currently estimated cost of the 'critical level', although we had assumed that we had been able to disengage from them all. The next meeting would take place as soon as possible after the General Election, which, although not at that date announced, it was clear was going to be held shortly and which Ministers assumed they would win, as they did, although not as easily as they had thought.

The next and final meeting was held on 23 October after the election. It confirmed the decisions of the previous meeting and was primarily designed to establish what was to be said publicly and how to handle it internationally and in Parliament. As the prospect of facing the Americans became real, there was a tendency to allow some back-pedalling on the firm line taken over withdrawing from Cyprus and Masirah, the barren island at the mouth of the Persian Gulf where the RAF leased an airfield from the Sultan of Muscat. The Treasury remained unrepentant and reserved its position. They maintained that our economic position demanded much greater reductions; that, if NATO were prepared to revise its strategy, these could be effected without detriment to our security, and Cassandra-like prophesied that we should find ourselves having to do the same exercise all over again in a few years' time. It was decided that a statement would be made both to Parliament and to NATO on 21 November. Before then John Hunt and I would go first to Washington and then to Bonn to explain the Review to their governments and seek their views before we made firm proposals to NATO, preceded by letters from the Prime Minister to the American President and the German Chancellor to seek agreement to our mission.

After I had played my part at the Remembrance Sunday Service at the Cenotaph on 10 November, John Hunt and I left on the weekly RAF VC10 flight to Washington on the afternoon of Monday 11th. The clock being against us, we arrived in Washington at cocktail time and went straight to the embassy, where, after dinner, we conferred with the ambassador, Peter Ramsbotham, and his staff, which included Richard Sykes as Minister, later to become the extremely effective head of the Foreign Office defence department and to be tragically murdered by the IRA when ambassador at The Hague. The following day was a full one. It started with that terrible American institution, a working breakfast in the State Department, the host being Dr Kissinger, whom I was most interested to meet. Jim Schlesinger was also, clearly reluctantly, present. He made it clear that he did not take kindly to being dragged over to the State Department to meet us and to be kept waiting there for his breakfast, playing second fiddle to the famous Henry. Other principals present included William Colby, the head of the Central Intelligence Agency, and our own ambassador. John Hunt opened the bowling with the economic and political background and left it to me to describe briefly the military aspects. Kissinger listened very carefully, asked some pointed questions and then stated clearly his initial reactions. These were of concern that our action might spark off similar movements in other members of NATO, especially in the Central Region, which would not be affected by our reductions. While not challenging our priorities, he nevertheless made clear that his main anxiety was the virtual abandonment of any capability to take military action, however limited, outside NATO, because this would leave the USA as the sole western nation with such a capability, and for political reasons he did not like the idea of having to act entirely alone. His one positive objection was to the proposed withdrawal from Cyprus. To this he was strongly opposed, not so much on the grounds of the loss of the facilities there, but because it would give the Russians the impression that the West was weakening its position and interest in the Eastern Mediterranean. When directly questioned by John Hunt as to whether, given our problems, the USA attached importance to our retaining our nuclear strategic deterrent force of ballistic missile submarines, he stated very firmly that he was strongly in favour, to which, less strongly, Schlesinger gave his support. The latter had not contributed much to the breakfast discussion, but reserved his fire for a much longer meeting held directly afterwards in the Pentagon. Here I took the lead, first with Schlesinger himself present, and subsequently covering matters of greater detail with his senior officers and officials. They asked a large number of searching questions, the general theme being that, if we did not try to be so self-sufficient in development and procurement of our own equipment, and if we and other European members of NATO were prepared not to duplicate what each of us and the USA provided in terms of operational forces, we could make economies without reducing our forces. This of course was a familiar argument which I had had already with Schlesinger on my visit in March. On the whole it was clear that they were relieved that the result had not been worse. They promised to study our proposals in detail and comment on them in the short time available before an announcement was made in Parliament and to NATO, hinting that they felt that a greater degree of consultation at an earlier stage had been expected.

We flew back to London that evening, having breakfast, a wash and a shave in the VIP lounge at Heathrow, before flying straight on to Bonn, arriving in mid-morning of 13 November. We were met by our ambassador, Nicholas Henderson, and went straight into a meeting with the Defence Minister, Georg Leber, and his officials, including Admiral Zimmerman. We received a sympathetic hearing. They were clearly much relieved that our reductions did not affect our contribution to NATO's Central Region. We did not at any time reveal either to them or to the Americans that we had assumed that we would be able to reduce the strength of the army in Germany by 5000 men as part of the second phase of MBFR.* We stood

* Mutual and Balanced Force Reductions, see p.384

pat on the line that we would make no reductions in our Brussels Treaty commitment of 55,000 men outside the context of MBFR. They accepted a slowing down of the planned rate of production of the MRCA† for the RAF, reassured by our statement of continued commitment to the project as a whole. Leber was clearly pleased that we had chosen to consult Germany and the United States in advance of explaining our proposals formally to NATO. After lunch we flew back to London, feeling a trifle weary, but that we had satisfactorily done what had been required of us.

The next step in the process was the announcement to Parliament on 21 November. On the same day I went to Brussels and explained our proposals to the NATO Military Committee in permanent session in the morning and, in company with our permanent Council representative, Edward Peck, to the Council in permanent session in the afternoon. We explained that at that stage the conclusions of the Review were proposals, and that their implementation was subject to consultations with and comments by our NATO partners; but that any changes suggested must not increase the overall cost. On the whole our proposals received a sympathetic hearing, and the fact that we gave NATO a full two months in which to consider them was appreciated. We were thought to have done better than the Dutch. The final act in the process was the publication of the Defence White Paper in March of the following year, 1975, after the comments of NATO had been received. The main concern expressed was our proposal to abandon virtually all force contributions, even of a contingency nature, other than to the Allied Mobile Force, to the Mediterranean area. In reaction to this, we undertook to reconsider the possibility of a small air force and army deployment to north-east Italy. This whole process had hardly been completed when we faced the 1975 budget, in which Healey, faced with the need to reduce public expenditure, decided to cut the defence budget in the following financial year, i.e. 1976/7, by a further £110 million. We had advised Roy Mason that, difficult as this was to accept, we believed that it could be

† Multi-Role Combat Aircraft.

handled without going back on the assurances that we had
only just given in the Defence White Paper, largely because
the after-effects of the 1973 three-day week, caused by the
miners' strike, were still being felt in considerable short-
falls and delays in delivery of equipment and spare parts.
Nevertheless it appeared as an early warning of Healey's
self-fulfilling prophecy that the Defence Review and all that
had been put into it was not going to be allowed to be the
final answer.

17

Last Post

Although the Defence Review had taken up most of my time, there were several other important matters which occupied the attention of the Chiefs of Staff. The most critical was that of Cyprus, where the events of July 1974 resulted in the Turkish invasion. Early in the morning of Monday 15 July news reached the Ministry of Defence that a coup had taken place in Nicosia, in which the Presidential Palace had been attacked apparently by ex-supporters of Grivas in the Greek Cypriot National Guard, which was officered largely by mainland Greek Army officers. The fate of Makarios was not known. Air Marshal John Aiken, Commander British Forces Near East, had put the whole British garrison of the Sovereign Base Areas on alert, while trying to discover what the situation was. He was much concerned with the position of the four and a half thousand families living outside the base areas, principally in Limassol and Larnaca, whose husbands were at work in the bases. The situation at Episkopi was complicated by the fact that the main road from Paphos, the stronghold of Makarios's support, to Limassol, always a centre of pro-Grivas elements, ran through the base. By late afternoon it had been fairly reliably established that Makarios was alive and in Paphos. The Bishop of that place had asked the United Nations Force in Cyprus to assume responsibility for Makarios's protection. Bitter interfactional fighting went on throughout the night, centred on Nicosia, Famagusta and Limassol. In spite of this, escorted convoys of husbands had been able to rejoin their families in those areas without serious incident.

On the morning of 16 July Makarios moved into the protection of the UN Force in Paphos, which was provided by the British contingent of the Force and was a detachment of the Coldstream Guards. At 12.30 p.m. Cyprus time (11.30 a.m. British Summer Time) the Bishop of Paphos's palace was under fire from a Cypriot National Guard patrol boat and a National Guard force from Nicosia was approaching the town. Makarios, fearing that the small UN force at Paphos would not be able to protect him, asked the British High Commissioner in Nicosia to arrange for him to be rescued by the British and taken to the safety of the Episkopi–Akrotiri base. This request was passed by 'Flash' message to the Foreign Secretary, Aiken being warned at the same time by the High Commissioner, Stephen Olver. Fortunately a contingency plan to rescue the Archbishop had been in existence for a considerable time. While Aiken alerted the helicopter squadron and also his personal Argosy aircraft, in which the Archbishop could be flown out of the island at least as far as Malta, he anxiously awaited authority to proceed. He was strongly opposed to allowing Makarios to stay in the base for even the shortest time for fear that this would turn the National Guard, who were now the *de facto* authority in the island, against the British, with all the implications this would have, especially for the families in Limassol and elsewhere outside the bases. Ministers in London, however, took a different view. The last thing they wanted was to be saddled with Makarios in London. Meanwhile the situation at Paphos was becoming critical, and Aiken judged that, if he did not implement the plan immediately, it might not be possible to effect the Archbishop's rescue. At 3.45 p.m. Cyprus time, three-quarters of an hour after receiving Olver's warning, Aiken was on the secure radio-telephone to Air Marshal Pete Le Cheminant, my deputy, urgently demanding permission to proceed, pointing out that there would still be time after the Archbishop's rescue to reach the final decision as to his destination. I therefore gave him authority without further reference to Ministers, although they were immediately informed. Makarios was rescued in the nick of time and was about to be transferred to the Argosy, when the Foreign Office said that he was to be held at Akrotiri while Ministers discussed his future. Aiken protested vigorously against this. Reluctant agreement was given by officials to Makarios taking off en route to Malta, while his final destination, or even perhaps his recall to Akrotiri, was under discussion by Ministers. As a result of intense and rapid diplomatic activity, Dom Mintoff was prevailed upon to persuade Makarios to stay in Malta until further plans had been made. The RAF Wing Commander accompanying the Archbishop had done his best to persuade him not to expect immediate onward flight to London, although he could clearly see a RAF Comet at Luqa airfield on his arrival there.

During the next few days it became clear that the executors of the coup were the mainland Greek officers serving in the National Guard, and the instigators the 'hawks' of the Colonels' government of Greece, notably Brigadier Ioannides. They had installed Nicos Sampson as puppet head of the Greek Cypriot government, a choice which discredited them with all but their most fanatical supporters. Turkey called upon Britain, as a co-guarantor of the 1960 constitution, to intervene, either on her own or in cooperation with Turkey, to restore the 'independence and integrity' of Cyprus, even though in principle this would have meant the reinstatement of their arch-enemy, Makarios. Turkey made it clear that she expected us to allow her to bring additional troops into the island through our bases and to act together with her: failing that, she would act alone.

This put the British government on the spot. If we acted in cooperation with Turkey, and even more so if we let them make use of the bases, the whole Greek Cypriot population would turn against us. This would not only prejudice the existence of the bases themselves, but would immediately put at risk all the service dependants and British citizens living in the island. If however the Turks intervened alone and we did nothing to prevent them, we ran the risk of being almost as unpopular with the Greek Cypriots as we would have been if we had cooperated with the Turks. We might then end up equally unpopular with both elements of the population, with risks as great as those involved in active cooperation with the Turks. I sympathized with the Foreign Secretary's dilemma. I remembered how, as the peacekeeper ten years before, I had felt hamstrung by the vulnerability of our families in the island and the need to avoid antagonizing the Greek Cypriot population.

By Friday 19 July the threat of a Turkish invasion was appearing imminent. All the Turkish troops, aircraft and ships needed had been brought to a high state of readiness. It was still however impossible to judge whether they had taken the decision to invade or were merely bringing pressure on us to intervene as the only means of preventing them from doing so. On several occasions in the previous ten years they had come as close as this to invasion, and indeed, on more than one, had actually set sail, only to return under cover of darkness. When, therefore, in the early afternoon of 19 July, we had definite intelligence from the RAF airborne radar of two separate groups of ships sailing south from the Turkish port of Mersin, it could not definitely be forecast as an actual invasion. The number and size of the ships detected did not appear to be sufficient to do more than land a brigade-sized force, probably at Kyrenia, and the smaller force (two ships only) was perhaps designed to seize the port of Famagusta in conjunction with the Turks of the old city. I was due to go with Edith and friends to a performance of *Idomeneo* at Glyndebourne that evening. I discussed with Roy Mason whether I should go: it would take me two and a half hours to get back. Pete Le Cheminant would remain on duty, and, as there could be no question, as we saw it, of active intervention against the Turkish forces, there was not likely to be any decision, other than one to reinforce the bases, for which my presence at a shorter time interval would be needed. I therefore set off, taking the precaution of taking my own car as well as our friends', so that, if I were recalled, the others could stay. On arrival I warned the box office that I might receive a call and told them where I was sitting. Just as the first act was about to begin, an anxious attendant summoned me out and asked me to ring Le Cheminant. He told me that he was having difficulty with the Foreign Office, as they wished to threaten the Turks with action and to make some military moves, perhaps naval, which might lend substance to this. He had pointed out all the implications of finding ourselves actually engaged in hostilities with the Turks, NATO and CENTO allies, and of the dangers, particularly at night, of aircraft and ships approaching their forces. Even if we intended our threats to be empty, the Turks might take a different view. *In extremis* they could muster stronger forces than we could in the area. He thought that his arguments had been accepted and hoped that it would not be necessary for me to return. By this time the first act had started, and I had to listen to it through the speakers in the organ room. I was able to return to my seat for the second act, but, when I went again to the box office at the start of the dinner interval, there was a message for me to ring again. Le Cheminant told me that the Foreign Office was still in a bellicose mood, and asked me to return to lend my weight to the argument. Snatching a slice of pâté and gulping a quick drink, I dashed for the car park and drove like the wind to London. When I reached Le Cheminant's office, he told me that good sense had prevailed and that the Foreign Office had calmed down. However it was clear that the invasion was on, and it took place at dawn on 20 July, limited to the area of Kyrenia. Reinforcements for the bases, which had already been brought to short notice and which included 41 Commando Royal Marines, on board HMS *Hermes* offshore, were set in motion.

Within the next two days the Turkish forces had linked up with Nicosia, but, by the time that a precarious ceasefire had been established on 21 July, they had merely secured a 15-mile-wide corridor between the city and Kyrenia. They had bombed Nicosia airfield and the Greek part of Famagusta, known as Varosha, and had also bombed and sunk one of their own frigates which was off the south of the island, most of its crew being rescued by the RAF. The Greeks, overflying our Episkopi base, landed about 200 soldiers at Nicosia airfield on the night of 22 July, which provoked further Turkish bombing of the airfield, making life very uncomfortable for the headquarters of the UN Force which was stationed there. While all this had been going on, John Aiken had successfully carried out an escorted evacuation of families and British citizens and some others from Limassol, Larnaca, Famagusta and Nicosia, generally with the full cooperation of the Greek Cypriot National Guard. The western base area at Episkopi received 8,500, and the eastern base at Dhekelia 1500. The plight of British and non-Cypriot residents and tourists in the area of Kyrenia now caused

concern to the High Commission, whose office in Nicosia
was in the front line of the fighting, to Aiken and to Ministers
in London. About 2000 persons were involved and it was
decided that they should be rescued, making use of HMS
Hermes and her helicopters. In the evening of 22 July this
was agreed by the Foreign Secretary Callaghan, who sent
a message at 9.20 p.m. to our ambassadors in Greece and
Turkey, asking them to obtain assurances that it would not
be interfered with. These assurances were not forthcoming,
and at 2 a.m. (Cyprus time) on the 23rd Aiken was woken
up and informed. He decided to continue with the operation
and consider it again at 4 a.m. Meanwhile Callaghan had
sent a personal message to the Turkish Prime Minister, Mr
Ecevit, saying that he expected full cooperation and would
hold Ecevit responsible for any incident caused by Turkish
forces. Aiken decided to proceed with the operation to the
accompaniment of a series of 'Flash' telegrams from our
embassy in Ankara advising postponement, and warnings
from the Turkish General Staff, to which we replied direct.
In the event the operation went without a hitch and was not
interfered with. By the early afternoon over 1500 people
of twenty-three different nationalities had been rescued in a
very well conducted operation in which high risks had been
faced, which fortunately did not materialize.

The next crisis arose over Nicosia airfield. It began by
rumours on 23 July that the Turks were about to attack and
seize the airfield, on the north-western side of which the UN
Force Headquarters and the Force reserve armoured car
squadron, which was British, had their camp. The Turkish
forces overlooked the western end of the runway. In the
next 24 hours tension rose to a high level. The Turks
maintained that the UN Force had abandoned the airfield
and that they now controlled it. General Prem Chand, the
Indian commander of the UN Force, reacted to this by
announcing that the UN Force had taken over the airport
temporarily and that it had thus become an internationally
protected area. Ankara continued to maintain that they had
already taken it over, which their ambassador in Nicosia, no
doubt embarrassed, kept on insisting that they would shortly
do. Callaghan kept on warning the Turkish Prime Minister
and Foreign Minister of the very serious consequences that

this would have, while trying to call in Kissinger to his aid in putting pressure on the Turks. It was clear, however, that in no circumstances would the Americans threaten military action against them. Callaghan was anxious to stiffen the threat against the Turks and to strengthen the hand of the United Nations. The UN Secretariat in New York were therefore persuaded to ask us to accede to the request that Prem Chand had already made for reinforcements and air support. This was forthcoming on the evening of 24 July, and overnight we sent up two armoured car squadrons and two companies, the latter from the Coldstream Guards, from Dhekelia to Nicosia, and flew out eight RAF Phantoms, which, having refuelled in flight, were ready for action at Akrotiri on the morning of the 25th. There had been keen competition between the Royal Navy and the RAF to provide the aircraft, and the former were disappointed that the latter were able to prove that they could get there first, although HMS *Ark Royal* was near Gibraltar. The political and military problems involved in a direct attack by RAF aircraft, operating under British national command, in support of the UN Force against the forces of a co-guarantor power, which was also a NATO and CENTO ally, the UN Force having itself been established primarily to protect the Turkish Cypriots, were intricate to say the least, not covered by the Security Council Resolution, and certainly best not put to the test. By this time political events in Greece and Cyprus had taken charge. The Greek Colonels' government collapsed and was replaced by Karamanlis. In Cyprus Nicos Sampson was thrown out and the reasonable, pro-Makarios Glafkos Clerides replaced him.

No sooner was tension over this tricky problem for the moment relaxed than a new version of the same type of problem arose again: that is of making threats, if the consequences of implementing them are such that one could or should not carry them out. The Turks had occupied only a small area. The change in the political scene in Greece and among the Greek Cypriots meant that the pressure for intervention by us came now, not from the Turks to overthrow the coup, but from the Greeks to throw out the Turks. Although we had successfully evacuated all the families, and British citizens who wished to move, into the safety of the bases, which had been reinforced and were much less vulnerable to Greek Cypriot action or pressure than before, the short- and long-term arguments against becoming directly involved were still strong, particularly against getting involved in a direct military confrontation with the Turks, both on the widest politico-military grounds and on the narrow military one that they could bring much stronger forces to bear, especially in the air, to which the overcrowded bases would be vulnerable. The possibility of our establishing a naval and air blockade of the north coast to prevent further Turkish reinforcement and resupply was considered and rejected for these reasons.

For a fortnight there was an uneasy peace. A ceasefire agreement was signed on 30 July and service families were allowed to return to their homes outside the bases. Tension rose again on 11 August when it appeared that the Turks were intending to expand the area they held, having used the previous two weeks to build up their forces. At this time talks were going on at Geneva under Callaghan's chairmanship. On 12 August the Turks tabled proposals demanding as a Turkish Cypriot zone the area which we had from the start assumed that an invasion would be intended to seize, amounting to one-third of the island, the area they did eventually secure. They threatened to walk out of the conference by midnight, if this were not agreed, and to take military action next morning to secure their demand. The familiar pressure from the Foreign Secretary, the UN Force and others that we should do something to prevent or deter this came to the fore again. With the families unfortunately outside the bases again, the arguments against any action, and therefore against empty threats, were stronger than ever. We dared not do anything until we had got the families back into the bases again.

This was still being deliberated at UN Headquarters in New York when the Turks struck, opening hostilities with air attacks on Nicosia at dawn on 14 August. They did not however make any move to attack the airfield, where the small UN Force showed great resolution. The difficult decision that we should have to take about air support for them, if they were attacked, did not fortunately arise; but by this time Callaghan had reluctantly accepted that we should not, in such an event, intervene, reinforce or support the UN Force. A meeting that afternoon, chaired by the Prime Minister, decided that the government's policy should be one of a long diplomatic haul, and that we should continue to maintain a low-key military posture, concentrating on the security of our base areas and nationals.

While this had been going on, the families once more packed up and sought refuge within the bases, from which most of them were evacuated to the United Kingdom. After this experience, coming on top of that of ten years before, I was determined that we should not again find our freedom of action in Cyprus so totally restricted by ,the vulnerability of large numbers of women and children living outside the bases. The disadvantages of being involved, without any real power to influence, had been clearly demonstrated and thoughts began to turn to extricating us from Cyprus altogether, when it became politically possible to do so. This excitement having calmed down, we went off on holiday to the Île d'Oléron again, this time taking my Gull dinghy on the roofrack.

The Defence Review being, for the moment at least, behind us in the spring of 1975, attention could be turned to other matters which had been held in abeyance while it had been in progress, as well as to the practical problems of implementing it. I had felt unable to leave the country for any length of time while the Review was in progress, and had planned to make 1975, the middle year of my term, the year of travel. In March I set off to visit Muscat, where the Sultan's forces, assisted to a high degree by British soldiers and airmen, both within his forces and in British units, were fighting an interesting campaign in the Dhofar against tough opponents in rugged country, a campaign successfully concluded by the end of the year. I went on to Hong Kong, meeting the Chiefs of Staff of Sri Lanka at a refuelling stop at Colombo, followed by a short visit to Kuala Lumpur for a brief reunion with Malaysian colleagues, and to Brunei, where I saw the Gurkha battalion and the Sultan's own force, the Royal Brunei Malay Regiment. In Hong Kong the main topic of discussion both with the Governor, Murray Maclehose, and the Commander British Forces, Edwin Bramall, both old friends, was naturally the proposals in the Defence Review both to reduce the garrison and for the Hong Kong government to pay a greater proportion of its cost. A protracted process of negotiation lay ahead, which was successfully concluded by Bill Rodgers on a visit a year later. On the way back we stopped in Singapore – a nostalgic visit – where I discussed with all concerned the plan to implement the Defence Review decision to withdraw totally from Singapore within a year, an operation which in the event went very smoothly. We returned on the normal RAF VC10 flight via Gan, also to be evacuated in the same time scale.

April saw me heading east again to attend a CENTO Military Committee meeting in Islamabad, my first visit to Pakistan, the only important aspects of which were a long discussion with my Turkish colleague, General Sançar, on the intractable problems of Cyprus, an interesting tea-time discussion with the Prime Minister, Zulfikar Bhutto, and a sight-seeing visit to Lahore. At the end of April I paid an official visit to Yugoslavia, in the course of which I celebrated my sixtieth birthday at a 'partisanski' lunch, an open-air banquet in the Sutjeska valley, scene of a great battle between the partisans and the Germans and Italians very soon after the first British officers, one of whom was killed, had joined Tito. We received a warm and friendly welcome wherever we went, and I would very much have liked to stay longer. Immediately before this I had paid a short visit to Gibraltar, stopping off in Portugal at the request of the Foreign Office to make the acquaintance of and try to give some support to the senior officers of the Portuguese armed forces, who were locked in a struggle with the communists. It was a fascinating experience and I came away with the feeling that they were overwhelmed by the number and intensity of the problems they faced. To them, getting out of Africa clearly came first in priority: after that the problems of Portugal itself would have to be tackled.

May brought the usual crop of NATO meetings in Belgium. In June I paid a visit to the missile range in the Hebrides, which included an exciting flight by helicopter in very strong winds to St Kilda. Later that month I paid an official visit to Norway, cementing the good relations I had established with my Norwegian colleague, General Zeiner-Gundersen. The build-up of Russian military facilities in the

Kola Peninsula, east of Norway's frontier in the extreme north, the increased Russian naval activity in the Norwegian Sea, and the problems arising in the field of rights on, over and under the sea in the Barents Sea and around Spitzbergen showed signs of bringing about a more realistic and robust Norwegian attitude towards the Russians and to defence generally. I was at pains to stress both that, in spite of the reduction in reinforcements available as a result of our Defence Review, we attached high importance to providing support to Norway in emergency, and also that its availability and development would depend very much on the attitude of the Norwegians themselves beforehand and at the time. This caused no offence: it was made clear to me that of all the allies the British were the most welcome in Norway. Unfortunately when we visited the North, the weather was overcast and wet, but it did not prevent Zeiner-Gundersen and myself and members of our staffs from walking, much of it in marshland, for some five hours along the Russian frontier towards the end of a most interesting and very long day, which culminated in a glimpse of the midnight sun through clouds as we dined. A visit to our forces in Germany in July and to The Netherlands armed forces in September completed a busy year's travelling, the highlights of the visit to Holland being attendance at the state opening of the Dutch Parliament, a visit to the impressive Delta project controlling the mouths of the Rhine and Waal, and an afternoon sailing in the state yacht of Friesland, very similar to a Norfolk wherry, on the Friesian lakes.

But life was not all travel. There were a number of major issues to face, mostly connected with future equipment projects. At the heart of them lay the fundamental issue: should Europe continue to attempt to maintain its own independent defence industries and the research and development facilities to back them, or resign itself to becoming at best sub-contractor to the immensely powerful American defence industry, backed by all the research effort that had been devoted to their space programme with its fall-out in the miniaturized electronic industry, which had many military applications. Behind this choice lay the major issue as to whether one could or should remain dependent on American support indefinitely, and, if not, whether it was prudent to build up as high a degree of European independence in the defence field as possible. The French took the latter view, and in the days when Michel Debré had been their Defence Minister and Lord Carrington ours, Carrington and Heath had shown considerable sympathy with it.

I had for some time wished to put these issues squarely to Roy Mason, but was reluctant to do so until the Defence Review was out of the way. The opportunity arose when Mason became chairman of the Eurogroup for 1975. Eurogroup was a grouping of the European members of NATO, less France who refused to participate, which met to try and coordinate their views before NATO meetings of Defence Ministers. The first 1975 meeting was to be in London, and Mason wished to appear more than just a routine chairman. The Americans, led by Schlesinger, were laying great emphasis on standardization as essential, if better value was to be obtained from the resources that European members of NATO devoted to defence, which were clearly not likely to be increased. This pressure derived both from the plight of the US defence industry, its order books drastically reduced with the end of the Vietnam war, and from Congressional concern over stationing US forces in Europe or planning to reinforce them in war, if the Europeans were not prepared to make sufficient effort themselves to provide conventional forces strong enough to resist the enemy for long enough both to make American reinforcement worthwhile and also to avoid an immediate call for the use of tactical nuclear weapons, which could quickly escalate to a strategic nuclear exchange in which Russian nuclear weapons landed on the USA. I was convinced that it was necessary for Britain and for the other European members of NATO to clear their minds as to the policy they wished to pursue, to agree on it, and, having done so, to put their house in order to make it possible successfully to follow the policy. It was clear to me that it would only be possible to resist American pressure (if it was decided that it was right to do so) if at least France, Germany and ourselves agreed a common line and cooperated fully. This would not be possible as long as the defence industries of Europe were so fragmented and were continually competing against each other. I believed that a first step was to agree in general terms which countries should be accepted as the 'leaders' in development in certain fields, however production might be shared. The general aim should be for Europeans to agree on the fields of weapons in which they had reason to feel that they could or must preserve a European independent development capability, and those in which it was not worthwhile or not sufficiently important to attempt to compete against the USA. In the end the aim should be that, when the Europeans agreed to go for European equipment, they should all accept the same one and try and persuade the Americans to accept it also; and equally that, when they agreed to go for American equipment, they should all go for the same one and ensure that it was also going to be in service with the US armed forces – a simple enough aim, but far from easy to achieve, as results were to show.

Although Mason did not accept all the implications, tending to take a more nationalist and less European view as far as industrial aspects were concerned, he accepted the idea and flung himself into promoting it with enthusiasm as 'The Two Way Street', helped by an American report (the Callaghan Report) which had already made similar proposals. One of the results was to alarm the French, smarting under the rejection of their entry in the competition for an aircraft to re-equip the Belgian, Dutch, Danish and Norwegian Air Forces in favour of the American Northrop F16. This left the French aircraft industry with little or nothing on its military order books, while Britain, Germany and Italy had the Tornado MRCA ahead of them. If the Two Way Street were to be successful without French participation, they would be left out in the cold. They had consistently refused to participate in the Eurogroup and, to accommodate their sensibilities, a new body had to be invented, called the Independent Programme Group, to try and establish a European end to a dialogue with the Americans in this field. At its early meetings at the beginning of 1976, it showed distinct signs of promise, which is more than could be said for any practical sign of American sympathy towards the Two Way Street, perhaps too much to expect in a Presidential election year, which was also the 200th anniversary of the Declaration of Independence. By the time I left the Ministry of Defence much of the steam had gone out of the concept, and it looked like running into the sand of narrow national interests on both sides of the Atlantic.

In our own equipment programme, the major issues were the Maritime Harrier, the air defence version of the MRCA, guided weapon projects and the future airborne early warning aircraft, all affecting the future of the British aerospace industry, in which the two remaining aircraft and guided missile firms, the British Aircraft Corporation and Hawker-Siddeley, were due to be merged into one nationalized firm. It had long been clear to the Ministry of Defence that our own future orders of aircraft and guided missiles could not support the research and development staffs of two different firms, and successive governments of both political colours had pressed for a voluntary merger, which should incorporate close links with other European firms in the same field. Nothing had come of this, and enforced nationalization was the result. The Chiefs of Staff had consistently shown reluctance to support projects which appeared to us to be uneconomic, or inferior in quality, or later in time-scale than equipment available either from European, generally French, or American sources; but we continually found ourselves forced by Ministers, under pressures, the origins of which were commercial, even if they were voiced by officials within the Ministry, to accept package deals which balanced acceptance of foreign designs or production against British projects which we would have preferred to reject. The guided weapon projects were a case in point. We were allowed to accept an American guided weapon to be fired from a submarine and a Franco–German anti-tank missile, provided we accepted a British missile to be fired from naval helicopters against surface targets (not a high priority in some naval eyes) and indefinite postponement of a future anti-tank guided weapon for army helicopters. Although not a strict parallel, the Maritime Harrier owed its continued support to similar influences. The adaptation of the RAF's vertical take-off aircraft, to enable it to operate from the navy's new anti-submarine cruiser or carrier, had become an emotive issue. It was the last hope of preserving fixed-wing flying for the navy, and was suspected by others to be justified solely as a last ditch attempt to preserve the Fleet Air Arm. Critics, who included myself, doubted its operational effectiveness, particularly as so few of them would actually be available at any one time. Under the Conservative administration Carrington had had serious doubts about whether to proceed with the project, and no decision had been taken when their government fell. Now the issue had to be faced again. As before, the pros and cons were finely balanced, and the tilt in favour was provided by the industrial argument: the need to keep Hawker-Siddeley in the aircraft business while nationalization was brought about.

If there had been doubts about the navy's Harrier programme, in which a comparatively small sum was involved, there were equally grave doubts about the air force's commitment to the air defence version of the Tornado, in which very large sums of money were involved over a long period. This fighter version of the MRCA was required only for the RAF, our German and Italian partners in the project intending to rely, probably, on US aircraft for this role: in our case, it was intended to replace the ageing and unsuitable Lightnings as well as the American-made Phantoms. The problem was that its performance was little better than that of the Phantom; but the latter would need new avionics and the air staff had doubts about its fatigue life. My deputy who dealt with these matters, Air Marshal Michael Giddings, a man of rigid, puritanical devotion to his profession, was a convinced opponent and a firm supporter of choosing an American aircraft. Extracting a coherent policy on air defence from the air staff proved a tough, prolonged and frustrating process, which, after a year's effort, was only partially successful. Nevertheless it did clarify some of the issues, even if it did not lead to clear conclusions. It proved, to my satisfaction at least, that one could not replace or significantly reduce the fighter aircraft programme by investment in a medium or high level surface-to-air missile system. Ideally one should have both, but we would never have the resources. The number of aircraft planned – 110 – was clearly an absolute minimum. The operational argument raged round the endurance required and the ability to engage multiple targets and ones at long range. In the end the decision turned on whether or not it was possible to cancel the air defence variant without fatally affecting the MRCA programme as a whole, just as we were approaching the difficult time at which the three nations involved had to commit themselves to a firm production programme, and in a year when two of them, as it turned out, were to be involved in general elections. I myself became convinced that this was not possible, and, in the face of considerable reservations on the part of the army and the navy, as well as on Giddings's part, it was accepted.

At the time we were discussing this, the French Minister of Defence, Monsieur Bourges, paid a visit to Roy Mason and sprang on us the prospect of a deal, by which, if we collaborated with the French on a fighter developed from the design they had been pushing as a rival to the F16, they might be interested in buying the interdiction and strike version of the MRCA instead of going ahead with their own *'avion de combat futur'*. It did not need a deep or long examination of this proposal to realize that it would not suit us, and the French themselves seemed apologetic for having suggested it. There did however seem to be some possibility of cooperation on a future aircraft, which, for the RAF, would succeed the Harrier and the successful Anglo–French Jaguar, just coming into service with both our air forces. The difficulty was that this lay a long way ahead, and would not help the French aircraft industry meanwhile. Our air staff was changing its mind about what sort of aircraft this should be, partly under the influence of the 1973 Israeli–Arab Yom Kippur War, partly as a result of studying developments in the Warsaw Pact air and anti-aircraft forces. Both indicated that employment of aircraft in the ground attack role in close support of the army was likely to prove a highly expensive and not very effective use of resources; and also that, to survive in the air above our own forces, our tactical aircraft would have to have a better air-to-air combat capability than had been envisaged for the Jaguar/Harrier successor. This was a conclusion that was not welcome to the army, and led to considerable discussion. Ever since lessons, too hastily and readily accepted without examination, had been emerging from the Yom Kippur war, I had been trying to get underway an authoritative study and consideration of all the information we had acquired and could acquire about it. I had charged Pete Le Cheminant with this, an area in which he had exceptional personal experience. He had a difficult time getting his colleagues, the single service Vice-Chiefs of

Staff, to reach agreed conclusions, and I had equal difficulty in persuading the Chiefs themselves to accept them, even when hedged about with qualifications and provisos. However the study was valuable and did bear fruit in agreement on the air staff target for the Jaguar/Harrier replacement and in decision by the army to go for an anti-aircraft multiple cannon in addition to its missiles.

The other major equipment problem arose over the airborne early warning aircraft required to replace the RAF's very aged Shackleton and the navy's equally aged Gannet, the latter designed to operate off carriers. We were in the early stages of developing a version of the Nimrod (itself a derivative from the Comet) with a completely new British electronic fit for this purpose, when the Americans launched a major sales drive for an integrated NATO force, based on the Boeing E3A (a derivative of the well-known commercial 707), known as AWACS (airborne warning and control system). After careful consideration, and in spite of considerable doubts about its suitability both for detecting ships at sea and for dealing with the dense concentration of aircraft tracks expected in the Central Region of NATO's European Command, we concluded that, provided it was subscribed to by all the NATO nations and was large enough in total numbers to cover the whole area, in particular the Eastern Atlantic and the air approaches to the United Kingdom, it would be cheaper than the Nimrod solution, available earlier and in some respects more effective. Thus began a long and complicated process of negotiation within NATO, in the course of which the number of potential contributors dwindled until it appeared that only the USA, ourselves and possibly the Germans would be prepared to foot the bill for the force, the main base of which it was agreed in NATO should be in Britain. In the end the Germans were not prepared to lend their support, and, as no contribution was forthcoming from other NATO nations, we reverted to our original project of developing an airborne early warning version of Nimrod*.

Another major equipment problem running at a slower pace during this period was Anglo–German cooperation on

---

* The Government had to revert to the Boeing solution in 1986.

a future tank. At the time I had become CGS in 1971, Carrington had already agreed with the Germans that neither should allow their armies in future each to have their own tank: they must collaborate. We were then only just completing the re-equipment of our 1000-strong tank fleet with Chieftain in place of Centurion. The much larger German fleet, some 4000, was replaced in two stages: the first would take place in the late 1970s, and was likely to be based on a new model of the German Leopard, unless they agreed to standardize with the USA on an American tank, of which two different models were under development. The Anglo–German project was intended to meet the second phase which would coincide roughly with our need to replace Chieftain in the mid-1980s. As we fully realized, there was a fundamental difference of outlook between us, the Germans laying great stress on the need for a low silhouette and a very high degree of mobility. To achieve this, they were prepared to accept thinner armour, fewer rounds of ammunition and did not demand penetration of the enemy's armour at ranges beyond 2000 metres. We placed considerable emphasis on the need to ensure a high degree of survivability of the tank on the battlefield, and doubted the practical ability of the tank to make use of the theoretical mobility for which, in our opinion, the Germans were prepared to sacrifice characteristics of higher priority. We believed that the Yom Kippur War had confirmed our views. Discussion between the officers of both armies concerned with these matters greatly narrowed the difference of outlook to a degree which would undoubtedly have made possible an agreed concept. But by that time other factors were bringing pressure to bear to produce divergence, one being the determination of the Germans, both official and commercial, to break our monopoly in tank gun design, another the competition between them and the Americans for the tank to replace the first half of their fleet. The delay looked like leading to a postponement of the date when they would want the Anglo–German tank to one that was too late for us. On our side, a large order from Iran, to be met by an improved Chieftain, opened up the possibility that the latter could lead straight on to a Chieftain replacement. In the end each country went its own way.

After the Defence Review, there were some sufficiently naïve to imagine that, having struggled through it, we would be able to plan on the assumption that the levels of defence expenditure resulting from it would be maintained. I was cynical or realistic enough to realize that we would not escape the annual haggle in the Public Expenditure Scrutiny Committee, in which the Treasury and other major spending departments would continue pressure to reduce defence expenditure, if only to make politically acceptable reductions in politically more popular areas of public spending. We had, of course, to absorb into our estimated cost of the 'critical level' a number of commitments of which we had assumed we could be rid, notably Cyprus. These added up to a total of £75m a year at 1976 prices. The 1974 PESC exercise had lopped a total of £170m over three years from our budget targets. In his 1975 budget Healey had made a further cut in the 1976/7 target of £168m (at 1976 prices). Following this there was a long and bitter struggle over the 1975 PESC exercise, the Chancellor demanding a total reduction of public expenditure of £2000 to £3000m a year, to which defence was expected to provide £1200m over the three years to 1979/80. This could clearly not be done without both cuts in the front-line forces and major cancellations in the equipment programme. After heated discussions between the Ministry of Defence and the Treasury, the amount to be found by defence was settled at about half that figure. We managed to accept this without affecting force levels and making major cancellations, by planning major reductions in overheads, principally in establishments which we had wished to close in any case, but had been prevented from doing by political objections, and also by major reductions in civilian employment. Whether in the event resistance from the trade unions involved would make it possible to effect the economies in time remained to be seen. As usual the Chiefs of Staff had to undertake and undergo the painful annual process of serving up a shopping list to the Secretary of State to illustrate what the effect of such cuts might be, a delicate process in which the rivalry between the service departments in defending the allocation of money to their own programmes became the dominant factor. My last summer saw the process under way again, by which time we had already had to absorb cuts totalling £1300m at 1976 prices since the Defence Review. The longer we appeared to be able to absorb these cuts without affecting force levels, the more suspect became our protests that the process could go no further; but, if we took a stand and said that it would involve certain very distasteful steps, our bluff might be called and we could find ourselves having to put them into effect, when in fact they could have been avoided. This was the dilemma that faced us every year. I considered it to be of considerable importance to preserve the credibility of the Chiefs of Staff. If our judgement was proved wrong by events, the pressure to disregard our advice, always latent in many different quarters, ministerial and official, within and outside the Ministry of Defence, would increase.

This general issue was to be raised in the process of a 'Management Review' of the Ministry, which was initiated at the request of the Prime Minister immediately after the Defence Review. It was a process which had been applied to other government departments, including the Treasury, and was intended as a searching reappraisal of the functioning of the department with the aim of both increasing efficiency and producing economies. Since the Ministry of Defence had incorporated the old Admiralty, War Office and Air Ministry in 1964, there had been several further inquiries, committees and investigations into its organization and working. In Healey's time as Defence Secretary there had been strong pressure for further integration of the service departments. The general principle was accepted that the primary functional organization must be based on sea, land and air forces. The principal change in Carrington's time had been a radical reorganization of the procurement field, based on the report of a special committee, headed by Derek Rayner of Marks and Spencers. This had resulted in the concentration into one Procurement Executive within the Ministry of Defence of the responsibilities for research, development and procurement, including production in Royal Ordnance Factories, formerly exercised by the Admiralty, the War Office (which had taken them back from the Ministry of Supply some years before) and the Ministry of Aviation and Technology. On the whole this reorganization had proved successful. The establishment of the Management Review

opened the doors again to all the well-known criticisms of
the Ministry: that it was too large; there were too many levels
of consideration; there was not enough decentralization
of responsibility; there were too many military officers of
excessive rank (by the civilians); there were too many civilians
with excessive status and power (by the military); that too
much power was retained in the hands of the military and
especially by the Chiefs of Staff, who were concerned only
to preserve the interests of their service at the expense
of the overall needs of defence; that it took too long to
extract an answer from the staff, and that working methods
were laborious, too dependent on committees ensuring that
every interest was represented, and too little left to normal
staff work by individuals. A good deal of this criticism was
justified, but much was exaggerated.

In drawing up the terms of reference for the review, the
PUS, Michael Cary, had tended to draft them in a way that, in
my view, prejudiced the outcome in favour of one that would
conform to the ideas common to Ministers and civil servants;
that is that they should exercise greater power of decision at
an earlier stage, wresting it away from the Chiefs of Staff.
Supported by my colleagues, I succeeded in getting the terms
of reference made much more general, and in ensuring that
the team charged with the task of carrying it out should have
an entirely free hand and should not have to work towards
any preconceived pattern. In any case they had to report to
a steering committee, chaired by Cary, of which the military
members were myself, Admiral Ray Lygo, Vice-Chief of
the Naval Staff, General John Gibbon, Master-General of
the Ordnance, and Air Chief Marshal Neil Cameron, Air
Member for Personnel, who became Chief of the Air Staff
before the Committee had finished its work, and Chief of
the Defence Staff later.* Michael Cary, a gifted and attractive
character with considerable experience in the defence field,
died suddenly in March 1976 on the evening of the day on
which he and I together had attended the passing out parade
at Sandhurst where his youngest son was a cadet. His death
was a severe blow to us all, but his successor, Frank Cooper,

* After his retirement, he was made a Life Peer, but died soon afterwards,
in January 1985.

was equally experienced and had held the key post of Deputy Under-Secretary (Policy) in Healey's day. Not surprisingly he tended to support the Ministerial/official line. Fortunately I got on as well with him as I had with his predecessor, but I detected early on a determination on his part to see that the PUS played a more forceful and independent part in advising the Secretary of State than either of his predecessors had done. The Review recommended a number of improvements, none of them involving drastic change.

1976 had suddenly brought a change of prime minister, when Harold Wilson resigned and was succeeded by James Callaghan. This seemed likely to be helpful to defence, as Jim Callaghan was favourably inclined towards us and particularly to the navy. Throughout the Defence Review, he had been a strong supporter of Roy Mason in his fight against Denis Healey. If anything, he had been rather too keen to employ military forces wherever and whenever possible. Wilson had never seemed interested in defence, although he had proved very helpful over the Defence Review, particularly in handling those Ministerial colleagues who were not sympathetic to our case.

A matter in which I played an important part was the choice of Chairman of the NATO Military Committee to succeed Peter Hill-Norton, who had been appointed to the post after he had handed over CDS to me, and whose term had been extended to April 1977. I was keen that his successor should be a soldier, and I also considered that it would be a good thing if it were not to be considered a prerogative of the British and the Germans to fill the post. While walking along the coast of Northumberland during the NATO Military Committee's visit to Britain in 1974, I had asked Zeiner-Gundersen whether he might be a candidate. He said that, subject to his government's approval, he would be glad to be considered. Having obtained the support of the Foreign Office, my colleagues and Roy Mason, I asked the Norwegian Minister of Defence, Mr Fostervoll, at a NATO meeting in Brussels if I could propose Zeiner-Gundersen. He promised to give me an answer on my visit to Norway in June 1975, when he told me that he was happy to let me put his name forward, provided that it would not meet with opposition. During the next six months, therefore, I approached most of my NATO colleagues to seek their views. I found general support, although some were non-committal, notably my German colleague, Admiral Armin Zimmerman, who hoped himself to succeed Hill-Norton. The affair became entangled in the German desire to occupy more senior posts than they did in NATO; but, having with some difficulty negotiated my way through the intrigues which Zimmerman employed to frustrate the appointment, I was glad to be able to arrange Zeiner-Gundersen's unopposed selection by his colleagues on the Military Committee, leading to a successful term in office; from then on, however, the relationship between Zimmerman and myself was cool. Not long afterwards he suffered a stroke, from which he subsequently died.

My last year as Chief of the Defence Staff had also been an eventful one for me personally. In 1975 the Royal Tank Regiment commissioned a portrait of me and allowed me, in cooperation with General Pat Hobart, to choose the artist. We selected Michael Noakes and were very pleased with the result. In 1973, when I was on leave between the posts of CGS and CDS, I was approached by the publishers, Weidenfeld and Nicolson, with the proposal that I should edit a book of short biographies of the major military figures of the twentieth century, to be called *The War Lords*. I agreed to this mainly with an eye to keeping in touch with the literary world as an occupation for my retirement. I enjoyed the task, which involved an extensive correspondence with over 40 different authors. The book was published in June 1976 and sold well both in Britain and in America, where it was published by Little, Brown and Co.

The major family event was Alice's engagement and marriage. After leaving Durham University in the summer of 1975, she had gone out to Iran with the intention of earning enough there to make it possible for her to travel round the country. However, soon after arriving in Tehran, she met a young Captain in the Grenadier Guards, Claude Walters, who was helping the Iranian army to establish a junior leaders' battalion. They quickly became engaged; she returned with him after Christmas, and they were married on a very hot day in June 1976 in the chapel of the Royal Hospital, Chelsea, the reception being held in the lovely Council Chamber.

We had planned to spend part of our summer holiday in a barge on the Oxford canal, but the drought was so severe that there was not enough water, and we hired one on the Thames instead, going down and then upstream from Abingdon. John and a French boy were with us for the whole trip, and Andrew and Anne for a few days. On 22 October, after a round of farewell visits and a dinner given for me by the Army Board at Chelsea Hospital, I handed over to Marshal of the Royal Air Force Sir Andrew Humphrey, confident that he would prove as excellent a Chief of the Defence Staff as he had Chief of the Air Staff. Tragically he died early in the following year. He was temporarily succeeded by Admiral of the Fleet Sir Edward Ashmore, the First Sea Lord, until Neil Cameron assumed the post towards the end of the year. A guard of honour from the Royal Tank Regiment was drawn up outside the Ministry of Defence as I left, and two days later Edith and I crossed the Channel and drove to Bonnieux to help Antony and Elizabeth move from France to my mother's old cottage at Chilmark. I had served in the army a great deal longer than I had intended or expected to, when I entered Sandhurst forty-three years before.

18

Ex Africa

Ex Africa semper aliquid novi.
There is always something new from Africa.
                    Pliny (AD 23–79), *Historia Naturalis*

For a long time it had been my aim to keep myself occupied in retirement by writing, and, at the time of the publication of *The War Lords*, George Weidenfeld had asked me what I was intending to do when I retired: if I hoped to write, he would like to plan my literary activity over, say, the first five years. He suggested a two-book contract, one of which might also form the basis of a television series, and for this he suggested a history of the British army. For the other I suggested a biography of Field Marshal Lord Harding, for whom I had great admiration and whose career I felt had been a full and interesting one, or of General Erskine, whose son Philip had approached me with the proposition that I might write it. I told George Weidenfeld that I could not commit myself until I was nearer retirement. We met again in September and agreed to go ahead, starting with the biography of John Harding.

I began work on the book in January 1977 with two weekends of talking to my old divisional commander, then coming up to the age of 81, and taking notes of his reminiscences. I had discovered that he had observed the rules and kept no diary and hardly any personal papers. His memories therefore had to be filled in by a description of the historical background to his career, the research work for which I found of much interest. My writing was interrupted in April,

not only by John's Easter holidays, but also by a visit to Israel
at the invitation of their Minister of Defence, Shimon Peres.
In January the Israeli Defence Attaché in London had asked
if I would lecture to their resuscitated Defence College which
was shortly to open, and, not having visited the country since
before it became Israel, I was glad to accept. However, after I
had arranged to go at the end of April, the reopening of the
College was deferred until October, but they kindly kept the
invitation open and I lectured instead to their staff college,
augmented by the attendance of most of their senior officers,
my subject being 'The British Armed Forces: their tasks and
problems'. The most interesting parts of the visit were a tour
of Jerusalem, escorted for part of it by the forceful Mayor,
Teddy Kollek, a visit to the Golan Heights and the troops
occupying them, and one to the frontier with the Lebanon,
where they were in contact with the Lebanese Christians. The
vital military importance of the Golan Heights to the defence
of the Jordan valley was clearly impressed on me. I did not
visit Sinai, where at the time an extensive exercise was in train
in reaction to Egyptian movements. General Tal showed me
their new tank, which they had designed and were building
in their main tank workshop, an ambitious project.

Towards the end of May I received a letter from the Prime
Minister, James Callaghan, saying that 'he had it in mind to
recommend my name to The Queen for a Life Peerage'.
Would I accept? I found it very difficult to make up my
mind. At that time I had no high opinion of the influence
of the House of Lords. However good its debates might be,
what was said there, it seemed to me, hardly ever had any
effect on the acts and policies of government. I disliked the
snobbery and flummery of aristocracy and also felt that some
retired or serving members of the forces might regard it as a
reward for, in their eyes, being too ready to cooperate with
the Labour government over the Defence Review. The first
person I consulted was Peter Carrington, who was entirely
sympathetic to my doubts, but urged me to accept, saying
that a refusal would be misunderstood. After long discussions with Edith, I also sought the view of my elder brother
Antony. Rather to my surprise, he was entirely in favour.
That finally convinced me and, still not without hesitation, I
accepted. It was announced in the Birthday Honours at the

beginning of June and I was introduced into the House on
19 July, my sponsors being Field Marshal Lord Harding and
Marshal of the Royal Air Force Lord Elworthy.

I had by then got well on with my writing in preparation
for John's summer holidays, a period when I did not expect
to have much time or inclination for scribbling and for a
week of which we had hired a boat on the Llangollen canal.
Towards the end of the month Denis Greenhill* asked me to
a dinner at Brooks's club that he and George Jellicoe† were
giving on 25 July for a prominent Rhodesian, C. G. Tracey.
Peter Carrington and John Davies‡ and some others were
also being invited. Rhodesia was much in the news in those
days and, as I thought it might be an interesting evening,
I accepted. At the dinner Tracey said that he believed
that Ian Smith had accepted in his heart of hearts that
majority rule, based on one man, one vote, was inevitable,
but thought that he could achieve it in cooperation with
Bishop Muzorewa and the Reverend Ndabiningi Sithole,
and excluding Joshua Nkomo and Robert Mugabe's Patriotic
Front. Led by Peter Carrington, all impressed on Tracey
that Smith himself was the real obstacle. No deal with him
would ever be acceptable in African eyes and the first
step towards a peaceful settlement must be his departure.
Tracey did not argue against this, and there then ensued a
general discussion of how elections leading to independence
could be achieved, on the twin assumptions that Smith had
been removed and that power should not fall into the
hands of the pro-communist Patriotic Front. I suggested
that, although very difficult, it ought to be possible to
establish some sort of international organization to arrange
the election and provide security for it. We concluded with
a general agreement that it was not much use for Tracey to
talk to the Opposition: he should see the Foreign Secretary,
Dr David Owen. Carrington and Davies agreed to make an
approach through 'the usual channels', while Greenhill and
I undertook to put the suggestion to Michael Palliser, PUS
of the Foreign Office.

* Lord Greenhill of Harrow, PUS Foreign & Commonwealth Office 1969–73.
† The Earl Jellicoe, Lord Privy Seal 1970–74.
‡ Rt Hon John Davies, Secretary of State, Dept for Trade & Industry, 1970–74.

Next day I was unable to get him on the telephone and wrote him a letter instead, giving him a resumé of the discussion and suggesting that he arrange a meeting between Tracey and the Foreign Secretary. I received a brief acknowledgement of this from Sir Antony Duff, acting for Palliser, who was on leave, and a few days later a call from David Owen's private secretary saying that the Foreign Secretary would like to see me on the matter before, as I understood it, he saw Tracey. At midday on 3 August I met David Owen for the first time, and for over an hour he talked about Rhodesia, saying that he had difficulty in obtaining sound military advice on the difficult question of the future of the Rhodesian armed forces and what to do with the Patriotic Front guerrillas. Denis Healey, then Chancellor of the Exchequer, had suggested that he should talk with me about it: did I think it a practical possibility to integrate guerrillas with the regular forces? I said that, in certain circumstances, it could be. It had been done on a small scale in Kenya and Malaya and more recently in the Dhofar in Oman. Having sent his private secretary, Ewen Fergusson, out of the room, he asked me if I was interested in becoming personally involved. I replied that I would be 'very, very reluctant'. I explained that I had put official life behind me and was enjoying being a private citizen, living at home dabbling with my pen. He said he quite understood and we parted.

I had a lingering suspicion that I had not heard the last of it, and, when we set off on Sunday 14 August to pick up the boat at Whitchurch, the only person who knew how to contact us was my daughter Susanna. On the morning of 16 August we were nearing Chirk aqueduct when the hirer of another boat from the same yard, having seen the name of ours, hailed us and told me that police were looking for me and wanted me to telephone Oswestry police station. Having passed through the long Chirk tunnel, we tied up and Edith and I walked into Chirk, found a telephone box, and rang the police, who gave me a number to ring. This turned out to be the Treasury doorkeeper, and eventually I established contact with Stephen Wall, one of Owen's private secretaries. He told me that Owen wished to see me urgently and we agreed that I would be at Llangollen police station at 9 a.m. next day, and that the police would have to get me to an agreed rendezvous. To add to the drama, almost as soon as we had started off again to find somewhere to tie up for what was by then going to be a very late lunch, the boat broke down. However, we got to Llangollen next morning and Owen and I met at 11 a.m. in a bedroom of the Officers' Mess of the RAF station at Shawbury, to which Owen had flown. David Owen went over again his reading of the Rhodesian situation and then explained what were to be the Anglo–American proposals; that is that Britain, with the agreement of both Ian Smith and the Nationalists, would assume responsibility for governing Rhodesia during a six-month transition period, which would lead to free and fair elections based on universal adult suffrage, male and female; all executive and legislative power, on behalf of HMG, would be vested in a Resident Commissioner, who would also be Commander-in-Chief of all the security forces, including those of the Patriotic Front. To supervise a cease-fire and assist in the maintenance of security, there would be a United Nations Force under its own commander. Owen explained that he regarded it as essential that both the USA and the United Nations should give their support. Britain must not accept responsibility on her own. It was obvious that he wished me to accept the post of Resident Commissioner, but before he actually made the proposal, I asked a number of questions in elucidation, concentrating on what was to happen to the security forces, including the police, and on the position of the Resident Commissioner both in relation to the British Government and in law, Owen being very vague about the latter. At 12.30 he asked if I would take on the job, saying that the Prime Minister was very anxious that I should and that President Carter and Secretary of State Vance of the USA had been told and fully approved the choice. He stressed the advantage of appointing a military figure and explained that he and the Prime Minister wished to announce that I had accepted being designated Resident Commissioner at the time that the proposals were published, as they believed that this might help to make them more acceptable to the White Rhodesians and to the Rhodesian security forces. I had of course been turning the possibility of this over in my mind ever since I had first met David Owen, and by this stage I had concluded that I could not refuse.

I was unable to think of somebody else, and the fact that I had recently accepted a peerage seemed to me to increase the obligation to undertake a duty which I certainly did not approach with any enthusiasm. I therefore said that I would accept, on the understanding that there was no question of disbanding the Rhodesian armed forces. Owen reassured me on this and, while we both ate an excellent cold lunch provided by the RAF, I read a number of reports about the Rhodesian situation. At 1.15 p.m. we parted – nobody else had been present at the meeting – he by aircraft for London and I in a police car to join Edith and John in the pouring rain at the northern end of the Pontcysyllte aqueduct, which we crossed in a strong westerly gale, a somewhat unnerving experience in a light fibre-glass boat with only a low step of metal between one and the valley of the Dee 120 feet below.

I had never had anything to do with Rhodesia and had to set about familiarizing myself with the situation. A brief summary of its history since 1945 sets the background. High hopes had for a time been raised by the formation of the Central African Federation, bringing together the colonies of Northern Rhodesia and Nyasaland and the *de facto,* if not *de jure,* self-governing dominion of Southern Rhodesia. This had broken up in 1963, ten years after it was founded, as the former colonies, as they became independent, disliked the domination of the Federation by the whites of Southern Rhodesia and the hard-liners among the latter saw the break-up as a way of escaping from the apron-strings of Westminster. This was followed, in 1965, by Rhodesia's Unilateral Declaration of Independence. Since then a series of meetings had taken place between successive British Governments and Ian Smith's rebel régime, centring on means of satisfying the five principles on which both Labour and Conservative governments had insisted before independence could be agreed. They were:

1 Unimpeded progress to majority rule.
2 Guarantees against retrogressive amendment of the constitution.
3 Immediate improvement in the political status of the Africans.
4 Progress towards ending racial discrimination.

5 Acceptability to the people of Rhodesia as a whole.

Harold Wilson's talks with Smith on board HMS *Tiger* in
1966 and *Fearless* in 1968 had failed to reach agreement; but
Alec Douglas-Home's talks in 1971 had succeeded, on a very
complicated formula which would have gradually increased
the black electorate until it became a majority. However this
failed the fifth principle, when the Pearce Commission set
out to sound out Rhodesian African opinion.

At that time the African nationalist leaders were in detention. There had originally been one movement, ZANU
(Zimbabwe African Nationalist Union), led by Joshua Nkomo
with Sithole as his deputy. In 1961 Nkomo had split off,
forming ZAPU (Zimbabwe African People's Union), leaving
Sithole with ZANU, Robert Mugabe being his secretary-
general. In 1971 they were all in detention. Somebody had
to represent African Nationalist opinion to the Pearce Commission and the mantle fell on Bishop Abel Muzorewa, who
hitherto had not taken an active part in politics. He thereafter
came to be regarded as a man of peace and goodwill, capable
of uniting all the nationalist factions, which were loosely
brought together under his titular presidency as the UANC
(United African Nationalist Council).

In December 1974, under pressure from South Africa,
Smith released Nkomo, Sithole and Mugabe from detention
and attempted to negotiate a settlement with the UANC, but
failed. This was partly because of a fundamental difference
between the two sides, which persisted for as long as I was
involved, Smith insisting on real power remaining in the
hands of the whites, conceding only the participation of
blacks in its exercise, while the nationalist leaders sought
a genuine transfer of power to their hands. But it was
also partly because of disagreements among the nationalists
themselves, some of it based on the tribal rivalry between
Matabele, represented by Nkomo, and the majority Shona,
to which the others belonged. Finally, also, it failed because
they all felt that they were negotiating under the threat
that, if they did not settle, they would return to detention.
Following the failure of these talks, Smith attempted to reach
agreement with Nkomo alone, Sithole and Mugabe having
left the country for Mozambique, by then independent of

Portugal, with the proclaimed aim of starting an armed struggle. Under renewed pressure from South Africa, whose Prime Minister Vorster cooperated with Zambia's President Kaunda to bring them together, Smith and Nkomo engaged in discussions between December 1975 and March 1976, in which Nkomo was prepared to agree to a qualified franchise giving the whites 25 per cent of seats in Parliament and an entrenched Bill of Rights. But Smith foolishly was not prepared to agree, and Nkomo, realizing that Smith was not going to accept a genuine transfer of power, went into voluntary exile in Zambia and declared that ZAPU also would resort to armed struggle. Muzorewa refused to relinquish the leadership of the UANC within Rhodesia, and at about the same time Mugabe split away from Sithole, taking the bulk of ZANU, certainly its most militant and communist element, with him.

Meanwhile the Foreign Office was trying to evolve a policy by which HMG could hope to bring about a settlement. The first essential seemed to be that Ian Smith must somehow be removed. Some other white Rhodesian, more acceptable to African opinion, should then form a caretaker government committed to the acceptance of majority rule within two years, in which the African nationalists would participate. Agreement would have to be established on the fundamentals of a future constitution and on the interim arrangements, while the details of the constitution were being worked out. Discussion should start on the basis of Nkomo's proposals. These interim arrangements would last until elections were held and independence guaranteed, and would be based on there being a majority of black ministers. The British Government would help with advice and with financing a scheme which it hoped would persuade whites to remain in the country. While these proposals had got no further than discussions within the Foreign Office, where Antony Crosland as Foreign Secretary was reluctant to burn his fingers by tackling Rhodesia, America's Secretary of State, Henry Kissinger, after the failure of his policy over Angola, decided to take the initiative in dealing with the problems of Southern Africa. In June 1976 he met Vorster in Geneva and as a result came to the conclusion that Vorster could deliver Smith. He suggested that Britain should reassume its authority over Rhodesia and install a Governor, although Smith might have to remain as political leader of the whites, a proposal which Callaghan and Crosland rejected. In September Kissinger went to South Africa to see Vorster and saw Smith also while he was there, with no British representative present. They agreed on five points:

1 Rhodesia agreed to majority rule within two years.
2 Representatives of the Rhodesian regime would meet immediately with African leaders to organize an interim government which would function until then.
3 The interim government would consist of:
   a A Council of State, half-African and half-European with a European chairman, who would not have a casting vote. It would be responsible for legislation, general supervision of government business and supervision of the drafting of the constitution.
   b A Council of Ministers with an African majority and an African First Minister, in which decisions would be taken by a two-thirds majority. The Ministers of Defence and for Law and Order would be European. The Council would have delegated legislative authority and executive responsibility.
4 The United Kingdom would enact enabling legislation to establish the interim government, as would also the Rhodesian parliament.
5 On the establishment of the interim government, sanctions would be lifted and all acts of war, including guerrilla warfare, would cease.

Kissinger flew on to Lusaka on 19 September and discussed these proposals with Presidents Kaunda and Nyerere. He then sent a message to Smith giving him the impression that they had agreed them, as a result of which Smith announced them in a broadcast on 24 September, also giving the impression that they had been agreed. This put HMG in a very embarrassing position. Not only had Kaunda and Nyerere not agreed them, but HMG had not either, and they had not even been discussed with, let alone been agreed by, the other Front Line Presidents, Machel of Mozambique,

Seretse Khama of Botswana and Neto of Angola, nor with any of the Rhodesian African Nationalist leaders. The Front Line Presidents called on Britain to convene a conference to arrange the transfer of power, and Ted Rowlands, Minister of State at the Foreign Office, set off on a tour of Africa to discuss who should be invited and where it should be held, while Kissinger impatiently pressed HMG to hold a conference.

The result was the Geneva Conference held from 28 October to 14 December, presided over by Britain's representative at the United Nations, Ivor Richards. It was doomed from the start. Smith assumed it was required merely to determine how the five points he had agreed with Kissinger should be implemented. It was up to the African nationalists to agree among themselves how the African-held portfolios would be distributed. The nationalists, however, were ill-prepared for negotiations. Nkomo and Mugabe, under pressure from the Front Line Presidents and the Organization for African Unity, had come loosely together in an association they called the Patriotic Front. Initially Sithole had not been invited, but Muzorewa, not wishing to find himself alone with the Patriotic Front, said he would not go unless Sithole came also, and he was then invited. All of them made clear that they did not accept that the five points were agreed. As it appeared impossible to get agreement on how the country should be governed during an interim period, covering the two years leading to majority rule, it was suggested that Britain should assume direct responsibility during the period; Smith was adamantly opposed to this. When the conference went into recess on 14 December, it was intended to resume on 17 January, Ivor Richards spending the interval in travelling round Africa in an attempt to find a basis for agreement. He was unsuccessful in bridging the gap between Smith's determination that the real control of events during the period should remain with the whites, while the Africans demanded real and irrevocable transfer of power to them, although they could not agree among themselves about who should receive it. Crosland therefore decided that there was no point in reconvening the conference, and, before any further progress had been made, he died and was succeeded by David Owen in February 1977.

Owen not only felt that Britain had a moral obligation to bring about a settlement, but he was prepared to involve himself personally, as Crosland had not been. He attached great importance also to involving the Americans. In March 1977, it was agreed that the two governments would cooperate in an attempt based on taking the initiative in proposing a solution, rather than just presiding neutrally over a negotiation. As a result John Graham of the Foreign Office and Stephen Low, the US Ambassador to Zambia, set off in May to Africa, seeing all the parties concerned, including the Front Line Presidents. They discovered that the differences between them on such matters as a future constitution, bill of rights, abolition of discrimination, etc. did not appear to be very wide. The biggest hurdle remained the method of exercising power during the transition period, especially in terms of security forces. Initially thoughts had turned to a Commonwealth or even a British force to ensure security, the former being preferred; but neither were real starters (as CDS I had vehemently opposed any suggestion of using British troops in Rhodesia). The final proposal based reliance on the Rhodesian police* backed by a United Nations Force. They went round again in July to try and sell their proposals, receiving a rebuff from Smith, who, a week after they had left, announced that he would hold a general election preparatory to making an attempt to reach a settlement with the internal African Leaders, Muzorewa, Sithole and Chief Chirau, for whom a somewhat bogus political party, ZUPO (Zimbabwe United People's Organization), had been formed. In August David Owen himself took over the baton and had held further talks with Vance and Vorster before he had met with me at Shawbury.

The week after my return from holiday, I went up to London to get myself briefed and had another meeting with Owen. He told me that unfortunately, following a visit by Nyerere to Washington, President Carter had written Nyerere a letter in which he confirmed that, under the Anglo–American proposals, the future army of Zimbabwe would be 'based primarily on the liberation forces'. Owen

* Still known as the British South African Police, having originally been the private police force of the British South Africa Company recruited by Rhodes to escort the original Pioneer Column.

realized that this would never be accepted by Salisbury and probably not by Pretoria, but said that the best he had been able to do had been to get American agreement that in all official papers the word 'primarily' should be omitted, although he had to accept that, if Nyerere chose, he might reveal it. He also told me that Nkomo, in a recent conversation with him, had repeated the assurance he had previously given that he wished to see the existing Rhodesian armed forces maintained as an effective force after independence. I pointed out to him that even 'based on the liberation forces' was an entirely different concept from that I had understood was intended when I had accepted the appointment at Shawbury, and he acknowledged this. I had to consider whether or not I should now back out, before my appointment had been announced. It would clearly be very embarrassing to the Government if I did, and it was no fault of theirs – neither they nor even the State Department had been consulted about the wording of Carter's letter, which had probably been written on the advice of Andrew Young, the black American ambassador to the United Nations, who thought the British much too inclined to favour the whites. With great misgivings, therefore, I confirmed that I would carry on. I was given a draft of the White Paper* announcing the proposals, which it was intended to publish on 2 September, the day after Owen planned to see Smith at the end of a tour of African capitals in company with Andy Young, which itself would be the day after the Rhodesian elections. I was also given a paper on Law and Order, which I only had time to glance through before leaving. It was a revision of a draft, supplementary to the White Paper, which I had seen at Shawbury and in which I had suggested some changes. I raised one personal problem with Owen. I had long promised Edith that I would take her on holiday to Greece after I had retired, and we had planned to leave in mid-September, visiting Jordan beforehand to stay with our ambassador, John Moberly, and his wife Patience, who was Edith's first cousin. We did not plan to return until 7 October. My first involvement would be discussions with whomever the UN Secretary-General appointed as his representative, and after

* Comd 6919, 1 September 1977.

that joint talks with 'all the parties concerned' in order
to try and bring about a cease-fire; but, before this could
happen, the proposals would have to be presented to the
Security Council and the Secretary-General authorized to
act. Although Owen was optimistic about the speed with
which everything would go forward, he thought it unlikely
that I should be required before mid-October. He encouraged me to go, saying that he would call me back if necessary.
On 31 August, the day before Owen, then in Nairobi, was
due in Salisbury, I was summoned to London to comment
on the press statement Owen had drafted for himself to
make in Salisbury next day, before it was submitted to the
Prime Minister. It would be accompanied by an announcement that I had been designated as Resident Commissioner
under the proposals, which would be published at the same
time. The best part of the statement was a sentence saying
that the British government and parliament would not formally appoint the Resident Commissioner unless they were
satisfied not only that there would be an effective cease-
fire, but that the outcome of the preliminary negotiations,
in which I would engage, was 'generally acceptable to the
parties concerned and will provide a climate in which free
and fair elections can be held and a stable independent
government of Zimbabwe can be formed within six months
of a return to legality'. I was still far from happy about the
wording concerning the future Zimbabwe National Army,
which ran: 'Enrolment in this army will be open to all
citizens, but it will be based on the liberation forces: it will
also include acceptable elements of the Rhodesian Defence
Forces.' However Owen had signalled that this formula had
only been negotiated with the greatest difficulty with the
Front Line Presidents and that any attempt to alter it would
forfeit even the limited support they were prepared to give
the proposals 'as a basis for negotiation'. I felt that I could
just live with it, and that it should be possible somehow to
find a solution which would at least meet the letter of the
undertaking, but which also had some hope of acceptance
by the Rhodesians and of working in practice.

The Prime Minister approved the statement, which would
be made at 1 p.m. Salisbury time, 3.30 p.m. London time,
next day, 1 September, immediately following the meeting

of Owen and Young with Smith. I was to meet the press at the Foreign Office at 6 p.m. When I did, the main point of interest was naturally my views on the practicability of an integration between the Rhodesian armed forces and those of the Patriotic Front. I pointed out that the formation of the British regular army was an amalgamation, carried out by General Monck at the Restoration in 1660, of elements from Charles II's Royalist forces that had served with him in exile and those of Cromwell's New Model Army, a comparison which I admitted was far-fetched. Ian Smith's immediate public reaction had been to describe the concept as 'crazy'. In fact, I was told, he had spent so much time arguing against the appointment of a new Commissioner of Police that this key problem appears to have been little discussed, one reason, no doubt, for his being taken aback by the prominence given to the subject and the exact words used in Owen's press statement.

Owen telephoned me soon after his return and, in a long description of what had passed, said that the views expressed in private were much more hopeful than the public statements; that he had been impressed with General Obasanjo of Nigeria, President Machel of Mozambique and Prime Minister Vorster of South Africa as 'tough realists'. Over the weekend C. G. Tracey telephoned me from Rhodesia and suggested a meeting between myself and General Peter Walls, Chairman of the Rhodesian Joint Operations Committee. I said that it would have to be an official invitation and that I saw no objection to a meeting on neutral ground somewhere in Europe, and suggested the following weekend. However, when I saw Owen again on 7 September, he was not in favour, thinking it would give the impression that I was in collusion with the whites, if I got together with Walls before the UN Secretary-General had appointed a Special Representative. By that time in any case Smith had vetoed it. At our meeting Owen outlined future procedure as he saw it. The UN Security Council would be asked to authorize the Secretary-General to appoint a Special Representative, whom he hoped would be the UN Force Commander designate, in his preference a Nigerian. I would discuss with the latter the future of the Zimbabwe National Army, the means of bringing about a cease-fire and the function of the UN Force and other forces in the transition period. We would then both set off together round the perimeter, concentrating on those who could bring pressure to bear on the Patriotic Front, i.e. Nigeria, Kenya, Tanzania, Zambia and Mozambique, and then go on to South Africa and Rhodesia. If our discussions appeared to lead to the basis of a cease-fire, HMG would ask the Security Council to form a UN Force, and, if Smith had still not accepted, South Africa would be asked to pull the rug out from under him. If they refused, and not till then, they would be threatened with sanctions themselves on oil and arms supplies. He expected the whole process to take two or three months. His visits had given him the impression that it might be easier to make progress on military matters than on political. In the six days between then and our departure for Jordan, I assembled a military staff, which the Military Secretary, Robert Ford, had been most helpful in providing at very short notice. They were all first-class officers, Colonel Jeremy Reilly, Lieutenant-Colonel Willie Rous, Major Roger Wheeler, Captain Mike Weedy and Captain Chris Price. Johnnie Graham himself was nominated as my future Deputy to oversee the civil government and political side, while Michael Weir, an expert on the Middle East, was lent to me as a political adviser and James Allan appointed as our liaison officer in the Rhodesia Department in the Foreign Office. As Commissioner of Police designate I had my eye on Roy Henry, then Deputy Commissioner in Hong Kong, who had been such a great success in Sarawak during and after 'confrontation' and in Fiji before he went to Hong Kong. In spite of the difficulties the Hong Kong police were facing at the time, the Governor, Murray Maclehose, was prepared to release him and Roy Henry himself was willing to take it on. As guidelines on which to work while I was in Jordan and Greece, I gave my staff an outline of my ideas for the future Zimbabwe Army, the essentials for a cease-fire and the principles on which maintenance of law and order should be based. I envisaged the disbandment of all specifically anti-terrorist units (that of the Selous Scouts had already been specified) and of purely European units, the regular Rhodesian Light Infantry and those in the Territorial Army, but the retention of the three battalions of the Rhodesian

African Rifles and the Africanization of the supporting arms. 'Based on the liberation forces' would be catered for by the formation of four regular battalions from the Patriotic Front and 'all citizens'. The regular force would be backed up by two forms of reserve, one of about 4000 to bring the regular forces up to war strength, the other of about 10,000, which I suggested should be called the Zimbabwe National Guard. It would be distributed throughout the country in infantry and pioneer companies, its arms held in central armouries, guarded during the transition period by the UN Force and after independence by the regular army. I saw this body as the principal method of absorbing the ex-guerrillas and, while in practice disarming them, letting them retain the status of soldiers and, if they wished, employing them on 'hearts and minds' schemes for the development of the Tribal Trust Lands. This plan would give the future army a regular strength of 10,000 and a reserve of 14,000. On the assumption that the regulars would have to be paid at least as much as the Rhodesian African soldiers were currently receiving, and the reservists something when they were called up, this was certainly as large an army as Zimbabwe would be able to afford; on the assumption that independence had been peacefully achieved and that the country would be at peace with its neighbours, she would not need a larger one. While this army was being formed – and I had no illusions about the extreme difficulty of obtaining genuine agreement on it, achieving and maintaining a cease-fire and thereafter implementing the plan – the task of keeping the peace in a period when emotions and tempers would be running high, would rest fairly and squarely on the police. However distasteful to the nationalists their image might be, and there was no doubt that it was, it would not be possible to govern the country, hold free and fair elections and effect a peaceful transfer of power to an independent Zimbabwe, based on majority rule, if the police were to undergo a radical transformation at the same time. Apart from a change at the top, which I regarded as essential, I set my face firmly against being committed to any changes in the police in the transition period that were not recommended to me by my own choice of Commissioner. Although the White Paper had envisaged a role for the UN Force in 'support of the civil power', I realized from my own UN experience that both the political restriction which the UN would impose on it and the nature of the force itself would severely limit its effectiveness in that field. I laid particular emphasis on the importance of seeing that no body of armed men, of whatever kind or origin, should be able to bring pressure to bear during the transition period which could prejudice the freedom and fairness of the elections, which were to be its culmination and its main purpose. This was the main reason for insisting that all armed forces during this period should be under the orders of the Resident Commissioner and no one else.

Having assembled my staff and outlined my ideas to them, I left them in the suite of offices which had been provided in the attics of the Foreign Office near the Rhodesia Department, and set off for Jordan and Greece. I had originally intended to stop for a few days in Cyprus also in order to talk to Makarios about his dealings with Lord Harding, when the latter had been Governor of Cyprus and had exiled him to the Seychelles. He had said he would be very happy to do so and I had fixed a day, but he had died earlier in the year and we only spent one night at Episkopi with the army commander, Brigadier John Acland, having flown out by RAF VC10 on an indulgence flight, continuing next day by Cyprus Airways to Amman.

We had a marvellous holiday. The Moberlys gave us a rushed but comprehensive tour of the sights, including Jerash and Petra, which we toiled round on foot and which I had always longed to see. Official engagements were limited to a call on the Chief of the Armed Forces, who gave a dinner party for us of all the principal figures. King Hussein was away in Amman and I did not therefore call on him. I had met him twice before, once at a private dinner given to him by Julian Amery when I was CGS, and later at a dinner at No. 10 Downing Street when I was CDS. On 18 September we flew by Royal Jordan Airways to Athens, where we spent the next three days sightseeing very energetically in considerable heat, including going to Sounion and back by local bus.

On 22 September, hiring a small car, we set off for the Peloponnese, following much the same route as I had done in 1938. At Mycenae I was delighted to find a room at the Belle Helène, which had not changed much since I had stayed there then, apart from the erection of a large patio restaurant in front. We were the only guests in the hotel, and, after dinner, I managed to carry on a primitive form of conversation with old Agamemnon, the proprietor's father, who had run the hotel when I had been there before and had originally worked with the British School in excavating Mycenae and other nearby sites. In spite of his having forgotten his English and I most of my Greek, we managed to communicate. Having visited Epidaurus, which I had missed on the previous occasion, we made our way to Mistra, which, although greatly changed, impressed me as much as before.

Next day the clouds were well down over the Taygetos mountains and I therefore decided to go the long way round by Githion and Areopolis instead of straight over the top. It took us through the desolate country of the Maniotes before we turned north again up the coast road between the mountains and the sea to Kalamata, stopping to see the ruined castle of Zarnata on the way. By this time the weather had improved and, after a good cheap lunch and a visit to the citadel at Kalamata, we motored on to Pylos, a beautiful little harbour with its citadel overlooking the Bay of Navarino, where in 1827 Admiral Codrington's Anglo–Russo–French fleet of 26 ships destroyed 53 ships of the Turkish and Egyptian fleets without losing one of their own, a decisive step on the way to Greek independence. The citadel itself with its impressive walls and attractive Byzantine church and its view over the bay was a delightful spot. After a glorious bathe on a sandy beach south of Mount Kaifa, we reached Olympia and revelled in its beauty.

We spent two nights there, Willie Rous ringing me up from London to say that he saw no need for me to cut short my holiday, although things were beginning to move in the UN. On 29 September the Security Council adopted Resolution 415, calling on the Secretary-General to appoint a representative to enter into discussions with me and with 'all the parties' on the military and associated arrangements considered necessary to effect the transition to majority rule in Rhodesia. However, I decided to start back earlier. We had originally planned to go north after Delphi to see the monasteries of the Meteora before returning to Athens via the island of Euboea, but it would have meant a lot of driving and money was running short. As it looked as if I might be needed earlier in any case, we decided to return to Athens after Delphi, to which we set off next day. There we stayed in a simple bed and breakfast hotel, recommended to us by the hotelier at Olympia, where, from our room, we had a wonderful view over the valley to the south. We had glorious weather in which to admire the sanctuary and the striking view from it. On our way back to Athens, we visited the monastery of Osios Loukas and the ruins of Amphiareion, tucked away among the pine trees, spending our last night at the seaside resort of Vougliameni for a final bathe.

On my return I was delighted that the UN Secretary-General, Kurt Waldheim, had appointed the Indian Lieutenant-General Prem Chand as his representative under Resolution 415. He had been Commander of the UN Force in Cyprus all the time I had been CGS and CDS and I had always visited him on my visits to Cyprus. I saw him at London Airport on his way through to New York and put him in the picture, and, after seeing the Secretary-General, he returned to London. We then had very useful discussions with him, his political adviser, James Jonah of Sierra Leone, and his military adviser, Lieutenant Colonel Gerry O'Sullivan of Ireland. We found ourselves in full agreement on almost every issue. In previous discussions with US State Department officials, led by Dick Moose, we had had some difficulty in persuading them that our plans met the requirement of 'based on the liberation forces' and I came under considerable pressure to amend them to make them more acceptable to the Patriotic Front and the Front Line Presidents. In resisting this, I had the firm backing of David Owen, although I was under pressure from him to accept modifications to the Anglo–American proposals over replacement of judges and in extending the numbers and function of advisory councils.

Ian Smith had by then adopted a less scornful attitude to the proposals and had invited Prem Chand and myself to visit Rhodesia 'to see the situation for ourselves'. However it was thought preferable that our first meeting should be with Africans and a meeting with Nyerere and the Patriotic Front in Dar es Salaam had been fixed for 1 November. After that we would go on to Salisbury to see both the internal nationalist leaders and Smith's military men, hoping to include other Front Line capitals as well. Meanwhile Graham would return to Salisbury to discuss matters such as the independence constitution, which did not relate to the transition period. Prem Chand was restricted to 'military and associated arrangements' under Resolution 415, whereas I was empowered to discuss all aspects of the transition period, with Michael Weir as my political and Henry Steel as my legal adviser. David Owen hoped that we would make progress and expected that I might find myself shuttling to and fro, out of the country for some time. I needed an aircraft which would hold all my staff and be able to go almost anywhere. After discussion with the Ministry of Defence we agreed that, taking all factors into account, a RAF Hercules, fitted up to be as comfortable as a Hercules could be, which was not very, would be the best. My unfortunate staff had to fly all the way to Dar es Salaam in it, while Michael Weir, Henry Steel and I flew British Airways to Nairobi, where we were picked up by the Hercules and taken on to Dar es Salaam, arriving in time for an interview with Nyerere before lunch and our first meeting with Nkomo and Mugabe and their delegations in the afternoon at the residence of our High Commissioner, Mervyn Brown. Prem Chand and his staff had arrived separately, as had Steve Low, who was to accompany me throughout. Nyerere was in affable mood. He said he had only two questions to ask me, neither of which he expected me to answer: how was I going to form the Zimbabwe army and how were we going to get rid of Smith. I gave him an outline of my plan for the former, with which he appeared content, and said that the latter was not my business.

I was in uniform for my meeting with the Patriotic Front in order to emphasize that we were supposed to be discussing 'military and associated' matters. Nkomo, who had difficulty extricating his vast bulk from a Volvo car, and Mugabe did their best to appear in harmony, Nkomo taking the lead in discussion. He opened by challenging me about what we were there for, quickly moving on to object to my proposing to discuss 'military and associated' matters with Muzorewa and Sithole, who had no military men and were not fighting the war for liberation. They made clear that they did not accept the proposed position of the Resident Commissioner

or his powers, and were not prepared to discuss matters
of substance. I explained the outline of my plans for the
Zimbabwe army, the conditions for a cease-fire and the
functions of a UN Force, as well as the general concept of
government during the transition period. They refused to
comment, taking the line that nothing could be done unless
Britain, who remained responsible for Rhodesia, got rid of
Smith and negotiated direct with them. Having been warned
that Nkomo could easily be provoked to rage, I kept the
atmosphere as cool as it could be in the heat, Nkomo shaking
with laughter rather than rage at one point, although Prem
Chand's emphasis on 'all the parties' threatened storm. It
was clear that they were in no mood for progress, almost
certainly having had considerable difficulty in agreeing a
common line between them. However I managed to extract
their agreement to a further meeting, preferably in Malta,
with ourselves and representatives of the Smith regime, if
all matters relating to the transition period were on the
agenda and if Smith's representatives were, at least for
appearance's sake, regarded as members of the British delegation, a point of principle which I did not concede. We
had allowed for two days of discussion, but had little more
than two hours, the press remarking on the brevity of the
meeting. Nkomo, who had concealed his destination, left for
Moscow that evening. Next day we gave a description of what
had occurred to Nyerere's able and sympathetic Foreign
Minister, Ben MKapa, lunched with Prem Chand and his
staff at their seaside hotel, had a swim in its pool and walked
about the beach.

On Wednesday 2 November we flew to Salisbury, Prem
Chand travelling separately by charter aircraft to emphasize
his independence. I chose to wear uniform and for my
military staff to do so, partly to assert the right of a British
Field Marshal, travelling in one of Her Majesty's Royal Air
Force aircraft, to do so in Rhodesia, partly because we were to
meet the Rhodesian Joint Operations Committee (JOC), who
would be in uniform themselves. We were greeted correctly
by the head of protocol and by Jack Gaylard, the Secretary
to Smith's Cabinet. Willie Rous and I then left in an ancient
pre-UDI hired Rover, driven by an African chauffeur in a
garish yellow and green uniform, to Mirimba House, which

had been the British High Commissioner's house and was
still retained by the British government. It had recently
been opened up by Jeremy Varcoe, detached from the High
Commission in Lusaka. The police did not officially escort
us, although they were everywhere about, looking glum and
rather embarrassed. A few, including those at the gate of
Mirimba, saluted. By the time I left four days later, they all
did. A feeble demonstration of Chirau's supporters greeted
us at the gates, one banana being thrown which bounced
on the roof of the car. That afternoon Prem Chand and I
and our staffs met the JOC, led by General Peter Walls. I
reminded them of the basic principles of the Anglo–American proposals and explained my proposals for the Zimbabwe
National Army and the essential elements, as I saw them, of
a cease-fire. Prem Chand described his ideas (many of which
we had in fact suggested) for the function and organization
of a UN Force. Apart from a brief discussion of the suggestion for integration of the Patriotic Front forces, in which
General Hickman, the army commander, made it clear that
he would only agree to accept them if they enlisted in
the Rhodesian forces in the normal way, they made no
comment, making it clear that they were not allowed to do
so. They said that they would report all I had said (which was
tape-recorded) and we arranged to meet again the following
afternoon. The atmosphere was formal but friendly, and at
the end the Commissioner of Police (in whose officers' mess
the meeting was held) invited us all to have a drink. Although
it was only 5.30 p.m. I judged it would be impolite to refuse.
While we were drinking, Walls told me that they had all been
summoned away (the news had come in while we had been
talking that a rocket attack had taken place on a hotel near
the Victoria Falls, which had caught fire). I thought that we
should therefore leave as well. As I passed the prominently
displayed Visitors' Book, I hesitated to see if I were asked to
sign it. As I was not, I continued on and got into my car to
return to Mirimba. Later that evening our contact with their
head of intelligence, Ken Flower, told me that Flower had
complained that I had given offence by being in uniform
without seeking Rhodesian permission, by leaving the Mess
after only a short period and by not signing the Visitors'
Book, an indication of Rhodesian touchiness. In fact, several

months later Walls told Peter Carrington, when he visited Salisbury, that he had been impressed with the courteous and sympathetic way in which I had behaved.

Next morning, in plain clothes this time and for the rest of my visit, we had a meeting with Gaylard and some of his colleagues in the government buildings. As I was going in, a journalist asked if we were making progress, to which I replied 'Oh, yes'. Unlike the JOC, Gaylard and his colleagues, as well as asking questions, were prepared to discuss in depth and detail. The problem of the future of the armed forces was clearly the key issue, and they also raised the question of the replacement of the Police Commissioner. But they also made it clear that they had no authority to budge on any issue. Gaylard took the line, with which we were to become very familiar, that, if they made a settlement with the internal leaders, support for the Patriotic Front would fade away, Nkomo would join the settlement and Mugabe be left out in the cold. In answer to my request that their representatives should come to a meeting with the Patriotic Front, probably in Malta, to discuss 'military and associated matters', Gaylard said he would have to ask Smith, and I asked him to arrange for me to see him also. Back at Mirimba House for lunch, I received a message that my meeting with the JOC, arranged for that afternoon, was 'cancelled'. The reason given was that, as they had not been given authority to discuss matters in any further depth, there was no point in our meeting. However, on the following day, they agreed that Colonel Reilly and Major Wheeler of my staff could visit theirs in order to explain in further detail any question they might have. This led to an invitation by General Hickman, which was accepted, for them to stay behind for a few days after I had left to be briefed about the Rhodesian Armed Forces and the general situation. That evening I gave a small drinks party for those considered to be among the more influential of the 'liberal' whites. It included Hector McNally and Alan Savory of the National Unifying Force, Evan Campbell, C.G. Tracey and David Lewis from the business community, Dr Craig, Rector of the University, Roy Welensky and others. Roy Welensky was pessimistic. He warned me not to believe that Smith was held back from being more progressive by his reactionary colleagues. He was as hard-line as any of them.

He also correctly predicted that, to solve their manpower problems, the Rhodesian Army was about to increase significantly its recruitment of Africans. McNally and Savory emphasized how little influence they were able to wield, particularly in the face of the combination of government censorship and control of television and radio.

On 4 November Bishop Muzorewa came to Mirimba with a large delegation, supported also by a crowd of demonstrators, mostly female, who had walked from the centre of the city and chanted outside the gates, while we were talking. After I had recited my piece, with which by now I was becoming very familiar, Muzorewa read out a series of prepared statements, setting out his party's position, which in most cases demanded rather more than the Anglo–American proposals were prepared to give. His attitude to my proposals for the future army was noncommittal. He was in favour of the integration of 'liberation forces', but claimed that few ex-guerrillas of the Patriotic Front would wish to join, as they had been recruited under duress and would want to return to civilian life, school etc. He claimed that 85 per cent of their fighters within Rhodesia would support him and that, if there were a settlement, he could persuade them to stop fighting. His main concern was to claim that he had as much right as the Patriotic Front to be included in discussions on 'military and associated matters', including a cease-fire. I tried to distinguish between talks about a cease-fire, which could only be with those who were actually fighting, i.e. the Rhodesian security forces and the Patriotic Front, and those which concerned the future of the armed forces and other matters affecting the transition period and independence, in which he, as leader of one of the nationalist movements, had every right to be represented. This did not satisfy him. When I asked him if he would accept that separate talks should be held, one set with the Rhodesian regime and the Patriotic Front, and the other with the Rhodesian regime and the internal leaders, he asked for a recess to consult his colleagues. He had throughout appeared unwilling, perhaps unable, to reply directly to any question without whispered consultations with them. After a long break, we reassembled and he replied that his party would be prepared to accept my proposal for separate talks. When I tried to obtain his views about my proposals for the future Zimbabwe army, he said that he would need time to study them: when pressed as to whether or not he would regard the Rhodesian African Rifles as 'acceptable elements', he said that they were 'probably all right', but other units would have to go. I was far from impressed with the Bishop and not pleased that, after he had left, his flock outside the gates increased their tempo, the ladies threatening to bare their breasts if something, unspecified, were not done. Having sent a delegation of my staff, with members of the police and the Rhodesian security service, down to talk to them, they dispersed fully clothed.

The other nationalist cleric, the Reverend Ndabiningi Sithole, came in the afternoon with a smaller delegation and no chanting supporters. He made a very different impression, suave, eloquent, reasonable and intelligent. He expressed himself more fully a supporter of the Anglo–American proposals than the Bishop, but took the same line over 'military and associated matters', i.e. that he had his own fighters, that they would answer his call if a settlement could be arrived at, and that he was therefore entitled to participate in military talks, including any concerned with a cease-fire. When I cast doubt on this, he offered to take me to meet his guerrilla leaders 'in the bush', an invitation I could clearly not accept, although Prem Chand nearly did so, until persuaded by James Jonah and Gerry O'Sullivan that it would have unacceptable implications. He raised no objections to my proposals for the future army, but concentrated his criticism on the lack of any representation of the nationalist parties in the Resident Commissioner's transitional government. He made the point, which impressed me, that it would be difficult to persuade the liberation fighter to lay down his arms, if the only change were from a White Rhodesian regime to one headed by a white British Field Marshal. He advocated an advisory council on which he and other nationalist leaders would sit, as would a representative of the whites. I did not reject this, pointing out that the proposals empowered me to appoint advisory councils, but I was careful not to commit myself, as the principal aim of the proposals was to avoid the arguments about who should participate, in what proportion and with what powers, during such a period. Apart from his claim to control guerrillas, Sithole impressed me.

I had intended to leave on the Saturday for Botswana and was hoping therefore to see Smith either next day, Friday, or at the latest on Saturday morning. He had gone to Bulawayo to attend a Rhodesian Front rally and the message I received from Gaylard was that he wished me to see Chief Chirau and his ZUPO delegation before he would commit himself to seeing me. I resisted this. Not only was HMG at that stage reluctant to accept Chirau on a footing equal to the other four nationalist leaders, seeing him largely as Smith's puppet, but it would even further complicate the problem of getting 'all the parties' concerned to a conference table. Chirau could clearly not claim in any way to have an army of his own and therefore to be concerned with 'military and associated matters'. While not refusing to see Chirau, I did nothing about it and had to be careful to keep to Mirimba House and not be seen to have time on my hands. I therefore fell back on the argument that Chirau was not concerned with 'military and associated matters' and that, as John Graham was in Salisbury and was discussing matters concerned with the constitution and post-transition affairs, there was no need for me to see him.

That evening we gave a buffet supper at Mirimba for Walls, Gaylard and their colleagues, a valuable evening in a relaxed atmosphere in which Prem Chand and I were able to have a fairly uninhibited talk over dinner with Walls and Gaylard. The principal division of opinion was over the future of the armed forces and the police, the need to maintain standards in government generally, if the whites were to stay and the economy of the country be maintained, and their advocacy of the view that an internal settlement would itself bring about a cease-fire. Whether or not they really believed it, I could not say. They recognized that it was unlikely to work unless Nkomo were included. Both made much of Shona–Matabele rivalry and the danger of a civil war between the two if the regular forces and police were emasculated or politicized. Almost all the Rhodesian whites to whom I spoke agreed that Nkomo was the only African who had the standing and the ability and character to dominate. Mugabe was widely regarded as an outcast, having thrown in his lot with communism and relying on intimidation for his support. Before this supper, Smith in a speech in Bulawayo had scornfully rejected the idea that my talks were making any progress. My laconic 'Oh, yes' had prompted him to say that he was surprised that I tolerated on my staff someone to brief the press who was 'a bloody liar'. I was informed that he could not see me on the Saturday, as he would not return to Salisbury until late that evening. I had to consider for how long I ought to postpone my departure. I could clearly not hang about indefinitely at his beck and call. On the other hand to go off in a huff without seeing him would also be to play into his hand. Whether or not it was a deliberate ploy of his, partly perhaps to try and force me to see Chirau, I do not know. As the engagement which kept him in Bulawayo was watching a cricket match, it looked like a deliberate brush-off. I had said that the latest hour to which I could postpone my departure was 10.30 a.m. on Sunday.

On the Saturday morning I saw Josiah Chinamano, a Shona who was the representative of Nkomo's ZAPU inside Rhodesia. Although not departing in principle from the official Patriotic Front line, he was much more reasonable in his approach and clearly favoured a meeting between 'all the parties'. I found him a charming and *sympathique* character, a judgement which was confirmed by my next visitor, Mr Connell of the Rhodesian Red Cross. His message was that what the African wanted above all was human dignity, not to be treated as a second-class citizen in his own country. A peaceful settlement was urgently needed, as health services were breaking down in the Tribal Trust lands, contributed to by the lowered standard of nutrition.

It was finally arranged that Prem Chand, with James Jonah, and I, with Steve Low, Michael Weir and Willie Rous, should see Smith at his official residence at 8.30 a.m. on Sunday. He was accompanied by Van der Byl, Minister for External Affairs, Hilary Squires, Minister for Law and Order, Hawkins, Minister for the Armed Forces, and Gaylard. The atmosphere was correct and cool. Smith opened by asking why I had not seen Chirau, and, when I had given my reason, he complained at the way HMG treated Chirau, and we passed on to other matters. I rehearsed my familiar part and gave him a resumé of the discussions we had had. He said we were putting the cart before the horse.

He could not discuss transitional arrangements until the main political decisions had been made. As a soldier I should not get involved in political matters. I said that it seemed to me that the principal political decision was for him to make: did he or did he not accept the principle of majority rule based on universal adult suffrage, one person, one vote? He sharply replied that he had never committed himself to this 'without safeguards', and that one of the principal safeguards was the preservation of the security forces. He made clear that he rejected any plan 'based on the liberation forces'. I said that the difficult problem of how to get those who were fighting for what they regarded as their freedom to stop fighting could not be wished away. Somehow or other they would have to be satisfied that they had achieved what they had been fighting for, and that, if they laid down their arms, they would not be cheated of it. I quoted Sithole in support of this. He trotted out the Muzorewa line and went further, maintaining that, once an internal settlement had been reached, 90 per cent of the guerrillas outside the country would desert the Patriotic Front and stop fighting. It was the support of the Front Line States that kept the war going. At one stage he said that my task was to control the Patriotic Front. I cast doubt on this view, and said that I thought that any settlement which did not include them would mean that the war would go on for a long time. I then asked him if he would send his military representatives to a meeting in Malta with the Patriotic Front, which we had provisionally arranged for 16 November. He said he would not, as political matters would be involved, Hawkins chipping in to say that they could not possibly leave the country while there was a war on. I then suggested that, in that case, he should send political representatives. He replied that he would only consider it if HMG were prepared to send political representatives to confer beforehand in Rhodesia with his representatives and those of the internal leaders. I said I had no authority to agree to this, but would inform the Foreign Secretary. I then drove straight to the airport, where I spoke to the press before flying off. I said that I had found a wide measure of agreement on several fundamental matters, but that there were still differences to overcome.

My next stop was at Gaborone, my RAF Hercules being

the largest aircraft ever to land on its small airfield. Next morning I met President Seretse Khama and his colleagues, including his son Ian, dressed as a brigadier and then second-in-command of Botswana's small army. All I had to say was met with warm approval, and the whole atmosphere was friendly, informal, cooperative and full of common sense. Although my next port of call was Lusaka in order to see President Kaunda, we had some problems over flight clearance to enter Zambian airspace, but it was eventually sorted out and we went on there, lunching in the air. My first meeting was with Mr Mwale, the External Affairs Minister, and it did not augur well. We then went on to see Kaunda, the meeting to be followed by a dinner for us all in State House. I and Prem Chand played over the now well-worn record and I gave a summary of the discussions I had had in Dar es Salaam and Salisbury. Kaunda listened carefully to what I had to say and then declared that he would have to think and talk it over with his colleagues and meet again next day. This was disconcerting as I had planned to leave early to fly to Lagos and we had already had difficulty in obtaining flight clearance over Zaire. However I had no alternative but to agree to some hours' postponement. When we met again at a fairly early hour next morning, he was in sombre mood. He kept reiterating his demand for Smith's removal, maintaining that Owen and Young had undertaken to effect this, and that nothing could be achieved until it was done. 'Who will bell the cat?', he kept on saying. He went on to urge that elections should be postponed until some years after independence. If they were held after a transition period of six months, the man who came out ahead of the others would not command allegiance and the result would be civil war. Smith should be removed and power handed over to the Patriotic Front, who should be encouraged to form a government of national unity to include the other nationalist leaders. This of course was a radical departure from the Anglo–American proposals and I could only say that I would report what he had said to the Foreign Secretary. We left feeling that we had not got any further in hoping that he would bring pressure to bear on the Patriotic Front to take a more accommodating line.

The long flight (seven and a half hours) in a Hercules to Lagos was not the ideal form of air travel. Prem Chand was

able to look down at various places in Zaire where he had
been engaged in the UN Force there. At Lagos, I spent the
night with our High Commissioner, Sam Falle, whom I had
known in the Far East, and we went, together with Prem
Chand and the US Ambassador, to see President Obasanjo
and his principal colleagues next morning. Prem Chand and
I repeated our well-worn performance and I described the
discussions we had had. A number of questions were asked
and I gained the impression that Obasanjo and his colleagues
thought that our proposals were reasonable. The problem
was to get them implemented and the obstacle was Smith,
the discussion returning to the question of how he was to
be removed, a matter I said was not my business. But as
long as the Patriotic Front took an unreasonable line, it was
difficult to bring pressure to bear for Smith's removal. If they
accepted the proposals, it would be another matter.

On my return to London, I reported to David Owen
both in person and in a written note. I said that I had
found two radically opposed views. The first, those that
recognized the Patriotic Front as the only organization which
could validly claim to fight for freedom for the Rhodesian
African, and took the line that those who had compromised
or would compromise with Smith were traitors: HMG should
get rid of Smith and hand over power to them. 'Apart
from political and emotional reasons,' I wrote, 'such a policy
would suit Zambia and Mozambique in ensuring that they
would cease to bear the burden of supporting Patriotic
Front forces in their countries and of facing hostile forces
across their borders.' The opposing view, held by most white
Rhodesians as well as Muzorewa, Sithole and Chirau, was
that the majority of Rhodesian Africans did not support
the Patriotic Front, which was an artificial creation of the
Front Line Presidents: that the vast majority would support
an internal settlement and feared that, if the Patriotic Front
came to power, they would take their revenge both against
all Africans who had been associated with the government
and the administration in any way and against their political
rivals. HMG could not support either view. The first was
morally unacceptable. It would be fought to the bitter end
by the white Rhodesians, who, if they lost, would abandon
the country. Talk of 'belling the cat' and bringing pressure

to bear on Smith through South Africa led down this road. But HMG could not support the other view either. For one thing, it would lead to an intensification of the war, not an end to it, with the OAU turning further towards support of the communist bloc. The argument was about who should wield real power. As I wrote:

> Power in Africa derives from popular, emotional support, affected more by tribal affiliation than by political ideologies, from possession of the machinery of government and from the barrel of the gun. The white Rhodesians are not prepared to hand over the last two, unless they are satisfied that the rivalries over the first are not going to tear the country apart and undermine the security of which they require to be assured, if they are to remain physically and commercially.

Smith and Kaunda both feared the division of the country after independence; the former tried to insure against it by preserving white control, while trying to give it a credible black façade, the latter by a handover to the Patriotic Front, which incorporated both Matabele and Shona elements, in the hope that support would swing to the man who held the real reins of power in his hand. The only way out of the dilemma I could suggest was for HMG to be the agent through whom Nkomo and his followers were weaned away from the Patriotic Front's extreme element and brought together with the internal leaders, while keeping the international pressures against it at bay. 'The bait will have to be,' I wrote, 'to satisfy him somehow that the machinery of government and of security will fall into his hands, and that it must be, in its essentials, the machinery which exists today. It would be a hollow victory for him, if he achieved power only in a country of which the machinery of government and of security, as well as the economy, had collapsed into the sort of chaos which occurred in Algeria, the Congo, Angola and Mozambique.' I suggested that the first step was to build on the proposal for parallel talks which emerged from my discussion with Muzorewa and with Smith; but the attempt to separate military and political talks was artificial. They should be presided over by a Minister with myself present.

19

All Africa

There is all Africa, and her prodigies in us.
Sir Thomas Browne (1605–1682), *Cyrus's Garden*

When Nkomo learned that Smith had refused to take part in the talks we had provisionally arranged for 16 November in Malta, he refused to attend and announced that the Anglo–American proposals were dead. On 24 November Smith announced his intention of seeking a settlement with the internal leaders, and shortly afterwards carried out a major raid on Patriotic Front camps in Mozambique, of which Muzorewa expressed his disapproval by abstaining from talks with Smith for a week. The period up to the end of the year was spent in meetings in London with the Americans, the Nationalist leaders and others on their way through, and Brand Fourie, the Permanent Under-Secretary of the South African Ministry of External Affairs. All of them gave me an opportunity to explain in greater detail my proposals, which were further elaborated and which I always made clear were not a blueprint, but a basis for a negotiated agreement. At no time did any of those to whom I explained them disagree with them or suggest alternatives, although American State Department pressure to modify them to make them more palatable to the Patriotic Front continued. I felt, and Owen said he agreed with me, that, unless I had been installed as Resident Commissioner by 1 April 1978, I never would be.

Pressure continued to get the Patriotic Front to come to a meeting at which we could at least discuss on a bilateral basis

all aspects of the transition period. David Owen had hopes
that President Machel of Mozambique, whom he recognized
as a realist, could bring them to the table, and, as he had
not been able to see me on my November tour, it was
arranged that Prem Chand and I should go there in January,
accompanied by Steve Low, Michael Weir and Henry Steel.
We flew British Airways to Johannesburg and on from
there to Maputo in the aircraft of the US Defense Attaché
from Pretoria. On the day of arrival, Friday 6 January
1978, I had a meeting with Machel and his colleagues, at
which I explained our proposals, answered Machel's questions and emphasized that we could make no progress if
the Patriotic Front refused even to discuss them. Machel,
who was cheerful and friendly, stressed the importance of
getting a settlement quickly and having myself installed in
Salisbury instead of Smith. It was agreed that we should
meet with his colleagues the following day to discuss in more
detail the questions and comments raised by Mozambique
back in October, which had never been answered. In fact
their questionnaire was the only intelligent and formal commentary on the Anglo–American proposals that had been
received. Meanwhile Machel undertook to put pressure on
Mugabe to agree to attend a conference. Next day we had
a valuable discussion which lasted all morning. We felt we
had cleared up several points of doubt or misunderstanding,
and the Mozambicans expressed themselves satisfied with
my proposals for the army. They said that they suspected
that, although the Americans were sound on the issue of
'based on the liberation forces', we were not; my explanation
had satisfied them. They made much, as Machel was to
do at our meeting on the Sunday, of the need for the
transitional government to have the 'moral authority' of
the nationalist movements behind it. These must therefore
be actively associated with and participate in it. They cited
their own experience in which, during the transition period,
the forces of Frelimo, although kept separate, had been
'made available' to the Portuguese Transitional Governor in
emergency. 'Don't think,' said Machel, 'that, just because you
are a Maréchal de Campo, people will obey you. You will
want them to do things they won't want to do and not to do
things they will wish to. You are bound to disappoint their

expectations, which will be pitched high. You will need the authority of the nationalist leaders, if you are to persuade them. The only alternative will be to shoot them, and you will not want to do that.' It was much the same point as Sithole had made and I appreciated its validity, while being careful that I did not commit myself to acting only through them. Machel gave a stern warning against recognition of a Smith-organized internal settlement, which he feared we would be tempted to accept as a *fait accompli*. It would not bring the war to an end, but lead to a worse civil war, which would be hailed as one between the West and Communism. He would then be unable to resist pressures for his country to become a base for the communist side. It was the last thing he wanted; he was too involved already. He wanted a settlement and a friendly, prosperous and stable Zimbabwe as his neighbour, with whom he could do business and thus restore his economy. He promised that the Patriotic Front would come to a conference. I found Machel and his colleagues straightforward, intelligent and reasonable people to deal with. They listened to one's arguments, clearly took in what one had said, and, even if they disagreed, which they did, finished by saying that they were not the negotiators; they had made their point and it was up to us whether or not we acted on it. There was none of the emotional ranting we had met in some other places. Maputo itself was seedy and down at heel, the walls plastered with communist slogans, but life seemed to tick over fairly normally as far as one could tell. No doubt it depended on toeing the line. We were certainly treated with every courtesy, although not allowed to go anywhere without an escort.

To fly straight from there to Pretoria to the office of Pik Botha, the Minister of External Affairs, in Herbert Baker's imposing Government Building, slightly reminiscent of those of New Delhi, was an interesting contrast, and my first introduction to South Africa. Pik Botha gave me a lecture on South Africa's general attitude, her belief that progress should come gradually, political advancement depending on educational and economic development. We should give Smith's attempt to reach an internal settlement a fair wind, letting it lead to a wider, internationally acceptable one. South Africa wanted a Rhodesian settlement quickly, in

1978. They did not want things to go wrong there, as it was they who would have to pick up the bits. His lecture took up most of the time. I gave him an account of my talks in Maputo and briefly recapitulated the main points of our proposals for the transition period, including those affecting the armed forces. Even though we continued for longer than had originally been scheduled, there was little substantive discussion. I then had to face a large press conference at our embassy. After hurried consultation with our Minister (the Ambassador was away) and the American Ambassador about what I should say regarding our attitude to Smith's attempt to reach an internal settlement, the Americans pressing me to be more negative than I wished to be, I said: 'The British government's view is that any agreement that does not involve all the parties concerned is unlikely to be accepted internationally, is unlikely to be lasting and is unlikely to end the war.' I then paid a rapid visit to Gaborone, where I put Archie Mogwe, the delightful External Affairs Minister, and one of his colleagues in the picture (Seretse Khama and most of his colleagues were up-country at their cattle-posts) and flew back to Johannesburg, where I had a few hours before our flight back to London was due to leave. I had hoped to see there my son Andrew, who was working in Lesotho for their Development Corporation, but he could not come the 300 miles or so, as he could not get back over the border at Maseru before the South African Police Post closed it for the night; so I had to be content with a telephone call.

Machel was as good as his word, and, as a result of pressure by him and his fellow Front Line Presidents, Nkomo and Mugabe accepted David Owen's invitation for them to meet with him and Andy Young in Malta on 30 January. Prem Chand and I also attended, the meetings being held in a hotel on the highest point of the island near Medina. Our proposals for the transition period were again explained and those for the military aspects evoked little comment. Discussion centred on the machinery of government during the transition period, the Patriotic Front demanding a dominant position and rejecting what they called the 'dictatorial powers' of the Resident Commissioner, which they said amounted to re-colonization. They sought a Governing Council which they would control and from which the internal leaders would be excluded, except as part of Smith's representation. In an attempt to meet them, David Owen accepted the concept of a Council, provided that defence, law and order and foreign affairs were reserved for the Resident Commissioner, and suggested that its members should be those who led the delegations to the Geneva Conference. On that basis Chirau would be excluded, and the Patriotic Front would only have to win over one of the other nationalist leaders to outnumber the others. This was not accepted by the Patriotic Front. The general atmosphere of the meeting, in spite of basic disagreement, appeared to be one of understanding and cooperation, helped by the fact that the delegations, with observers from the Front Line States, spent the whole day together and joined each other's tables for lunch. I found myself usually either with Chinamano or the Mozambicans. I asked Mangena, Nkomo's chief military man (later killed by a Rhodesian mine in Zambia), if he regarded the Rhodesian African Rifles as 'acceptable elements' of a new Zimbabwe army, and he said he did. When I put the same question to Mugabe's equivalent, Tongogara, he was noncommittal. Andy Young and his delegation stayed in the same hotel as the Patriotic Front, sitting up late at night, talking into all hours and staying on with them after the end of the conference. Although the Patriotic Front had made it clear that they did not accept the Anglo–American proposals and insisted on a dominant position in a transition period, Owen and Young were not prepared to accept a breakdown at that stage and proposed that both sides should go away and consider the result of discussions, and meet again when they had thought things over.

On the flight back on 1 February, David Owen likened the atmosphere that had been created to that said to be evolved between kidnappers and their hostages, to which I replied: 'Who is the kidnapper and who the hostage?' I had already told him that I thought we were in danger, under pressure from the Americans, of being dragged along at the heels of the Patriotic Front, who would demand concessions to their aim of dominance which we should not give, if only because they would never be accepted by the Rhodesians. I said that I could not see the Anglo–American proposals, as originally published, ever being implemented, in view of the positions adopted by both the Rhodesian regime and the Patriotic Front, and suggested that I should resign as Resident Commissioner designate. David Owen asked me to stay on until it was seen whether or not follow-up talks were going to take place. During the rest of the month there was considerable pressure from the Americans to make further concessions to the Patriotic Front, which they described as 'confidence building measures', intended to give them confidence that the scales of the proposals were not weighted against them. In particular I had to resist pressures for changes in the police and on other law and order issues. In the event I was always supported by David Owen, who recognized that I would not accept arrangements which I was certain would not work. Neither the British nor the American government would be prepared, quite rightly in my opinion, to back the authority of the Resident Commissioner with force. My authority would depend on its acceptance, even if grudgingly, by 'all the parties concerned'. Maintenance of law and order would be difficult enough in any case, impossible with a police force at odds within itself. Now that my proposals for the military aspects of a cease-fire and of the transition period had been elaborated, I turned my attention to what would be required on the civil side, my staff and that of the Rhodesia Department, in collaboration with the Ministry of Overseas Development, producing an extensive check-list of all that would have to be done, if the moment ever came when it was agreed to go ahead with the proposals. It seemed to me as important to be clear about what one should not attempt to do, as what one should. Clear and prompt moves to end discrimination and detention, and to bring Africans into more responsible posts in the administration would be of great psychological importance, but it would be wrong to attempt fundamental changes in such fields as agriculture and education. Not only was six months far too short a period for this, but there were basic principles of policy involved, which would be for a future independent government to decide.

Agreement to a further round of talks with the Patriotic Front had still not been reached when, on 3 March, Smith announced that he had reached an internal settlement with Muzorewa, Sithole and Chirau, which would lead to majority rule at the end of the year. Although it had not been worked out in detail, it fell far short, not only of the Anglo–American proposals, but more so of the demands which Muzorewa and Sithole had themselves made in the discussions with Graham, which had led to them, and subsequently. David Owen was under pressure from the Front Line Presidents and from the Americans to condemn the settlement, and he had to remind the latter that, in his discussions with President Carter when the Anglo–American proposals had been formulated, the President had said that, if Smith could make a genuine success of an internal settlement which looked like meeting the Fifth Principle (acceptable to the people of Rhodesia as a whole), he would go along with it. Owen took a strictly neutral line in Parliament, welcoming Smith's acceptance of the principle of majority rule and proclaimed intention to work towards it, but pointing out that the settlement as announced, with its entrenched position for the whites, was 'seriously defective'. HMG neither endorsed nor condemned it: the test would be that it should prove acceptable to the people of Rhodesia as a whole.

Hoping that I should know one way or the other by then where I stood, I had provisionally planned to go with Edith and John, as soon as the latter's Easter holidays from Winchester began on 22 March, to stay with Andrew and Annie in Lesotho for three weeks. To get the cheap APEX fare, we had to book three months in advance and could not change the dates. To get there involved going through South Africa, and we had hoped to visit the Kruger National Park at the end of the holiday. I discussed with Owen whether or not I should go, and he agreed that I should, subject to recall if necessary. Flying economy class, and as a private citizen to Johannesburg and on to Bloemfontein, was very different from my official travels, as was the journey with ourselves and our luggage crammed into Andrew's ancient Volkswagen. Passing through the South African police post at the border in the crush of Easter traffic, caused by South Africans hoping to enjoy the forbidden fruits of gambling and pornography at Maseru's Holiday Inn, was a revealing experience. The fact that we were in a Lesotho-based car enabled us to get through more quickly than others, but did not help us over the filling in of forms and the glum scrutiny at the police post itself. We spent two and a half weeks in that beautiful, friendly country, its poverty-stricken economy totally dependent on the earnings of almost all its male population in the mines of South Africa. There was more rain than normal for the time of year, which affected some of our journeys up into the hills, and meant that wading across rivers and streams, normally the only method of crossing, was sometimes hazardous. We rode, walked, tried to fish, watched birds and visited the diamond mine over 10,000 feet up in the Drakensberg mountains. Andrew met with many frustrations in his job and the news came while we were there that, in the summer, he would move to a new one with the East Africa Development Division, attached to our High Commission in Nairobi. At the end of our visit he drove us in the Volkswagen to Johannesburg, our attempt to visit the Golden Gates Game Reserve on the way being frustrated by rain. As we passed through immigration control at Jan Smuts airport on 11 April, I was intercepted by the South African government protocol official, whom I had met in January, who told me that a call from London would be put through to me in the VIP lounge. It was to tell me that, on arrival at Heathrow in the morning, I was to go straight to the Foreign Office to see David Owen, and that, after one night at home, I should be returning to Africa with him for a round of meetings. This had resulted from President Carter's visit to Nigeria at the beginning of the month, at which he had proposed a conference of 'all the parties'. Preliminary separate bilateral meetings by Secretary of State Vance and David Owen with the Patriotic Front and the Salisbury regime were to lay the foundations for this.

On 14 April therefore Prem Chand and I were with Owen, Vance and Young when they met Nkomo and Mugabe and their delegations, all of us housed and the conference held in a hotel overlooking the harbour at Dar es Salaam, where we noted that hardly a dock crane stirred all the time we were there. Hopes were placed on pressure being exerted on the Patriotic Front by Nigeria and the Front Line States, all of whom had senior representatives present as observers, prominent among them being the flamboyant Brigadier Joe Garba, the Nigerian Minister for External Affairs. We went through the familiar explanations and arguments, my exposition of plans for the Zimbabwe army being received with close attention and no comment. The Patriotic Front reserved their fire for the police, maintaining that they could not accept their oppressors and that they had men trained to take their place, an argument I refused to accept. That and the question of how power should be exercised during the transition period were the main bones of contention, the presence of a United Nations Force being another. After Vance and Owen had persuaded Nyerere to exert pressure on them, Nkomo and Mugabe gave way to the limited extent of accepting a Resident Commissioner and a Governing Council, with reserved powers for the former over defence, law and order, provided that he acted through Ministers who would be their men, a proviso that was not agreed. They also said they would accept the presence of a UN Force, provided that its task was agreed with them and involved control of the Rhodesian armed forces, a proviso again that was not agreed. Although the conditions attached to their acceptance were not agreed and they continued to demand a dominant position in the Governing Council and at least parity in the police with the existing force, the impression was left that they had made important concessions and that progress had been made, certainly in the minds of the Front Line States. They had at least agreed to the main object of the meeting, to attend a joint conference with Smith's Executive Council, although it was left in the air whether Chirau would be accepted as a participant in his own right or only as a member of Smith's party. The conference ended with a banquet given by Nyerere in States House. In the margins of it I tackled Nkomo and Mugabe separately on the issue of the Zimbabwe National Army, noting that they had not commented on my proposals: did this mean that they were content with them? Nkomo's reply was that it gave him 'no problem', Mugabe's that 'of course (as I myself had said) it would be a matter for negotiation'. I found myself seated at the top table at dinner between Sam Njoma, leader of SWAPO, the Namibian liberation movement, and an attractive lady who was a junior Minister or State Secretary of the Angolan Ministry of External Affairs.

That company was an interesting contrast to that in which I found myself the following evening, Sunday 16 April, when, without Prem Chand, we were gathered together in

Pik Botha's house in Pretoria for a meeting, followed by
dinner, to discuss both Namibia and Rhodesia. Botha's main
concern was to reach a settlement which would have international approval and bring the war to an end, so that the
international pressures on South Africa would be removed.
Johnnie Graham and I, and I suspect Owen also, were
surprised at the extent to which Cy Vance went to reassure
Botha that, if South Africa cooperated on these two issues,
pressure on her would be lifted, and this in the presence
of Andy Young. We flew into Salisbury next morning, an
historic occasion, being the first visit of a US Secretary of
State to Rhodesia, Kissinger having seen Smith in Pretoria.
We went straight to meet the Executive Council, Ian Smith,
Muzorewa, Sithole and Chirau, the Africans each with one
colleague, Muzorewa with Chikerema, often suspected of
trying to oust him, Sithole with Gabellah, and Chirau with
Chief Ndewini. Ian Smith had David Smith and Van der Byl
as fellow Ministers and Gaylard and Claypole as senior officials. The atmosphere was cool and reasonable, Smith and
his colleagues asking the awkward question of what they were
expected to do to prove that their settlement was 'acceptable
to the people of Rhodesia as a whole', apart from having an
election, which was what they were aiming to do and were
only too willing to have help and an external presence to
observe. They asked if the Patriotic Front had accepted the
Anglo–American proposals, and, both at formal sessions
and informally between them, harped on the theme that
they had invited Nkomo (and in lower key Mugabe) to join
them, but had had no response. We should persuade them
to join, but they could not expect a special position and must
stop their guerrilla activities. Vance handled them tactfully
and sympathetically, a bit too sympathetically perhaps, while
Young made a gaffe which played into their hands. When
asked what he thought the motives of the Patriotic Front
leaders were, he replied 'personal power'. We lunched at
Mirimba House, Vance having invited the Executive Council
to join us, an invitation they refused so that they could use
the interval to consult each other over their reply to the main
object of the visit, the invitation to come to a joint meeting
with the Patriotic Front. When we resumed in the afternoon,
there was some discussion of law and order problems and

the likelihood of the war coming to an end as a result of appeals by the Executive Council to the 'men in the bush' to give up. Sithole offered to take one of us to meet some of the guerrilla leaders with whom he was in contact, and, with the agreement of Owen, I left Colonel Reilly behind to do so. It was a sign of where the real power lay that, although one of Sithole's men was co-Minister for the armed forces, on that occasion Reilly was side-tracked into merely visiting the Rhodesian security forces in the Kariba dam area and given another briefing. He was to meet one of Sithole's contacts in this way on a later visit. Smith's answer on behalf of his colleagues was that they could not see much point in attending an all-party conference, to do so running a serious risk of undermining confidence and progress in the internal settlement, which they hoped the British and American governments would support, even to the extent of lifting sanctions. They did not reject the invitation and would think it over. David Owen made clear that sanctions could not be lifted until elections had been held to meet the Fifth Principle.

In discussion with Vance and Owen at Mirimba House before departure, Owen said that we ought to see within a month or two whether or not the internal settlement was going to work in terms of its support by Rhodesian African opinion and in persuading the guerrillas to give up. I said that I thought this unlikely. I thought that nothing very much would happen, while the positions of both the Patriotic Front and of the internal settlement would gradually deteriorate as a result of their respective internal troubles. Meanwhile the economy would also deteriorate and the war get gradually, although not very significantly, worse. It was a pessimistic judgement, which was unfortunately to prove correct. It was clearer than ever to me that there was no hope of the Anglo–American proposals, as originally conceived, being implemented. In his (Owen's) acceptance of a Governing Council for the transition period, which would exercise executive and legislative powers in all fields except those reserved to the Resident Commissioner, a fundamental change in the nature of the latter's position had been introduced, and Owen had agreed at Dar es Salaam that I could not be expected to be bound to accept the post

under those conditions: indeed it would be important that
its holder should be an individual agreed as acceptable to
those forming the Governing Council. By the end of the
Salisbury meeting I had decided to propose to Owen on
the flight back that I should terminate my appointment at
the end of May. I had originally contracted for six months,
and since the end of February had agreed to renew month
by month, the decision being taken about the middle of the
previous month. Prompted, I suspect, by Steve Low, who
knew this was in my mind, Cy Vance said to me that he
hoped I would continue. I told him of my intention and
said that I did not think it should embarrass his or my own
government. He said that he thought the end of May was
much too soon and pressed me to continue until at least the
end of July. I told him I would discuss the matter with Owen
on the flight back to London and, of course, take into account
what he had said. I had high respect for Cy Vance, whom
I had first met when, as Commander of the 3rd Division, I
had arranged a demonstration of one of our first anti-tank
guided missiles, Malkara, for him when he was US Secretary
for the Army. More recently I had attended a Ditchley Park
weekend conference on NATO, over which he had presided.
Although not apparently a forceful man, he was quick in the
uptake and an excellent negotiator, a welcome change from
the over-talkative and unreliable Andy Young. Young, like
Owen, was too apt to speak before he had thought out
what he was going to say, which sometimes produced some
startling results.

David Owen was clearly relieved that I was prepared
to soldier on for some months longer. Hopes were now
based officially on bringing about the all-party conference,
and Johnnie Graham and Steve Low were sent off on semi-
permanent exile to try and bring the two sides closer together, while the familiar procession of nationalist leaders and
representatives of the Front Line States through London
continued. David Owen had no illusions about the chances
of obtaining results from an all-party conference, unless
behind the scenes the two sides could come closer together,
and significantly Smith and Nkomo. On his way through
London Nkomo had secret and private talks with Owen,
in which he revealed that his aim was simultaneously to

make private approaches to the other nationalist leaders, while being prepared to meet Smith personally, protected by the presence of Garba of Nigeria from being accused of doing a private deal and from being misrepresented by Smith. Meanwhile the Graham–Low mission should continue its work independently and the two approaches should not be linked.

Owen saw this as a hopeful move and was prepared to cooperate with it. At the same time Smith was becoming disillusioned with Muzorewa and Sithole. The dismissal of one of Muzorewa's team, Byron Hove, as co-Minister for Law and Order for publicly demanding a speedier and more radical change in fields such as the police, and Muzorewa's indecisive attitude to that and other incidents, had lost him much support. As a second visit by Colonel Reilly confirmed, the scheme to win over or at least neutralize guerrillas by declaring certain areas 'frozen' was producing meagre results. In these areas the guerrillas were left alone, provided that they agreed to suspend active operations. To the Africans the internal settlement did not appear to be leading to any change. Discrimination continued and the whites were still firmly in control in spite of the presence of some blacks in the government. To Smith and his white colleagues the internal settlement was clearly not bringing the hoped-for result, an end to the war: in fact it was getting worse, the murder of 13 British missionaries and some of their pupils near Umtali on 23 June producing a sharper shock than the gradual deterioration in security which was leading to a position in which the government's writ had ceased to run in many areas of the Tribal Trust lands, and movement on roads, particularly at night, in European-inhabited areas was hazardous. The major towns however remained virtually untouched by the war, apart from the involvement in army or police service of almost all the able-bodied European male population.

After the incursion of guerrillas from Angola into Zaire, leading to the occupation by them of the important mining town of Kolwezi and the murder of 97 Europeans there, attention was given to the possibility of having to evacuate Europeans in an emergency from Rhodesia. Although it was no real concern of mine, Owen sought my advice on

certain aspects, which was to the effect that I thought it
unnecessary, undesirable and indeed impracticable for the
British Government to make any such plans. The white
manpower and its firepower available in Rhodesia was far
greater than any we could deploy there quickly and would
be sufficient to protect their dependants in a real crisis.
How was one, in any case, to decide who was entitled to
be rescued and who was not? If such a critical situation did
nevertheless occur, the South Africans would be forced to
intervene before we could send anything but a token force
from Britain. If public pressure forced our intervention, it
only made sense to do so in cooperation with South Africa.
To plan this in advance raised great political difficulties. If
we did intervene, being on our own and in international eyes
responsible for Rhodesia, we would find it very difficult to
limit the action of our troops solely to rescue operations, a
situation which clearly had very serious implications. I kept
the Chief of the Defence Staff, Neil Cameron, unofficially
informed of the advice I had given, for which I believe he
was grateful. Owen said he agreed with me, but that public
pressure on the British Government would be such that they
would not be able to stand aloof. The initial pressure came
from the Conservative opposition, and, at that time, there
was much speculation about the possibility of an imminent
general election. Letting the kith and kin down could have
lost votes.

Meanwhile the Americans kept on pressing for concessions to make the proposals more acceptable to the Patriotic
Front, in response to the argument from the Front Line
States that they had moved towards us at Dar es Salaam,
while we had done nothing in return. All I was prepared
to concede over the police was the suggestion that the UN
police observer element should be accompanied by representatives both of the Patriotic Front and of the internal
regime, as an insurance against police discrimination. This
satisfied the Americans, although it was unlikely to meet the
Patriotic Front's demand. Attention was also concentrated
on the Governing Council. By this time Owen's aim was
somehow or other to bring about a situation in which Nkomo
was accepted as leader of a transitional government, under
the umbrella of a Resident Commissioner with reserved

powers for defence, law and order and external affairs. Smith might be brought to accept this, if the composition of the Governing Council were such as to see that the Patriotic Front did not have a dominant position in real terms. In July I had received a visit from a retired British army officer who worked in Flower's intelligence organization in Salisbury, with whom I had dined privately on my first visit there. Flower had asked him to contact me to sound out my views on how Nkomo could be brought into the settlement. Could he be bribed to abandon Mugabe? I said I was convinced he could not. He needed Mugabe, until he was certain of being firmly and irrevocably in power himself. When he had achieved that, he would probably hope to win over the less extreme followers of Mugabe to his side, isolating the remainder. Only assurance of a position similar to that currently held by Smith would satisfy him.

By August the combined efforts of the Graham–Low mission and other contacts led to the formulation of three options for the composition of the Governing Council. Owen favoured membership being based on the Geneva Conference participants, but thought that we might have to settle for parity between the Internal Settlement leaders and the Patriotic Front, giving each four seats. Under Option A the permanent chairman would be one of the members agreed on in the negotiations beforehand, the preferred candidate being Nkomo. A rotating chairman, as the Salisbury Executive Council had, was ruled out as leading to chronic indecision. Option B would introduce a radical change in the proposals. The governmental structure would be as for Option A and in all respects it would be the same, except that instead of a six-month period, leading to elections and independence, the Resident Commissioner appointed by Britain would only remain until a referendum had been held on three questions: the acceptability of the transitional arrangements, the outline of the constitution and the date for the elections. If the answer to the referendum were 'No', Option A would continue in force: if it were 'Yes', the Resident Commissioner appointed by Britain would be replaced by one chosen by the Governing Council, and independence would be granted there and then. Option C would be the same as Option A, except that the Resident Commissioner

would himself be chairman of the Governing Council and
have a casting vote. Under all three options, the problem of
the constitutional relationship of the Resident Commissioner
to the British Government was left in the air. The attraction
of Option B was that it would make easier a 'fix' by which
Nkomo was accepted as *de facto* leader of the country, all
the members of the Council would have a vested interest
in obtaining an affirmative answer to the referendum, and,
once it was over, HMG could honourably wash its hands of
the whole affair, leaving the Rhodesians themselves, black
and white, to sort out all the intractable problems like the
future of the armed forces and the police, agriculture, education and social policy generally, hoping that the lifting of
sanctions and the end of the war would restore the country's
ailing economy. To the British government all the options
had the attraction that they would be less, if at all, responsible
for the direction of the affairs of the country, while it met
the demand of 'all the parties' that they should not only have
a say in, but control events. The loser was the unfortunate
Resident Commissioner, who would find himself in practice
at the mercy of a Council which, except perhaps in Option B,
would be bitterly divided within itself. I told Owen that I did
not consider myself bound to serve under any of the options;
that, provided I was satisfied that the basic pre-conditions
of the Anglo–American proposals were met, i.e. that there
was going to be an effective cease-fire and that the parties
concerned genuinely intended to support the proposals, I
might work under Option B, but would almost certainly not
do so under the other options. He understood and accepted
this, going so far, in a meeting with the Americans, as to say
that 'no man in his senses would take on the job under those
options', a remark he may have had cause to regret later,
when Option B was opposed on the grounds that it was
abandoning the commitment to free and fair elections and to
leaving the choice of a leader to the Rhodesians themselves.
Owen had always realized that it would be criticized on that
score, but felt, as I did, that the advantages outweighed the
drawbacks. The Americans disliked it, as did Nyerere and
the Conservative opposition, who regarded it, not without
justification, as a patent way of fixing Nkomo as the future
leader of the country.

The end of July 1978 had come and gone while all these discussions and manoeuvrings behind the scenes were in train. It was also by then clear that there would not be a general election until the autumn at the earliest, 11 October being the forecasters' favourite date. At my monthly meeting with Michael Palliser, the PUS, to decide whether or not I should agree with the Foreign Secretary to sign on for another month, it was clear that it would be irresponsible to try and go while it still appeared as if the all-party meeting was on the cards, and I told David Owen that I would serve on 'until 11 October'.

Nkomo, accompanied by Garba, had met Smith secretly in Lusaka on 14 August. It was reported, almost certainly incorrectly, that Smith had offered Nkomo the permanent chairmanship of the Executive Council in the transitional government, but that Nkomo replied that he would not return to Salisbury unless a significant role was found for Mugabe. It was understood that a further meeting would be held at which Mugabe would also be present, and the Nigerians set about trying to persuade him to join in, although he had not been told beforehand that Nkomo was to meet Smith. It was also thought that Smith had not forewarned his colleagues, although he later claimed that he had, Sithole and Muzorewa denying it. While this had been going on, the Rhodesian Joint Operations Committee, certainly Walls and Flower, had become increasingly dissatisfied at the lack of progress towards a political settlement and disillusioned with the internal settlement and its failure to improve the security situation. They held a private meeting at which they considered the possibility of ditching Smith, renouncing UDI and putting themselves under the authority of the British Government, putting out feelers as to what the reaction of HMG would be. Owen and Johnnie Graham took the view that, in such a situation, no British government could refuse to accept responsibility. My firm view, backed by Michael Palliser and Henry Steel, was that HMG should refuse, unless all the pre-conditions of the Anglo–American proposals were fully met; that is to say that there would be an effective cease-fire and that *all* the parties concerned had genuinely accepted them. This would mean that a Renunciation of UDI (RUDI as it was dubbed) should not be accepted, unless at least the Front Line States agreed and undertook to cut off support to the Patriotic Front, if they opposed it, and the Security Council authorized a UN Force. If we accepted responsibility without these pre-conditions, we should merely have taken the place of Smith's government and find ourselves with a war on our hands, the Patriotic Front and the Front Line States turning to Russia for support. The Front Line States had a crucial part to play, as also had South Africa. I appreciated that, if such a situation arose, the Patriotic Front would smell victory and be even less inclined to accept any lessening of their demands, but the psychological effect of Smith's downfall, combined with the very real interest of the Front Line States in ending the war and reaching a settlement might turn the scales. In general my views were accepted. The answer, given through the same channel as that on which the question had been raised, was that it would not be as simple a matter as they appeared to imagine, and that they should lend their weight to getting Smith to reach an agreement with Nkomo. However the possibility of RUDI was taken seriously, and it was decided that Britain's reaction would be to go immediately to the Security Council, seek an immediate cease-fire, the implementation of the Anglo–American proposals, as modified by the Options (B being favoured at the time), the appointment of a UN Special Representative, and the establishment of a UN Force. We had always envisaged a period of some six weeks passing between the time when the parties agreed that they would accept the Anglo–American proposals and the full implementation of a cease-fire, coinciding with the start of the transition period. This would be necessary, partly to meet UN procedures and establish the UN Force, partly to pass all the necessary legislation through the British Parliament and partly to take all the detailed steps necessary to establish an effective cease-fire. Under a RUDI, this would clearly have to be drastically telescoped in spite of the risks involved. The officers who had originally been earmarked for my staff, apart from Reilly and Rous who were still with me, were not now all available, nor was Roy Henry, being about to take over the appointment of Commissioner of the Hong Kong Police. I had taken no steps to find a replacement, but immediately did so and was fortunate in obtaining the agreement of Sir James Haughton that he would act as my Police Adviser, replacement of the new Commissioner of the Rhodesian Police not being appropriate in the circumstances of RUDI, in which presumably he would have voluntarily placed himself under the authority of HMG.

While we were hastily making contingency plans to meet RUDI, the Smith–Nkomo–Garba plan had come unstuck. The Nigerians had put pressure on Mugabe, who, backed by Machel and Nyerere, resisted it. Relations between Nyerere and Kaunda were strained at the time for other reasons, and, while the Front Line Presidents were divided over the desirability of Mugabe and Nkomo doing a private deal with Smith, Sithole on 31 August leaked the news that the previous meeting had taken place and Muzorewa accused Smith of betraying Sithole and himself. While the the future of this carefully laid plot was in jeopardy, an incident occurred which put paid to all progress. On 3 September an Air Rhodesia civil aircraft, taking tourists from Kariba back to Salisbury, was shot down soon after take-off, almost certainly by a SAM 7 missile. It crashed, killing 34 of the passengers, 18 surviving. Ten of them were then killed in cold blood by a gang of Nkomo's ZIPRA terrorists who happened to be in the area. Even that might perhaps somehow have been got over, but Nkomo, in a radio interview, claimed responsibility for shooting the aircraft down, justifying it on the grounds that he had information that Air Rhodesia flights in and out of Kariba were used to carry military personnel. He maintained that the subsequent murder of the survivors was a fabrication, and made matters worse by treating the whole affair in an offhand and jocular manner. It is probable that he felt the need at the time to defend himself against accusations of doing a deal with Smith, but the effect was disastrous to all hopes for progress towards a settlement. Rhodesian white opinion was understandably incensed and Smith reacted to it, calling Nkomo a 'monster'. Any idea of RUDI vanished overnight.

A few days after this, the British Cabinet had its first meeting after the summer recess, and the Prime Minister decided that he was not going to have an autumn election. I had to think again. The all-party meeting was still supposed to be on the cards, and, with the whole situation in disarray, it would only have added fuel to the fire if I had resigned. I decided therefore that I would continue until I saw the result of the debate on the Queen's Speech at the start of the new parliamentary session in November. It was possible that the government might suffer a defeat, the Liberal–Labour pact having been terminated, which would be an appropriate reason for me to resign also. The next event was the invitation by a group of right-wing US Senators to the whole of the Rhodesian Executive Council to visit the USA and the American decision to grant Smith a visa to do so. This predictably was resented by the Front Line States and the Patriotic Front, who feared, correctly, that American public opinion was veering away from support of Carter's policy in Southern Africa, which appeared to appease, if not actually favour, communists. While there, Smith clearly realized the significance of the Senate resolution, as amended by the Case/Javits amendment, which resolved that 'the United States would not enforce sanctions after 31 December, provided that the Government of Rhodesia had by then demonstrated its willingness to negotiate in good faith at an all-party conference and that a government had been installed, chosen in free and fair elections in which all parties had been allowed to participate.' On 19 October, while still in the USA, Smith announced that he and his colleagues would be prepared to attend an all-party meeting 'provided that there were no pre-conditions'. This did not help much, as the Patriotic Front, whenever they had agreed to attend, had always insisted that it must be to discuss the Anglo–American proposals, and both they and the Front Line States had been very sensitive to any hint that we might be backing away from them and enticing the Patriotic Front into joining the Internal Settlement in some way.

Even if these differences of approach had not themselves been an obstacle, the Rhodesians made certain that Nkomo would not accept by a severe air attack on ZAPU camps in Zambia, one very close to Lusaka, in which heavy casualties were inflicted. This was as much a slap in the face to Kaunda, who had recently had to ask for the re-opening of rail links through Rhodesia to South Africa in order to obtain urgent supplies of fertilizer, as it was to Nkomo. Following on the

Viscount incident, it appeared finally to shut the door on
any further attempt to bring Nkomo and Smith together.
Not long after Smith's return from the USA, he announced
that the elections, which the internal settlement agreement
of 3 March had fixed for 31 December, had been postponed
until 20 April 1979. By now it was quite clear to me that there
was no point in my hanging on any longer. The Government
survived the debate on the Queen's Speech, and in that part
of it which dealt with Rhodesia, Owen made public for the
first time the modifications made by the Options (they had
already been given to 'all the parties', as had my papers on
the Zimbabwe National Army, the cease-fire and UN Force).
In referring to the position of the Resident Commissioner,
he said: 'We envisage an agreed figure as Resident Commissioner being appointed to hold executive authority for all the
forces of law and order.' In his summing-up speech, Ted
Rowlands, the Minister of State, said: 'We have not said that
it should necessarily be a specific person, although we have
had the valuable advice and efforts of Lord Carver. However
an agreed figure to be in charge of security issues would
be a fundamental aspect of the discussions either before
or during the course of an all-party conference. That vital
aspect must be settled.' This gave me my cue. The House of
Lords held a marathon debate on the issue of the order to
renew Rhodesian sanctions a day or two later. As it began,
I went to see Owen in his room in the House of Commons
and said that, in the light of what both he and Rowlands
had now publicly said, I though it inappropriate for HMG to
designate anyone as Resident Commissioner in advance, and
suggested that I should resign at the end of the month. If he
thought this would be too embarrassing to the Government,
I would be prepared to hang on until the end of December,
but definitely not a day longer. He accepted this, but did
not commit himself over the date. I returned to the Lords
to sit out a debate in which 41 peers spoke, finishing at
2.15 a.m. in a thick fog, through which I had to drive home
to Shackleford, having cast my vote for the Government.
A few days later Owen told me that the Prime Minister,
who in the House of Commons had said, under pressure
from the Opposition, that he might himself preside over an
all-party conference, if he thought it would have any chance

of success, was sending Cledwyn Hughes* out on a tour of Africa to report on the prospect for such a conference, to be held probably in January. He did not wish to announce my resignation until Cledwyn Hughes had at least started on his mission. At the annual Diplomatic Reception at Buckingham Palace on 23 November, I suggested to David Owen that, after already one postponement, 30 November should be firmly fixed for the announcement. He agreed to try and persuade the Prime Minister, and was successful. On that day he and I went together to see Callaghan and I spent half an hour discussing with him the unpromising prospects, after which I held a press conference in the Foreign Office, and finally, with an immense feeling of relief, shook myself free. Among the messages I received, when I did so, was one from Dick Moose of the US State Department, which read: 'I had hoped for many months that we would provide the cat and you would provide the bell. It still may happen, but in the meantime we will miss your wisdom and sage counsel.'

In May 1979 Margaret Thatcher's Conservative administration came to power, with Peter Carrington as Foreign Secretary. In spite of their attitude when in opposition, they were prepared to go farther and faster than their Labour predecessors, and at the Lancaster House Conference in September reached agreement that Britain should temporarily resume authority over Rhodesia, in order to supervise elections which would unequivocally hand over power to the black majority of the country's inhabitants. A monitoring force, provided by troops from the Commonwealth, the great majority British, would ensure that the armed forces of both sides did not interfere. Lord Soames was appointed as interim Governor with full powers. Willie Rous, who had been my invaluable military assistant when I had been Resident Commissioner (Designate) and was then commanding 2nd Battalion Coldstream Guards, was in charge of the monitoring force at Umtali, near the border with Mozambique, and kept me informed of events. One of the principal differences between the Lancaster House settlement and the Anglo–American proposals was that no attempt was made to disband or disarm any of the military

* Later Lord Cledwyn of Penrhos.

forces on either side until the new government came into power after the elections. This ran the risk that the result of the election might not be accepted by one or other element, leading to a further civil war. If Mugabe had not clearly been the victor, this might have happened, and it was to be a long time before the problem of what was to happen to all the armed men was satisfactorily solved. I had always realized that it was a key question in the search for a solution. It had been an interesting experience, but I was glad that I had not actually had to grapple with the task of trying to make the Anglo–American proposals work in practice.

20

A Continuation of Policy

War is nothing else than a continuation of
state-policy by other means.
Karl Maria von Clausewitz (1780–1831), on War

Before I had become involved in Rhodesia, I had been
approached by Evelyn Shuckburgh* to ask if I would be
prepared to be considered as his successor as Chairman of
the Executive Committee of the British Red Cross. Having
discussed with him, Lady Brabourne† and the Director what
it would involve, I said that I would be very glad to be
considered. All seemed to be set fair for this to take effect
in 1978, when I became involved with Rhodesia, and when
I had finished with that, Shuckburgh had other ideas, and
I heard no more from him. Harold Caccia§ had also made
a vague suggestion that I should become involved with the
St John Ambulance Organization, but, as his proposal was
extremely vague and I was at the time committed to the
Red Cross, I did not pursue the matter further. I had
also received an equally vague suggestion from the General
Electric Company, conveyed to me by Toby Aldington**;
but, although Arnold Weinstock‡ referred to it once after

* Sir Evelyn Shuckburgh. Distinguished diplomat, ambassador to Italy, 1966–69;
see also p.233.
† Daughter of First Earl Mountbatten. Became Countess Mountbatten on his
death in 1979.
§ Lord Caccia. Distinguished diplomat, PUS Foreign Office and head of Diplo-
matic Service 1962–65.
** Lord Aldington. Banker and ex-MP; see also p.15.
‡ Later Lord Weinstock, Chief Executive of GEC.

I had finished with Rhodesian affairs, no more was heard of that either.

I was quite content to restrict my activities to writing and to work in the house and garden. There was a great deal to do in the latter field when we moved house in February 1979. Although Shackleford Old Rectory had served us well, we did not want to spend the rest of our days surrounded by stockbrokers and rhododendron bushes. Ever since I retired we had been looking for something to suit us better in the general area of Hampshire and Wiltshire, and eventually found Wood End House, near Wickham at the southern end of the Meon valley. Originally a cottage, dating from at least the mid-seventeenth century, it had been enlarged at various times, notably by an Admiral Knight, who had added an attractive Georgian extension towards the end of the eighteenth century. Both house and garden needed a lot doing to them, and it kept us both very busy. I disliked being indoors if it was not raining, and devoted most of my time to the fairly large kitchen garden, while Edith planned the resurrection of the flower beds. My literary output tended therefore to be related to the rainfall in south Hampshire.

I had finished writing *Harding of Petherton* at the end of 1977, just as I was getting involved in Rhodesia, and it was published in September 1978, receiving fairly favourable reviews. Meanwhile my agents, David Higham Associates, and I had been discussing with the BBC the possibility of a television series about the history of the British army. I had produced an outline framework of *Seven Ages of the Army*, and had written the first Age, that of Cromwell, before I had started my life of John Harding. The other Ages were to be those of Marlborough, Wellington, Roberts, Haig, Montgomery and Templer. The BBC were not enthusiastic, which did not surprise me, but indicated that they might be interested in a series on twentieth-century warfare. I was attracted by that idea, as I had agreed to give the Lees Knowles lectures at Cambridge University in February 1979. I had chosen as the theme of these the relation between the theory and the practice of armoured warfare, a subject that derived from a suggestion by George Weidenfeld for a book on the contrast between the theories and the conduct of warfare, and he himself suggested producing the lectures as a slender book. It was published as *The Apostles of Mobility* in August 1979. In further discussions with the BBC, they said that a number of programmes covering both the First and the Second World Wars had recently been shown; but they might be interested in a series covering wars since 1945, the Templer Age of my original concept. Weidenfelds agreed to accept the change, and I began work on the book towards the end of the time I was concerned with Rhodesia. I completed the typescript in January 1980, and it was published in October of that year under the title of *War Since 1945*, and in April 1981 in the USA by Putnams. It received generally favourable reviews and sold quite well. I had produced draft TV scripts for two of the wars described in the book, the campaigns in Palestine and Kenya, but the BBC was pulling in its horns and was not prepared to go ahead. As a form of compensation, I was the subject of a long Profile interview by Desmond Wilcox, filmed in May 1979 and shown in August, which produced quite a fan mail.

It was probably as a result of this that I was asked to give an interview for a Panorama programme in November on the controversial subject of the replacement of the Polaris ballistic missile submarine force. In preparing this, the producer had read the evidence I had given to the House of Commons Select Committee on Expenditure. The committee had started to examine the subject in the last days of the Labour administration, and published an incomplete report in April 1979. I had been somewhat reluctant to accede to the committee's request that I should give evidence, but, after consulting Frank Cooper at the Ministry of Defence, I wrote the following, which was published as an appendix to the report.

The rationales for Britain's possession of a strategic deterrent weapons system rests on the need to be able to threaten such unacceptable damage to the Soviet Union that the latter would be deterred or stopped from action that was so unacceptable to Britain that she herself was prepared to accept the damage that Russian retaliation would involve.

Such a need would arise if Britain had reason to believe that the Soviet Union was not or would not be deterred from such action by a threat of strategic nuclear action from the United States. It is therefore a form of insurance policy against the withdrawal of United States support for the defence of Western Europe, including Britain.

Given that the circumstances in which such a need would arise must be regarded as very unlikely and would inevitably mean the end of NATO, the decision as to whether or not to embark on the provision of a new weapons system must depend, in military terms, on a judgement as to whether or not it is worth paying the premium to meet a risk which is so unlikely to arise. An important factor in making that judgement will be the cost and the priority it should be given in relation to other forms of defence effort. In political terms the questions that must be faced and answered will be whether it would be acceptable to a British government to make clear to the world that it no longer intended to insure against that risk and to allow France to be the only Western European country to do so.

The contribution of such a weapon system in military and political terms to that of the United States in support of NATO or outside it is of secondary importance and would not in itself justify the expenditure involved in the provision of a new system.

The Panorama team thought that those views were not exactly what they would have expected from an ex-Chief of the Defence Staff, and I was interrogated keenly on the issue in their interview. I made it clear that I had never believed in the need for Britain to have its own, independent strategic deterrent force, regarding the American nuclear capability, based in Europe, at sea and in the USA, as more than sufficient; and that I had never been able to envisage a realistic scenario in which a responsible British Prime Minister would order a British force to fire its own weapons, in circumstances in which the American President had decided that it was not right to use theirs. This was consistent with the views I had held at the time when I had discussed these matters with Liddell Hart, as described in chapter 12. The programme as a whole was critical of the Conservative administration's decision, soon after it had taken office, to produce a new force of submarines, equipped, if the Americans agreed, with their Trident missile, for which we would produce our own multiple, independently targeted warheads.

My appearance on the programme and speeches on the subject in the House of Lords attracted a good deal of attention. I had not thought it right to speak in the House while I was involved in Rhodesian affairs, and made my maiden speech on 22 May 1979 in the foreign affairs and defence debate on the Queen's address at the opening of the new session. Convention dictated that a maiden speech should not be controversial, and I therefore limited my remarks on the subject to stressing the overriding importance of maintaining American support for European defence, warning that too much emphasis on the necessity for a nuclear balance within Europe could lead to some weakening of the deterrent value of that support, and saying that I hoped the government would link the problem of replacing the Polaris system to that of what was then known as the 'modernization of theatre nuclear weapons' in Europe. I was hinting that any future system of ours should be regarded, not as an independent strategic force, but, as it had been consistently described in successive Defence White Papers, as a 'contribution to SACEUR's theatre nuclear forces'. But a debate in December of that year on a question raised by Lord Kimberley, asking the government what its plans were for replacing Britain's existing nuclear deterrent, gave me an opportunity to speak out more decisively on the subject. After having made clear that I was not opposed to nuclear weapons as such, that I believed them to form an extremely important part of NATO's armoury in keeping the risks of war low, and that Britain should continue to man nuclear delivery systems, whatever the origin and ownership of their warheads, I dealt with all the various arguments advanced for our having an independent strategic system, and, countering the one favoured at that time, said:

> A more valid argument, although I would prefer to say a less invalid one, is one in which war had started in Europe, NATO forces were engaged, but the United States feared escalation to the stage of strategic nuclear

exchange and refused to authorize the use of nuclear weapons at all, or refused to escalate beyond either the tactical or the theatre. In those circumstances, would it be right, would it be reasonable, let alone would it be likely that the United Kingdom should decide to go it alone? It is very doubtful that we should have the support of our allies in doing so. Indeed, in those circumstances did we think that it would stop the Russians in their tracks? I believe that the answer to all those questions is 'No'.

I had followed Peter Hill-Norton, who had also been ennobled and who strongly supported the replacement of the Polaris submarines by a new force, but found myself lined up with the authoritative voices of Solly Zuckerman* and Alun Chalfont,† and in line both with the Liberals and most of the Labour peers, whose leader Fred Peart,§ said that he was 'nearly converted' to my view, although still a believer in such a force.

The replacement of the Polaris system, and the choice of system, was not the only nuclear weapon issue under public discussion. The others were the stationing of US cruise missiles in Europe, as the main feature of the modernization of theatre nuclear forces, and the neutron or enhanced radiation warhead for shorter-range delivery systems. In principle I could not object to either, and certainly did not support the emotions they aroused in their opponents.

Cruise-missiles would perform exactly the same function as the longer-range aircraft, the British Vulcan and the American F1-11 bombers, had been performing for some time. In some respects they were preferable to aircraft: their launchers were mobile and not dependent on fixed bases, making them less susceptible to pre-emptive attack. The popular objection to the neutron bomb — that it killed people and left property intact — was ridiculous, considering that existing warheads did enormous damage to both, as

* Lord Zuckerman. Chief Scientific Adviser to the Secretary of State for Defence, 1960–66, and to the Government, 1964–71. A close associate of Lord Mountbatten.
† Lord Chalfont. Regular Army officer, 1940–71. Defence Correspondent of *The Times*, 1961–64. Minister for Disarmament in Labour administration, 1964–70.
§ Lord Peart. Former Labour MP and Minister of Agriculture.

well as producing fall-out, if burst near the ground, and that the enemy's riposte to their use would not necessarily be as 'clean'. My objection to the cruise missile, which I only voiced occasionally and in low key, was that it was yet another new system, involving new warheads, and that the reason given for its deployment was false: that it was a counter to the Russian SS20 mobile ballistic missile. As the latter was mobile, the cruise missile could not destroy it either before or after it had fired. My objection to the neutron bomb was that the very reason why it was produced – to cause less 'collateral' damage and therefore be more acceptable to use on NATO territory, especially West Germany – blurred the distinction between conventional and nuclear weapons, and made it appear that NATO envisaged fighting a nuclear war. As I had said in my maiden speech, the concept of a European nuclear balance was a dangerous one, in that it tended to create the impression that a nuclear exchange or war confined to Europe, west of Russia's frontiers, in which the Russian and American homelands would be spared, was something that could be accepted. I had realized that there was an inescapable dilemma in nuclear deterrent strategy. The aim of it was to make the risks of going to war at all so unacceptable to one's opponent that he would not embark upon it, whatever the political, economic or military pressures might be. However, in a world in which one's opponent could answer back in kind, to pose an unacceptable risk to him was to confront oneself with the same danger; and when, in reaction to this, strategies were devised that reduced those risks, making the use of nuclear weapons appear more acceptable, they undermined the deterrent value of the strategy, while retaining the danger that, if, as a result of the weakening of deterrence, a war did start, the use of nuclear weapons, even of limited yield and on a limited scale, would result in appalling destruction.

I had to admit to myself that I had not seriously considered the basic principles of nuclear deterrence in any depth since I had been Director of Army Plans and had discussed them with Basil Liddell Hart 20 years before. The only aspect of them which had come before the Chiefs of Staff, while I had been CGS and CDS, had been the project for the 'improvement' of the nuclear warhead on the Polaris missile in the navy's existing ballistic missile submarines. This, according to the intelligence experts, the scientists and the navy, had become necessary as a result of the Russian construction of an anti-ballistic missile defence covering Moscow. The project had been started in the time of the Conservative administration and continued under its Labour successor. It had run into difficulties, financial and technical, the latter causing the navy to suggest a fundamental change in design for safety reasons, which would have given it only a marginal advantage over the existing warhead, while reducing its range. The latter was a very significant factor, as every alteration in maximum range meant an enormous variation in the area of ocean in which the submarines could cruise on patrol. Clearly, the larger the area, the less the chances of detection. The first time that the issue was raised, when I was CGS, I had questioned the need for an independent strategic force, and therefore for improvement, and had received a severe lecture from Peter Hill-Norton, who had said that, if it became known that those were my views, I would certainly not be appointed his successor as CDS. I replied that that was my affair and I would make my own judgement. The Chiefs of Staff took the view at that time that they favoured the project, as long as it was not at the expense of conventional forces, a view I was content to go along with. The technical problem arose when I was CDS. I then took the line that, the government's policy being to maintain an independent strategic force, but to make no plans for its replacement, the sensible thing to do, provided that the cost was not totally out of proportion, was to improve the warhead for the existing system. If that involved unacceptable disadvantage, either on the grounds of safety or of finance, and therefore of its effect on conventional forces, we should abandon the concept of an independent strategic deterrent and accept that our ballistic submarine force was no more than a contribution to SACEUR's theatre nuclear forces. In that case no improvement of the warheads was needed. The navy, under the influence of the US Navy, was, I thought, exaggerating the safety problem. The air force and army did not contribute much to the argument. When I was CGS, the air staff had favoured a weakening of the criteria for an independent strategic force. In taking this view, they were suspected by some of modifying the criteria so that a replacement system could be provided by aircraft. I took the view that such a change in criteria would amount to abandonment of the claim that our force was one that could effectively deter the Russians on its own. I would not object to that personally, but it would be a major change of policy with significant political implications. When Andrew Humphrey succeeded Denis Spotswood as Chief of the Air Staff, he abandoned that view and took the line that it was a naval affair, and that, if the First Sea Lord, Edward Ashmore, and his experts wanted a particular type of improvement, it was not for him to argue against it. The scientific and political arguments were strongly in favour of continuing with the original project, codenamed *Chevaline*, and the navy reluctantly gave up pressing for an alternative. The existence of the project, and its cost which had escalated to £1000m by then, was first revealed by the Conservative government in 1980 at the time that they announced their decision to ask the Americans to supply the Trident missile for a new force of British submarines, for which we should have to provide yet another design of nuclear warhead, this time delivered by multiple independently targeted re-entry vehicles (MIRV). *Chevaline* had provided multiple re-entry vehicles, but all aimed at the same target.

These announcements, coming hard on the heels of the government's favourable response to the American proposal to base cruise missiles with nuclear warheads in western Europe, including Britain, fanned the flames of a renascent concern in this country, as well as in West Germany, the Netherlands, Belgium and the Scandinavian members of NATO, about nuclear weapons and the danger and likelihood of a nuclear war. It was added to by the government's intention to breathe some life into civil defence, a commitment pressed upon it by its grass-roots supporters. Unfortunately this also created the impression that they envisaged fighting a nuclear war and being prepared to accept a nuclear attack on this country as something not fundamentally different in scale from the bombing blitz of the Second World War. A number of inept and unfortunate statements were made by Ministers, which played into the hands of the pacifists and nuclear disarmers. Events in Iran and Afghanistan, and the advent to power of Ronald

Reagan's hawkish, Republican administration in the United States, made a war between Russia and America seem a real possibility to many people. Since the Vietnam war, the puritan, radical urge to protest had had little outlet, other than Chile, South Africa and Rhodesia, and the nuclear issue provided a fertile ground for its activity.

My attitude to the government's decision to provide a replacement system for Polaris, based on Trident, at a then (1980) estimated cost of £5000 billion, which I saw as bound to affect adversely the strength and flexibility of our conventional forces, and the view I had expressed publicly about nuclear war and weapons generally, led to invitations to speak at university union debates on that and related issues, and to lecture to many different audiences, in universities, at schools and to political and other bodies. I took the line that I had followed in the House of Lords. I did not agree with the alarmist view that the increasing number of weapons, warheads and delivery systems meant that we were bound to be engulfed in a nuclear war in the near future, in support of which the nuclear disarmers quoted a speech* Mountbatten had made in May 1979, four months before his death. In it he had said:

> I have never been able to accept the reasons for the belief that any class of nuclear weapons can be categorized in terms of their tactical or strategic purposes ... In the event of a nuclear war there will be no survivors – all will be obliterated ... I cannot imagine a situation in which nuclear weapons would be used as battlefield weapons without the conflagration spreading ... The real need is for both sides to replace the attempts to maintain a balance through ever-increasing and ever more costly nuclear armaments by a balance based on mutual restraint. Better still, by reduction of nuclear armaments, I believe it should be possible to achieve greater security at a lower level of military confrontation ... The world now stands on the brink of the final abyss. Let us all resolve to take all possible practical steps to ensure that we do not, through our own folly, go over the edge.

* At Strasbourg, on the occasion of the presentation of the Louise Weiss Foundation Award to the Stockholm International Peace Research Institute.

Although I thought to describe us as being on the brink of the abyss was an exaggeration – the likelihood of Russia and America misunderstanding each other's moves had been significantly lessened by the introduction of satellite photography – I agreed with almost all he had said, and with the similar line being taken by Solly Zuckerman: that it was the vested interests of the scientists and engineers involved, especially in the USA, which had driven the nuclear arms race forward to the grotesque situation in which there were some 50,000 warheads more or less equally distributed between Russia and America. As I said in my lectures, they could not possibly be used. I stressed the awful dilemma that we faced. There was no doubt in my mind that the possession of nuclear weapons by those two great powers, coupled with the fact that both were clearly committed to European defence by the presence of their forces there – the USA to the West, the USSR to the East – had preserved peace in Europe for longer than in any previous century. It was the fear of the terrible consequences of war between them which kept the peace; if that mutual deterrence were, tragically, to fail, the presence of very large numbers of nuclear weapons on both sides would mean that, even if only a small proportion of them was used, our civilization would be destroyed. Hence my emphasis on the need for strong and flexible conventional forces which would provide the only hope of bringing events under control before one side or the other was tempted to use them. From that position I went on to point out that for NATO to initiate nuclear war, if its conventional forces were facing defeat, would be disastrous. Geography and the balance of forces would inevitably mean that NATO would come off worse than the Warsaw Pact in a nuclear exchange, whatever assumptions one made about the number and type of weapons used. For Britain alone to do so would be certain suicide. These were all arguments that Liddell Hart had used 20 years before, and his widow, Kathleen, wrote to me to say how glad she thought Basil would have been to know that I was continuing to employ them.

Many people – both those in favour and those opposed to nuclear weapons – gained the impression that I was much more opposed to them than I was. This had the advantage that I was asked to address audiences who would not normally have thought of inviting a Field Marshal to do so. As over Rhodesia, I found the position of being on neither extreme, but supporting a position which it was not easy for the uninitiated to understand, an uncomfortable one. I had to make certain that I was not represented as, or thought to be, a pacifist or nuclear disarmer. But it was just because my point of view was not a simple black or white one that I felt it important that I should persevere in putting it forward, sometimes to fairly hostile audiences, both doves and hawks. However, I was heartened and given greater confidence in my views by finding strong support for them among many well-informed and responsible people, as well as a significant cross-section of the more intelligent officers of all three services. They were closely in line with the policies of the Liberals, the newly formed Social Democrat Party and also the right wing of the Labour Party. I was not popular with the Conservatives, although several Conservative peers and Members of Parliament told me that they agreed with me.

I became more involved than I wished to be in this issue, but took part also in wider discussions on defence matters. At the suggestion of General Bill Rosson, who, after his retirement from the US Army, was working for a post-graduate doctorate at New College, Oxford, Michael Howard, then Chichele Professor of War Studies, invited me to talk to the University's Strategic Studies Group on Strategy. In preparing my lecture, I re-read what Liddell Hart, Beaufre* and many others had written, finding Beaufre's *Introduction to Strategy*† particularly valuable. Writing *War Since 1945*, involvement in the nuclear debate and rethinking strategy took me back to the central issue, posed by Clausewitz, which had dominated Liddell Hart's thinking after the Second World War. In the nuclear age, was war acceptable or effective as a "continuation of state policy by other means", as Clausewitz had defined it? In his great study of war, Clausewitz had come to the conclusion that the key to victory was to concentrate the maximum force to defeat the enemy's armed forces in battle, not to let operations drag out in

* General André Beaufre. Distinguished French soldier and writer on defence matters; see also p.253.

† Translated by Richard Barry, Faber & Faber, London, 1965.

marches, countermarches and sieges, as they had in the eighteenth century before Napoleon appeared on the scene. This he called Absolute War. But the destruction and misery such a war was likely to cause could frustrate the object for which one had gone to war in the first instance, as it had in Napoleon's case. It would be 'divorcing war from political life'. 'When that happens in our thinking,' he wrote, 'the many links that connect the two elements are destroyed and we are left with something pointless and devoid of sense.' He died of cholera before he had resolved this fundamental dilemma. If that were true in his day, it was clearly infinitely more so if nuclear weapons were used.

In the concluding paragraph of *War Since 1945* I had written:

> To the final question – does war, the resort to force or violence, achieve its aim, 'the continuation of state policy by other means' – there can be no definite answer. In some cases, it clearly has done; in others, it has achieved its political or military aim, but at a cost to some or all of the participants, or to the inhabitants of the country over which it was fought, that calls into question whether it was worth the effort. In few of the countries involved can one say that the majority of the population lead a better life as a result. But, if the alternative is to give in without a fight to whomever threatens or uses violence to obtain power for himself or for those with whom he is associated, society would collapse into anarchy. It is as well to remind those who quote the injunction in the Sermon on the Mount to 'turn the other cheek also' to him 'who shall smite thee on the right cheek', that, in the version in Saint Mathew's gospel, this is preceded by the words 'I say unto you that ye resist not evil.' The sad fact of life is that, if evil is not resisted, it will prevail. That is the justification for the use of force to deter, and if necessary, defeat those who turn to it to further their own ends, the justification for maintaining in the service of the community and the state forces who are trained, skilled and well-equipped to meet that challenge when and wherever it arises. Their profession is an honourable one.

In none of the wars described in that book were nuclear weapons used, although the Americans considered the possibility of their use in the Korean War and at the time of the siege of Dien Bien Phu in France's Indo-China war. I drew all these thoughts together in a lecture which I was originally invited to give to the Department of Human Ecology at Edinburgh University in October 1981 on 'A Military Strategy for the '80s and '90s', and which I repeated elsewhere both under that title and that of 'War as a Continuation of Policy'. In it I said:

> I believe therefore that war is an acceptable means, in the last resort, after all other forms of persuasion and pressure have failed, to resist evil: to prevent what one believes to be an evil system being imposed on oneself, one's family and one's community, especially if it is imposed, or threatened to be imposed, by force. I also believe that it is acceptable to use war as a means, in the last resort, of preventing one's community from being deprived of the essentials of life, from being reduced to starvation or abject poverty. But, even in those cases, if to engage in it, or to continue it, once embarked upon, would produce greater misery, then it would be wrong to resort to it; but that decision will always be a very difficult one, especially if there is strong popular pressure for war, as there often has been.

And later on:

> To continue to rely on the fear of nuclear war to prevent war in Europe is a high risk policy; but the fact must be faced that the higher the risks of war, the less likely is it that anyone will take the risk of going to war. The policy of appeasement in the 1930s was a low risk policy, and it led to the Second World War. To follow what appears to be a low risk policy now could lead to a Third World War, which, inevitably, sooner or later, would turn nuclear. A low risk policy in the short term means a high risk in the longer term. I believe that nuclear weapons must not be abolished, but must be kept in the armouries of the major powers to deter them from war against each other, which

would inevitably involve us all, whatever we did or didn't do. It is one of the ironies of the whole business that every attempt to reduce the horrors of war, or the burden of providing armed forces, tends to make war appear more acceptable, and it therefore becomes more likely; and once it starts, all the experience of history goes to show that it is extremely difficult either to limit or to stop it.

My final paragraph ran:

NATO's strategy must rely on the fear of the consequences of nuclear war to deter war; but it must give equal importance to the vital need to bring hostilities to a halt by strength and flexibility in conventional forces, if, tragically, deterrence fails. This will not be achieved by reductions in defence effort. What NATO must discard is the concept of fighting a war with nuclear weapons, on land, in the air or at sea. It is illogical, because the West would lose such a war. It is impractical, because in practice it could not be fought; and it is immoral, because it would make life for us all – in the world as a whole, and for our descendants – far worse than the life we now enjoy. I for one enjoy it immensely, and I hope that my children and grandchildren will enjoy it as much as I have done and do.

To have to face the arguments of intelligent, humane men and women, who believed with passion and conviction either that one should not contemplate resort to war at all, or that only the abolition of nuclear weapons, and our own voluntary abandonment of them, could save Britain, Europe and the world from a holocaust, was a sharp challenge. I had to think out again for myself both the underlying principles and the methods of conducting war, in a way that one seldom did while busily employed in the day to day affairs of the armed forces. I had to ask myself if what my life had been devoted to had not been fundamentally wrong. I was glad to be able, with a clear conscience, to believe that it had not; although I had to admit that many wars had been unnecessary; that their results had not always been worth the sacrifices and misery they had caused, and had often left the participants, even the victors, worse off than if they had not embarked upon them. I concluded that the bombing of cities, which were not military targets, had been a fatal step in the wrong direction, although I also recognized the dilemma inherent in the fact that every step designed to make the conduct of war more acceptable made it more likely that nations would accept the risks of going to war. In a world in which nuclear weapons had been invented, the consequences of going to war at all, certainly in Europe or between the major powers, could be disastrous. The real folly was to imagine that nothing had basically changed, and that, even if war was no longer thought of as a source of honour and glory, it could be embarked upon with the sort of resignation with which we had faced the prospect in 1939.

My involvement in the public discussion of nuclear weapon policy led not only to requests to give lectures to many different audiences and participate in university debates and discussions, but also to a suggestion, in January 1982, by Matthew Evans, managing director of Fabers, that I should write a short book on the subject, which I agreed to do. It forced me to read through the key books, mostly American, covering the development of nuclear weapon policy from 1945 to that time. As I did so, I found that they reinforced, rather than challenged, the attitude I had taken. I finished the book, *A Policy for Peace*, in April and it was published in September, the grim photograph of myself on the cover never, to my annoyance, having been submitted for my approval. It was a fair success, selling over 6000 copies in the first six months after publication. I received many appreciative letters, one of the most significant being from the German General von Senger und Etterlin, C-in-C of NATO Allied Forces Central Europe, who wrote: 'I am almost in complete agreement with your views.' It also led to an invitation from Professor Carroll Wilson, formerly of the Massachusetts Institute of Technology, to participate, as a member of the steering group, in a study, known as the European Security Study (ESECS), of how to improve NATO's conventional capability. He first approached me in October 1981, and, impressed by him and Professor Kosta Tsipis, who was initally concerned but took little active part, I readily agreed. The other British members were eventually Michael Howard, Lawrence Freedman, Hugh Beach and Alasdair Steedman. Hugh by that time had retired from the army after being Master-General

of the Ordnance, and Alasdair from the RAF, having been
the UK Military Representative at NATO Headquarters. I
suggested both in order to have representatives who had
experience of equipment matters and of the air force. One of
the weaknesses of the group was that, although strong in
academic and army representation, it was short of naval and
air force advice. The study was limited to NATO's Central
Front and participation to Americans, British and German,
with one Norwegian. An attempt to associate the French .was
unsuccessful, the two distinguished Frenchmen invited insisting that they could not be held responsible for the conclusions, whatever they might turn out to be. Carroll Wilson had
envisaged an ambitious programme of 'workshops', but,
sadly, he died after the first had been held, for which a
number of valuable papers were written. His declining health
and death affected the possibility of raising funds for further
'workshops', and the study was completed after a meeting of
the steering group at the Aspen Institute in Maryland in
January 1983, chaired by Robert Bowie of the Brookings Institute. The final report was agreed* over two days of intense
drafting by Bob Bowie, Milton Katz, McGeorge Bundy, General Franz-Josef Schulze and myself at Cambridge, Massachusetts, in February and was unanimously agreed by the
26-strong steering group. Among its recommendations was
that 'Our present reliance on possible early use of nuclear
weapons threatens to undermine the two main purposes of
the Alliance: the need for credible deterrence of adversaries
and effective reassurance of our own peoples. We find ourselves in strong and unanimous agreement that the Alliance
should now move energetically to reduce its dependence on
such early use.' It called for a determined effort to improve
the capability of NATO's conventional forces 'which would
enable NATO to use conventional weapons systems to strike
targets for which it now relies on nuclear systems', and
estimated that the cost of the report's recommendations
could be met within a 4 per cent annual growth in NATO's
defence expenditure. A follow-up report by a small group,
in which Alasdair Steedman was the British representative,
reconsidered the report and its costing in 1985.† It was

* Published by Macmillan, London, 1983.
† Published by Westview Press, Colorado, 1985.

a very interesting and stimulating experience to discuss these important matters in such a distinguished group, and reassuring to find how wide the agreement was on most of the major issues, which were the subject of hot debate in all our countries at that time.

Another by-product of involvement in public discussion of these issues was an invitation to take part in the 'Edinburgh Conversations'. These, initiated by Lord Ritchie-Calder and Professor John Erickson, consisted of an annual meeting with senior officials of the Soviet Union for informal discussion of subjects of mutual concern. At the 1980 meeting, the Edinburgh team had found itself without anyone who could speak authoritatively on defence matters, and I was pressed to join them for 1981, when the conversations were to be held in Scotland. I agreed, but at the last minute the Soviet team insisted on a change of date and I was otherwise engaged. I was then urged to participate in the 1982 conversations, due to be held in the Soviet Union. With some misgivings, but with encouragement from Frank Cooper, then Permanent Under-Secretary in the Ministry of Defence, I agreed on condition that, at my expense, Edith could accompany me and visit Leningrad while we were talking in Moscow. John Erickson assured me that there would be no difficulty about that, but he was wrong. As the date approached, excuses were produced that space was so limited that wives could not be allowed. They also tried to change the place of the meeting to Tashkent, throwing in a day's sightseeing at Samarkand. I was delighted at the prospect, and annoyed when I discovered not only that the Principal, Dr Burnett, had turned it down on the very reasonable grounds that none of the officials we hoped to meet would go so far from Moscow, but also that the Soviet authorities had been told that it was I who would not wish to be exposed to such a long flight in both directions. However, I was by then committed, and we arrived in Moscow on Sunday 26 September 1982, travelling by Aeroflot, met by Dr Mayanaev, Vice-Chairman of all the Soviet Friendship Societies, and André Parastayev, Secretary-General of the Soviet–Great Britain Friendship Society, who co-chaired the meetings with Dr Burnett. He spoke good English, having been Consul-General in Calcutta and having served in the Soviet Embassy in London from

1971 to 1979. He was ably assisted by a charming younger man, Anatoly Kuzmenko. We were housed and had our meetings and meals in a modern two-storey building in the south-western suburbs of the city, intended as a conference centre for senior trade unionists. I was given a huge suite, complete with TV set, on which I watched a clearly ailing Brezhnev read the wrong speech in Azerbaijan.

The participants on the Soviet side came from the Foreign Ministry, the General Staff, the Institute for International and Economic Affairs and Georgi Arbatov's Institute for US and Canadian Affairs. To balance the presence of Hugh Beach and myself, they produced an elderly retired general, who was head of the War Veterans Association, and an admiral who had been the Soviet naval representative in London in the Second World War. Neither took any part in the discussions. We were subjected to the usual Soviet lines on most subjects, Arbatov trying to persuade us that Europe could now stand on its own feet in every respect without being dependent on the Americans. Over meals or between sessions one could sometimes obtain a more relaxed and open-minded view. Lev Semeiko, a retired colonel of engineers in Arbatov's institute, appeared to be one of the most reasonable. They were clearly obsessed by the fear that the Americans were ceaselessly trying, by every possible means, to undermine 'the Socialist system' and still entertained the idea that they could do so by means of a first strategic nuclear strike. Even if that were not so, they were forcing an arms race on the Soviet Union to prevent it from establishing the 'New Society' at which they had been aiming ever since the 1917 revolution. The Soviet representatives dismissed as unwarranted the argument that the USA had almost exactly the same fears about the Soviet Union. I found it very difficult to make up my mind whether or not they really believed all they said, generally coming to the depressing conclusion that they probably did.

We were shown the sights, the Kremlin looking much less grim than I expected, and attended the ballet (not the Bolshoi) in the huge theatre there and a performance of Bach's 'Mass in B Minor' at the Conservatoire. Both were of high quality and packed full. The most interesting part of the visit was to meet Russians and find them human beings like ourselves, some very charming and amusing, others much less so. The audiences at the ballet and the concert could have been similar audiences anywhere else, although nobody was smartly dressed. The same could be said for the crowds in the street; there was a drabness about everything. I was surprised to discover a remarkable collection of French Impressionists in the Pushkin Gallery, where there was an exhibition of Picasso on display, as well as a permanent collection of Chagall, very different from his well-known pictures.

It was a contrast to go almost directly from a week in Moscow to New York to give a talk at a conference held by the Council for a Livable World, followed by attendance at a huge lunch in Washington at which Robert McNamara was presented with the annual Einstein Peace Prize. He, McGeorge Bundy, Gerard Smith and George Kennan had recently published their famous article in *Foreign Affairs*, in which they had called on NATO to reconsider its reliance on a policy of first use of nuclear weapons. It was a great pleasure to be collected from the lunch by Joanna Woods, wife of Richard Woods, the Minister in the New Zealand Embassy. She was a cousin of Edith's through her father, Claud Proby, and of mine through her mother Patricia, née Pearce. I spent the night with them before flying back to London.

1982 was also a busy year of writing. Nothing having come of the idea of a TV series about *The Seven Ages of the British Army*, which had become diverted into *War Since 1945*, Weidenfelds agreed in January 1982 that I should revert to the original concept as a book, the two years in between having been spent in compiling this one, which I put into cold storage. I completed *The Seven Ages* in April 1983, the final text, after some changes, being accepted in August. It was published in April 1984 and sold nearly 4000 copies by the end of June. It was published in paperback by Collins in 1986. At the lunch he gave for me to celebrate its publication, George Weidenfeld asked what I proposed to write next. Provoked by a rather critical review by Correlli Barnett, who complained that I had failed to deal with the struggle between continental and maritime strategy in our history, I suggested a book on that theme and was asked to produce a synopsis of it. That involved delving into naval history, my knowledge of which was slight, as well as expanding my knowledge of European history generally and the activities on the continent of armies other than our own. After six months of reading, most of which I found of great interest, I produced my synopsis, but received no reaction from Weidenfelds for some time.

Meanwhile I had become involved in another project. In November 1983 I was approached by General Neil Ritchie's nephew, Alistair Ritchie, to whom he had entrusted his papers, with the request that his own version of the circumstances leading to his appointment as Commander of Eighth Army in 1941, his time in command of it, and his subsequent removal should be made public. He had suggested that his nephew should consult me. Neil Ritchie died a few weeks later. I undertook to read through his papers, which, on my advice, Alistair Ritchie deposited with the Imperial War Museum, to see if there was enough material in them for a book. I came to the conclusion that there was not, but undertook to write a piece which would, if possible, do something to restore Ritchie's reputation which had suffered at the hands of Auchinleck's admirers and others. Owing to the paucity of the material in his own papers, it involved several sessions in the Public Record Office at Kew, thumbing through the war diaries of all the formations of Eighth Army and the voluminous piles of signals attached to them, some of them, and of the operation orders, having been signed by myself. It brought the desert scene vividly back to me. My final product came out too short for a book (35,000 words), but too long for anything else. However Christopher Dowling of the Imperial War Museum thought that it should be published and Batsfords agreed to do so, in association with the Museum, if I expanded it to take a fresh look at the whole desert campaign up to and including El Alamein in the light of what had been written or revealed in the 20 years since they had published my two previous books on the campaign. The result was *Dilemmas of the Desert War*, which I finished in June 1985 and which was published in April 1986, receiving generally favourable reviews. By the end of the year it had sold nearly 3000 copies, 1000 having been taken by the Indiana University Press in the USA.

By the time that I had finished writing it, I had received Weidenfelds' reaction to my synopsis. In March 1985, at a meeting with George Weidenfeld, John Curtis and Mark Collins, they said that, although it would be an interesting book, its appeal would be limited, and they persuaded me to undertake instead a book about 'The Great Armed Forces of the World in our Century'. I produced the synopsis within a month, and it was accepted in June, with a target date at the end of 1986, which I met. The result was *Twentieth Century Warriors: The Development of the Armed Forces of the Major Military Nations in the Twentieth Century*, the nations being Britain, France, Germany, Russia, the USA, Japan and China. It was fascinating to cover the same events through several different eyes, and particularly to view the military history of the century from new angles. I was fortunate in persuading distinguished academics, who were experts on the different countries, to read and comment on the chapters concerned with their expertise. It inevitably came out longer than the 120,000 words contracted for. After some discussion, I managed to avoid major cuts in return, reluctantly, for having no illustrations. It was published in November 1987 and sold over 2000 copies in the first six months. It was published by Weidenfelds in the USA in June 1988. It received some excellent reviews. In addition to writing books, I contributed to others: one on 'Getting Defence Priorities Right' for *Alternative Approaches to British Defence Policy*, edited by John Baylis; another on 'Conventional Warfare in the Nuclear Age' for the new edition of Princeton University Press's *Makers of Modern Strategy*, edited by Peter Paret, to celebrate the publication of which a seminar was held at Stanford University, which I attended; another for *Disarmament*, edited by Julia Neuberger, published by Macmillans on the eve of the 1987 General Election; one on Field Marshal von Manstein for *Hitler's Generals*, edited by Correlli Barnett, and another on Montgomery for *Churchill's Generals*, edited by John Keegan, as well as forewords, articles and book reviews, most of the last for the *Times Literary Supplement*.

Writing, and doing the reading for it, were not however my only activity. Although my attendance at the House of Lords was not as constant as that of peers who looked on themselves as politicians, I attended when defence, or other matters in which I was interested, were under discussion: 38 occasions in 1983. At the beginning of the 1984/5 session,

Lord Sherfield asked me to join the Select Committee on Science and Technology, of which he was the chairman. When I protested that I had no appropriate qualifications, he replied that the same applied to him and pressed me to accept, which I did. In 1985 the sub-committee on which I served, under Lord Gregson's chairmanship, studied Marine Science; in 1986, under Lord Nelson of Stafford, Surface Transport; and in 1987, under Lord Shackleton, who succeeded Lord Sherfield as chairman of the main committee, Space; in 1988, under Lord Nelson again, Civil Nuclear Power. It was an educative process, to which I hope I made some contribution, however unscientific. A pleasant aspect of my duties as a peer was to carry the Sword of State at the State Opening of Parliament. This is normally the privilege of a peer who is also a senior officer of the armed forces, the Queen herself nominating which one is to have the honour. I was fortunate to be granted that honour in 1980, 1982, 1983, 1984, and 1987, the last establishing a record: the first peer, so I was informed by the College of Heralds, to have carried it five times.

We had also found time for travel, except in 1979, when we were too busy getting our new house and its garden into shape. In 1980 Edith spent several weeks early in the year in Kenya, staying with Andrew and Anne to see our first grandchild, Gordon. In August I helped Freddy and Johnny Coates sail their yacht back from Sweden. I joined them at Gothenburg and, after negotiating the Lin Fjord through northern Jutland, we were stuck in the fishing port of Tybörn for a week while gales raged in the North Sea. After a good sail from there to Den Helder, we had to take refuge again at Scheveningen, where the two young members of the crew had to leave to get back to work. From there we had a good sail, crossing the shipping lanes in the Channel on a clear moonlit night, to Brighton, where I had to leave Freddy, Johnny and the other member of the crew to sail on to Poole. In May 1981 Edith and I flew to Crete and hired a small car, travelling all over the island, looking for the small mediaeval churches with their frescoes, bathing and walking down the great gorge of Samaria, eleven miles long. In September 1982, before I went to Moscow, we joined Clare and Tony Dorman for ten days in a farmhouse near Moissac in the southern Dordogne, doing some leisurely sightseeing on the way there through the Massif Central. In September 1983 we drove through Germany and Austria for a holiday in Yugoslavia, sightseeing and bathing down the coast and visiting Peç in Kosovo, returning by the lovely uplands of the Durmitor mountains. We came back through Trieste, northern Italy and France, another greatly enjoyed holiday, in which we saw some lovely buildings and scenery. That Christmas we drove to Crans-Montana in Switzerland, where Andrew joined us from Botswana and Gordon from Hong Kong. I thought that I had had my last skiing holiday when John and I joined the Moberlys at Hochsölden in Austria in March 1977, and was glad to find that I could negotiate most of the excellent long runs in my very unstylish fashion and derive great pleasure from it, following Andrew's more polished performance, while Gordon took his first lessons in a children's ski class.

We had hoped that John would come too, but he was busy looking for a job, having returned in June from a trek which had taken him from Botswana in August 1982, to which he had flown to join Andrew, through Zimbabwe, Zambia, Malawi, Tanzania including Zanzibar, Rwanda and Uganda to Kenya, where he revisited the African school at which he had taught in 1979 between Winchester and Durham, and then back through Uganda and the Sudan to contact a friend working in the north. His journey back to Kenya from there was as exciting as his return flight from Nairobi by Aeroflot via Moscow was tedious, although cheap. He had already crossed the Sahara twice, once with Alice and Claude in their ancient Landrover, the second time on an expedition he organized with fellow Durham undergraduates, starting at Dakar and travelling by public transport or lorry-hopping via Timbuctoo and Tamanrasset. In 1984 he joined Procter and Gamble as a trainee cost and management accountant. While we were away on this ski-holiday, we received the sad news of my brother Rodney's death. The polio which attacked him in 1950 caused him great difficulties with his breathing as he grew older, and every winter had become a severe struggle.

The fortieth anniversary of the Normandy landings occurred on 6 June 1984 and Freddy Coates suggested that we should sail over there to mark the occasion, to which I readily agreed, having at that time received no invitation to attend any of the ceremonies. A few weeks before the anniversary, Philip Moore, The Queen's Private Secretary, rang me up and said that The Queen had decided that she would like a senior officer from each of the armed forces who had participated in the operation to accompany her in the Royal Yacht and at the ceremonies in Normandy, and hoped that I would be able to come. I said that I had landed on D + 1, but he explained that it was the general operation and not just the D–Day landings that was the qualification. I explained my quandary: that I had committed myself to Freddy, and that I doubted if he would be able to get another crew at such short notice. Philip said that The Queen would quite understand, and asked me to suggest other names, which I did. It was with great fervour that, just before dawn on 6 June, we lined the yacht deck at the entrance of the locks at Ouistreham and gave three cheers for Her Majesty as HMS *Britannia* passed close to us, acknowledged from the bridge by Paul Greening, Admiral Royal Yachts, a near neighbour at Wickham. A month before that, Edith and I had spent a short holiday with Graham Hill, a friend of Singapore days, in his lovely villa in Sardinia.

In October I attended a conference at Caen, organized by L'Institut de L'Histoire du Présent, the subject of which was the reaction of the local population to the landings in 1944, and its effects on them. I had been asked by its director, Professor François Bederida, to contribute a paper on the Anglo–American strategy which lay behind the campaign. We all spoke in our own languages and there was no interpretation. It was interesting and good for my French. We took the car, visiting Paris and staying with Don Cook at L'Étang-la-Ville on the way. Edith had to return from Dieppe before the conference, as Susanna, living in London, was not well. On the day after the conference I lunched with Erik de Mauny and his wife in their charming farmhouse near Thury-Harcourt. He and I were both involved in supporting the Salamander Oasis Trust, the moving spirit behind which was Victor Selwyn. He, as a bombardier Royal Artillery, and others had produced a volume of poems in Cairo in the Second World War, and the Trust was formed to revive appreciation of poetry written by serving members of the forces during the war, to recover and publish it. I became involved through Dan Davin, who had written the chapter on Freyberg in *The War Lords*. On my way to lunch, I had revisited the area where I had taken over command of 4th Armoured Brigade and tried to identify the orchard near Villers-Bocage where I had lost my lunch 40 years before. Although I had a clear picture of it in my memory, I was not certain that I had found it.* When I explained what I was doing to a Frenchman, who had regarded my activities with some suspicion, he told me that he clearly remembered the battle, when he had been a boy of 14. After an excellent lunch with the de Maunys, I drove to Cherbourg to face a very rough passage to Portsmouth.

A few weeks later I found myself in France again for a meeting of the Franco–British Council, a body set up by President Giscard d'Estaing and Mrs Thatcher to foster Franco–British understanding. For the first time the French had agreed to include defence on the agenda, and Alistair Horne had asked me to attend. The meeting was held at the end of November in the conference centre established in the Palais des Papes at Avignon. The British assembled a high-level and well qualified team for the defence sub-committee, chaired by Denis Healey. Unfortunately the French produced a second-rate team, principally composed of civil servants of the Ministries of Defence and Foreign Affairs. All we achieved was a clarification of the basically different attitudes of our two countries towards European defence, but with a saving clause that a special meeting to consider defence issues would be arranged in the following year. We were splendidly entertained, including a great dinner in the palace, attended by the French Prime Minister, Laurent Fabius, and Margaret Thatcher. Most of the guests who were supposed to be at the table at which I was placed failed to turn up, with the happy result that Monsieur Fabius's entourage finished up there, and I had an extremely interesting conversation with his *chef de cabinet*.

At the end of January 1985 we went on a Swann's tour of the Nile, Edith's first visit to Egypt. Cairo was very different

* See p. 183.

and much less attractive than when I had last seen it 42 years before. After seeing the sights, we flew to Luxor and continued by bus to Aswan, where we stayed in a hotel as the boat could not get above the Esna barrage, which was closed. Having flown to see Abu Simbel, we visited the ruins of Philae at Aswan, and Kom Ombo and Edfu on our way to join the boat at Esna to sail down to Luxor. Thereafter we saw all the sights and were excellently guided and looked after, as we made our way downstream, getting seriously grounded on one occasion, as the level of the river was very low. I had paid little attention to Egyptian antiquities when in Cairo before the war, preferring Muslim art and, above all, the desert. I found this trip fascinating. It was our first experience of a package tour, and we were greatly impressed by the efficiency with which it was organized, and pleased by the opportunity to share the experience with a variety of people, mostly British, American and Canadian.

Having attended another conference of the Council for a Livable World in San Francisco, I had sworn never to cross the Atlantic again unless my fare was paid at a class above Economy. That was the reply I gave to Professor John Koumoulides of Ball State University, Indiana, when he asked me to lecture about my peacekeeping experiences in Cyprus to a group interested in Greek history. When he readily agreed and offered any date, I could not refuse and was very warmly welcomed there in March 1985. That summer, Andrew, having finished his contract with the Botswana Development Corporation, began a Master of Business Administration course at INSEAD at Fontainebleau. We visited him there, paid a nostalgic visit to Féricy, and did some sightseeing in Burgundy on our way to Lyons to attend the special meeting on defence of the Franco–British Council. This time the French fielded a more impressive team and we had some interesting discussions, which once more highlighted the very different political approach to European defence of the two governments, resulting in different military strategies and equipment policies. Unless the political approaches changed, the French towards NATO and the British more towards an independent European defence organization, there was little hope of greater integration of military doctrine and equipment procurement.

From Lyons we drove straight to Castiglioncello, near Livorno in Italy, where I was to participate in an international conference organized by the Italian Association of Scientists against Nuclear Weapons. There were speakers from both sides of the Iron Curtain, as well as from neutral countries. Some of the talks and discussions were interesting, the hardest line being taken by the East German delegate. The delightful Finnish participant confided in me that his first military experience was in the cadet corps of Worcester Cathedral Choir School, to which he had gained a scholarship just before the Second World War. Being welcomed by the council of the local commune, which had been dominated by the Communist Party since 1945, was also interesting, the speeches, all in Italian, apparently being entirely devoted to argument about why the proceedings were not being translated for our benefit. One of the most impressive participants at the conference was Professor Sidney Drell of Stanford University, a firm opponent of President Reagan's Strategic Defense Initiative, whom I had met at a Ditchley Conference on that subject the previous year. After the conference we spent a week sightseeing in Tuscany, at San Gimignano, Siena and Florence, before driving back through Switzerland and France, visiting Vinci, Lucca and Parma on the way.

We were not the only members of the family to have travelled. While John and Andrew had returned from Africa, Alice had spent a year in China, establishing an English language training centre at the Central China College of Agriculture at Wuhan, after which she visited various places of interest, including Kashgar, before rejoining Claude, when he had qualified as a vet in June 1984, on a holiday in Thailand. Spain was our next choice. Apart from our holiday at Tamariu on the Costa Brava at the time of the Coronation in 1953, Edith had seen nothing at all of the country. She had not been able to accompany me when I gave a lecture in Madrid in 1981, nor when I was the guest of the Gibraltar Chamber of Commerce, founded by my grandfather, Benjamin Carver, on the occasion of its 150th anniversary in December 1982. We therefore planned a round trip in May 1986, taking the car by ferry to Santander and visiting all the major cultural centres, spending a few days, after we had visited Granada, at Mojacar with Charlotte and Peter Fraser, who had been on my Political Adviser's staff in Singapore. The tour brought back memories of my visit to Antony and Elizabeth in Spain in 1946. Sadly Antony developed lung cancer on holiday in France a few months after we had returned, from which he died in November.

On the way back from Spain we joined up with Andrew, who had just successfully completed his course at Fontainebleau. We went on to stay with Don Cook at L'Étang-la-Ville, visiting Monet's garden at Giverny on our way back to the ferry at Ouistreham. I had passed the garden a month earlier, when I helped Ralph and Patricia Serocold sail their yacht across to Le Havre and then chug up the Seine to Paris. The following year we covered the north-west corner of Spain and northern Portugal, driving from St Malo and back to Ouistreham. We spent a few nights at the extraordinary hotel at Busaco and picnicked near the spot from which Wellington had commanded the battle against Massena in 1810. In between, I had attended another conference about nuclear weapons in Italy, somewhat similar to that at Castiglioncello. This one was held in Florence in December 1986, and was organized by a group of professors of its university in association with the Department for Disarmament Affairs of the United Nations. It was supported by the Italian Government and the city of Florence, and the participants were drawn not only from both sides of the Iron Curtain, but from Africa and Asia also, the audience consisting largely of people connected with the university or the city. We were sumptuously housed and entertained. I escaped one evening to dine with the British Consul-General, Ivor Rawlinson, in his delightful villa in Bellastuarda, Harold Acton being among the guests.

Having never visited Prague or Budapest, we decided to do so in 1988, driving in our own car and staying on the way there and back with Willie and Judy Rous in Germany. He was then a major-general, commanding the 4th Division. The only problem proved to be booking hotel rooms, as the Spring Music Festival was on in Prague and the Trade Fair in Budapest, but our defence attachés in both capitals helped us to solve the problem. We saw all the sights at both places, and some in between, and were glad that we had decided to go there and to travel on our own. We stayed in Austria between the two, on the way out with Countess Gabriele

Seefried at her Schloss near Gresten and on the way back in Vienna. In July I went to Brunei as a member of a parliamentary delegation, invited by the Sultan to attend the ceremonies on the occasion of his forty-second birthday, 21 years after he had come to the throne. We spent a day in Singapore on the way there, and I was astonished to see the developments since I had last been there in 1972, as I was at the changes in Brunei, where the general prosperity was impressive. We were very warmly welcomed there and shown recent developments in housing, education and health. We were received by the Sultan and by two of his brothers, one the Minister for Foreign Affairs, the other of Finance. On our way back through Singapore, we enjoyed an interview with Lee Kuan Yew, who was as stimulating as ever. We had seen his son Brigadier-General Lee Hsien Loong, Minister for Trade and Industry, in his office as Deputy Minister for Defence in the old British Officers' Mess at Tanglin. I was particularly interested to meet him as he had been at Cambridge with Andrew and had been attached as an officer to 1st Royal Tank Regiment.

Finishing this account of my life to date, I realize how extremely fortunate I have been: in my origins, in my up-bringing and education, in my family, relations and friends and all those who have helped me in so many different ways, in my good health and in the opportunities which chance has presented to me. I felt this most deeply when Edith and I celebrated 40 years of happy marriage with our four children on 22 November 1987, and again, sadly, when I was left the sole survivor of the four Carver brothers with the death of Paul on 21 March 1989, a month before his seventieth birthday.

Index